EVOLUTIONARY PLAYWORK

Play is a crucial component in the development of all children. In this fully updated and revised edition of his classic playwork text, Bob Hughes explores the complexities of children's play, its meaning and purpose, and argues that adult-free play is essential for the psychological well-being of the child.

The book is divided into fourteen chapters that together examine the fundamentals of evolutionary play. First, Hughes examines the very earliest ideas of playwork and its impact on brain growth and organisation today. He then goes on to explore and explain the key theoretical concepts underlying playwork. These include discussions on free play and creating suitable play environments alongside more thorny issues such as safety and consultation. Finally, the book offers up some of Hughes' most recent research that reveals how his approach to play and playwork in global society has continued to evolve throughout his career to meet new challenges and needs. Throughout this book, Hughes has included his fellow practitioner Mick Conway's vivid observations of children at play to bring the facts and arguments in the text to life.

This revised edition reflects important recent advances in our understanding of the evolutionary history of play and its impact on the development of the brain, of the role play in the development of resilience and of the impact of play deprivation. *Evolutionary Playwork* is still the only book to combine the reality of playwork practice with the fundamentals of evolutionary and developmental psychology, and it is still essential reading for all playwork students, practitioners and researchers.

Bob Hughes has been a theoretical and applied playworker for nearly forty years. He is widely published on the subject of Play and Playwork and was the first Editor of the *International Play Journal*. He has been the National Coordinator of PlayEducation, an independent playwork agency providing training and research services, since 1982.

EVOLUTIONARY PLAYWORK

REFLECTIVE ANALYTIC PRACTICE

SECOND EDITION

BOB HUGHES

Routledge
Taylor & Francis Group

LONDON AND NEW YORK

First published 2001
by Routledge

This edition published 2012
by Routledge
2 Park Square, Milton Park, Abingdon, Oxon OX14 4RN

Simultaneously published in the USA and Canada
by Routledge
711 Third Avenue, New York, NY 10017

*Routledge is an imprint of the Taylor & Francis Group, an
informa business*

British Library Cataloguing in Publication Data
A catalogue record for this book is available from the British
Library

Library of Congress Cataloging in Publication Data
Hughes, Bob, 1944–
Evolutionary playwork: reflective analytic practice/by Bob
Hughes. – 2nd ed.
p. cm.
1. Play. 2. Recreation centers. 3. Child development.
I. Title.
GV182.9.H84 2012
155.4'18–dc22

2011009796

ISBN: 978-0-415-55084-0 (hbk)
ISBN: 978-0-415-55085-7 (pbk)
ISBN: 978-0-203-87383-0 (ebk)

Typeset in Melior and Univers
by Wearset Ltd, Boldon, Tyne and Wear

MIX
Paper from
responsible sources
FSC
www.fsc.org FSC® C004839

Printed and bound in Great Britain by
TJ International Ltd, Padstow, Cornwall

To Rob, Maf, Tom, Fin and Elijah with deep love and gratitude.

Dedicated to the memories of
Frank King and EJ 'Ted' Beattie

CONTENTS

FIGURES

PREFACE TO THE SECOND EDITION

Although the pace has significantly slowed down now, the ten-year period since the first edition of *Evolutionary Playwork* was published saw an almost continuous flurry of Government and Assembly activity, set in train in the early years of the Blair administration.

The Dobson Review (2004), instigated in part by the National Voluntary Council for Children's Play, and the Children's Play Council, was the first sign of a change of fortunes, bringing badly needed, although hardly overwhelming, financial resources into the 'play' field from the Big Lottery.

This was followed in 2006 by a vastly more serious cash injection of £155 million via the Big Lottery Fund, followed by £235 million funding from Central Government. Regrettably the Coalition Government (2010) cut £20 million of this when it came to power, so the eventual grand total was £370 million. £50 million of this was allocated to the five-year Play England project, whilst the rest went directly to local authorities (apart from a £1 million adventure playground grants programme) (Source: PlayEngland).

In Wales, the National Lead Body, PlayWales, initiated the development of the first ever National Play Policy, supported by the Welsh Assembly. Since then PlayWales has developed materials, books, films and training initiatives which have revolutionised the field's presentation of play both here in the UK and internationally. PlayWales is also responsible for underpinning the work that produced The Playwork Principles, and the groundbreaking First Claims 1 and 2.

The Scottish Government became a champion for Children's Play in 2008, when it created a policy framework for play. Play Scotland and other partners are currently developing training and provision initiatives as a part of this.

In Northern Ireland, as well as delivering seminars and conferences, the lead organisation for Play, PlayBoard, has continued to develop its playwork, cross-community and cross-border initiatives. It has also developed a Play Policy for Northern Ireland with the support of the Assembly there.

During this time-frame play, and provision for play, were frequently in evidence on TV and the other media, and it was not unusual to see a Government Minister or 'play person' talking about the subject.

The recent general election (2010), however, has brought that to an abrupt halt. And the current financial crisis is resulting in the rigorous pruning, and in some cases the decimation of play services all over the UK. Where before it looked as if governments had at least understood the significance of some of the play message, and were prepared to explore and experiment with it, that message now looks redundant, relegated to the annuls of 'what if?'.

One could lay the change of fortunes for our children, their play and their future, firmly at the feet of the current Coalition Government, but that would be unfair. They too have their priorities; that play and play provision, and the main subject of this book, playwork, are not included, or, to be fair, may not be included, is perhaps more the fault of the continued convolution of the argument, and the inability of the 'field' to present it coherently and consistently. My own position is that the agenda presented is far too unwieldy and unfocussed.

Like astronomy, play is a huge subject and like astronomy, more is unknown than is known about it. As playwork, or, as it is called in this book, *Evolutionary Playwork*, is suffering, what is hopefully only a temporary decline, the scientific disciplines that explore play are producing findings that demonstrate that the claim made about the centrality of play to human evolution by Jerome Bruner in 1976 were a bull's-eye of prediction.

There is no doubt that we are passing through a period of setbacks with regard both to our collective understanding of play and our contemporary strategies for utilising that new understanding, but let us hope that they will be short-lived and that parents and other concerned adults will soon begin to voice their desire once more, to ensure that all children have access to free, unbridled play as an integral part of our contract to civilisation.

ACKNOWLEDGEMENTS FOR THE SECOND EDITION

As well as thanking Routledge and my editor Simon Whitmore for their continued support, I also thank Rob, Maf, Annie, Liz, Domi, and my three grandsons Thomas, Finnian and Elijah, who provide me with constant wisdom, wonderful insights, and great laughs.

As well as all the children I have had the honour to work with over the years, I want to thank especially those I have worked with most recently in the Borough of Islington, London, together with their play-workers. They gave me endless hours of learning and pleasure in the period 2005–2010. My thanks also go to Islington Play Association who made the work possible, especially Anita Grant, Paul Hacker and Steve MacArthur, and the IPA staff. My gratitude is also due to Kelda Lyons and Mick Conway who have both contributed expertly to the text, to Professor David Ball who advised me on safety, and to my friend and valued colleague Gordon Sturrock, who as well as providing books and discussions, acted as the representative of a far wider group of play people who offered help and support and friendship to me. You know who you are.

I would also like to acknowledge the work of Claudette Barnes, Mick Conway, Kelda Lyons, Sandra Melville, Eddie Nuttall, Julia Sexton, Gordon Sturrock, Tom Williams and Adrian Voce, for taking my original work on Bio-outcomes and Magic onto the next level.

My thanks also go to UNESCO for their permission to use Roger Hart's Ladder of Participation, and to the University of Toronto for their permission to use their diagram of MacLean's Triune Brain. My continued thanks also go to the staff at the following libraries: University of Cambridge Library, Departments of Experimental Psychology and Physiology and the Faculty of English, University of Cambridge, The British Library and the National Play Information Service at the National Children's Bureau – in particular Anna Kassmann-McKerrell.

INTRODUCTION

■ A boy, perhaps nine years of age, is playing right beside me, using small farm animals in a pen. He is moving them about and making mooing and other animal noises. He is immersed and seems oblivious of everything around him. Suddenly the general noise level drops and he looks up. Then he lays down and begins the imaginative narrative again. Now he is bringing it out into the centre of the room, still making mooing and other noises. He is transporting the whole thing to the sand-play area. Eventually he lays in the sand-pit himself with the animals, burying them in the sand.

■ Joe had been singing the praises of playwork to a friend. The discussion had been about trusting children. He had said, 'Playwork teaches us that, if children are playing near water, don't be too protective by hanging onto their coat collars. Stay close, if you are worried, but trust the child to be aware of the dangers and take the necessary precautions'. The friend took notice of playwork's wise words. And the next time he took his child to the lake in the park, instead of hanging onto her coat collar as he normally did, he let her play freely close to the water's edge. Trusting her, but at the same time keeping a close eye on her. Obviously not close enough – she fell in!

What is happening in these two events? What are they telling us? That children play with toys and get so absorbed that they endow inanimate objects with human and other living characteristics, and are oblivious to the world around them? That there is something called playwork that gives parents bad advice about risks, encouraging them to let their children fall into water?

The first, every one of us will recognise. We have all played and if we are young enough may still be able to evoke that strange dissociation from reality that is imaginative play. And if we try we may still be able to recall endless play memories of events, other children, pets, places and feelings that we unconsciously filed away as children.

These precious memories and the emotions that accompany them are the only real link as adults we have of the particular kind of experience that we call play. As children, we navigated a seething children's reality populated by the synergy between our evolving minds and bodies and the world we were growing up in and adapting to. An interplay so powerful, so internalised, so highly personal and intimate that years later we would still be able to recount detail with a clarity that we would be hard pressed to remember about events that happened last week or even yesterday.

Thinking about playing we might also revive moments of wincing embarrassment, of genuine pain or nerve jangling fear as we explored and experimented and challenged the previous limits of our experience.

The second example although less familiar, may have no less powerful resonances, although for very different reasons. As adults, as parents, we want our children to play too. We want to let them out, to experience the fun and challenge we remember. But for many of us the fear of injury or abduction, of traffic, strangers or even other children, means that they either end up playing where we can see them, when we can supervise them or when they are under camera surveillance.

One problem about this, as this example tries to illustrate, is that all to often, when we *are* there we become a controlling and restrictive influence on what they are able to do. Not only do we supervise and protect, as one would expect of say a master craftsman overseeing an apprentice. All too often we over-supervise and over-protect, and stifle life-learning and experience. It is as if we are not just frightened by the potential threat posed by traffic and strangers, but are afraid of everything when it comes to our children. In one sense this is understandable, but in another are we not simply attempting to avoid reality?

2

It is a natural expression of the bond between parent and child that we do not want our children to come to harm, to experience pain or fear. But herein lies a dilemma. Should we adults be there at all when children play, and if the answer is yes, we cannot avoid the question 'For how long?'. How long do we expect this to go on for? Until our children are ten, fifteen, twenty-five?

And what impact might this hyper-level of supervision and surveillance be having? Is it possible that the supervision described in the example, rather than protecting the child, actually had the effect of disabling her, and that the reason she fell into the water was not because she had not been supervised enough, but that she had been supervised too much in the past?

Could the lesson in that example be, that we must make it possible for our children to take more, rather than less, risks? That to be able to explore and navigate the world with the minimum of harm and injury throughout the whole of life, children must experience and learn to deal with, at least a version of the real world as early as possible? Could that be what play is for?

And remote camera surveillance is becoming at least as great a menace to children's competency as is anything other than the most tenuous supervision. To be and become well-adjusted and skilled human beings, children are driven to explore and experiment. This drive is not only directed at the physical environment and at the non-human species that also live there, it is also directed at any other children. Communication, a complex soup of words, emphases, facial expressions and body-postures, to be effective, has to be tried out.

So too does sex. Sexual competency in later life ideally requires gaining some level of basic experience during childhood, which in turn anticipates privacy and respect for the child's innocence, something which in modern society, particularly with the advent of CCTV, is increasingly rare. This is a hugely serious and significant development in the modern world, and one which may render increasing numbers of adults.

Research discussed later shows that the effects of play deprivation on primate's sexual skilling is so devastating that the affected animals are incapable of mating. This has real and serious consequence for the continuation of any affected species, including human beings.

There are difficult and vexed questions for us all here. They appear to throw into relief the ability of parents and society at large to look after children's development. Although perhaps all they really highlight is a contemporary schism between the experiences many of us had when we were children and those we are prepared to allow our own children to have. Although this in itself begs many questions.

And yet the suggestion that children should be left to encounter risk and interact with other children and species without the continual emotional/moral editing that comes from adult over-supervision, still implies a genuine concern for children. That playing – whether in an imaginative narrative, or in close proximity to, say, water or height – is such a vitally important component of childhood – that it is viewed as essential that children experience it even if it does put them at risk of harm and injury. And that without play they will certainly come to harm. Where do these notions come from? The answer is, from something called *Evolutionary playwork.*

EVOLUTIONARY PLAYWORK

Supervised and organised spaces for children's play have been around for years. Until the late 1960s the adults who supervised and organised them were known as 'playleaders', and there were hundreds of them around the UK and elsewhere. However, at the beginning of the 1970s a new generation of playleaders, with different views and who preferred to call themselves play*workers*, began to emerge. Uncomfortable with their supervisory, organisational and socialising – what I would call 'domesticating' roles – they began to turn to the scientific/academic/ political literature to underpin what they did and why they did it.

What they found there caused a revolution in their thinking and formed the embryo of what is now called 'evolutionary playwork'. Prior to this paradigm shift, playleaders had depended primarily upon the tension between their own intuition and common sense on the one hand, and the prevailing political and community realities on the other, to guide what they did and how they did it. Now, they had discovered an Aladdin's Cave of concepts, ideas, outcomes and mechanisms, along with a growing body of empirical data, that they believed could be taken from the mainly biological literature and applied as the underpinning principles for the practice of the new discipline of

4

playwork, a discipline that would provide a service which although less civically biased might be of infinitely more value and relevance to the children they worked with – particularly from the perspective of their physical and mental health, their ability to weather the storms of life and continue to successfully adapt to the evolving social and climatic changes that face them.

For the past forty years, this is what playworkers have struggled to apply and to share with everyone else.

EVOLUTIONARY PLAY THEORY

What did playworkers find in the literature that so captivated and motivated them? Their initial discovery was that, for many years natural scientists – psychologists, ethologists, ethnologists, evolutionists, ecologists and primatologists and others including historians, writers, clinicians, architects, educationalists, sociologists and even poets – had been studying play in humans and non-humans; that there were a vast array of data, ideas and analyses surrounding these studies, and that whilst some (for example, Schlosberg 1947) argued that as play could not even be properly defined, let alone be a manageable topic for scientific research, there were others who were pondering its possible centrality in evolution (Bruner 1976: 13–14; Sylva 1977). Every playworker interested in the scientific study of play had their favourite influences. For some it was the psychologists, Lorenz, Fagan, Sylva and Bruner. For others it was the work of evolutionary ecologists like Clutton-Brock, ethologists like Hinde, anthropologists like Bateson, or primatologists like Lowick-Goodall whose work at the Gombe Stream Reserve went on to fascinate television viewers for over twenty years. But choices were more preferences of style and accessibility, for many playworkers at the time were not university graduates and often found the scientific literature difficult and inflexible.

However, what each of the different texts demonstrated in their own way was that play's existence was virtually universal among mammals; that its diversity and duration was linked to that species evolutionary history, and that its complexity, in any given species, was an indicator of their level of evolutionary development. Bruner (1972), for example, analysed the manual behaviour of different species as less to do with the evolved structure of their hands and more to do with the nature of the programme that controlled the use of those hands (pp. 36–37). This idea of an evolutionary 'programme' becomes increasingly central to the evolving idea of playwork as it moves from its genesis to the contemporary period, whilst the universality of play in mammals has extended to avians, reptiles and even some species of fish (Burghardt 2005).

For some playworkers, viewing children as the young of a species – albeit their own – rather than as 'children' or young (or even 'incomplete or unfinished') adults was and still remains a problem. For them their analysis was and is probably still drawn more from 'human rights', welfare reform, cultural or day-to-day care issues. However, for those who felt more able to make the transition, they had access to a wealth of data about play in non-humans, that could then be juxtaposed with knowledge from their personal and professional experience of play in humans. Not withstanding anthropomorphic considerations, this comparison made it possible to both explore and experiment with the practical implications of the non-human studies, by applying them to practical playwork circumstances. (Playworkers were also beginning tentatively to assert that their experience was, in many cases, more long-term and in-depth than any scientific study of human children to date.)

The evolving playwork practice continued to integrate the literature on genetics and socio-biology, as it too evolved. Reading Wilson (1975), for example, when he stated, 'Human genes have surrendered their primacy in human evolution to … culture', it was inferred that because genes were now seen to be affected by 'non-biological, super-organic factors', if playworkers were to comprehensively provide for children's evolutionary needs – which was how playwork was beginning by some to be perceived – play spaces had to mirror 'culture' as well as biology.

For a period of time there was lull. The 1980s and early 1990s were comparatively quiet periods for this developing relationship, although playworkers had more than enough to contend with, attempting to unpick the implications of the various scientific works already in existence and clarify their implications for practice. This unpicking resulted in, for example, work by King on play environment criteria, King and Hughes, and Hughes and Williams on the play process, Battram on possibility space, Gordon on Riskogenics,

6

Rennie on the ethics of confrontation and Sturrock on the play-worker as shaman.

From the mid 1990s until the present day, research on play and related areas began to be viewed as highly pertinent to the development of playwork theory as well as practice. In particular neuroscience, ecology, evolutionary psychiatry, neurology and evolutionary biology. For example:

- **Neuroscience.** See Stephen Siviy's (1998) chapter in *Animal Play* on the Neurobiological Substrates of play behaviour.
- **Ecology.** See Heinrich and Smolker's chapter on 'Play in Common Ravens', in the same publication.
- *Hermeneutics.* Defined as 'the theory and practice of interpretation and understanding, some knowledge of this discipline becomes particularly relevant when playworkers want to advocate on behalf of children – speak with "their", voice'. In 'Spots of Time', by Louise Chawla (2002), there are several useful signposts regarding the how's and why's of hermeneutics applications, including reference to what is described as Schleiermacher's astounding phrase, because 'each person contains a minimum of everyone else' (p. 205). How pertinent this phrase is to the underpinning evolutionary history of our own species.
- *Quantum Considerations.* Although this is a new and developing field, quantum evolution already has some relevance to our practice, and there are some links to the neurological processes described by McLean's Triune Brain Theory. Briefly it alludes to the duality of some of the organism's functions, that like subatomic particles themselves we are neither one thing nor another. For example, 'Consciousness appears to be parallel, in the sense that we can be aware of many items at once, but serial in the sense that we just have one stream of consciousness – we can't think two thoughts simultaneously' (p. 289). Thus, thought occurs in simultaneous series and parallel processes, not unlike the wave/particle duality. This quantum mechanical paradox, explained in the Copenhagen interpretation by Bohr, may go some way to providing a partial explanation of difficulties inherent in researching play – that because it contains ludic ambiguities, it defies – like the electron in quantum theory – definition, because the observer, and observational instruments actually impact on the phenomenon of play being observed.

There is also something about how play manifests itself that seems dual/quantum in nature. McFadden (2000) says, 'One part of the mind – the unconscious – is matter based; the other – the conscious mind – is an energy field. Both aspects of the mind are equally real; they just have different manifestations.' If this is so, I find myself asking if it is the same with play; that there is matter-based play, that which is mediated by the brain and which mediates brain growth, and energy based play, that which is not quite 'of the body'?

I have also long wondered if as children play, they give off an energy field, and apparently recent bioluminescence experiments show that this may be possible! (Kobayashi *et al.* 2009).

- **Cortical Maps.** Referred to primarily in Brown's chapter in *Animal Play* (although they are also explored by Damasio (1994), which he calls 'dispositional representations'), they are the outcome of the child's increasingly conscious engagement with its play environment. Brown suggests that regular visits to a particular spaces or place, where children engage each time in 'a slightly different choreography', 'provide the player with a continuous series of value laden scenes', which he says, 'may form our consciousness' (p. 254). He also describes play as 'this adaptive, flexible and pleasure laden action'.
- **Evolutionary Biology.** See Burghardt's 'Genesis' in *Animal Play*, or his chapter on the evolutionary origins of play, in *Animal Play*.
- **Evolutionary Psychiatry.** Read an excellent discussion on the role of archetypes and the environment of evolutionary adaptedness in good mental health, in Stevens and Price, *Evolutionary Psychiatry* (1996).
- **Neurology.** See various papers by Huttenlocher and McEwen. The former cited by Brian Sutton-Smith in *The Ambiguity of Play* (1997).

In Sutton-Smith, citing Huttenlocher, he suggests that 'the infant's brain's ability to constantly undergo physical and chemical changes as it responds to the environment is taken to suggest enormous plasticity', and that, 'Play's function ... may be to assist the actualisation of brain potential ...' (p. 225).

Citing Kotulak (1996), Sutton-Smith also states that 'an over abundance of cells and synapses is produced and the brain has to use them to make itself work' (p. 223). In fact Huttenlocher (1990, 1992), having

8

suggested that children under ten years of age have the potential to grow brains that are twice the potential size of children over that age, has proposed a sensitive period for plasticity, which far exceeds infancy, spanning from about eight months to eight years in length.

The playwork corollary of this is that anyone working in any way with children in early or middle-childhood cannot escape the potential importance of play in those children's lives during that time-span, given that 'children spend more time playing than any other waking activity' (PlayBoard 1990: 8).

EVOLUTIONARY PSYCHOLOGY

Evolutionary psychology is a fusion of two fields, cognitive psychology and evolutionary biology. Christened 'evolutionary psychology' by the anthropologist, Tooby, and psychologist, Cosmides (Pinker 1997: 23), its basic premise is that the design of the mind must have evolved by a process of natural selection. Central to evolutionary psychology is the premise that the mind, operating like a piece of computer software – a program – evolves new mental modules, as it solves the adaptive problems of survival and reproduction each organism is presented with in the environment in which it finds itself.

The role of genes in the evolution of the mind was felt to be a significant although not an exclusive factor. Evolutionary psychology accepts, for example, the work of behavioural geneticists, that environment as well as genes determines the mind and that 'genes often build different minds in response to different environments … changing the way in which the mind causes behaviour' (Evans and Zarate 1999: 159–60).

They continue, 'Indeed this flexibility is an important part of the way we are designed. Natural selection has programmed human development to be contingent on various environmental triggers' (ibid.: 160).

So evolutionary psychology offers a model in which a flexible mind – determined by the rigours of natural selection – triggered by various environmental factors, determines behaviour.

How does this happen? Naturally evolutionary psychologists have their own explanation but play is no stranger to genetics nor the playworker

9

to the notion of adaptation or flexibility, so could play be at the centre of the evolutionary psychology equation? And if so, could playwork have a pivotal environmental role? There are other similarities between these two areas, too.

For example, at the beginning of the last century, Hall's theory of recapitulation 'maintains that the play of children reflects the course of evolution from prehistoric hominids to the present' (Garvey 1977: 9), alluding to the role of genes in the recapitulation process. Several psychologists and ethologists, including Loizos (1967), Eibl-Eibesfeldt (1967, 1970) and Bruner (1972, 1974, 1976), claimed that the essence of play lies in combinatorial flexibility, requiring the restructuring of thought or action (see Sylva 1977: 60). Hutt *et al.* (1989) linked the idea of combinatorial flexibility to innovation (p. 225), whilst Sutton-Smith (1979) viewed these 'new combinations of thought' as providing 'an increase in the cognitive alternatives available' (p. 316).

Thus, there is a possibility that it is through the medium of play – itself a characteristic of many species and determined by the process of natural selection – that the evolution of mind may be facilitated. That the play drive exists to bring the human child into contact with the various features of its environment and that then, via playful recapitulation, the mind and genes are adapted as a consequence. Is this simplistic or useful conjecture?

Sutton-Smith offers this:

> 'play as novel adaptation, may have developed in two stages: the first as a reinforcement of potential synaptic variability through the performance of variable antics [flexibility], and the second as a fuller imitation of the evolutionary process itself, in which the organism models its own biological character [recapitulation]' (p. 229).

This suggests a relationship between the drive to play and the development of mind. However, in Konner (2010) Byers, in a far less circumspect quote, says 'The idea is that natural selection designed play to *shape brain development*, and most likely they are *directing their own brain assembly*.' This suggests two complementary processes are mediated by playing. One, the physical generation of brain, i.e., neurological material, and two, the organisation of that material in line with the child's immediate play experiences.

Perhaps this is what Byers is suggesting. That playing, perhaps drawing from what Panksepp (1998) identified as the thalamus area in the brain, is designed by natural selection to construct and organise a human brain that 'fits' and 'anticipates' as Dennett (1997) said, the organism's evolutionary needs. In other words, play is evolution's gift to those species that manifest it, simply because it enables them to not only adapt their brains as they play into adolescence and adulthood (Kroodsma 1981), but it also enables them to create, that is, construct and organise a brain that is created specifically for the world the child is in as it plays – a brain that may, for example, anticipate change; the need for adaptive potential; a flexible self, a migratory self!

So while play may not enable us to see into the future, it may still be ahead by years, of any scientific predictive mechanism of forecasting, because it provides an evolved interface between the complex internal human processes that keep human's functioning and the environmental changes that one day might lead us towards their extinction. Or to put it another way, play is an evolved conduit, a portal through which evolution has anticipated a bi-directional flow of needs and responses. The needs being what the body and mind want at any time, and the responses being what the universe can offer. If these are in synch then the species can continue, if not then perhaps time is limited. It is play itself that has evolved to take the pulse of both the organism and the planet, and it is this knowledge on which the theory and practice of evolutionary playwork is predicated.

ON THE ROLE OF THE ENVIRONMENT

Needless to say, the nature of environment is a vital factor in play-work – that is where we ply our trade, but it is also a vital factor in neural plasticity too. Whilst Sutton-Smith (1997) has drawn our attention to the role of environment in the plasticity phenomenon more recently, work by Bennett *et al.* (1964), Rosenzweig (1971), Rosenzweig *et al.* (1972) and Ferchmin and Eterovic (1979) discussed the implication on brain growth of different kinds of environments, suggesting that interaction with 'enriched' environments resulted in brain growth whilst interaction with 'impoverished' environments did not.

Bruner (1972) gave a fascinating pre-emptive analysis of this later work on brain growth, when he suggested that the evolutionary backdrop to rapid brain growth after birth was related to anatomical design, stating 'If a bigger-brained creature is to get through a smaller birth canal, there is required, of course, a smaller initial brain size and therefore, greater initial immaturity – the human brain grows from approximately 335 to 1300 cubic centimetres during development' (p. 37).

Whilst Bruner's figures may have been overtaken by more recent findings, e.g., Huttenlocher (1990), the implication of what he says is very interesting. For if, as a part of human evolution, a larger human brain becomes an outcome of natural selection, but a fully developed brain will not fit through the birth canal (Grof (1975) gives us a fascinating insight into the struggle human babies may endure during birth (pp. 95–153)), then nature's answer is to provide enormous potential for growth prior to birth, which is only realised once birth has taken place.

I take the Sutton-Smith and Huttenlocher material to imply that it is play that is the realising medium.

Sutton-Smith (1997) encapsulates this stating 'humans are born with more going for them than they will ever have again' (p. 225), emphasising the importance to development of the period described by Huttenlocher (1990, 1992) as 'the sensitive period'. Bjorkland and Green (1992) add to this by describing the key neonatal cognitive characteristics of children up to the age of five – i.e., during this period of massive brain growth – as 'unrealistic optimism, egocentricity and reactivity', or to put it another way, play (Sutton-Smith 1997: 226).

Thus a useful relationship between play, brain growth and environment begins to materialise. Play, described by Gould (1996) as a 'flexible, quirky, unpredictable, evolutionary potential for creative responses' (p. 44), interfacing with an 'enriched' environment, facilitates plasticity and 'actualises' novel connections (Sutton-Smith 1997).

However, later research by McEwen (1999), Balbernie (1999) and Perry (2001) also emphasises the potentially negative role of the environment on brain development, concluding that factors like stress can have a negative impact upon what McEwen terms 'adaptive plasticity' (p. 118). Analyses relating to the impact of 'impoverished' environments have also been available in the literature over the years. Its conclusions not only highlight the serious consequences of the

12

'play-deprivation' caused by them, but invites environmental reflection on what the defining characteristics of 'enrichment' might be, and clinical reflection on how the effects of 'play-deprivation' might be eliminated (Suomi and Harlow 1971; Huttenmoser and Degan-Zimmermann 1995; Chugani 1998).

Fox (1989) also discusses his concerns about the impact of modern technological environment on humans who are only adapted to what Bowlby called 'the environment of evolutionary adaptedness', the Palaeolithic environment of 20,000 years ago, inferring that human children, forced to play in an environment that dismisses millions of years of evolution may encounter problems. He says '[modern] society is only made possible by the grasping hand, binocular vision, and hand-eye co-ordination shaped by 70 million years in the trees. [But] it is as though only the last few thousand years are particularly privileged and the rest can simply be written off as pre-history' (p. 219). Fox suggests there will be consequences to this short-term view of what being human is. '[Our brain] is not an organ of cool rationality: it is a surging field of electrochemical activity replete with emotion and geared for a particular range of adaptive responses. Force it to try to work outside of that range for long enough, and it will act, it will rebel. It will regress to those pristine behaviours (including the very necessary aggressive ones) surrounding its primary functions, survival and reproduction.' This transformation is vividly demonstrated by Harlow's work in the early 1970s and in Stuart Brown's chapter 'Play as an Organising Principle', in *Animal Play*.

THE CHALLENGE FOR THE PLAYWORKER

The challenge for the playworker, posed by the literature, was and is considerable. For whilst yesterday's playleaders may not have felt strongly that they needed to be guided by the literature, today's playworkers cannot avoid it, and this development is highlighted by the almost exponential growth of playwork training in the 1980s and the subsequent development of NVQ and higher – Dip. HE, Degree, Masters and PhD – education outlets in the years that followed.

Now, not only does the prospective playworker need a better understanding of what play is, what it does and what facilitates it, she also has to wrestle with the enormously complex environmental and ethical issues I have alluded to above. A further complication for the professional has arisen as the designated and supervised play space has increasingly been identified as a compensatory medium for those children, who because of a whole raft of social and environmental factors, are playing *less*, are playing *outside* less, or are only able to play in a context when there are *adults present* (Hughes 1996b).

Playing less, as we have seen above, may negatively affect children's development and capacity to adapt. Playing outside less may similarly affect their development, but may also have the effect of dissociating children from the natural world, a dissociation which Orr (1993) suggests means 'that we will have cut ourselves off from the source of sanity itself' (p. 437). Playing in a continual adult context generates similar concerns, for there are numerous examples of adults making arbitrary judgements about what constitutes allowable, politically correct, safe and sanitised play (Hughes 1999c).

From an evolutionary perspective any development that creates in children a dissociation between the present and the past could cause enormous problems for them. Wilber (1996), discussing the evolution of human consciousness, highlights the problems that may result if human beings start, in the words of Ruse (1979), 'to control and direct their biological evolution' (p. 222).

Describing the human individual as a 'compound individual', Wilber states, 'compounded, that is, of all levels of reality that have unfolded prior to man's present stage, and capped by that present stage itself' (p. 169). Paraphrasing Hall's Theory of Recapitulation, Wilber continues 'We begin by repeating that each stage of evolution transcends but includes its predecessor ... that each stage of human evolution, although it transcends its predecessors, must include and integrate them in a higher unity'. He finishes with a stark warning: 'Failure to do so equals neurosis' (ibid.). In other words, if adults interfere with play, if they stop children engaging in certain types of play, then those children may become ill.

So the major lessons I can draw from the literature of the past thirty years are that play is critically important to human development and evolution; that it takes place most effectively in a variable, enriched environment, and although perhaps created by and operated by a team of adults, must not be adulterated by them, or contaminated by their non-play agendas.

14

WHY EVOLUTIONARY PLAYWORK?

Darwin is quoted by Gruber (1974: 54) as saying, 'Survival depends upon the organism remaking itself'. What I interpret this to mean is that at birth human children contextualise themselves in the here and now, as Byers suggests, but that playing enables this complex compound individual to continue to adapt as conditions dictate.

By interpreting the biological literature and integrating it into their principles and practice, those playworkers who perhaps more accurately designate themselves as evolutionary playworkers can begin more effectively to:

- facilitate play that shapes brain development, and enables children to directing their own brain assembly;
- create environments that enable children to construct and organise a brain that 'fits' and 'anticipates' their evolutionary needs;
- create and apply a practice that enables transcendence whilst avoiding the experience of play deprivation.

This book is called *Evolutionary Playwork* because it differs from *playwork*, as defined in Bonel and Lindon (1996) as 'managing the play environment and providing the resources which enable children's play' (p. 15), for example, by identifying and emphasising play as a powerful biological force which, I believe, may only be subsumed into any particular social model at the expense of the children it is attempting to serve. What the scientific literature says clearly is that, from an evolutionary perspective, we should not view our children as having been born into a static social preconception,but rather into a developing continuum. Children play to change, thus change rather than comfortable predictability must be the overriding characteristic of the play space.

Else and Sturrock (1998) get much closer, by defining playwork as 'work[ing] with children in the expansion of their potential to explore and experience through play'.

I would only add: 'in a context which always prioritises their biological nature and their need for flexibility and adaptive potential'. This is in line with what Johan Huizinga (1939) stated in *Homo Ludens*: 'Play is older than culture, for culture however inadequately defined, always presupposes human society, and animals (or children) have not waited for man to teach them how to play'.

15

The structure of this book

Evolutionary Playwork is divided into fourteen chapters, ranging from a history of its development, to an exploration of what is Evolutionary Play, along with chapters focussing on its more technical aspects. It examines Evolutionary Playwork, and the Evolutionary Playspace and asks 'Is the Playspace working – How will we know?' It also provides some previously unpublished Conference presentations under Deeper Considerations.

In Chapter 10, 'The Evolutionary Playworker', we have an input from playworker, Kelda Lyons, who has provided an up-to-the-minute fix on what practical playwork involves.

MICK'S STORIES

Most of the chapters now have what I have called Mick's Stories from Mick Conway – another highly talented observer of children's behaviour, with a long track record in playwork. They include some 'laugh out loud' accounts of his observations of children, although those of a nervous disposition should be warned that some of them contain swearing.

After growing up on a farm in Co. Tyrone, Mick started his life in playwork on Bermondsey Adventure Playground in London. In 1985 he joined Hackney Play Association, and became its Director in 1996. Mick co-authored *Quality in Play* with Tony Farley, and worked with Bob Hughes on what became the Playwork Principles. At the time of writing he works for Play England.

Chapter 13 is entitled 'Some Deeper Considerations', and includes various papers, articles and presentations I have written over the past decade. My intention by including them, is to help the reader to access my thinking from a number of directions in the hope that if one presentation is not clear enough about a particular point, then another one may be.

MY REASONS FOR WRITING THE SECOND EDITION

My primary motivation is my awareness of how much has changed in the decade since the first edition was written. Knowledge has evolved, and where possible I have incorporated at least a fleeting reference to what I think are important developments. The context for Evolutionary Play, Evolutionary Playwork and the kinds of spaces in which they might take place have also changed dramatically for many children. The number of natural spaces operated by playworkers has declined, whilst those dominated by expensive, entertaining but essentially evolutionarily irrelevant fixed play areas has increased dramatically. There is a lesson there.

Governments became interested during the 1990s and 2000s, and then lost interest again, as the point of the exercise was buried in a shambles of trivial politics and badly thought through strategies. Certainly the play movement must come of age, but as a cutting edge leader of new opinion, rather than becoming again subsumed into the social quagmire of ChildCare, Early Years Education, After School and Sports and Recreation. If there is not enough within the pages to justify such a stance then I have not done my job.

I doubt there will be a third edition, this is my best shot, to try and say something about perhaps the most wonderful and incredible gift humankind has ever been given, save the gift of life itself. For although there is much to be doomy and gloomy about in the short term, and this probably dominates the text, this book is really a celebration of our good fortune at having randomly evolved such an incredible mechanism as play. All I have tried to do is to argue why ensuring that we utilise that gift to the best of our human ability would be a good and civilised move. Of course it is up to the rest of our species to do the 'ensuring'. Not only are the outcomes of playing a miracle, the effects of playing are too. It makes us feel good, happy, at one, excited, not just in a fairground way, but as if all our ancestors are joining in. For unlike most of what we do, *play* is something we have always done, the laughter of new brain growth and increased flexibility echoing through primeval forests, in caves, across savannas, on cold ice and hot sand, in sierras and underground. Now as we move from a world of industrialisation, to one of micro technology and beyond, might we be laughing less, or less spontaneously, as the emphasis shifts from the simple, child-controlled interactions – climbing, skipping, singing – to those controlled by commerce and sedentary consumerism? I don't know, it seems like it and it does worry me. Maybe that just comes with growing old!

17

I hope you will find what is contained within these pages, interesting and useful?

Bob Hughes
PlayEducation
Spring 2011

CHAPTER 1

A SHORT HISTORY OF THE DEVELOPMENT OF EVOLUTIONARY PLAYWORK

Evolutionary Playwork has a development history of over forty years, which has seen it evolve from the point of view of a small number of practitioners to what we call an 'application', with a growing theoretical base, and a whole range of different and unique practices.

The following chronology and explanation was originally developed around February 2004 (revised February 2010) as part of the support material being prepared by Gordon Sturrock, Mick Conway and I, for the development of the Playwork Principles. It is included in this text to give the reader a flavour of the 'main' events that have occurred during the development of *Evolutionary Playwork* up until the present day.

It charts my own playwork experiences and as such is a personal view of playwork history; it is an undeniably subjective and partial view and does not pretend to be anything else. On no account should the reader assume that this is a comprehensive account of everything that went on in generic playwork. Individuals, events and publications that they may judge deserving to be prominent features may not even be included.

As I write (March 2010), playwork is moving in several different directions simultaneously. It has become a subject of academic study. It is becoming an arm of government social policy – albeit a rather small arm – immersed to some extent into a new primeval learning soup of working with children – a soup containing all manner of professionals, and where studying playwork will be one of several options. It is becoming part of the explanation of how we should deal with the alienation and illnesses caused by the proliferation of institutions and technologies that dwarf most human beings, and it is seen by a growing number as a potent factor in creating bonds between current and future generations of children and the Earth itself. I have some concerns about the direction some of these developments are taking and the impact they are having on the child's essential, individual evolutionary drive to freely interact with the world and the universe – a vital component of evolutionary play itself.

I have long stated that for playwork to flourish, a new mind-set that is able to see the difference in these global warming times, between bio-evolutionary bases and socio-economic ones, is needed. We have yet to reach the point where the development of our species' children through adult-free unrestricted play is viewed as our most important social objective.

In the future we may look back and see this as a period of missed opportunity. The problem though is that it has always been a human failing not to see the wood for the trees, and that blindness – that our salvation, our resistance to extinction lies in the child's world, and not in the adult's – may be what marks us out as unable, perhaps incapable of resisting the pressures of extinction in the end.

Having said that, whatever else this book is, it is a celebration of childhood and play. I hope the reader will sense that to be an evolutionary playworker is a privilege and an honour. We are members of a fortunate group who, as well as seeing the worst that humanity can throw at its children, have also had the opportunity to re-visit the world of our own childhood, by looking, and sometimes even passing through the mirror, or as it was called in 2009, 'the wee gap' (O'Neil) between the world we inhabit and that inhabited by the child.

TRACKING THE EVOLUTION OF OUR MEANING: A PERSONAL CHRONOLOGY OF THE DEVELOPMENT OF PLAYWORK CONSCIOUSNESS AND THE EVOLUTION OF THE IDEA OF PLAYWORK

1   1969–1979
The genesis of playwork
The playworker as role model
Playwork as manifest[1] objective

20

Playwork as a generic vocation
The NPFA as the lead organisation, Abernethy and Satterthwaite
APWA, LAPA and Thurrock
It's Child's Play
Berg, Goodman, Holt, Illich, Neill and Colin Ward
Joe Benjamin and Jack Lambert
JNCTPL > JNCTP
Notes for Adventure Playworkers

2   1980–1985
Playwork derives its own definition of play.
The ethnicising and genderising of playwork
The playworker as victim
Playwork as manifest[2] subjective
Playwork as social intervention
Manchester and the health and safety agenda
Talking about play
From Riots to ACPR Ltd and PlayBoard
PlayEd 82, 83, 84, 85

3   1986–1995
Swansea and Blencathra
Playwork as child centred and co-operative
Playwork as ChildCare/PlayCare
Risk as a health and safety issue – birth of the litigious culture
The playworker as facilitator, the child is in control
The playworker as shaman – The genesis of 'deep' playwork
Playwork as manifest[3]
PlayWales, The NCPRU, PlayBoard (NI), Play Scotland, The Sport's
Council and SPRITO
NVQ/Dip HE in playwork
Leeds Metropolitan University
The PlayMovement
The National Voluntary Council for Children's Play and National Play
Information Centre
International Play Journal
PlayEd 86, 87, 88, 89, 90

4   1996–1999
Playwork has a scientific rationale
A playworker's taxonomy of play types

1   1969–1979

The genesis of playwork

Until about 1972, playworkers were called playleaders, and although they worked in play settings, the assumption by employers was that they were rather like the youth leaders of the day. Jess Milne, formerly of Hackney Play Association and now freelance, is probably the longest serving/surviving playworker in the UK. He started work at Ampton Street AP in the Kings Cross area of London in 1966.

The playworker as role model

In the early days, playworkers/leaders saw a large part of their function as providing children with a stereotypical model of socially responsible behaviour. However, that view soon began to change. This was partly due to our evolving perception and understanding of what play was and what play provision was for, and partly due to our intense immersion in the lives of the children we were working with – an immersion that often made our professional expectations unrealistic, when so many had life-chances that were limited by poverty, unemployment and poor health.

Playwork as manifest[1] objective

Playwork practice at this time was dominated by predictable reactions to the children's playing context. A lack of trees, hills and countryside prompted structure building. A lack of the opportunity to engage with new experiences created the justification for community artists and the use of scrap materials. The perceived lack of depth of interest in children in society in general created a desire to advocate for them and to represent them. Playworkers at the time were very objective about what they were observing and what they were doing about it. However, what they saw were the obvious economic and geographical manifestations of life in the 1970s and they and most of their employers and funders reacted to that with a type of play-orientated class analysis, i.e., that play provision was a 'working-class' amenity that would cut down truancy, vandalism and crime. There was also, at this time, a developing move by communities themselves to squat on unused land and to develop it as playspace.

Playwork as a generic vocation

As a consequence, not only was there an expectation that the playleader/worker would be all things to all people, there was also response from the leader/workers themselves that that was how they expected to be perceived. It was not uncommon for playworkers in the mid 1970s to describe their job as part parent, teacher, social worker, policeman, advocate and so on. This is almost a classic description of a community worker.

The National Playing Fields Association (NPFA) as the lead organisation, Abernethy and Satterthwaite

During the 1970s and early 1980s the NPFA was the lead national play organisation in England, providing advice, guidance and some grant aid to voluntary and statutory bodies who made provision for children's play (although in London and elsewhere, local authorities and charities also provided grants). The NPFA was headed by Lt. Col. R. G. (Bob) Satterthwaite, and its Children and Youth Department (headed by Drummond Abernethy) had a regional staff of eight experienced play people, some of whom are still involved or on the periphery of playwork, including Rob Wheway (freelance), Tony Chilton (retired), Fraser Brown (Leeds Metropolitan University), Bob Hughes (PlayEducation), Paul Eyre (retired), Felicity Sylvester (freelance).

As well as providing a Regional Officer Team and *PlayTimes*, an authoritative magazine (Peter Heseltine was its editor), the NPFA ran lively playworker meetings all over England. Not only did this give playworkers the chance to debate issues they felt were important, it gave them the opportunity to meet other playworkers, a very important development at a time when playworkers were very isolated.

The NPFA also had a smaller presence in Scotland, Wales and Northern Ireland, but this waned as they developed their own National Organisations. Different forms of play provision, including adventure

24

playgrounds, also existed in different population centres including Belfast, Cardiff and Glasgow.

APWA, LAPA and Thurrock

The Adventure Playworkers Association was also formed in the early 1970s to facilitate the discussion of professional issues. LAPA, the London Adventure Playground Association and precursor to PLAY-LINK, was also formed around this time. A Playleadership Course was also operating at Thurrock College, the genesis of the NVQs, Diplomas and Degrees which dominate our current FE/HE educational perspective. It also breathed life into all of the 'off the shelf' training in playwork which pervaded the 1980s pre-qualification period.

It's Child's Play

In the mid 1970s a new playwork charity arrived called 'Make Children Happy', run by the late Ian Fletcher. It produced *It's Child's Play*, a playwork newspaper, and several publications on working with children, including my *Notes for Adventure Playworkers*.

Berg, Goodman, Holt, Illich, Neill and Colin Ward

Playwork's early academic roots are not in Bruner and Sylva as one might expect. They are in the more anarchic, libertarian works of the time that extolled creativity, community, educational justice and freedom.

Joe Benjamin and Jack Lambert

Although the late Joe Benjamin's *In Search of Adventure* and Lambert and Pearson's *Adventure Playgrounds* captured some of the essence of 'play', they also acted as a catalyst for the transition from playleaders into playworkers. The books were viewed as romantic and did not reflect the reality that many playworkers were having to deal with in their daily lives. *In Search of Adventure* is currently being translated into Japanese!

JNCTPL > JNCTP

The playwork politicians had arrived. The Joint National Committee on Training for PlayLeadership was formed and then mutated into The Joint National Committee on Training for Playwork. Later JNCTP was instrumental in creating the PIEG, the precursor to SPRITO (Playwork), which then became SkillsActive.

Notes for Adventure Playworkers

Notes was written by Hughes in 1975 as a 'warts and all' exploration of the Adventure Playground ethos at the time.

Commentary

Although many veteran playworkers are as guilty as each other for the generic identity of early playwork (see above), its developmental direction was equally to do with the social and political climate at the time. As now, many of the children early playworkers worked with, experienced repression, abuse, neglect and being misunderstood, and playworkers wanted to show them that they cared about them and advocated for them. It would be some years before a truly play-based analysis for playwork was available. What this early period began to establish was that although part of the root meaning of playwork lay in a genuine affection for the children playworkers worked with – creating an almost parental defensiveness of their right to exist, tinged with a rejection of the kind of society that smothered their creative impulse and corrupted their world with a controlling adult agenda – the driving force of playwork came from the gradual recognition that their own childhood had been a hugely significant period for them, and that play had been the single most important component in it, One they would draw from daily in their adult lives.

In other words, one of the insights for the early playworker was in the realisation that to the children we worked with, play, its freedom, its diversity and quality, was a far more important influence than we had ever thought. Play was not something to exploit, manipulate or corrupt as they had felt playleadership had done. Play was a cosmic force that we all had a share in and were all hugely influenced by. Along with this realisation, came another. If playwork was going to successfully facilitate or enable 'play' – the play we were having insights about – then there would be many ethical, practical and political dilemmas that would need to be identified and overcome.

It may seem odd now, that the gradual dawning of the importance of play in children's lives only came after many playworkers had been practising for years. However, playwork then (or playleadership to be more accurate) was more about behaviour management and citizenship than it was about acknowledging the power of play and facilitating that. What changed that was the opening up of the opportunity for playworkers themselves to challenge ideas through discussion and debate.

2   1980–1985

Playwork derives its own definition of play

In the period 1982–84 PlayEducation developed a definition of play incorporating the features of free choice, personal direction and intrinsic motivation. One articulation of it was included in the JNCTP Recommendations on Training for Playwork, October 1985.

The ethnicising and genderising of playwork

Until at least the late 1970s the great majority of playworkers were white and male. During the next five years, however, playwork's demography was 'transformed' by a huge influx of white women playworkers, together with male and female playworkers from other communities. This change was infinitely enriching to us all, but it wasn't without its problems.

The playworker as victim

This new influx of playworkers brought to a tired and debilitated workforce assertiveness and confidence that served to invigorate the whole field but there was a price to pay. Whereas certain communicative modes (name-calling, physical competition, and other forms of what might now be termed oppressive behaviour) had previously been interpreted as the normal way in which children learned about a world containing both diversity and power, and about their position in that world at any given moment, with greater awareness of the impact of racism and sexism, many new playworkers would not tolerate either. In many cases this analysis stemmed directly from the experiences of the workers themselves, who then assumed that what they had felt, was what the children felt in similar circumstances.

Playwork as manifest[2] subjective

So playwork's analysis shifted during the early part of this period from manifest objective to manifest[2] subjective. Manifest[2] because although playworkers were still basing their intervention upon observable material, it had changed from the socio-economic impact of poverty to 'the impact of gender and race oppression'.

Subjective, because the intervention rationale of this new playwork was not based upon an objective view of the child in a socio-economic and/or political context that often had little to do with the playworker, but on a subjective view that had everything to do with the playworker's own experiences.

Playwork practice, which had been personal but detached, now became just personal.

This was a hugely important growth period for playwork, for, as with the previous period, it faced all playworkers with issues that needed dealing with – personally, socially and professionally. As well as raising awareness and confronting prejudice, this was also a period when on the ground the relationship of play (the biological phenomenon) to playwork (the means of facilitating that phenomenon) was subverted by these other non-play based rhetorics. It wasn't long before policies relating to racism, sexism and general behavioural management began to be applied to children's behaviour when they were playing, in what up until that time had been regarded by most people, as the children's space.

Playwork as social intervention

And so play provision began to be seen as an extension of embryonic social policies that were, as they had been in the previous period,

28

more to do with youth crime, violence and stereotypes than about play and playwork.

Manchester and the health and safety agenda

Playworkers were not a particularly diplomatic group – their work was often physically hard and the context violent and difficult. In the early day this physically could result in explosions of verbal and sometimes even physical violence during confrontations between workers and older children. Playwork's natural enemy were recreation departments, which playworkers saw as lazy, adult orientated and wasteful, particularly in the context of improving the level of resources applied to work with children. The latent animosity between these departments and playworker or adventure playground, boiled over in the late 1970s and early 1980s when local authorities took drastic action against adventure playgrounds around the UK in the changing health and safety climate. In the late 1970s, Puddlebrook Adventure Playground, which had earlier been run by Bob Hughes, was dismantled, and in Manchester in the early 1980s, seven Adventure Playgrounds lost their funding. In 1982, NPFA published 'TASAP', 'Towards a Safer Adventure Playground' written mainly by the now sadly deceased playworkers Bill McCullough and Frank King. Quite obviously confrontation would not work, but neither would the argument, continually put forward, that the child's need to play was obvious. Playwork needed a more evidence-based analysis.

Talking about play

At about this time (1982), Bob Hughes and Hank Williams were commissioned by the NPFA's Play Times to write a series of articles entitled 'Talking about Play'. The articles talked exclusively about play and playwork, which was very unusual given the current political context. However, the reason for writing them was a deep-felt concern about the drift playwork was experiencing, as a consequence of having social rhetorics but not having a tangible theoretical base, from which to derive and articulate strategies and practice. For, although sexism and racism formed an important part of the context both for play and playwork, they were neither, so what was?

The analysis contained in Talking about Play provided for the first time in playwork a link between play, the development of survival strategies and the first use of the term *flexibility* in a playwork context.

From Riots to ACPR Ltd and PlayBoard

Also in 1982, England* experienced a high level of social unrest particularly in Brixton (London) and in Toxteth (Liverpool 8). One of the many reasons given for it at the time was the lack of opportunities for children and young people. Michael Heseltine, the then Secretary of State for the Environment, set up a task force headed by Ed Burman who ran Interaction. In cities and towns with significant ethnic minority populations, play provision received greatly-increased 'Urban Programme' funding with little in the way of strings attached.

One outcome of the task forces' deliberations was that in 1983–1984, the Association for Children's Play and Recreation (ACPR Ltd), was created, together with the appointment of a lead Minister who would take responsibility for children's play. ACPR was eventually renamed PlayBoard. It died in England a few years later, but its name still lives on in Northern Ireland, where it is still the lead organisation for children's play there.

The other part of the ACPR equation was the demise of the NPFA's Children and Youth department, which ceased to exist when ACPR came into being. Most of its Regional Officer Team found work with the newly formed ACPR.

> *I am aware that Northern Ireland's population were enduring the Troubles, and that there and in Scotland and Wales, important playwork developments were occurring too. But, from the perspective of the development of playwork *per se* I judge that the Inner City riots in England at that time probably played the most significant role. BH

PlayEd 82, 83, 84, 85

Another innovation was the appearance in 1982 of the PlayEd Conferences. Organised by a small independent agency, PlayEducation, to

30

bring playworkers, academics and especially scientists together. These conferences still occur from time to time.

Commentary

The main lesson from this period was that, although other rationales could be applied to playwork, playwork's basic purpose could only be drawn from the play literature. Playgrounds were destroyed under the guise of health and safety irrespective of their value to children. One reason the authorities got away with what would now be seen as an attack on children's rights was because the playwork field argued the value of provision for children on the same grounds as local and central government did, rather than from an original playwork perspective rooted in the literature.

However, this was not an easy time to be developing a theoretical base either, Compared to its heyday in the 1970s when *Play: It's role in Development and Evolution*, and *The Biology of Play* were published, the early 1980s were rather unproductive, although a few groundbreaking publications demonstrated that this was just a temporary blip.

Playwork was also suffering from internal divisions and that too left it vulnerable. The development of ACPR demonstrated in government, a clearly perceived need for play provision for children. But instead of offering government playwork's expertise and evidence regarding what worked, and even what that meant, ACPR increasingly saw its role as carrying out government instructions, rather than advising it from a position of knowledge and experience of working directly with children. (There are parallels with how other more recent National Bodies have also seen their role in their relationship with Government, here.) The perceived difference between evolutionary insight on the one hand, and societal collaboration on the other, created a schism, which still exists today.

Having said that, this tranche of playwork development indicates that playwork was evolving and that questions relating, perhaps as much to British society as to playwork, were being explored through debate and changes in working practices. Nevertheless, playworkers were beginning to realise the importance of a professional ownership of playwork wherever that ownership took it. That what constituted the theory and practice of playwork was increasingly viewed as the remit of those with first-hand experience of playwork rather than those with management, financial or political – local authority and voluntary organisation – expertise.

3 1986–1995

Swansea and Blencathra

During this period PlayEducation held a number of ground-breaking teach-ins exploring practice and policy. The first batch was held at Swansea University, in the mid-1980s, whilst the second took place at the Blencathra Centre in the Lake District. More about Blencathra later.

Playwork as child centred and co-operative

As usual, the Playwork field continued to reflect on its contemporary identity. Like the sexism and racism it had sought to eradicate, it began to see the identity it had fostered as potentially adulterating and repressive and began to return to a more child-centred and more caring articulation of playwork, than had been manifested in the early 80's. Perhaps playworkers felt that whilst they still had to bear down hard on these manifestations of intolerance, they had swung too far in the other direction. During this period, a set of values and assumptions were developed for the field, to inform the newly evolving NVQ and to provide the field with an articulation of its perceived values base. This articulation was a valuable step in the field's development, but because it was not derived from, or grounded in either a theoretical or philosophical base that was rooted in the authentic evolution of playwork itself, many viewed it as problematic.

Playwork as ChildCare/PlayCare

Childcare organisations began to articulate playwork as a form of child-care or what they called 'playcare' practice. This analysis was disputed by many playworkers as both childcare and playcare were parent-, not play- or child-driven services. This development arose mainly from the implementation of the Children Act (1989).

32

Risk as a health and safety issue – birth of the litigious culture

Increasingly during this period another basic premise of playwork – that children need to be able to access and assess risk – suffered significant erosion, primarily from the punitive and often incorrect application/implementation of health and safety legislation. One reason for this was that parents were becoming increasingly willing to sue local authorities if their children had accidents whilst playing at play projects/grounds or on fixed equipment. Not only did this undermine the very nature of play, their action was frequently unjustified and not down to negligent behaviour on the part of playworkers or anyone else. But employers preferred to settle out of court, rather than risk losing the enormous sums that would accrue from losing cases. However, although by then, there were a few expert witnesses for the defence, Peter Heseltine (UK) being one of them, and Paul Hogan (USA) being another, the outcome was that for years to come, many children became increasingly wrapped in cotton wool by parents, unable to risk the kind of injuries children had always suffered when playing, in order to experience the joys of play itself. However, the real culprit were the local authorities who thought it better to eradicate playful risk taking than risk expensive litigation themselves. At the time of writing (2010), although one senses change in the air, this is still generally the case even though an increasing number of parents want their children to experience risk.

The playworker as facilitator, the child is in control

During this period, however, other more positive developments also came about. Play was increasingly being perceived in playwork as a process that the child might be genetically programmed to engage in and that the playworkers' function was that of facilitator – in two senses. The first was that the playworker facilitated play by providing an environment in which children would know intuitively that play was anticipated. The second was that the playworker facilitated play by 'refereeing' the space between groups of children in order to ensure that the artificial nature of the play spaces and the wide range of children they attracted did not detract from children engaging in play in the first place. During this crucial period playworkers also began to return power back to children by recognising that whilst at play children should, where possible, be in control both of what they did, and why they did it.

The playworker as shaman – The genesis of 'deep' play work, the loss of Frank King

The 1989 Played Conference in Cardiff saw the first articulation of the playworker as shaman (by Gordon Struck) and began what is now a familiar journey for play work into the depth psychologies. Frank King died.

Playwork as manifest[3]

This is the final period for playwork as a manifest discipline. Having evolved from manifest objective, through manifest subjective it has finally become manifest external, experiencing the dictat of government (although not of specific legislation), for the first time, particularly through the development of the NVQ and the influence of the Sport's Council. Playwork was being told what to think and what to do. Needless to say, the field of playwork did not react well.

PlayWales, The NCPRU, PlayBoard (NI), Play Scotland, The Sport's Council and SPRITO

From the development and subsequent demise of ACPR, a number of new playwork organisations developed. Wales developed Play-Wales, Scotland, Play Scotland and Northern Ireland, PlayBoard. In England things became complicated. The development of ACPR had linked play to recreation (a completely unrelated idea in the scientific literature). After the demise of ACPR, another organisation was created, The NCPRU (The National Children's Play and Recreation Unit). Although it attempted to walk the wire between the two ideas – play and recreation. Play was also being subsumed into sport, as the Sport's Council had more influence in the governance of play.

34

The NVQ and Dip HE in playwork

Until now formal playwork education had not existed. But the desire of the 'field' for a formal qualification, and the creation of conducive academic conditions by NCPRU, brought about the development both of a competency-based, and academic qualification (see Leeds Metropolitan University).

Leeds Metropolitan University

Also in 1989 the Dip HE in Playwork was launched by Fraser Brown, Stephen Rennie and Sue Palmer. This has since blossomed into courses that go as far as Masters. Now LMU also playworkers studying to PhD level.

The PlayMovement

The creation of The PlayMovement was an attempt at bringing the disparate factions of play/playwork together under an appropriate political umbrella. It was initiated in the late 1980s at a PlayEd Conference in Bolton. My memory is that it was colonised by a confused 'green' lobby mentality, and although it lasted for a couple of years and held meetings in Newcastle, Bristol and London, it finally lost its way and disappeared.

The National Voluntary Council for Children's Play and the National Play Information Centre

The demise of the NCPRU was also not long in coming, and it was followed by the creation of the National Voluntary Council for Children's Play, housed at NCB, this heralded the crucial development of the National Play Information Centre (now the NPIS).

International Play Journal

Sadly the *IPJ* suffered a similar fate to the Play Movement and NCPRU although it lasted longer than both. Three issues a year for three years established that an international Journal exploring play and playwork was feasible and viable: even though the publishers disagreed.

PlayEd 86, 87, 88, 89, 90

PlayEd Conferences continue to offer the cutting edge view of playwork throughout this period, often acting as a lightning rod for the raw emotions that many playworkers felt.

Commentary

This was the period in Playwork's development when it exercised its existential angst and asked who am I and what do I stand for? The previous period had been dominated by hammer-wielding white male adventure playworkers, but in a relatively short space of time white women and women and men from minorities had replaced many of them. Predictably the new face of playwork asked, 'Where to now?' Perhaps inevitably the exploration was routed through personal perceptions of injustice and abuse, and playwork became a feminist and multicultural projection. This broadened playwork's own internal analysis, it had the effect of softening terminology (like child-centred) and woke male playworkers in particular up to the reality that female children might be getting very little out of provision as it was then constituted. 'Girls only' nights were tried, and religious festivals from around the world were celebrated. I don't remember them being particularly successful, and it's certainly my perception that these 'tweaks' were tried without any genuine interest in their relevance to the evolving prism of playwork. Brown and Lomax (1969) talk of play deprivation being as damaging to females as to males, meaning perhaps that the problem is not male but human. The question was, 'Can playwork identify play experiences that apply specifically to to female children, and by offering them ensure that girls are as protected as boys against play deprivation, or should we assume that an enriched play space that incorporated the spirit of, for example, the playwork menu (see Chapter 4), would provide an appropriate play backdrop for girls and boys alike?'

In *Homo Ludens*, Johan Huizinga, states, 'Play is older than culture, for culture, however inadequately defined, always presupposes human

36

society, and animals have not waited for man to teach them their playing'. What this implies is first, that adult culture is irrelevant in the play setting. If a culture does exist it is the mutating culture created by the children themselves; second, that the level of intervention being tried during this period is adulterative; and third, that the play needs of all children, irrespective of parental background, are always the same, give or take some emphasis. Perhaps the best way to describe this era, is that it was the one in which playworkers had to check out some important principles and feelings and that meant chasing some developmental red herrings, and going down some dead ends and blind alleys. It was a time when the world inside the wire and outside the wire became blurred, and not for the first time, an adulterating agenda was allowed to hijack play and dominate the playspace for a while.

4   1996–1999

Playwork has a scientific rationale

Although this period, like the others, is one that reflects a remarkable level of change, the changes which took place are of a type and magnitude that are not reflected in any other period save the current one. For most of its existence playwork had to rely on a manifest analysis which as well as having the effect of positioning playwork's *raison d'être* inaccurately, left playwork continually vulnerable to the charge that it was ineffective. It was effective within its own perceived parameters, but not within those posed from without. Almost from its inception, playwork had suffered from imposed identities which had been defined either by the agendas of its funders or by individuals, groups or organisations with power and a willingness to adapt their own reasons for existence to mirror the current political or social policy climate. Needless to say this was a continually debilitating and diversionary experience for those with an analysis of playwork, which although continually evolving as knowledge and experience dictated, was rooted in the specifics of play as a manifestation of biological evolution and development.

However, during this next period something changed, and playwork's power and confidence grew as a result. What that was, was that whilst playworkers had long known intuitively of the links between children's play, species evolution and well-being, it wasn't until this period that it could be shown that the scientific evidence agreed, and that, that made a convincing theoretical articulation of playwork possible, which made sense from a funders' point of view and from that of the practising playworker.

A Playworker's Taxonomy of Play Types

Now a component of playwork practice could be articulated as the facilitation of playtypes, for example, a phenomenon well documented in the scientific and playwork literature and which had proven links to the notion of play as a developmental medium for social skills, problem solving, therapy, imagination and fantasy, coping with metaphysical issues, physical fitness and so on, and all of it was cited in the scientific literature.

This is more important than may at first be thought. Many playworkers knew from their own experiences, and from those of their children, how important play was to development, but what they needed was more accessible literature that would make it possible to take the lessons from the literature itself and apply them to their own practice. Playwork was not only a 'made-up' profession, it was almost as many 'made-up' professions as there were playworkers. What the science did was make it possible for all playworkers to have the same rationale for what they did. It provided a comprehensive basis for sound theory and intelligent practice that all playworkers could learn. It meant that there was such a discipline as 'Playwork'.

Playwork as compensatory

Playwork was also being described as a compensatory discipline. Meaning that playworkers could learn to identify any perceived deficits in children's experience of play types, for example, and make compensatory responses for them, using environmental modification (see Chapter 11).

38

The playworker as observer, analyst and preparer

How playwork was performed was also coming under increasing scrutiny as playworkers were being described more as observers of children's behaviour, as analysts of it and of the preparers of the play space, rather than as interveners in children's play. Until now it had been felt as legitimate by some, when asked 'What is your job?', to answer 'To play with children'. With a growing scientific basis for playwork's evolving analysis this view was seen as increasingly inappropriate, both from the perspective of what playwork existed to address, and from the new perspective of the potential for the contamination or adulteration of children's play by adults. For not only was the practice of adulteration viewed as moving the ownership of their play from children to adults, it was also viewed as diverting the normal flow of the child's play away from the direction of its biological/evolutionary drive and into one more suited to the needs of the adult and of contemporary society.

Playwork as latent[1]

Until this period playwork had mainly been concerned with the manifest content of facilitating play, like knowing first aid, being able to build structures, staff and site management, arbitrating between groups of children and being a source of advice and guidance within and between genders, cultures and abilities. Now playwork was beginning to explore the hidden, symbolic, latent nature of play and ask, what is our role here? One response – in the embryo of its development – was that of therapy. (See the Colorado Paper, below.) Another was in the facilitation of play as an evolutionary mechanism.

Play is a biological mechanism?

Although this was hardly an original conclusion – playworkers were well aware that the great volume of research on play had been done from the perspective of play as a biological phenomenon – what was new was that playwork and playworkers were increasingly articulating their professional analysis in this form, as the language became more familiar and the power of the processes involved became clearer.

39

At last the hugely complex nature of play was revealing itself – much as the constellations had revealed themselves to astronomers – and playwork's articulation was maturing as a consequence.

Children's Play Council

The Children's Play Council developed out of the NVCCP. Like its predecessor the CPC never really developed into a voice for playwork. Although it did publish the rather derivative 'Best Play', used at the time by many local authorities, to review their play services.

Play as SPNs

In 1999, the term Stereotypical Play Narrative or SPN (Hughes, 2000) was coined to describe the effects of a particular kind of adulteration. The term SPN was used to describe the impact that adults can have on manipulating children's play behaviour. Either by depriving children of free choices through their (adults') colonisation of the play space, or by the forceful contamination of the child's experience by that of the adult. The result being that the child felt it had continually to frame its play from the perspective of the adult's potential reaction to it. The overall effect being that the child's play content was determined by an adult who had power over it. This has two effects. The first was that the child's play becomes stereotyped and as such bore little relation to the spontaneous, goalless behaviour that is authentic play. (Given the later revelations regarding play deprivation this is probably very harmful in itself.) The second was that while the child was engaged in an SPN it was not engaged in authentic play, with a consequent loss of any of play's benefits.

Although SPNs potentially exist in every manifestation where adults work with children, they are more likely in custodial, i.e., child care situations, where children cannot freely leave.

The Colorado Paper

Although somewhat complex and concentrated, this is without doubt one of the most important and analytical papers to come out of playwork

40

since its genesis. The Colorado Paper, written by Gordon Sturrock and Perry Else for the IPA/USA Triennial Conference in June 1998, under the title 'The Playground as therapeutic space: playwork as healing', explores both the play process and playwork at a depth unimagined a decade or even five years earlier. The paper introduces many terms that are commonplace with theorists and practitioners today, including 'the ludic ecology', play frame, containment, play cues (although the notion of meta-communication had been recognised for some time, it had not been put into such an all-embracing context before), the meta-lude (although this had appeared in the *International Play Journal* earlier), issue and return (of play cues), termination or decay (of play cues), the ludic cycle, dysplay and adulteration. More than anything else the Colorado Paper demonstrated that authoritative work regarding the relationship between playwork and the phenomenon of play could be written by and for playworkers without reference or apology to other more established disciplines.

The Ambiguity of Play

Brian Sutton-Smith's book *The Ambiguity of Play* (1997), also represented a watershed in the development of playwork, primarily because, among other things, it alerted playwork to some important developments in neurology's understanding of the human brain, which had powerful implications for playwork practice.

Like Bruner's (1972) *The Nature and Uses of Immaturity*, and Sylva's (1977) *Play and Learning*, the *Ambiguity of Play* is a text that playworkers will gain insights from, regarding the beautiful complexity and essential nature of play to human beings for many years.

Play Environments: A Question of Quality

At the same time as the publication of *A Playworker's Taxonomy of PlayTypes*, I made an attempt to tackle the difficult subject of the quality of play environments in *Play Environments: A Question of Quality* (Hughes 1996, PLAYLINK). It suggested quality practice indicators, and introduced the notion of IMEE (Intuition, Memory, Experience and Evidence) as a method for assessing quality, and offered a means of assessing play environment quality from a child's perspective.

PlayEd 94, 95, 96, 97, 99A, 99B

After a short break (PlayEducation had folded in 1990 when I ran out of money, and didn't restart until 1993), PlayEd Meetings were resumed – first in their birthplace, Horwich, near Bolton, and then in Wolverhampton, Leeds, Ely and Sheffield. The Ely PlayEd (1999) marked the first meeting to explore a theoretical playwork agenda, using the theme 'Theoretical Playwork and the Research Agenda'.

Commentary

Although a very difficult period for many involved in playwork as it became increasingly subsumed by the political and economic might of child-care and its agents, this is also perhaps one of the more creative period for playwork. Its lack of identification with Childcare and Play-care both as services and political operations enabled playwork to further clarify its own identity, by exploring what it was not. Questions like, 'Could children ever play freely in a custodial care framework? Could childcare workers ever be playworkers? Is open access provision more effective than closed access provision, and What was meant by more effective? Was child-care more likely to adulterate the child's play experience, either with pre-conceived adult agendas or by the impact of SPNs? Could a service driven by adult economic needs ever serve the needs of children?' and so on. Many followed the childcare route. There was money and jobs in it, and kudos. Conferences at the time, demonstrating the seamless transition from the Thatcher to the Blair mindset, were populated by the power-dressed and beautifully presented icons of the time – proposing, if my memory serves me – Sainsbury's' After School Clubs, and BHS Adventure Playgrounds. But there was little of creativity or interest to talk about, save the next Government initiative, and of course children were hardly ever mentioned as the political agenda gained momentum. Soon playwork was all about employment, jobs and the New Deal. So the focus was no longer just on whether playwork and childcare could be merged, it was also on whether we had learnt anything in the preceding twenty-five years

42

and whether the projected 80,000 new playworkers promised by the New Deal needed to know any of it. The field did expand, but in general any fear of a cyberplaywork takeover did not materialised and playwork's development continued to draw from its own learning and experience supplemented by developments in the relevant sciences.

5   2000–2004

Play as a neurological architect/Animal Play

In 1998, Cambridge University Press published *Animal Play – Evolutionary, Comparative and Ecological Perspectives*', edited by Bekoff and Byers, although it didn't come to playwork's notice until four years later. This groundbreaking book provided playwork with awesome insights into the role of play as an evolutionary engine and the devastating potential for 'play deprivation' to wreck and even to destroy human and other species' lives, although the latter had been known, in primates, although not acted upon for over 40 years! See for example the work of Harlow and Suomi.

What *Animal Play* did for playwork was finally to enable it (playwork) to demonstrate the vital importance of what it had been attempting to provide for children, their families and their communities since its inception. Namely, supporting an essential biological process that was continually under threat from ignorance, the economic exploitation of children and a genuine misunderstanding of the essence of childhood, and offering protection from the effects of play deprivation.

Although most of the book draws from literature derived from evolutionary studies of species other than humans, from a theoretical perspective at least, it is fascinating to play 'What if', and see that the implications of findings relating to other species could apply equally to humans as well. (This has recently been further highlighted in presentations given by Marc Bekoff and Bob Hughes at the IPA Triennial Conference in Cardiff 2011.)

Evolutionary playwork

This term was coined in Hughes (2001) to re-emphasise that the growing body of scientific evidence confirming a direct relationship between play, evolution and brain growth, demonstrated that playwork should never have been viewed either as a social engineering, a socialising or citizenship tool, but rather as a comprehensive support for deep biological processes – expressed through mechanisms like adaptation, flexibility, calibration and the different play types – that enabled the human organism to withstand the pressures of extinction. In short, playwork was about helping the species to survive extinction and adapt to change, by ensuring that wild adult-free play in diverse environments was still a choice for its children.

Therapeutic playwork and psycholudics

Although terms claimed by several different groups/individuals the former probably originated in conversations between Stephen Rennie (Leeds Metropolitan University) and Gordon Sturrock (The Play Practice). It was first seen in print however in Else and Sturrock's Colorado Paper. Therapeutic Playwork was developed on the premiss that if many/most of the neuroses that trouble adults and children develop during childhood, then playworkers work at the very genesis of neurosis and with its most powerfully curative medium, play.

The term 'psycholudics' meaning the study of play from the perspective of the depth psychologies was first coined around 1998 by Gordon Sturrock.

Quality playwork – Quality in play

Although rarely previously applied to playwork the term 'quality assurance' began to be used in the 1980s to assure parents of the quality of service their children were getting from Child-Care and related services. Playwork quickly realised the way the wind was blowing and began to explore the notion of quality in playwork services too. This process had already begun with Hughes' (1996b) *Play Environments: A Question of Quality*, and various child-care agencies throughout the UK brought out a variety of quality assurance packs throughout the 1980s and 1990s mainly concerned with satisfying their various legislative responsibilities. However, it wasn't until 1999 when Hackney Play Association published 'Quality in Play' composed by Mick Conway and Tony

Farley, after extensive consultation, that a comprehensive playwork process for assuring the quality of professional playwork practice was made available to the field. The process was rooted in the new playwork ideas of the time – playtypes, loose parts, cues, returns and frames – and provides assurance frameworks for 'the play environment' and for 'managing playwork projects'.

Reflective playwork

The work of Damasio and other neurological investigators helped playworkers during this period to understand that the process of reflection may be concerned with creating a connection between the emotional 'old' brain and the rational 'new' brain, so that issues relating to our individual and collective survival are always included in any reflective computation. This would imply that reflective analytic thought can tap right into the roots of who and what we are, which may explain why Grof (1975) proposes that we can access individual and species biological processes during deep reflection.

What this means is that when the playworker reflects, she is passing current observation/experience along ancient neural pathways, and through the prism of evolutionary history – a process that make reflection a deeply emotional (spiritual) as well as a rational experience.

Playwork as hermeneutic

Rorty (1979) and Gadamer (1975) maintain that all knowledge is interpretive. Hermeneutics is defined as 'the theory and practice of interpretation and understanding in different kinds of human contexts' (6: 63).

Playwork is normally about our interpretation of the words and physical behaviour of the children we work with. In that sense it is not only reflective, it is also hermeneutic.

Work in Chawla (2002), in particular, supports playwork's assertion that because of the ludic immersive nature of what it is, playworkers can legitimately act as advocates and spokespeople for the playing child.

Playwork as a 'transpersonal' journey

In his book *Realms of the Human Unconscious*, Stanislav Grof (1975) referred to a particular characteristic of human experience as 'the transpersonal', meaning, that level or area of affect that relates specifically to all human beings throughout time rather than to that experienced by one individual through its personal existence.

Grof's work suggested that it is possible to access this collective strand of our being, using focussed thinking or reflection, or what one author called 'an inverted stare'. Hughes (2003a) suggests that if this was the case it would be a useful tool that would enable playworkers to more closely identify with what children were experiencing/feeling in a given set of circumstances, and thus react more appropriately to those feelings. What accessing this strand would also mean is that playworkers would be able to locate 'a commonality of experience', an articulation of 'an affective common denominator', that would apply to any human child in that particular set of circumstances. It would mean perhaps that playworkers would become more skilled at locating in themselves types or levels of feelings that would more closely approximate what others felt in similar circumstances, enabling them to propose remedies to address some children's perceived needs.

In Hughes (2003a), searching for this commonality was described as 'The Journey'. A journey which, as well as attempting to locate affective commonalities, might better equip playworkers to explore their own rationales and motivations for engaging in playwork and for intervening in children's play.

Playwork as latent[2]

'The Journey' brought evolutionary playwork to its most advanced/esoteric application of the work. For if a psychic interface was created, as the result of deep and concentrated, almost shamanic channelling of thought between the playworker and the child, then the playworker would become capable of engaging in hermeneutic interpretation at the bio-evolutionary level, rather than simply at the level of social or personal motivation. This would be helpful, as some diseases and dysfunctions manifested by children are less caused by manifest circumstances like home, school and relationships, than by latent circumstances like

46

anxiety or depression, brought about by certain evolutionary imperatives not being met – what in Stevens (1982), is called the 'frustration of archetypal intent' – in playwork terms, not being able to engage in enough fire, recapitulative, or imaginative play for example.

More than any other, this period of evolutionary playwork development charts a dramatic move from a socio-economic analysis of working with children at play, to a bio-evolutionary approach.

The First Claim Parts I and II

Although the issues of playwork language and conceptual development had been addressed theoretically for some time (Sturrock, Taylor, Battram, Russell, Lester, Gordon, Else and Rennie) and less theoretically by Conway, Palmer, Hughes and Farley, it was PlayWales who made possible the creation of a structured process, by commissioning and publishing two quality assessment manuals with the overall title of *The First Claim*. Initially intended to develop a quality assurance process, these publications demonstrate the more than semantic difference between the terms assessment and assurance. Although many bodies had sought to develop criteria that assured quality in the provision they operated, the qualitative tests they employed tended to be derived from processes dictated by certain legislation, like Health and Safety, Hygiene, Equal Opportunities and the Children Act. What *The First Claim* attempted was the creation and testing of specific playwork criteria, firstly to create a 'base-line', for professional assessment, and from that begin the journey towards developing criteria that would assure the 'appropriate' level of quality that would address the needs of most children at play. But first, the meaning of quality itself in the context of play, play environments and playwork had to be clarified.

'*The First Claim* – A framework for playwork quality assessment', contained a set of graduated criteria for measuring what its creator regarded as appropriate qualitative indicators. Many of these were generally viewed as controversial (like playing with fire and taking risks), but were still thought to be an integral part of what playwork was and what it represented for the playing child. It also formally introduced a notion – which Sturrock had been articulating for some time – that playworkers themselves must explore the impact of the affect of their own childhoods and what he called their 'unplayed out material', on how they conducted their own practice, in particular their rationales for intervening when children were playing. It had long been felt that many playworkers used the play environment and the children themselves to exorcise issues relating to their own childhoods and to their own play experiences. *The First Claim* did not so much condemn this, as invite playworkers to be more 'authentic/ honest', firstly by recognising that they had these issues, and secondly by doing something positive about them.

The second part of *The First Claim*, entitled, 'Desirable Processes', invited the more experienced playworker to observe children's play using a number of 'play mechanism' templates, and analyse their intervention rationales using a number of intervention templates. Both processes were designed to enhance both the observational, analytical and modification skills of playworkers (Modification = Changing physical environments to better address the play needs of the children there.) and enable them to improve their critical faculties both of their own and of others' practice.

Playwork Theory and Practice

Published by the Open University Press in 2003 and edited by Fraser Brown, now Reader in Playwork at Leeds Metropolitan University *Playwork Theory and Practice* provided a snapshot of the nature and range of thinking in playwork at the time of its publication. It shows a field much changed from its inception in 1970. Still creative, thoughtful and diverse, but perhaps more academic, rational and less emotional. This may be the model for the future of playwork too as those who interface with Government on playwork's behalf articulate a vision of playwork's responsibility, authority and maturity. An obvious concern is that as playwork comes of age, its legacy of anarchic, refusenik, loose cannon spontaneity and timelessness will disappear and the child-like essence of its work will disappear with it!

PlayEd 2000, 2002, 2003

This last grouping of PlayEd's still attempt to reflect the variety and diversity of interests and approaches in contemporary playwork. 2000,

48

'New Playwork – New Thinking', was held in Ely, 2002, 'One Heart – Many Pulses', was held in conjunction with Cardiff County Council in Cardiff, and 2003 Playwork in Normality and in Extremis, was held in conjunction with Belfast City Council at the Waterfront Hall in Belfast.

National Play Information Service

A major development during this period was the creation of the NPIS. Employing two expert librarians, and managed by NCB, the NPIS offered playwork an impressive resource that included regular literature and book reviews, new books and a wide range of journals.

Spirit of adventure play

Organised by PlayWales and run in Cardiff, 'Spirit' as it soon became known provided an annual opportunity for adventure playworkers and others from throughout the UK to come together and discuss their work.

Commentary

Although this period contains far-reaching developments, like the relationship between play and brain development, it is also a time of consolidation. After a long period where playwork had worked to establish its authenticity, by moving from intuition to evidence, the longed-for bridge between science and practice was at last developing.

6   2005–2010

Gordon Burghardt (2005)

In his contributions in *Animal Play* and his book *The Genesis of Animal Play*, Burghardt describes play as an almost ever-present drive and behaviour in humans and other species. He suggests the revolutionary idea that there are different sorts of play that evolved at different times in our evolutionary history for different reasons and which do different things, when particular conditions converge. He also demonstrates the link between play and brain growth.

Evolutionary Psychiatry

Evolutionary Psychiatry (Stevens and Price (1996, 2001) and Brune (2008)) draws our attention to two particular ideas. The first is that human beings are predisposed to satisfy certain archetypal needs; the second is that if the environment does not fulfil those needs, then psychopathology will result. This has huge implications on both the role and content of the playwork environment.

Play rangers

The term relates to those undertaking peripatetic playwork. I am not aware of any theoretical rationale for the term play rangers other than that which already exists for 'playworker'.

Play England

During this period Play England evolved from the Children's Play Council. Although it had a membership and a network of Regional Representatives, it was less an independent national lead organisation, than, for example, were PlayWales, Play Scotland or PlayBoard (NI), and more a conduit of Government policy relating to play in England. Along with its predecessor the Children's Play Council, Play England successfully attracted significant funding for play in England, although as I write (winter 2010–2011), the organisation has been subjected to significant cuts, that may be due to three different factors. One, its 'broad brush – generic' approach to provision for play, two, its (perhaps too) close relationship with the Blair/Brown Government, and three, its failure to create a credible bond between itself and the 'field' as a whole. There is still no lead organisation representing the professional views of playworkers in England.

50

Distance Learning

For all those playwork students who for whatever reason could not go to University to study, the University of Gloucester offers a distance learning package for playwork students. Its most visible academics are the ex-playworkers, Wendy Russell and Stuart Lester, authors of the landmark report 'Play for a Change'.

PlayEd 2007

This PlayEd Conference, held in Wolverhampton, is particularly notable for the contributions made by Gordon Burghardt and Louise Chawla.

More playwork books

This period saw the continuation of a prolific exploration of playwork ideas. New books included *Foundations of Playwork*, edited by Brown, *PlayTypes – Speculation and Possibilities* from me, Perry Else's *The Value of Play*, and Kilvington and Wood's *Reflective Playwork*.

Adventure playground criteria

Play England commissioned a group of play people to analyse what it was that made adventure playground, special. Although this will be dealt with further in the text, one radical outcome was the notion of 'magical play'.

Commercialisation

One striking indicator of the deskilling of playwork and playworkers was the proliferation of commercial companies building structures for play spaces. These spaces were not just of the 'fixed' variety, or the traditional 'platforms' developed out of 'consultation' (see Chapter 12), they were also unique, artistic entities that were intended to be viewed as an intrinsic part of a total playground experience. Although sometimes they were beautiful and very interesting, they still took the development of spaces – as an important component of their play experience – away from children, and as such represented a negative development from the evolutionary playwork perspective.

Blencathra revisited

Built on the side of Saddleback Fell just outside of Keswick, The Blencathra Centre had been an Isolation Hospital. Since then it has been a Field's Study Centre. Because of its isolated location, PlayEducation had hired it since the mid 1980s for playwork seminars and courses. During 2005–2010, it was used again by playworkers from throughout the UK to facilitate thinking, theorising and problem solving on playwork issues.

Commentary

From its intuitive genesis in the 1970s to the present day, evolutionary playwork has evolved steadily by applying the new thinking from the scientific literature, to its own theory and practice. During that period the world for children has changed dramatically. In 1970 little would have been thought of a child going out to play alone – and certainly without an adult present – of children having fires and dens, and climbing high into trees. Now, many children are not allowed to play and those that are often have to do it in sight of the house or a parent/carer.

Although many approaches have been tried, playworkers have resisted playwork becoming a compensatory discipline, preferring rather to provide children with a welcoming, vibrant and more or less free space in which to play and decide for themselves what their needs are.

Whether this can continue to be the case, when the relationship between playing and crucial developmental issues like brain growth is proved – particularly, if children are playing less, or less diversely.

But even a more compensatory approach will be difficult to provide if today's level of cuts to play services becomes the norm for the foreseeable future. For whatever its drawbacks, PlayEngland's close relationship with government did offer a basic level of protection for play which has gone, now replaced by a new narrative, rooted yet again in socio-economics, rather than bio-evolution.

With luck children will still thrive, in spite of society's general lack of understanding of the importance of playing to individual children and to our species as a whole. But I am concerned that without the necessary freedom to play, or access to the diverse environments in which to play, children will begin to manifest psychopathologies in increasing numbers – signs of the malfunctioning that will result from play deprivation. Perhaps the process has already begun.

This personal history highlights the complexity of the problem, in particular the need for facilitation rather than interference; love rather than domination and generosity rather than spite.

The spaces exist, both in our cities and in our national parks. Any thinking adult knows that the situation for children today when compared to most of the rest of us is dire. For not only are they threatened with poor health and obesity, and an increasing alienation from the natural world, because they are playing less, parents seem to view their children's need to play, without them there, as though it has evolved to annoy them personally, and as such is something they can give or take away – in short, it is a choice. This is patently not the case. As I imply throughout the following text, this is a dangerous judgement.

Parents, extended family members, local authorities, voluntary bodies and Central Government must do more, rather than less to ensure that all children have regular, free access to a wide range of different environments in which to play and where they can learn about each other and the world they inhabit. Without manifesting this generosity of spirit towards our children, their future and ours is in doubt. THE CLOCK IS TICKING ...

CHAPTER 2

EVOLUTIONARY PLAYWORK VALUES

What do playworkers believe? What should they believe and where should those beliefs come from?

For the thinking evolutionary playworker, there will inevitably come a time when she asks, 'Why am I doing this?' 'What is it that I am trying to do, what is it that I want to change, and into what?', and 'If I were to write a Mission Statement, what would it contain, and why that?'

One of my motivations for writing this book in the first place was to clarify in my mind my own responses to these questions, whilst at the same time providing the reader with what I regarded as some of the basic evolutionary playwork knowledge that might help them in their own quest towards making informed and clear choices regarding their own motivations.

There is no one definitive, commonly held, answer, to 'Why Playwork?'. My own conviction is that an evolutionary analysis, rooted in, although not exclusively derived from, human biological data, is the most rational; not only does it explain why children play, why they need to play, and why that play needs to be under their control; it also addresses what the impact of modern life is on play's frequency, duration and content, and how we can compensate for that using different forms of playwork provision and intervention. In other words, a response derived from evolutionary ideas gives practical playwork more meaning than do other analyses, whether they are socio-political, economic, educational or recreational. And in general terms I think that is the field's current position too, but that could change.

On reflection, when I first became a playworker in 1970 my personal analysis was both shallow and naïve. I wanted to help, and I wanted

54

to do good. Having already volunteered in the local Youth Service, and trained to be a teacher, I thought I had something to offer, although the truth was, I had little idea of what that meant. This view of 'playwork as a kind of public service' was reinforced when I realised that the children at the playground, and their parents, came from exactly the same background as me and my parents – secondary modern educated, estate dwellers, and factory people who could perhaps do with a hand, either to maximise their life chances, or to consider different alternatives.

For my first couple of years as a playworker, I did my 'good', as different situations arose. I fielded crime, behavioural issues, parental neglect and abuse, the attitudes of the authorities towards the children and their parents, violent outbursts, and community politics. But increasingly I found myself asking those difficult questions I started with. 'Why am I doing this?' and 'What is it that I am doing?'

I remember my epiphany well. This first playwork experience was as an adventure playworker, on a site that had been a farmyard when I had been a child, but which was now on the edge of a large and dense housing estate. I had played in the farmyard, and the surrounding countryside was well known to me. One day, whilst standing on the top platform of a tower, the children and I had built – surveying both the surrounding area and the playground, with the children going about their business – I had my first genuine insight of the context that I was working in, and that the children were playing in. What struck me initially was the change that had taken place in the twenty-six years since I had been born in that town. Where there had been fields, now there were houses and factories. Where there had been allotments and a pond, there were just more houses. Where there had been birds' nests, birds' eggs, birds' songs, newts and cattle, there were cars, parking bays and shops. And where there had been a farmyard and a pathway to the woods, there was now this adventure playground. I wondered, 'What difference these changes might have made to the children, and to their play? What was happening, what was going on, what was the real reason for the playground being there?'

I began to think more about play as a need, about playing as behaviour, as an interaction of the child's internal world with the external, as what I now call a 'bio-evolutionary' phenomenon; I began comparing what I had done as a child – how I had been able to do it, why I had done it – with the situation that the children on the playground were experiencing. This period and that process, together with later arguments and evidence presented in numerous texts, formed what is the basis of my own beliefs and convictions about play and playwork, as outlined in this book. However, we should remember that everyone, playworker or not, has their own valid story to tell about what play means to them.

And as well as our personal bases, government has also become involved from time to time to provide its own spin on why as a society we should provide for play and how we should go about doing it. Since the 1970s, these political initiatives have mostly been directed at youth crime, anti-social behaviour and vandalism, normally by either overtly or covertly using the child's need to play for the purposes of socialisation and citizenship training. Not surprisingly, most of them have failed dismally.

So what do we know about playwork values?

Although as I said earlier, in recent years much of evolutionary playwork's professional rationale for existence has been derived from Darwinism and psychology, that is not the whole story of playwork's internally generated values bases. From its genesis in the 1960s and 1970s until recently, playwork has undergone what can only be described as a continuous series of tortuous examinations of what playwork is for, and how best to do it.

Today playwork's Mission Statement is encapsulated in what are known as The Playwork Principles, developed in 2003/4. But the Principles are only the latest in a long line of attempts to encapsulate playwork's role and practice. The Principles – together with two other 'mission statements' that first appeared in Hughes (1996b) – are explored in this chapter.

1   THE TEN NEWCASTLE POINTS

In 1985, I was invited to undertake a series of training sessions for a group of experienced playworkers in Newcastle upon Tyne. We decided to use the opportunity to construct a statement of playwork's main objectives and to explore their implications.

56

Our main conclusions were that quality play experiences are important because they will help children to:

1 think for themselves
2 make their own decisions
3 have confidence in their own abilities
4 develop empathy
5 develop personal values
6 test out strategies without the stigma of failure
7 resolve contradictions and inconsistencies
8 communicate their needs, beliefs and desires more clearly
9 have an understanding of the life process
10 develop an understanding of the interrelationship of everything
11 question everything

Each of these conclusions was not only felt by the group to describe a skill that was important for children to have, but that each of them would only evolve through engaging in good play experiences. I was very pleased with the result of these sessions, although on reflection they are biased towards the social and egocentric. The final outcomes were useful, and perhaps more importantly, the playworkers had – perhaps for the first time – acknowledged the importance of clear and accurate language to describe them. (At that time, although composed of many educated, articulate individuals, the playwork workforce was unwilling to expend much effort on defining what playwork was trying to achieve. Perhaps because they felt that it would make them even more vulnerable to cuts and closures than they already were. Whatever the reason, the mantra was 'It's obvious!'.)

Of course it wasn't obvious. It wasn't obvious to the workforce undertaking it, let alone the wider population, and it was essential that playworkers themselves could clearly and concisely say what they did, and why it needed to be done, if only for their own professional survival. If they didn't then someone else would define playwork for them, and they would be professionally, perhaps even ethically, compromised.

This was the height of the Thatcher Government, and just after the end of the Miners' Strike. There was incredible pressure on local authorities to cut their spending, and unless playworkers and their managers could argue their case in terms that were both intelligible, professionally accurate, and could be perceived as a societal priority, they would become the cut's targets. After all, only four years previously seven adventure playgrounds in Manchester had been closed for much the same reasons.

So I was very pleased that the group were trying to make statements that were clear, concise and authoritative. What I wasn't so pleased about was what they were actually saying. Certainly the implications of much of what they said, would later be proposed as social outcomes for play (see for example Best Play), the problem was that the Newcastle Points failed to both demonstrate that play was more than a social phenomenon, and that playwork could have a role in facilitating it.

Instead, what they gave us was a selection of fairly limited observations, that if children played, then these things would happen. At no time did they make the link between these intuitive outcomes and the 'quality play experiences' they as playworkers provided, or explain what they meant by 'quality play experiences'.

If we assume they meant 'high' quality play experiences, that assumes that such a thing as low quality play experiences also exist! The question people would ask is 'How do you tell the difference?' 'How do you know that these low quality experiences don't facilitate the same outcomes as the "high" quality ones?'. We will, of course be addressing this issue later.

Certainly opinion had value, particularly opinion derived from face-to-face experience, but opinion was not evidence, and to alter the likely course of the tide of cuts, although not guaranteed, evidence could offer more protection than intuition or conviction.

Having said that, the 'Points' were a striking demonstration of high values, and showed the degree of affection, concern and care the playworkers had for the children they worked with, during that period of playwork history. They wanted the best for the children, and they wanted to praise their potential and their developing social consciences.

However, perhaps the main issue I had with the Points' agenda, was that like others that were considered over the following few years, it was born more from an adult perspective of 'good' social values – that is, it was a 'political' construct – than from a deductive perspective regarding what specifically playwork values might say. In that sense, their mind set was more youth work than playwork, more social intervention than biological facilitation. Compare it for example with what was also being written in 1985 at the Merseyside Playwork Training Project.

> Play is nature's major developmental key to the future evolution of our species. Both the opportunity and ability to play are increasingly under attack from the environments in which we spend our lives, mainly because of our lack of understanding of the effects of them upon us. We should always struggle to understand and control those aspects of the human environment that can adversely affect us (MPTP 1985).

However, having said that, as an articulation of belief, where there had been none before, we were pleased with what we had achieved.

Sadly though the clouds of confusion were gathering, rendering clarity of purpose even less achievable, and playwork's identity increasingly fudged, as every conceivable diversion from group dynamics, to body language and feminism, and from racism, to equal opportunities, health and safety, and other 'adult issues' based thinking, was tacked on to practical playwork, by the playwork 'field' itself, in what seemed like a continuous attempt to force an identity on it, that suited the prevailing revisionist political climate.

I felt that a more robust, child/play-focussed articulation was needed to counter this development, if children's play needs were going to continue to be the dominant component of playwork. What follows was my contribution to that.

2 PLAYWORK BELIEFS AND PLAY ENVIRONMENTS

A Question of Quality

I wrote *A Question of Quality* for PLAYLINK in 1996, shortly after the *Playworker's Taxonomy*. My main object in writing it was to provide a practical environmental context for the use of the Taxonomy. Among its features, I included a nine-point set of conclusions derived from a synthesis of the literature at that time and my own playwork experience. It was intended to be a statement of where I believed playwork ideas should be situated.

The conclusions stated:

- **Trust the child.** (It is children themselves who, when playing, will best be able to determine their own evolutionary needs.)
- **Children's interactions with one another are essentially non-competitive.** (At play children are only in competition with themselves to improve their own performance.)
- **The content and intent of its play is determined by the child.** (Because in 'free' development, only the child can sense its own play needs, what is done and why has to be the child's decision.)
- **Children are whole environment citizens.** (Children have no concept of borders, countries, cultures, religions and so on. Play should always reflect that sub-cultural position, rather than be used as a means of induction into a particular defined perspective on life.)
- **Children are independent beings with human rights.** (Like other playing species, children have ludic integrity. At play they belong to no one, and nothing. This independence is their right and should be respected especially in their play, and their needs should be respected as theirs alone.)
- **Children are lone organisms.** (With integrity comes personal responsibility. In the first and second instance, everything is a problem that the child has to learn to solve by playing with it.)
- **Children are individuals deserving of respect.** (Children have life-generated perspectives that impact on their play. These should be taken account of when considering intervening.)
- **Playwork is child-empowering.** (Playwork's goals, both in terms of its interventions and its environment modifications, is to enable the child to make himself more physically and psychologically adaptive and flexible in every way. If playwork does not in some way provide children with opportunities to discover additional insights, skills, strengths and opportunities, to achieve these goals, then it is failing the child.
- **Playwork and equal opportunities are inseparable.** All children are ludically disadvantaged in some way. Playwork does not differentiate between the play needs of one child, and those of another.

What I had wanted to achieve with these 'conclusions' was to create a statement that not only avoided plunging playwork further into confusion about what playwork existed to do, by focussing specifically on

60

the child and on play, but which also countered the prevailing ascendancy of adult orientated input that was adulterating playwork thinking and action by contrasting it against something more play and child focussed something that might have the effect of counteracting the 'free for all' interpretation of playwork that was occurring in the field at that time, and demonstrate that what we were witnessing was an unconscious colonisation of the playspace by the very adults who were employed to protect it.

What seemed paramount was a declaration that children were more than helpless and dependent, immature social entities. Scientists described children as engaged in an epic struggle for survival, no less threatened to them, than it was to their parents or any other adult. Their primary defence was the scope and depth of their childhood play experiences in enabling them to be flexible enough to adapt to whatever changes befell them. In other words, their survival was their problem, not their parents or society's, and their main defence was play. This had to be playwork's focus, not spurious mumbo-jumbo about group work and cost-effectiveness.

The other thrust of this statement was that to do this, to be able to be equipped to defend themselves against the pressures of extinction for example, children had to have the power to make the decisions about what they did when they played. This was simple really. All it meant was playworkers would work to create 'good' play spaces where there were none, but what the children did on them, would be guided primarily by the children. I add 'primarily' simply because the playworker's experience is also important, it just isn't as important as the child's.

The problem for playworkers at the time was not that they weren't experienced and knowledgeable, but that they were continually under pressure politically and socially to apply a different interpretation of playwork, one that was more an extension of teaching or social work, one that showed that children were being inducted into modes of citizenship and appropriate behaviour while at play. (See also the 2009 Labour Government's Play Policy for a good example of this.)

Like others, I rejected this. After all, children were already being socialised at school and at home. There was no reason – and it was immoral and damaging anyway – to invade their playtime too, and diminish the huge benefits of unrestricted play. It was not their fault that they had few places to roam and to play freely. What we had to ensure was that new provision, like adventure playgrounds, remained free-play areas and did not become extensions of home or school. There had to be somewhere, where children could be the biological organisms that they were, too.

This notion of play belonging to the child was of crucial importance in the development of a discrete playwork identity. Of course playwork was not anti-society, it was just that its purpose was, like astronomy perhaps, more long-term and less day-to-day than people assumed. Playwork was certainly not about suffocating children with societal control and paranoia. Rather it was about returning the freedom and joy of life in a very challenging context (planet Earth) to them. Humans had existed on this planet for millions of years, but were rapidly losing the skills they needed for that existence. Quality play provided those skills. Play reminded them that as well as being modern, they were from ancient beginnings, atavistic and primeval, like the environment they inhabited. This was a strand of their being that needed to be kept both intact and activated, if the flexibility and adaptability so essential to survival were to be retained

In John Steinbeck's beautiful book, *To a God Unknown* (1935), one of the characters experiences this primitive, animist interface first-hand when he happens upon a glade containing a large rock with a stream of water flowing from it. The book impressed me deeply, reminding me that what we call civilization is only a recent veneer, that attempts to cover over many millions of years of different, formative and, in many ways, more important development.

What the story suggested, was that although human beings come together to form social groups for reasons of safety and security, they are much more than just social or gregarious entities. Their evolutionary history roots them in all aspects of human existence – of the Earth, and of the irrational as well as in the rational. It implies that quality and comprehensive play, if allowed, will be mythical, elemental and ritualistic, as well as technical, locomotor and social.

The incident in Steinbeck's book gave me an insight into a deeply spiritual side of myself too, that I had not acknowledged previously. What is worrying is that although human beings are these multi-faceted, spiritual and animist beings, it is our modern social nature, our societal success, which is valued as the primary moulder of our

62

identity, even though it creates harmful addictive layers – money, qualifications, position, prestige – which the other human qualities do not, and by so doing, it stifles other equally important human characteristics, that are perceived as less instantly gratifying, less convenient and more demanding.

The story provides a metaphor for a comparison between our modernity and our species' long existence. Human beings have been around a long time and today's children carry much of what has happened during that period in their genes. Their play needs to reflect the totality of what human children are, but increasingly it is unable to, because the physical and legal environment, and the children's parents, frustrate that. Children are members of a species among other species, this is an interdependent relationship, and it requires a component of our humanness that is all too often buried beneath our apparent desire to commercially exploit natural space, even if that is at the cost of the other species that depend on it. Comprehensive, child-empowered play can reactivate that relationship.

These conclusions drawn from *Play Environments: A Question of Quality* were intended to bring the debate about playwork's role back from an increasing risk of adult contamination to the child and to play. But increasingly I find myself posing the question, If there are such things as genuine and authentic play experiences, then surely by definition there must be children who may not have experienced all or any of them, and may be adaptively disadvantaged as a consequence?

I find myself wondering, given that so many prominent members of society seem to have attended private or public schools, and may have been boarders too, whether if we had a conversation about play, we would even be talking about the same type of experience? Whether when a Minister or his/her Officials imagines play they picture ranging, adult-free, mixed-gender, risky, feral behaviour or something else entirely? Of course the question might simply highlight my own prejudices and ignorance, but it is intended seriously, because it is these individuals who are often responsible for resourcing those local authorities and voluntary agencies who provide play settings for local children.

My interpretation of the literature is that it is primarily discussing free-play, when it identifies play's neurological and adaptive benefits, because the focus is ethological and applies primarily to wild species. So *play* takes place when children range without adults through urban or rural landscapes, exploring the experiences they encounter by themselves. Is it that, that those who frame and administer government policy also draw from or might this be an alien or even abhorrent concept to them?

This is an important question for anyone concerned about the link between experience and neural development in particular. For if those who frame government play policy do not recognise the play I describe in these pages, what is it that they do recognise and what construct are they driven to support – both or their own or evolutionary playwork's?

If the answer is both or their own, then that would mean that increasingly, the free natural play overwhelmingly preferred by children and supported by playwork, would be continually at risk of being subsumed into a more adult construct, perhaps of homework clubs, piano and ballet lessons, 'productive' hobbies and pastimes, simply because these adults would have a greater level of influence on backing their own choice. The problem with this is that it is difficult for we adults to be objective and detach ourselves entirely from our own childhood 'play' experiences. Even if they were bad or adult dominated, some might be unable to resist defending, even propagating them, simply because there would be nothing else to draw from. This is further complicated by changes over the past fifty or so years in how parents view their own children's play. Many parents, whilst not detaching themselves from their own play memories, apply completely different rules to their own children, either constricting their free play both in terms of ranging and risk taking, or allowing it to become adulterated as I believe is the case in many care and after school situations.

However, although there are many routes and just as many outcomes to this inevitable values debate there is one question that has not been asked. Should playwork have a formal set of 'agreed' values? In 2005 this is exactly what was created.

3 PLAYWORK PRINCIPLES

This final values statement is called The Playwork Principles. It was developed by a Principles Scrutiny Group, following foundation work

64

by Conway, Hughes and Sturrock for Play Wales, and was intended to establish a comprehensive professional and ethical framework for playwork in the noughties. The Principles describe what is currently viewed as unique about play and playwork, and provide a contemporary playwork perspective for working with the young.They articulate a belief that a child's potential to develop the skills essential to staving off the pressures of extinction will be greatly enhanced if given access to a range of environments and play opportunities that reflect both the EEA*, playwork applications and the assertions of the Taxonomy. They are:

1   All children and young people need to play. The impulse to play is innate. Play is a biological, psychological and social necessity, and is fundamental to the healthy development and well being of individuals and communities.

2   Play is a process that is freely chosen, personally directed and intrinsically motivated. That is, children and young people determine and control the content and intent of their play, by following their own instincts, ideas and interests, in their own way for their own reasons.

3   The prime focus and essence of playwork is to support and facilitate the play process and this should inform the development of play policy, strategy, training and education.

4   For playworkers, the play process takes precedence and playworkers act as advocates for play when engaging with adult-led agendas.

5   The role of the playworker is to support all children and young people in the creation of a space in which they can play.

6   The playworker's response to children and young people playing is based on a sound up-to-date knowledge of the play process, and reflective practice.

7   Playworkers recognise their own impact on the play space and also the impact of children and young people's play on the playworker.

8   Playworkers choose an intervention style that enables children and young people to extend their play. All playworker intervention must balance risk with the developmental benefit and well being of children.

*The Environment of Evolutionary Adaptedness

The Playwork Principles are the most recent of playwork's articulation of its values and as such it is a very interesting statement. They are undoubtedly influenced by individuals, playwork publications and research data, and demonstrate how the scientific literature, particularly evolutionary studies, have impacted on our understanding of play. I am going to explore each one briefly.

1 All children and young people need to play. The impulse to play is innate. Play is a biological, psychological and social necessity, and is fundamental to the healthy development and well-being of individuals and communities.

This first principle provides a strong affirmation both of the source of play and of its importance to physical and mental health. I expect that it is an attempt to begin the articulation with the conviction that play is not something we can do without or control, but it is vitally important. It is a powerful statement, except at the end, when it moves from individuals to communities. I am not clear at all how play benefits communities, unless what the authors means is that children are diverted, or that healthy children do not cause as much disruption.

2 Play is a process that is freely chosen, personally directed and intrinsically motivated. That is, children and young people determine and control the content and intent of their play, by following their own instincts, ideas and interests, in their own way for their own reasons.

As a statement of value the first line is impressive although hugely difficult to define. What it means in practice, is that as far as is possible children should be able to choose what they do, choose how they do it, and do it for their own reasons. What is most important in this principle is the word instinct. Instinct can be notoriously difficult to provide for in the normal scheme of things. Take sex for example. Sexual activity is instinctive and vitally important to us all. But the question of how children get their experience is very vexed. We know through the studies of Harlow and Suomi/Harlow that species that do not engage in immature (proto) sexual activity when young, are at least physically disabled, when attempting to procreate as adults. Although this is not totally the case with humans, it does mean that they may be disabled emotionally or physically without a degree of sexual interaction as they grow up. Should playworkers let it happen, pretend it isn't happening; turn a blind eye or prohibit it? What is the effect of adult or camera surveillance too?

What I am saying is that although playworkers genuinely believe that the content and intent of its play should be determined by the child, the reality is that there is always a struggle taking place about where to draw the line. Playworkers' judgement calls are influenced by funders, managers, parents and legislation as well as by the children themselves, and children can be very conservative.

3   The prime focus and essence of playwork is to support and facilitate the play process and this should inform the development of play policy, strategy, training and education.

My most fundamental concern with current and recent government intervention/support is rooted in this principle. What it is implying is that all playwork education, training, policy and strategy is embedded in and derived from an acknowledgement that playwork only exists to facilitate play, i.e., behaviour that is freely chosen, personally directed and intrinsically motivated and so on. Playwork has no agenda other than play. The question is, can the temptation to introduce agendas, or exploitations, or manipulations into play for adult society's sake be resisted?

4   For playworkers, the play process takes precedence and playworkers act as advocates for play when engaging with adult-led agendas.

This principle suggests that my concerns with point 3 were premature. In a way it is a stronger re-articulation stating very clearly that for playworkers, it is the play process and that alone, which they exist to support both in the play context and in the political arena, where other issues – like equal opportunities – may be introduced. I have to say, though, whether this Principle works in practice, this is an area where playwork has tended to give ground in the past.

5   The role of the playworker is to support all children and young people in the creation of a space in which they can play.

I'm not clear if what this Principle is saying is that one of the playworker's professional functions is to help/support children to create a good play space? If it is then it contains a contradiction which I think it is important to expose. Playwork first and foremost is about the creation of good playspaces in which children can play. Playworkers who create good play spaces, and the good play spaces they create, are needed because for an increasing number of children either there aren't any good play spaces left, or children are only allowed out to play in spaces that are supervised, meaning that good spaces have to be created artificially. Where I don't agree with the tone of this Principle is the term 'creation'. It is the playworker's job to create play spaces, not children's – that is why we go to all the trouble of writing books and studying play. It is the children's job to playfully modify – a term we will revisit later – the space created by the playworker. I will deal with its depth later, but I suspect that those who created this Principle were conscripts, perhaps volunteers in the army of Consulting with Children, developed from The Ladder of Participation, itself developed in a paper by the eminent psychologist and geographer Roger Hart in 1992. I am not clear whether Hart actually meant that children should engage in the design process of play spaces? If he did then he obviously wouldn't agree that play should be an unconscious process! As I write, in the UK we have reached a situation where everyone feels compelled to consult with children prior to the creation of play spaces. Before I go on I should explain that I have no problem with children participating in and being consulted on all issues that concern them. I hope that would go without saying. However, I do have one exception and that is play environments, simply because children cannot consciously contribute to the design of a space and then unconsciously use it. It's like being told how a magician does a trick and then trying to forget that information when the trick is being performed. No, play and play spaces are so important to children that they must only 'chance' upon them, use them and then move on. Their interest is not in their creation, but in their playful exploitation. And where there is no longer a naturally occurring space, hopefully they have playworkers to create good spaces for them to play in. Playworkers should be adept at wringing the highest possible play value out of a modest space.

6   The playworker's response to children and young people playing is based on a sound up-to-date knowledge of the play process, and reflective practice.

This is a straightforward Principle that says 'Always do your homework', and think about what you observe and why you do what you do in the way that you do it. I think homework should not only include keeping abreast of developments in the literature, but also how children's culture is evolving. The latest developments in music, technology, clothes, concerns, food and so on are all components of the playworker's judgement call arsenal.

7   Playworkers recognise their own impact on the play space and also the impact of children and young people's play on the play-worker.

The thrust of this Principle is so obvious that it shouldn't need stating, but it does. As Else and Sturrock (1998) demonstrated, the playwork-er's impact can be minuscule, but it can also be disruptive and over-bearing. They used the term 'adulterating', which implies that we risk contaminating both play and the frame within which it takes place, if we are unaware of how we operate within the play space. The play-worker who just joins in a game – who doesn't either wait to be invited or who doesn't just ignore the game – may be quite unaware that 'joining in' will alter, perhaps destroy, the dynamic the children have created.

8   Playworkers choose an intervention style that enables children and young people to extend their play. All playworker interven-tion must balance risk with the developmental benefit and well being of children.

A comprehensive review of intervention styles can be found in Hughes (2002). Intervention styles refer to the different ways a playworker might engage with children when they are at play, for reasons of safety, or management of difficult situations. I can't say I understand the first part of this Principle, because quite obviously, there will be circum-stances in a supervised space when an intervention will not extend a child's play. Banning them, or stopping them doing something, are just two examples of the realities of playwork, when some semblance of order needs to be maintained, because the playworker is an employee and responsible for children's safety. This is one of the real disadvant-ages of supervised spaces over spaces discovered when the children are ranging. In discovered spaces children have to deal with problems and issues themselves. But in supervised spaces, the playworker is expected to mediate between warring factions, between bully and victim, between 'racist' and recipient, between boys and girls and every other conceivable interface, simply because it is an artificial space attracting an artificial constituency. So I actually think that the first part of this Principle is impossible.

The second part is clearly about the balance between stopping children doing things that may hurt them, and allowing them to do those things so that they learn how to risk assess. This is a very typical example of the judgement calls that face the experienced playworker. Given the risky nature of growing up in the different environments we have created for ourselves, with all the trapping of the modern built environment – traffic, electricity sub-stations, drainage gulleys, railway lines and so on, together with different conflicts, dangerous adults and animals, not to mention that all of this is happening on an unstable planet, which is itself vulnerable to various cosmic issues like meteorites and different rays – children obviously need to experience risk and become skilled at dealing with it. They do this in the normal course of their play. The playworker may need to judge whether a child is taking unnecessary risks or whether the child is being encouraged by other children to go far beyond what it is capable of doing. No-one wants children to injure themselves, so judgements are normally down to common sense.

CONCLUSION

Surprisingly perhaps, these different values statements spanning more than twenty-five years of playwork's evolution, are remarkably similar in tone, and echo the need for respect for children, for an acknowledgement of the importance of play both to our biology and to our ontology and for a degree of common sense, so that children are able to play normally, but are not put in danger.

What these different values statements also map is the development of playwork itself, from a fairly timid, almost apologetic articulation of what playworkers felt were necessary social consideration, to a confident articulation of what playworkers expect from society as we move into a more bio-evolutionary age, where we can no longer take our survival as a species for granted, and where increasingly, the impact of playing in fighting off the pressures of extinction, sees play as an integral, if not imperative, component of our species' future.

MICK'S STORIES 1

Here Fred, have some cornflakes

A boy aged about five was playing with a knobbly piece of wood and pieces of the crushed bark safety surface, chattering away to himself and his play objects. A playworker came by and asked 'What are you doing?', 'Nothing' he said, shrugging his shoulders – end of conversation. She shrugged in reply and went about her business of putting up the swings. About five minutes later, another playworker asked him 'Who's that?'. This time he said 'This is my dog. She's called Fred! And she's very, very naughty. But she's hungry too. Here Fred, have some cornflakes' as he fed bits of bark to Fred. The conversation continued for several minutes, curling and spiralling fantastically around animals and favourite food and all sorts of stuff I can't now remember.

Both playworkers had asked open rather than closed questions, but his responses were very different. He was an exceptionally bright and playful child, but his mum and dad were having serious relationship problems at the time and he could often be solitary and quiet in his play. Both playworkers knew what was going on in his life, but it was the empathy and understanding of the second playworker that I think encouraged him to extend his play. He was happy to let her into what we now understand to be his play frame – her more playful approach encouraged him to respond with verbal play cues in a way he didn't to the first playworker.

Beans

The playworkers heard hysterical laughter and came out of the building to find about ten children, mostly girls, facing a girl sitting on the playground 'throne' – a brightly painted massively oversized chair built out of poles and planks. The girl on the throne called out 'Mexican!' The children jumped up and down. 'Baked!' The children pretended to fart, holding their noses. 'Black-eyed!' They pretended to punch themselves in the eye. 'Runner! They ran madly on the spot. 'French!' They shook hands and bowed politely saying 'Bonjour' to each other. 'Has!' They mimed limping with walking sticks or shuffling along with Zimmer frames.

Throughout they were watching and outdoing each other in ever more ridiculous acting out and movement. The game had never been seen on the playground before, lasted for about 15–20 minutes and has never been repeated as far as we know. When asked how it had come about, the children said they'd made it up.

Just think about the imagination and wit (has-beans!) involved in this one-off wonder that had absolutely no playworker or other adult intervention apart from creating a space on and around which it could possibly happen. This for me is an example of the essence of play and playwork, and evidence, if any were needed, that children are the experts in their play.

Archaeology

The children had been enjoying digging and mixing clay to make a wood-fired mud oven based on a traditional Turkish type, but with added play features like having real grass growing on the outside, populated with plastic toy animals. Another story in itself was the look on the Ofsted inspector's face when told it was actually used. By children! To cook pizzas! Which they made themselves! And actually ate! And nobody died!

Although the oven was finished, the children kept on digging in a corner of the playground, because making mud was good fun, and they were increasingly intrigued by the broken crockery, rusty nails, bones and the other bits and pieces they found. This developed into a full-blown archaeological dig complete with careful excavation in an area they roped off with all sorts of dire warning signs: 'Keep Out! Danger! Deep Excavation!'. Items were carefully uncovered and brought to finds tables where they were painstakingly washed in a series of old margarine and ice cream tubs with old suede brushes, toothbrushes and paintbrushes, most of which were smuggled from their homes.

The finds were then carefully labelled in plastic bank cash bags: broken crockery = Ming dynasty; rusty nails = Iron Age; the bones of buried playground pets and pigeons = Roman or Viking or dinosaur remains; pre-decimal coins = pirate treasure etc and carefully placed in a multi-drawer cupboard they 'borrowed' from the playground office. Children aged from about six up to about thirteen changed roles over the days, dropped in and out of different elements, and eventually abandoned the whole thing when interest waned after a couple of weeks.

And there's a postscript. A flyer from the Museum of London arrived offering free hands-on archaeology sessions. Everybody got quite excited, the playworkers arranged to take a group of children to the museum, and I tagged along to help out. We were given a very boring and patronising lecture about how to behave in the museum and use our worksheets. Worksheets? 'This is even worse than school' one child muttered. After what felt like an age, we were led into a room containing boxes of sand in which real ox bones, bits of genuine Samian pottery and (very obviously) fake fibreglass representations of Roman and Saxon foundations were buried. It was nothing like the playground dig. The verdict of one older child, shared by all of us, was 'That was the most boring trip out ever!'

I like several things about this story. The children spontaneously developed the mainly playworker-led mud oven project into something else entirely, and the playworkers had no involvement apart from simply enabling the children to use the space, tools and materials to extend their play. Well, up to a point – one of the playworkers couldn't resist burying interesting things like foreign or pre-decimal coins in the excavation after closing time, to be discovered with great excitement when the archaeologists returned the next day.

Many of the children had been watching and enjoying the *Time Team* TV series and had picked up a lot of knowledge of archaeological dig techniques: the concepts of layers with older stuff lower down; systematically brushing, sifting, cleaning and labelling finds and so on, but they used this knowledge in a purely playful way. I don't think any of them, even the youngest, saw it as a real archaeological dig, though they were genuinely fascinated by the stuff they found. The *Time Team* programme gave them a conceptual frame that enabled them to play around with a rich repertoire of rules and ideas. What Sandra Melville has described as 'the implicit permission' given by the playground environment, both the physical space and the playworkers, was what made the whole thing possible. In comparison, the Museum of London was an inauthentic play experience because of the much narrower range of permissions and possibilities. In fairness to the museum, they were doing their best, but were coming from an educational or instructional rather than a playful mode.

What does this story illustrate about some of the play concepts and theories? The children were engaging in lots of play types to a greater or lesser extent, singly or in combination. I would include symbolic, social, creative, exploratory, mastery, object and role play. A fairly complex play frame (various children over several days digging clay and mixing it into mud for the oven, plastering it onto the chicken-wire frame, sowing the grass seed and arranging the toy animals) expanded and changed into a much more complex and longer-lasting series of play frames. These were instigated, maintained, developed and changed by hundreds of play cues and returns over the following two weeks, all within an overall archaeology or *Time Team* play frame. However, not all the children all the time would have been in the archaeology or *Time Team* play frames – most dipped in and out, or went off to do other things on or off the playground. All this happened within a series of full play cycles that were destroyed or abandoned as individual children from time to time, and then eventually all of them, lost interest and moved on to other things.

And I'll leave it to the reader to think about how many of the criteria for an enriched play environment were afforded to the children by the playground.

Granddad's job description

My partner Sue and her grandson Charlie, who was then about six, were driving back to London from a weekend away when I was somewhere else. 'Sue, can Mick be my granddad?' he asked out of the blue. 'I'm sure he'd love to be your granddad.' Charlie was quiet for a minute or two. 'But if he's my granddad can he still be my best friend?' As you can imagine, my heart just melted when Sue told me about what he'd said – the best job-share offer ever!

But what's it got to do with play? Over the years Charlie and I had all sorts of adventures together – exploring Highgate woods looking for imaginary tigers, climbing hills and trees, burying 20p pieces or hiding them in a hole in a fallen tree (mysteriously, we never found any of them again), learning to ride his bike and investigating every (and I

74

mean every!) nook and cranny of the neighbourhood, having complicated conversations about why the moon was sometimes big and orange but mostly small and white 'with a dirty face', whether the London moon was the same as the one in Devon, how rainbows and what he used to call 'thumberstorms' were made.

He'd had minimal contact with his biological granddad, and wanted to be able to say to the other primary school kids 'that's my granddad' when we turned up to collect him for a weekend away with his extended family. He was working out his social relationships, and needed to know that he'd got them right. This was sophisticated questioning at all sorts of levels: if Mick becomes this can he still be that; would his real granddad still be his granddad; where exactly do he and his mum and dad fit into the extended family; would my Irish nieces and nephews he'd not yet met really be his cousins? Our next big adventure was Charlie's first ever plane flight to Ireland to meet them, and they got on like a house on fire. In a delicate resolution of the thorny problem of my being divorced, their Catholicism and Charlie's relationship to us all, the Irish children and Charlie decided to their mutual satisfaction that they were 'kind of step-cousins' in a diplomatic peace deal as subtle as any negotiated in Northern Ireland.

CHAPTER 3

WHAT IS EVOLUTIONARY PLAY?

All play is evolutionary. By that I mean each of the different behavioural routines that we call play has evolved at some time during our evolutionary history.

But play is also a very personal experience. For some it is dolls and rough and tumble, for others it is skateboarding or computer games. It is what children do when adults are not there or what children do when the adults that are there are perceived as honorary children. When my five-year-old grandson Thomas catches my eye, gives me a manic stare and rushes off to dive into a pile of leaves, that is play. When, as a woman described recently to me, that as a child she would dig up worms so that she could wash them and put them back into the ground, that too was play. Play, as Kent Palmer describes, is an 'ecstasy of variety' (Sturrock 1997). It is the infinite expression of the human soul in communion with its universe (see also Palmer 1994).

It is painting, acting, experimenting and exploring. It is risking and it is death defying. It is the child at its most immersed in the fantasy of other worlds where she may be transported into what Winnicott called a 'potential space', to become a horse or a space alien (Ogden 1993: 223).

It is where he imagines he is so tiny that it is possible for him to disappear between the roots of a tree or voyage into the flames of a fire.

Play is damming streams, fighting back the tide, nicking apples and making dens and caves. It is spiritual, creative, locomotor, dramatic, archetypal and precious. It crosses species boundaries and gives life to inanimate objects and voices to ideas.

Play is what happens when children are propelled by a desire to know and understand, or by the thrill of attempting to transcend their

76

previous limits. Except for the few, who by force of circumstance or lack of opportunity have not been able to play, it has happened to every child in the past, as it is happening to every child currently on this planet, whether that child is living in the high Andes in Peru, with Bedouins in the Sahara, in Japan, India or in Europe. It is one of the single most profound forces we share as a species but one most of us knows little about, although our memories of playing, what Sobel (1993) calls our 'touchstone' memories, live with us throughout our lives. It is, on the whole, what children do, and historically what children do has tended not to be particularly important to adults, as long as they do it quietly and preferably somewhere else.

Play is regarded by many as trivial, as a waste of time or as a way of using up excess energy. But, as I have said, we have all done it, and it has often had a profound effect upon us. Yet as adults we often only value it as a sanitised and adulterated experience for our own children. It certainly is an enigma.

Having said that, if play is so diverse, so personal and so universal how can it have any meaning, why should it be important? How, for example, can we pin down what it is? How can we say it even exists, let alone define why it has any relevance to us?

WHAT IS PLAY?

Play is a personal experience. For each of us it happened where *we choose to* play, with *our* friends, with *our* toys or *our* other play props. These are the things *we* consciously remember as players. But for those who observe and investigate play there are, even with this huge diversity, many characteristics that were as common to my play as they are to everyone else's. And it is these defining characteristics which tell us what play is and, importantly, what is not.

According to the literature, behaviour has to satisfy the following several criteria to be acknowledged as play. For example it has to be:

- freely chosen, i.e., a voluntary activity (Neuman 1973);
- personally directed by the child (Hughes 1996b);
- intrinsically motivated, i.e., performed by the child for no external goal or reward (Koestler 1964).

But to be play, behaviour also has to be:

- spontaneous (Patrick 1914);
- first-hand experience and include struggle, manipulation, exploration, discovery and practice (Bruce 1994);
- goalless – it is often described in terms of process rather than product (Bruner 1972);
- where the child is in control of the content and intent (Hughes 2000);
- a performance of motor patterns in novel sequences, like gallumphing, or movements out of context, like the cat that runs sideways with its tail at an odd angle (Miller 1973);
- repetitious, to facilitate the learning of complex skills (Connolly 1973);
- neophilic, i.e., drawn to the novel, new, fun or interesting (Morris 1964, 1967);
- non-detrimental (King 1987);
- contain play cues or meta-signals, like eye contacts, facial expressions and body positions that start processes of many social *and* non-social engagements (van Hoof 1972, Bateson 1955; Else and Sturrock 1998);
- a balance of different experiences (Hughes 1988).

And if a behavioural routine does not satisfy most of these criteria, particularly those relating to free choice, personal direction and intrinsic motivation, then it is not play and any benefits that are said to come from playing, will not apply.

As we can see, play is a very complex phenomenon, where a number of conditions that seem to be less about what the player actually does and more about how and why s/he does it, have to be satisfied.

PLAY AND RISK

Like the young of other playing species, children often take enormous risks when they play The content of their everyday playful routines often flies in the face of what would be regarded as acceptable socialised behaviour. Burghardt (2005), echoing Geertz (1972), says that there are some forms of play whose costs seem to outweigh their benefits. Some adults have actually called what children do when they

78

play irresponsible, or pointless, even dangerous – and to allow them, even to encourage them, to take control of what they do, even if it is during their *playtime*, they regard as the height of irresponsibility.

One is tempted to ask, why children seem to need to interface with the world in ways that are so risky? To the evolutionary playworker the answer is obvious, 'How else can they learn to survive life in such a hostile place, if they do not explore it and experiment with it?'

Both the science and playworkers' personal and professional experiences confirm that the urge to play freely exists in us all – it comes from deep within, as if we already know intuitively what play is and what it is for. When young children play they have an agenda independent of anything we adults might want to do. It is as if they are embarking on a research programme, where they are collecting and analysing data, and constructing and testing their own theories of what life is all about (see Eibl-Eibesfeldt, 1967, 1970, Gopnik 2002).

WHERE DOES PLAY COME FROM?

> ... play is a primal activity. It is preconscious and preverbal – it arises out of ancient biological structures that existed before our consciousness or our ability to speak.
>
> (Brown, S. 2009: 15)

Increasingly play is believed to be the outcome of a biological drive, in much the same way as eating and sexual activity are the manifestations of other such drives.

Drives are like genetic rivers, whose primal forces come from sources deep within our central nervous system and, which, in flowing through us, give us the energy and focus to attempt to satisfy our most basic desires for life and understanding, often in the most difficult of circumstances.

The play drive may have evolved to ensure that as vulnerable and naïve young organisms, children engage with the world they live in, in ways that are in tune with their immaturity but which are also highly efficient, so that they are gradually able to interpret the sensory experiences gained whilst at play – most of which, as we shall see – are vital to their continued development, their capacity to adapt, and to their longer-term survival.

In other words, play is the result of a drive, or what a BBC film about play (*Horizon* 1998) called an 'urge', and like other drives, play *has* to happen, it is irresistible, it is something that, as the same film suggested, will normally happen later if it does not happen sooner, or, if it does not have an outlet, will result in physical or psychological damage or both, to those who suffer that restriction.

So, when we see a child playing with a flower, or in the dirt, or skipping or playing tag, we should remind ourselves that what we are looking at is the childlike result of a deep and irresistible urge to explore, experiment with and have knowledge of the world, the universe and everything.

Our drive to play is hugely important. Playing has a pivotal role in increasing our ability to adapt both in general terms and to changing environmental and atmospheric conditions in particular. A major reason why we have not become extinct is that we play. The psychologist Lorenz (1972) said that we have become 'specialists in non-specialisation' because we play; and that because of that we are good at lots of things rather than expert at just a few. Having access to this *diversity of behavioural choice* Wilson (1992) is a vital component of our adaptive processes.

ARE THERE DIFFERENT TYPES OF PLAY?

Another reason that play is vital to us and to numerous other species is that it provides us with a range of different ways to interact with and learn from experience. In fact, play is not one thing, but several different things.

Burghardt (1998) said that play is 'most certainly' a heterogeneous category and that different [playtypes] may have 'different causal bases, functions and phylogenies...' (p. 6).

What Burghardt is saying is that during our evolutionary history different kinds of play evolved at different points in evolutionary time; they evolved for different reasons and to do different things.

Let's have a closer look at this statement.

80

During our evolution, all sorts of behaviours appeared as a result of the process of mutation. However, when these mutations were tested against the different conditions that prevailed, some worked – that is they helped the organism survive for longer – and some didn't – the organism died before passing on its genes.

What Burghardt is suggesting is that play is a mutation and that different sorts of these play mutations evolved over time; that different conditions caused them to evolve, and that they were successful at doing different 'survival' jobs, i.e., different kinds of play have had, and continue to have, the effect of helping human beings – during childhood – to stave off the pressures of extinction, so that they can survive long enough to pass on their genes.

A STORY OF PLAYTYPES

Perhaps there was a time, long ago, when our ancestors did not play at all. But then as conditions on Earth – the atmosphere, food availability, landscape, population size – began to change; C1, dangerous life-threatening pressures were created (see Figure 3.1). To address this, organisms began to evolve 'playful' behaviours. These playful behaviours mutated into different forms. Some of these playful mutations supported the organism's need to adapt to the dangerous changes, and some did not.

If the mutant 'playtypes' helped their 'host' organism to adapt to the changes, then the organisms survived and passed on their genes to the next generation, including the mutant playtypes. Others, which hadn't evolved any playtypes or had only evolved unsuccessful ones, perished without passing on their genes.

The organisms that adapted, helped by the mutant playtypes, passed on the mutant playtypes to future generations; pt1 was created.

Conditions changed many times over the years moving from C1 to C7 and beyond.

The conditions that caused the very earliest of the playtypes mutations, C1, etc., still exist today. So even though the playtypes that overcame these early conditions are very ancient, it is still essential that children engaged in them.

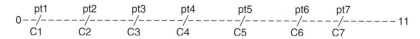

Figure 3.1 Different playtypes evolved to stave off the pressures of extinction.

The conditions to which I refer and which were responsible for testing our playtypes mutations may have been caused by numerous factors. Burghardt (2005) said playlike behaviour may be the result of the convergence of different life-history (genes), ecological (environment), physiological (body) and behavioural (activity) conditions (p. 360).

WHAT ARE THE DIFFERENT PLAYTYPES?

Although there may be – and certainly have been – many more, sixteen different playtypes have been identified from the scientific literature. In this text, those identified in Hughes 1996a are used. They are:

- communication play
- creative play
- dramatic play
- deep play
- exploratory play
- fantasy play
- imaginative play
- locomotor play
- mastery play
- object play
- recapitulative play
- role play
- rough and tumble play
- social play
- socio-dramatic play
- symbolic play
  (See Hughes 1996a, Hughes 2002 and Hughes 2006 for a more comprehensive discussion of play types.)

82

These sixteen playtypes enable children to experience the w
variety of levels. For example:

By engaging in:	Children experience the worl
Communication Play	through the mediums of talking, singing and meta-communicating.
Creative Play	by exploring materials and different permutations of colours.
Deep Play	by interfacing with death and mortality.
Dramatic Play	by experiencing events by playing them out.
Exploratory Play	by ranging and investigating new spaces.
Fantasy Play	by exploring ideas that are unconnected with reality.
Imaginative Play	by exploring ideas that are connected with reality.
Locomotor Play	by engaging in three-dimensional movements.
Mastery Play	by attempting to exert control over the physical environment.
Object Play	by exploring the tactile and cognitive properties of objects.
Recapitulative Play	through our previous evolutionary stages.
Role Play	by experiencing adult functions by engaging in them.
Rough and Tumble Play	by calibrating one's own and others' tactile and muscular capabilities.
Social Play	by investigating and applying social protocols and rules.
Socio-Dramatic Play	by experiencing catharsis by dramatising difficult experiences.
Symbolic Play	by using materials and symbols to represent abstract ideas and concepts.

BUT WHY IS PLAY IMPORTANT?

What we can deduce from children's engagement in these playtypes, and from our own observations, is that there is a direct (i.e., causal) link between the various playtypes they enter into and the development of their capacity to symbolise, to create, to imagine, to communicate and so on.

It is as if each of these types of play is a kind of lens through which the child sees the world differently. If the child experiences its world through a symbolic lens for example, it perceives the world as being full of props that represent other things – flags, numbers, drawings, and models for example – allowing the child to appreciate that life is full of abstract ideas. However, if the child experiences the world through a locomotor lens, it perceives a different view, a world full of different sorts of three-dimensional movement – climbing, swinging and running – allowing the child to appreciate that on that level, life is a dimensional experience to move through and to navigate. And if the child experiences the world through the lens of mastery, it perceives a world of elemental challenges – damming streams, building dens, growing things – that allow the child to appreciate that life is dynamic, a constant struggle with powerful forces.

So the evolution of different kinds of play during our long evolutionary history – as well as making it possible for us to survive the pressures of extinction – has also made it possible for us to navigate life on numerous levels, as a multi-dimensional experience, via everything from imagination to communication. This powerful capacity for experience, and therefore learning and application, has probably provided the foundation for the numerous scientific and cultural developments that have occurred in most human societies over thousands of years.

PLAY AND BRAIN GROWTH

However, perhaps of even greater importance is the more recent discovery that when children play their brains do two things: they grow and they become organised and usable.

84

In his book, *The Ambiguity of Play*, Sutton-Smith (1997), drawing from the neurologist Huttenlocher's brain imaging work, makes an astounding suggestion, that

> 'children under 10 years of age have at least twice the potential brain capacity of those over 10 years'.

Meaning that the brains of young children, from babies to those in middle childhood, say 0–8 years old, are incredibly sensitised to growth, when compared to older children and adolescents.

The human brain's capacity for 'plasticity' as a consequence of the ascendancy of the birth of neural material (synaptogenesis) over synaptomortality (the death of neural material), has been known for at least fifty plus years as a consequence of Rosenzweig *et al.*'s work in the 1960s. Although then, it was thought that brain growth/plasticity was only the result of the effect of an 'enriched environment', rather than of play too (Rosenzweig *et al.* 1962, Ferchmin and Eterovic 1979, Zuckerman 1984).

Sutton-Smith (1997) suggested that any additional neurological material created by the plasticity process might be taken up by play, and this stimulated the notion that play (Hughes 1999) might act as a sub-operating system, or an interface between the immature brain and the flood of experience encountered by the playing child.

However, it was *Animal Play* (1998), edited by Marc Beckoff and John Byers, that arguably provided a huge stimulus for playwork theorists to begin to understand the impact that play might be having on brain growth. The book contained a series of seminal chapters that threw light on the evolution of play, brain growth, and the impact of play deprivation.

In it, for example, Burghardt (1998) stated:

> 'These authors presented evidence suggesting that play behaviour in some juvenile mammals may permanently modify muscle fibre differentiation and cerebella synapse distribution … the changes posited are permanent and unlikely to be induced by other behavioural means' (p. 18).

I interpreted this to mean that in the species he had studied, play itself permanently increased brain size and organised neural material. If we apply this to human children, then Burghardt is suggesting is that when children play their brains and muscles are modified by the play experience, and that that modification or change is permanent.

PLAY AND THE SENSITIVE PERIOD

The reason this happens is because human children play during what is known as a sensitive period.

> 'A sensitive period in behavioural development refers to a window in development during which specific types of experience permanently alter the course of development of the brain or of other systems that support behaviour. The experience-dependent development is not possible at ages before or after the window'. The author goes on to say, 'it is reasonable to postulate that play with its discrete age range of expression, may be another example of performance-dependent development' (pp. 210–11).
>
> Kroodsma (1981), Byers (1998) in Beckoff and Byers, *Animal Play*

This would also help to explain what Huttenlocher discovered during his brain imaging work too. My interpretation is this: different play behaviours have mutated over millions of years. Some of them – perhaps sixteen, although probably more – have had a successful effect on humans' capacity to withstand the pressures of extinction and have been selected and retained, as part of our behaviour. However, mutations that benefit play itself have also occurred, namely a sensitive period that favours brain growth, play *and* childhood, in that it is at its most effective between the ages of 0 and 8. As a species we are indebted for our continued existence to a process of natural selection, which, through random mutation and genetic selection on the basis of survival, has given us:

- different types of play which enable us to perceive and explore existence on multiple levels;
- a sensitive period which is active during the childhood age range of 0 and 8;
- a relationship between play, the sensitive period between 0 and 8, childhood and brain growth.

This indicates that over millions of years an evolving relationship between playing and neurological development or the development

86

of what are called substrates, i.e., underpinning developmental mechanisms, may have occurred. The great benefit of this may be, as Sylva (1977) also alluded, that playing stimulates 'not [just] specific behavioural routines' (p. 18), but the general mechanisms that enable thought and behaviour to happen in the first place. This powerfully reinforces the argument that play should never be exploited to train or educate children into specific ways of being, for in so doing the adaptive power of this mechanism may be compromised.

Playing during a sensitive period provides children with a general adaptive predisposition, which enables them to move fluidly between cultures, languages, technologies, climates and landscapes. Specialisation (Lorenz 1972), which is what any exploitation is inevitably about, may advantage affected children in a short-term vocational context, but it could have far-reaching adaptive consequences, which have the overall effect of disadvantaging and even disabling children in the longer term.

What this reveals is the large number of convergences that play and evolution have. It suggests that because play has not been discarded by natural selection; because play took place primarily from birth to about 8 years; because that period related to Huttenlocher's sensitive period; and because play was seen to be instrumental in or participant in brain plasticity and muscle development; playtypes may have evolved independently of one another over evolutionary time. Perhaps this is because they have advantaged the organism by both enabling the playful exploration of a perceived threat to a species continuation, and the comprehensive analysis of that threat, using the behavioural repertoires play contains, thus demonstrating that play has both a major anti-extinction capability and a developmental capability in the human evolutionary process.

However, that is not all. In *Animal Play*, Byers (p. 205) also states:

> '... in these three species, play is turned on when there is an opportunity for experience-dependent modification of the cerebellum, and it is turned off shortly after the architecture of the cerebellum is complete'.

Suggesting that playing is a deliberate, albeit unconscious choice on the part of the human organism, to accelerate brain growth, and that children play as an unconscious but deliberate act, to stimulate brain growth, and only when that growth is accomplished, do they stop playing.

Why is it useful to use the term organism rather than child? Although all children are an amalgamation of many influences – some cultural, some biological – many of the basic play processes are mainly biological in nature, uninfluenced by culture. And whilst the different manifestations of play may be overlaid by culture and experience, the actual mechanism is not born of culture but of biology. I am inferring from what Byers is stating above, that 'biological' processes do not relate to children as cultural entities but as biological entities, as organisms, experiencing processes over which they have no control at all. If different forms of play have mutated and been selected by our evolution, and if play is something our bodies do to generate neural tissue among other things, then children have little or no control over that process – although they may have control over what they do – it is probably regulated from within their central nervous system. In fact, Panksepp (1998) suggests as much by stating that play resides in the thalamus area.

However, what is just as intriguing is the role the different types of play might have. If, for example, children do engage in play to increase the size of their brains, might it be that different kinds or types of play have been selected because they have an influence on the growth of different parts or locations of the brain? In other words, might what children are doing when they play, actually influence the kind of brain they create during the sensitive period, *and* the efficacy of that brain to affect survival? For example, Lorenz (1972) writes of us as being successful because we are specialists in 'non-specialisation', but what of the child with a football brain, a computer games brain, a reading brain, a gun brain, a ballet brain or a virtual brain?

PLAYTYPES AS PREDICTORS AND SOLVERS OF EVOLUTIONARY PROBLEMS

Animal Play stimulated my speculation about the role of different types of play. However, in stating that play was 'most certainly' a heterogeneous category and that different playtypes may have 'different causal bases, functions, phylogenies and ontogenies' (p. 6), Burghardt (1998) begs a number of hugely important questions. For

88

example, when in our evolution did different playtypes appear, why did they appear then, in what order did they arrive? And working from the premiss that for them to still be such a prominent part of our behavioural repertoire *and* to have perhaps existed for many thousands, perhaps hundreds of thousands of years, they must still have and have had a significant evolutionary role or they would have disappeared as a result of natural selection. I wonder, as it was with the Periodic Table, to predict hitherto undiscovered elements, if it is possible to predict future playtypes; might – as I have suggested above – playtypes evolve as an evolutionary response to problems that would otherwise (without the evolution of a particular playtype) have resulted in our extinction as a species? Needless to say this implies that we are able to link the evolution of earlier playtypes to potential extinction events, and as yet we have not.

The enormity of these questions and the subsequent importance of providing a comprehensive evolutionary play experience to human children whose play opportunities might otherwise be lost or subsumed into an edu-care or pedagogical service for children is frightening. The need for playwork practice that emphasises the importance of unhindered (although intelligently supervised) access to play has never been more urgent or more heavily underpinned by evidence.

SO PLAY HAS A GENETIC COMPONENT?

Although it is likely that much of what we actually observe when children play is learnt or acquired through contemporary experience, the template on which that observable behaviour sits, the play 'jig' if you like, has been retained and passed on genetically through successive generations since the time it originally evolved.

In fact Hall's 'Theory of Recapitulation', which was the originating stimulus for recapitulative play, actually requires that simple or compound evolutionary memory be passed on generationally. The notion that different play types may have evolved independently and years apart, and are yet present in the play of every child, also implies a genetic component. That children engage in meta-communication and play cues which they can both emit and recognise in other emissions also suggests that play has genetic as well as learned components. That there is a synergy between the above 0–8 sensitive period, brain growth and play also indicated a genetic component to play. Finally, that play may significantly influence the type and timing of neurological and muscular construction, or the substrates that underpin them may also suggest a genetic component to play.

PLAY, ACTUALISATION, ORGANISATION AND CORTICAL MAPS

> The very fact that play contains so much nonsense, so much replication, and is so flexible certainly suggests that it is the prime domain for the actualisation of whatever the brain contains.
>
> (Sutton-Smith 1997: 226)

Play may have other important neural functions too. For it may not only create extra brain capacity, it may 'actualise' it and makes it usable. Sutton-Smith theorises about the 'enormous plasticity' of the infant brain, suggesting that the creation of an over-capacity of brain material ensures 'enough extra wiring for adaptation to any kind of environment in which the child is reared' (Huttenlocher (1990, 1992), Sutton-Smith (1997)). He also suggests that at birth, human infants have more going for them, than they will ever have again. Given the plausibility of the connections between infancy, play, the sensitive period, and plasticity, one could hardly argue!

However, he also draws our attention to another of play's possible functions. 'Play's function', he writes, 'may be to assist the actualisation of brain potential…its function [being] to save, in both brain and behaviour, more of the variability that is potentially there …' (p. 225).

What can we deduce from what Sutton-Smith is telling us? First of all that initially, as brain matter is produced, it is formless and not usable, even though the young infant makes 1000 trillion synaptic connections, they are likely to attenuate – die off – if they are not used (Huttenlocher 1990, 1992). My reading is that as the infant begins to play, so synaptic connections relating both to the actuality of the child's behaviour (what it is actually doing), *and* to the general applicability of the behaviour (increased flexibility, adaptive potential), begin to become organised into what we recognise as the functioning organ. Having said that, this is not a final or hard-wired state. The brain is like the sea, in a constant state of change, forming and reforming.

90

Brown (1998) adds 'Perhaps play functions as an "attractor", a stabiliser ... offering an alternative to what he calls "rigidification"'. What this implies is that ordinarily when neural material has formed and become organised, that is it. It and the behaviour it informs become rigid and inflexible. But as Gould (1996) suggests, 'We have evolved an extended childhood, presumably for the advantages imparted by prolonged flexibility for learning. And we retain some of this crucial flexibility into the adult stage that in most mammals entails rigidification of behaviour' (p. 54).

So perhaps play does act as an organisational jig (see previous section) on which minutely different behavioural mutations can sit – preserving both the flexibility, randomness and unpredictability of the play we see children engage in. Gould suggests quirkiness too, which may be a better term.

This should be no surprise. Children need both generalities and specifics from their playful interactions with the world, and with so little obvious knowledge or experience, given they can still perform awesome tasks like pick up languages, locomotor in three-dimensions, symbolise and fantasise, evolution may have provided a one-stop shop, which whilst not providing the means, offers a partnership between itself and the organism in which it dwells. Far from being parasitic, play joins with the human child not only to extend its life but also to offer it a level of fulfilment that it would otherwise never know (see Edelman 2006, Lewis 2005).

However, the developmental continuum starting with over-capacity, actualisation and organisation does not quite end there. For Edelman (1992) in suggesting that what he calls 'perceptual categorisation, memory, affect and [senses]' combine to form cortical maps one after the other. Brown (1998) adds, referring to two playing lionesses, that [their] rough and tumble play [could be] establishing new and dynamically interconnected maps each time they play. And that 'although', he says, 'the play signals given and received are real and unambiguous, the interplay between maps, the scenes they contain are highly individualistic' (Brown 1997, Damasio 1994, Edelman 1992), meaning that as they play, these lionesses are engaged in mock combat, which has both real survival (behavioural) benefits, whilst at the same time laying down a multilayered map of the experience. Brown adds that these maps remain present and available for modification throughout life and accumulate most rapidly in infancy and [adolescence] as the major cartography of learning.

These 'maps' are neurological representations of real recent events. They help children to navigate present and future events on numerous different and simultaneous levels. They contain virtual stored visual, kinaesthetic, emotional and spiritual experiences that record and store detailed representations of events (Gopnik 1993, Beckoff and Allen 1999).

Brown (1997) citing Edelman (1992) suggests that cortical maps may contribute to the formation of the human consciousness. 'These maps possess what Edelman describes as "re-entrant connectivity", which is the means by which the brain brings percept (something that is sensed) and concept (an abstract idea) together, allowing the emergence of a high order consciousness in human beings' (p. 255).

WHAT DOES PLAYING DO?

As well as having an intrinsic role in brain development, it is generally agreed both in the literature and more practically by playworkers that play has an important role in the development of the following essential skills:

- movement and balance
- communication
- social interaction
- perception
- emotional expression and reciprocation
- problem-solving and abstraction
- logic
- aesthetics
- creativity
- motor skills (Bruner 1972)
- communication skills (Chomsky 1965, van Hoof 1972, Bateson 1955)
- problem-solving skills (Harlow 1973)
- social skills (Arlitt 1937, Pribram 1967)
- perceptual and cognitive skills (Kohler 1937, Wolfgang 1974)
- creative skills (Harlow 1973)

- emotional skills (Wilson 1975)
- aesthetic skills (Klopfer 1970)
    (See Hughes 1996b for a more comprehensive explanation.)

This suggests that if we do not behave playfully, or if we cannot, because we are play-deprived for example, then we may not gain these skills, or we may not gain them with the same degree of competence and effectiveness as we otherwise might have, or they may be corrupted or dysfunctional in some way.

Simpson (1976) and Connolly (1978) suggested that because they play children are able to adapt more easily to new physical surroundings, using the skill of calibration; whilst Suomi and Harlow and Suomi (1971) proposed that not playing made calibrating our physical surroundings difficult, if not impossible. '*When these monkeys reach physiological maturity they are incompetent in virtually every aspect of monkey social activity.*'

Others, including Loizos (1967), Bruner (1974), Sylva (1977), Sutton-Smith (1979) and Hutt *et al.* (1989), have written about the importance of play in terms of the flexibility it affords the player, suggesting that what was becoming known as combinatorial flexibility (Bruner 1972, Sylva 1977) leads to new thought, which in turn leads to new combinations of thought, a prerequisite of the problem-solving process. More on this later.

PLAY, MIRROR NEURONS AND RESILIENCE

In their groundbreaking and eminently readable review and analysis, Lester and Russell (2008) highlight a possible role undertaken by play as both an outcome of mirror neuronal activity and a 'primary behaviour for developing resilience' (p. 47).

Citing Rizzolatti *et al.* 2001, Gallese *et al.* 2004 and Burghardt 2005, they suggest that the 'mirror neuron system' provides a conduit, a bridge, between the actions of others and similar matching, imitative or imagined actions. That as children watch each other, so, 'the same neurons fire as those that fire when they actually perform the actions observed'. They see the mirror neuron system as a potential pathway to further understanding and the integration of physical, affective and imaginative behaviours, and suggest that 'this amazing ability to imitate is one way of opening and maintaining interaction, leading to shared activity, dialogue or play' (p. 46).

This certainly has resonance with Bekoff's (1997), Bekoff and Allen's (1998) and Gopnik's (1993) analysis of play bows and behavioural intentionality, arguing that 'certain kinds of information that comes, literally, from inside ourselves is coded in the same way as information that comes [from] observing the behaviour of others'. Gopnik claims [for example] that others' body movements are mapped into one's own kinaesthetic sensations, based on prior experience of the observer ... (p. 110). This view adds support to Brown and Damasio's suggestion that play enables the formation of cortical maps (see above).

I think what is both interesting and perhaps anticipated is that play and its impacts are both whole body and whole species experiences. That there does exist an evolutionarily selected synergy between individuals within the same species that creates, for example, psychosocial similarities. Anticipation for example, where the potential for a shared experience is not only acknowledged, but also imagined, may be a powerful precursor to some forms of bonding.

Lester and Russell also suggest that children's play provides a primary behaviour for developing resilience, and regard this as a key and fundamental finding from the evidence presented. Resilience is defined as 'the capacity of dynamic systems to withstand or recover from significant challenges' (Masten 2007: 923).

'Resilience', write Lester and Russell, 'marks the ability to spring back from and successfully adapt to adversity', although in those who are less flexible, there may be a cost. Stevens and Price (2000), for example, say that children are not resilient, but malleable, that experience changes brain structure and this has echoes of the work of McEwen and Balbernie. In a sense they are talking about different intensities of the same thing. *Roget's International Thesaurus* cites changeability, lightheartedness, rebound and flexibility as major characteristic of resilience – each of which is also a major characteristic of the trial and error nature of the play experience.

Anyone who as a child built dams to hold back the sea, or water from a stream, will appreciate the need to be able to 'get over' the disappointments inherent in every play experience, whether it be trying to make friends, understand something new, falling out of a tree, or even lighting a fire in the wind and rain.

The broad lesson that playing teaches children is that having the capacity to bounce back is necessary – even though it is accompanied by a degree of desensitisation. For although, from the adult observer's view-point there may be a sense in which play is unreal and not serious, for the child – whatever the context – it is both real and serious at the time, even though its life may not depend on the success or otherwise of what it is engaged in.

Perhaps resilience is more a product of the unrealistic optimism, egocentricity and reactivity to which Bjorkland and Green (1992) alluded. Commenting, Sutton-Smith (1997) said, they (children under five years of age) 'overestimate their ability to function skilfully, despite continued negative feedback'. Furthermore they tend, as Piaget has said, to see things rather selectively, from their own perspective. And they are highly reactive to whatever stimuli are placed before them, regardless of the relevance of the stimuli to whatever else is going on, a characteristic Werner (1957) spoke of as their 'lability' (p. 226).

My reason for including this passage from Sutton-Smith's *Ambiguity of Play*, is its clear articulation of features similar to those considered by Lester and Russell. Lability describes the capacity of an organism for change. So does malleability and so does resilience. What Sutton-Smith seems to be suggesting, however, is that in their mad dash for experience of whatever kind, which, as we have seen, may be directly related to plasticity and neural organisation, young children are unrealistically optimistic. What Sylva (1977) described as 'treating everything as being of potential biological significance' (Lorenz 1972). Demonstrating, if not proving, that play has been selected because it is so effective at acting as the interface on the world.

CHAPTER 4

PLAY TYPES AND THE PLAYWORK MENU

WHAT ARE PLAY TYPES?

Perhaps one of the more beautiful evolutionary mutations is that of the different kinds of play – each with its own reason for mutating, each with its own reason for being selected, each with its own time of genesis, and each with its own discrete, normally visible identity.

Without the different types of play, human childhood – and that of numerous other species – rather than the excited leap in a diverse unknown which it is, would be a cloning period, where identical copies of parents, mirroring their knowledge, beliefs, values, emotions and perceptions, would simply move humanity onto a conveyor towards extinction. Quite simply, without play, we wouldn't be here. What playtypes give us is access to the infinite diversity of experience that is life on Earth, and of course the flexibility both in brain and behaviour that comes from that.

Although we now acknowledge the current existence of sixteen different types of play – there may be more – there have almost certainly been others, that may have enabled children from past ages to interact playfully with the world as it then was, and adapt to it as they experienced the changes brought about by massive volcanic explosions, life-extinguishing earthquakes and apocalyptic tsunamis.

An understanding of playtypes not only gives us a deeper insight into the complex processes of adaptation; it also provides us with a retrospective (anthropological) view of our past evolutionary story, and a forecasting tool, that helps to extrapolate our future.

Before playtypes, playworkers used to describe what they observed children doing under one umbrella heading, 'play'. Obviously they knew that within that overall term children did different things like talking, running, swinging, climbing, creating and dramatising, but these were all regarded simply as different parts of the same homogeneous act, playing.

However, more recently, because of new research and the application of more thought to the complexity of play in the field of playwork itself, play has begun to be broken down into different sub-headings which according to Burghardt (1997) have an identity and uniqueness all of their own. In other words, rather than seeing play as one thing with different facets, play is now seen as a collection of unique behaviours. These sub-divisions of play have become more generally known as 'play types' (Hughes 1996a), and they represent behavioural routines, or modes of thought, which are quite separate from one another and which serve different purposes (Burghardt 1997, 2005).

In 1996, *A Playworker's Taxonomy of PlayTypes* (Hughes 1996a) was published. The taxonomy or 'scheme of categorisation' was produced to enable those who worked with children to call similar playful routines, by the same names, to 'sing from the same hymn sheet', and to be clearer and thus more specific about what they were observing when they watched children playing.

This was by no means the first categorisation ever produced, there are others (Parten 1932, Piaget 1962, Smilansky 1968, Mitchell 1990, Fagan 1995). However, unlike them, the *Playworker's Taxonomy* focussed on the use of everyday language to describe the various play-types that playworkers were observing on a daily basis where they worked.

Initially, fifteen discrete sub-categories of play were identified in the literature for inclusion in the taxonomy. They were:

Symbolic; Rough and Tumble; Socio-Dramatic; Social; Creative; Communication; Exploratory; Fantasy; Imaginative; Locomotor; Mastery; Object; Role; Deep and Dramatic Play.

This was increased to sixteen in 2002 to accommodate *Recapitulative Play*, which it was judged not only described a unique set of playful routines, but also was particularly prolific in play in the wild, particularly where other species, myths and rituals were concerned.

Each of the sixteen playtypes included within the *Taxonomy* have a unique behavioural signature. For example:

Play Type	What you see
Communication Play	talking, singing and metacommunicating.
Creative Play	exploring materials and permutations of colours.
Deep Play	interfacing with death and mortality.
Dramatic Play	experiencing events by playing them out.
Exploratory Play	ranging and investigating new spaces.
Fantasy Play	manifesting ideas that are unconnected with reality.
Imaginative Play	manifesting ideas that are connected with reality.
Locomotor Play	engaging in three-dimensional movement.
Mastery Play	interacting with the physical environment.
Object Play	exploring the tactile and cognitive properties of objects at close hand.
Recapitulative Play	recapping on previous evolutionary stages.
Role Play	exploring adult functions by engaging in them.
Rough and Tumble Play	calibrating one's own and others' tactile and muscular properties.
Social Play	investigating and applying social protocols and rules.
Socio-Dramatic Play	experiencing catharsis by dramatising difficult experiences.
Symbolic Play	using material and symbols to represent abstract and conceptual ideas.

Several benefits came from the development of a specific taxonomy for playwork. The first – outlined in Hughes (2006) – was that it made possible improved communication and understanding about the source, construction and complexity of play. Like any other discipline, playwork has to be funded and that means convincing people who may not be expert in play, that the application for funding is valid. In the past, play has been considered a difficult to define, even

98

esoteric phenomenon. The *Taxonomy* was intended to help this situation by clearly defining different playtypes and most importantly, grounding each one in the scientific literature. (Further discussion of the benefits of a knowledge of playtypes can be found in Hughes 2006, pp. 29–31.)

However, from a practical perspective, perhaps the greatest benefit, both of the *Taxonomy* and a better knowledge of the different playtypes, was that they helped to ensure that what the playworker offered in terms of accessible play experiences was comprehensive, i.e., that the experiences that were made available to children were sourced from one of the known playtypes, and that experiences from each of the playtypes was available. For example, playing chase was sourced from locomotor play, and making collage was sourced in creative play. The reason for drawing from all of the known playtypes, is that we cannot assume that one type of play is more or less important than another, and avoid those we are less attracted to. So to ensure that it is the children themselves who make the choice regarding which game to play or which activity to do, we provide for every type of play.

How do we know what types of play exist? The short answer is we don't, or to be more precise, we're not sure. Certainly by exploring the scientific literature for references to different types of play, which we then categorise, we can build up a list of known or recognised types, and then we can use the list we create to ensure that we are working with each one. But of course there may be other types of play that are currently unidentified; if that is the case, we will have to find ways of incorporating them into our practice if and when they are identified.

Much of the thinking initially contained in the *Taxonomy* was eventually confirmed by findings in two later publications. *Animal Play* (Beckoff and Byers 1998), and *The Genesis of Animal Play* (Burghardt 2005), whose texts then helped stimulate the more advanced playtypes ideas in Hughes (2006).

Both texts presented revelatory suggestions, which until that time had only existed in the intuition and imaginations of practitioners. In *Animal Play*, for example, Burghardt states, 'Play [is] "most certainly" a heterogeneous category and different playtypes may have different causal bases, functions and phylogenies' (p. 6).

Let's look at the first part of this statement, Play [is] 'most certainly' a heterogeneous category. This is reaffirmation of what the *Taxonomy* suggests; that the word PLAY is a grouping term, that it is not *one* thing – PLAY – but several different things. In the second part of this powerful statement he takes this further. 'Different types of play', he says, 'may have different causal bases, functions and phylogenies'. This was new thinking for playwork.

Burghardt seems to be suggesting a number of startling characteristics for play. Not only are the different 'things' that make PLAY, actually different types of play, or different playtypes – that although they differ in terms of what you see, they still satisfy the same identifying criteria of free choice, personal direction, intrinsic motivation, spontaneity and so on – but each of these different playtypes may have different causal bases (there may be different reasons why they have evolved), they may have different functions (they may do different things), and they may have different phylogenies (they may have evolved at different times in our evolutionary history).

And as well as suggesting new functions for play, Burghardt also implies that once there were no playtypes at all, and thus no play in the behavioural repertoire of our ancient ancestors, or other playtypes have evolved and come and gone over time. In other words, different ancestors played differently.

As I have written above, in the taxonomy I suggest sixteen different playtypes: Symbolic; Rough and Tumble; Socio-Dramatic; Social; Creative; Communication; Exploratory; Fantasy; Imaginative; Locomotor; Mastery; Object; Role; Deep; Dramatic and Recapitulative. (A more comprehensive analysis of each playtype can be found in Hughes 2006.)

My interpretation of what Burghardt is saying is that each of these different types of play has evolved or appeared at different points in our evolutionary history, for different reasons and to do different things. Meaning each different playtype has a job, which is different from any other playtypes. What could these jobs be?

```
     pt1      pt2      pt3      pt4       pt5       pt6     pt7       ptn
0--/-------/--------/-------/--------/--------/-----/------/---201·
   C1       C2       C3       C4        C5        C6      C7        Cn
```

Figure 4.1 Different playtypes evolved to stave off the pressures of extinction.

100

In Chapter 3 I presented a brief analysis for the development of play-types to date, and the kinds of conditions under which the different playtypes may have evolved – Burghardt (2005) – conditions that may have also included population bottlenecks, extreme meteorological or astronomical events, food shortages or even factors to do with good mental health and happiness, like communication and attachment.

The picture that Burghardt's (1998) earlier statement conjures up is of a mammal (existing long before homo erectus), which does not play at all. Then, as certain [threatening] conditions – perhaps territory or threat related – converge over time, play behaviours begin to evolve. One type of play, out of a number that mutate, is successful at staving off the threat, and is selected. Could this be perhaps how our first playtype appeared?

Applying this conjecture to play in general, we can say that under different sets of circumstances, different behavioural routines that we call playtypes evolved to do something. What, we aren't yet sure! Neither can we be sure which playtype was the first one, although locomotor play is a good bet, simply because without the evolution of three dimensional movement, attack and escape would have been impossible, death would have occurred and other playtypes would not have evolved. A possibility with which Burghardt (2005), Hughes (2006) and Byers (1984) agree. 'The conclusion that locomotor play is the earliest appearing type of play is supported by the findings in marsupials' (p. 224).

If each playtype does have a function, it probably relates to a potential threat to us, either individually or as a species. This suggests that each of our current playtypes evolved as balancing mechanism to aspects of behavioural or intellectual underperformance in the prevailing conditions – low mobility, poor flexibility, inefficient problem solving, ineffective communication and so on. The evolution of playtypes to address what had become comparative inadequacies had the effect of enhancing our potential to adapt and survive, i.e., communication play helped human beings to better understand one another, whilst symbolic play helped them to think more conceptually.

It may even be, as it is with atoms in the molecular world, that *all* human behaviours are compounds of different playtypes, and that playtypes or the precursors to full-blown playtypes, i.e., proto-playtypes, are evolution's behavioural atoms and molecules.

Of course, this is all just speculation, but it does lend support to the earlier contention that all playtypes are equally important, and one should not be provided for at the expense of another, even though some playtypes are judged as problematic in some playwork contexts.

Imaginative play, creative and fantasy play, for example, are normally viewed as totally innocuous to most adults engaged in working with or providing for children's play because they're easy to manage. Loco-motor play on the other hand needs a lot of space, and many spaces given over to play are far too small for it, and this can create obvious problems. Rough and tumble play is another difficult area. Although regarded by researchers as 'the cause of social bonding' and having a positive affect for children (Baldwin 1982), it is still often banned, for fear that children might hurt one another. Deep play is also frowned upon in many settings, even though it provides a conduit for acquiring and honing many skills that benefit children, and is also a mechanism for children to access an understanding of mortality. Deep play may even enable children to devise risk-assessment strategies as a way of dealing with what Stanislav Grof (1975) called the 'agonising existen-tial crisis', resulting from an increased awareness of the nature of death and dying.

Until we know more, we playworkers should exercise great caution about depriving children of the kinds of playtypes children have always experienced when adults have not been present. The scientific literature, although not conclusive, suggests that all forms of play have an important role in the development of human children. In fact highly respected researchers, including Burghardt and Byers, agree that play has one overriding benefit – it makes children's brains grow bigger.

The downside of this for playwork, is that if we arbitrarily omit par-ticular playtypes from a child's experience, then the brain generally, or the different parts of the brain to which those playtypes may relate, will not manifest their optimum growth potential, and the child will be disabled, relative to other children who have experienced those playtypes.

102

TRIUNE BRAIN THEORY

The structure of the brain has undergone particularly interesting evolutionary analyses, which could also throw light on the chronology, evolution and purpose of playtypes.

In the early 1960s, the neuroscientist Paul MacLean put forward the idea that the human brain has evolved in the three quite separate stages, and that the resulting three parts are radically different from one another. These different parts, three brains in one, are shown in the now famous diagram of MacLean's Triune Brain.

MacLean (1985) suggested that although these three brains communicated with one another (Stevens and Price 2000) 'each one had a different phylogenetic history, its own special intelligence, its own sense of

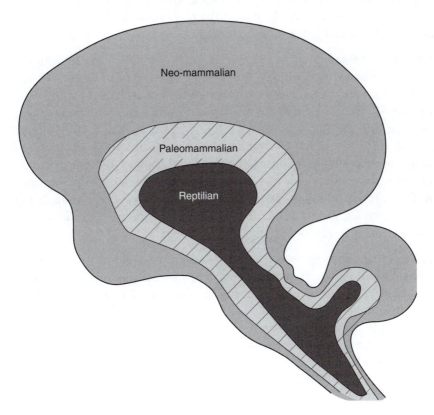

Figure 4.2 MacLean's Triune Brain.

time and space, and its own motor functions' (p. 15). Furthermore, the three brains were 'radically different in their chemistry and structure, and in an evolutionary sense, aeons apart' (p. 219).

As the diagram illustrates, the central or oldest part of MacLean's Triune Brain he called the 'Rc' or reptilian complex. It mediates a spontaneous reaction to the world (Hughes 2006) that was basically composed of attack and defence behaviour. The layer covering the Rc, he named Paleomammalian Brain. It was made up of those 'sub-cortical' neuronal structures which comprise the Limbic System and which are responsible for emotion. Stevens and Price (2000) say that MacLean (1985) particularly draws attention to three forms of behaviour that most clearly distinguish the evolutionary transition from reptiles to mammals. These are, they say, nursing and maternal care, audio vocal communication for maintaining mother-offspring contact, and play (p. 16), although he is not clear what he means by play. The final or most recent layer he called the neo-mammalian or neo-cortex, which is responsible for rational thought.

One might reasonably ask, is it plausible that what we see as different types of play in our children, are in fact visual manifestations of the different stages in our brain's evolution? That as well as recapitulating playtypes that have appeared at different points in evolutionary time, we manifest reptilian play too, or at least a reptilian component? Could different playtypes actually derive from different parts of MacLean's Triune structure (Hughes 2006), not as Burghardt might have suggested after all – as a linear progression mediated by our need to fight off the pressures of extinction – but as a visible manifestation of the complex neurochemical mixture in our brains, communicating its needs as it interacts with the world, instead?

Consider this paraphrase of Stevens and Price (2000) to illustrate this 'When a child enters a play space she brings with her, in a manner of speaking, a crowd of people from her past. What evolutionary play-work has recognised is that as well as her modern self, she brings the hunter-gatherer, the primate and the reptile from her ancestral past too. The play space is crowded with this menagerie, each member of which has a right to have her needs addressed and, if possible, to have her play needs fulfilled' (p. 242).

104

PLAY TYPES AND THE PLAY ENVIRONMENT

Although from a management perspective some playtypes are problematic, it is relatively easy to provide for most of them and on the whole what they need is straightforward. Disposable and scrounged materials, loose parts, dressing-up clothes and props, landscaping including naturally occurring features like rocks, trees, bushes and water, and of course open space, will cater very adequately for most of them. However, thought does need to be given to the location and layout of different features and materials, and the playworker may need more than one, perhaps several, of some things. A variety of different materials – fabrics, household items, art materials, stationery, furniture – will certainly facilitate symbolic, creative, fantasy, role, dramatic and imaginative play, although dramatic play may benefit from a specified raised area like a stage, too,

Rough and tumble can take place on any surface. But if there is genuine concern that some children will hurt themselves, the playworker could provide a softer play area with mats and mattresses for it. The playworker can also ensure that any rough and tumble that happens does not cross-over into a real fight, by being aware that play spaces are not only artificial in their content and construction, they do not accurately reflect how children behave towards one another outside. For example, individuals or groups who find themselves in the same supervised play space might never choose to mix outside, choosing instead to avoid each other. When they do find themselves in the same place, playworkers should be sensitive to any potential dynamic, and whilst not over-managing healthy interaction between what might normally be competing groups, should also recognise that that interaction may lead to physical competition or even fighting, which may need a different approach.

Socio-dramatic play is more the realm of a therapeutic or psychotherapeutic environment, although children will always dramatise and play-out what is happening to them in 'real-life'. As with dramatic play it is best to provide a specific area where children can engage in both dramatic and socio-dramatic play. Because of the potentially explosive nature of the socio-dramatic narrative, I would expect that area to be a particular focus for the playworker. Like the rough and tumble space, this area could also contain softer materials to protect children if a highly emotional incident does occur.

Social play can also take up lots of space and playworkers should try to ensure that children have enough space to run about and let off steam. Adequate levels of social and locomotor interaction are crucial to health and well being, but without social play children cannot understand what and how they are feeling in social situations, or decide on their own rules of engagement with other human beings. As well as enabling children to socially calibrate themselves, i.e., How close do I stand? How hard do I touch? How loud do I speak? Can I look directly at that person? etc., they are also faced with learning to solve the puzzle of what other children's faces and bodies are communicating about mood and motive, when they are playing. This particular form of what is known as meta-communication (Bateson 1955; van Hoof 1972; Else and Sturrock 1998) is a very sophisticated device we humans have evolved. It has the effect of either topping up what we say with words – using emphasis, pitch and volume – with body movements or stances, and complex facial expressions, involving our eyes, our eyebrows and our mouths, or – perhaps as the triune brain theory suggests – that language (rational) may be what we have evolved to mediate our more primitive responses to the world, like aggression (reptilian) or fear or repulsion (limbic).

Meta-communication is a very interesting area for evolutionary playwork. Children are invariably socialised to trust and believe adults and they rarely question whether what adults say is true or false. However, in the child conducive atmosphere of a good play setting, children will immediately challenge adults when they detect a conflict between what the words are intended to convey, and what that adult's face and body tell them. This is hardly surprising given that it is both a developmental and a survival advantage to be able to read the actuality of situations involving other human beings or even other species, quickly and accurately. A detailed understanding of the language of meta-communication will help any child better to decode and encode the complex interactions that go on between adults, and between adults and children, and help them make decisions on appropriate courses of action in different circumstances. This has obvious advantages if children are approached by strangers who might also cause them harm, but it can also be useful in understanding how to deal with manipulative, exploitative, bullying or oppressive older children and adults. Needless to say, the observant playworker will identify instantly the child who has been ill treated or over-indulged by their body and facial expressions, whether that is unsolicited flinches and fawning, or inappropriate swaggers and inconsiderate behaviour.

Games like tag and hide and seek, which have a locomotor as well as a social component, and adolescent games like Spin the Bottle and Knocking Down Ginger, all contribute to a better understanding of how children network and relate to one another. So much of human relationships involves what Wilber (1996) calls the 'subtle' realm, and require in the child acute skills of observation, memory, mimicking, rehearsal and hearing co-ordination.

There are arguments for and against a specific space for creative play. If one can only provide for painting and model making, this can probably happen anywhere and should be happening wherever the children are. But some play projects make it possible for children to engage in more sophisticated creative activities like making jewellery and candles and so on, which require specially designated areas and tools and have health and safety implications. I have often wondered whether this kind of highly specialised activity, which invariably has to be supervised and taught to children, belongs in a play space, or whether it would be better kept in the school environment, which is more suited for it. Specialised activities may provide adults with 'products' to show off, but the price for the child may be that the playground loses spontaneity, and the natural tendency to destroy which is the normal final chapter of a creative session is eradicated.

However, if it is there and children do engage with it, a special area specifically designed to cater for the use of hot, sharp, delicate and expensive materials and tools is an essential. However, I would still ask myself, who is this for, whose needs are being met? Is it for me, or for a more artistically inclined worker, or is it really for the children, because I have assessed a deficit in the level and type of creative play they can engage in?

Resources are always under pressure and they may be needed elsewhere. If they are used to fund access to a particular play type, be clear that it is the children's needs that are being met. I remember visiting a play project some years ago, and was concerned to see twelve table-tennis tables in their indoor accommodation. When I asked, 'Why so many ping-pong tables?' I was told the senior worker liked to play table tennis!

A great deal of communication play will happen without any facilitation at all, although prompts like nursery rhyme murals, music and books, may stimulate it. Perhaps the most important point to make is that the playworkers should try not to censor how children communicate.

In Hughes (1996a) I described communication play as the way we access vocabulary, nuance, fun and rude words and dual meanings. Sometimes we forget that language itself is not just words, it is the meaning of those words in different contexts and with certain emphases. And as I describe above, communication is not just about the spoken word but includes body posture and metacommunication too. In my experience, children are not conscious of the meaning of many words until they are made conscious either by the reaction those words get when they are used, or by the reaction they get from others when they use them. Children are rarely intentionally offensive, but if the use of words creates a reaction, they will use them again and again to get that effect. The following two extracts were overheard from two small children at an open-air festival:

■ Willy-bum, willy-bum, poo, poo, fart pants.
■ What's the message? Fart, fart, that's the message.

These words were probably picked up individually in other contexts and were not seen then as particularly funny. It was only when the children strung them together that they discovered that they made sounds that made them (and the rest of us) laugh.

Sometimes, children learn words or phrases that adults regard as offensive. Dealing with this conundrum needs great sensitivity on the part of the playworker. The play space is where children come to play, ideally to experience adult-free play, if the play space is compensating for a lack of space elsewhere. In this context the playworker's main function is to facilitate that. However, some professionals still argue that one of the characteristics of good play provision is that it offers protection to the children using it. That is generally taken to mean protection from dogs, traffic, and dangerous hazards like electricity or predatory adults. However, in this specific context, it may also mean protecting children from other children's language by actually stopping those children using certain words or terms. I am not sure how appropriate or even ethical that level of intervention is, even if the words do cause we adults offence. It may be an intervention too far and certainly requires a careful and thoughtful judgement call.

Children have to sort out language and other forms of communication as they go along. Discrimination of meaning and intent is after all, a very necessary survival skill. If one child calls another child 'four eyes', for example, should we step in and stop the child saying that? If that is the case when do we stop intervening? If a child uses 'racist' language, which it has clearly learnt from a parent or relative, should we step in, and if so, on what basis? Some adults believe that racist language is a special case that should always be confronted. But surely we are not in the business of confronting four- or five-year-old children in their own play space, who are behaving perfectly normally, first by absorbing their local language and secondly by using it. If that child had been playing out in the street or in the wild, a playworker would not have been there to intervene, so why do it in the child's play space just because the space is artificial and contains playworkers? Generally language should be left to children to sort out. On the whole they will make it clear when they are offended, intimidated or embarrassed by what another child is saying. Of course – and this refers to another important playwork judgement call – if a child is being harassed, if a child is suffering a barrage of language over time, if a child is being persecuted, then of course we should intervene and protect that child, but that is less about language per se and more about persistent intimidation. But we should not act as linguistic arbiters and react as soon as a child says something sensitive to another child. To do that places us between the two and destroys any opportunity they might take to resolve the situation themselves.

Personally, I restrict my intervention to when it all begins to be less about communication and more about persecution. When the perpetrator is apparently enjoying the discomfort of his target, when the target is obviously feeling uncomfortable and showing it, when an innocent remark escalates into a linguistic feeding frenzy. We have to use common sense.

The language and communication issue can be very complicated. At one play setting, I heard a child shout, 'Fucking Paki', only to turn around to see two brothers, both from a Kashmiri background, squaring up to each other, with one of them shouting this 'racist' insult at the other.

At another play space, local middle-childhood boys, six to ten years of age, frequently used homophobic terms like gay and poof to insult one another. Whilst I didn't consider it my role to provide gender orientation education there, I did judge that part of my role was to insert metaphorical question marks where children perceived something as correct or obvious when it might not be. To address the homophobic issue, I went and bought an old bicycle – a model with no cross bar – to ride from home to the playground. In that location, where status was very important and where to have the latest mountain bike, trainers, stereo, iPod, Wii or whatever was an absolute esteem essential, to arrive on an old bike was bad enough, but to arrive on a model normally chosen by women was total heresy and threw my own sexuality into question. The point I made to them was, 'Do you understand what any of this homophobic stuff is about?' Their reaction was firstly amazement, then laughter, and then a real decrease in the homophobic language.

All too often, what with peer pressure, TV fashion pressure, music business pressure, this pressure and that pressure, small children in particular do not have a clue about the meaning, or more importantly the impact, of much of what they are saying. It is vital therefore that they be given a chance to discover meaning and impact, before we pile in team handed to 'teach or correct' them, perhaps leaving them feeling inadequate and humiliated as a consequence, simply because we perceived ourselves as better editors of their language and behaviour, than is their own experience.

Exploratory play requires loose parts, puzzles and space. A playwork colleague in Belfast always kept a big box containing clocks, locks and other things like old radios, so that the children she worked with could pull them to bits, see how they worked and then try to put them back together again. Another interpretation of the term exploratory play might be playfully exploring the play environment, and that has other playwork implications. It is a good idea from time to time to look at the environment being offered to children and ask, perhaps at a team meeting, 'Would we have wanted or been stimulated, to play here ourselves?'. Or, 'Would my children want to play here?' The answer would probably be a resounding 'yes' to both questions if the play space was an interesting place to be. Visual effects, pictures, projections, structures, planting and building all change a bland space into one to explore. Mazes are great, so is landscaping. Simply being able to move from a busy area to a more secluded one is interesting. Moving from a flat area to a high area, or shielding off part of the environment with cloth or paper will attract the curious mind. Anything that means the only way the child will find out about where s/he is, is to explore it.

Mastery play is also vital, and access to it is crucial because of its contribution to good mental health (Stevens and Price 2000, p. 7). In many of its manifestations it could just as easily be called elemental play, because it is so often about mastering the elements.

Mastery play is actually quite difficult to provide for indoors, unless you have a large space to work in. This is because it is about the child interacting with the natural world; learning the effect/affect of trying to master different aspects of the natural environment. I use this term 'trying' deliberately, because mastery is about trying things out, it is about process, about trial and error when interacting with all aspects of nature. It is about discovering what can be controlled (a garden), what might be controllable with more knowledge, practice or information (a dam), and what, despite every effort, is beyond control – the weather, for example.

From a play perspective the term Mastery describes a very effective and enjoyable, although not altogether risk-free, process, where children interact with whole range of geological, botanical, elemental and atmospheric aspects of their habitat, in ways which often have a basis in engineering, science and construction.

Mastery play is a vitally important way of engaging with the world in a 'child-scale' format, and learning important lessons by doing, observing and reflecting. Mastery is a great deal about asking questions of the natural world and exploring what can be controlled, what should be controlled, how things can be controlled, and so on. The fun is often in losing control or in never having had it in the first place, rather than in any form of environmental domination.

Trying to hold back the tide and by so doing playing with the notion of futility is a good example of mastery play. Mastery is also about working with nature in interdependent ways. Building a camp out of natural materials, for example, not only tells children it can be done, it enables them to acknowledge the assistance that the natural environment can give. This is a hugely important environmental, as well as a play, lesson, but it is one increasing numbers of children are never going to learn unless they are given the opportunity to engage in mastery play in a play setting.

Mastery play not only provides information and questions about the context that is being played in, it encourages children to question. In his book *Play* (2009), Brown quotes Isaac Azimov saying 'The most exciting phrase to hear in science...is not Eureka, but, that's funny' (p. 143), meaning that's strange, I wonder why that happened? That's what Mastery play makes children ask. Other play types do much the same in their own particular area of experience. Children should not need to be taught to question, their play should contain such unexpected and unimagined experiences, i.e., experiences that contain what Koestler (1967) called the 'aha reaction', that questioning should be a natural corollary to play.

Object play, or problem-solving play as it is also known, needs loose parts, and an interesting environment that throws up problems for children to solve.

Deep play, although vitally important, is another of the play types that is losing ground, partly, I think, because of our litigious culture, but also because playworkers have become over concerned with safety in recent years.

The received wisdom seems to be that children should never get hurt when they play; never graze their knees, or get the odd bang on the head! But these 'accidents' are unavoidable in Deep play, and there is a reason for this. As implied by Burghardt (1998), each play type has a unique function. Geertz (1972) implied that Deep play's function might be to bring [children] alongside mortality so that they can learn not to fear death. Fear of death is probably human's most dominant neurosis, and certainly one of humanity's most ubiquitous sources of psychological instability. Given that the instability caused by neurosis is bad for human survival, it is possible that evolution has addressed this by selecting behaviours like Deep play that have the effect of balancing fear against reckless enjoyment.

That doesn't mean that Deep play exists so that children can kill, or nearly kill themselves, quite the reverse. Instead it is a playful acknowledgement that although death and dying are real, and that they will happen to us all, we should not allow them to dominate our lives. In this sense, Deep play helps children to come to terms with knowledge that is difficult to comprehend and to accept. Like the other play types, engaging in Deep play is good for children's mental health, and to stop or restrict them from engaging in it impoverishes their experience and their ability to cope with the realities of life. One of the other major aspects of Deep play is that it makes it possible for children to play with risk and learn how to risk assess. This is dealt with in some detail by Gill (2007).

The great majority of children are neither stupid, nor suicidal. They will not deliberately go far beyond the limits of their known skills. But to develop at all, they need to take some of what they do beyond its previous limit, simply to see if they can. When we see a child engaged in something 'dangerous', we are making that judgement from our standpoint, not from theirs. For them, what they are doing may be exhilarating or fun, and they are certainly not going out to deliberately maim themselves. It might, however, be a part of their computation that injury, whilst not a probability, is a possibility. All human beings have to learn to risk-assess, and where better than a play setting – a space devoid of hazards, which is supervised/operated by someone who understands what is going on and who will almost certainly have a first aid qualification and be in touch with the emergency services – to do this experimentation? It is not often I would sing the praises of artificial play environments over the natural environment, but in the case of Deep play I would. To understand caution, to compute risk, to respect the built and natural environments from the perspective of the risks they contain, but not to be afraid of them, is essential to personal survival and a happy life. It is need-to-know material and most of it can be accessed in a high-quality playwork space.

However, a huge change needs to take place in parenting before this can happen more generally. Today's Mums and Dads seem even more frightened for their children's safety, than were past generations of parents. Parents are so petrified of their child getting hurt or injured, that in over-protecting them, they do exactly what is required to almost guarantee that an accident will happen.

Play is nature's way of training children to successfully navigate the environment they find themselves in. If we stop them playing – if we stop them interacting with the world without a parent constantly telling them to be careful – then they cannot learn that navigation, and a simple operation like crossing the road, becomes a huge ordeal. Like any other loving parent, I never wanted my children to get hurt or injured or hit by a car or either. But whilst I recognised that feeling this was normal, what was also normal was the acknowledgement that these things might happen, as awful as they are. There is a point in a child's life when the child has to be – to a greater or lesser extent – allowed, and even encouraged to get on with it, as there is in the lives of the young of every other species. Children cannot be carbon copies of their parents. They will have their own friends, their own relation- ships and, importantly in this context, their own ups and downs, including illnesses and accidents. The more equipped they are to deal with life's problems, the better they will be at dealing with what life throws at them. Wrapping them in cotton wool does them no favours at all, it just makes the inevitable more painful when it occurs. Siviy (1998) says playing is important because it enables children to learn to 'roll with the punches of life' and by so doing, keep sane and balanced.

It's worth reminding ourselves from time to time that we live on a planet. It is a dangerous place, and in the end, it is we as individuals who have to deal with the experiences we encounter. I had a serious car accident some years ago. The injuries were bad enough, but what was really awful was the realisation of how simple it was, that this could happen at any time. I had to get my own head around that. Nobody, not my mother or anyone else, could do it for me, and it is the same for our children. There is a point when we have to say a kind of metaphysical goodbye to our babies. That does not mean we do not love them and will not support them, but it is a recognition of reality.

So where better to do this than on a happy, exciting, vibrant, colourful space full of all sorts of wonderful experiences, and other children who are also unconsciously going through the same process?

There is a phrase currently in vogue, 'Go for it'. Whilst all too often that can be interpreted as do what you want and do not worry about who you tread on to get there, it can also mean: 'this is not a rehearsal, if you don't do it now, it may not come around again, so go for it.'

There is a wonderful optimism in such a sentiment. Deep play makes it possible for children to make the most of their lives. Not necessarily vocationally or in terms of status – although it might indirectly do that too – but rather in terms of increased awareness, higher conscious- ness, improved well-being and a greater appreciation of what it is they are involved in.

So, like all other types of play, Deep play is vital for children. However, the playworker should ensure that the Deep play experiences that are offered are what they purport to be. They do not contain any hazardous 'surprises' that are the result of negligent practice or shoddy thinking.

I am not highlighting this just to protect children. Playwork is nothing if it does not honour and respect the children it serves, even if it does appear a hard-nosed friend at times. But if children do come to a play space operated by a playworker, not only is it essential that risk is accessible, it is also essential that danger/hazard are not. Then there can only be two potential sources of injury to children:

1   A genuine freak accident, and these can happen anywhere at anytime.
2   When a child is reckless and tries to perform far outside of his or her known range of ability.

There will be children who, because of play deficits or disabilities, may not be aware of their limitations. At a swimming pool, for example, there is always the possibility that a non-swimming child will jump into the deep end.   We should be aware of similar possibilities in play spaces and must always be vigilant. But for those children who use the play space regularly, they will know the limitations both of the environment and of themselves, and if they get hurt, hopefully they will have learnt a valuable lesson from the experience.

A knowledge of play types is useful for two reasons. The first and more practical reason, is that by sub-dividing play into its constituent playtypes, we can more effectively provide for it in total; we can also address the issue of deficits in the availability of particular playtype experiences.

Second, by sub-dividing play into its component parts we are better able to theorise about the mechanisms of the play drive. Earlier I compared the play drive to a genetic river and that is a useful analogy, but perhaps a better one in this context is that it could be seen as a high-energy cable with sixteen cores, each of which energises a particular play type. At one end of each core is the playing child, while at the other is a monitoring mechanism that computes which play type, or combination of play types, is most appropriate for a. the successful navigation of a particular experience, and b. the further development of skills and characteristics common to most play types. For example, aspects of balance, flexibility, communication and problem-solving.

AMALGAMATED PLAY TYPES

Playtypes may also develop with ontology, beginning with partially formed proto-types in early childhood and finishing in late childhood with the most advanced and complete forms. They may also appear as amalgamations, forming behaviours like football, painting and tag. It is likely that only the very young manifest play types singularly, as they struggle to master locomotion or communication, unable perhaps to perform more than one difficult act at a time. But as experience grows and perception becomes more complex, so the way they interact with the world through play types becomes more amalgamated.

This does not necessarily change the notion of play as a drive, or an energy source, but it does suggests that any drive or source is very complex; that either the drive can exist in sixteen different forms – which can manifest themselves simultaneously or in different numbers of permutations, all of which may be relatives in a particular neurochemical family – or that the delivery mechanism for each play type is different in some way. For example:

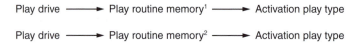

Figure 4.3 The simultaneous manifestation of different playtypes.

For a fuller explanation of the sixteen playtypes, see Hughes (2006).

THE PLAYWORK MENU

Another useful way of organising practice is by using what is called the '*playwork menu*'. This subject has been looked at briefly before (see Hughes 1996b) under the title the 'Playwork Curriculum'. The *playwork menu* is designed to enable playworkers who view their practice as a series of unrelated activities to use its simple organisational method to more clearly collect what they offer children, under four overall headings. It is designed to make it easier for practitioners to analyse and prepare the play environment, by using these headings in advance of the children's arrival. So when the play setting is in use, the playworker is free to generally oversee what is happening, rather

116

than having to engage in programming activity and risking dominating the children's choice of activity and methodology for engagement by doing so.

The playwork menu categorises applied playwork into four main areas:

1 The Senses
2 Identity
3 Concepts
4 The Elements

The rationale (Hughes and King (1987)) for creating the menu was this. Play is a fundamental mechanism for acquiring information. It begins with absolute basics like touch, where the interface between the child's skin and the world exists. Play is a process that is not motivated by external diversions like status or material benefits, instead, what is gained during play is beneficial to the child as a whole, as an organism. That is, play is not motivated by future career, or a particular relationship, by travel or in any conscious objectives, it is raw biology, where the organism is driven to gain knowledge of itself in its surroundings with the sole purpose of surviving. The play-work menu is intended to reflect that basic relationship.

DIVERSITY, BALANCE AND DEPTH

Play has been selected to enable the flexibility and adaptation that is essential to human survival, so it is not driven by specific end-products. Instead it operates most effectively in a context of diversity, balance and depth of engagement or through an intuitive understanding of its *raison d'être*. What I mean by intuitive understanding in this context is that one of the benefits we gain from playing is not under-standing as comprehension, so much as it is understanding gained from immersion in an experience, through a fusion with that experi-ence; what might be termed *learning though absorption*.

For example to playfully understand mud or water, it is necessary to have more than an appreciation of their chemical composition or their physiological benefits. There is a level to playful interaction, which is about a coming together, a combining or symbiosis between the play object and the player, that puts a value into the combination of child and object that becomes a 'whole' which transcends the sum of its parts. Physically playing with mud or water, for example, enables children to gain a whole other understanding of texture, viscosity, temperature, impact and so on. Playful immersion in toys develops this deeper special quality, so does immersion with places, people and other species.

Anyone who has ever owned a cat will know that they can study all sorts of things about them; their habits, history, psychology, their illnesses and so on, but no amount of knowledge will tell you about that cat as a living and breathing entity. Ask cat lovers about their cats and they talk about tactile sensations (stroking, etc.), auditory sensations (the purring and mewing noises they make), their movements and the fun and affection they give – this is more than understanding through knowledge, it is a transcendence of perception brought about by a level of immersion in the cat as a live reality. Like the cat lover, the playing child is also engaged in immersion. But where the cat lover is only engaged in immersion on a mono-dimensional level – the human and the cat – the child engages in immersion on a multi-dimensional, multi-medium level – the child and the universe. So the playing child is not just making factual sense of the world as it plays, it is also making sense of it on emotional, psychic, kinaesthetic and sensory, etc., levels too. The four parts of the menu are intended to help playworkers to ensure that whatever they provide for the child – be that experiences, props, toys, environmental foci, narrative stimulants, even respites and oases – it will fall into one of the menu's broad categories, enabling the playworker to make sound judgements regarding the experiential comprehensiveness of the environment they are offering children.

SENSES

The first category in the menu is *senses* – hearing, sight, touch, taste and smell. Each of these sensory interfaces certainly tells the child about different aspects of its play experience, but it is more complicated than that. To say, for example, that the *sight* sense enables a child to see what it is playing with is to totally understate the experience. What the child sees is shape, colour, context, potential applications, form, depth, perspective, size, and so on. I am not asserting that the child would be conscious of each characteristic in its early years, and I am not saying a child would describe things in this way. But what I am saying is that increasingly – over time, at an atomic or sub-atomic level – these are the building blocks that are being created and they *do* represent what the child is seeing, even though the child is unaware that the process is taking place.

Similarly, the importance of *sound* can be equally understated. Many play environments have music playing in the background for example, or just have the radio playing, perhaps tuned to an anonymous station, just to provide continuous background noise. If that is the case, given that music is so important to human beings and so diverse in its different cultural, instrumental, vocal and notational formats, it might be more valuable to the children if some thought were given to creating a musical environment in which surprise, drama, ambiance, rhythm and so on, are deliberate features. Not because questions will be asked later, but because music – every sort of music, from Hip Hop to Plain Song, from Electric Folk to Reggae and from Bangra to Orchestral – grounds, i.e., stabilises children by immersing them in an experience that resonates physiologically and emotionally.

Children should be enabled to experience music and other sound spectra as a total portfolio of what sound is and can be, including developing a consciousness of its overall complexity and the effort taken to create it. And, as well as having the opportunity to listen to music, children should have the opportunity to be able to make it. More importantly they should know that they can, and that the props for doing it are continually available to them.

Social play is also an important source of basic sound building blocks. During social play, by watching another child's meta-communication and body posture, children learn to recognise and understand intonation, emphasis and pitch, and to discriminate between the match and mismatch of the spoken word.

Tactile diversity is also a crucial experience, and its effect on the child can also be understated. After all, where do children first encounter the building blocks that make it possible to express their emotions, to gesticulate, or stroke, or tickle, even express anger by slapping a surface, if not through play?

Where do they gain the fine motor coordination required to differentiate between the pages of books and newspapers? Textures, pressures, palms, fingertips, manipulative movements, holding, acute motor movements, are all important characteristics of the tactile experience that a play environment should give the child the opportunity to engage in. Good play spaces offer a wide range of opportunities for tactile interfacing, so that children can begin to develop a tactile relationship with metals, woods, fabrics, ceramics, plastics, papers and even the touch pad of a laptop or a game consul.

Diversity, balance and depth in what they see, hear and feel when they are playing gives children an overview of their existence, which is awesome rather than ordinary. For each experience is not only valuable in itself, it also makes comparison and analysis possible. Why do I like that? Why do I not like that?

Why does that tune do that to me, and that one does that to me? Why does some music make me want to dance and some music make me want to sob? Why do some experiences make me feel better or worse, what do those terms mean anyway? Each play experience should provide interesting and useful additions to the child's experiential portfolio and the auditory experiences available in the play environment whether devised by the playworker or the children, should be assembled in ways that make that possible.

Children should always be able to play with the senses of smell and taste too. Whether that is through cooking on an open fire, or making 'perfume' from wild flowers, by trying new foods, or enjoying barbeques, or by evoking house, school or even cinema smells or the smell of animals, straw or cut grass.

Knowledge, awareness and above all, an appreciation of smells and tastes is an important prop for imaginative play, a subject for discussion in social play, and an introduction to cookery and chemistry, and it might be a lifesaver too. But more importantly for the playworker, playful access to each of these sensory universes helps children to appreciate the minutiae of each experience. It enables them to listen, look, feel, taste and smell with delicacy, discrimination and wonder, to transcend the 'take it for granted' way in which many adults live their olfactory lives, and be conscious of the reality of the sensory interface, that is 'the world telling them what it is'.

IDENTITY

The second menu category is *identity*. Identity is derived from at least two quite separate questions. Who am I? Who do I want to be? A good play environment can give children objective feedback on the first and facilitate decisions about the second.

I am particularly interested in the idea of identity. As a child I always thought that people were whoever they wanted to be. I do not recall ever being put under pressure to change who I was. I was called 'skinny' and 'four eyes', but I do not think anyone expected me to binge eat, or take my glasses off as a result. But in many places on Earth, being of a particular identity is viewed by some, both as a badge of exclusivity or of exclusion.

Whilst I appreciate that to many adults, inducting their children into a tribal, class, national, school, vocational or even a football team identity means a great deal to them in terms of their own traditions and heritage, there seems to be little accompanying awareness of what a human catastrophe this kind of categorisation can bring about, creating as it might both human and conceptual barriers between children, and a false and even tortured view of self in the children affected by it.

For playworkers, children can only be children, the young of our species. They cannot be perceived of as coming from a particular religious, ethnic, national or economic group. As Cairns (1987) wrote of children during the Troubles in Northern Ireland, if they are allocated a particular social role, then, 'children come under enormous pressure to take sides'. At one play setting I worked on, the children came from several economic, social, religious and ethnic backgrounds. Should we have treated them differently? Were their play needs different because of their parents' religion or ethnicity? Certainly, we were respectful of perceived differences. But from a professional playwork perspective we started from the premiss that every child's needs – not withstanding those with additional special needs – were the same.

I interpret Article 31 of the UN Convention of the Rights of the Child to mean that the Right to Play is the right to play freely, in diversity with other children, without the constant intervention of adults. A Right to Play must be seen as advantaging children and not empowering adults. I think it vital that the right to play is not confused with citizenship or with children becoming useful members of society either. Obviously insisting on this right being enforced will not make problems vaporise, but where divisions do exist, it would make life more difficult for those who would try to segregate and separate children from one another.

As with our senses, the development of the building blocks of being conscious of having an identity and comprehending what it is starts very early. If that start is censored in some way, containing only part of the available information – like a jigsaw puzzle with only half the pieces – the child will only get half the picture, and may never be able to overcome the disabilities caused by that deficit later in life.

Much of the hate crime that exists is not just the result of the institutionalisation of phenomena like homophobia, sectarianism or racism. Certainly they do exist in many institutions, but when children will not even cross the road to play with other children because of attitudes they are 'sensing' from parents, family or community, as is the case in many divided communities/societies, then something more powerful than propaganda is at work, something deep within the psyche of the individuals involved.

Children are not born racist, sexist, sectarian, homophobic or whatever else. These are things they learn from other people, but what is it they actually learn? The previous section on senses gives us a clue. Just look at touch. A parent only has to give a child a tiny anxious squeeze of the hand, a tiny, unconscious tactile cue, whenever a particular word is said or a particular context mentioned, for that child to quickly begin to associate feelings of anxiety or disgust with that word or that context. It only needs a consistent raising of an eyebrow or a disapproving twist of the mouth, for a child inadvertently to link that look to a particular person or group of people. It does not need a patronising manner or downright rudeness or violence to create the links; they are just the heavy guns that may come later. The *real* building blocks, as with everything in childhood, are much more subtle.

Children, particularly young children, are sensitised to tiny fluctuations in meta communication, because it is through sensitivity to these tiny changes, in how words are pronounced, emphasised or accompanied with gestures and so on, that the child as an organism is able both to sense *and* learn how to sense change and danger, and thus survive.

122

Children will use different props – mirrors, masks, make-up, dressing-up clothes – to play with the idea of identity and with their own version of it, but they are only that, props. Wearing an ostentatious hat, for example, does not actually say much about whether a child has an ostentatious identity or whether she is insecure, and from a playwork perspective it doesn't matter anyway. What matters is that she has the time, focus, opportunity *and* props to explore who she is and what that means to her, so that she can be both secure and happy with what she discovers or looks to ways of changing herself, if she is not. Playwork is not about making judgements about children's identities, and this is where I have problems with some of my playwork colleagues who feel that certain child identities are, by definition, bad or wrong. I cannot agree with that for the reasons I have stated. Their concerns normally lie with children who take on racist, sexist and similar identities. But what if a child takes on an identity which is viewed as disruptive, or negative, or irritating? Are these regarded as inappropriate identities too, and if not why not? Their impact may be equally hurtful. Why should some playful manifestations of identity be regarded as worse than others?

That does not mean that some behaviour will not be viewed as intolerable, and perpetrators asked to stop or invited to leave the play space. 'Civilisation', i.e., the workability of the space itself, has to be maintained. But these judgements should always be a last resort, based on safety rather than political or social correctness. Alienating children because they come from a particular background is only inverted discrimination. The play space is a raw environment, it has to be to facilitate much of the raw behaviour that is at the cutting edge of the play drive.

If a child has only just discovered a piece of information which, after time, could fundamentally alter his or her view of the world, playworkers have to acknowledge what is happening. Forget for a moment that some playworkers might actively display dislike for children from, say, a racist background. Imagine that a child from a racist context does begin to question its racist certainties because s/he has discovered that all children with 'pink hair' do not stink, in direct contravention to everything about children with pink hair that the child's family has taught. Whilst the inappropriate playworker might be saying to the child, 'See, see, you were wrong', the child is having to weigh up the pros and cons of the reality of this revelation.

How does one reconcile the discovery that one's parents could be wrong, particularly when you are young and seek certainties rather than surprises? That one's aunts and uncles, brothers and sisters, friends and their family's views are inappropriate and no longer coincide with ones own? What does one do with this knowledge now that one has it? For example, during the Troubles there, I met numerous people in Northern Ireland who seemed to find this kind of discovery about the 'other side' almost impossible to compute, because the meaning and value of everything, *everything*, every preconception, everything that made life worth living, membership, belonging, history, tradition, powerful symbolism, music, family, was thrown into question. 'If I am not that, then what am I?' That is a huge and destabilising question to have to ask when you are four or five years old, and one you might be forgiven for avoiding answering, particularly in a social context, where views of that nature are traditionally rarely subject to scrutiny or amendment.

Many children go into denial over identity, afraid to be who they are because of the preconceptions of others. The playworker's job is not to alienate such children but to help them to feel secure enough, both in the play environment and in themselves, to explore who they are, either on their own or in the company of other children. This is particularly important for children who find themselves growing up in a context where a particular identity is already a foregone conclusion, but where the impact of adult imprinting has not yet quite 'hardwired' that given identity into the child's perception of the universe.

Playworkers also need to hold in their mind, particularly when they are working with young children, that much of what they see as expressions of identity is actually work in progress, that they can help the child to move forward with – although they aren't concern themselves with the outcome of the processing – if they provide her with opportunities to engage with the concept of identity generally and personally and take any obvious obstacles out of the way.

Identity can be explored in any number of ways. Mirrors, dressing-up clothes, other props – hats, gloves, jewellery, bags, even guns, uniforms, musical instruments and clip boards could be made available. Photographs, personal stories, flags, hair dressing and historical viewpoints are also useful. However, we need to remain clear that as we are facilitating an exploratory process, there must be no subjective limitation on what is explored.

124

CONCEPTS

The third category of the playwork menu is *concepts*. My *Penguin English Dictionary* definition of a concept is 'an abstract or general idea'. I have just been discussing identity (which is a concept) in the context of racism (which is also a concept). We've mentioned death (which is a concept) and we've alluded to fairness and justice (which are also concepts). This section is not so much about what concepts are, as about acknowledging that they exist and making it possible for children to describe ideas that come to them, which might be shared and even valued by other children. The simplest means that come to mind is conversation – which ideally would be initiated by the child – and visual display, using drawings, murals, or putting something like a flag or sign on the wall of a den – e.g., The Posse, or Home Sweet Home, both of which could represent the idea of 'belonging'.

The notion of democracy, for example, is recognised by many human beings as representing a preferred way of being governed, of conducting debate and of decision-making. Most of us are not totally clear what democracy is, any more than we are totally clear about the notion of justice, or love for that matter. These are more the terrain of philosophers. But irrespective of our personal comprehension of abstract ideas, they are as important to us, as our sensory interactions, because they are at the very root of how we live our lives, of our beliefs and values, and how we perceive everything abstract, from 'Time to Numeracy'.

The playworker's contribution to facilitating play with concepts is relatively simple. Her function is to ensure that children are given access to concepts on a sensory level and on an intellectual level. That is, they are assured, by the playworker's behaviour, that exploring, discussing and having opinions or other obvious manifestations of conceptual thinking is expected on the playspace and anticipated intellectually and practically by the workers.

As with the previous section, it is essential that the playworker sees herself in a facilitative role. We exist to help children to access ideas, not to predetermine outcomes. The play space is exploratory ground, so in the playspace, democracy is not 'right' any more than is fascism. Islam is not more 'right' than is Buddhism. Vegetarianism is not 'right' any more than is omnivorism. What is 'right' and 'wrong' is more the philosophical and moral province of the world outside the play space, the play space is where children gather insights, and play with ideas and explore how they feel. Above all it is a place of discovery and reflection.

Because play is essentially an adult-free experience, if there is even a suspected relationship between that adult-free experience and the development of vital characteristics that aid children's understanding and evolving consciousness, it is essential that playworkers do not corrupt that relationship. It is essential, but in the real world it is probably also unavoidable – so the question really is 'How much can or should adults legitimately intervene in children's play?' My judgement would suggest a sliding scale from 'not at all' to 'as little as necessary'. Others might say, 'as much as is necessary to get the result adults want', irrespective of how child-centred, etc., they say they are in coming to that conclusion. Personally I feel that that would be an infringement of the child's biological and psychic integrity on the playspace.

Outside the boundary of the play space, playwork recognises that in general, adults' rule and children are not normally perceived in the way they are being described here. In the past, children have always been able to separate themselves from adults for long enough periods to form their own, often contradictory, views, of the world; an essential if we are to avoid not all becoming clones of some preconceived normality.

Currently though it is becoming increasingly difficult for children to do that. Often it is impossible. To counter the potentially disastrous loss of first-hand unregulated learning, playworkers have to learn how to accept and provide for non-conformity, and child-controlled behaviour, and play provision based on evolutionary playwork principles is a good start. If one accepts that the engine for our continued evolution as a species is play – and this includes social evolution – then if we do not support that assertion, the more the adult world will feel able to control and constrain the play drive, the more we will damage the very essence of our young, and the more likely it will be that their development, and that of our whole species, will be thrown into reverse mode.

Increasingly, children are manifesting dysfunctional behaviour. They are experiencing considerable discomfort in the narrow confines of what adults feel is appropriate for them – normally circumstances that are rarely what adults experienced themselves as children. A growing parental obsession with safety over the past thirty years has turned many children's lives into little better than that experienced by animals subjected to battery farming (Huttenmoser and Degan-Zimmermann 1995). Having access to quality play experiences can help these children to overcome the effects of their confinement, but their parents have to accept that there are inevitable risky consequences, the potential for which will increase the longer the situation drags on. A psychic shift in the current perception that many parents have of their children's sensitivity to confinement, security, safety and lack of freedom is long overdue. All children have a desperate need for adult-free play experiences, far more than they have for safe and controlled ones. It is the parents who say children have to be safe, and who transfer that neurosis onto their children, not the children themselves.

Fox (1989) encapsulates the impact of confinement on the human brain. 'Force the [brain] to work outside its range of adaptive responses for long enough, and it will react, it will rebel' (p. 209).

What seems important is that the children have the opportunity to sort these ideas out for themselves by learning to make conceptual judgements about safety and security on the one hand, and freedom and risk on the other. My experience is that most children, taking into account where they live and the risks that are a feature of their everyday lives, will opt for a balance between the two that will allow them to have fun and have a sense of achievement, whilst at the same time feeling relaxed and not under pressure or feeling anxious.

I did not know there were such disciplines as philosophy or economics until I was in my mid-teens. But if, after a conversation for example, a child knows that things exist, even if that child does not know what they are or what they mean, the child's own curiosity may drive him or her to investigate (Morris 1964). One cannot investigate if one cannot imagine. And one cannot imagine if one does not know. Imagination is limited by experience, and that includes experience of the conceptual and the abstract.

ELEMENTS

The fourth category of the playwork menu is *elements*. The elements, in this context are earth, fire, air and water. Although I have discussed this in some detail elsewhere (Hughes 1996b), I would like to spend a little more time exploring one aspect of playful elemental interaction further. Elemental interaction is another crucial experience for the playing child. For as well as bringing children into contact with life-giving materials, like air and water, and through this contact reinforcing the importance to human beings of free and unpolluted access to these essentials, our need to engage in it may have deeper evolutionary significance.

There are at least a dozen theories analysing why human children play. One of them is Hall's *Recapitulation Theory* (1904). G. Stanley Hall, its author, was significantly involved in the genesis of what is now known as developmental psychology, and his ideas about recapitulation are very interesting in the playwork context. Put forward by numerous researchers, particularly Haeckel in 1866, under the term the Biogenetic Law, the original notion of the recapitulation 'lobby' was that ontogeny recapitulated phylogeny. That as each individual human embryo grew, so it chronologically manifested the physical characteristics of its earlier human ancestors, in the form of growing gills, fins, a tail and so on. This particular interpretation of the idea of recapitulation has since been discredited.

However, Hall's idea was that as they developed children would recapitulate evolutionary stages of human development, and that there was a one to one correspondence between childhood stages and evolutionary history.

Reaney (1916), who later expanded on Hall's work, offered a more play orientated slant, i.e., that a child's play is a recapitulation, or a re-cap of what children's ancestors did; not in their play, but in their adult life. I will be exploring possible reasons for this later. Hall's and Reaney's thinking is explained further in an interesting examination of their work in Helen Schwartzman's book *Transformations* (1978). In it, Schwartzman says the following:

> What she [Reaney] proposed was that the various stages of childhood could be divided into 'play periods', that corresponded with the various stages of human evolution. For example, she suggested that the animal stage or period (birth

128

to age 7) was reflected in swinging and climbing games; the savage stage (7–9) exhibited hunting and throwing games; the nomad stage (9–12) was reflected in skill and adventure games and 'interest in keeping pets', and the pastoral and tribal stages (12–17) were characterised by doll *play, gardening and finally team games* (p. 47).

What Hall's and Reaney's ideas imply is that when children are playing, some of what we see is a re-run of different stages in their evolutionary history, a recapitulation of some of their ancestral past, in the form of Reaney's model of children's evolutionary play stages.

My interest in this theory is that some of what we witness as play-workers may be a demonstration of the process of recapitulation at work. Why this is pertinent to playing with the elements is that elemental play, which can involve anything from digging, sowing seeds, cooking over open fires and children's rituals and ceremonies, has always struck me as very primeval and instinctive, not of this time at all. Yet children engage in it quite naturally and spontaneously without prompts or encouragement.

In my own play, elemental interaction was a big part of what my friends and I did. We often had fires and built shelters, in the form of tree dens, straw-bale dens and caves.

But on reflection what impressed me most about my elemental play is the way we exposed ourselves to the elements by playing outside a lot of the time. I can remember, on windy spring days, playing with my shirt open to the wind and I can still evoke the feeling of exhilaration, virtual flight, and importantly what I can only describe as the feeling of 'looking through the eyes of ancients', that came with it.

It is true to say that we carry our past with us in our genes. For example, Jones (1993) writes of Freud's belief that behaviour was controlled by biological history (p. 227). It may be that recapitulative play is a manifestation of all our genetic echoes, a recap, certainly, perhaps a reconnection, with our own ancestors. We are, after all, the most advanced form of the amalgamated genes of many generations of human beings, whose life experience was encoded into their genes and passed on through the ages. As the Hall/Reaney models suggest, each of us is standing on a pyramid of our own past, going all the way back to the beginnings of time.

Whilst I don't claim that play is only about recapitulation, I do believe that some of play is playing back through time. That a particular mode of playing – what I call recapitulative play – activates a mechanism for an unconscious reconnection with what may now be only faint imprints of times long gone. In fact, these days, recapitulation may carry a highly symbolic, even metaphysical, role for the human child. That it is not alone on the frontiers of time, in an alien technological culture, but is connected to a personal and unique history, which it may feel driven to play out, to actualise, in order to derive some stability, comfort and feelings of belonging and control, in what may be an unsettled and alienated period in our own evolution.

Whatever the realities of recapitulation, it is too important an idea for us not to give it attention, and in the play space it is easily accommodated, if the props are there. In this case they should include a fire area and water buckets; elevated areas that enable children to view panoramas and experience wind; there should be puddles, stand pipes and paddling pools, even small streams, to enable children to engage in water-play; and timber, cloth and digging tools for children to build dens and shelters. If recapitulative play is allowed to be a significant feature of the play space, children may well begin to play out rituals using body paints, fires and music, too.

A more detailed exploration of the idea of recapitulation can be found in Chapter 13.

MICK'S STORIES 2

Brazil v Brazil

In Ireland, the boys were playing computer football games, but the two older ones decided to go outside to play real football – mainly because Barney could not believe his luck when Charlie said he didn't mind being in goal most of the time. Padraig, who was aged about seven, continued playing alone and after a while came running out in great excitement. 'It's Brazil v Brazil, and we're losing 7–4!' The boys (and the girls) raced in to see and play this new and bizarre game, and to Padraig's immense pride told him that he was completely mad and a total genius.

130

Padraig had manipulated a rule-based electronic environment to create new and quite paradoxical play frames, firstly with the machine, then with the children. It suddenly dawned on me that he had controlled the content and intent of his play to a large extent, both within and outside the given parameters of the game. He was engaging in at least some elements of creative, exploratory, fantasy, imaginative, social and mastery play.

For the first time I began to get interested in thinking about how children use and interact with computer games. I'd always been bored by them, because they didn't exist when I was a child and I'm useless at playing them. No doubt this is why I uncritically joined the consensus that they were probably bad for children through reducing active play outdoors and contributing to obesity or poor mental health. I suppose I'd forgotten about the endless hours that I and other children from my generation spent in equally sedentary play activities like reading comics and books, painting and drawing, watching TV, making models or playing with dolls.

Bob and others have posed the question of whether new play types could emerge from changes in the environment and particularly technological development. I've certainly seen how Charlie has used his mobile phone, MP3 player and computer to build social networks that include real cousins, friends and people he's actually met with more virtual people, including playing with his own identity in online social networks. I have no idea who he is in contact with or what he gets up to in his electronic world and I've had my worries and moral panics about this – until I remembered that my parents had no real idea what I was up to at his age when out playing or on the phone to friends.

It will be interesting to see how internet-based social networks change and develop, and whether more physically interactive Wii and dance mat type technology will spread into other areas. Or perhaps they will disappear like the Airfix models that took up so much of my childhood.

Some play equipment manufacturers have devised solar-powered outdoor interactive electronic games where the children have to hit buttons at different heights and locations around the equipment in various sequences to rack up scores, which are then uploaded to the internet. The idea is that this encourages physical activity, but I was intrigued to hear that children in Holland have subverted the system. Instead of individual children running around frantically hitting the buttons in the correct sequences, they worked out that they could get massive scores by working as a team to hit the buttons while barely moving a muscle!

When a mobile phone is not a good idea

We rang Charlie to see how he was enjoying his holiday in Devon. 'I'm having a great time, thanks, but we're playing hide and seek, and you've just given me away!'

I need my bones!

Crumbles Castle is an adventure playground in Islington, so named by the children because the play building was constructed from recycled granite sets and cobbles and looks like … well, a crumbles castle. The roof with its battlements is a play area, and one wall has short sections of telegraph poles set into it horizontally as a climbing feature.

Charlie came up to the roof with me and we looked over the battlements at the poles and the potential drop below to some crash mats. 'Fancy a go?' I said. 'No way man am I gonna do that! Noooo waaaay – I need my bones!' So we had a look at it from the bottom of the wall, and Charlie decided he would have a go at the less scary-looking climb up – from down here the crash mats looked a lot bigger and much more bone-friendly.

Twenty minutes later he raced over to where I was taking photos: 'Did you get a picture of me jumping from the very top one?' I certainly had got several, of his first tentative efforts and his increasing mastery play, climbing up, down, horizontally, diagonally, finding easier routes first and then working out the harder ones. Two old hands, also about eight, but playground regulars, gave him tips. Then they asked one of the playworkers if they could pile up the crash mats, plus a few more from the storeroom and jump from the top poles – a good four metres high.

This brilliant playworker didn't say no or yes straight away. She reminded the old hands about the rules they had previously agreed:

132

that jumps must be strictly one by one, the mats had to be straightened up by the last jumper if they had moved, and no jumps if somebody was climbing up.

Finn McCool v the Giant Volcano

Charlie has always loved climbing and in loads of my photos of him he's high up in trees, rocks, cliffs and climbing walls. The Giant's Causeway in Ireland was a particular hit – he just couldn't believe his eyes when he saw it and was convinced that someone must have built such a perfect climbing and jumping adventure playground.

We were there with my sister, who is a teacher. She told me about taking her geography class to the causeway as part of the curriculum, but secretly also as a great day out. She'd taught them how a massive volcanic welling up of lava millions of years ago crystallised into the thousands of polygonal columns as it poured into the sea and was cooled.

She'd also told them the myth of the Irish giant Finn McCool who built the causeway to have a fight with his opposite number in Scotland's Staffa Island, which has the same geological forms and is the other end of Finn's causeway according to the legend. On the coach back to the school after the visit, one of the children said to her 'Miss, you don't seriously expect us to believe that volcano lava story?'.

CHAPTER 5

COMBINATORIAL FLEXIBILITY, NON-SPECIALISATION, CALIBRATION AND CONTEXTUALISATION

Play is a very complex phenomenon, as the following chapter demonstrates. It needs sensitive and informed playwork practice to ensure that its benefits are fully realised.

COMBINATORIAL FLEXIBILITY

I first came across the idea of combinatorial flexibility in the late 1970s in a chapter in *The Biology of Play*, called, 'Play and Learning', by Kathy Sylva. In it, she writes '[Another] hypothesis of the benefit of play ... focuses on the *flexibility* it affords the player. The playing animal is free from the tensions of instrumental goals and can borrow bits of behaviour from survival patterns such as feeding or fleeing.' Loizos (1967), Eibl-Eibesfeldt (1967, 1970) and Bruner (1972, 1974), she says, 'claim that the essence of play lies in such combinatorial flexibility. Play trains the animal [or the child] to string bits of behaviour together to form novel solutions to problems requiring restructuring of thought or action. Eibl-Eibesfeldt suggests that some animal play is "scientific research" performed by non-humans.' And finally Sylva states 'What is acquired through play is not specific information, but a general [mind]set towards solving problems that includes both abstraction and combinatorial flexibility' (p. 60).

Bruner (1972) threw light on the idea slightly earlier, stating 'The flexibility of skill consists not only of this constructive feature, but also of the rich range of "paraphrases" that are possible ... for there is, in a sense, something language-like about skill, the kind of substitution rules that permit the achievement of the same objective [meaning], by alternative means.'

134

Sutton-Smith (1979) had his own spin on the concept, describing it as responsible for '... new thought, [leading to] new combinations of thought'. Adding that combinatorial flexibility leads to '... an increase in the cognitive alternatives available', as well as their flexible management.

Sylva (1977) takes care to differentiate between play and problem solving, implying that the difference is in the 'salience of the goal itself. In the latter, the goal is all-important, whereas in play the essential activity is the process of assembling the components'. Whilst Hutt et al. (1989) see combinatorial flexibility as one of the outcomes of what she calls 'innovative' play. 'Play that involves the repetition of certain actions, but also introduces some novel elements may be called "innovative", and in such play the child may be considered to be consolidating some skill or knowledge, while introducing some novelty to prevent the execution of such skill from becoming monotonous, as well as perhaps to extend "combinatorial flexibility".'

Sylva (ibid.), however, also adds a note of caution about the validity of the idea. 'Evidence for the role of play in promoting flexibility is sketchy. The evolutionary data, although appealing, are correlative, i.e., the species who most "need" flexibility demonstrate the most play', and then goes to provide 'some evidence for the theory' citing studies by Kohler (1926), Birch (1945), Sutton-Smith (1967) and Bruner (1972, 1974).

What has this got to do with practical playwork?

If we imagine the child as a young organism surrounded from birth by a huge range of puzzles, which she has to gradually learn how to solve if she is going to survive and develop, one question that comes to mind is 'How does the child go about solving these puzzles?'

First of all, the child does not see them as problems, but as experiences to be played with. That is, as experiences to be explored, investigated and experimented with.

For the infant, these puzzles are mainly sensory. 'To what does that tactile feeling relate, what is that smell, whose voice is that?' Later, as well as sensory problems, issues around co-ordination, locomotion, and so on, also begin to be explored and, as the child's horizons move from its carer, to its living environment, and then to the outside environment. The experiences and the child's means of playing with them become increasingly complicated as the child becomes more skilled. Eventually, the child is able to communicate, build relationships, navigate risk and make sense of the complex realities of being alive.

What the play process does in this context is bring the child and the world together gradually. This enables the child to start, for example, with very basic information about touch and tactile experiences, until she has built a tactile map that helps her to know where she is in her surroundings. Similarly, the child builds maps of smells, tastes, sights and noises, each of which helps him or her to have a more accurate fix of where she is and what and who else is there. This is the embryo of the cortical map (see Chapter 3).

Just developing knowledge about touch requires the playing child to engage with and absorb hundreds, if not thousands, of tiny pieces of information about different surfaces, different hand movements and different finger pressures, all of which tell her something different in tactile terms. If this is broadened to include all the senses, then we are talking about many different packages of information – tiny insights, reminders and confirmations, about feelings, colours, heights, weights, temperatures, volumes, tones – millions of tiny, different sensory snapshots of the world around the child, which when run together form the child's perception of reality at any given moment. Gopnik (1993), Beckoff and Allen (1999), Brown (1997) citing Edelman (1992) suggest that these cortical maps may contribute to the formation of the human consciousness.

In very early childhood two main processes are occurring. One is information gathering, the other is information processing, both of which, inevitably, have an effect on how the child sees the world. For example, if I start today with no tactile information and by the end of today I have a great deal of tactile information, my view of the world as a tactile space will have changed greatly by tea time, from what it was at breakfast.

Initially, each tiny experience is totally new, but gradually the child begins to develop a sensory memory and then other memories, each of which can be drawn from, to help the child as it encounters new places, spaces, objects and, of course, new and more complex problems to solve.

Many puzzling problems can neither be perceived nor solved until a relevant bank of knowledge has been developed. Each piece of knowledge,

136

like a tiny piece in a vast jigsaw, can then be utilised to discover whether it has any role in the solution of more complex problems, and this is where I surmise the mechanism of combinatorial flexibility comes into play.

What the term 'combinatorial flexibility' describes to me is a process where the child immerses itself into a problem and then using a high speed scanning/testing and accepting/rejecting mechanism explores its memory for tiny pieces of information that have been learnt from experience, to see if any of those pieces, or any combination of those pieces of information, might contribute to a solution of the problem it has immersed itself into.

Children are not born with solutions to the puzzles or problems they encounter. Solutions are frequently arrived at through a process of trial, error and elimination. But this process can be greatly speeded up if the child has a large reservoir of information, which if always being accessed and creatively used, might result in a large but up-to-date reservoir of unused but possible combinations of solutions to new problems.

In other words, the more a child plays in a diverse and novel environ-ment, the better she will be at performing those complex combinato-rial tasks, and solving the puzzles and problems essential to her continued adaptation and development.

From a playwork perspective, I see the child as an organism that is 'energised' or 'animated' by the diversity and variety of available experience. That is, the greater the range of experiences available to the playing child – the greater the depth, the more exciting, stimulat-ing and interesting the choice – the more the child is motivated to play. The more the child is motivated to play, the more she becomes immersed in the experiences available, and the better she immerses herself in their individual components. The playworker's dilemma is how she judges what constitutes an appropriate range and depth of available experiences, what constitutes optimum choice?

Choice implies access to everything, or at least to a diverse range of experiences. Needless to say, this requirement is instantly breached if some play types are disallowed or if the play environment emphasises one sort of interaction, say social interaction, over another, say loco-motor play.

So the relationship between combinatorial flexibility – as I understand it – and a good play environment, is that because in a good play environment – enriched, diverse, comprehensive, authentic and elemental – the knowledge reservoir is infinite and novel, the processing speed and potential range of solutions of the combinatorial process are greatly enhanced. It also means, as it does in evolution, that there will often be more than one solution to any given problem. This is particularly the case if the child has free access to diverse experience that it can explore in its own time.

Take, for example, the problem of seeing something brightly coloured on a shelf just out of the child's normal reach. The child extends her reach by standing up straighter or standing on tiptoe, or by finding something to stand on – a book, a chair or a ladder – to add enough additional height. However, she will only generate these solutions if her previous experience contains each of their component parts.

The young child starting from scratch will have to work out, solve, what is going on. She may try to do this by crying, hoping that someone else will solve it for her. She may get angry or frustrated. Almost certainly, she will return again and again, until she has enough of the pieces of the solution and enough of a drive to solve it, to enable her to fit enough parts of the solution together to achieve the required result.

Perhaps a better example of the power of combinatorial flexibility is the complexity of driving a car, which calls on thousands, if not millions, of tiny pieces of information to come together in a whole variety of flexible combinations, to make the act of driving possible.

When I am training I sometimes invite playwork students to imagine driving to a meeting on a Friday – a rainy, winter's night – with three other colleagues:

> 'You are driving to a meeting, it is Friday night, it's dark and the roads are busy and it's raining. You are making judgements about the distance of the car in front by the changing size and intensity of its brake lights. You have got your headlights on, you have got windscreen wipers on, you are looking out through the windscreen at traffic in front, which because the roads are crowded, is speeding up and slowing down all the time. You are steering the car using the steering wheel, your

right foot is on the accelerator and you are making tiny movements to make the car go faster or slower, your left foot is responsible for the clutch – which you need to change gear, for which you use your left hand – or the brakes, which have to be used cautiously because the roads are wet and slippery. As well as looking out of the windscreen at the cars in front, you also have three mirrors, one just above and to the left of your head and one on each door to tell you the speed and location of vehicles coming up behind you. You have an indicator which you use to inform other drivers of your intended movements to the right and left. You have got the car sound system on and you are changing the stations or putting CDs on instead. You are having an argument with your colleagues, whilst unwrapping sandwiches. You are looking out of the front and the back of the car virtually simultaneously. You are making complex judgements about the location and speed of traffic, in difficult conditions. Your hands and feet have got several jobs to do and require a great deal of co-ordinated movement to do them. And so on …'

This is a far more complex example of the same combinatorial flexibility process that eventually solved the problem of the brightly coloured object. It is just that instead of one complex problem there are many hundreds – all occurring at the same time. There is no right way to combine all the skills necessary to drive. There are legal requirements, of course, but the actual process of driving can be totally idiosyncratic. That is because flexibility in this process tailor-makes the solution to our experience – we just have to have the necessary knowledge in an accessible form to arrive at our own solution.

Another way of looking at the combinatorial process is this. Imagine the brain as a space made up of billions of little compartments – like pigeon holes – into which each of the tiny pieces of knowledge learnt go when we are interacting with our world. When we encounter a problem, it makes sense to assume that a solution, or a part of a solution, might lie in what we already know, i.e., somewhere in all of these tiny pieces of knowledge. But how can we find out? Evolution has constructed a fantastic tool, which is able to selectively plug into any number or permutations of these knowledge boxes, at any one time, and compare what they collectively represent as a possible solution to the problem (see Figures 5.1 a–d).

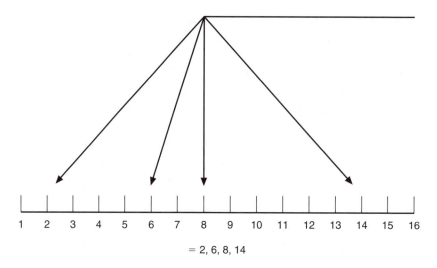

= 2, 6, 8, 14

Figure 5.1a Stages of combinatorial flexibility.

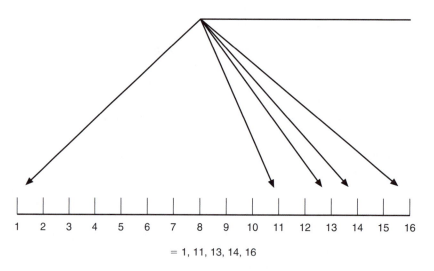

= 1, 11, 13, 14, 16

Figure 5.1b

140

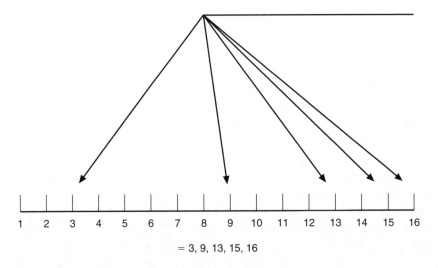

= 3, 9, 13, 15, 16

Figure 5.1c Stages of combinatorial flexibility.

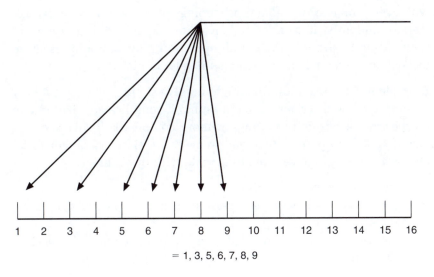

= 1, 3, 5, 6, 7, 8, 9

Figure 5.1d

The image I have is of an old-fashioned telephone exchange, but instead of having one person doing the plugging, it is like having thousands, perhaps millions, of people doing it, so the process is incredibly fast, as it would need to be. Think, for example, if we were faced with a problem that had immediate survival implications. Instantly our combinatorial flexibility faculties would kick off on a multiple search of what we know. Practice would teach it not to bother with all sorts of information, which we would know to be irrelevant in that context, so the mechanism is quite specific, i.e., it has a rough idea of where to look. Having accessed the information area where it is judged that a solution to the problem might lie, it tries numerous permutations of boxes – permutations of types of information, permutations of numbers of boxes – until solutions addressing the problem to a greater or lesser extent begin to materialise. (How this might work is not the province of playwork, although some of the questions it throws up are fascinating. For example, are the millions of tiny packages of information we absorb with every single physical and psychological operation we undertake stored randomly in the brain, are they organised into types of information to simplify the search operation, how is the information located and recognised, i.e., who is the telephonist?)

A problem requiring a solution might involve simply working out how to jump over some water; it might be more complicated, like how to escape from a burning building; or more complex still, like locating food. What I propose is that the process, the skill of combinatorial flexibility, seems to have something to do with three things:

- how we perceive problems;
- how we access a vast and increasing body of knowledge as we evolve;
- how we explore that knowledge in a way which is both selective and comparative so that the search process is able to locate permutations that have some relevance to the problem being looked at.

When one thinks how much we know, when one breaks down much of what we do unconsciously – walking, cooking, driving – into their component parts, it is fascinating to reflect on how we know where to look for information to address a problem we may have only just encountered.

142

As I have said above, we need to know what sort of problem it is, then we need to find where relevant information might be stored and then analyse that information in any number of different combinations, until we find an answer – it is a truly awesome human characteristic, and its implications for practical playwork are considerable.

The foundation of mental flexibility lies in the experiential diversity and cognitive novelty with which the playworker initially furnishes the play space. Neither flexibility, nor combinatorial flexibility in particular, can develop in a sterile and non-malleable space. Both the plasticity and actualisation required to generate and organise the neural material essential to a complex flexible neural network rely on interaction with interesting, challenging and evolving environments for their existence, Without a careful analysis of the novelty and malleability of a play space on the part of the playworker, this will probably either not happen at all, or not be sustainable.

The notion of the development of combinatorial flexibility as an essential part of playwork intervention invites the question 'What sort of environment would best facilitate combinatorial flexibility?' I would propose 'Those environments in which there was graduated access to increasingly complex experience'.

For example, on one playspace I operated, I developed an under-5s area. My premiss being that when young children first came to the playground they would have access to an 'initiation' zone, i.e., a zone in which they could become familiar with what a play environment was, what it felt, looked and sounded like, prior to actually engaging in the more challenging and authentic playground proper.

Today's children, particularly the growing number who for whatever reason are experiencing play-deprivation of one kind or another, would also benefit from access to one or more of these initiation or 'graduated' zones; but it should not stop there. Children who were already combinatorially flexible at one level could move into other parts of the space which had been deliberately modified to be even more demanding in terms of the intellectual and other challenges they offered. This may sound like a model of a school, and in a sense it is. However, there are some huge differences. The 'curriculum' is drawn from the fundamentals of our biological existence and not just those to do with a social or civic analysis of what and who we are. The methodology for learning is totally directed by the individual child's developmental agenda as perceived by that individual child. The teachers are mainly responsible for the preparation of the learning environment. Their interaction with the children is very limited and governed almost exclusively by the child and not by the adult.

Human beings are organisms that operate interdependently with, and dependently on, their environment, as the application of combinatorial flexibility graphically demonstrates. But to operate at maximum effectiveness, children need to be able to integrate themselves with other, non-human, systems, by playing with them. I fear that this is happening less and less, and that as a consequence our species is moving inexorably away from identifying with its ancestral evolutionary roots – what Bowlby (1958) called the Environment of Evolutionary Adaptedness – treating its habitat and the other species that depend on it with them as commodities and property rather than as vitally important occupants, both in their own right and because we are totally dependent on many of them for our own continued existence.

Orr (1993) says 'If we complete the destruction of nature (i.e., if we separate ourselves from the natural world) we will have succeeded in cutting ourselves off from the sources of sanity itself'.

We are already some way down that road. However, if children are given access to the best we can give, in terms of authentic play spaces, then as Harlow and Suomi (1971) and Einon *et al.* (1978) both imply, play in a quality space can positively affect the impact of play-deprivation, and enable children to develop a more flexible, and probably more sensitive, relationship with the planet itself and with all its occupants.

NON-SPECIALISATION

Although originally proposed by Morris (1964), this idea was in the Sylva (1977) chapter too. Quoting Lorenz (1972) she proposed that 'Man and other species had become specialists in non-specialisation, because they play', and that 'natural selection would favour the most playful individuals in the specialist species for they have acquired more useful information about the potential of the environment and their actions on it' (pp. 59–60).

Importantly, non-specialisation – which I take to mean being good at many things instead of being expert at a few; having a large portfolio

144

of 'good enough' skills, rather than a small portfolio of 'expert category' skills – is being cited here as being responsible for our continued existence as a species, and that play is central to our continual struggle against extinction.

This makes a great deal of sense and provides a powerful argument for ensuring that the children who come to spaces playworkers operate have personal control in accessing what one hopes will reflect both the planet's and our species' huge diversity. None of us knows what is around the corner (as I write, China has just experienced another powerful earthquake and most of Northern Europe is experiencing a dust cloud generated by a volcano in Iceland that has caused the grounding of almost all aircraft. No-one was prepared for either), but as children play they are being continually reminded of where they are, and of the changes that can take place at any moment, so that as organisms they are in a fully adaptive mode. So by ensuring that children have authentic and playful access to the world, the adaptive processes deep within them, perhaps neural, genetic, chemical or molecular processes, are as up-to-date in terms of global and species intelligence as is possible.

Obviously it is important here that the playworker does not make this a conscious process – playing is not a conscious act – and the consequence of trying to make children conscious of why they are playing, rather than for fun for example, would be that they would become anxious and neurotic, and this would have a serious anti-play effect.

What non-specialisation means to me, is that it is better from an adaptational perspective to touch every base little and often, rather than touching a few bases over a prolonged period. It means having a continually updated overview, taking the temperature and checking things out, but doing each of these things from a biological, rather than just a social, perspective, as individual organisms rather than as young members of a pre-determined social structure. When children play what we should see is raw biology. However, all too often, those charged with a responsibility for play or children or childhood do not draw from the bio-evolutionary analysis that would focus on that, but on a social analysis that inevitably focuses on all manner of non-play outcomes to do with predetermined social targets – like cutting crime, vandalism, even teenage pregnancy and drug taking. Such an analysis may conclude, for example, that children need to be socialised at play, that play facilities should be developed to provide employment, that play facilities should be developed to cut crime, or provide child-care facilities, rather than for the benefit of adaptation or good physical and mental health. Where is the child as an 'organism' in these considerations? What about what the child needs?

There is an on-going debate in playwork about the nature of the play drive; my contribution is that as well as being manifested through sixteen different playtypes, the play drive also has three separate but interlocked and simultaneous modes that activate different genetic characteristics. The first is that play operates in a contemporary mode derived from a need to interact at the contemporary interface, to play in the now, today, engaging in play that has immediate impact in enabling children to make sense of their immediate context. This mode is demonstrated by a child's inclination to explore, to range, and to investigate everything around it.

The second is that the play drive operates in a recapitulative mode, derived from a need to connect with one's personal ancestral past, by recapping what our own ancestors experienced in their lives: this is called epigenesis and demonstrates that maintaining a live connection with our individual past is as important as maintaining one with the present. Wilber (1996) suggested that each one of our evolutionary stages must be integrated into our contemporary 'self' or neurosis will result. In other words, recapitulation – recapitulative play – is a necessary prerequisite for good mental health. This mode is demonstrated by a child's inclination to engage in apparently redundant routines like making fires, den building, ritualising and growing things.

The third mode is the play drive operating as a collective, pan species process. That whilst the contemporary and recapitulative modes demonstrate variations in our individual evolutionary histories and in our immediate contemporary contexts, transpersonal play, that is the mode of play that describes our similarities, our collective identity, is driven by a transpersonal or species component. Almost irrespective of culture, geographical location, economic circumstances and so on, human children reflect general similarities in their play, as well as recapitulative and contemporary differences. This aspect of the play drive is mirrored in children's general tendency to engage in similar games, dressing-up, role-playing, jokes and rhymes, and interact with loose parts.

146

Each of these currents is running through children simultaneously. However, although they can be theoretically differentiated from one another – we can describe them separately – this does not mean that they should be dissociated from one another and supported as if they were individual entities – they are not. Children are not modern or ancient, neither are they individual or collective, they are all of these things, all of the time, and any attempt to separate the different modes will result – as Wilber so rightly implies – in 'lost children' who are neither of the above, detached from both the phylogeny and the ontogeny of human identity, which has been evolving over millions of years.

Equally, practical playwork must take care not to bring about separation either. Nor should it emphasise or facilitate one strand because it is socially acceptable, and not another because it is judged as primitive. The great value of play lies in the sum of each of these different phylogenetic and ontological manifestations; where the child is able to move back and forth between the 'now' and the 'always' state, from the immediate individual biological state to the species' biological state, and back again, in free-flowing modulations, engaged in a connection between what is happening in current reality and what has happened during our species' history, each mode informing, advising and updating each of his or her internal adaptive computations.

What is worrying is that I suspect that increasingly today's children exist primarily in a contemporary technological mode, without the influence of the recapitulation or transpersonal modes to balance here and now individuality, with the perspective of long-term and species' interests.

The above discussion demonstrates how a part of the adaptive mechanism might work, but more importantly, it provides us with an explanation about why it is so important to ensure that play is not seen as a mechanism for socialisation or formal education. In play, children have to be able to move freely between the primeval and the contemporary. Unless that is able to happen, the child's identity will be distorted, and more important, the child will sense that something is not right. This genetic connection, this direct line between now and then, is essential for mental stability (Stevens and Price 2001, Fox 1989). If the child is not able to engage in a comprehensive and authentic play experience, then it may become dysfunctional, and only make the connection when it is older, and far less able to go with the flow, being too aware by then of what is happening and trying to control it. These phylo-ontological aspects of playing should occur during childhood, when they are not felt by the child to be either significant or extraordinary, but normal and ordinary.

I agree with what I understand Lorenz (1972) to be saying. Adaptational intelligence needs a broad brush approach, where children need to be able to access the widest range of experience when they play, if they are going to be able to analyse the maximum number of situations requiring an adaptational view. The playworker will have realised that she cannot teach adaptational interaction and computation; it has to happen spontaneously, i.e., as play is actually happening. Every child is equipped to do it, and it is why human beings continue to survive. However, if play becomes marginalised, or treated as if it is dissociated, i.e., split into its three component parts and one or two parts left to wither, then as a species we may well begin to experience problems with the pressures of extinction.

I believe that world governments are currently making grave errors about where their young should be in their list of priorities and thinking. Rather than being increasingly viewed as immature recipients of services and being smothered by adults' neuroses, children need to experience the elements, know the freedom to range, have insights into the lives of other species and take lots of risks. That is a parental as well as a governmental responsibility. It is a *species* issue, like global warming, water shortages and mass migration, and we all need to consider it.

For example, in the UK, much of the formal educational process is geared towards specialisation. Everything is constructed to channel children into knowing more and more about less and less. Exam grades are everything. That may be appropriate in terms of specialist jobs markets and status and prestige, but it is a problem on the adaptation front. Money, for example, is no help in terms of biological adaptation. We cannot hire someone to do our adapting for us, it is something that as individual members of a species we have to do for ourselves. If we do not, if we continue to focus on 'superficial' social priorities rather than on our 'deep biological' needs, then like many other species that were unable to adapt and became extinct as a consequence, so we increasingly risk the same fate. All the effort and

148

sacrifice of our ancestors would have been for nothing simply because we failed to acknowledge our vulnerability to change, and allowed ourselves instead to sleepwalk into the evolutionary cul de sac that is extinction.

CALIBRATION

Calibration is not just another interesting idea, it is a functional reality. It happens to us on a daily basis and is developed and applied when we play. I understand 'calibration' to mean 'the measurement of one thing in relation to another'. The *Concise Oxford English Dictionary* defines it as:

> i. correlating the readings of an instrument with those of a standard; ii. adjusting results to take external factors into account or to allow comparisons with other data.

Much has been written over the years about this subject. Simpson (1976) discusses calibration in the context of mounting behaviour in monkeys, implying that if a monkey does not put the necessary building blocks together that tell it (a) how to mount and (b) where to mount, then it will not be a player in the procreation stakes.

In human terms, what the skill of calibration does is make it possible for children to update their physical relationship with the physical environment both as they and it change. Imagine, for example, a baby who is just beginning to crawl. In the middle of the room is a chair. This chair has a number of unchanging features. It is a particular shape, a particular weight, it is a particular height, in a particular position in space and so on. These features are fixed. The chair will remain the same shape, weight and height, unless forces external to the chair move it, or change its shape.

The baby is smaller than the chair, it cannot sit on it and cannot move it. The baby will learn these things by interacting with the chair. However, after a period of time has passed, say six months, the baby will have grown significantly. In relation to the baby's size and strength now, the chair has changed, for example the baby will be able move it, she may even try to sit on it. Obviously it is not the chair that has changed, it is the baby. Every so often the baby will return to the chair and to other household features she has calibrated her strength

149

and height against, to check out her current calibration relationship with them.

So, one aspect of calibration is about comparing physical changes against a fixed physical environment. Children need playfully to explore their physical environment and map it, in terms of a whole range of different characteristics. For example, as they grow, they will need to know how much muscular pressure they need to exert to close doors, turn on light switches and turn water taps off. Children are not born with this knowledge and unless they are well calibrated, they will be unintentionally clumsy and noisy, banging doors shut, leaving them open when they thought they had closed them, not turning lights on and turning taps on too full and spraying themselves with water. The other aspect of calibration is that as well as continually calibrating oneself against the physical environment as *they* change, children have to calibrate themselves again when *it* changes. So, if they move to another environment, they have to learn it all over again. For example, part of the excitement of going on holiday is that we go to new places, with new spaces to explore and map. However, it can be very frustrating when light switches are different and turn in ways we are not used to, or when the hot and cold taps are reversed, or when door handles are not where we're used to locating them. Having said that, with constant playful practice, as children upgrade their knowledge of their physical selves against a known environment – a swing, a tree, a particular jump – calibration soon becomes a continuous feature of their playful routine.

For the playing child, it is not so much about learning or mapping static or changing spaces, as it is about learning how to learn. Play is about developing the building blocks that make learning possible. So from an early age, as biological players, children need an environment which interests them enough, so they will actually want to explore it and learn how to calibrate it. But they also need an environment that is changing, so that they learn about re-calibration – this is one reason why a play environment should be in a changing rather than a stagnant state.

I first came across the term 'calibration' in Bateson and Hinde's *Growing Points in Ethology* (1976). In it, Simpson (1976) states, 'I suggest that play may ensure not only the initial calibration of the infant's skills, but also a continuous re-calibration of these skills as he

150

changes in size relative to the fixtures of his surroundings, and relative to his peers, who are also changing size and strength.'

One day the child cannot pick up a chair, then its strength increases fractionally and then it *can* pick the chair up. One day she is smaller than someone else, then she is bigger, then she might be smaller again. Each of these changes, and each of these subsequent re-calibrations, alters the dynamic between the child and his or her environment.

Engaging in the process of calibration not only gives children an awareness of the relationship they, as physical objects, have with every other physical object in their play frame, it also has an affective, i.e., emotional, component that informs how children feel about their own physical characteristics. Most of us have seen a baby getting frustrated when it cannot move something. But that interaction is telling the baby that there will be things in the physical universe that it cannot control and it needs to come to terms with that.

Repetition is also an important ingredient both of playing itself and specifically of calibration. Connolly (1973) and McFarland (1973) both suggested that repetition of particular kinds of actions is important in order that complex skills may be learnt. What they may be saying is that complex skills are the sum total of many less complex proto-skills and that for the integration of both the less and more complex skills into our brain pathways, we need to repeat them many times for the appropriate circuitry to form. This is certainly borne out on the playground where children will often do the same thing over and over again and then vary what they do slightly, and then repeat the variation again and again.

Simpson (1976) also re-emphasises the point made earlier about muscular force, what I called muscular pressure. He says 'The organism may in this repetitive behaviour test the variations in force [muscular force] necessary to perform a particular behaviour'.

He also states 'there is a point at which early extensive calibration of numerous situations can be termed experience, which can then be extended into new situations, so that repeated calibration in a different environment or set of circumstances becomes less necessary or unnecessary'.

Eye + Action = Calibration(1)
Calibration(n) + Memory = Experience

So if children engage in enough calibration and re-calibration activity early on in their lives, they may be able to navigate new spaces more successfully as they grow up.

CONTEXTUALISATION

Contextualisation is a variation on calibration and refers to a more psychic than physical version of calibration. Contextualisation is more about gaining a 'sense of place', about having a developed view about where one is in the scheme of things, about one's place in the universe.

The idea of contextualisation came to me after I had been working on a particular play project for some time. When, following a distressing bereavement, several of the older children became emotionally sensitive and very detached from the rest of the children for a few days.

Contexualisation is a 'What is the meaning of life?' version of calibration. It helps children to develop perspectives and values. Experience tells me that deep play is primarily a feature of the child's play repertoire in middle-childhood and is both an expression of their realisation of the fact of mortality and a way of encountering it in their own world. However, even a genuine realisation of mortality is not a potent enough preparation for the experience of real loss, which tends to throw children into a metaphysical spin, because it requires thought of a kind children are quite unused to prior to this kind of event. When someone disappears out of one's life, it is difficult for most of us, particularly children, to comprehend. 'How can people just disappear?', 'Where do they go?', 'How do they get there?', 'Where is Heaven?', 'How do you know?'

Suddenly, from the secure, or relatively secure, reality of the unconscious, children now have all these questions, which those who should know everything, i.e., adults, do not have answers to – that is both scary and perplexing. It signals to them that death is a big issue and one people know little about, except, of course, that it will come to them too, one day.

Dealing with this new dimension in which people disappear and never come back, where people children love and care about just seem to evaporate, requires a total re-evaluation of what they think life is

152

about and what their priorities in it should be. If this experience is badly dealt with by the playworker it can leave children feeling confused, betrayed and worthless. It is easy to take life seriously and even easier to take it personally. A child who may have already had a hard time can evaluate the loss of a loved one as the final confirmation that life is pointless and that ideas like concern and respect are meaningless. The playworker's approach to this type of event in children's lives should be much like their approach to every other aspect of the child's emotional life – to be there, to make sure the child knows that, but not to crowd – ensuring that they do not hijack the child's experience, and colonise it with their own.

Throughout their lives, children have to make sense of experiences like death, whether a near death of their own, the deaths of thousands in natural disasters or the abomination of other children being massacred. How they deal with both the notion and reality of death as children will determine how able they will be, as time goes on, to deal with it as adults.

The relationship between metaphysical issues and play is an important one, for play is about life in its entirety. This must include the realisation and experience of death for it to be a complete experience.

Hall's (1904) notion of recapitulation is an interesting one in this context. For what Hall suggests is that play is also a reliving of our ancestral pasts, which must mean, if Hall is correct, that play is genetically programmed and that today's play is actually coded into the genes of today's children to be passed on – with all of the other ancestral information – via procreation. The implication here being that humans not only pass on the 'height and hair colour' sorts of characteristics through their genes, they also pass on evolutionary events, of which one would expect death to be a significant part, which would then be played out in the future. As we know, this is the case in a whole range of children's play narratives.

So, perhaps the best way to understand contextualisation is to see it as the calibration of real-life events and experiences, against the preconceptions and expectations one has developed from parents, siblings and experience to date. 'Is it worse or better than I expected?' 'Do I feel more or less let down than I thought I would?'

CHAPTER 6

STIMULATION THEORY AND PLAY DEPRIVATION

INTRODUCTION

If play is as important to human development, adaptation and survival as recent evidence suggests, then what happens if children don't play? This question was being posed in playwork as early as the late 1980s, and theoretical outcomes of chronic play deprivation were tentatively modelled in a developing Stimulation Theory (Hughes 1984, 1996). However, it wasn't until empirical investigations by Huttenmoser *et al.*, Chugani and latterly Brown and Lomax, and then Brown, were published that the devastating impacts of play deprivation predicted earlier were actually realised.

THE STIMULATION THEORY MODEL

The premisses of Stimulation Theory are very simple. Human beings thrive on environmental stimulation. Whether they perceive it as positive or negative they incorporates it into their picture of the world. Weather, cooking, art, relationships, work and play all contain the sensory highs and lows that are the backdrop to life on Earth.

However, optimum environmental stimulation is more or less a balance between the negative and the positive, between the pains and pleasures of existence.

What Stimulation Theory asserts is that although most children experience this 'balance', as positive and negative affect, many children (and it may be an increasing number) do not. Instead they experience one or more extremes of environmental stimulation. It further

154

asserts that chronic exposure to these extremes changes children, and moves both their behaviour and expectations in the direction of the extreme.

Stimulation Theory posits four extremes to which children might be drawn.

- **Over-positive:** positive stimulation not balanced by a corresponding level of negative input.
- **Over-negative:** negative stimulation not balanced by a corresponding level of positive input.
- **Z1:** positive and negative stimulation coming from an erratic or unreliable source.
- **Z2:** an absence or very low level of any kind of stimulation.

Rather than enabling children to develop strategies for dealing with them, as balanced and predictable stimulation would for example, these extremes corrupt children, offering not the optimism drawn from balance, but either continuous unrealistic positive affect, or the bleak prospect of never ending negative affect, or unreliable stimulation where positive and negative are interchangeable, or stimulation of such low level that it provides more an absence of anything rather than a presence of anything.

Stimulation Theory suggests the following extreme outcomes:

- Over-positive children will use violence to protect what they have.
- Over-negative children will use violence to get what they don't have.
- Z1 children unable to predict what will happen next become anxious and withdrawn.
- Z2 children unable to access necessary levels of environmental stimulation develop fantasy existences, constructed from whatever experiences they have had.

I will explore each of these four categories later. Suffice it to say now, that theoretically they suggest that play deprivation – caused by inappropriate types and/or levels of environmental stimulation – could be responsible for the development of behaviour that is either lethally violent, withdrawn and neurotic, and/or fantasy driven, or even a mixture of all of these.

This model was constructed to clarify what might go wrong for children chronically exposed to inappropriate levels and types of environmental stimulation, and to offer stimulus-based suggestions about providing balanced, reliable and optimum levels and types of environmental stimulation in play settings.

A deeper analysis of this idea

Selfishness, aggression, confusion and withdrawal are normal human states which are usually subsumed into each child's total personality, only showing themselves on rare occasions. Most children, most of the time, are playful, stable, optimistic and friendly individuals, and because of this predictable norm, playworkers are able to develop particular operational criteria for their work with children. However, not all the children playworkers meet are like this. Some are very angry and highly aggressive. Others seem lost, existing only on the fringes of groups. Some appear spoilt and arrogant, communicating their apparent contempt at every opportunity, whilst others are nervy, frightened and constantly lacking in confidence.

When these children come to play spaces, playworkers may need to adapt their operational criteria accordingly, but what might this mean? How do children become extreme in their behaviour and what can playworkers do to contribute usefully to these children's play experiences?

By exploring the theoretical impact of different types and levels of environmental stimulation on how children might view the world, this chapter not only offers an analysis that provides tentative insights both into the development of extreme behaviour and the prognosis for the children affected, it also provides the playwork genesis of an exploration into both the cause and the impact of what we now call play deprivation.

ENVIRONMENTAL STIMULATION

Human beings rely on different kinds of environmental stimulation for their playful interaction with the world to have any sensory content. With every contact we have, whether visual, auditory, olfactory or tactile, we rely on the world providing us with information about its nature via the type and intensity of the stimuli we receive.

When a child is playfully interacting with the world, it is because it is sensitive to the world of different stimuli, that it is able to develop a sensory picture of the world around itself.

Hard things, soft things, things that are warm, others that are cool or cold, things which smell or taste good or bad; pleasant and unpleasant sounds. The child must develop a sensory memory where it learns to discriminate and make judgements between different temperatures, between different tastes and smells, and begin to build up the ability to understand that in order to understand anything about what is happening around it, or to be able to predict and forecast, the child must learn to analyse and evaluate the information arriving as stimuli and try to develop an increasingly informed view of what things mean and what to do about them. For example, what clothes to wear, what food is favoured, what music to like, do I believe what the person is saying to me?

Although these stimuli are normally described purely in sensory terms – smells, tastes, tactile feelings, sights and sounds – they can be described as two different stimulus types; positive stimulation (which I will sometimes abbreviate to '+ve' in the text) and negative stimulation (which I will sometimes abbreviate to '-ve' in the text).

Positive stimuli are the ones humans would normally describe as pleasant, negative ones as unpleasant, and because to some extent, which is which, is dependent upon individual perception and mood – for example, I like that colour, I do not like that taste – they are open to subjective interpretation. However, we sense many stimuli in more or less the same way. We all either like them, or dislike them. If someone hits us, in general we humans tend to find that a disagreeable experience, whoever does the hitting. Whereas, if we get a smile or a hug, we generally like it. However, later models of stimulation theory predicted that in the extreme, both positive *and* negative stimuli could actually be very harmful, particularly if exposure was chronic (Hughes 1996b).

Positive and negative stimuli are opposites, like tickles and nips. And in general, for each nice, beautiful, interesting stimulus experience, there are equivalent nasty, ugly and boring ones. When children play, the potential for one acts as a balance for the potential of the other, thus encouraging children to keep playing.

For example, if a child wants an exciting swinging experience she might choose to go on a large American swing. She will have watched other children and will be aware that the higher she goes, the more she will hurt herself if she falls. Although of course, like everything, the child needs to experience the reality of the situation before that calculation has any real meaning. Nevertheless she will risk the negative to experience the positive. Some experience of physical and psychological pain and pleasure is essential to making informed and balanced life judgements. It is when the child is at play that she can learn this. It is also when she is at play that the spectrum of pleasure and pain can be most effectively evaluated. This is why risk is such a vital component in authentic play. It is the potential or reality of the negative – fear, fright, pain – that encourages the child to risk assess and apply a degree of caution to unknown experiences.

SO WHAT PLEASURE IS WORTH WHAT PAIN?

This is a vitally important 'curiosity versus realisation' computation for the child at play to make. It provides her with a basic, push/pull, attraction/repulsion mechanism, which is at the heart of intrinsically motivated play. For even without any external goal or reward, the playing child still engages in what Sylva (1977) calls a 'dialectic', weighing up the pros and the cons, before undertaking action.

The playworker should be aware of the importance of her role in facilitating this dialectic. For example, how the play environment is presented to children will have a significant impact on their curiosity (Morris 1964). The range of both positive and negative experiences on offer will act as a limitation on it, or as an attraction to it. The narrower the range, the more impoverished the play space, the greater the limitation imposed on the child's neophilia or love of the novel; the higher the level of novel experiences, the more enriched the play spaces, the greater will be the child's neophilic drive.

For the child, play should be both a discovery and a balancing experience, so that the child is constantly able to update its perception of where it is. When the child is playing, she is constantly engaged in a process of 'deepening' her understanding of the spectrum of reality into which she has been born – a spectrum that stretches from the sub-atomic to the cosmic – whether that experience is visual, like looking at sunlight as it passes through the leaves of a tree, or tactile, like the feel of air on skin, as the child is in motion on a swing.

158

Children need balancing experiences to be able authentically to evaluate the nature of their everyday play and other experiences in their home context, and they also need access to experiential contrasts that enable comparisons to take place. If the play space offers access to a balance of both positive and negative stimulation, that will enable the child to experience a form of 'stimulus normality'. Although this will not affect the child's general circumstances, it will enable her to be conscious of alternatives to feeling hard done by, or to feeling privileged.

Experience has led me to conclude that a majority of the children I have worked with already inhabited this 'stimulus middle-ground' of play. Their everyday experience of the world, although diverse and deep, fell within the comparative parameters of, say, plus or minus 5 on the Stimulation Spectrum.

As play environments, their homes and the areas around their home were moderately stimulating and varied, and offered much of what they needed both in terms of experience and novelty. My playwork contribution to these children was to offer alternatives and supplement some deficits – like accessing new friends, interfacing with new risks, and engaging in water and fire play. But for many of them, the play space's greatest attraction was that it provided somewhere where they could do what they normally did, but away from adults. This is probably the case for many of those children who already live in 'playable environs' where they have access to dirt, trees and water, but still choose to use supervised play spaces, like adventure playgrounds. The attraction is not just the neophilic and elemental, it is also the notion of playing freely and independently, of engaging in the norms of the culture of the young rather than having to continually adjust behaviour to satisfy the preconceptions of the adult world.

However, there was also a significant, and growing minority of children who attended each of the play spaces I operated, who did not experience this 'stimulus middle-ground' of play. Instead their everyday normality was either more extreme (they experienced high levels of negativity or positivity, on a daily basis), or the levels of stimulation they were

Extreme			Extreme
++ve	+ve Balance −ve		=ve

10 – 9 – 8 – 7 – 6 – 5 – 4 – 3 – 2 – 1 – 0 – 1 – 2 – 3 – 4 – 5 – 6 – 7 – 8 – 9 – 10

Figure 6.1 The Environmental Stimulation spectrum.

subjected to fluctuated wildly (making it impossible for them to predict or forecast what was going to happen), or the levels of stimulation were unhealthily low (causing them to experience a degree of sensory deprivation). Frighteningly, for some, normality was a mixture of all three!

THE FOUR DOORS

Imagine a wall with many doors and behind each door is revealed a new, vibrant, interesting, although perhaps difficult, and even risky, play experience. This is the world many children inhabit. A world of diversity of experience, of unpredictability, a world which requires children to be endlessly flexible and adaptable, learning from each experience and evaluating its value and meaning in the light of what she already knows from the experiences she has already had.

Now imagine a wall where there are only four doors. Where each door opens onto a world representing a stimulus extreme.

The over-positive or indulged door

This door gives entrance to a world that is always positive, where the sun always shines, and where children are indulged, protected and get every plaything they want. When a child knocks on this door s/he is always welcomed and feels special.

The over-negative or de-sensitised door

This door gives entrance to a world that is always negative, where it's always cold and raining, and where children are disliked, shunned, even threatened, and have to struggle to get anything they need. When children knock on this door they are ignored and feel unwelcome and inferior.

The Z1[1] or erratic door

This door gains entrance to a world of contradictions, that can be anything from frustrating, to very frightening. Children in this world can be indulged or rejected for doing the same thing. They can experience love and hate only moments apart, promises are made, broken and made again. Playthings are provided and withdrawn without explanation. When a child knocks on this door, sometimes it opens, sometimes it does not, and the child feels insecure, unable to trust her own judgement or trust the word of others.

The Z2[1] or de-humanised door

The final door gains entrance to a world in which very little happens, where at best it is boring and at worst, numbing. Where children are ignored, left for hours and have to invent what they need from within their own imagination. When a child knocks on this door, the door opens but nothing else happens, no welcome, no rejection, just feeling lost, ignored, superfluous and alone.

Of course most children experience each of these metaphorical doors and the worlds they give access to at sometime in their lives, and from the perspective of healthy development in an environmental context that is probably all to the good. Experience of each of them is probably useful to the development of skills that make it possible for us to survive and thrive in a whole variety of different situations. However, it is also likely that a proportion, and perhaps an increasing proportion, of the children with whom the playworker works will come from home and living environments all too often biased towards one or other of these doors/ worlds. These will be children whose experiential balance and diversity will have been so limited, that most of their judgements and strategies will have been computed from one sort of experience and one sort only.

STIMULUS EXTREMES

The over-positive or indulged door = extreme +ve bias

Play behaviour(1)+ (+ve) stimulation(1) = Reinforced Play Behaviour(1)
Reinforced Play Behaviour(n)+(+ve) stimulation(n) = ++ve biased play
world view

1 In Hughes (1996b), categories Z1 and Z2 were referred to as 'Zero A' and 'Zero B' respectively.

What these equations suggest is that for play behaviour to do its job, children must evaluate the experiences that present themselves to them as they are playing. The idea being that as the child randomly engages with different experiences, and as they explore them with their senses – propelled by their evolving movement, co-ordination and dexterity skills – they take those experiences and consider them in the light of what they know already.

For example, if a child hurts itself, if she receives a bang on the head, initially she may ignore it, if it did not hurt much. She may have done it before. If it did hurt, or if she keeps on doing the same thing, she will eventually look to the source of the pain and begin to make the connection between it and herself, and she will begin to calibrate herself not to do it, by working out how far she can lift her head before it contacts the surface she is banging it against. It may take a large number of knocks – for example, some young children spend an inordinate amount of time banging their heads by standing erect when they are under tables, with all of the accompanying noise and tears – before the calibration lesson sinks in. But it is a vitally important and essential lesson on many levels and, if not experienced, will deprive that child of necessary life knowledge.

Children need to know about pain. Pain not only tells them about their mortality, but about their relative fragility too, and like it or not, it is a huge feature of what makes us all human. Lady Allen – one of the pioneers of Adventure Playgrounds – is reported to have remarked 'Better a broken bone than a broken spirit'. Pain is an important part of our day-to-day survival mechanism. Little cuts and bruises when we are children, particularly if we get them from vigorous and enthusiastic play, form a vital interaction with the world, and are essential indicators of the nature of that interaction. Too many cuts and bruises and we moderate the impact of the interaction; we become more careful. If we do not, then we get bigger cuts and bruises, until we do moderate our behaviour or we really hurt ourselves; in which case, we have to evaluate our behaviour in the light of that experience, or we have a survival problem.

The child's need to learn about pain is not helped by over-eager or inappropriately-timed adult intervention, or by only playing in an environment that is overridingly positive. Understandably, most parents/carers do not want their children to hurt themselves, and most

162

of us do not like the sound of children crying, but it is essential that we understand that without a lot of knocks, our children will be less well equipped to survive either physically or psychologically, in what is after all a very dangerous world. Some parents/carers cannot or will not accept this and instead of giving their children access to balancing experiences, do everything they can to protect their children from everyday scrapes, disabling them as a consequence.

The over-positive or indulgent adult may see the child as their life's greatest accomplishment, or as a kind of ornament. The child might be the focus of huge amounts of 'transference', if, for example the adult has either been badly hurt themselves, or has a vivid imagination when it comes to injury or distress. In wanting to forgo the experience themselves they project this onto the child's world and intervene continuously to stop the child experiencing either what she, the adult, has experienced in reality, or what she is fearfully imagining is possible. Alternatively the adult may see the child as a piece of property, where the child's free interaction with the world undermines the feelings of power the adult gets from controlling the child's behaviour.

Whatever the reason for the intervention by the adult, if the child is overprotected, it will become an unwitting accomplice in a process of biasing its own worldview. On the other hand, indulgence might not just be about protection, it might also be about the constant need to reinforce the perceived 'specialness' of the child by the parent or relative. Specialness – favouritism, spoiling, indulgence – suggests to the child that it can do no wrong; that it is always the other children who make mistakes or act inappropriately. The child may be the recipient of a constant stream of smothering, and undeserved positive stimulation, perhaps in the form of food, or other treats, hugs, or compliments, at a time when pathways in the child's brain are being formed that set this as an anticipated default position. In other words, because the stimulation the child gets is excessively and unrealistically positive (++ve), and because there is no balancing negative stimulation to moderate the child's expectations, it will learn to expect what is in fact over-positivity as its balanced norm or default position.

An over-positive play worldview can be described on a spectrum ranging from a *naïve view* of what that child might expect from playful interaction, to an *egocentric protective view*.

The naïve view

Because it has always been protected by its over-anxious carer and may never have experienced a fall, or banged its head, the naïve child will not have developed the survival building blocks which link personal safety to the calibration processes that are reinforced by the negative stimulation of pain. This child may be spatially clumsy or even reckless, when it comes to height or speed, risking personal injury, because s/he is unaware, or not aware enough, of the risky nature of the environment.

The egocentric protective view

At the other extreme, the child's anti-social behaviour may have been positively reinforced by an over-indulgent carer, or its aberrant behaviour explained away as 'cute'. Consequently, without the balance of reprimand, or social rejection, she will not have developed the building blocks that link successful social interactions, to behaviour which is perceived by others as reasonable. Because of this deficit, the child may become selfish, perhaps bullying, unable to understand why other children, or even adults, do not give in to her every demand. And, depending on its physique and guile, the child may begin to use physical force to get her own way, thus, reinforcing her perception of her 'specialness' or superiority, or alternatively retreating, angry, embarrassed and bewildered at not getting her own way.

The child who is always protected at home may find the demands of the play experience daunting, in which case she may get a negative reaction from children who have experienced less protection, which she may not like. Alternatively she may find play exhilarating, and take silly risks, perhaps hurting herself or other children. Either way, whether she finds play daunting or exhilarating, because the initial building blocks for calibration and social interaction are missing, or not fully formed, like a computer with a half-formed operating system, she will not be as able to function as she anticipates, and may become resentful or perpetually critical as a result.

Children who are over-indulged will find the play space a difficult place to navigate socially. Although most groups of children have

164

some kind of in-built hierarchical view, much of what is decided is through negotiation and agreement. Children know that each of their peers has a parental, school and behavioural context, and consideration is given to each of these when decisions are being made about where to go, what to do, for how long, etc. However, this system breaks down or is undermined by the entry of an over-indulged child into the group, who, because she knows no better, will expect every decision to go her way. That is, if the child's early stimulus experience has been primarily positive, if she has not experienced contrary views, which act to persuade her that her judgement can be wrong as well as right, then she will not be familiar with negotiation, and may continually attempt to force her view on the rest of the group. The result being that she will either begin to dominate the group by force or be jettisoned by it. Either way, this child's view of the other children will be diminished. The term force in this context does not apply to the won power derived from having to fight to survive from an early age, it is the unbalanced force of relative size, or ability to intimidate, or use tactics like crying to achieve desired ends.

Children whose play environment is over-ridingly positive, where they always get what they want, and whose play experience is not governed by a 'real' world curriculum of danger, disappointment, frustration, poverty and potential injury, are also at risk of a positively biased view of the play world. They will find it difficult to operate with children whose expectations have been lessened by experience, who have learnt to do without, to compromise or to share. The child from an over-positive environment may well find it easier to function in the over-positive, predictable world she inhabits at home, to the one in which she has to 'give ground' to other children. This child's discomfort might be such that she begins to dislike the children who do not get everything they want, perceiving her world as somewhere that is special and which needs to be protected from them, growing up into an adolescent whose world view is at least disparaging of those with materially less than her.

Taken to the extreme, these over-positive children (++ve children) have a considerable potential to become embittered with the real world outside of their cosseted space. The reaction of the world to them will be to either reinforce that view, in which case they may become more reckless or violent, or it will reject them or attack them back, in which case they will feel vulnerable and become increasingly overtly or covertly violent, as a result.

Theoretically it should be possible with concentrated opportunity for good, balanced play experiences, for these children's play deficits to be addressed. They should be able to recover the building blocks without the experiential gaps – rather like re-recording a badly recorded song with a better recording – particularly if they are enabled to re-engage in early/middle play again, but this time with a programme designed to address the deficits and their symptoms. However, Huttenlocher's (1992) imaging findings on brain plasticity imply that this would need to be done at a relatively early age to be totally effective. The additional synaptic potential to which he alludes (p. 64), and which the child would need to utilise, would only be available for a few years, during the 'sensitive period' referred to in Chapter 3, and by ten years of age much of this potential will have been lost.

Less recent material from the literature, including Harlow and Suomi (1971), Novak and Harlow (1975) and Einon *et al.* (1978), support this, implying that short periods of quality play can have the effect of overcoming serious deficits in social skills, for example. Although whether this is as true for human children as it is for other species is unclear.

Good supervised play environments have a lot to offer ++ve children. They are happy, fun and welcoming places to be. Children have the freedom to do what they want, within a context of some compromise and negotiation. They are reasonably well resourced. They are normally staffed by experienced and knowledgeable playworkers who, by ensuring that the space is interesting and novel, and that it addresses the range of different play types, facilitate a considerable diversity of experiences. Like other 'normal' children, over-indulged children may find the supervised play space attractive and interesting and find it relatively easy to adapt to their new situation. Giving ground or playing less recklessly may be perceived by them as a small price to pay for friends and happiness. In other words, fundamental human needs might over-ride dysfunction and have the effect, at a neurological level, of replacing incomplete circuitry with a more complete version drawn from the missing experience.

What can the playworker do when over-positive children come to play?

Some proposed indicators of an over-positive play bias:

- inability to navigate the play space;
- difficulties with other children;
- reckless or clumsy behaviour;
- high expectation of immediate access to materials;
- always has sweets, the latest toys, the latest fashions;
- smokes at home;
- engages in destructive behaviour;
- has bodily adornments including tattoos, studs and particular hair cuts from an early age;
- expects favours;
- talks loudly, intrudes into others' space;
- is obese;
- looks through other children;
- adopts a particular tone when s/he wants something, but ignores or dismisses children the instant s/he gets it;
- egocentric – expects to be the centre of attention;
- sulks, has tantrums;
- walks through other children, never around them;
- rarely says 'thank you';
- exhibits cruel or bullying tendencies.

It is important that playwork practice is just not focused on addressing specific indicators of indulgence, but on recognising the root causes of the child's situation. The child should be enabled to play through her difficulties, rather than be criticised for her behaviour. She will be more socially competent and less of a danger to herself and others as a result. More importantly what might have been serious experiential deficits that could have led to de-sensitised, and perhaps, eventually, to de-humanised behaviour, may have been repaired by the child's own engagement in the 're-play' process.

This means that one's expectation of the indulged child should be exactly the same as those of any other child, with perhaps one exception, that because one is aware that she may have some serious experiential deficits, any supervision should take place initially at fairly close range to enable fast intervention if there is a dispute between this child and others, or if this child's behaviour represents a danger to herself or to other children.

The level and nature of any necessary intervention will also differ. As indicated earlier, the playworker's presence in the general vicinity is enough to make some children re-evaluate what they are doing, whereas others may need more direct intervention where materials, tools or other children are removed with the minimum of disturbance to that child, so that the 'frame' of the child's behaviour is changed (Else and Sturrock 1998).

However, playworkers should always remember:

- that change may be slow, and that dysfunction may return several times before it is overlaid with new behaviour;
- the playworker's most important function, for that child, is to engage with her in such a way that she continues to come to the play space. If she is confronted directly or embarrassed, she may never return.

The over-negative or de-sensitised door = extreme-ve bias

Play Behaviour(1)+(-ve)stimulation(1) = Undermined Play Behaviour(1)
Undermined Play Behaviour(n)+(-ve)stimulation(n)=ve biased play world view

The problem for the over-positive child is that whatever the strategic choices she makes when she plays they are either:

- confirmed as appropriate or correct by her over-indulgent carer, or
- made to appear to be correct by an over-protective carer.

The problem for the over-negative child is the reverse. Far from being indulged, this child's self-image and perception of self is continually being battered and undermined by the events that are occurring in the home/living/playing environment.

When a child playfully interacts with the play environment, he is receptive both to positive and negative experiences, sensing them as either pleasurable or unpleasant. The child has evolved to expect a range of experience, and if those experiences are of only one type, i.e., only positive *or* only negative, the child will begin to adjust his expectations of what he gets from playing. These expectations will become manipulated by his experiences. The child who experiences predominantly positive affect will anticipate play experiences that continue to confirm that, that are manipulated towards the positive, i.e., the more positive effect he derives from playing, the more he will learn to expect. Similarly, a child playing in an environment that only contains negative experiences will anticipate negativity, and have his expectations manipulated towards the negative, i.e., the more negative effect he derives from playing, the more negativity he will learn to expect.

Just as with the over-positive child, where a child's expectations are manipulated by a bias of negative experience, serious consequences ensue, both for the affected child and for other children.

A positively-biased child will expect things to be positive, to go her way, and she will make all sorts of assumptions about the world to ensure that is the case. The impact of her experience upon her neurological structures and brain chemistry leaves the child with no other alternative. When she plays, if her view of the world is not confirmed, and she realises that – for example she may discover that many children do not have what she has and do not share her preconceptions – her reaction may initially be confused, but will eventually result in fear of loss and eventually *defensive* anger.

Alternatively, a negatively-biased child will expect things to be negative. This child's neurological structure and brain chemistry is also determined by experience. His worldview is that bad things always happen and he adapts to that perception, adopting either 'a shoot first and ask questions later' view, or a 'keep your head down' view. When he plays, this child will expect the experience to contain verbal and physical violence and anticipate that. However, if, when he plays, his view of the world is not confirmed, if for example he sees that not everyone has been treated as he has, then whilst his initial reaction may be shock, perhaps even shame, this will eventually turn into *offensive* anger.

So for children experiencing an extreme negative play bias the prognosis is more or less the same as it is for the over-positive child, violence, although for *offensive* rather than *defensive* reasons. It is my belief that the older these children become, the less effective will be any attempts to enable them to balance themselves by playing with experiential alternatives.

What can the playworker do when over-negative children come to play?

Some proposed indicators of an over-negative play bias:

- taking over equipment or materials from other children;
- ignoring the playworkers;
- flinching or ducking when playworkers or other adults are in close proximity;
- looking physically or materially neglected;
- punching or pushing with little or no provocation;
- bullying behaviour;
- being 'old before their time';
- exhibiting high levels of attention seeking;
- stealing;
- violent interactions between siblings;
- very defensive;
- trying to make playworkers fearful – manifesting threatening behaviour;
- destructive behaviour.

It is very tempting to create a self-fulfilling prophecy with over-negative children. Having said 'You do that again, and you're out!', one should not be surprised that they do indeed do it again and that they do have to be excluded. These children know they are going to fail and they know that the consequence of failure may be being shouted at or hit. So if the playworker gets angry, that instantly reinforces their preconception. It is better to recognise that the negativity they bring to the play space can be a force for good – these children often like to help adults. However, because of their violent potential, the playworker should still intervene at fairly close range. This does not mean that they should be crowded but rather that a playworker should be in the vicinity until she is content that they will not attack other children, and other children may not need to be re-located. The playworker's strategy should be one of kindness and positive reinforcement. Children so affected have a right to know that they are

170

loved. However, they may have been so damaged that it might take many attempts and many failures before an over-negative child is able to discriminate between what happens at home and what happens at the play space and begin to be able to appreciate the difference.

The Z1 or erratic door = unpredictable levels or types of stimulation

Play Behaviour(1)+erratic levels of stimulation(1) = confusion(1)
Play Behaviour(n)+erratic levels of stimulation(n) = repetitious implementation of unworkable survival strategies = low levels of self-confidence and self-esteem

This model is particularly applicable to children whose carers are experiencing difficulties with domestic violence, mental illness, alcoholism and/or drug addiction, and whose behaviour is unpredictable, as a consequence. In this context it is not unusual for a child to ask a carer a question, and get a 'yes', then ask the same question a short time later and get a 'no'. Or worse still, get a 'Yes my darling' first and then a 'What the fuck are you doing now you little ***?!', only a short time later.

Even though one of the main evolutionary reasons for playing is to be flexible and adaptive, continually trying out strategies for adapting to situations that themselves keep changing randomly does not make biological sense. Children need some level of consistency, to be able to judge how to be, in a whole variety of circumstances. Take that consistency out of their situation and they are forced to conclude that everything is an illusion and act accordingly, i.e., that nothing matters and that nothing they do matters either. They may spend an inordinate amount of time trying to second guess their carer's reactions to things, devising complex and convoluted strategies to 'guarantee' required outcomes, only to be continually thwarted by the carer's continued random, patternless behaviour.

Eventually, if the carer's behaviour is only mildly erratic, children may just avoid them, hoping that by the time they, the child and carer, are in contact again, the situation will have stabilised. But, if the carer's behaviour is widely erratic, incomprehensible or verbally or physically violent, the child may begin to show symptoms of neurosis, increasingly unable to predict or second-guess, in such a fluid and unpredictable environment.

What can the playworker do when 'erratic' children come to play?

Some proposed indicators of an 'erratic' play bias:

- disbelief;
- neurotic behaviour;
- over-protection of siblings;
- fear or nervousness of adults;
- isolating or withdrawn behaviour;
- unexpected knowledge of symptoms and treatment of mental illness, alcoholism and/or drug abuse;
- imitation of parents during socio-dramatic or role-play episodes;
- tiredness/hunger;
- poor play 'performance'.

More than any other of the extreme groups considered so far, 'erratic' children risk being out on the margins, lonely, friendless and neglected. Over-positive children will attract other children because of what they have materially and because of the confidence the positive reinforcement gives them. Over-negative children will attract children similar to them as friends and their confidence will feed from the impact their combined presence brings, wherever they are.

But 'erratic' children have had their trust dented or destroyed. Their reaction is always to not quite believe or trust what is happening because their experience is that it will soon change again. So, if the playworker says, 'I promise', she will not only need to keep that promise on that occasion, she will need to keep it many times, before children so affected can benefit from the synaptic overlay which says that, at the play space at least, things can be relied upon. In an ordinary, as opposed to a specialist play space, these children will be difficult to work with simply because chronic exposure to erratic stimuli makes them very unpredictable, fragile and nervy. The playworker, expecting tantrums and arguments initially, should try to be patient and build on the reliability and hence the predictability of the space. But playworkers should also be warned that unless they are able to

172

maintain the opening hours, session durations, visits, or whatever they promise, they should not build up these children's expectations, or they themselves will actually contribute to the level of damage these children experience. Having said that, although playing with other perhaps, non-erratic or non-extreme children will have its difficulties, simply engaging in play that is not continually fragmented by a carer's erratic behaviour will, at least, tell these children that the erratic environment is not the only environmental type to exist.

The Z2 or de-humanising door = sensory deprivation

Play Behaviour(1)+low-level stimulation(1) = decrease in behaviour and increase in imagination
Play Behaviour(n)+low-level stimulation(n) = play extinction+fantasy driven behaviour

For this part of the model I use the similarity human beings have with electrical appliances. They need current i.e. stimulation, to function. From the point of view of the basic human organism, it doesn't really matter whether that current is positive or negative. What is important is that there is stimulation. If human beings do not get an optimum level of stimulation they cannot function properly and begin to fall into a kind of sleep state induced by this sensory deprivation.

Sensory deprivation experiments on human beings, in Heron (1957) for example, have shown that without the stimulation which keeps them in contact with current reality, human beings hallucinate, sleep and lose all track of where they are. It is a very powerful type of deprivation.

It is likely that a significant number of children are exposed to various levels of this type of stimulus deprivation. Shut away, ignored, lied to, battery rather than free range, these children's exposure to diversity and depth of experience will at best be lower than is healthy, and at worst will be lower than the optimum necessary for them to function as normal human entities. At the extreme edge, children may experience an ungrounded internalised dream state where their behaviour is driven more by their imagination and the fantasies it produces, than by their current, marginalised reality. The two worlds, the real and fantasy, may begin to merge, leaving the affected child unable to distinguish, for example, between a doll and a human baby.

Serial murderers are often profiled as lone and secretive players for much of their childhood, bereft of normal extended human social contact, often playing alone, using 'road kills' as their toys. Perhaps there is a link between the dead animals used as play props and the nature of the subsequent relationship they have with their victims (see Hickey 1991).

Children who are alone and without the stimulation other children get when playing in a diverse and interesting environment are forced to create their own play reality, although the term unreality is probably more appropriate. Where can this come from but from their limited past experience, their dreams and fantasies? And what happens to these children if their play is drawn from this limited source for months or even years?

It is not beyond the bounds of reasonable extrapolation to suppose that chronic exposure to such a way of playing would gradually override the existing brain circuitry, with affective pathways that relied totally on the child's made-up fantasies, modelled by the isolation, loneliness and rejection such children may have experienced. The problem might be that the more the fantasy mode is the preferred mode, the more the child's emotions will integrate themselves into it. In other words, the brain will search for an operational norm that incorporates behaviour with affect. If the child begins to associate good feelings with its fantasy world, particularly if it is already associating bad feelings with much of its real world, then fantasy may increasingly become the child's preferred state. This in itself is not necessarily dangerous, although it could be problematic. But if the child draws violence, blood and death into that fantasy – if, for example, she plays at murdering a baby, by 'murdering' a doll – it is not a huge step, if the affect she experiences is strong enough, for her to consider trying the real thing, if the opportunity to do so presents itself.

This may be the point that children who kill other children reach. Once involuntarily trapped inside a play fantasy, they may predate on other children, and unaware of reality, or insufficiently grounded in it, and driven on by the gratification of affect, may involve them in their violent fantasies. Recent incidents including one at Finland, Germany, in the US and elsewhere lend real credibility to what might otherwise be regarded as wild speculation.

174

What can the playworker do when sensorily deprived children come to play?

Some proposed symptoms of sensorily deprived play bias:

- secrecy;
- preferred isolation;
- withdrawal;
- whispering to toys and objects;
- curiosity with death, dead things, blood and gratuitous violence;
- attending to non-existent stimuli;
- very plausible and persuasive;
- decline in social skills;
- lack of interest in general play activity;
- no friends or friends only with younger children;
- sexual protocol naïveté;
- giving other children scary insights.

In everyday playwork this is still uncharted territory. Depending upon the circumstances, sensorily deprived children may prefer their chosen isolation to the bustle of the play space. If their isolation has been imposed, on the other hand, they may be so damaged that specialist help is needed.

However, if the child seemed willing to socially interact, if she was giving signals of trying to join in with the general play space activity, but appeared to be encountering some difficulties, like trying to talk to other children, but is not easy to understand, talks too quietly, does not make eye contact with those she is speaking to, or trying to join in a game, but obviously does not know the rules, or any of the children, is clumsy, or even if she articulated inappropriate violent or sexual examples from her imagination, I would still hold-back from intervening in order to give her time to gradually immerse herself in the play space activity, or use the perceived indifferent mode I describe in Hughes 2002.

Over time, this approach would allow for some form of child/child, child/environment, child/playworker interface to develop, which may have the effect of re-skilling the child and helping her to re-join the full play space reality. And while there must be children who, for a whole variety of reasons, are suffering the effects of sensory deprivation at one level or another, they are not being formally assessed or engaged as such from a playwork perspective, simply because such procedures are not yet in place. My intuition is that children who are chronically and seriously deprived in this way are taken to a psychic space by that experience, where their original personality is all but lost and where, instead, they become an amalgam of images and related affect drawn from their earlier unconscious childhood experience.

Seriously affected children – those who show most of the signs above – could pose a danger to themselves, to other children and to society at large, simply because their interface with other human beings is so dominated by the images generated by their own imagination and supported by internally generated effects. Such children are to all intents on emotional 'auto-pilot', unaware/numb to the impact of their behaviour on child or adult alike.

Andrew Vachss, a children's lawyer in the US, once spoke of what he called 'freezer children', who grew up with little adult contact, love or affection, whose only real human interaction was with children like themselves, who spent each day sitting on roadside fences or on the kerb, staring blankly into space, maybe smoking dope or drinking, unaware of the world passing by. They would remain that way until some internal clock went 'ding – food time', and only then would they begin to attend to the people passing by. Then they became like sharks, first identifying their prey, getting into the swim to follow it, waiting until the timing was appropriate and then going in for the kill, for money or food.

Vachss, who worked with young offenders (see Vachss and Bakal 1979), said, that all too often these children, who would hurt somebody without remorse or empathy, when asked what they most wanted in the world, would say 'A pair of shoes, or a McDonalds'. They were lost children.

Conclusion

Whilst there is little hard scientific evidence for the theoretical ideas proposed above they do seem to ring true to many of the practitioners I come into contact with when I am training. The implied antidote to

stimulation theory and play deprivation

deprivation and extremes of stimulation, of addressing them with their opposites, also meets with some agreement although there is no evidence of any strategy being devised to research this further.

However, research cited later, including McEwen (1999), Huttenlocher (1992), Perry (1994), Balbernie (1999) and Zuckerman (1969, 1984), together with my own professional experience, leads me to conclude that children are highly vulnerable to experience in the form of whole environmental stimulation, and that when that stimulation is extreme – whether positive, negative, erratic or deprived – the impact upon the playing child can be severe.

Every embryonic behavioural filter the child needs to draw upon, whether moral, humane, civilised or legal, is affected by the experience the child is having of such stimulus conditions. Experience in this context implies not taught information, but that which is absorbed through long-term immersion in certain kinds of situations. The antidote to which I allude simply describes the provision of alternatives in which to also become immersed, but providing another different template for the child against which to judge its actions and attitudes.

And whilst this proposition may be beyond the means of many play projects in any sophisticated sense, providing for alternatives generally, rather than specifically, is relatively easy and can be achieved using the spirals and other tools outlined in Chapter 10.

PLAY DEPRIVATION

The previous section is a revised version of the theoretical analysis of Stimulation Theory originally contained in the first edition of *Evolutionary Playwork*. It describes how different types and intensities of environmental stimulation might affect children's behaviour. Each of the scenarios over-positive, over-negative, erratic and deprived could, in their own way, contribute to a child experiencing a level of play deprivation. The first two, in biasing children's experience, depriving them of the opposite; the third, erratic, simply by its unpredictability and unreliability might render affected children incapable of trusting their own or others' judgements with regard to playing and make actively engaging in play too difficult a choice, the child preferring instead to watch from the sidelines; but it is the fourth category – Z2

Deprived – that forms the foundation for the play deprivation I have modelled since the early 1980s. With little or no stimulation, experiencing chronic physical or psychological isolation or both, the affected child gradually loses her attachment to reality and creates a reality of her own instead – one in which her rules and her games and her friends (if she has any) prevail, played out in a potentially dangerous and violent drama.

Although by the time the first edition of *Evolutionary Playwork* was published in 2001, some evidence supporting the predictions of the theoretical model had also been published, especially the study by Huttenmoser and Degan-Zimmermann (1995), it wasn't until the early 2000s with the publication of Beckoff and Byers' *Animal Play*, that evidence relating to now famous play deprivation research, in the late 1960s, eventually came to light (Brown 1998).

Although only currently under evaluation, the effects of the lack of interaction with the world, which play-deprivation implies, may be catastrophic. Studies on other species record aggression and social incompetence.

Harlow and Suomi's (1971) study *Monkey's without Play*, concluded:

> 'no play makes for a very socially disturbed monkey. When these monkeys reach physiological maturity they are incompetent in virtually every aspect of monkey social activity. They are antisocial and will viciously attack a helpless neonate or suicidally attack a dominant male in the absence of social agents they will attack themselves rendering skin and muscle to the bone.'

Whilst children, especially from 'economically disadvantaged backgrounds, showed less frequent and complex fantasy and socio-dramatic play' (Smith *et al.* 1998).

However, it is in more recent studies in Romania and Switzerland that clearer insights into the potential impact of this phenomenon become available. Huttenmoser and Degan-Zimmermann (1995), for example, referring to what they describe as 'battery children', attribute play-deprivation to the effects of traffic and parental fears of predatory adults.

Battery children, they say, are 'often aggressive and whine a lot. By the age of five they are emotionally and socially repressed, find it difficult to mix, fall behind with school work and are at much greater risk of obesity'. Studies on children who have been without play and who have become stimulus deprived report 'mental problems, physical desensitisation, and restrictions in brain-growth' (Chugani 1998), and severe learning difficulties, erratic behaviour, difficulty in forming bonds, depression and withdrawal resembling autistic children or hyperactivity and loss of control, like children with ADD. 'The neurological cost [being] that regions of children's brains are utterly devoid of electrical activity' (Tobin 1997).

Because play is cited as a major influence in the development of skills – from communication to creativity, and from social interaction to problem solving – it is reasonable to propose that the effect of play-deprivation would be to diminish the ability of the children affected to communicate, be creative, to problem solve and to socialise. In other words, if we create a play-deprivation matrix, for example, we can see that because their environment was apparently totally devoid of stimulation, *and* because they were unable to search for stimulation elsewhere, the children to whom Tobin and Chugani refer may have been suffering chronic, i.e., long-term, play-deprivation and the reported damage may have been the result.

Play type	Intensity of deprivation									
	1	2	3	4	5	6	7	8	9	10
Communication play										x
Creative play										x
Deep play										x
Dramatic play										x
Exploratory play										x
Fantasy play										x
Imaginative play										x
Locomotor play										x
Mastery play										x
Object play										x
Recapitulative play										x
Role play										x
Rough and tumble play										x
Social play										x
Socio-dramatic play										x
Symbolic play										x

Figure 6.2 A play deprivation matrix.

Because the deprivation suffered by Huttenmoser's battery children is less severe – the environment is less stimulus deprived, and they are able to go elsewhere, even if they have to be transported by parents – it may have resulted in acute, rather than in chronic, symptoms. Perhaps their matrix would look something like this: see Figure 6.3.

By definition, most children will suffer some level of play-deprivation of most play types at some time during their childhood. I have no idea, and I doubt whether anyone else has, what the effect of being mildly deprived of, say, creative play might be. Although I would hazard a guess that children so deprived would initially feel frustrated at not having a creative outlet. In fact, symptoms of frustration might be the Level 1 warning signal for every form of play-deprivation. (I choose the term frustrated, because the child would be unaware of what it was his or her warning systems were communicating, or even that they *were* communicating, and might just feel mild annoyance, frustration or unease because of the embryo of a deeper feeling of being unfulfilled.)

Some say the play drive will manifest itself under all conditions, and they cite, for example, that children were known to have played in the concentration camps of the Holocaust.

Play type	Intensity of deprivation									
	1	2	3	4	5	6	7	8	9	10
Communication play					x					
Creative play					x					
Deep play					x					
Dramatic play					x					
Exploratory play					x					
Fantasy play					x					
Imaginative play					x					
Locomotor play					x					
Mastery play					x					
Object play					x					
Recapitulative play					x					
Role play					x					
Rough and tumble play					x					
Social play					x					
Socio-dramatic play					x					
Symbolic play					x					

Figure 6.3 A 'battery-child' play deprivation matrix.

180

I agree that as a basic human urge, the play drive in children, like the sex drive in adults, will be potentially active the whole time, but equally, like the sex drive, without the appropriate conditions – in the case of play, time, security, permission and novel foci – it would probably remain potential rather than actual.

Certainly children will consider playing in any environment in which they find themselves, and frustration and boredom will result if that environment is sterile or restrictive. But if the gradient of deprivation increases, if movement is restricted, for example, or if the period of deprivation moves into hours or days, we can imagine that any latent desire to engage in some play types, e.g., locomotor, social, rough and tumble, symbolic, mastery and deep play, may just evaporate. Other play types might linger much longer as children so deprived played to entertain and stimulate themselves. Gradually though, these – socio-dramatic, creative, exploratory, object, role and dramatic – would also decay. With silence, and without sensory stimulation, the child would be left to talk to itself for comfort and engage in flights of fantasy and imagination. I wrote earlier of my concern that children chronically deprived of company and sensory stimulation, but who still have some props in the form of toys, may begin to dwell in a world in which fantasy/imagination and reality become indistinguishable.

There are probably many hypotheses about the factors surrounding the murder of children by children. Mine begins in this realm, the realm in which some children, for all sorts of reasons – some obvious, like sexual abuse, some less obvious, like loneliness, or low self-esteem – find themselves in a space inside their heads where they can freely manufacture fantasies, and having found this space, find it difficult to leave, perhaps even preferring it to their reality.

I imagine that if the phenomenon of a fantasy-driven reality does exist, that children in such a state, unable to know the difference between projections generated by external experience and those generated internally, would be capable of committing acts of great cruelty and violence. The human mind, even in childhood, is quite capable of concocting fantasies of nightmare content, which, if transported into the external realm, may not only be responsible for murders by children, but for certain types of violent crimes committed in later life. Obviously this is only conjecture, but childhood is a delicate time and enormous damage can be done then, which may emerge later in life, not necessarily as conscious vengeful acts, although this may happen too, but as violent games that confuse fantasy and reality.

I once interviewed a man in Belfast about his childhood. He was from a Catholic background, but in his early years, he had lived in a predominantly Protestant area. I asked him to draw me a lifeline. (A lifeline is a device many trainers used to help those they are training to organise their memories and their recall.)

His lifeline from 0–14 years was divided into three pictures. The first 0–5 years contained a large flaming bonfire, a house, three adults and a small child sitting on a trike, a toddler's tricycle. The second picture, 6–9 years, contained a miniature Gaelic football pitch, a bike, a church and a school. The final picture, 10–14 years, contained a drawing of a soldier, an army barricade, a gun and a corpse.

0–5 years. The interviewee told me that on his third birthday his parents had given him a red trike. Two months later, on the 12th July, a number of adults – he said they were Protestants – had lit a large bonfire so close to his house that the glass in the windows cracked. At some time they took his trike and threw it onto the fire, where it was destroyed.

6–9 years. Shortly after the 'Troubles' started he and his family moved house and he found himself in a Nationalist enclave where he was free to play and to express his culture.

10–14 years. In the early 1970s, he joined a paramilitary organisation. During the 'Troubles' he was imprisoned for long periods for his paramilitary activities. He told me it was 'Get even time, them bastards burnt my trike'.

While I do not know for certain if this man was telling me the truth about anything I have described, I do know that it is possible. I have known many children who have images imprinted on their brains of the great cruelty, neglect, abuse and humiliation they have suffered at the hands of adults. They then want to get even, and some, as this example demonstrates, do.

Whether this man would have done so without the onset of the 'Troubles' is anyone's guess, but I believe that his story was true and I also believe that deep down, the burning of his birthday trike created a time-bomb that the 'Troubles' themselves only exploded.

Depending upon the severity of the conditions of deprivation, eventually even the child's capacity for communication, fantasy and imaginative play would also disintegrate. For Chugani's (1998) children this would probably happen in their early infancy, as neglect and an almost total lack of contact with anything outside of their imagination took its toll.

However, for Huttenmoser and Degan-Zimmermann's (1995) battery children, it would take many years and may never happen completely. These children would just continue to whine and suffer the discomfort of an unsatisfactory relationship with the world, becoming socially and environmentally disabled as a result. But it is doubtful that the play drive would begin to dry up, although they would probably experience increasing difficulty in initiating play and could end up needing help to start the play process off.

Although my theoretical model, the evidence of acute play deprivation recorded by Huttenmoser *et al.*, and the impact of chronic sensory deprivation reported by Chugani (1998) and Tobin (1997), lead inexorably towards a conclusion that play deprivation is a malign scourge, it wasn't until Brown (1998) published in Beckoff and Byers (1998) that evidence supporting the serious implications of Z2 children in particular came to light.

In his erudite chapter, Brown describes the story of Charles Whitman who in the late 1960s went on the kind of killing spree, which more recently has become so common.

> 'Whitman, a 25 year old architectural engineering student at the University of Texas, at Austin, had, after killing his wife and mother, mounted the campus tower, and with deadly accurate fire, killed 17 and wounded 31, before being gunned down ...' (p. 246)

Whitman had classic over-negative and Z2 credentials. A violent, over controlling and abusive father, over-negativity, playlessness, 'three months before the Tower tragedy he was having homicidal fantasies', he had a 'sense of powerlessness, humiliation and entrapment' and was friendless, isolated and withdrawn at school.

Brown said:

> 'his [Whitman's] inability to find coping techniques through play ... were striking findings agreed upon as extremely

December 1986	Bogota	August 1987	Hungerford
July 1989	France	November 1990	New Zealand
October 1991	Texas	October 1992	Sydney, Australia
July 1993	San Francisco	December 1993	New York City
June 1995	Sweden	September 1995	Southern France
March 1996	Dunblane	April 1996	British Columbia
April 1999	Columbine High	April 2007	Virginia Tech
November 2007	Finland	December 2007	Omaha
December 2007	Las Vegas	February 2008	Chicago
June 2010	England (Whitehaven)	July 2010	Norway

Figure 6.4 Lone gunman attacks 1986–2011.

significant by their team'. 'We had originally expected to discover a brain tumour and drugs as primary causal agents, but our intensive investigation weighted abuse and playlessness as the major factors placing him and his future victims at risk'. (p. 248)

In a further study of twenty-six young murderers, Brown and Lomax (1969) concluded the following: 'Findings we were not expecting were play deprivation and/or major play abnormalities for example – bullying, sadism, cruelty and extreme teasing, which occurred at the 90% level' (p. 248).

And in a study of twenty-five drivers who had either killed someone or else had died in a crash – most were driving drunk – it was found that 'Their play histories, were very similar to the murderers and very different from the comparison population' (p. 249).

Brown concludes, 'What all of these studies repeatedly revealed and what struck our separate research teams as unexpected, was that normal play behaviour was virtually absent throughout the lives of highly violent, anti-social men regardless of demography' (p. 249).

The volume of evidence for both the phenomenon and impact of play deprivation will grow and hopefully that will herald an age where all children are able to play regularly and by so doing 'find coping techniques through play, humour, safe reciprocal friendships and other distancing and stress-lowering habits' (p. 248) and 'be better equipped at a neural level to "roll with the punches" associated with daily social interactions' (Siviy 1998: 236).

184

However, before we leave play deprivation, there is still one question that deserves a brief exploration, and that is 'Why does play deprivation have such lethal consequences?'

I suggest it is because of something I call *Evolutionary Anticipation*.

Whilst acknowledging that evolution itself is blind and random, I still suspect that if a particular human trait, like play, has manifested itself in countless generations of countless individuals, then newly born babies, as organisms, still anticipate play as much as they anticipate food and breast feeding. If it doesn't happen, as it didn't with Whitman, then children will initially become distressed as in the Huttenmoser *et al.* study, and if their play deprivation continues, they will begin to manifest symptoms of de-humanisation – lethal, arbitrary violence, for example, as in the Brown chapter. Here's what I wrote a few years ago for a Conference in Belfast.

> 'If a child suffocates through a lack of anticipated oxygen, or starves through a lack of anticipated nutrition, or misses the love and attachment it anticipates from its mother, it becomes highly distressed. And this reaction would escalate if the deficit were prolonged as demonstrated by a baby's heart-rending separation call (McLean 1985), the most primitive and basic mammalian vocalisation. I imagine that the same thing would happen if a child were play deprived, because like oxygen, nutrition and love, the human organism has evolved to expect play, and now its life and sanity may depend upon it. We have evolved for millions of years with the help of the powerful mechanism, which we call play. If children are suddenly unable to engage in play then many thousands, perhaps millions, of years of anticipated groundedness, adaptation and playful mutation will come crashing down around them ... and they will experience what Grof (1975) calls "an agonising metaphysical crisis"...'
>
> Hughes (2005)

Evolutionary Anticipation is an idea, nothing more, but it provides an indication at least of why play deprivation appears to have such a catastrophic impact on those apparently affected by it. It says, play is a humanising force. It not only tells children about what and who they are, it tells them when and where they are too. Without play, without a daily, hands on, optimistic experience of a sensory reality, children soon become lost, unable to make any sense of the emotions, and involuntary attachment yearnings they feel. Play deprivation, or the resulting frustrated evolutionary anticipation, appears to take away their evolutionary compass, leaving them drifting helplessly in a meaningless cosmos.

EVOLUTIONARY PLAY AND EVOLUTIONARY PSYCHIATRIC CONDITIONS

The potency of play in furthering our understanding of the sources and treatments of psychological conditions (Stevens and Price 2001) may in part be due to another of its important roles – as a mechanism in the development of our identity. Thomashow (1995) wrote that play, by giving children a sense of place, a sense of self, enables them to realise that they have a unique perception of the world, through the prism of their own identity.

Normally we tend to think of identity as a socially endowed concept, but as some theorists (Hart 1979; Chilton-Pearce 1980; Shepard 1982; Cobb 1993) say of middle-childhood play, 'this is the time that children establish their connections with the earth ... which is crucial to their personal identity'. This suggests that identity has a biological facet too; that we have a bio-identity (p. 10). Sutton-Smith (2007) goes further. Play, he says, is a consultation with deep-seated evolutionary emotions (p. 12).

Many of the psychiatric difficulties humans experience today may be due to the escalating loss of this bio-identity in recent years (Stevens and Price 2001, Brune 2008). A bio-identity is not just the creation of contemporary social interaction, but of our evolutionary history, and of the relationship we have with everything which is not human, but which is still a huge part of what makes us who and what we are. If the continuity of our view of ourselves as animals as well as sophisticated humans is fractured, or if our relationship with the planet and the other species that live here becomes imbalanced, then we become less grounded in the reality of our biology, and more dependent instead on artificial constructs of identity, constructs that diminish our humanness and our emotional foundations and make us dissatisfied and unhappy.

Sobel (1993) wrote 'as we bonded with our parents in the early years, so we bonded with Mother Earth in middle-childhood' (pp. 159–60). Stanley Hall (1904) and Ken Wilber (1996), develop this theme too. Hall's Recapitulation Theory suggests that play enables a vital re-enactment of the various stages of human evolution to re-forge the links that may be fractured. Wilber describes what those stages might be in terms of an evolving consciousness and includes the reptilian, savage and ritualistic stages, which playworkers see on a daily basis when children are able to dig, build dens and play with fire. This is a theme I will be returning to later.

MICK'S STORIES 3

Rhododendrons

I first got the point of rhododendrons in Tilgate Park in Crawley. Along one side of the lake they have been planted in a series of strips about five metres wide and up to fifty metres long which form natural three-dimensional climbing mazes. Charlie and his cousins loved climbing in them from a very young age, because they could often stay off the ground for dozens of metres at a time as there were nearly always more branches within reach, just the right size to grasp or step on to get to the next bit.

The renowned Copenhagen play space designer Helle Nebelong believes that designing climbing structures where rungs and other elements are evenly spaced actually de-skills children. 'How are they to cope with the knobbly and asymmetric forms they will encounter in the real world?' she asks. And a girl she worked with summed it up perfectly, 'The branches tell me where to put my hands and feet'.

One adventure playground designer tries to eliminate uniformity apart from the elements that encourage running. Elsewhere, just one step, rung or other feature out of place in a regular sequence could be a hazard, but where all of them are irregular 'then from the very start children are watching where they're going'.

INVISIBLE

The playworker turned round in pretend surprise and asked 'Who tapped me on the shoulder?', 'Me'. 'But there's no-one there!', 'I'm invisible', 'Oh no! It's invisible Daniel again!'.

Daniel loved being invisible on the playground, where most of the children and adults went along with his fantasy. He was academically gifted, had only recently arrived in the area, and his mother (a single parent) seemed to me to be very over-protective. She was particularly anxious about him playing with some of the children that she considered were bad influences and I used to see her quizzing him on their way home each day about who he'd been playing with and what he'd been doing. To me, his invisibility was his strategy to enable him to play with whoever he wanted to while telling his mum with a straight face that he hadn't been – if they couldn't see him, how could he have been playing with them?

That was my story and I was sticking to it – until I did a reality check with the playworker, who readjusted my rose-tinted spectacles. What had actually happened was that one day Daniel's mum had agreed that he could invite a couple of the playground children (who were also close neighbours) round to their flat, and they'd stolen a £20 note. She challenged their parents, who first of all completely denied that their kids had stolen the money, and then said that it shouldn't have been left out in plain view where it was a 'temptation' to them. Daniel completely stopped playing with the perpetrators, and when they came anywhere near him in the playground, he would get up and leave. Yes, he still loved being invisible in his fantasy world with the other children and playworkers, but what I thought was him dissembling to his mum was actually him reassuring her that he was genuinely staying away from the perpetrators.

Cursing and swearing

I was up a ladder at the top of the big tyre swing, checking and greasing the swivel and fixings, level with the children's camp in the adjacent tower. I suddenly realised that for the last few minutes I'd been overhearing every swear word imaginable being used by a number of different children, and immediately assumed they were being directed

188

at one or more victims of bullying or were the prelude to a serious fight. I called out 'Oi! What's going on in there you lot?' There was an instant silence, and as I started down the ladder to investigate, the next thing I heard was giggling and stifled screams of laughter. A grinning face with two hands joined in mock contrition popped out of a little window of the camp and said 'Sorry Mick! We was just practising cussing. Don't tell the playworkers or our mums! Pleeeeease? Really, really, really pleeeeease?'.

From time to time around the estate where I live, two girls aged about 8 or 9 years old wheeled their dolls in toy buggies loaded with plastic supermarket bags hanging off the handles, stuffed with doll paraphernalia, drinks, sweets, and all sorts of bits and pieces. They constantly chattered to each other, 'I can't fucking get him to sleep, he's such a moany little thing'. 'Mine's just the same, she's cry, cry fucking cry'. 'The price of Pampers is bleedin' disgraceful'. 'That organic baby stuff's the same. Tell you what though, I got her onto them mashed bananas they throw away in Chapel Market'.

Was this just sad copying of tough life on inner city estates? I'm not so sure. The children were utterly immersed in their play roles, effing and blinding away in perfect mimicry of their parents and neighbours. They had created their own secret subversive bubbles of playfulness in which they were acting out real life situations and experimenting with the language they heard every day at home and out in the world.

In the playground the children themselves had agreed a strict rule forbidding swearing, but the camp tower was a place where they could break their own rule playfully with little chance of being overheard and told off. The two girls were probably out and about on the estate and neighbourhood for the same reasons – I've often heard mums screaming at kids 'Fucking stop that fucking swearing!' And while the two girls mostly kept straight faces and acted out their parts, sometimes they couldn't help dissolving into helpless giggles as their subversion and mockery of adults overwhelmed them.

Mike Greenaway once asked a brilliant question at a Play Wales Spirit of Adventure Conference. 'If a child on a playground tells you to fuck off, what should you do?' There was a lot of knowing laughter, but no one really came up with an answer. Mike's answer to his own question was that you should think hard about why they said it. In my experience children said it to me in all sorts of situations. Sometimes it was their blunt and disappointed answer to my explanation of why the playground had been shut, or opened late. Other times it was an expression of real hate because I'd done something like banning them or one of their mates. But mostly it was a self-deprecating and friendly verbal nudge when I told them how much I appreciated them for something they'd done (or more often, not done, come to think of it).

You won't let go?

The big day had arrived. Charlie had decided he was going to 'properly' ride his bike and we cycled off to the park. We unbolted the stabilisers and I held the back of the saddle as he got onto his suddenly very wobbly bike, his bottom lip characteristically jutted out in concentration, determination and quite a bit of uncertainty. 'You won't let go until I stop wobbling?' he asked me. 'Not until you're ready'. Off we went, and within a few seconds I realised he'd got it, and let go. After about twenty metres he called out 'Let go now!'. Fifty metres further on he eventually looked round to check, and of course promptly fell off the bike. He lay there for a second or two (my heart was in my mouth) then he got up, turned around and a huge grin spread across his face when he realised that he'd ridden well over seventy metres on his own. 'Yessssss! I did it! I did it! I can ride a bike!' he shouted.

Getting back on the bike, he wobbled a bit, then pedalled furiously straight towards me and fell off again just beside me – this time because both his hands were punching the air instead of holding onto the handlebars. A pensioner sitting on a nearby bench laughed and said 'Well done mate. You got to fall off a couple of times and take the knocks before you get it. Go on my son, get up and have another go, we all had to do the same'. Within weeks, Charlie and I were writing our names by skidding our back wheels in straight and curved lines in the loose surface of the nearby all-weather pitch, riding down flights of steps (scary at first for me, because this was something that I had never had the chance to do as a child) and generally mucking about on our bikes in the neighbourhood and beyond.

It was Charlie and the Hackney pensioner who gave me the idea of using learning to ride a bike as an example of getting the balance between risk, safety and benefit right in Quality in Play. It dawned on me that parents, neighbours, communities, institutions and the media accept that there is a positive balance between the risk and benefit of learning to ride a bike, while in virtually every other aspect of children's play, there was a constant focus on the risk side of the equation.

Robin Sutcliffe told me an interesting story about this. When lecturing playwork degree students at Leeds Met he asked whether they thought that breaking a bone was an acceptable consequence of risky play. About half said yes, and half said absolutely not. His next question was who had broken a bone as a child, and it turned out that virtually all of those that thought it was ok had actually broken a bone playing, while those who thought it was unacceptable had never done so.

CHAPTER 7

AN INTRODUCTION TO EVOLUTIONARY PLAYWORK

SETTING THE SCENE

Evolutionary playwork is a new and developing discipline. As yet it has no agreed theoretical or practical base. Typically there are any number of conflicting views of what it is and what it is for, some of which differ fundamentally. Some of these views, including those contained within this text, are derived from long-term personal and professional experience and reflection. Others are more political or pragmatic in their orientation. Each of these different views has been influenced by a number of factors:

■ **The ethical base** each of us uses to determine what we believe is right or wrong, good or bad, appropriate or inappropriate, and the process by which that base has evolved. For example we might have been taught ethics at school or university. Or perhaps, our ethical judgements have come from an amalgam of life experiences.

■ **The memories and emotions that come to us when we recall playing when we were children.** Was playing a good experience, was it fun, was it interesting, did we miss out on bits of experience, did we have experiences we could well have done without? Was our play narrow, structured and full of 'do not', or was it a broad experience, where we did more or less what we wanted, and where we took responsibility for whatever happened? Are our memories of playing accompanied by feelings of warmth, worth and amazement, or varying degrees of pain, bewilderment, loss or disconnection?

■ **Our rationale for working with children at play.** Is our involvement, and more importantly the interventions we make, driven by our needs or the children's? By 'our' I mean as individual adults and as adult society. Are we engaged in socialisation and citizenship training, or even indoctrination, are we playing out as-yet-unplayed childhood material of our own, or are we stepping away from our adult agendas and instead utilising our own life experience as a resource for children? Is our motive more sinister? Are we driven to control, bully or abuse?

▪ **The impact that the increasing volume of scientific literature has had upon our perception of play and children.** Over the years, and particularly in the past two decades, a great deal has been written about play, about its importance to human development, species survival, personal well-being, self-esteem, sanity and our collective evolution. Some may feel that the scientific findings are irrelevant, too difficult or an attempt to dehumanise play, or professionalise playwork, or mystify and exclude people from it, whilst others may see it as a source of inspiration and confirmation.

Aware of and sensitive to each of these influences, *Evolutionary Playwork* attempts to navigate a course that puts children, their play drive and their need for appropriate spaces in which to play at the forefront. It does not claim to be definitive, but rather attempts to provide the reader with an authentic view of some of playwork's thinking, through the experiential prism of one playworker.

PLAY LEADERSHIP

Until the early 1970s, playwork as it is currently interpreted did not exist. What did exist was 'play leadership'. Over the previous thirty years play leadership had been developed as society's response to a perceived need for different forms of supervised play provision, after the school day and during school holidays. These different forms included prototypes of what are now called adventure playgrounds.

On the surface, this provision existed to provide children with somewhere to go and with something to do, but below that there was a presumption that it would address problems of crime and other social and moral issues to which the young, i.e., children and adolescents, were felt to be particularly vulnerable.

By the time I began work as a playleader on an adventure playground in 1970, play leadership had long been established as the dominant approach for working with children in supervised play projects.

However, it did not take long for the unspoken expectations of citizenship training, moral education and crime reduction embedded in play leadership's underlying philosophy to make me and others who were also new to the field feel uneasy.

Although my own play experiences had not been idyllic – I had had my fair share of bullying, fights and lucky escapes from rivers, railway lines and trees for example – it had been a period of intense and diverse first-hand experience. I had learnt to survive without my carers. I had experienced privacy and solitude; I had utilised my personal power; I was becoming conscious of beauty and imagination and I had not only had experience of fear and risk, but had learnt to overcome and control them so that they did not rule me.

Certainly, a lot of what I experienced at play was negative, and some of it was awful and still affects me today, but balanced against the powerful feelings of freedom, personal narrative, self-reliance and in my case a love of and affinity with nature, which increasingly accompanied it, I still felt generally at ease with the ups and downs of life as a playing child (see Siviy 1998). By the time I was nine years old, I had experienced street games like skipping and different ball games, built dens and played hide and seek and tag, experimented with sex, killed frogs and rabbits, raised baby pigeons, stolen apples, and begun to reflect on those experiences, and form a view of life, and of myself, which changed and moulded me.

Play was a substantial and hugely significant part of my life, which represented the totality – both positive and negative – of my interactions with other children, other species and other systems, on every level of my being, in a time and a space which was almost exclusively adult-free, uncontaminated by their agendas and their myths and neuroses. I would not have been the 'me' I am without it. By 'adult-free', I mean just that. My friends and I did not avoid adults at all costs, but we did tend to go where they were not. Not because we disliked or hated them particularly, but because our collective experience of them was of prohibition, interruption, interference, repression and highjacked exploration, experimentation and discovery. Our experience of parents, teachers, the police, and the general public was that they were always stopping us doing things, or worse still, telling us how to do them, or even worse, doing them for us.

We hid, ranged, climbed, camouflaged and imagined invisibility, to get away from their influence and, perhaps more importantly, from their perception that the world belonged to them; that at best we should be patronised and humoured, and at worst, be treated as their subjects, their property, with no rights or original thoughts of our own. Without adults, we created our own rules, adapting them to suit our changing seasonal, developmental, chronological, domestic and cultural circumstances. We conversed continually, making our decisions along the way, negotiating and compromising as and when. Thus we survived long, dark, freezing cold winters using dens, fire and cookery; explored landscapes and developed our local topography; taught ourselves about the flora and fauna, created myths and adopted the gods (Roman, Viking and Native American) philosophies and symbols that excited us and felt relevant to the world we inhabited.

Of course we knew that our play was not our only reality. There was also the one we left when we were playing. Reluctantly we had to go home to refuel and sleep. We had to go to school too, and we had families and siblings. But playing was our *preferred* reality. At play we had choice, it was up to us. Its landscape drew from our experiences, our imaginings, our drives, even if we were still ruled by our stomachs, by time, and by our physiological limitations. Play was the magical realm, where you could fly and disappear, where you battled with fear and the elements, and where the genesis of a moral identity, necessarily sculpted by cringing error and blushing apology, guided our utterances and forged our beliefs.

Embedded in this perspective, I found play leadership's agenda covertly manipulative and patronising.

Certainly I wanted to ensure that the children I worked with, had access to the widest possible range of really authentic play experiences in as adult-free an environment as could be created on the adventure playground I operated. But that did not include fitting the parameters of those choices into a predetermined civic or societal framework. This was not school after all, and it was my opinion that children would gain the most from a play experience that was restricted by their own limits and limitations, rather than those imposed by what I termed the '*world outside the wire*'.

195

The world of play leadership seemed content to cast itself as the legitimate agent for a societal invasion of the child's private world as I saw it. As well as feeling that that was intrusive and repressive, it also felt that reducing children's play to a form of entertainment and post-delinquency training was not only crass, it interrupted something of far greater importance, even though I didn't know what that was. I also believed that play leadership's objectives could have been more easily achieved, and their achievement more legitimate, in an out-of-play, school setting.

Although I could see that training in citizenship might be necessary to enable children to more effectively function in what was fast becoming a multi-cultural, technological democracy, and that all kinds of inputs might be needed to equip children for life in a complex and overcrowded world, it seemed the oddest of misfits to use children's play and what might be, for some children at least, their sole play environment, to achieve what were adult social objectives. Like others at the time, I felt that children's play was best left to children.

Increasingly too, I felt that there was convincing external evidence of an important biological process in operation during play. That uncontaminated, unadulterated play might be a developmental and survival essential, and that my primary professional function should be to help and support the play process in as transparent and authentic a way as possible, rather than to exploit it for personal, political or for social ends. Others were feeling this too. Here was the genesis of *Evolutionary Playwork*.

Now, as I write in 2010, the reasons for this original reluctance to apply an exclusively social intervention model to working with children at play have become much clearer with the advent of so much new evidence, but at the beginning of the 1970s they were intuitive, and regarded as naïve, rather than as mature and informed.

Nevertheless, an alternative to a socio-political model was evolving: I certainly felt that a space dedicated to supporting playful development could not be operated successfully using social or political parameters. Rather it had to be informed by the more subtle and long-term imperatives from the biological and evolutionary evidence from human and other playing species research. Play was increasingly being interpreted as a generic species experience, which enabled the young to develop a unique view of life, which was not pre-determined

196

by having to be viewed through an adult prism, unlike home and school. This was an acknowledgement that at play, children might be very different beings to the ones they were when under the scrutiny of adults, and children were finding it increasingly difficult to escape that scrutiny. I viewed this increasing lack of autonomy as a dangerous development, dangerous not only for the individual children but for our species as a whole.

For millennia, because it had either been out of sight, or had taken place at a distance, most play had occurred without adult interference. This meant that knowledge of everything from negotiating skills, sexual knowledge and power transactions, to the development of topographical skills and elemental applications like fire, had developed from first-hand experience. Consequently, every new generation of children would have the effect of infusing society and community with new perspectives and creative ideas, thus refreshing them and avoiding social atrophy. Play that was constantly overlooked by adults and manipulated by them, as we were beginning to find out, might result in a narrow and impoverished version of the original, which instead of injecting vigour and energy into society could have the opposite effect, rendering children anxious and disabled instead.

I saw playing as that part of childhood which enabled each child to develop an independent and adult-free view of who they were and of how they wanted to proceed. Of course it would only be a part of the total view they would have, but it was the part which had the effect of counterbalancing the thrust of adult hegemony, the part which said 'I am an individual in my own right too, I am also a unique member of our species on this planet'.

It was in about 1972 when I and others began to feel unacceptably uncomfortable with our play leadership designation. Increasingly we were being expected to engage in what was an uneven rapport with police, probation and social services, and schools, which, although instructive and useful on one level, was creating dilemmas that verged on professional ethical issues.

I felt increasingly that the play space (by then I had been operating an adventure playground for two years) I operated should be a sovereign space, which belonged to the children who attended it. It was their space, the only one they had on the planet. They needed it; the way they used it was proof enough of that. Needless to say, the other services did not agree and assumed that because the space was operated by an adult, and a local authority employee at that, they would be able to have easy and legitimate access to the children, who used it. I simply thought that in different circumstances, these same children would have been miles away in adult-free spaces, as I had been when I was a child. All too often, their innocent proximity and vulnerability to the influence, intimidation and sheer power of the adult world left me feeling personally guilty and professionally inadequate.

There was nothing particularly sinister in the authorities' desire to have access to the children. Usually it was just for a chat about a stolen car, a break-in or a runaway child. It was not what these adults did, or how they did it, that so troubled me, it was that they assumed that because they were adults they had the right to invade the children's play space, without any preconditions or negotiations. They didn't respect the children's integrity and the children knew that. My fear was that if they got away with it unchallenged, the children would simply leave the playground to find other spaces which, although adult-free, might also be hazardous or leave them vulnerable in other ways.

This marked a professional and personal epiphany for me, and a vital piece in my consciousness of the playwork jigsaw fell into place. I realised that although it felt as if I was just becoming emotionally involved, what was really happening was that I was allowing my own childhood play criteria to merge with my evolving professional perspective, and this was creating a practice of professional judgement calls that made sense not only to me as an adult but to me as a child too. I have since learnt that being able to take this dual perspective is essential to 'good' playwork practice, although for a whole variety of reasons (Hughes 2001) some people still find it impossible and cannot avoid overriding it with a mainly adult perspective.

I wanted children to want to play in the spaces that we operated on their behalf; not just because they found them attractive, stimulating and interesting, but because they were mysterious and challenging too. The alternative were the roads, the spaces in and around the houses, and in the case of my first playground, the fields used for growing crops, all of which were not conducive to groups of playing children. I also wanted them to choose what they did there and how and why they did it. My reasons are outlined below.

198

Because of my own childhood experiences, I still retained the perception that until relatively recently at least, it had been safe for children to locate their own ideal play places. That they would be away from adults, away from the noise, dirt and danger of traffic, and away from bullies and dogs. Invariably these spaces were the children's secret areas they had chosen because they were not overlooked, and often incorporated wild space, dirt and undergrowth.

Increasingly, however, these wild, private areas were becoming less and less available to children. Farming and industry were rendering many of them dangerous and polluted. Roads and road-building programmes were destroying them or isolating them near main roads and motorways, putting children in mortal danger. Other transport developments like trams were having the same effect. Typically the built environment was not being developed with the needs of children in mind. Of course, they still played in the wild areas they could access, but the price they paid was often high.

The problem now was, how could children still access natural, non-adulterated experiences, experiences that would enable them to form their own unique relationship with the world and the universe, as they had for millennia, if the only spaces available to them were either hazardous or even dangerous?

One solution was to make dedicated provision for play. To provide spaces for children to play in. But for such provision to work, for it to be effective and authentic, it had to reflect, as closely as possible, the essence of those private, unadulterated spaces that children had always been naturally attracted to. My view was that, although many of them possessed the necessary physical characteristics, spaces operated along play leadership lines would not satisfy this criterion. A new perspective had to be developed, both on what a good play environment was and how best to operate it.

The rationale underpinning the embryonic notion of evolutionary playwork was not that children should be separated from adults, but that for a period of time every day, they should, if they wished, be able to play without parents or carers present and that there should be a play space specifically catering for that need, for them to go to.

By offering this, *Evolutionary Playwork* was arguing, that to support children's uniqueness, and their individual and collective integrity, in the face of an unprecedented encroachment by adults into their physical and psychic domain, ideas and applications urgently needed to be developed that focused on addressing the child's free-play needs rather than on the needs of adult society to control play.

Needless to say, there were problems with this overridingly play-centric view. One was that adults voiced concern that children were able to experience risk, fire, relationships and an exclusively child-based culture. Another was that many parents believed that they alone should be the arbiters of what their children experienced. There were practical difficulties too. When would a playworker intervene if there was a problem? What would a playworker do if adults came and expected entry to the play environment? What about smoking, or swearing or sexual activity? And what about drugs, bullying, racism and violence? These professional questions, together with the inevitable pressures from employers and other adults to impose adult solutions on them, made us all realise that there was not only a great deal to learn, but a lot to think about and to decide.

Like many of my peers at the time, I felt that playworkers had a primary duty to the children they worked with to resist anything that gave power over play back to adults. And whilst trying to remain employed, continued to explain what I saw as the alternative view. After all we were only attempting to protect the children's right to play, in ways and for reasons determined by them – although we did not have a scientific rationale for doing so. What did that mean in practice? That in specifically dedicated spaces, where evolutionary playwork's rationales applied, children would, for good developmental reasons, be free to do and say things, which some adults might find objectionable.

Now, years later, the importance of such designated spaces for children to play in, together with knowledgeable playworkers to operate them, is obvious to most if not all, and playworkers are better equipped to argue a case, which is growing less tenuous by the day. There is a growing body of scientific evidence that play is a vitally important component in adaptive, developmental and evolutionary processes and that being deprived of play has a catastrophic impact on children. Playworkers are also gradually uncovering the subtle criteria behind what makes 'a good play space' and there are other initiatives relating to play space quality also taking place.

200

By acknowledging the importance of human evolutionary criteria, like:

- flexible responses;
- connectedness through recapitulation;
- non-specialisation through diversity and novelty;
- risk assessment,

and trying to ensure that they form the bedrock of its practice, evolutionary playwork is attempting to realise one of its core beliefs, that children who are regularly able to access spaces that enable them to play naturally, uncontaminated by social, political or even parental prescription, will not only have happy and fulfilled lives, but will be better equipped to adapt to the problems resulting from planetary, global, climatic and population instability, and the potential scarcity of life essentials like food and water, in the future.

POLEMIC

Several theories (see, for example, Hall (1904) and Wilber (1996)) contain the implication that we should be concerned, that a vital feature of human phylogeny can, and perhaps is breaking down – namely the connectedness of each of our evolutionary stages to one another.

The disintegration of extended families, the decrease in shared family myths and rituals, in shared holidays, the preferred isolation/separation created by technology, distancing from the realities of discomfort, death and disease, the expectation of instant olfactory and emotional gratification, inconsiderate mobile phone behaviour, feeling personally affronted when volcanic eruptions, extreme weather or wars disrupt travel plans, unbridled consumerism and recreation without acknowledgement of the domestic or environmental cost, and so on, each suggest that as individuals, and perhaps as a species, we may be changing, losing touch with what and where we are.

In a conversation with a team from PlayWales, a few years ago during which we explored this, this 'lost touch' phenomenon became known colloquially as the 'Not the e bubble syndrome'. The syndrome referred to an imagined/extrapolated evolutionary stage where human beings had become so disconnected, both from their recent history, and more importantly from their animal, pre-cultural and mythical past, that they had begun to view themselves not only, not as animals, and thus morally permitted to dominate all other species, but also as potentially immortal, as long as they protected themselves and their offspring from life itself, by creating an hermetic eternity in which risk, danger and death, and even the weather, were avoidable realities.

The problem is that this is not so far away from how many people actually perceive themselves today, and it is the potential for dis-connectedness that rings extinction bells very loudly in my evolution-ary playworker ears. If human beings are becoming immersed in a mind set in which they feel invincible – a very plausible fantasy in our virtual and technological world – then they are in great danger. These days a simple incidence of adverse weather conditions can render individuals, communities, even nations, paralysed, confused and bemused not so much about why this is happening, but about why this is happening to them. As I write, (Spring 2011) parts of Brazil, Australia and Sri Lanka are under water, with hundreds dead and missing. In March a huge earthquake, followed by a massive tsunami devastated parts of Northern Japan. The simple fact that we are living on an unstable planet, surrounded by an unstable atmo-sphere, in the middle of a dark and lonely universe, which means that we are all at risk of catastrophe the whole time, seems to be bypassing great swaths of the human population, locked as they are in a dream world created by the markets and media.

What *Evolutionary Playwork* is attempting to return to children is the direct line into the reality outside of that dream world, the shopping mall, the TV or games console, and safe armchair. Real weather, real risk. If today's children do not access reality or enough of it, I fear that not only will they be disadvantaged, even disabled in terms of survival, but their perceptions of reality will be manufactured, not by experience – irrespective of where that experience derives – but by the lack of it. A disturbing case study of the impact of play deprivation documented by Stuart Brown, in the previous chapter, describes by its very absence how important play is, to our sanity, mental stability and grip on reality.

The tools of *Evolutionary Playwork* (see below), although rudimentary and obvious to anyone who has played without the constraints imposed by materials, props and adults, still appear to cause problems for many adults. Some are experiences, whilst others are more about context and conditions. What each of them exists to do is replace a link in today's children's evolutionary chain which appears either to be missing or unactivated, by providing access to that experience in conditions that replicate what we judge would have been 'normal' once for the great bulk of the human population.

Until about halfway through the last century, many children would have played out in the fields and streets much as children had done for millennia. What they did was neither supervised, nor contaminated by an adult input. Their play would simply have been an integral component of a child-created culture.

Increasingly, from about the 1960s, because of rising traffic levels, industrialisation and fear of abduction, young children particularly have been forced to play in and around the houses where they live. This has meant not only an increase in surveillance to the intolerable levels children experience nowadays, but an increasing input from parents and carers regarding what is and is not permissible or desirable in play. This has also effected a decrease in the richness and diversity of children's play habitats, and an over-reliance on bought 'play' things where the packaging is often more interesting to children than the equipment or toy itself.

A likely outcome from the gradual impoverishment and decreased volume of child-controlled play is that today's children will be less skilled and less capable of dealing with the issues that experience would normally have prepared them for. These skills and capabilities won't have been either learnt *or* activated, because each child will not have sufficiently engaged in those experiences at first hand.

This is why *Evolutionary Playwork* is so crucial now. Hopefully it will have the effect of reversing the tide of disconnectedness, for the children who experience it, and create the real interface they need to avoid the very real possibilities of extinction and/or species insanity through play deprivation, and instead return them to a more optimistic life trajectory which, although it unavoidably incorporates difficulty and unpleasantness, also gives them access to the priceless human experiences of achievement, hope, beauty, culture and love.

SOME OF THE MORE CONTENTIOUS TOOLS OF EVOLUTIONARY PLAYWORK

Giving access to fire back to children

For over 400,000 years (Zhoukoudian–UNESCO) human beings have relied on fire for warmth, light, protection, creation and community focus. A vital component of the human psyche, fire has been used to symbolise everything from the supernatural, change and purification to chaos and war, and is included symbolically in both alchemy, wicca and other religions. Suddenly it is unavailable to children, or only accessible under strict supervision. 400,000 years of use and belief deleted from the playful experience of current and future generations virtually overnight.

During my own childhood (1944–1956) fires were common components of my play ecology, both at home and as I ranged. They were things one sat by in solitude, feeding the flames, staring into the embers and watching the smoke drift; they were a focus to dance around and sing by – ritual places which facilitated rites, conversations and reflections; they were feeding places where beans were heated, spuds baked and bread toasted; they were places where everyone had a job – to fan the flames, add fuel or get water. Fires created a communal focus where childhood culture was passed on often through imaginative conversation and myth making, and they were places to learn of life's dangers and thrills using story telling and even lies. Fires kept us warm, dry and cheerful, and gave us heat and light, in winter's freezing days and dark evenings after school.

We jumped them, swung over them, stood around them, rode our bikes through them, urinated on them – producing vast clouds of steam – built them into bonfires and burned rubbish on them. Mostly we burned wood, but occasionally our fuel would include roofing felt, and even coal. Sometimes our fires burned us too, if we became too lairy or incautious, or if we lost concentration, but aware that inexperience or lack of care begat injury, we took that as a lesson from life and remembered that in life we must pay attention!

Now, many adults who work with children are not happy or confident about the combination of children and fire. It may be a matter of trust, or the lack of experience, but all too frequently, it's just that the adult, not the child, does not trust fire and has little or no experience of it. We also live in an age when many adults seem to operate from the premise that if children are protected from fire, then somehow they will never experience injury or – god forbid – death through fire. The reality is that they are more, not less, likely to experience burns if they do not have knowledge of fire from an early age.

Evolutionary Playwork asserts that most children can be trusted to learn how to interface with fire without overbearing supervision. After all, experience of fire can only grow from exposure to it. Better, surely, a fire at six years of age in the more controlled confines of playwork and the risk of a burnt finger, than no playful childhood experience and the use of petrol or fireworks with catastrophic consequences at fifteen?

In these predominantly fireless days, perhaps it is prudent to give children graduated access to this lethal element as many will have no experience of it at all.

1   Fire can be gradually introduced using a campfire scenario, in a designated fire area (a fire pit is too permanent) where an adult is both responsible for the children's safety and for the fire itself. The children are allowed to be close to the fire but that is all. At all times a metal bucket of water is close to the fire too, and this is used to extinguish the fire.

2   The second level allows for the children to use the fire to cook toast and to light sticks. The situation is still supervised by an adult who is also responsible for the fire.

3   On level three the children are shown how to light a fire using paper, twigs or kindling and increasingly large pieces of fuel. They are then allowed to use the fire and extinguish it with water. The adult supervises from a distance.

4   At level four the children gather fuel and light a fire under an adult's distant supervision. They are left alone with occasional supervision about how to use and extinguish the fire.

5   Finally, children are allowed to have as many fires in the designated fire area as there are fire buckets – one fire to one or more children. They are able to construct, light, use and extinguish their fire.

Giving access to risk back to children

In palaeolithic times, about 20,000 years ago, children played in what Bowlby (1958) termed the Environment of Evolutionary Adaptedness. The term describes the environment to which we are most recently adapted, rather than the one we live in today. Such an environment would have been full of risks that would have needed to have been overcome by children as they played. If not, the result might have been fatal. Wild animals, reptiles, poisonous snakes, insects, berries and fungi, fast deep water, cliffs, high trees, warlike communities, getting lost and so on are just a few of the risks they would have faced.

Human beings have always had to deal with risk as a normal part of surviving. We live on an unstable planet, with an unstable atmosphere in the middle of a universe that is saturated with life-threatening possibilities from infrared and X-rays, to meteors, asteroids and comets. Every generation must develop a fairly fatalistic mind-set to be able to cope with such conditions, it's that or consciously suffer panic, fear and anxiety throughout life.

Of the many outcomes of playing, this mind-set is one. As children play with the environment and other children, experiencing height, speed, balance and the occasional fight and inevitable accident, so they develop an experiential hard shell that enables them to still feel optimistic about life and continue to strive rather than giving-up.

Because risk is all around us, experiencing it and learning how to assess and control it is an essential component of life for children, and all children will take risks if they are not physically stopped from doing so. Encountering and overcoming a whole range of risks – height, speed, sharpness, poison, hostile animals/people – is a normal and vital part of a child's day-to-day life education. However, the perceived nature of those risks will be less or more extreme depending on the previous experience and current perceptions of the child. Whether the risk involves jumping from a foot-high step, propelling a wheelchair at speed down a ramp, climbing a high tree or riding a bike on the parapet of a bridge, children will engage in it. It is evident in the traditions of everything from exploring and science to mining and extreme sports, that as a species we acknowledge and often enjoy risk; but all too frequently now, as with fire, children are stopped from undertaking activities that have an element of risk, unless the activities, are perceived as safe, by adults – that is that they contain the illusion of risk, without actually carrying much risk. Obviously, in reality they cannot be both safe and risky, but there is a more important point, and that is, if the risk is to be real and not an illusion – if it is going to be a source of valuable insight and experience to the child – it has to have a *real* element of potential physical harm attached to it. That means if the child does not concentrate or if the activity overstretches his or her abilities, then the child could get hurt; this is essential knowledge for life. *(Recently, a member of the British Royal Family, commenting on the death of a young person undertaking the Duke of Edinburgh Award in Australia, suggested that the event would make the scheme more attractive to young people because it meant that it was real, 'I could really die doing this!')* I agree that children and young people expect real experiences both on awards of this kind and more particularly when they play and feel that something is lacking, and not right, if they do not get them. Play, like life, is not safe, and if it is, it is not play.

However, this is not to confuse risk with danger or what some professionals call hazard. Risk is something children can recognise. Something they can be aware of or conscious of, if they are attending to their context, i.e., roads, mountains, bad weather, height, etc. Risk is something children should know they are entering into, like choosing to climb higher, swing faster or balance more precariously. Danger, on the other hand, is not obvious to a child – however careful they are. Pollution, poisons, high-tension cables, rotting timbers, radioactive waste, dog faeces, even disguarded fridges are all dangers and should not be present on any play space.

There is a developmental legitimacy in injuring ourselves as we attempt to stretch our limits and evolve our skills and abilities. Lessons can be learnt from such experiences. A broken arm now might save a life later. The planet Earth is risky but it is our only habitat, so children need to be aware of the risks it contains – from the seas to the mountains, from the underground caverns, to the species that live on the surface, especially their own – and where they can learn to assess, avoid and manage them, and where they cannot, to confront them with the skills and mind-sets they have learnt through their play.

Evolutionary playwork embraces the proposition that experience of risk, interacting with the elements, creating ritual and myth, and engaging with other species and systems, are what human children the world over are anticipating when they play, together with interfacing with other children and having fun. Where possible, evolutionary playwork tries to compensate for the erosion of all or much of that experience for many children, by identifying the criteria, props and values necessary to create environments where those experiences and their component parts can be available in forms which, whilst providing authentic challenge, do not expose children to unknown dangers, fears or feelings of failure.

Evolutionary playwork views children not only as young organisms, but as the apex of human evolution and seeks to create appropriate spaces where they can playfully explore and experiment with their world and universe.

Children are given access to risk using bridges, swings, towers, slides, aerial runways, other structures and so on, constructed by adults. If there are trees, children are permitted to climb them, although unaided and without the adult encouragement which might tempt them to go higher than their own risk assessment would normally allow. Children may also be allowed to access playground buildings' roofs.

Giving access to privacy and space back to children

For even longer than they have used fire, human beings have hidden, taken refuge, lived and died in caves and structures that afforded them shelter, privacy and protection. Like their ancient ancestors, endless generations of playing children have constructed shelters, for much the same reasons. A table and a blanket, tents, caves, dens, camps and tree houses have all become iconic indicators of the presence of children. With the advent of roads and traffic, and the decrease, even disappearance, of vacant spaces, wild areas and accessible farmland, for most children this recapping of our evolutionary history has virtually disappeared and the vehicle for the creation and perpetuation of children's culture has almost vanished with it. This is more than a loss of somewhere to go. Privacy is lost too. Proto-sex is under threat as is proto-criticism, negotiation and debate. However, perhaps of greatest importance is the loss of the identity and knowledge of continuity, which creating and spending time in shelters has given human beings for many thousands of years. Without continuity, without

208

first-hand experience of human evolutionary history, and the integration of those experiences into their psyche, children may be forced to re-identify, perhaps even reinvent, themselves, and may settle instead for a manufactured identity like consumer, or customer, or a virtual one supplied by a games manufacturer. We are what we are – evolving animals – and to be re-branded so that the experience that our evolution has given us is eroded, even erased, would be both tragic and dangerous, leaving us, as it would, even more vulnerable to the ever present pressures of extinction than we are now.

Children will always build if materials and tools are available. Making sure they are is one of the functions of the playworker.

Giving access to diversity back to children

Evolutionary play spaces are normally artificial spaces – spaces that are firstly designated for children's play, and then created. Although the children who use them will significantly change them by digging, building and other forms of activity, in a macro sense, the spaces are constructed by playworkers. In order to ensure that when the children use them they are able to control what they do, it is essential that much of the 'behind the scenes' work is done when children are not actually present. This process of preparation is known as 'environmental modification' and, as the term suggests, it is about changing or modifying the play space in ways that will engage children and stimulate their play drive.

The diversity – from landscaping, to structure building, to planting, to painting, to bringing in new experiences (see 'The Barrel', Chapter 8) which results from modification is important for two main reasons. The first is that children's imaginations thrive on novelty. The more interesting the space, the more it will generate different play routines. The second, however, is even more important. Modification is an ongoing process that never ends. Novelty, and the imaginative stimulation that comes from it, will soon die away as children engage in a high-speed exploration of the initial modification's possibilities. If modification is not continuous, the play space will become stale. This may explain why the usage of manufactured playgrounds – fixed equipment playgrounds – may drop away, following the initial flurry of activity (*International Play Journal* 1:2: May 1993).

In fact modification is not only the adult's prerogative. Modification is what children are doing continuously when they play, to make things more novel. With fixed equipment, this is more difficult and so, although this may save on maintenance bills, the lack of additional novel possibilities may limit their appeal.

Playworkers do not escape this problem either, and must work hard to keep the space both interesting on the surface and open to further possibilities, as children 'mine for novelty'.

The reason this is so is that when children could range as they played, as they wore out an area of its novelty, they would move on nomadically until they found their next metaphorical waterhole/oasis – a space that had new novel features. In my own case this might have been an old tree, somewhere with a good view or vantage point, somewhere hidden with endless imaginative or mythical possibilities (see 'The Valley', Chapter 8), or an old building or ruin.

Now, as many children are less able to range, to ensure that they still have access to novelty, artificial spaces must fill that ranging, nomadic, novelty gap. This is a huge task when children can exhaust the novel possibilities of some modifications in hours.

Of course some modifications continue to modify themselves. Growing plants, bushes and trees, even if picked or broken, will continue to propagate. Because of this, planting is an invaluable source of modification. However, most modification relies on the creativity, ingenuity and inventiveness of the playworkers (see the 'Playwork Menu', Chapter 4.).

EVOLUTIONARY PLAYWORK AS INTERVENTION

Whilst applying evolutionary playwork tools to spaces designated for play may provide a high level of attraction to even the lowest concentration span, because of their interesting and stimulating effects, if a child is going to get the maximum bio-evolutionary benefit from playing, it also needs to feel that the play space is authentic, i.e., where the child can do what it wants and has control over what it does, without overbearing or inappropriate interference from playworkers.

210

That said, there will inevitably be times, for a whole variety of reasons, when playworkers have to, or decided to, engage with a particular child or group of children. This is known as 'intervention'. Ensuring that the type and intensity of intervention is both necessary and appropriate, and does not unduly or unnecessarily interrupt the flow of play, is a judgement of considerable skill. Judgement and knowledge of why, how and when to intervene will be affected by a number of factors which playworkers need to be aware of. Knowledge of the purpose of, and rationale for, evolutionary playwork are obviously crucial, but playworker self-awareness and their own childhood play history are equally important.

Modification and intervention are discussed more fully in Chapter 10.

THE DISCIPLINE OF PLAYWORK

There is beginning to be a totality of playwork thinking and practical expertise, that will, for the time being at least, represent what we currently know. However, this does not mean that all play projects should look the same, or emphasise the same approaches. This may dismay those who prefer a more ordered approach, but although there is a generality of underpinning rationales, knowledge and methodology which I believe to be correct, this does not distil down into absolute specifics on the ground – the playing child and its play environment are just too complex for anything other than general guidance. An example might be that all play spaces should have at least one fire from time to time, but that does not mean that fire will be a major feature of all play spaces, any more than water fights will, or swings, painting, ball games or off-ground tag.

A play space is the play equivalent of a good restaurant. You can have any amount of culinary or cultural diversity as long as there are good, wholesome, nutritional basics on which to build it. The play space will be good as long as the experiences it offers are diverse, malleable and risky and encourage a flexible, experimental and exploratory approach. It does not have to have giant telegraph pole structures, or allotments, and even if it does have them, it doesn't have to have them forever. The playing child who ranges stands to discover an infinity of diversity as long as the environment is fertile with experiences and ideas. So it should be with dedicated play spaces, that she should be able to encounter predictability and surprise, the mundane and awesome together with the funny, exciting, emotional and moving. In short they can be anything at any time.

It is depressing if spaces all look and feel the same – and it misses the point of having them. Rather they should be a celebration of diversity and a hub of excitement, fun, activity, reflection and learning through absorption. Generally they should not be sedate (although they can be) or well behaved, they should be frantic lively spaces filled with the joy of newness and discovery.

THE PLAYWORK APPROACH

Not everyone who applies playwork's rationales, knowledge or applications will be a professional playworker. Often dedicated spaces rely on volunteers, parents and community members to operate them, whilst professionals like doctors, architects, teachers, artists, early years and care workers and scientists often apply playwork's under-pinning principles and methods in their own work context.

This is hardly surprising, for although the number of playworkers has been growing rapidly, it has never been big enough to claim success for what has been a play/playwork revolution both in the UK and further afield in the past decade. For whilst playworkers are refining and clarifying issues around play and the play process, and around intervention and experiences, others, for example Furedi on risk, Byers and Sutton-Smith on brain growth, Chawla on hermeneutics and Brown on play deprivation, have been moving the whole play debate forward internationally, whilst central government, particu-larly in the UK, has done its best to support play initiatives within the confines of their own preconceptions and childhood baggage.

More and more human beings from all over the globe appear to be rec-ognising the importance of play to human beings, particularly during that all-important period we call childhood. And more and more people seem willing to lend their voices and pressure to improve things for children. However, we must also learn from what is happening.

Imagine the world's children's play as a field of delicate flowers not yet in bloom. Weeds and weather threaten to overwhelm it. But if we act without knowledge, without sensitivity we risk destroying the embryonic flowers with the weeds. If we water too much, they drown or rot, if we water them too little they die or dry up.

In their Children's Strategy Document (2009) the Government demonstrated their own two-edged sword of caring about play, by funding a range of projects, but also stating that 'children should treat each other with respect when they play'. A sound social sentiment perhaps, but completely inappropriate and a good demonstration of the potential power of politics over knowledge. If children are forced – either by government or playworkers, for that matter – to behave in ways that do not reflect the reality either of their internal or their external play context then they will not be playing, simply because play is spontaneous and goalless and can contain fighting, spitting, name calling in its repertoire. I am tempted to ask where the report's author experienced this play that was so unlike any play that I have witnessed?

That error aside, it has been hugely encouraging to see government interfacing with play and discussing it, and making provision for it, as a serious subject/discipline. Time is running short and we depend upon this level of interfacing to bring about essential changes in opinion, learning and provision.

The whole adult world community should be encouraged to apply a playwork approach to their lives. In every sense they would be enriched, but perhaps more important, their awareness of the increasing pressures on our species might itself increase along with sympathetic actions, at a rate faster than those pressures, and perhaps we can pull out of the lethal dive we are currently in, although Gaia (Lovelock) predicts no such escape. We lose nothing by trying and children gain a great deal.

CHAPTER 8

WHAT IS EVOLUTIONARY PLAYWORK?

What kind of environment would most suit the needs of evolutionary play? Well, given that human beings have evolved little since the Palaeolithic period, say 20,000 years ago, it is reasonable to suppose that examining the characteristics of the kind of environment that was predominant then might be a useful starting point.

Via the work of Bowlby (1958), etc., this paleolithic environment has become known as the Environment of Evolutionary Adaptedness (EEA), or the ancestral environment. The EEA is assumed to be the last environment to which we truly adapted as a species, and that since then, right up until today, we have not been in-tune with our environment. From a playwork perspective this presents two concerns. One, that the modern environment offers little opportunity for evolutionary play, and two that the modern environment contains numerous different psychological and physical ingredients to which we are not adapted as a species and that are harmful.

Examples of harmful physical features are fairly obvious – population density (more people/less space), traffic, weapons of mass destruction, anonymous, monolithic institutions, pollution, electricity sub stations, railway lines, toxic/radioactive chemicals, drugs and so on, until we come to global warming and food and water depletion. Examples of harmful psychological features may be less obvious, but what about stress, the manifestations of certain mental illnesses, low self-esteem and insignificance. Or the feeling of powerlessness as TV news overload informs children of yet another disaster, which they can do nothing about. Or the feeling of uselessness when faced with so many technological 'advances' that they have no comprehension of how they work – cars, aircraft, fridges, TVs and computers. Reading this list, you would be forgiven for wondering when it was written, given that it is already so out of date.

214

The problem, as Robin Fox (1989) points out so well, is that 'modern characteristics' from the agricultural and industrial revolutions, right up to the current technological revolution, have continually been in collision with the 'needs of our paleolithic hunter gatherer selves'.

The play environment's contents and ambiance should never have the effect of diminishing children with characteristics that either only a few will either comprehend or master. Some level of playful success should be available to every child when it plays. That is the evolutionary point of playing. It enhances each child with adaptive advantages they would not have had without playing. But today's environment – the scale of architecture, the dominance of vehicles, private land, the exploitation of resources, the pressure to buy the latest gadget, piece of clothing, DVD or game – reduces children to consumers, but not just that, it also reduces them to consumers who *know* (both intuitively and because their schooling tells them) that what they are doing is damaging the very habitat on which they depend for their physical and genetic survival both now and in the future.

What evolutionary play helps to return to today's children is the chance to re-establish the symbiotic relationship that once existed between their paleolithic ancestors and their environment. Not, as Fox emphasises, 'because it represents some kind of utopian ideal, but because it is what we are' (pp. 221–22).

To this end we can begin to construct what our evolutionary play environment might look like, although it is perhaps necessary here to explore two avenues rather than one.

The first avenue looks at the play environment as a *pseudo-paleolithic space*. By this I mean a space that contains many of the components playworkers have long advocated as desirable and which represent the cultural space that children normally inhabit when they are both able to freely range, fantasise, imagine, and interact in ways that preclude any form of adult intervention. They may use matches, knives and other tools, they may light fires and cook foods in modern containers, there probably won't be the odd appearance of a wild animal, but inasmuch as it is possible to frame an evolutionary play space, this will be close. Stevens and Price (2000) describe the Ancestral Society in this way: 'They shared the same values, rules, customs and mores. Their beliefs were sustained by myth, ritual and religion'. This could be a description of the generality of most of the populations of children I have ever worked with.

The second is the play environment as rooted in *palaeolithic pre-sumptions* but this time containing evidence of the real modern world. Although this would represent a less natural world it would be much closer to the current reality of good authentic play provision. For while children would have access to trees, streams, darkness and privacy, so too might there be modern toys, computers, computer games and music downloaded onto iPods.

I suspect that from the perspective of alleviating the symptoms of ill-nesses mediated by our inability to adapt to modern pressures, the first example would be most effective. And here I am not talking about the current love affair with forest schools that have a high level of adult intervention and organisation. However, the second example is very definitely nearer to where we are at the moment. The problem with the former is, will children be attracted by a play space that bars them from bringing with them their childhood trapping of contemporary times?

The golden rule however is that every play environment can be different and still satisfy important basic design ideas that fulfil children's evolutionary play needs. Ideally an evolutionary playwork environment would provide, as a minimum, access to:

- different kinds of outdoor and indoor spaces;
- the elements – fire, earth, air and water;
- height, depth, motion, balance, co-ordination;
- creative experiences like making music, inventions, discovery and arts;
- mastery experiences like building, planting, digging and damming;
- other species and different systems, like domestic species, rocks and sand;
- compensatory alternatives and choices like new foods, music, views, noises, and perspectives;
- landscaped areas with flowers, fruits and berries that give children access to private moments out of the gaze of the general flow of the space.

What I should stress is that evolutionary playwork is not about compulsion or coercion, it is not even about encouragement. It is about provision and preparation. And if the experiences or props provided are appropriate to the needs of the children, then they will be driven to engage in them spontaneously and without any further adult prompting. As soon as children are invited to 'Come and join in', or asked, 'Will you do it for me?', the child's play is being adulterated and s/he may not be engaging in the experience for their own, intrinsic motives. It is absolutely crucial for successful playwork that we do not lead play but facilitate it. This is a particularly difficult idea to apply where playworkers are being pressurised by a manager to *do* things. Before children arrive playworkers prepare the space with materials and props. However, when children are present the playwork's job is only to mediate when necessary, to observe and record, and to intervene only when it is unavoidable. For example when a child is about to injure itself – and this requires the playworkers to have an appropriate level of knowledge about the physical and psychological capabilities of each child – or when it is about to injure another child – which again requires in-depth information about how different children interact with one another.

The new playworker's first impression of this kind of environment might be a wall of sound, or a chaotic tangle of activity. Authentic play tends to be noisy, messy and anarchic, if it is not, there is probably something wrong. That is not to say that children do not relish seclusion and privacy, because they do – as they would have in Palaeolithic times, but a great deal of play is either about vigorous interaction, or animated communication, either with the physical environment, with other children, or both.

DEPENDENCY

For young children play is a new and exciting discovery and it is nearly always accompanied by squeals and shrieks of laughter which are contagious and often uncontrollable. They are into everything and will expect the playworker to watch, to help, even to take part. Obviously s/he will, but s/he must remember the playworker's facilitative function and resist becoming part of the gang, or a playmate on whom the children may become dependent. It is very easy for this to happen. It is equally easy for the playworker to become dependent on them. If the playworker does the thinking, then they as children do not have to. As a consequence the playworker may start to feel needed or valued and so a cycle of dependency starts to evolve between play-worker and children.

There is a sense in which the evolutionary play environment is managed wildness. But the wildness will not really manifest itself whilst the playworker is a prominent feature of the space. S/he must withdraw, or adopt a stance that says 'I am doing this. Unless some-thing happens to change things – the noise level drops, someone screams, a fight breaks out – just carry on'. The playworker's participa-tion in the child's world must be minimal or s/he will become a source of the contamination that playworkers call 'adulteration' (Else and Sturrock 1998, 25–26).

PERIPHERAL VISION

Perhaps one of the most important skills playworkers need is highly developed peripheral vision. There are many things children will not do if they think they are being watched, and to alleviate this, periph-eral vision is a valuable tool. Although scanning the play space with eyes and ears is a vital defence against injury and insecurity, it is essential that the playworker learns to be sensitised to what s/he needs to see and hear. It is important, for example, that s/he does not overtly stare either at individuals or groups as they play – hence, peripheral vision. The skill of looking in one direction whilst keeping children elsewhere in view, ensures that they feel safe from excessive unpleas-ant attention from other children and secure from external threats, but do not feel overtly overlooked or monitored, whilst they engage in what is, after all, their private behaviour. The opportunity to be without being watched is particularly important at a time when we are all under increasing surveillance, as we go about our daily lives.

MOVING IN AND OUT OF THE PLAY STATE

Feeling safe and secure, even when engaged in risky activity, is essen-tial for children at play. Safety and security makes it possible for chil-dren to relax, to switch off or moderate their natural vigilance enough to make engagement in fantasy or imagination more likely than it would be otherwise.

218

IMMERSION

For example, noisy or physical interruption by another child or adult can destroy the natural process of becoming immersed in fantasy, which is almost a dream-like state. Alternatively, when they have become deeply immersed in play, I have known children to be deaf to calls, shouts, even whistles, and oblivious to taps on the shoulder. One group of relatively older boys, who had never been to the seaside, at one play project I worked on, got so 'lost' in fantasy play in our large sand pit – building tunnels and castles, and making rivers from the water stand pipe – that it took me minutes to make the appropriate 'sensitive' contact with them and let them know that we were closing.

Knowing that children become immersed – what someone called 'going through the wee gap' (O'Neil, 2009) – is a crucial piece of play-work knowledge too. When children are engaged in particularly potent play narratives, i.e., when they are deeply immersed in an imaginative or fantasy experience, either with other children or alone, they are effectively somewhere else – in an immersed reality – inhabited by people or things in a landscape we cannot even imagine. So it is vital when closing time is approaching that adequate time is given to enable 'immersed' children to leave their immersed land – which might be a highly preferred alternative to their reality – and return to 'now'. For the child who is immersed it can be both painful and disappointing to be 'juddered' out of the play state too quickly. My preferred approach is to facilitate a natural, gentle transition, first using soft cues, like a quiet voice or a gentle touch, only gradually building up to louder or firmer cues, if necessary. Using whistles, or shouting at closing time, hurrying children out of the door, forgetting what some of the children may be going home to, is not good playwork practice.

THE VISUAL ENVIRONMENT

Play environments can be visually very different. Adventure playgrounds, probably the most advanced play environments to be developed so far, are a good case in point. In their early days, as Junk Playgrounds, they were more like children's allotments; whereas, in the UK in the 1950s and 1960s, they became more like children's settlements, with dens, shops, small farms and fire- and water-play.

In the late 1960s and 1970s large structures began to predominate on adventure playgrounds. Huge flags appeared, massive swings, slides, towers and walkways constructed by playworkers and children, took root and altered the skyline of many towns and city districts. To some extent this was just an attempt by playworkers (playleaders then) to inject more adventure into the adventure playground, but it also signalled a new and disturbing trend that continues up to the present day – not just the domination of the physical space by adults – in this case playworkers – but more problematic was the colonisation by them of the play agenda itself. Not only did adventure playgrounds facilitate play, they began to dictate what that play should be – adventurous, macho, physically risky and male. Of course this is not wrong in itself, it is just partial and incomplete!

RESOURCE CENTRES

From the mid to late 1970s evolutionary playwork environments also saw some other important visual changes. For example, until then, what a play space looked like had depended upon the use of materials like timber, paint and boxes, which had often been scrounged from skips, homes, local businesses and factories. The development of the Play Resource Centre meant that a whole new range of creative play materials were made more accessible, particularly to the large number of small community play organisations springing up around the country.

COMMUNITY ARTISTS

Community artists were also making their presence felt by the mid 1970s, creating attractive murals on bleak playground walls and depicting cartoon, political, industrial and cultural scenes on gable ends. Community artists also gave the play world the 'inflatable', arguably the most important piece of interactive community sculpture ever conceived. However, these inflatables were not the bouncy castles that came later which were just pale imitations of what had existed originally. Action Space, an inflatables company based in London and Sheffield, for example, produced the most incredible inflatable structures. In 1976–77, they created a huge internal maze, made from different

220

coloured plastic, that an adult could actually walk around inside. It was inflated with an electrical pump and kept inflated using a network of valves, not unlike the valves in the heart, but these were huge. It was possible to crawl through them with the pressure of the inflated air in one's face.

Not only did this maze contain a network of enormous tubes, it also had a number of dead-end cubes people could sit and rest in. It ended in an inflated 'big top', where there were huge figures children could dive on and wrestle with. It had everything – thrills, mystery, fear (of getting lost), colour (lights playing on the plastic), sound (the squeals of the children, mixed in with music) and laughter, as they all bumped into each other. I spent many hours crawling about inside this thing, playing my own version of calibrating the weird world it created and enjoying the laughs and excitement of the social interaction the maze stimulated.

LEGISLATION

Legislation – in particular Health and Safety legislation – also had an impact on the visual nature of play space, as did the playwork field itself in this context. The publication of *Towards a Safer Adventure Playground* (NPFA 1982) had a massive impact in professionalising playwork, but at the same time, it had the effect of inhibiting some of the visual inventiveness and creativity that, until then, had been the hallmark of the unique interaction between playworkers and children.

INNOVATIVE PLAY ENVIRONMENTS

Many of the play spaces I have visited recently have all but lost this spontaneous and original visual identity. They look like play spaces I would recognise from years ago. They have not moved on in any visual sense. That saddens me. Thirty years on, play spaces should not still be modelling themselves on the examples of the 1970s, frozen in time, ossified by a perception that 'they had it right then'. Certainly flags can be exciting, as can structures, allotments, landscaping, planting, painting and decorating, building, swings, loose parts and so on. But perhaps most exciting of all is that none of it has to be fixed, or permanent. It can and should be changing and evolving on a daily basis – not just to create a new, surprising and visually interesting space but to generate energy and stimulate action. A major problem with many of our contemporary play spaces, whether supervised by playworkers or not, is that they are fixed, permanent, inflexible, unchanging and boring to the experimental and exploratory children who are looking for 'good' spaces for their play.

There is some evidence, particularly in London, that new thinking is affecting what some play spaces look like. There is a developing aesthetic of different structures that has moved them away from the generic towers, platforms, giant swings and bridges, to more unusual forms, influenced by arts design as well as by applying playwork learning.

In them more attention is being paid to the combined silhouettes of the play structures, so that they look different against the skyline. Poles are being used more creatively both as cross beams as well as uprights, and one 'playscape' designer is using local industrial artefacts as playful installations, and perhaps most importantly, children are able to access authentic risk by having structures to climb and balance on, that take them up to three or four metres above the ground.

However, even in these innovative spaces there is one major flaw, from the perspective of what play is for. Like the old-fashioned fixed play areas with the generic swing, slide and roundabout, they are still not malleable, not alterable or changeable by the children. They still represent an adult colonisation of unpreconceived minds, and that makes them light years away from the spaces and contents that children would have naturally been drawn towards in Palaeolithic times. Then play would still have been dominated, but it would have been dominated by nature. And it would have been through an exploration, interaction, exploitation, experimentation, conversation, etc., with nature, that evolution (mutation and natural selection) would have crafted human beings to become what they have.

The problem with a heavy-handed adult input, whether through fixed equipment or, far worse, through the commercial promotion of addictive technology – to which we have yet to adapt and as a consequence remain highly vulnerable – is that they distort the purpose of playing from the child's ends to their own. This is important to remember when any of us is considering the content of any space intended for play.

All play spaces that attract children organically, i.e., by word of mouth rather than by commercial advertising, have special features that matter to children on some level or another. For example, silent or wooded areas, where only the wind through the trees or the odd bird-call can be heard, give urban and rural children insights into the experience of solitude and separation. This matters, because they make it possible for children to sense something tangible of the spirit-ual nature of their existence, adding another dimension to their own preconceptions of the world. Similarly, befriending other species – farm animals, cattle, goats or horses, wild birds, like jackdaws and pigeons, rodents like polecats or ferrets, insects like bees and even domestic cats, dogs, guinea pigs and hamsters – all provide children with foci for love, care and friendship, demonstrating, perhaps under-lining, that human life is about life on a planet containing many species, rather than one.

THE UNPREDICTABLE SPACE

One intended effect of evolutionary playwork as a compensatory inter-vention is that it should enable children to increase their adaptability – their adaptive responses to different situations – by enabling the child's developing physical and mental agility to be used and expanded at every opportunity. No play space – whether it provides problem solving, engaging in risk, social interfacing or simply enjoy-ing sensory experiences – should be so predictable, so forecastable, that any surprise and novelty it once contained is lost. To be that obvious – as many play spaces are – is more anti-play than play, because the uniqueness of the experience, the process, is lost.

Going to a play environment that is always the same, that never evolves, or is never subject to continuing modification – even destruc-tion – sends out an adulterating message of inertia that most children will interpret as boring, and will only use as a last resort. Obviously, there will be times and places when stability and predictability are more important than change. If, for example, the area in which the playworker's work takes place has high levels of damaged children, who as a result of extreme poverty, deprivation, abuse, racism or sectarianism, need a sanctuary or an oasis just to gather their thoughts and sort out how they feel and who they are, then they will need a space that offers just that, so that they are able to focus on the life issues affecting them, rather than creating new ones born out of the stress of the unpredictable. So although this will not be the norm, rigorous modification here will have to be a more tentative process, using a more therapeutic approach.

But for most UK children, already faced daily with the predictability of an adult agenda, including their preconceptions of youth culture/consumerism, the nature of citizenship, the content of the national curriculum and their parents'/carers' apparent obsession with low-quality safety rather than high-quality risk, the play space is the only place where the biological bottom line that predictability, although comforting, is also unreal, is being addressed. Human society may be a 'global village' – we might be able to communicate globally in seconds by e-mail, and whatever is invented in the future – and we may feel the dominant species in a predominantly human landscape, but we still live on a piece of matter in the middle of space, which can be the subject of internal or external change at any moment. Children need to know that, and to develop the skills through playing that will enhance their chances of surviving those changes that will inevitably occur (for example, Haiti recently suffered a massive earthquake and tens of thousands, if not hundreds of thousands, have died).

Children need experiences of things, events and concepts, to even begin to be aware that these things are there. And knowledge and experience of the reality of their impermanence is vitally important to them. Firstly because having knowledge of the transitory nature of existence may motivate them to engage with the play environment in ways that will enable the skills of adaptability and flexibility to grow, and secondly so that the notion of death does not surprise and undermine them and affect their mental health. By responding to this metaphysical need, by creating a temporary, transitional play space, which children can engage with in an infinite numbers of ways, the playworker will be facilitating in the children, both an awareness of the fleeting nature of everything and the temporary sense of loss that may accompany that, *and* the up side of temporary – change, innovation, creativity and new possibility – and from that a realisation that existence has many facets.

VISUAL STIMULATION

A good play space will also be visually stimulating. So it must also be subject to regular visual change or it will become stagnant. One playground I used to visit had had the same murals on the walls of its play building for over ten years. Not only had the available colours moved on, and painting techniques evolved, but the images were totally antiquated. The whole thing sent a message that said, 'we're too tired to bother' – quite the reverse of the message it should have been sending out, which I would articulate as 'consider doing everything'. (You might ask why I didn't say anything? I did, frequently. But this space was like that for a variety of factors, which neither the staff, parents or management seemed able to address. I was just a visitor and wasn't able to do anything directly – that's why I'm referring to it here.) What they could have done was revitalise the space with fresh colours, different images, lights, posters, photographs and so on.

Obviously there is little that can be done for a staffed play space where people are unmotivated, perhaps unskilled, perhaps even uninterested. Even in the most remote, poorly funded after school club on an estate somewhere, the children attending both deserve and need a sensorily attractive space – by that I mean a space that children find interesting, not the stereotype that attracts adults and therefore by definition *must* attract children – in which to play. After all it might be the only outlet they have for their play drive during their formative years. A good space will be busy, colourful, diverse, noisy, surprising, friendly and imaginative, it won't be quiet or tidy or offer just the predictable diet of 'play activities'.

THREE CASE STUDIES

The best way to get an idea of the potential of a particular space is to look at it from the perspective of a playing child. There are good places to hide. I can run about. We can light fires, make camps and dens, build, and make a mess, and a noise. We can have fun. If the space doesn't offer these experiences, then it could be restricting children's locomotor, mastery, creative and imaginative choices, and may actually have a damaging impact effect.

Among the locations I have managed over my forty-plus years as a playworker are three adventure playgrounds. Even though some of my practice at the beginning was below the supposedly 'high' regulatory standards applied now – particularly in terms of health and safety and intervention – it might be helpful to provide some insights into why I took certain decisions, and made certain visual and other choices about the appropriateness of different environments and about the modifications I undertook to improve the space for the children who came.

Where possible I will use what I call the *IMEE Protocol for Reflective Practice* described in detail in Hughes (1996b) as a guide. The IMEE protocol is a simple reflective tool that enables playworkers to organise any environmental analysis of the quality of a particular play environment against four criteria. Their own *intuitive* judgements of what a 'good' play environment should be like; their childhood *memories* of play environments they were frequently attracted to; their *experience* of what kinds of play environments work from their professional perspective, and what scientific *evidence* might exist to support their conclusions.

IMEE helps us to do two things: to look at the science from the perspective of personal and professional experience, and to look at personal and professional experience from a scientific perspective.

Because these case studies are intended to throw light on some of my playwork decision-making, I have deliberately not identified where they are or when I worked on them.

PLAYGROUND A

Playground A was developed out of an initiative by the local Round Table and District Council following a proselytising visit by Drummond Abernethy, one of the founders and main advocates of adventure playgrounds in the UK at the time. He was the then Director of the Children and Youth Department of the National Playing Fields Association, the lead national play organisation of the day. The space, one-third of an acre of chain-link fenced land, had been landscaped with horseshoe-shaped mounding on three sides of a flat area and contained two wooden sheds. I was appointed shortly before it opened.

226

Intuition

My first feeling, my intuition, was that it was a beautiful space and a wonderfully diverse environment for playing. It had a small coppice at one end, and the fence was intertwined with hawthorn and elder, which created an enclosure, a secret space, a sanctuary, rather than an enclave. It felt safe too. Not necessarily safe from injury, but safe from things children would not know, or would not understand. Here, children could and did deeply immerse themselves in the pursuit of playing. Here butterflies and hide and seek, could act to balance the realities of bullies and some of the negativity of some children's home lives. It felt a good place to go, to me, somewhere the child in me would have chosen to play too.

Memory

When I was a child I was a member of a gang of boys whose ages ranged over six years. I was in the middle, so some of them were three years older, some three years younger. A number of girls were transitional members too. The gang, all children of working parents, who were not encouraged to go home – except in exceptionally inclement weather – until their parents came home from work, spent their time in a number of different locations. First there was Annie's, a piece of farmland used for cattle and horses, that had a river with pools and fast bits, some streams, undulating grassland, old high trees, a railway line, bridges, and clay banks. Then there was The Valley, which led on over the railway line into the fields beyond. The Valley was an old steep stream bed that had cut a deep groove into the Suffolk clay. Along its length were fallen tree trunks, pools, and beaches of tiny flints and sand. At its source perhaps two miles as the crow flies from my house, and near the fields that flooded and froze over in our harsh winters, it was just a stream bed, perhaps eighteen inches deep, with six inches of water flowing along its bottom. But at the other end, at the bottom of the incline down which it flowed, it was twenty feet deep and the stream at its bottom was perhaps two feet wide – quite a jump for little legs! Going to Tinny Meadows incorporated the long walk there, along the railway line, where we would hunt for slow-worms to race, and the meadows themselves with a fast-flowing small-ish river where the races were held. Then there was the Vine Wood and Bluebell Wood that were in different locations at least two miles apart. Another main play venue was The Café, a classic transport 'caff' on the edge of town, where we would congregate and listen to the newest rock and roll releases. The music was a very important play prop, and we used it, and our vague knowledge of the performers – black, white, male, female, and mostly American – to dance, and mime, and display and impress. I never remember actually buying anything from the café.

Fast forward to 2010. Although I'm not looking for play spaces that mirror my own, I am searching for certain commonalities with them.

Nature. Childhood is the time when we bond with our planet. For although we may have homes and parents, it is the earth and its manifestations to which – although we take them totally for granted – we most naturally gravitate. This process, which incorporates both feelings of familiarisation (love), and competition (hate), reflects a human dilemma rooted on the beginning of our time. Ever since we have been conscious beings, we have recognised that earth is not just our home, it is also our prison, from which there is no escape save death. It makes sense then that a play space should contain a large portion of the natural world, with all of its diversity, beauty, and awesome splendour. In my childhood play spaces, we had fires, dug caves, built dens and tree houses, caught and raced slow worms, picked wild flowers, and identified birds by the flight patterns and eggs. For many children, those days of scenic plenty must seem like ancient history. But ignoring the slow worm racing, the wild flowers and the birds' eggs, children who attend a supervised play space should still be able to build dens, have fires, plant and grow wild flowers and vegetables and, if the conditions are right, keep hens, and other species.

When I played, we also spent a lot of time climbing, swinging, and building on trees, and we used to scrump too. The equivalent artificial play space today might have mature trees and saplings, and contain fruit trees, so that children can still have the pleasure of having direct access to certain fruit.

Each of the different places we went to was very different. Some were close to home, others were much further away, and because of that they felt different too, remote, isolated and mystical. Some had water features that dominated them, others just had a tinkling stream that

228

stimulated imagination and sensuousness, rather than physical challenge. Combined they offered an experiential diversity that was never equalled at school. Artificial play spaces should also offer richly diverse alternatives. Quiet places, overgrown places, activity areas, water, hills, banks, pools, with nothing in straight lines.

The Real World. I don't actually mean 'real', it's all real. What I mean is the human-made bit of experience. We had a jukebox and rock and roll, and now children have other things, which they will also expect to be a part of the landscape where they play. I won't say what they should be because by the time this is read it will all have changed. Suffice it to say that a children's space, a space that is truly a play space, will integrate the natural and human worlds and children will play with both. However, I would add one proviso, that because human children have a biological need for immersion in the natural world, the space should emphasise it with plants, water, undulation, wildness and above all growing things. I know that councils can't abide uncut grass, but in a play space they must resist this compulsion and allow it to grow.

The human world should not be emphasised or encouraged, but simply allowed to enter. Even without encouragement or advertising, football and micro-technology will take up the time of many children. This should not present a huge problem, as long as there are natural alternatives to them, available too.

Experience

Playground A turned out to be a very diverse and popular environment for the local – and sometimes, the not so local – children. The wooded area was popular for dens, although I had not banked on little children – unable to build and only beginning to become adept at tool use – hammering copper nails into the trees and killing many of them over the years. A protective sleeve would have helped. The blind side of the landscaping was a popular location for building and games. I played hide and seek there with the children, many times myself, balancing on the chain link fence, masked by a hawthorn or immature ash, to get away from the hunters. Not only feeling very smug that they could not find me, but experiencing the excitement of the chase that I thought I had lost years before.

Any prospective playworker should be warned, however, that if the children like you at all, and you get involved in 'catch' type games, it will often be you they try to catch first. This is not only exhausting, but also impractical when you have to be free to react to whatever else might arise. One game is fine, but a whole afternoon may mean that you are not available if other children need you. I had half expected the blind side to be used as a toilet too. It was occasionally, but we had toilets nearby and it was only rarely that a child was 'taken short'. However, the blind side did need clearing of rubbish from time to time. This was partly due to flotsam blowing from the local rubbish tip, which was next door, and also to the effects of time and weather on frail dens, that meant that furniture, mattresses and plywood, sometimes with nails in, had to be cleared from the area to keep it both hygienic and hazard free. The public – visible – area was initially used as an activity space – except in bad weather and during the winter when we went to an adjacent building. In the early days this space provided our main focus for dens, fires, water-play and general games like tag. But gradually, as we constructed a network of towers, bridges, walkways, swings, a slide and an aerial runway – known there as 'the death slide' – the children were able to access different and more complex experiences that incorporated height and motion, like high tag (chase played 'at height'), and swinging games, which enabled those at different developmental stages to engage in graduated risk and incrementally challenge themselves to go further. This area was constantly evolving and growing in complexity and provided a third dimension to the playground – a second tier – an 'off-ground' playground, or play space on legs!

The barrel

We had a good relationship with our local community and got a great deal of 'scrounged' materials from them. On one occasion we visited a local chemical plant, to see if they had anything interesting for us. They had a plastic reactor which they had used to make the basics of perfume, which they said we could have. I suppose this would nor-mally have been graciously refused by most playworkers, but I had previously been a chemist and was confident that I could make the reactor safe to use, although I had no idea how it would be employed. Standing on its end, the reactor was about seven feet tall, six feet in

230

diameter and it had a hole in one end. We took it back to the play-ground, half filled it with water from a standpipe with a hose, and washed it out for some days. When there was no trace of perfume, i.e., when we could not smell it anymore, we cut a hole in the other end and placed the reactor on its side. The first thing the children did was roll it, and compared to them it was huge. Needless to say, it did not take them long to compute that it would be more fun to roll it down the hillside provided by the landscaping, than along the flat. And it did not take much longer to work out that it would be even more fun to be inside it when it rolled. What followed was a piece of pure invention. The children deduced that if, say, six of them got inside it, on top of the landscaping and aimed it down the hill, by rocking it increasingly violently, it would eventually roll down the hill with them inside it, pressed against the sides. This provided thrills and spills for weeks, for hundreds of children and as far as I know was the earliest – and in my view the best – example of the 'puny' play barrels that came later, and that even one child would be hard pressed to get inside. It was used so much that it eventually wore out!

Evidence

A huge amount of what the literature forecast should happen when children are engaged in play did happen on Playground A. This is just one example: Locomotor play has an important role in the development of our skills of hand–eye co-ordination, balance and so on. However, at that time, I could never have predicted both the skill and grace which even the most ungainly, clumsy children would exer-cise on the whole variety of swings we built at Playground A. One, a gibbet swing, for example, required children to launch themselves on a wide arc, which, at its extreme, came close to a tall and very solid structure. The children showed skill on this swing that would have warmed an instructor at the Moscow State Circus. Their acrobatic skills were amazing, their judgement incredible. They could gauge avoiding the structure's massive uprights by centimetres, when to have collided with it would probably have meant painful injury. They were very brave. And although the drive to engage in this form of Deep locomotor play is probably irresistible, some of them *were* very young. It was a privilege to know that this was possible – not taught, not cajoled, not for reward, not out of fear, not just for fun either – it was far more than that. It was a kind of ecstasy, a natural exuberance, an immersion in motion, because they wanted to experience it. Certainly that was how it looked to me. Playground A was an example of a 'good' evolutionary play space.

PLAYGROUND B

It is not my intention to offend anyone who was associated with it, but Playground B was a dreadful place.

Like so many playgrounds in the UK, its siting was a classic demonstration of the appalling status many adults in power give children and play. Although it was not on or next to a rubbish tip – a not unusual siting for children's spaces– it was far too small, like many play environments today, and only occupied the space that would have accommodated, say, two small houses. It also attracted a large number of local children, who then became frustrated when they could not even exercise their most basic need to run about. The local population, although economically varied, typically contained some 'hard' families whose children used the playground. The children and adults from these families could be violent and we, the workers, were constantly suffering the 'what if' anxiety and were frequently pelted with stones and earth whenever we left the playground to go home.

The playground consisted of a fenced rectangle of grass and a shed. There was no planting, landscaping, indoor accommodation or space to do creative work. And there was little room outside to modify the site and make it more interesting. In addition, when I arrived, the other playworkers were 'at war' with a large group of the local children and their parents.

Intuition

After Playground A, my heart sinks when I think of Playground B. It was tiny and boring. My first reaction was, what is this playground here to do? What do adults expect to happen here? It was minimal, it had no points of interest, and nowhere to get another perspective. The children were constantly overlooked by adults, always in strong light and always exposed to the weather. There were no natural features. It was a bleak place, that only served to reinforce any negative precon-ceptions the children may have felt that adults had of them. My intu-ition said that the children would have been better off with nothing, rather than with this, because it raised their expectations but gave them very little of what they would have biologically anticipated. It was a bad site and location. It was violent and unfriendly. It was boring, and presented no playful challenges. I wondered how children could be expected to have an attraction to such a place? Unless, of course, they were damaged and saw the playground as a useful and local focus for their aggression, projecting their anger either towards the playground's physical fabric or towards the playworkers.

Whenever I see a play space, like this one, now – a grudging reaction to parental or political pressures to do something for children, how-ever inappropriate it may turn out to be – I realise how far playwork has yet to go, both in terms of developing and articulating its own knowledge base, and in terms of changing public perceptions (this is still the case in 2011). Even with 'good' playworkers, I have seen how great is the qualitative chasm between what they experienced as chil-dren themselves and what they are prepared to accept for the children of today. Playground B was such a space. For although it was managed by good-hearted, well-meaning non-play professionals and parents, typical of many voluntary committees today, they were incapable of addressing the fundamental needs of those local children, many of whom, without a convincing demonstration of commitment to them, would never view their childhood as a period to cherish and to draw from throughout their lives.

Memory

My own childhood experience of such spaces was limited. The play-ground at my school had been barren too, devoid of any natural fea-tures that I can recall now, although it was on a slope, which made for great games of attack and defence and incredible ice slides in the winter. But the school day gave that particular space a momentum and a structure, which it did not have after school – then it was dead space. The 'green' outside my friends' houses on our council estate was also barren, but it carries powerful memories into the present for me. We could have been overlooked, but then the great majority of mums and dads would have been out at work, and so would have had little impact on what we did. My strongest memory there, probably at around eight or nine years of age, is of fixing metal bolts to the heads of arrows we had made from elder or beech saplings and, using bows we had also made, firing them vertically into the air, dodging them as they hurtled back to earth!

However, if this had been the only space we had access to, and if there had been adults there supervising us, particularly if they had been adults who showed fear – as we must have on Playground B – who talked differently, and who traditionally had been the butt of attack for many summers, it would have been a very different experience for my friends and I.

That is not to argue against playwork or playworkers when they are needed– when there is no viable or appropriate alternative – quite the reverse. Rather it is intended to emphasise the need for careful consideration of what kind of provision it should be when it is made. Thought must be given to where provision is to be placed, how it will be operated and by whom. Importantly, consideration should also be given to whether it will represent – in the minds of the local children – a lasting recognition by adults of the children's fundamental needs and rights, or an imposition on their space, or worse still, a theft of that space and a colonisation of it by adults.

As a child, I had been lucky, and would probably not have benefited much from access to playworkers or play spaces – although this would be far less the case for children growing up in the countryside now. But then, the lack of traffic, and open access to fields and streams, meant that we had endless choices and opportunities to range and engage with a whole spectrum of diverse flora and fauna (although, even then, we had our fair share of hostility from local landowners). But for the children who used Playground B, no such choices were available. They were trapped by traffic and territorial demarcation, and pressurised by a lack of adult-free space. And as a response to the experiential deficits these conditions caused, Playground B was just an adulterated and, in my view, irrelevant solution.

Perhaps the most negative feature of Playground B was that it acted as a pressure cooker. During my own childhood we had choices of experiences and environments, which meant we were rarely bored, or frightened by sustained violence. For the children there, Playground B was all they had. It was go there, or stay at home, which for many was not a choice. A cycle was created by its history, which meant that many children went to Playground B reluctantly, spent all day in fear of being bullied, and left terrified that they would be attacked on the way home. The impact of this was that children were depressed, or became violent themselves, either fighting the bullies or colluding with them.

Experience

Thinking of this playground now still fills me with anxiety. For even though I am convinced that 'good' playwork can make a significant contribution to children's development and to their potential to develop, I would still have to ask, in this particular context, if the children experienced a net gain or a net loss from our intervention. And, on the whole, the answer must have been the latter. It was not that we did anything that was particularly bad practice, rather that we could not do anything that was particularly good practice either, although we tried. It had just been too bad, for too long.

However, as we will see with the next example, it is possible to turn a bad situation around, if the time and experience is there to develop an appropriate strategy. But at Playground B, I still believe that nothing would have worked. Everything was wrong. I remember many incidents, but two stand out.

First, Playground B was included in the 'round' of summer play-schemes, which would now be called Playdays. On these occasions, as well as being able to use the normal site, the children also had the use of an inflatable, which the playworkers were expected to supervise. The inflatable was not of the bouncy castle variety, it was more like a large mattress with no sides, which, when inflated, was about a metre and a half high – quite a fall-height for the small children who might be expecting to use it, along with their sisters and brothers. Access to this inflatable always brought out a variety of different behaviours in children. Most of them were relatively benign, but some of them inevitably became wild and dangerous. On this occasion, twenty to thirty children at a time, boys, girls, three-year-olds and eleven-year-olds, invaded the inflatable, wildly drop-kicking each other. One could be forgiven for asking why we did not separate them by gender, or by age? That, however, would not have been possible. As the thing became inflated, the children just mobbed it. We had no control and were only able to contain the situation and engage in some damage limitation. Instead of serving the children, we had simply been reduced to providing an outlet for their aggression. We should not have been made to have the inflatable in such a supercharged atmosphere – it was a wonder that children had not been seriously hurt – but that was not our decision!

Second, the other incident involved another imposed visit by the same inflatable. On this occasion, only little children were playing on it and they were having a nice, gentle moment. Nice and gentle, that was, until a group of several of the local mothers came along. One, who was heavily pregnant at the time, decided that she wanted to have a go on the inflatable, too. She gave us no warning and no permission was asked or granted. She just threw herself onto the inflatable, oblivious of the children already playing there. As she landed – she must have been quite heavy – the inflatable caved in and the little children all fell and rolled into the dent she had made. And as she bounced back out, they flew in all directions. Luckily again, no child was seriously damaged, but they had been badly frightened. What would we have told the child who might have been injured, or its parents, or our employers or managers? In the real world, at this cutting edge, whose fault would that have been? Playground B should either not have been there, or if it had to be, it should have been enabled to operate in a way which was much more sensitive to its social context. Unfortunately, the mixture of playworker naïveté, inexperience, lack of team work and the apparent management ignorance and disinterest that existed at that time more or less guaranteed a painful failure for everyone involved.

Re-reading this in 2011 I am horrified, but it is all true. Notwithstanding the tiny size and boring nature of this playground, the primary mistake was not with that year's staffing but with the playground's staffing history. Every year the local authority had hired cheap student labour to operate the playground. Although well meaning, these young people were no match for the savvy and street-wise kids from the locality, whose older male siblings regularly engaged in knife fights and robberies. And so a modus operandi had evolved each summer where the 'fucking students' did what they could to survive the summer, and the local children did what they could to try and ensure they didn't. We came along after years of this, and it *was* scary. Perhaps it would have worked better with more trained staff to supervise things. But with a clientele consisting of feuding extended families – where everyone from grandparents and uncles to young children would turn up en-masse it was a hopeless task, which eventually was recognised, and the playground closed.

Evidence

I could have considered the work of the American architect and educationalist, respectively, Talbot and Frost (1989). They recommend the application of certain classical design ideas to enhance and contextualise children's play spaces. Using, for example, changes of scale, the suggestion of other beings, archetypal images, placeness, line quality and shape, sensuality, novelty, mystery, brilliance, the juxtaposition of opposites, and so on, they believe that the spaces so adapted will both stimulate and facilitate play of all kinds. Whilst I agree that spaces containing these characteristics will provide children with interesting and sometimes fantastic experiences, I am also aware that the reality of size, resources and support for many play spaces renders their consideration somewhat unrealistic. Playground B would have been too small to make any significant physical change to it, even if it had had the necessary finance and support, which it did not.

I could have invoked the lessons of Nicholson's *Theory of Loose Parts* (1971), in which is stated 'In any environment, both the degree of inventiveness and creativity, and the possibility of discovery, are directly proportional to the number and kind of variables in it' (p. 30).

But that would not have made any difference to the effectiveness of this playground either. By the time I arrived, the children were using the play space to exorcise their domestic angst and any attempt to introduce interesting and stimulating features would only have resulted in their subsequent destruction by fire or other means. And even if I had known what I now know about the therapeutic potential of playwork, as described in Else and Sturrock (1998), Rennie (1997), and Taylor *et al.* (1999), in hindsight, I still do not feel Playground B would have provided much of benefit to its constituents.

The only strategy that might have worked would have been to close the playground and only re-open once the cycle of usage had been broken, but that would probably have taken two or three years.

These kinds of playgrounds should only exist where they can be operated by qualified and experienced playworkers, and where they are supported by knowledgeable management, convinced of their value. Anything less, and even well-run spaces risk descending into the support and knowledge vacuum that was Playground B.

Compensation

Although it is now widely agreed that one of the functions of play projects, playgrounds, play environments and play spaces is to compensate, that is, to address the play deficits that local children are experiencing, on Playground B at that time we did not know about compensation. Thus, no analysis of the children's local 'play' situation was ever undertaken. If it had been, we may have discovered that the playground's users, the local children, were perhaps generally play-deprived, or that they were emitting hyperactive play cues, or were caught up in a cycle of debilitating violence or abuse, or were only engaging in a limited number of play types which were biasing their experience, and perhaps we could have done something useful to address this.

Superficially, compensating for play deficits means providing children with play experiences they might otherwise not have, like giving them access to creative materials, or taking them out on trips. But in the context of evolutionary playwork, compensation also means designing a large part of the operation and development of a play space around the assessed play deficits in the local area, deficits that have been arrived at as the result of an audit or a diagnosis (see Chapter 10).

Compensation is a way of ensuring that children have access to those ingredients of the play experience they need for their development as biological organisms, but which they may not have, because of the nature of their living or cultural environment. One of the problems with Playground B, for example, was that it was far too small and as a consequence it was frequently overcrowded, making it impossible for children to play games or experience solitude or talk quietly with their

238

friends. It was also always frenetic and laden with layers of anxiety that had been generated over generations. Quality compensation, because it addresses assessed deficits, should help children to feel better, more at ease, less anxious, more balanced and contented and certainly less angry.

On Playground A, I had been highly valued by my managers. They never claimed to be experts, but always made sure that I was properly resourced, and they were interested in the children, and in the work we did with them. Playground B, on the other hand, 'felt' like a nuisance, a begrudged drain on resources as far as the local authority was concerned, and a means of satisfying a personal psychological need as far as the voluntary managers were concerned – a toxic combination, particularly with a group of inexperienced or unworldly students caught in the middle.

Perhaps it was just designed to act as a space that contained and managed the local child population? Certainly no interest was taken in the work we did there, that I ever saw, and as the incidents with the inflatable demonstrate, the playworkers had little or no strategic say in what happened there, even though they bore the brunt of any violence or abuse that resulted. Like so many playgrounds I have known of, Playground B was the victim of a policy which was manifested in long periods of denial of its existence, interspersed with brief periods of uninformed imposition from above. Needless to say, it was not a happy experience.

PLAYGROUND C

My introduction to the users of Playground C was being called a 'motherfucker', having sand and stones thrown at me, being spat at and having my car kicked. However, although this is certainly an accurate reflection of my early experience there, it is not a fair indicator of the real humour and character of the local children, or for that matter, of the adults of the area.

Every play space is different, and every play space population is different. At Playground A, most of the children came from white, working-class families who were part of the London overspill programme. Many of them had lived in cramped, impoverished housing, with no access to gardens or secure open spaces. Their main play needs, as I perceived them then, were to be able to navigate an unusual volume of space, particularly three-dimensional space – like trees – and gradually to be able to integrate themselves into what was a new and very strange rural environment, which would probably necessitate interactions with domestic species, wild flora and fauna, darkness and stars. At the playground we tried to address some of the implications of these needs by creating somewhere which had, on the whole, a fairly relaxed and welcoming ambience, where the children felt ownership and belonging and where, above all, they could express the diversity of their newly stimulated drive to play, in as many formats as resources and reasonable safety would allow.

Playground B, on the other hand, had a mixed white population with a high proportion of children who had experienced instability, insecurity and prejudice, together with a whole raft of other socioeconomic and health problems. None of us was prepared for the ways this context would manifest itself, and the levels of violence and aggression that would result. This was one reason why this particular play space proved to be unsuccessful.

Playground C was different again. The major group of users were first- or second-generation children from either Pakistan or Kashmir. I was told that many of the children's parents and relatives had come from very rural parts prior to coming to the UK. Most of the children who came were from a Muslim background. Initially, most of the users were also male.

Other groups, although smaller in number, also contributed significantly to Playground C's diversity. There were families from Eastern Europe, Italy and India; a large representation from the Caribbean; and a small number of white British and Irish families, and local travellers' families.

At that time, the area where the playground was sited was economically quite disadvantaged, its housing stock was run down and some of it overcrowded, and there was also a drugs issue, although nothing serious by today's standards. There were race issues too, which, because of mixed population, were very complex. There were also religious and cultural issues, particularly around how parents viewed the playground and the concept of play in general. Needless to say, like Playground B, Playground C had had a long and quite turbulent history, but for quite different reasons.

what is evolutionary playwork?

As a playworker, who by then knew a lot more about the practice and theory of playwork than I had at Playground A, this seemed an ideal place for me to apply what I had learnt, and to see which theories would stand the test of a real play space. I was beginning to feel that the children on this playground, unlike those on B, would at least get my best shot, however far short of the ideal that turned out to be.

Three days after I started, however, there was a 'riot', an alleged sexual assault by a user against another playworker, there was some criminal damage, and the police – whom I had not called – arrested several of the users and the playground was closed. The reasons for these events are complex and attempting to unpack them probably unproductive. My perception is that they were the inevitable culmination of a period of what I can only describe as inappropriate playwork and management input.

Whatever the reasons, Playground C had gone through a period of considerable turbulence. The children seemed very unstable and untrusting, and this manifested itself in some anti-everything behaviour, which came to a head around the time of my arrival. I was just left reeling, and wondering what was going on. In order to clarify the situation I talked to a lot of people, including many of the children, workers from the local multi-cultural centre, youth and community workers, teachers, my own colleagues and managers, and parents and councillors.

I suggested that we should close the playground for three months, whilst I tried to develop and implement a playwork strategy, which hopefully, with their help and support, would salvage the situation.

However, before I could do anything, I needed to gather some intelligence about the children's context. I had only been there for a week and knew little about the general area where the children lived, or more importantly about their play patterns, or how they interacted with one another and their play environment. So I did two things. Firstly, although I didn't live there at that time, I made sure that I was visible in the general area of the playground, particularly when children were going to and from school. I went to the local shops, I said hello to everyone I met, and I did that for several weeks and for several hours of every day. Initially I was met with blank faces, but gradually people started to say 'Hello' back and were as friendly as people who do not know each other can be. The children knew I was from the playground and did not appear to hold a grudge, not in the street anyway.

Secondly – because I assumed that children might still want to use the outside area of the playground, even though we were closed – I put a small amount of water in the playground's little paddling pool and left a few bits and pieces around, that could be played with – some paper, a pencil and so on. I did this every evening. Then, every morning I looked for evidence of use of the area and materials. I was aware that leaving even a small amount of water in the pool all night did represent a risk, but judged it to be so tiny and that the chances of anyone getting hurt were almost non-existent. This proved to be the case. What the first part of this strategy told me was, although I had been the object of a number of frightening incidents, these were not remotely representative of the general atmosphere in the area, except in periods of high tension. It also served as a reminder that I knew little or nothing about growing up either in an inner-city area, or in a predominantly Muslim community. And although every community I had worked in had had its fair share of life's problems, this situation was very foreign to me, and that needed to be rectified.

The second part told me that a range of children of different ages were still using the outside play area in the evenings. I would find grass floating in the water in the morning, chalk drawings and graffiti of different levels of maturity were on the walls, heavy pieces of wood had been moved, children had been seen on the roof, and the play materials had been used. I also noticed new cigarette ends, evidence of joints being smoked and, on one occasion, I found a hypodermic needle. So some children and presumably adolescents and adults still viewed the playground, or at least its outside area, as a place to go.

Although it could sometimes be tense after dark, in daylight the area was reasonably friendly and not at all threatening. Children liked, and still used the play space, and from this I deduced that the main barrier to a successful re-launch of the playground would be me and how I dealt with the situation.

One thing I also did early on was go to the playground in the evenings and 'appear' in the outside area. Without a word, I would put more materials out and go back inside. Initially this meant that I again became the focus of their attention, and doors and windows were banged and abuse hurled, but gradually any children who were there ignored me as much as I ignored them and an unofficial truce was declared. My reason for doing this was to demonstrate to children that

I was there to serve, rather than to intervene. That as a playworker, my presence was to enable their play, not to invade their space or privacy. I viewed that as a particularly important statement to make, given that I was white and not from their community, and therefore a potential catalyst to overreaction. For example, these children had had to endure marches by racist organisations through the areas they lived in. Who was to say that I wasn't one of these racists?

Suffice it to say that at the end of three months we re-opened with two assistant playworkers from the local Muslim community, one male, one female, which transformed the children's behaviour.

Language

I have a theory about why this was. Although almost all of the children spoke English, for many of them Urdu was their first language. And although most of these Urdu speakers could communicate fluently using English, there seemed to be some circumstances – particularly those in which emotions or long explanations were involved – where English appeared an inadequate medium for communicating how the children felt. In fact during arguments, the use of English seemed to be almost counterproductive, inhibiting expression and causing further frustration.

To better understand the significance of this, I tried to put myself in their place, in the place of a child from a displaced minority population, where almost everyone else in the family only spoke Urdu. In this context, Urdu would be used to do most of the important and deep communicating, like expressing emotions and articulating other deeper ideas like religious and political concepts.

From this, I interpreted that children might find it difficult, even impossible, to communicate deeper feelings in English. For one reason they did not use it all the time and may never have used it when dealing with emotions or relationships at home. And for another, I had noticed that the form of English they spoke did not appear to carry the range of intonation and emphasis so essential to communicating accurately those things that matter, whereas their use of Urdu did appear to. What this told me was that more than anything else, these children desperately needed access to Urdu-speaking playworkers who were cognisant of their circumstances and the pressures they were under, and who could help me to provide an appropriately playful context that the children could engage in. If this analysis was accurate, imagine the relief any of us would feel at having access to someone – in this case two playworkers from their own cultural background – to communicate with, who could understand both the language and the context in which it was being used, and who would confirm that they did understand, and would respond to what was being said with equality and understanding.

Intuition

Unlike Playgrounds A and B, I had mixed feelings about the appropriateness of Playground C. Although it had its faults, for example the outside area was quite unmalleable and contained a lot of concrete, its indoor accommodation was good. There was a lot of space, a large hall, two smaller rooms, a kitchen and toilets. Upstairs there was an office. And although the echo in the hall could move one close to insanity on busy winter days when all doors were closed, the sense of space, with high ceilings and huge ground area, was probably a luxury to us all, especially those children who lived in cramped accommodation. The two smaller rooms made it easy to separate experiences, when that was felt to be necessary, i.e., if some children wanted to be quiet or alone, whilst others wanted to engage in their customary mayhem. The middle small room was used mainly for sitting, conversation, music, dancing, table-football, pool – which I hated for the trouble and angst it caused – and small board games. The small room next to the kitchen was normally used as a creative and artistic space and everything the children produced was displayed there, if that was OK with them. I did this to demonstrate a sense of valuation of everything the children did, without being judgemental. However, the outside area was a different matter entirely. It had previously been a builder's yard, and although it was a good size (about half the size of Playground A, and at least ten times the size of Playground B), there were still immovable traces of its previous life everywhere, which were quite hazardous. In the centre of the outdoor area was a concrete mound that had been built to cover up the concrete base of a crane, and everywhere, only a few inches – sometimes only a few centimetres – below the ground was builder's rubble, steel rods and slabs of concrete. (It reminded me of some of the early playgrounds in London and other cities, where digging often uncovered old cellars and the remains of bombed-out buildings.)

The playground was also adjacent to some sheltered accommodation and the relationship between the elderly residents and the children was not good. However, the playground was not near the road, it was well fenced, and although it did not have any genuine natural features, it did have landscaping and vegetation. In short, it had limited possibilities, although these had resource implications.

Memory

Even though I would not have been used to the numbers who used Playground C – it was not unusual to have well over a hundred children on Saturday afternoons – as a child I would have felt at home in this space, because it was generally friendly and vibrant. There were places to hide and climb, and lose yourself. There was water, albeit in the form of a small concrete paddling pool. There was indoor and outdoor space, lots of diversity of experience, there was a place for fires and space for building and the whole area had a feeling of enclosure, that it was hidden and private. Behind the outdoor area there was at least one mature horse chestnut tree, whose purple blossom in spring was an amazing and optimistic visual display.

The biggest advantage of the space was its size. It provided the children with room to run about after a day cooped up in school. Its biggest disadvantage was its proximity to the adolescents and adults who used the small park and community centre next door, and who sometimes intimidated or bullied children as they came to the playground.

Experience

Although the playground's positioning was ideal in one sense – it was away from traffic, convenient for the children's homes and near a shop – in another, it was awful. Its proximity to the elderly residents' accommodation, for example, was one constant headache. It was also close to an area constantly in use by older boys from a community that had a well-established male pecking order. To effectively facilitate 'adult-free' play, play provision needs to be separated from other forms of adult provision, from housing, sheltered accommodation and factories and offices. If it is not, there is constant irritation. Balls go through windows – some innocently, some not so – children climb over walls, they may shout things that feel, sound or could be insulting to others. They use physical gestures that intimidate the uninitiated. Older children are often out late at night, and may keep people awake and make them feel vulnerable. And none of this is either unusual or limited to this particular space, it's what children do and always have.

As a play space, Playground C would score perhaps 6–10, given its context. It had loads of room, and although historically den and structure building had been limited, we were able to make the most important sensory and elemental experiences accessible to the children who came.

For example, fire play was a popular, although vexed, activity. Many of the children had little or no experience of real fire – a very common phenomenon in these centrally heated times – and I believed strongly that they should have the opportunity to know the dangers and benefits of fire as early in their lives as possible, if only to ensure that their first experience of it would not be at the top of the stairs, when they were trying to get out of a burning house. Apart from the odd blister, which normally came from touching a piece of hot wood, or picking up a surround brick before it had cooled, there were very few accidents. I only allowed as many fires as there were fire buckets, and that limited the number of fires and ensured that there was always the wherewithal to put the fire out, as well as to light them. Fire play acted as the catalyst for one other memorable development.

Initially, it was rare to see any of the children's parents at the playground. This is not unusual, in my experience. But it was unheard of to see a mother from the Pakistani/Kashmiri community in the outside play area, at that time. Until one day, that is, when the mother of some of the regular users came, lit a fire and prepared and cooked chapattis in the open air.

With a mother in traditional dress doing familiar things, and with Urdu being spoken, for a moment the playground seemed totally focused on one important aspect of the area, and on many of the issues crucial to all of the children, about culture, identity, choices and future possibilities, which might never have been addressed in that way, if the playground had not been there.

The paddling pool was vital to the success of the external environment too. For many of the children, a visit to the seaside or a river was a rarity, and water, in its many forms, like every other element – earth, fire, air – is a vital 'interactor' for the playing child. We are evolved from sea-dwelling creatures and I imagine that, deep within our genes, is the source of that part of the play drive that forces us to search out water. This notion was first alluded to by Haeckel when he proposed that every animal re-lives its evolutionary past during its embryonic development (Jones 1993). However, it was Hall (1906) who proposed that children recapitulate their evolutionary past when they play. In every play setting I have worked on, water in the form of bombs, pails, hoses, puddles, pools, streams, etc., has always been a major play feature. The paddling pool meant that hot children could immerse themselves in cool water, it could be sat in, floated on, played with, and used as a prop for all sorts of imaginary scenarios. A stream would probably have been better, meandering across the outside area, with little waterfalls and pools, but the pool was a good second best.

Because of the concrete and mounding it was possible to get up relatively high, thus flying balloons and using windmills and model gliders was a possibility, so to a limited extent, the element air was also catered for. What did prove difficult was access to the element earth.

If the builder's yard rubble just below the playground's surface ensured that digging holes necessary for building structures – swings, towers, walkways – and dens was going to be difficult, growing things was going to be almost impossible. We overcame that by buying several tons of topsoil and moving it bodily with the help of the children, from the gate where it had been dumped to another part of the site, to construct a garden. Most of the children who came to the playground did not have gardens and many appeared unsure of what a garden could be used for! When all the earth had been moved, we planted fruit trees, shrubs and vegetables.

This experiment was a partial success, and gave the children access to tactile, visual and mastery experiences that they otherwise would not have had. But there was an important playwork lesson here too. If the playworker does create such a focus, she should try not to make it mean too much personally. Certainly she should not keep saying to the children how important this garden or whatever, is to her. For although, most of the time the garden will just be that, a garden – where things grow and children play – if things go wrong (and they will), the garden, or whatever other focus the playworker has created, may become a way of applying pressure on, or of attacking him or her. Luckily I had expected this and accepted that there would be times when to get at me or the other workers, some of the children would pull things up and destroy them, sometimes when we were closed and sometimes before our very eyes! My solution was to view the garden as just another experiment, and to buy more plants than we needed and simply replace what were destroyed. The garden was never intended to be perceived as something they had to like or had to want. Rather, it was intended to give the children access to alternatives and choices that would otherwise have been absent from their lives. From that per-spective, it had to have the effect of providing a balancing mechanism to other, more de-sensitising experiences freely available in the local area. Therefore it was essential that we did not see the garden as some-thing that had to be defended. Quite quickly the children got bored and stopped using the 'garden' as a stick to beat us with.

Evidence

I return to Talbot and Frost (1989) and Nicholson (1972) for a brief final critique of Playground C. The underlying message in both of these excellent articles is that the ideal play environment – whatever else it is – must be a place that is conducive to playing. That is, it must be a space where children not only feel secure and stimulated, but one in which important aspects of their drive to play can be freely expressed. This may seem obvious, but in many of the play contexts I have known over the years, playing has been the last consideration of designers, managers and, sometimes, even playworkers!

Construction and mastery were not really possible in Playground C. In most other aspects the outside area was certainly above a qualitative bottom line, but as with spaces too small to be able to play games that involve a lot of running, because of its builder's yard history, Play-ground C's impact on digging and building was inhibitive and frustrating.

248

It is my experience that if an environment is recognised by children to contain the ambience and props for play, the play drive begins to take over and their behaviour changes. They stop being the result of whatever socialising forces they have been subjected to and instead become those embryonic engineers, architects, builders, cave dwellers, hunters and gatherers that Nicholson (1972) and others have alluded to.

The researcher Eibl-Eibesfeldt (1967, 1970) even described the play of the young as 'scientific research', whilst the educational psychologist G. Stanley Hall (1904) called the expression of these different roles 'recapitulation'. While there is little hard scientific evidence that this 'transformation', as Schwartzman (1978) calls it, is developmentally significant or has an impact on individual evolution, the fact that all children, except those who are stopped from doing it, seem to undergo this change when the environment is appropriate for play, is enough reason to continue to facilitate it. More research needs to be done in this area. Playground C's impact on the local children was very positive, particularly after the addition of the two local play-workers. Attendances rose, violence all but disappeared and small children and girls started to attend in increasing numbers. There were odd clashes along the way, but these were more a consequence of cultural 'crossed wires' than of significant problems. Most importantly the playground gave the children the opportunity to broaden their experience, and said there was a world out there to explore and experience that was not all racist and threatening by any means. Working at Playground C was one of the most enriching experiences I have ever had.

MICK'S STORIES 4

Imagination TV

Most days on the playground we lit a fire. Like millions of children today, a majority of the Bermondsey children lived in homes where they had no experience of a real fire. Before coming to the playground, most didn't know how to set up and light a controlled fire and were amazed and delighted to find out that you could slowly bake potatoes in the embers or quickly fry sausages or boil eggs or roast marshmallows over the flames.

They loved both the excitement of big bonfires showering sparks into the night sky and the quiet companionship of just sitting chatting around a small fire gazing into its ever-changing heart. One night a girl said 'It's like imagination TV. You can see anything you like in it'. This started off weeks of gentle musing about what they could see in the fire.

Frankie loved fires – of all sizes. His eyes blazed if a playworker lit up a cigarette (this was in 1979) and he was obsessive about helping with starting and tending the playground fire, but this wasn't enough for him. Other children told us that he was responsible for a series of arson attacks on parked cars, vans and lorries in the area and a major fire in a derelict factory. Then he nearly killed a family because he hadn't considered that someone might be living above an empty shop he torched. Oddly enough, the children were adamant that he'd had nothing to do with a fire on the playground that burnt out the building.

So what to do about Frankie? He was around ten years old. The police had no idea that he was the 'Bermondsey Arsonist Strikes Again' in the local headlines and his mum and dad were serious alcoholics who'd been rehoused in what was then called a sink estate for rent arrears – council housing policy at the time. Back then we playworkers saw the police and social services as at best remote and unfriendly, and at worst as the enemy. Also, the playground, or rather the playworkers, relied on the support of the local community and 'grassing' was by far the worst thing you could do in Bermondsey in those days.

I talked to Frankie about the possible consequences of his fire obsession, but he just shrugged and said he didn't care what happened to him. I had a word with a brilliant local detached youth worker, who had a chat with Frankie and discovered that he had been setting fires not just because he loved them, but also because he hoped that if he was caught he would be taken away from his extremely neglectful and often physically abusive parents.

He persuaded Frankie to talk to the Educational Welfare Officer at the school he had rarely attended and he was eventually placed in foster care with a family in the Kent countryside. Frankie rang us at the playground a few months later to tell us 'It's like heaven, only better, except there's no Addie round here'. Everyone in the local community knew our adventure playground as 'The Addie'.

Petty officer

We were huddled around the playground fire for warmth on a freezing night in January 1980 because the play building was still burnt out, as the insurers hadn't yet paid up. We were talking about the armed forces, I think because recruitment officers had been around the local secondary school. Fourteen-year-old Dan pensively stirred the fire with a stick and said 'My uncle was a Petty Officer in the Navy'. He stirred the embers again and with a sly look, gave us the punchline 'Now he's just a petty thief!'

Easter houses

An annual ritual in my rural Irish childhood, which now sadly seems to have died out, was building an Easter house. Basically it was a typical children's camp or den, but with some extras. It had to have a working fireplace and chimney, traditionally built with clay sods, though anything that came to hand would do. I remember the huge excitement when we found a milk churn with a base that had rusted away – the perfect chimney. Next we had to collect hen's eggs, light the fire and hard-boil them in an old saucepan with yellow whin (gorse) flowers – this was compulsory, though nobody knew why. Finally, we had to roll the eggs down a stony hill to crack the shells, and then eat them. They looked and tasted marvellous with the shells and the outer surface of the egg white stained yellow. And nobody died, as far as I know!

Many years later I mentioned the Easter houses to a Professor of Social Anthropology at Queen's University in Belfast. She told me that the ritual of building a temporary shelter, and particularly cooking yellow-dyed eggs and rolling them down a hill, had been a tradition for millennia across northern Europe. It was almost certainly the surviving remnant of a prehistoric fertility cult, connected to the Germanic dawn-goddess Oestre, from whom we get the word Easter.

Along with many other traditional children's cultural or seasonal celebrations, much of the creative content has now almost completely disappeared or been co-opted by consumerism as in chocolate Easter eggs. But egg rolling survives as an annual event in several English towns and villages, and also as a high profile event on the White

House lawn ever since an eighteenth-century American law banned it as a children's play activity on the terraces of Capitol Hill. If you Google Easter Houses or egg rolling you'll find fascinating memories and details of where the traditions survive.

Marble races

Our English cousins often came to stay on our farm in the summer holidays in the late fifties. To their astonishment, we rural Irish children had little or no tradition of playing marbles, didn't know the rules or even that there was a marble season starting around Easter. We were equally puzzled by their lack of an Easter house tradition and their fear of cattle, sheep and hens. We had a healthy respect for cattle, but sheep? Hens? They did love our game of jumping on the crusty tops of cowpats to splatter anyone nearby, and quickly became experts at it.

One rainy day we went into an outhouse that had timber off-cuts, lengths of copper piping and other bits and pieces of every size, shape and length along with tools and workbenches – and best of all, as it turned out, a pipe bender.

Over the next few days we built and endlessly remodelled ever more complex marble racecourses with chutes, jumps, slaloms, tunnels and 'death drop' traps. Rules were invented, argued over, modified and frequently broken. What I most remember is the sheer fun of experimentation, trial and error, and our delight in someone's flash of genius in designing a new challenge for the marbles to negotiate. Which marble won what race was important up to a point, but most of the enjoyment was in building and remodelling the courses – that pipe bender meant that perfectly curved bits of copper pipe at all sorts of angles made for endless permutations.

CHAPTER 9

THE EVOLUTIONARY PLAYWORK
CONSTRUCT OF THE CHILD

These days children are often described as gene carriers, or as cultural entities, and more 'cosmic' views of children that describe them in terms of their planetary, astronomical or psychic/spiritual context tend to be unfashionable. And yet, children are members of one of many evolving species; their only habitat is a living planet and they look out onto a galactic backdrop that is as overpowering as it is beautiful; as unknowable as it renders humans insignificant. To provide an analysis of anything children do, without putting their actions into that context not only marginalises them, it also avoids a great deal of what makes children what they are. So, whilst most forms of out-of-school provision use education, containment and entertainment rationales to describe their purpose, evolutionary playwork attempts to use this 'cosmic view' as its starting point, as a way of determining what support children need, if any, and how that support should be delivered.

The term 'child' does not mean the same to everyone. To the United Nations, it means anyone under nineteen years of age, but to many others, 'child' would probably mean someone who was under the age of twelve or thirteen. From that age on, the term 'adolescent' would be seen to be more appropriate.

For the playworker, the meaning of the term 'child' has a particular resonance, because how we describe children in a general sense gives us insights into what our job is, and informs how that job should be done.

Reading the literature and reflecting on what it offers, gives us a particular insight into the child's dilemma, and into a description of 'child' that is perhaps more helpful to those whose function is to facilitate play. It is this dilemma that I intend to briefly explore in this chapter.

In Hughes (1996b) I suggested that the most useful 'construct' of the child for playworkers was that children are lone organisms, on a hostile planet, in the middle of nowhere

This does not mean that this is the only construct of the child that would be accurate and sympathetic to what play and playwork are. What I am attempting to do by using it is break down the idea of a child into a very basic format and stimulate insights into:

- what a child might need to address in order to survive and develop;
- what play's role is in addressing those needs;
- what playwork's function is in facilitating that play.

A LONE ORGANISM

Birth is the beginning of a lone journey for us all. Although we may spend much of that journey surrounded by family and friends, and colleagues and acquaintances, what these terms mean, the value we put upon them, the help they are to us, the nature of the bonds we forge and the quality of relationships we share, depend on what we do as individuals to communicate and to establish those relationships. Only then, assuming that there are family or friends or whoever to make friends with, can we establish relationships. In other words, whether or not these relationships exist at all is down to each one of us.

So the first part of this playworker's construct – the lone organism – is stating that playwork is predicated on the assertion that the default human state is a solitary one, and a number of things need to happen, to move from that solitary state to one which is more gregarious. For example, children must do things to establish links with other humans, or with other species and systems, and they also need some luck. Perhaps the notion of luck in this context sounds silly? But for many children born into the old stereotype of a Romanian orphanage, or into a civil war somewhere, or into any number of circumstances that could exist in any part of the globe, the suggestion that they could have had access to a loving, caring, supportive family structure is what really sounds silly. Although playworkers cannot assume that the life of any child with whom they work has any of these components, particularly in the context of practical playwork, what they can assume, by viewing a child through the lone organism prism, is that it will be driven to develop means of communication, of building relationships, and attracting other children or other species to it if it is ever to escape its solitary situation. And what are these means? Of course they are the spoken word, body language, meta-communication, being novel and being mobile. Without every one of these, *unfettered* communication is not possible.

The spoken word is what children are developing and rehearsing when they are engaged in communication play. It can take the form of simple noises, which form the beginning of deliberate sounds; it can be the formation of words themselves; it can be the repetition of fun noises and words, or songs, stories, poems and rhymes. But more than each of these, communication via the spoken word relies on expression, on intonation, emphasis, pitch, affective content, clarity and accent. Exploring, testing and absorbing these are the subtle content of much of children's communication and social play. For, in this context, language is not something children hear, rather it is something they interpret, in conjunction with other forms of communication.

Body language, for example, gives them an indication of the feelings and intent of the communicator. How they sit, where they put their hands and arms, where they place their legs, whether their head is back, forward or to the side will all go into the computation when a child is trying to understand what another child or adult is trying to communicate. What we try to communicate is vastly complicated. Communicating love, or hate, or gratitude, for example, requires children to attempt to express feelings that may be impossible using the spoken word alone. Nevertheless, the child still needs to learn how to express itself in these incredibly complex areas and, similarly, it needs to learn how to read others' expressions when they are being communicated. Body language is one method we have developed to add something to our language to express more than we are able to say.

Meta-communication enables children to add yet another layer to what we are trying to express, through changing facial expressions. Smiles, grins, grimaces, scowls, all communicate different messages which, when combined with the spoken word and body language, more accurately convey what children are actually trying to communicate. It is vital for each human child to be able to read what is being communicated to it via this triple prism, and to communicate to others using it.

Perhaps what is even more critical to the young child is the development of the skills that enable them to discriminate between, for example, what is being said, and the truth, or otherwise, of what is being said. The words say one thing, but the body language or meta-communication may say another. 'Of course I love you' may be the words, but do the eyes, the body or the face convey what the words imply?

In a training session I ran some years ago, a young male playworker described feeling that he had been sensorily deprived as a child by his parents, because of their persistent lying. He knew they were lying because he could read their meta-communication!

BREAKING OUT

Because play is the art of the experimental – because it is non-detrimental, because it is the mode of the explorer, because it allows for endless repetition and variation, because you can't fail and because it can be fun, and certainly interesting – so it is the tool human beings have evolved to embark upon a journey of breaking out of their hermetic bodily package and establish links with others.

However, another ingredient in the communication equation is mobility. For communication is all very well if everyone the child wants to communicate with comes to her. But what if she has to go to them? To reach another space from the one she currently occupies requires mobility, balance, co-ordination, calibration, spatial awareness, and even mental mapping skills. Each of these attributes is best acquired through a playful interaction with the world.

(Perhaps I should emphasise here that playworkers should not only be very sensitive to the need for children to have each of these communication skills, but they should be even more sensitive to the catastrophe of *not* having them. Honing communication skills is hard enough when one has sight or hearing, for example, but developing communication skills with a sensory or mobility deficit is many times harder.)

256

Communication requires effort, and the effort expended needs to be acknowledged in some way to justify its continuation. The good play environment, will enable and stimulate children to travel and traverse many interesting routes successfully, in their quest for communication and mobility skills. It will be a space in which it is acknowledged that children are exploring language and experimenting with it. It should be a space in which the complexity of mobility is acknowledged and facilitated in as many ways as possible.

Also, we must remember that children need to be able to make mistakes, to hurt each other and themselves, to see the look on the other's face and experience how that feels for themselves. Humanity is more about shared errors than it is about shared perfection, and the play space is the specified error ground in which that kind of learning can take place.

There will be times when children will actually prefer to return to the lone organism mode. Tiredness, frustration, a need for solitude, a time to think things through, the peace of tranquillity, all require separation from the crowd. However, most of the time these are moments of choice, times when children choose to separate themselves from those with whom they have relationships. For that choice to exist, the lone organism needs the opportunity to play, to develop the skills that enable it to make connections with others. Only then will it be able to control how lone it chooses to be.

From a playwork perspective the use of the term 'organism' is also very important. For, all too often, we forget that human children are biological as well as social or cultural entities. Using the term 'organism' helps to remind the playworker of a child's biological identity. It reminds us that as well as needing the social and cultural trappings of family, friendship, art and education, children also need energy and nutrition, warmth and shelter, clean air and especially they need to play. The term 'organism' also serves to remind us that much of what they need to engage with, and discover and explore through playing, is not so much to do with other human beings, as it is to do with sharing a planet with many other creatures, other living things and other systems. Finding a comfortable sense of place within that planetary diversity, particularly given our galactic insignificance, is crucial to mental health.

And unless children are able to perceive themselves as organisms too, unless they recognise that they are one among many, and act with

257

respect to non-human flora and fauna, they may unwittingly engage in the destruction of many of these things. And, as a consequence, they may be faced with an increasingly impoverished play space and an increasingly negative play prognosis.

THE HOSTILE PLANET

Although it is obvious that at birth, the human child is vulnerable to violence, disease, starvation, etc., what we may forget is that hostility is always present, and that because of that human organisms need to develop physical and psychological defences against it very early on in their lives if they are to survive and develop.

Something that is less obvious is that play is a generic human tool. Irrespective of where a child is born or what culture she is born into. It is a mechanism that makes it possible for her to adapt to wherever it is she finds herself, and in enabling her to interact with her local environment, to learn the in-depth nature of where she is. So, whilst gaining knowledge of tigers, snakes, spiders, earthquakes, tidal waves and changing meteorological conditions will be priorities for some human children, for others the major hostility priorities may be traffic, economics, pollution, guns, lack of space, or potential human predation, sexual abuse or even slavery.

In order to be able to overcome the problems associated with environmental hostility and develop the skills to enable adaptation – both to where they are, and to where they might subsequently go – children need to be able to play in spaces which reflect the various hostile characteristics in some way. Exposure to them will mean that children can explore them, gain an understanding of how they work and develop strategies for avoiding, confronting or, in some other way, solving the problems they present.

I do not mean that a play space should contain hazardous ingredients, but I do mean that children need to quickly become aware that 'hostility' exists in many forms and that they need to be prepared for them in a general sense. I am reminded of a quote in Sylva (1977), which says, 'What is acquired through play is not specific information, but a general [mind] set towards solving problems that includes both abstraction and combinatorial flexibility' (p. 60).

Through playing, the child is engaged in the following proposed equation:

Play + Environment + Experience + Evaluation = Molecular/ Atomic Building Blocks (applicable to most similar situations)

In short, playing in appropriate circumstances enables the child to do two things. First, it enables the creation of the neuronal networks that make high-speed computations about new situations possible. Second, it enables the application of the resultant potential for higher skills that make the analysis of problems possible in the first place. So play builds, as well as uses, the brain (Sutton-Smith 1997).

Another useful characteristic of a 'good' play space, in this context, is its unpredictability. If the space the playworker creates is predictable by children, it will certainly be a comfortable and secure space, which may be an asset to some children, but it may not present the hostile challenges or adaptational problems children also anticipate, and may not be very useful as far as adaptational skills are concerned as a result. Unpredictability injects the 'unknown' into the child's evaluation mechanisms – a kind of 'what if?' ingredient, that means children will learn not to put all their eggs in the one predictive basket, but will learn to hedge their bets, and draw their judgements from the numerous possibilities that present themselves, rather than from perceived certainties.

One great advantage of playing within a changing and unpredictable environment is that the child is able to build up a vast reservoir of different responses to different conditions and situations, some that are only slightly different to one another, and some that are markedly different. Then, if adaptation is required because of a change of circumstances, the child is able to use the facility of combinatorial flexibility (see Chapter 5) to mix and match potential solutions to her adaptational dilemma, until she finds a solution that fits most, if not all, of the requirements of her adaptational problem.

Children have to be able to develop the building blocks that enable them to address whatever problems and adaptational contexts that confront them. These may include wars, natural disasters, domestic violence and abuse, as well as the more mundane issues about growing up, moving house and learning to cope in a new class at school. One important feature of children having access to good play environments is that, if the adaptational problems they experience are simply person or place specific (i.e., they need to learn how to deal with a particular individual, say, a bully, or a particular place, say a housing development where there are lots of dogs, or cars) then they will develop a strategy for dealing with those particular situations. However, how they do that will not necessarily be applicable in other, even similar, circumstances. But if they are given a comprehensive, challenging and unpredictable play experience, it will not only equip them for their specific location but will provide them with a foundation for solving similar problems anywhere.

If a child is only adapting to a narrow range of local problems, she will get a very biased view of the world, which could be disabling in a broader context. For example, part of the play experience is about ranging, i.e., journeying to places outside of one's immediate area of experience. If ranging – whether physical or psychological – does not happen, then little of the variety and diversity of the world outside of the child's experience will be discovered and the child may, understandably, think that the world he or she knows, and his or her learned responses to it, are appropriate and applicable everywhere. Then she may discover that much of what is appropriate behaviour locally, given the circumstances that need to be addressed there, is totally inappropriate somewhere else, where nothing like those problems exist. A good play environment addresses this disparity early on, and whilst it may not be able to correct the experiential imbalance the child is experiencing, it can let the child know that the narrow world of, say, bullies, dogs and cars is not remotely representative of what is in the world, even a few miles away. People may speak with a different dialect, the topography might be different, customs and local culture may vary, even the micro-climate may be significantly different.

Obviously, this puts an onerous responsibility on the play space to continually address the child's need to range, to expand its depth and diversity of experience, and to see its own problems in a context of change and optimism, rather than in one of predetermination, narrowness and pessimism. However, this does require that playworkers are consistently active in attempting to evaluate the play space's effectiveness and developing and re-developing it, to ensure its continued relevance. As the earlier Sylva quote implies, play teaches children to expect the unexpected.

THE MIDDLE OF NOWHERE

Even if the child is successful in making friends and communicating successfully, and even if it does develop survival strategies appropriate to its needs, it still has one more very difficult problem to contend with. I refer to Grof's (1975) 'agonising existential crisis', and how it relates to the child's realisation that she is a 'vulnerable, impermanent and insignificant organism'. How can playworkers help children to deal with this psychic nightmare? Play and playwork can help children to address this problem on several levels simultaneously. For example, playworkers can ensure that both the resources and the atmosphere exist for children to engage in deep play, so that they can come to a realisation and analysis about what mortality is – not just the realisation of their own mortality, but that of friends and loved ones too. I am reminded of the horror on the faces of many playworkers I have trained when we have discussed the need for children to engage in deep play, where children are able to engage in different forms of risk-taking behaviour, as a natural tool for coming alongside the notion of death or near death. Yet without experience of factors that contribute to death – height, speed, strength, aggression – how can children learn to avoid it and perhaps, even more importantly, how will they learn to know the value of life? Adults forget, perhaps, that unlike old age, 'two point four' children, mortgages and jobs, which all come later, children need the metaphysical wherewithal to deal with death, their own death, from the moment they become conscious of it as a possibility. From relatively early on in life, nature provides them with the medium through which to explore this inevitable consequence of life. Deep play – as well as being thrilling and exciting – provides children with the closest possible access to real risk, whilst minimising unforeseen danger. The child is in control of how far the experience should develop – she is in control of her own level of fear.

Alternatively, perhaps, deep play is less about experiencing near death, than about experiencing, and thereby blunting, the impact of real fear, the cancer that eats away at lives, long before they become consumed by disease. The only difference between play-induced deep experience and life-induced experiential fear is that because it is play, the child is able to make stage-by-stage decisions about the development of a deep play experience, and her own immersion into it.

1   There is the tree, shall I try to climb it or not?
2   Shall I try to climb it today or another day?
3   After each foot of ascent, at each branch junction, as each new vista is revealed, the child is free to ask 'do I want to proceed?'. And free to decide 'No! This is as far as I want to go.'

However, the middle of nowhere is not only about death. Death is not the only ingredient of the 'existential crisis'. For as well as having to contend with the reality of its own and everyone else's mortality, the child also has to contend with the frightening realisation of being marooned on a planet, circling the sun, in the middle of the solar system, etc. Where the planet on which he is marooned is subject to enormous turbulence – both from without and within – and which, it is predicted, will eventually be consumed by its own sun. We only need to watch any of the many 'space' documentaries on TV to know that the crisis is also about insignificance, and about 'whether there is a point to anything'.

I am trying to outline throughout these pages my contention that, among other things, play has been selected because it provides support to human beings in coming to terms with what and where they are, and giving them some control over, and an understanding of what is happening to them. That, through their playful interactions with their physical and psychological environments, they develop an individual and collective relationship with them, which enables some meaning to be made of their existence.

However, if some children are play-deprived or if their play is adulterated, then these perceptions may not be able to be held by them. Wilber (1996) provides us with a scholarly analysis from which I infer that if one of play's effects *is* to enable humanity to feel 'at ease' with its situation, it has only met with partial success. In fact, he assigns a great deal of our history of conflict to our collective and individual inability to cope with the huge and devastating realisations of our circumstances.

The solution, Grof (1975) suggests, to the 'middle of nowhere' conundrum is that children 'transcend' it, and I certainly believe that access to diverse and authentic play experiences throughout childhood can help children to look further than their mortality. I also believe there is a spiritual or psychic dimension to play that enables an appreciation of life which is more than just rational.

262

Some years ago, on a working holiday in the Western Isles of Scotland, I stepped out of the caravan I was staying in, into the blackest night I had ever experienced. Then I discovered, as my eyes became accustomed to the darkness, that the sky was ablaze with stars, something I had never encountered to such an extent before. The feeling I experienced in the face of that void was one of great joy of being a part of a magnificent interstellar hologram, rather than simply a solitary member of an isolated species on one planet.

This incredible and vast context in which we journey through life offers us a perspective of what is valuable and important, as much spiritual as it is material. This marks an evolution in playwork itself. For, even as recently as a decade ago, to have mentioned the terms 'playwork' and 'spiritual' in the same breath would have been viewed by many as unacceptable. Yet now, primarily through the work of Sturrock and others, who have brought the depth psychologies into our frame of what playwork is struggling to facilitate, the spiritual dimension of existence is also a playwork consideration.

CONCLUSION

What this construct attempts to provide for the playworker is a contextual baseline, which helps to explain why play has evolved, and been selected in the first place. It does not claim to be the only construct or even the best, but from a playwork perspective it attempts to be the most helpful at setting the scene for different interventions should they be viewed as necessary.

CHAPTER 10

THE EVOLUTIONARY PLAYWORKER

What does an Evolutionary Playworker do, why that, and why in that way? What they do can be summed up as:

- Reflect
- Prepare
- Modify
- Observe
- Intervene
- Respond

These topics are the subject of this chapter.

REFLECT

This really means thinking about what is happening in the play project, and what if anything you and/or the rest of the team ought to be doing about it. Inevitably your thinking will not just be informed by the actual events, it will also be affected by other considerations like, is what is happening expected, if not what did you expect, what has changed, could you have done things differently, and so on? Reflection is just about staying connected with the general dynamic and ambiance of the project, *and* with the individual events that make them up.

First and foremost, you want the project to offer the children who come access to good, high-quality, diverse play experiences. So your first reflection is 'Is it?' The second is 'If it isn't, why not, and what can be done to change that?'

The real skill is in acknowledging that your main job is ensuring that a diverse range of play experiences is available and that the children

264

can access them. I say the real skill simply because it's very easy to get diverted from this core function by the thousand and one other issues that populate the playwork day. Parents, colleagues, managers, trainers, the children, safety and finance, all vie for your attention. It is essential that the actual point of the exercise is *not* subsumed by these secondary matters.

Spend at least thirty minutes reflecting on the day to come, and the same amount with the team, identifying and exploring any problems that have arisen – whether to do with construction, or behaviour or some other issue. Walk through the space, listen and look, and use your senses to trigger your memory of the previous day. Then write down what your priorities are for the day ahead.

Playwork reflection is a meditation that incorporates an immersion into both the play space, the children who play there, and into one's own childhood. Imagining that it is you at play in that space helps the playworker to assess how good the space is for play, by testing it against the echoes of the child within, as well as the needs of the child without. Here you are looking for recollected emotions – feelings that are fleeting, but still possible to evoke. The skill here is in being honest with what you do feel.

PREPARE

People will ask you, what do you do all day? You may be panicked into justifying your time and what you do with it. Don't be. Following reflection, the playworker must prepare the site for the day ahead. This happens in two forms, short term and longer term.

Short-term preparation is about removing hazards, cleaning-up, doing minor repairs, making tools and materials available, ordering things, warming the place up, checking the First Aid equipment, restocking the Tuck Shop, collecting scrounged materials, and generally getting the space ready for children to engage in what is, for them, a period of crucial behaviour, which needs to be as well serviced as possible.

Jobs should be allocated to other team members, and confirmation sought that they are clear about the day's priorities and the reasons behind them.

Preparation is always undertaken before the children come to the setting – certainly before they are let in.

Like reflection, preparation is also a meditative experience. Here you are trying to ensure that the setting presents itself in a way that children find interesting, stimulating and surprising, but also familiar and emotionally comfortable. This means being thorough, keeping promises, and ensuring that children are not disappointed. One of the most effective ways of doing that is to imagine playing there yourself, by going through it in your mind. Do not actually play – it will be phoney. This process will remind you of the previous day's events, and conversations you may have had, that have a bearing on today's preparation. Take care not to let children down by forgetting to do something which has been promised.

MODIFY

Preparation in the longer term involves modification. What this means is changing the setting in some way, and this can be done before the children arrive, or when the children are there – generally with the objective of involving them in it.

Modification can mean a minor or a major alteration. It might entail something you have decided to do in discussion with the children, something they want to happen. On the other hand it might entail major building or enhancement, that has arisen from your reflection, and could include structure building, changing an indoor environment, painting, digging a hole, or whatever.

The skill with modification is about scale and permanency, All too often, building – structures, swings, towers, slides – dwarfs the children and can make them feel overwhelmed and insignificant. Certainly some things can be huge, and a quantity of huge is OK. However, when it becomes anti the child, when huge is all or most of what there is, then the playspace has simply morphed into an extension of the playworker's own needs, and the point of the exercise has been lost. Remember, huge is a relative term. This is not referring to what you regard as huge, but what is huge relative to the size of the children attending.

Modification might mean undertaking and completing a job in a day; it might mean the gradual changing of an area over time, where the

266

playworker observes how the children use the modified area and bases further changes on what s/he observes. It all depends on the rationale for modification in the first place. Normally the point will be to create access to an experience that otherwise would be absent.

Modification is also used to make a space offer a more comprehensive range of certain experiences. So there won't be, for example, just one place where you can climb or swing but several places offering different climbing or swinging experiences.

Permanency is another issue. To reflect the diversity and novelty of experience that children would normally encounter when ranging, the play space must be continually evolving and changing. This is impossible if the modifications undertaken are big and permanent. With good creative design, children can get the same, if not better, experiences of risk, flight, height, movement and so on, from impermanent, smaller structures as from bigger more permanent ones.

Major modification where the target for change, or even demolition, may have an important history, should be accompanied by a goodbye ritual, which, depending on how the children feel, can either be dramatic or low key. In any setting, modification is essential if novelty is to be maintained, but be under no illusions about the power of such changes. In the wild, children will often frequently revisit sites of particular interest to them – an old tree, or riverbank – to reaffirm the link they have as they grow older. Such revisitation is not possible in an artificial setting, so the loss of treasured psychic icons must be recorded in some authentic way. The children will show you how.

What modification means is taking a space that has been designated for play and changing it so that the features which it then contains more accurately address the assessed play needs of the children who will play there. Environmental modification is a continuous process. It attempts to address the needs of the children as they change, as they grow up and as new children arrive. It is also a dynamic that the children themselves will engage in with the playworker or in their own right.

Part of the rationale behind modification is that, if children are an intrinsic part of a constantly changing space, then change will become a part of their own internal dynamic and this will positively impact on their ability to adapt. Their involvement not only makes an important contribution to some of the essential physical environmental change that keeps the play space interesting, it also oils the wheels of the child's own adaptation, a core essential of the play process.

Sylva (1977) described play as a dialectic relationship with the environment, which 'natural selection would favour'. Although this 'dialectic' could take a sensory form, it could also take the form of one or more play types, assuming of course that the modified play space facilitates them. This dialectic could be described as a continuously flowing exchange between the 'soul' of the child – in a whole variety of forms, depending on the play type in which the child was engaged – and the 'essence' of the environmental feature the child was having a dialectic with, whether that was a tree, a fire, the act of painting or a conversation.

What might happen during Sylva's dialectic is that as the child plays with its environment – remembering that play is a very particular mode of interaction that requires the child to freely immerse herself in the experience in which she is engaged – information about the nature and the changing nature of that environment is absorbed by the child through its senses, at an atomic or sub-atomic level.

In other words – and Jones (1993) deals extensively with this nature/nurture dynamic – one of play's functions could be that it acts as a kind of intelligence-gathering mechanism for adaptation. This means that sensory or immersion information absorbed whilst playing is not only used to enable the child to have an immediate forecast of its environmental conditions on many different levels, but that it is also used to provide the child with longer-term forecasts, stored genetically and utilised for adaptive purposes. Perhaps the child as a biological entity draws on the information it has gathered to make cellular changes or adaptations to its physiology and/or its behaviour, in order better to survive as environmental or other conditions, weather, for example, change. Perhaps *this* is why natural selection 'would favour the most playful individuals' (Sylva 1977).

In the last paragraph I used the term 'on many different levels'. This theoretical capacity to access information in numerous forms simultaneously is, for me, one of the absolute beauties of human play. Many scientific instruments can sense, identify and measure all manner of things, from colour, to wavelength, from mass, to pressure. But the human child at play probably does each of these and many, many

268

more at the same time – that is one of the reasons why working with children in playwork situations is as awesome as it is. For example, let us say that a child is engaged in creative play. What is creative play if we begin to unpick it? Let us say that the child is painting, with a brush and with a variety of colours. What can painting tell the child?

- There are different ways of holding the brush.
- The different holds create different strokes.
- Strokes can be deliberate and controlled.
- Strokes can be tentative and fragile.
- Strokes can express sensitivity.
- Strokes can express anger.
- Strokes can create images.
- Some images symbolise figures, like parents or pets.
- Some images symbolise places or spaces.
- Co-ordinated movement can form representations of reality and fantasy.
- There are different colours.
- Colours can differ fractionally.
- Colours can differ dramatically.
- Colours can be mixed.
- Mixed colours produce an infinite variety of other colours.
- Like strokes, colours can express anger and other emotions.
- Colours can express beauty.
- The sky can be painted using many different forms of blue.
- The sky can be other colours, too, and grass can be red.
- Houses can fly.
- The sun can be touched.
- Painting can be representative, impressionistic and abstract.
- To paint something 'good' requires a unity of physical discipline and psychological clarity.
- The act of painting is very satisfying.
- The act of painting is very exciting.
- The act of painting is very frustrating.

The list goes on. Painting tells the child a great deal about the nature of existence.

- There are many ways of doing things.
- There are no right ways.
- The child is in control.

- Painting has affective, i.e., emotional, content.
- Painting has representational content.
- Painting has symbolic content.
- The child can move from reality to fantasy and back again.
- There are many different viewpoints, there is no right one.
- Huge and tiny changes can have similar impacts.
- Affect can be expressed physically and creatively.
- No perception is the only correct one.
- Reality can be rearranged.
- Practice and application opens doors into rooms of greater complexity.
- Painting has cathartic qualities.

Even this rather clumsy exercise serves to illustrate that simply painting a picture can tell a child many things and enable the child to access life on many different levels. Less mature children will perceive these things at a proto level, whilst older will perceive them more on a more mature level.

On one project I worked at, children were able to access craft and creative materials at all times. One of our older girls painted a picture entitled 'Cut throat wedding dresses', featuring a bride with a cut throat with blood pouring down the front of her traditional wedding dress. Although this picture may have been a comment on marriage, or on the girl's own life, more than anything it seemed to be about personal control. I assumed she was stating that when she played, she should be able to access any form of information and put it into any new combination, however shocking or unusual. By doing that, by moving through what she perceived as her technical or creative limitations, she was genuinely able to engage in original exploration and experimentation. Not necessarily to shock, but to move into a space that was absolutely new. I think for this child, creating this picture and knowing that it was OK to do it, even though it was so obviously shocking, may have helped her to transcend her current domestic situation and move on.

I would contend that modification helps children to interact with the different facets of a play environment on many different levels. But the modifier, in this case the playworker, must be aware of the need for continuous evolution of that environment, if it is going to retain its neophilic attraction to children. An interesting but static environment may not retain a child's interest for long. Normally, children would range when they play, rather like many wild animals, moving on to a new space when interest – rather than food stocks – becomes depleted.

Desmond Morris (1967), then Curator of London Zoo, coined the term 'neophilia' in relation to play, suggesting that it is their instinctive attraction to novel things and situations that keeps children interested in playing. If this is the case then retaining that feeling of something being 'novel' requires alteration and change on the part of the play space. At another play project, we deliberately moved and hid equipment and props so that children would approach the space in a more exploratory and cautious mode, after we had noticed that their behaviour was becoming increasingly stereotyped. That is, every day they would come out of school, run to the play building and all head for the same piece of equipment, fighting each other off as they went.

I felt that the play space should not be contributing further to any of the children's anxieties and that this mono-directional flow had the effect of channelling all the children towards just one experience. I deduced that if they were given the opportunity to think, by removing some of the predictability from the site, they might be just as happy to go and do something new. Moving things around broke the flow, by slowing it down, and it did appear that children took more notice of the environment as a whole. The result was that the majority of children broke out of their previous 'tunnel thinking' and engaged in other aspects of the play space.

The lesson here for playworkers, play space developers and designers, is that it is not really enough to plant and landscape and build, if that process is just a 'one-off'. Planting, for example, should be continually changing the nature of the environment, perhaps on the basis of sensory characteristics. For example, the first tranch of planting might emphasise plants with smells or perfumes, the second, plants with interesting colours, the third, tactile characteristics and so on.

Landscaping could focus on hills, then gullies and then water, or a mixture of the three. All too many play spaces I visit are the same years later. However, that is not to say that the play space should be the subject of continuous and frenetic changes. Not because it would not attract children – it would – but rather because other facets of play, like socio-dramatic play and some mastery play, building, for example, might be discouraged.

As I have said, for children to engage in what I would consider 'authentic' play experiences, they need to be able to immerse themselves, and immersion is not conducive to the kind of environmental change which feels as if it is outside the children's control.

So change is essential, but it must be 'context sensitive' and should never be at the expense of the play processes that are being facilitated. Social play, for example, which often takes place as conversations interspersed with locomotor activity like tag, is actually helped by the stability of the setting for many children. It is the very sameness and reliability that enables them to relax and communicate on anything other than a dysfunctional level. Insensitive change would interrupt the delicacy of such interactions. It might also fragment the environmental familiarity, so essential to 'off ground' games.

Change as constant and gentle evolution seems most suited to the play space. Where change happens at a pace which is sympathetic to the child's need to adapt, it gradually integrates into their playscape. I would imagine a five-year evolving strategy, where the play space was completely transformed over each five-year period, with some less disruptive changes or essential maintenance taking place more frequently.

Needless to say, implementing this kind of 'strategic rejuvenation' has resource implications that will require the play space to be moved out of the 'begrudged grant' bracket, and into the 'perceived as essential' bracket.

Tools for modification and environmental assessment

Modification, can also be driven by the need to both assess and compensate for deficits in the children's general living environments. Some years ago, I developed some rudimentary tools for assessing children's play and living environments for features that would enable or disable children's opportunity for quality play experiences. They are primitive, and their measurements are comparative, but they do give playworkers a fix, what Sturrock (1997) called a 'North or South',

Sense	Play space A	Play space B	Play space C
Sight	7	5	4
Sound	7	4	6
Taste	5	2	7
Smell	3	2	5
Touch	7	6	4
Total (out of 50)	29	19	26

Figure 10.1 A sensory audit.

from which to begin to develop more accurate techniques. I hold the view that it is better to create a square football that can be kicked about and made round, than not to develop a football at all!

The first of these tools is a Sensory Audit. Initially this requires the arbitrary allocation of marks out of ten for the level of different types of sensory stimulation in and around a particular play environment. In time, various criteria will be developed for each of these tools which will help in their accuracy. Figure 10.1 gives us a simple example of a comparative basic sensory audit.

Where an environment scores less than a predicted norm, say thirty, then particular sensory deficits should be addressed. The second tool is called a 'Spiral', an early prototype of which was developed by the Merseyside Playwork Training Project nearly thirty years ago, from a primary school model. It can be used in several forms. Figure 10.2 shows an example of a Spiral, which can be used to make a comparative measure of the availability of different play types, either in children's immediate home locality, i.e., the estate, or road where they live, or on a particular play space.

Similarly this Spiral can be used to monitor change in three different ways:

- the availability of play types in the living environment;
- the availability of play types in the play space;
- addressing whether or not the play space is actually compensating for the non-availability of some play types in the child's living environment.

273

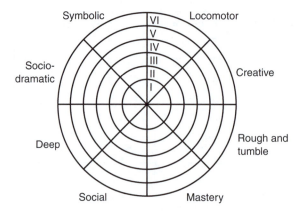

Figure 10.2 An example of the Play Types Spiral.

Other Spirals, Figure 10.3a–c, can be used to measure other factors that might facilitate or inhibit children's access to quality play experiences. Again they can be used to make measurements of the spaces the children are actually coming from, i.e., the home/play environment, and the play space they are coming to.

They can also be used to make comparative measurements to ensure that the play space is compensating for deficits in the general home environment.

Figure 10.4, the Dual Spiral, makes comparisons easier between the quality of more than one play space or more than one local environ-

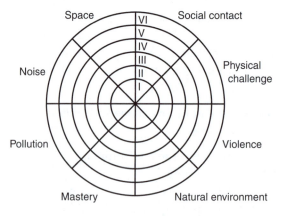

Figure 10.3a An Environmental Deficits Spiral.

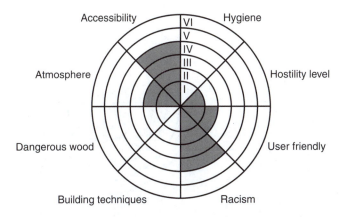

Figure 10.3b A spiral for other types of deficits.

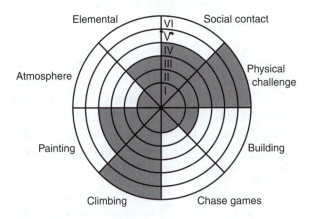

Figure 10.3c A spiral for different types of play experiences.

ment. For example, when trying to make a case for changes to provision on a particular estate, the Dual Spiral could be used to demonstrate that the deficit level of certain play-enabling characteristics was higher on estate A than on estate B.

Each segment on each Spiral provides a measurement (0 = absent, 5 = high). With frequent use, a playworker will soon get used to judging what levels to award each feature, particularly when making comparative judgements. The playworker will find it useful to note why a score of four has been awarded to one play space and a score of three or five to another. As these comparisons are analysed, so a clearer idea

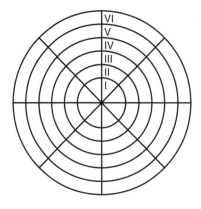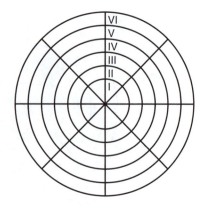

Figure 10.4 The Dual Spiral.

will emerge of what each of the categories means and what the criteria being used to make these fine judgements are.

Similarly, it will help if each playworker in the team measures living and playing environments independently, and then compares results, discussing why their measurements differ. The Spirals have been used on numerous occasions. The final tool is less visual but is preferred by some playworkers as it comes in list form and uses a scoring system of low/medium/high, rather than 0–5, or 1–10. There are two lists. One is called A Play-Enabling Environmental Indices Checklist, and the other, A Play-Disabling Environmental Indices Checklist.

As with the Spirals, scores from either Play-Enabling or Play-Disabling Checklists can be totted up, and total scores or individual compon-ent's scores can be used comparatively. With both methods, local factors, like the relative involvement of particular child populations, the relative pollution caused by a factory chimney, or the relative level at which local children engage in deep play activities away from the play space (e.g., playing chicken on a busy road) can be included for monitoring. Sharing and comparing results will enable these methods to be used with greater consistency and accuracy.

Analysing the results

These tools have been created to enable playworkers to improve the quality of the play environments they operate, by increasing their skill

INDICATOR

LEVELS

Low   Medium   High

1   Elements – water, etc.
2   Natural space – trees/vegetation.
3   Variation – landscaping, etc.
4   Open space.
5   Opportunities for height/movement – for co-ordination and games.
6   Opportunities for indoor/outdoor.
7   Opportunities for modification – tunnels/dens/gardens.
8   Opportunities for creativity – crafts/arts.
9   Range of play types – rough and tumble, fantasy, mastery, social, socio-dramatic, creative, etc.
10   Social opportunities – peers/adults/seniors.
11   Care/welfare.
12   Opportunities for other species.
13   Intellectual opportunities/problems.
14   Peace/quiet/privacy.
15   Security and safety – playwork, surfacing, lighting, design.
16   Visual stimulation – colour, etc.

Sub-total to be carried forward.

Figure 10.5 A Play-Enabling Environmental Indices Checklist.

INDICATOR

LEVELS

Low   Medium   High

1   Incidence of dietary/malnutrition/health problems.
2   Dogs.
3   Traffic.
4   Poverty, i.e., general socio-economic status.
5   Local fear of predators.
6   Long periods of school homework.
7   Noise.
8   Organised out of school activities.
9   Desolation, i.e., lack of visual/tactile stimulation.
10   Psychological referrals.
11   Poor housing stock, interior overcrowding, high density, high rise.
12   Isolation, i.e., auditory/social.
13   Inappropriate/hostile school boarding environment.
14   Compound abuse.
15   Lack of alternative experiences and attitudes.
16   Depressing or oppressive environment.
17   Concrete.
18   Sexual/physical assaults on children.

Sub-total to be carried forward.

Figure 10.6 A Play-Disabling Environmental Indices Checklist.

277

at making judgements during the process of environmental modification.

Applying the Audit, Spirals and Indices Checklists can all help this process, but a playworker's eyes and feelings about a particular space, although driven more by intuition than by methodology, will also be invaluable. A playworker should ask 'As a child would I have been attracted to play here?' and be rigorous with their response. They should ask 'What *specifically* do I like/dislike about the space?' Unless it is obvious – it smells, it is next to a main road, or it has electricity pylons going over it – they should ask 'What is it about *this* space that I do not like?' Sometimes places just have an intangible 'bad feel' and children will pick that up too. Playworkers who are also parents should also ask 'Would I want my children to play here?' If it is not good enough for their children, it is not good enough for other people's children either.

Designated play spaces are statements that say everything about how we view our children's play needs and what priority we give them in relation to everything else. Many serious problems in the adult population were either created or triggered during childhood – problems which access to a good play space or to a good playworker might well have reduced or alleviated.

It is every child's right to have access to good play experiences, but it also makes good economic and social sense. Proper investment in play and playwork could make all sorts of expenditure unnecessary in later life.

OBSERVE

The fourth stage is observation. The play space not only *exists* for the children, essentially they own it. And when they are playing, they will also be communicating not only how they feel about what is there, but also about what they need, which is not there. They will rarely do this verbally, partially because of their own linguistic inadequacies, although they may try (and if they do, you should take serious note), however, the more typical communication pathway is through their play, and this can be observed.

So, what should we be looking for? Play is an anticipated activity on the part of the child, it is evolutionarily programmed in, in this sense

278

– even though it can include cuts, bruises, arguments and the occasional fight – it should be registered by children, primarily as a positive experience. So we should expect happy smiling faces, laughter, shrieks of joy, banter, and calling (see also Hughes 2001).

Play is a drive that manifests itself in different forms that we call play-types. If the environment presents novelty, challenge, creativity, mastery and so on to the children, we should observe them engaging in the proto- and full-blown versions of all sixteen.

In a great deal of play provision, children are well known to the play-workers, so any deviation from, or extension of, their normal behaviour should be noticed and monitored. Play is very exploratory and experimental and children are continually pushing their boundaries, using the play environment as their exploratory medium. (Remember, play was described as [children] doing scientific research (Eibl-Eibesfeldt 1967, 1970).) Just now and again, children may need rescuing from a tree or a high structure.

Children are also driven to engage in games, whether traditional, like tag, or spontaneously made up. Where you notice missing props, or where the connectivity (connections) between the bases needed for the game are either absent, or don't work, review and improve them. A good example here is off-ground touch. Children should be able to chase each other whilst moving around the area chosen for the game. If there are insufficient connections, i.e., places where they can move to, whilst remaining off-ground, the game won't work. Likewise if the connections are unsuitable, i.e., too far apart, not easy to get to, or get on.

Because the point of the exercise is to make different kinds/forms of play possible, rather than to increase their frequency – so that what actually happens is the child's choice and as uninfluenced as possible by any other agenda – it is important that your involvement causes as little disturbance to what is happening as possible. You can see now why a lot of modification has to happen when the space is close, and the children are elsewhere.

Theoretical note

Children assess the play space in two different but simultaneous ways. As a total entity (the play space) and as a collection of individual experiences (water play, fire play, creative play). Thought appears to occur in simultaneous series and parallel processes, not unlike quantum theory's wave/particle duality. This is what has made some observers see play as having quantum characteristics (see, for example, McFadden 2000). This means that they use the play space in that way too – as a play space and as a collection of separate immersions.

As they play, they attempt to construct narratives that reflect this duality and anticipate it. Depending on how comprehensive is the anticipated experience, play should flow using the whole space, whilst dipping into the separate areas. The rate of flow will vary, depending on the novelty of the separate immersions, the scope for imagination offered by general landscaping for example, and the synergy between the two, the space and its component parts.

Observing this dual dance enables the keen eyed to see where the flow ebbs and flows, and propose alternatives or additions that may help perpetuate it.

INTERVENE

Intervention (see also Hughes 2002) means that for whatever reason, you make the move, not the children. Intervention is normally undertaken when there is a problem. That means either an immediate problem, like a fight, or something that might turn into a problem like name-calling or overt sexual behaviour.

Certain interventions can also be invoked for children who for whatever reason – perhaps illness or bereavement – need special support. Sophisticated models for intervention have been developed; for example, Else and Sturrock (1998) offer this four-part intervention hierarchy:

- play maintenance;
- simple involvement;
- medial intervention;
- complex intervention.

I would also offer the following guidelines regarding intervention. Intervention in children's play is appropriate under a number of

280

different conditions. The *first* being if the child asks for it. That is she indicates that she would like support from or interaction with a play-worker, either by saying so, or by using some form of meta-communication, or by issuing what is known as a 'play-cue'.

The playworker's skill, in this context, is to be sensitive to the fact that children may both expect and need some playworker intervention from time to time. Although I have stressed that the playworker's primary function is preparatory (prior to the children's arrival), and supervisory (when the children are there), children may need a game or a piece of equipment from the playworker, they may be lonely, or an expected friend might not have arrived, or they may just be bored or uncreative or having an off day.

However, there is another perspective on this level of intervention. Smith (1994) states: 'For example, Vygotsky (1978) postulated the importance of the "zone of proximal development" (ZPD) in under-standing how children enter into a social and cultural world. The ZPD is the difference between what the child can achieve unaided and what he or she can do with the aid of a more experienced, probably older person to help' (p. 189). He continues: 'This argument has been developed by Wood, Bruner and Ross (1976). Using the metaphor of "scaffolding" – (also used by Bateson and Martin (1999)) – they have described just how a more experienced person can help, for example, by pointing out salient features of a task, breaking up a large task into smaller components, helping with sequences and so on. If operating within the ZPD, or scaffolding slightly more difficult play, the adult can help the child learn more and play at a more complex level' (ibid.).

Whilst I accept this as a perfectly legitimate offer to practitioners, I feel that it could put the playworker into a contaminating frame. The play space is not school, and whilst learning may be an important playwork priority, what is even more important is how the child learns and whether she retains control over prioritising what is learnt. Play is a process of trial and error in which the error is as valuable to learning as is the success.

Within playwork we generally define play as behaviour which is 'freely chosen', 'personally directed' and 'intrinsically motivated' (PlayEducation 1984). The definition is seen as having authenticity by playworkers because it recognises not only the child-centredness of play, but its experimental nature (Eibl-Eibesfeldt 1967, 1970).

The Smith, Vygotsky and Wood, Bruner and Ross approach could have the effect of depriving the playing child of the valuable lessons that come from learning through playing freely – lessons that make play so unique as a neurological developmental medium (Sutton-Smith 1997, Burghardt 1998, 2005) – by proposing that 'someone older' points out salient features, breaks up large tasks and helps with sequences.

Certainly playwork experience suggests that this would, in general, be an unnecessary intervention. It is not what play seems to be for. It implies that children playing in adult-free spaces will, in some way, be disadvantaged without adult help. Certainly if the child initiates an intervention then limited help should be given, but the onus for learning in the play space should normally be on the child.

However, the biggest problem with the 'zone of proximal development' approach is that adult help will introduce 'short-cuts' to learning that will leave the child with gaps in its understanding or in the neuronal pathways that are formed as a consequence of new learning, that may make it difficult or impossible for the child to undertake similar tasks unaided.

The great strength of play is that, because the child chooses what to do, does it in his or her own way and for his or her own reasons, a task or object is learnt on every sensory level until the child has exhausted the thing's learning potential. This process may provide the child with many, many different pieces of information about that task or object, simply because the child is not aware of any pre-determined way to conduct its play.

If this awesome process is steamlined, if a solution is alluded to or its discovery simplified, what the child gains from that experience is also streamlined and simplified. This may not be a problem if all vital pieces of information from that experience are still learnt by the child, but who can know what 'scaffolding' an experience might omit or how important that omission might be in, for example, adaptational terms?

Certainly when a child asks for help we should respond, but we should be aware that the more help we give the more the experience is adulterated and the more the child may become dependent upon help that would not – in adult-free circumstances – have normally been available.

The *second* condition arises when the child has not asked for a playworker to intervene, but is clearly unhappy, distressed or isolated. An intervention here requires great sensitivity. Children, even when feeling bad, do not always want a cuddle or to be asked what is wrong with them, or 'Is there anything I can do?' An insensitive intervention in this context is often more about what the playworker needs than it is about what the child needs. It is quite common for children to come to the play space to be miserable in peace, when something has happened elsewhere – at home, for example.

One way for the playworker to check if she is welcome may be to move into another kind of zone, a 'support zone' – near enough for the child to be reasonably aware that the playworker is there, say three metres – and watch to see if the child is receptive to meta-signals or play-cues. If they are not picked up on the second or third attempt, and the playworker has cause to be concerned, i.e., she knows things are going badly for the child at the time, then she should move away, and observe.

Judgements in this context have to be very subtle. This child may have lost a friend, she may be distraught, she may be embarrassed and the playworker may be the last, rather than the first, person she wants to talk about it with. So the playworker should be respectfully, not intrusively, concerned. Having said that, movement into the 'support zone' will often be enough of a cue for the child – if she does want someone or some support – to make it clear that she would like to play or talk.

In artificial environments in particular, privacy can be a rare commodity, simply because of the lack of space and the number of children using it. So if a child does give the appearance of needing peace and quiet, playworkers should not draw attention to him or her unnecessarily, but observe from a distance (Hughes 1996b).

The *third* condition arises in more exceptional circumstances, when, for example, a child might be suffering from a condition that makes it difficult for other children to recognise or interpret the play-cues the child is issuing. Using the example of children with Attention Deficit Disorder (ADD), Else and Sturrock (1998) state:

'They issue play-cues to the containing environment as indicators of their commencing internalised gestalts. [If] these are
not picked up in the time the child allows, the return cannot
be framed and either dissipates or prematurely returns and is
annihilated. The child re-issues the cue, now laden with
increasing anxiety. These then repel the possibility of shared
gestalt (because other children or the worker sense that something is 'wrong' and do not play), and return to annihilation
before the internalised gestalt can be fully, or meaningfully
explored. The complete play cycle is truncated and the whole
activity becomes speeded up' (p. 23).

In this example the playworker is advised: 'intervention by a sensitive
worker, where the ... child, assured that the cues were being picked
up [and] as an almost immediate result, the firing off of cues, the
hyperactivity slowed down and adjusted to normal periodicity'
(p. 24).

The *fourth* condition arises when there are disputes between children.
These can be very complex and require great sensitivity on the part of
playworkers, as the situation – which might involve cultural, self-
esteem, status, racial, historical, or any number of other issues – could
be made worse by heavy-handed intervention. At Playground C, for
example, we had children from both genders and a whole range of cultural, economic and religious backgrounds and ages playing in the
same space.

In conditions of such obvious complexity, any intervention needs to
be moderated by previous continuous observation/scanning, hyper-
sensitive hearing and good intelligence. If the playworker is not up to
speed with what is happening in the play space, an initial and speedy
move into the 'support zone' will do three things:

- the playworker will be that much closer to the action, and will
  therefore be made more quickly aware of the current temperature
  of any dispute;
- the playworker's very presence might have the effect of restoring
  some perspective to the situation for the children involved;
- the playworker will have a better idea of the cause and therefore
  the likely method of resolution, i.e., is it a shouting match or is it
  likely to escalate and turn to violence?

Situations involving several children, and which should easily be resolvable by them, can become goaded into escalation and end violently. Once in the 'support zone', if my presence is registered, i.e., the noise level drops, or heads turn, I might lean over and say politely but formally 'Anything I can do?', which is often enough to take the sting out of a situation.

The playworker should try to remember that the dispute in question might be the result of a parental feud or a political event. Children, particularly from minority communities, may feel deeply emotionally driven to defend their (or their parents') country of origin against political ridicule, aggression and media attention. As I write, India and Pakistan are in a confrontational mode that may well be transferred to children where there is a play environment interface between the children of these two Asian communities. This certainly happens between children from communities adjacent to 'peace lines' in Northern Ireland.

Another complication arises if a dispute is being progressed heatedly in a language other than those understood by the playworker. What is being said? What are they shouting at each other about? Is either of them being deeply insulting to the other, saying 'Your Mum …' or something similar? In this situation monitoring and analysis of body language is essential and the playworker should be alert for weapons or a change of posture, which telegraphs an escalation in any dispute.

Abusive language can be another complex problem. Take for example the two Kashmiri brothers I mentioned earlier, who called each other 'Fucking Pakis', or the situation in which a child from a traveller background was surrounded by children from Asian and Afro-Caribbean backgrounds calling her 'a tramp'. These are not the stereotypical faces of racism we know, but in communities of children from many backgrounds, things are rarely straightforward.

Playworkers are taught to confront or challenge racism, but as I discussed earlier, my preferred route is to assume that most, if not all, young children are only following adult leads and have no idea of the possible meaning of what they are saying or what is being said back – it is a consequence of where they live, much the same as are traffic and pollution. I tended not to make a big deal of it until children were older and then I would take them to one side and provide an explanation. The little ones would normally get a 'Scuse me', a play-cue, and a game of chase, to take the heat out of the situation. Now and again playworkers have to take the brunt of racist language. It has to be seen as coming with the territory and not something to take personally.

The *fifth* situation arises when a dispute manifests itself as a fight or if it ends in violence. Children do engage in physical battles, particularly, although by no means exclusively, when adults are not around. The playworker needs to be able to acknowledge this and see it as a normal, although perhaps regrettable, manifestation of human behaviour. As with adults, children renege on agreements, their negotiations fail or are bypassed, and aggression is viewed as a legitimate means of settling disputes.

The frequency and intensity of violent episodes is often a function of the culture and the levels of affect being experienced locally. In each of the projects I described as case studies earlier, violence was a significant and relatively frequent feature. It normally took place between individuals or groups of children, but sometimes it could take the form of a confrontation between a playworker and a group of children, an older brother or sister, or one or more carers. Whatever form it took, it was unpleasant. In some situations playworkers and children can feel very vulnerable to attack.

Conflict resolution: a playwork perspective

Any intervention in a violent situation should be moderated by what I can only call 'graduated caution'. Implicit within that should be the recognition that the playworker's intervention is based on a predetermined strategy, which does not contradict the principles of playwork as facilitating play in an adult-free space. In other words, persistent fighting should be viewed as negative dysfunction manifested in anger, and intervention should be diagnostic and curative. Where possible it should be kindly, supportive, and never taken as an opportunity to be seen as the bigger bully.

Small children

Minimal caution should be exercised if small children (under five years) are involved in violent interaction. However, it should be brought to a halt immediately, with a one-to-one team intervention, i.e., a team member is allocated to each fighter and the children literally picked up and separated by, say, ten metres. Do not take little children to other spaces unless they have sustained injuries, in which case, first aid and perhaps an ambulance may be necessary – the playworker's employers will have a procedure. Taking them further than a separation zone may frighten them and make them feel totally, rather than just momentarily, out of control of the situation.

Older children

Exercise moderate caution. For children aged 5–12 years, my strategy would be that I either pretended not to see them immediately, or I reacted quite slowly. This may sound cruel, but those children who create friction, knowing playworkers will intervene, may become addicted to their protection. Intervention that is too early – and which has not allowed enough time to pass to let nature take its course – or which is perceived as unnecessary, will destroy the play space's credibility with those children who, although 'tough', are not generally bullies. In other words it is vital that playworkers are not seen to 'collude' (Sturrock 1999) with certain kinds of behaviour.

All sorts of children come to supervised play spaces and some of those who come will provoke others and then hide behind the playworker for protection. In adult-free space this could not happen and it is important that the playworker does not destroy the inevitable natural authority of some children in the play space and unwittingly replace it with a 'please Miss' attitude. If a fight continues for any longer than, say, 2–3 minutes, then it should be brought to an end, with something like, 'Excuse me, I think someone wants you over there', pointing in different directions for each protagonist and breaking the cycle the children are in. Only if it continues should the playworker resort to reason, or eventually to her own authority. I once separated two boys who were fighting by walking over to where they were with two fire buckets full of water, placing one bucket beside each fighter and just tipping the buckets over so the water went over each individual's feet – it was enough to completely defuse the situation.

Adolescents

Adolescent fighting, whether it is girls or boys, can be very different to the other two examples. It can be acrimonious, dangerous and unpredictable, and weapons can be involved or at least available, so maximum caution should be exercised. This is definitely my 2011 perspective given the high level of fatal and near-fatal stabbings in the last few years, and various knife and gun incidents on particularly incendiary play spaces.

Playworkers may need to draw on their local intelligence to ascertain what is going on, but they must not try to stop it on their own, whatever their principles. Adolescents fighting may be a matter of face or pride, and bringing a fight to a humiliating conclusion, just because the playworker has the power, simply amplifies in the children's minds that this is not their space.

If a fight is terribly uneven, if one child is on the floor, or crying or pleading for it to stop, it should be slowed down or stopped by direct intervention, appealing to the victor, 'She's had enough', or if that fails, by stopping them by restraint. But if it was fair and needed to be passed through, i.e., it would have happened even if it had not happened in the play space, it is vital that the playworker recognises that any intervention says at least as much about the playworker as it does about the children's behaviour – that we may need to intervene, that intervening may be important to us, for our own reasons.

The playworker should also be aware that because a supervised play space is an artificial environment, with an adult presence, it will attract some children into the vicinity of other local children, when normally that would not have happened. Sometimes the local children may unwittingly be exposed to a level of violence which has not been a part of their normal play experience in the past, and which may terrorise them.

The playworker should also be aware that such children might never have had to develop the survival skills that would enable them to defend themselves. This is a powerful argument for provision to be local. Where appropriate, move fighting adolescents out of the play space, in order to protect other children, particularly the younger ones. If weapons are involved the police should be called, for reasons of everyone's safety, not least that of the fighters themselves.

288

Siblings or relatives

Like other violence, sometimes this just has to happen and very often the only space where claustrophobic disagreements can be exorcised is the play space. These events should be treated in much the same way as violence between older children, i.e., with sympathy for both protagonists, and an assumption that this was probably the unavoidable result of dysfunctional affect between them.

Bullying

I was bullied a lot as a child. It is a thoroughly unpleasant experience, but personal experience of bullying is probably the best reason to resist intervening. I stress the word 'resist'. In the end, if bullying persists, if it is cruel, and a flagrant and continuous breach of the other child's right to play, then intervention is unavoidable. However, like so many intervention judgements it is essential for the playworker to ask, 'What are the valid playwork reasons for this intervention?' My response to that question is that like many of the forms of violence covered by the various headings above, bullying is a form of dysfunctional behaviour, i.e., something has happened to that child that has made bullying an acceptable strategy for her to adopt. I knew a child once who bullied other children unmercifully. I found out that the reason she felt safe to bully was that she had access to uncles who, if challenged by the playworker, she could call on for reinforcements. What I also found out, though, was that these 'saviours' bullied her, they were just violent people.

So some respite for the victims of bullying is essential, but some respite for the perpetrator of bullying is also a playwork necessity. Showing the bully the impact of their bullying, but caring about them too, can – in my experience – have the effect of inhibiting and reducing bullying behaviour. Perhaps except for the very young, it is an essential playwork requisite that children should be left to sort out their own problems and develop their own conflict resolution strategies. It is essential to their own skilling through play.

When this strategy is not so successful is when behaviour is dysfunctional, i.e., when it is driven by affect, and children are less aware of the reasons why they are doing what they are doing, and importantly, when they will have done enough. Then tempered intervention is unavoidable. What playworkers should always avoid is the personal desire to stop fights and disagreements, often because there is a high level of transference happening, i.e., the playworker, because of his or her own childhood experiences, is feeling the pain of the children. They should resist this identification by de-centring their approach in the same way as medical professionals do. That does not mean that they cannot have feelings – acknowledging feelings is also an essential component of good playwork – but in addressing the child's needs, the feelings of the playworker, although important, must come third or fourth to those of the child.

Violence against workers

Whilst this final piece is not really relevant to the notion of playwork intervention, it is a possibility and does happen, so I will look at it briefly. First of all, if children are fighting, particularly big children, then the playworker should take care not to become embroiled in the violence.

Second, whereas with the children the playworker should be flexibly interpreting the situation as it evolves, workers should always have contingencies for the possibility of violence directed against them, or more commonly against their vehicles. I am always reluctant to call the police. In some of the areas where play spaces are situated, the police may not be respected for any number of reasons, and calling them is tantamount to announcing the demise of the play space.

Calling the police also provides a vivid demonstration to the children of the playworker's loss of control and credibility. The most sensible strategy is for playworkers never to put themselves in that situation in the first place. They should not be prepared to work where they are vulnerable, especially after dark. If they are working in an area where violence is possible, they should leave when the children leave, at least until they have a better idea of what might happen.

Difficulties often happen at the most unlikely times. Saturday afternoons used to bring drunken older brothers to projects I have operated. One successful strategy I adopted was just to stay out of their

290

way until they got bored and went away. Another potentially difficult time is just before the play space closes. If problems arise then, the team should present a united front and remind possible aggressors that they are known and that the best thing is for everyone to go home. The reality is that playworkers can read all the books they want on 'dealing with violent behaviour', but behaviour is so diverse, and circumstances so unpredictable, that the situations they are confronted with will almost certainly not have been included.

The best insurance policy is to have playworkers on the team who are from the local area. That reduces the possibility of violence dramatically, simply because they are local, they know the culture and the language and therefore cannot be reduced to 'fucking students', or whatever other label might be used as a dehumanising justification for violence. More importantly, perhaps, is that a powerful link between the local community and the play project should be established, and that can mean that not only are playworkers less vulnerable to attack, but that there is a more comprehensive understanding of why the play project is there and why it needs to be there in the first place.

RESPOND

The final stage is respond. There will be many reasons why children come to play space you operate. Obviously one of them is that they come to play, but there are others that are more to do with their welfare. For example they may be lonely, they may be looking for security, or someone to talk to about difficult or sensitive issues. Whilst I do not see it as the playworker's job to ask children if they are OK – except in extreme situations, where for example a child is losing weight, or showing signs of physical or serious psychological abuse – they should use their intuition to ensure, for example, that their proximity or eye contact is telling the children, 'If you want to talk, I am listening'. Except in the extreme though, it is vital that the child makes the approach. Our job is to operate a play environment, not to implement policies of social engineering for outside agencies. So if the child wants/offers to talk that's good, but if she doesn't then that's OK, it's the child's space (see Hughes 1996b).

A contemporary sensory play audit

I want to finish this chapter with a contribution from Kelda Lyons, an experienced and very intuitive playworker from London. I invited her to submit her version of a sensory play audit, so that the process a playworker goes through prior to modification is graphically illustrated.

What is a sensory play audit?

This is an audit of all the sensory experiences that are available to children on an adventure playground. In other words, a summary of the sights, sounds, touches, tastes and smells. For example, a sensory experience is the smell of food cooking, or a child touching another child whilst playing on the swings. It is written from the perspective of a playworker.

Who is it written by?

I am a playworker with experience of working in varied play settings – estate/school based after school and holiday clubs, a children's centre, open access and disabled children's adventure playgrounds. I started by attending a playwork foundation course that gave me a solid grounding in play theory. I've also attended numerous playwork related short courses. I set up and developed an innovative inclusive project on an open access adventure playground. I have done a bit of structure design and build and lots of modification of play spaces. I have done focused outreach work, fund-raising, consultancy work and run training sessions in mastery and fire play. I have done lots of self-directed professional development including independent play studies, and have been mentored by experienced and knowledgeable playworkers. I have chosen to keep exploring my playwork practice in a mainly instinctive and self-directed way.

Why did I write the audit?

Two new playworkers on the playground I was working on introduced activities that gave the children opportunities to have tactile experiences with each other. I noticed how much the children enjoyed these

292

touch experiences and how it changed the whole environment – it became softer and friendlier. I started to wonder about how the experience of touch makes children feel, and how it affects their play. I then recorded all the instances of touch that I saw and felt. I followed by recording everything I could that relates to the five senses – you will see this on the following pages.

Why are sensory experiences important?

Because I saw that the sensory environment has a strong effect on children and their play. A dull or limited environment can mean that creativity and imagination are stifled and children are not inspired, or do not feel they are really allowed to play or experiment. I have seen children in a play environment where one type of culture and music dominated; they were fearful of listening to or liking other types of music apart from the accepted norm. In contrast, I worked in a centre where staff bought new music to listen to each week; the children there tried out lots of singing and dancing, which then led onto lots of different kinds of play (dramatic, fantasy, role, deep, communication). An environment where children don't get to touch at all (for example school playgrounds, where staff often say 'any touch leads to fighting') means that some children rarely have physical contact with peers, and miss out on the joy of physical contact with their friends.

The playground

The playground I did the audit on is an open access adventure playground, mainly for children aged eight upwards. It is in an area of London whose population has a very high percentage of children. Many families live in overcrowded homes and most children have very little access to green or outdoors space, with little opportunity to roam. There is a divide between the workers from the financial district and the rest of the residents, who are largely on low-waged jobs or unemployed. There are two main ethnic groups who do not mix very much. Schools have large percentages of one or the other ethnic groups. This playground offers a very different experience to the children's often geographically limited, overcrowded and racially divided surroundings.

Why is a sensory audit useful for playworkers?

Because it is the job of the playworker to create, stock and maintain an interesting play environment. Therefore the more informed and aware the playworker is of what that environment consists of, the easier it will be to keep the playspace interesting. The more interesting and varied the play environment is, the more opportunity it offers for children the more suggestions of possibilities there are, the more likely children are to try out new things.

Playworkers can use this kind of audit as a tool to make their playspace more interesting for the children. It can be used on any play environment to find out what the existing sensory experiences are. Once you have a good idea of what is there, you can think about what is missing and what else you could add into the play environment. For instance, if after doing your audit you realise that there are very few smell experiences available, you may want to burn some incense, plant some fragrant plants, cook some new foods or pick flowers and make perfume.

It can also be used to add to an existing audit of a play environment. You can do it to provide an overview, or to look at particular spaces/aspects of a site in small detail.

Let's work on the assumption that the playworker aims to create a compensatory environment, i.e., to create a playspace which aims to provide what children might normally get to encounter in the wild. You could also analyse what sensory experiences are missing in the children's local area and aim towards adding these into the play space. For example, if there are very little green spaces in the local area, you may want to make sure that there are some grassy areas, natural loose parts, plants and trees in your play space.

It may help you to consider what the experience of the play environment is like for individual children, especially when working with children with disabilities or special needs.

The sensory audit explained

I have written a page for each sense, listing the different sensory experiences I observed on the playground.

294

Next to each example, there is one of the following symbols:

*

**

***

These represent the amount of choice or control the child has over whether they encounter, or continue to encounter, that experience.

* The child has the least choice over encountering this experience. It is impossible/very difficult to move away from or avoid.

On this playground there is a very small indoors space. If that space holds an unpleasant sensory experience and it is raining heavily, the child may have to choose between being uncomfortable in the rain or putting up with the unpleasant experience.

Example – noise in cabin, from nearby four-lane road, or pile driving.

** The child has more control or choice than the above.

Example – a child banging a small drum, outdoors. If another child/ren don't want to listen to this, then they can either move away or negotiate with the drumming child to stop or drum somewhere else.

*** The child has the most or complete control over this experience. Whether or not they try it or are near it is completely up to them.

Example – eating a worm, or having a face paint done.

Italics – Sensory experiences which individuals are more likely to find intrusive or disturbing have been marked in italics. This will of course change with each individual:

smell of cake – (not in italics, so read as being a sensory experience that is tolerable for most children).

siren noise – in italics, so take as being a sensory experience that is more likely to disturb children in a negative way, i.e., stop them being immersed in play.

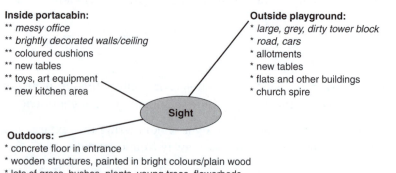

Inside portacabin:
** *messy office*
** *brightly decorated walls/ceiling*
** coloured cushions
** new tables
** toys, art equipment
** new kitchen area

Outside playground:
* *large, grey, dirty tower block*
* *road, cars*
* allotments
* new tables
* flats and other buildings
* church spire

Sight

Outdoors:
* concrete floor in entrance
* wooden structures, painted in bright colours/plain wood
* lots of grass, bushes, plants, young trees, flowerbeds
* colourful boat in sandpit
* shipping containers/portacabin
* lots of loose parts – toys, tyres, rope, dressing up stuff, buckets
* piles of wood
* swings
* chain link fence
** children's camps made with tarpaulins and boards
** fire pit made of mud and breezeblocks
** *floodlights/streetlights*

Figure 10.7 Sight.

Conclusions I came to after analyzing sight:

The visual aspect is more obvious than the other senses and immediately tangible. It tells you about what children get to do here and how people who work in and use the space regard it, and look after it. It's a very good indicator of any existing adult agendas.

The children have no choice about what they look at. So, along with sound, this is the sense where the children have the least control. The playworkers cannot control what the children see outside, but they have a certain amount of control over how the environment inside the site looks.

You could therefore say that when changing the visual aspect of the site, staff should consider what changes they make extremely carefully as it is very easy for adult agendas and ideas to dominate here. What is actually needed for a good play environment should be considered. If you are creating a compensatory environment, you will need to look at where else children go and what else they see in order to find out what you need to add into your play environment. How free the children are to alter the appearance should also be considered.

296

Here are some examples of adult agendas that I have seen/led myself:

'Adventure playgrounds should look bright, crazy, scrappy and messy and I'm going to MAKE IT LOOK LIKE THIS'.

'It needs to look more tidy or people will think we are a mess and won't come in'.

'Let's make it look bright and happy'.

'I can't be bothered to repaint that because I am lazy and don't want to get dirty'.

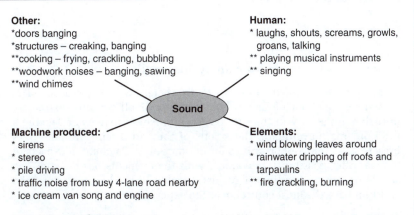

Other:
*doors banging
*structures – creaking, banging
**cooking – frying, crackling, bubbling
**woodwork noises – banging, sawing
**wind chimes

Human:
* laughs, shouts, screams, growls, groans, talking
** playing musical instruments
** singing

Sound

Machine produced:
* sirens
* stereo
* pile driving
* traffic noise from busy 4-lane road nearby
* ice cream van song and engine

Elements:
* wind blowing leaves around
* rainwater dripping off roofs and tarpaulins
** fire crackling, burning

Figure 10.8 Sound.

Conclusions I came to after analysing sounds:

Sound, along with sight, was the sense that the children had the least control over. They had very little choice about which sounds they encounter. After analysing the environment, I came to the conclusion that there are a lot of potentially unpleasant sounds on this playground.

It is also the sense that the staff had the least control over.

Along with touch, I found it to be the most personal, primal and expressive sense. For me it inspires the most joy. The noises that children make were the best to hear, with man-made music the second best. Child-produced noise is extremely powerful (think of a crying baby).

Machine-produced noise was the most intrusive (pile driving, drilling building foundations, the four-lane road near the playground, and sirens).

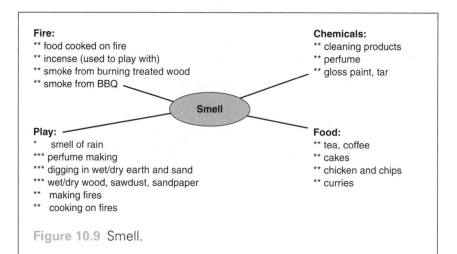

Fire:
** food cooked on fire
** incense (used to play with)
** smoke from burning treated wood
** smoke from BBQ

Chemicals:
** cleaning products
** perfume
** gloss paint, tar

Smell

Play:
*   smell of rain
*** perfume making
*** digging in wet/dry earth and sand
*** wet/dry wood, sawdust, sandpaper
**   making fires
**   cooking on fires

Food:
** tea, coffee
** cakes
** chicken and chips
** curries

Figure 10.9 Smell.

Conclusions I came to from analysing smells:

Smell is closely linked to taste. Smells change with the seasons. The contents of the above four headings overlap. Smell could be extremely intrusive, especially in the tiny portacabin. New smells were lacking a little on this playground. The smells of the earth, rain, fire and grass present good play opportunities for mastery play. The natural aspects of the site offer possibility to connect with the elements on this site. The smells under the heading 'play' also happen to be the ones where the children have the most control over the experience.

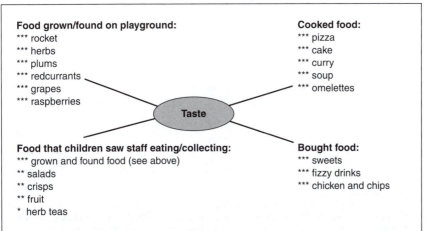

Food grown/found on playground:
*** rocket
*** herbs
*** plums
*** redcurrants
*** grapes
*** raspberries

Cooked food:
*** pizza
*** cake
*** curry
*** soup
*** omelettes

Taste

Food that children saw staff eating/collecting:
*** grown and found food (see above)
** salads
** crisps
** fruit
* herb teas

Bought food:
*** sweets
*** fizzy drinks
*** chicken and chips

Figure 10.10 Taste.

Conclusions I came to after analysing tastes:

The child always chose trying new tastes. It was therefore the sense that they had the most control over experiencing.

If the grown/found/cooked/staff food were not available on the playground, the choice of new taste experiences would be quite limited for some children. Some of them would be unlikely to experience the picking, cooking and eating of homegrown food.

Local shops only offer junk food or cheap chicken and chips.

Children are only able to try new tastes if they are offered or shown new ones, and it is made clear which new tastes are available.

Some good examples of this on the playground: I cooked with freshly picked herbs. Children saw staff eating plums off the tree and then started picking, eating and cooking with them. Staff and children bought and cooked foods that others had never eaten before and everyone had the chance to taste them.

Human:
** as part of role, fantasy, socio-dramatic, locomotor, imaginary, rough and tumble play
*** in blindfold games
*** makeup/hairstyling on themselves/others
*** touching staff out of curiosity/desire for affection
*** dressing self and others in fancy dress, henna and facepaints on skin
*** touch on swings – pushing, bumping, lying, sitting on, holding onto each other

Other touch:
** grass, rope, magnets, leaves, fruit, nettles
** weather and elements – earth, wind, rain, sun, water, sand, heat and materials from fire
** natural materials – wood, spiky plants, dead trees, clay, flowers, wool, stones
*** wax at various stages of melting/warm glue from glue gun
*** tools, knives, toys, wire, sellotape, synthetic cloth, heated hair curlers, dough, chalk

Figure 10.11 Touch.

Conclusions I came to after analysing touch:

After taste, touch was the sense where children had the most choice over whether they engaged in it or not. I observed very few unpleasant tactile interactions. I observed the children taking immense pleasure and having great fun with touch. Tactile interactions were also intimate, enthralling, calming and satisfying for the children. They explored trust and friendship with each other when touching. I thought that the children who have friends they can be tactile with are very lucky to have such relationships. I saw children connecting in a real way with each other (as opposed to having the same mp3 player).

Summary of the sensory audit

Sound was the sense that playworkers had the least control over. Taste was the sense that children had the most control over. Touch was the sense that children got the most satisfying experiences from. Sight was the sense that children had the least control over. Adult agendas and ideas dominate strongly when it comes to sight and what the playground looked like.

Even if unpleasant sensory experiences such as sirens and pile drivers could not be decreased, pleasant and interesting ones can be created and increased by the playworker; lighting fires, cooking different foods, providing incense and musical instruments.

What did I use the results of the sensory audit for?

First I should explain that the results of the sensory audit were used along with other general observations about the kinds of play that were happening on the playground.

1   To extend play that was already happening.
2   To provide opportunities that I thought should be available, but weren't.

Example of point 1

If I observed that the children were really enjoying a particular kind of play, for example having a go at making fire, I thought about which sensory experiences these included, then responded by providing more loose parts that they could extend this with. So, string, scissors, candles, boxes of sand and buckets of water, small pieces of wood, card, paper, lots of different kinds of matches, etc. I would put these things near the children, then stay reasonably close by. If children asked for help, then I might go and join in the play with them. If they didn't want help, then I might just stay nearby. Quite often I would start doing something relevant to what they were doing, near to them. This demonstrated something else they could do, or try out if they wanted to. For example, melting candle wax then pouring it into a bowl of water. In this case, the sensory experiences children were getting to experience were light and dark, heat from the flames, the cold outdoors, set wax, hot melted wax, textures and materials, sounds and smells. This means that the potential sensory experiences they were playing with were enhanced and extended.

Example of point 2

I observed that the children weren't getting to do some of the things I got to do when I grew up, because of where we were in the city; the kind of play that happens when you get to be in nature and go and explore by yourself.

I organised a 'night time treasure walk', making a big fuss about it for weeks beforehand. We made lanterns out of hand-painted glass jars, filled them with tea lights and hung them on sticks. One evening in December we walked along the canal in the dark with the lanterns and torches and had hot chocolate in a café in the docks. On the way there, I hid pre-made packs of treasure in the bushes. On the way back, the children used the torches to hunt for the treasure.

Why I responded in the way that I did

I wanted the children to be able to get immersed in their play. I thought they should be able to extend what they had been doing in the days/weeks/months before and continue the play they had chosen to do if they wanted to. I wanted the children to be able to expand upon what they were doing if they felt like it and have really satisfying play experiences.

I grew up in a narrow terrace house with a small back yard in central London. At school out of London and at relations' houses I got to play in the countryside and by the sea. At school we played in fields in the dark, had animals around us, got to build outdoors and experienced playing in the dark and fire on many occasions. I got to roam a little with friends in the countryside, and roam further with friends in London.

So I know how it feels to grow up in the middle of a city, having to be careful of who you talk to, where wandering is cut off by large roads and there are very few private safe spaces for children. Because of my school, I also knew the magical feeling of being able to run around in the dark near a fire, full of warm food and drink, without adults around, but knowing we could find them if needed. I wanted the children at the playground to be able to experience something as close to this as they could. I couldn't send them off into the night alone, but I could provide the treasure hunt experience that allowed them to be out in the darkness, eat and drink something hot and sweet, play with fire and light and explore their local area with friends.

On the playground I saw some frantic, unfocused children who found it difficult to play and found it hard to get satisfaction out of what

302

they were doing, whether that be a long game of cricket or one go on the swing. There was often an attempt to grab at playing, only to experience it in a way that didn't satisfy, before moving onto the next thing. I thought that if they had the choice to continue and deepen the kinds of play that they wanted to do, then they would have more of a chance of getting really lost in their play and having fulfilling play experiences.

The process between the audit/observations and actually adding new things into the play

I'll aim to describe the process, for me, between the results of doing the sensory audit/general observations and the actions of adding new things into the play environment.

I did observations and reflection on the play session as part of the staff team every day in a fifteen-minute end-of-day meeting. Other staff had perspective, knowledge and insights that were different to mine. This gave me another way to think about, and more importantly understand what I was seeing. Different staff had ideas of ways to do more on the playground. I learnt lots by watching and listening to the other play-workers and talking about play with them.

I did a lot of writing out of work time. If I thought something was interesting I would go home and write about it; my observations, what had happened in the days before and why I thought what had happened was so important. At the time I didn't always know why I was recording these observations; my instinct told me that they needed to be written down.

I was also lucky enough to have someone to discuss play with outside of work. We would talk about what had happened in the playspace. I was questioned about what I had seen and experienced. I was asked to explain how it made me feel and why I had found it so interesting. The understanding of why I found the play so amazing would then happen in a moment, like a spark. In this 'spark' moment, I also understood how the play that had happened on that day linked to the play that had happened in the past. So the things I added into the play environment were a response to the play of these individual children, in this place, at this time.

Behind this understanding of what was happening each day on the playground was everything I had learnt about play over the course of about six years, studying and working in different playspaces.

I was also studying local history. Parents and grandparents talked to me about the history of the area, the playground, their families and their own play memories. One playworker had a massive wealth of knowledge about the area. I had three years of my own knowledge of these individual children, their schools, youth clubs and families. I explored on foot and bike a lot because it was interesting and I like being outside and exploring. I knew about the roaming distances of some of the children, and also to some extent about their play experiences outside the playground. This meant I was able to look at the playspace in relation to and in the context of the rest of the children's world.

All this accumulated information-gathering, reflection and background knowledge gave me a clear understanding of the play that I saw happening, and how important it was for the children who were doing it. This understanding, along with the desire to make the play experiences more fulfilling for children, enabled me to make informed decisions about what were the right things to add into the playspace.

Some of the decisions were planned more in advance, some were more spontaneous and in response to what was happening in the moment. These spontaneous decisions were still informed by this body of knowledge.

What did I get from doing the sensory audit?

- More satisfaction from doing my job.
- A greater love of my work.
- Continued enthusiasm for the place I worked in and people I worked with.
- A deeper understanding of play, playwork and the consequences and effects of it upon the children I worked with.
- Better understanding of how adults can positively and negatively affect the play environment.

Points for the playworker to do and consider

1   Observe the play environment. Do your own sensory audit. Find out what sensory opportunities the place you work in affords each child. Think about what effect these sensory experiences might have on the children's play.

2   How do you think a lack of variety of sensory experiences affect the children in your play environment?

3   How do the current sensory experiences in your play setting benefit children with special needs or disabilities?

4   How do the sensory experiences affect the staff? This is important, because if the people running the play setting are constantly having bad sensory experiences, it might make doing their job stressful and difficult.

5   What can you do to ensure that the sensory environment/experiences are suitable, interesting, and further enhance the play opportunities? What are the sounds, smells, sights, touches and tastes that these children are unlikely to have experienced before? For instance, some children will never have tasted grapes. Others will have never seen, heard, tasted, touched or smelt the sea.

6   Look at Playwork Principle no 7: 'Playworkers recognise their own impact on the play space and also the impact of children and young people's play on the playworker'. What effect does each playworker have on the sensory environment? For instance, what if the playworker keeps going into the small indoors space and keeps shouting jokes and stories? Will it make it more fun or disturb the children? What if the playworkers allow one kind of music/food/culture experience to dominate? What if they constantly create new sensory experiences all the time?

MICK'S STORIES 5

The Addie Arms

Ten-year-old Laura had a condition where even the slightest bruise could be serious enough to mean extended stays in hospital, so she couldn't do many of the things that other children took for granted like 'boarder' swinging, rough and tumble play or camp and den building. In any case most of the dens and camps the children built became waterlogged swamps when it rained, or collapsed if someone 'borrowed' critical structural bits.

We decided to build a solid framework with a pitched watertight roof and a series of bays that formed a terraced street of camps within which everything except the basic frame and roof could be changed and modified. Laura bagged bay one and decided it would be a bar – her parents ran a pub in the area. The playworkers and children helped her with the initial construction of the walls and the bar counter, scrounging old office chairs and various bits and pieces and then left her to it. Every day her mum or dad would drop her off with a supply of squashes, juices, sparkling water, plastic glasses, a cool box full of ice, her cashbox and everything else needed to run what she named the Addie Arms, complete with swinging pub sign. She worked out a pricing scheme based on wholesale cost plus 10 per cent, far cheaper than the local sweetshops, while giving her some pocket money profit.

I passed it dozens of times a day, but never actually went in as I was 'too busy'. One hot August day she said to me 'Mick, just put the hammer down for a minute and have a nice cool drink'. From what was an amazing choice on the blackboard I settled for iced orange and passion fruit juice with sparkling water. I chose music from the offer of cricket, football, news or music on her transistor radio, sat back in the dimness in a salvaged leather office chair, and sipped my delicious drink while a cool breeze wafted through the net curtain, listening to the likes of Ghost Town and Stand Down Margaret.

Two of the dodgier older teenage lads came in and I tensed – we'd had problems with them for weeks, and I was pretty sure they had been responsible for recent playground break-ins, petty cash thefts and mugging children for their pocket money. Apparently completely oblivious to me, they ordered and paid for their drinks and stood at the counter quietly chatting to Laura in perfect mimicry of the chatter in the local pubs. After a few minutes, they drank up, turned round and with a grin and an 'Awright, Mick?' went peaceably about their way.

A play light bulb went on in my head that day, which remains one of my most blissful memories of being a playworker. Up until then, I'd mostly seen adventure play from a very narrow (and male) perspective of more, higher, bigger, faster, exciting structures and boisterous physical activities. Laura's oasis of calm and peace that was equally enjoyed by the older lads was quite literally an eye-opener for me.

And how not to do it

Many years later I was asked to design and build a camp structure on another playground and got it dramatically wrong.

This time the idea was to have a 'street' with a row of camps on each side. As before, only the roof and main frame would be fixed, while walls and so on could be changed and manipulated by the children. The design was more sophisticated with boarded floors laid on railway sleepers, and the frame uprights were on a regular grid pattern so that a range of wall elements (with or without windows, shop counters, hole in the wall 'cash machines', etc.) and hinged doors could be interchanged and moved around quickly by children. The idea was that they wouldn't need tools, nails or other fixings to build and take down their camp, though of course they could use tools and fixings to make creations in and around them. So what went wrong?

The scale was far too big. Though I'd used lightweight composite wooden boards for the walls and doors, the walls were too big and unwieldy for younger children to move around and the drop hinge tolerances were too fiddly for most of them to manage. The regular grid pattern meant that walls could only go here, and doors there. The wooden peg system that held the walls in place turned out to be a hopeless idea – most were lost within days. And last but not least, there was a huge amount of wasted roof space above the camps, which themselves were bigger than the children really wanted.

The camps were popular and well-used for the first few months, especially in wet weather, and a magical touch was added when the playground rabbits colonised the spaces between the sleepers under the floor – you never knew when or where a twitching nose might pop out. But the children eventually got bored with them. The penny finally dropped for me when I saw two children aged about eight or nine carrying a table over to a corner of the playground and draping an old sheet over it to make the perfect camp which could be moved more or less anywhere in minutes.

However, the playworkers managed to transform this white elephant into a structure that was used in all sorts of other ways for over fifteen years. On one side of the street they added levels, small swings hanging from the roof trusses and a scramble net leading up to an opening into an adjacent tower to make a mini indoor adventure playground, still with smaller areas for making camps and dens. The other side became a workshop area where the children could use tools and workbenches to make all sorts of creations.

Eventually the pitched roofs were replaced with platforms connected by a bridge and festooned with flowers in hanging baskets and pots. A full-width staircase was added to one end by the tarmac area and the playground entrance. This became a play and meeting and viewing space in its own right, as it doubled as a tiered seating area overlooking where ball games, hopscotch, wheeled play and playground puddle play happened and children could also see who was coming and going.

Apart from the obvious points that small is beautiful and less is more, on reflection this story tells me that I hadn't learned what I thought I'd learned from years of working on a playground. I certainly hadn't put it into practice, but skilled and experienced playworkers who observed what children actually did and then reflected on it made all the difference.

Costa Del Bermondsey

We playworkers were very proud of the sandpit with a small tower in the centre, complete with cranes, chutes and a rope-operated wooden JCB-type digger that all actually worked. We were also very proud of the splash pool with its water slide that we built nearby just before the summer holiday. They both became very popular with the children in that long hot summer, but for a reason that we never anticipated.

We came to work one Monday to find a queue of children outside the playground gate – not unusual – but there was something odd going on with an extra air of suppressed excitement. One of the children in a doom-laden voice said 'You'll never believe what's happened over the weekend!'. Our hearts sank – we'd had some quite serious damage to play structures recently. At first we couldn't see anything different, and then we saw the most amazing thing.

The heavy 12-by-12 timbers that surrounded the sandpit and supported the splash pool tarpaulin had been moved to join both structures. Around three tons of sand had been shifted and the tarpaulin carefully rearranged with a slope of sand on top of it to create a beach, complete with real seashells. The water slide had been carefully repositioned so that when the children came down it they would create smaller side waves rather than wash the beach away with big splashes.

We were gobsmacked and humbled because we so-called playworkers had never thought of combining the sand and water features. We found out that about twenty children had done most of the work over the weekend, with a bit of help from parents and the connivance of the management committee chair who was a keyholder.

Every day that long hot summer the Bermondsey beach was crowded with children and parents. This was the first time that so many parents had spent much time on the playground – I'm convinced because they were re-inventing and playing out their beach experiences. Generations of Bermondsey families had worked in the local dock and print trades that had now disappeared and could no longer afford to keep up a long-standing history of holidaying in seaside chalets on the Kent coast. The Bermondsey beach was their way of hanging on to a bit of their culture in hard times.

No logo

The Thatcherite market forces and Bermondsey duck-and-dive cultures memorably came together on the playground in the early eighties. Designer T-shirts with 'Bermondsey' printed diagonally across the back became must-have items for people of all ages across south London and beyond, but local children couldn't afford them – they were about £80 at present-day prices. My friend Robert, who worked at a local community print centre, came to the rescue. He brought his screen-printing equipment to the playground, the children brought their old T-shirts or dirt-cheap ones from the market and we printed dozens.

We soon had a visit from 'representatives' of the local company that had originated the craze, who told us in no uncertain terms that we were taking the piss and would have our legs broken if we continued printing them. They made the mistake of arriving when a dozen or so older children were on site. They were outraged and told our visitors they were taking liberties, that they knew exactly where their print works was, and that it might not be around much longer, lot of fires round here, know what I mean mate?

The owners turned up at the playground the next day, apologised profusely and it was agreed that we could continue to print one free T-shirt per child. About a year later, long after the craze died out, we were amazed to receive a cheque for £200 from the company as a donation to 'the second-best printing outfit in Bermondsey'.

CHAPTER 11

SAFETY, PARTICIPATION AND CONSULTATION

SAFETY

Of all the issues the playworker has to deal with, safety is one of the most contentious. Parents are fearful that their offspring will skin their knees, bang their heads or even break a bone. Whilst real accidents bring accusations of negligence and threats of litigation, and leave local authority officers, and those from voluntary agencies alike, with the blood draining from their faces at the thought of the huge figures involved.

Although I will leave it to others more qualified (see book list below) to explain the law as it applies to safety in play settings, the whole notion of safety, or risk-free behaviour, in the context of playing is a contradiction. The simple reason being that risk is an essential component of play. Without a degree of risk, it would not be an authentic play experience. Taking risks is essential if a child is going to learn about the true nature of life on earth. Risk, in play as in life, is not only unavoidable, it is everywhere, and as I wrote in Chapter 9, given that we live on a dynamic planet, in the middle of a dynamic universe, our best defence against serious injury is to understand the nature of risk from as early an age as possible – and that means incorporating it into our play.

There are huge benefits in engaging with risk too. Like circus performers, children's physical and psychological coordination and calibration become incredibly finely tuned when they play in risky situations; children learn to respect the elements, and become aware of their immense power when they play with them; they develop strength and agility; they bond and form relationships, increasing not only their own self-esteem, but their group standing; accessing risk during play not only produces neural matter and organisation, it will probably speed up some neurological processes related to flight and reactivity; it will aid certain kinds of problem solving; develop resilience, and retain play's behavioural plasticity. Playing with risk may alleviate neuroses caused by the fear of unexperienced damage and pain; it will also help children to 'roll with the punches' (Siviy 1997) and will help children to become more flexible problem solvers.

I would define risk as those parts of the physical environment that the child is aware of, which if engaged with may result in physical injury. The important distinguishing feature of risk is that the child is aware that the risk is there. Danger, on the other hand, is when the child is unaware of either the risk, or of the nature of it. The kind of threats that constitute visible, known risk are height, speed, balance and so on. With danger the threats are invisible – poisons, electricity, high-speed trains, fragile roofs, that sort of thing. Children should never knowingly be able to engage with dangers in play settings – although they will when they range more freely – because however skilled or cautious they are, the danger always remains life-threatening, simply because the child cannot reduce the problem.

Risk, however, is an essential part of what a play setting should be trying to offer, but there should be zero tolerance of anything danger-ous, like glass, dog's faeces or unsafe or worn-out ropes and structures.

My grateful thanks to Prof. David Ball, Middlesex University, for recommending and supplying the following reading list:

Ball, D. J. and Ball-King, L. N. (2011) *Public safety and risk assessment – improving decision making*, London: Earthscan.
Gill, T. (2007) *No fear – growing up in a risk averse society*, London: Calouste Gulbenkian Foundation.
—— (2010) *Nothing ventured – balancing risks and benefits in the outdoors*, Devon: English Outdoor Council.
Guldberg, H. (2009) *Reclaiming childhood: freedom and play in an age of fear*, Abingdon: Routledge.
Play England (2008) *Design for play: a guide to creating successful play spaces*, Nottingham: DCSF Publications. Available online at www.playeng-land.org.uk/resources/design-for-play.pdf (accessed July 2010).
—— (2008) *Managing risk in play provision – implementation guide*, Notting-ham: DCSF Publications. Available online at www.playengland.org.uk/resources/managing-risk-play-provision-guide.pdf (accessed July 2010).
PSF (Play Safety Forum) (2002) *Managing risk in play provision – position statement*, London: National Children's Bureau. Available online at www.

safety, participation and consultation

playengland.org.uk/Page.asp?originx_4178si_56947549249695b31j_200791
93740c (accessed July 2010).

PARTICIPATION AND CONSULTATION

The following paper was presented at two conferences. At the ICCP
Conference in June 2010, in Lisbon, Portugal, and the Speelom Conference in northern Belgium, in January 2011.

Pre-empting the punchline: consultation, participation and the death of play?

This short provocation is mainly intended to provide a moment of
reflection on a practice which is now endemic in the UK and which is
becoming increasingly popular in other countries.

My question is: is consulting with children and encouraging them to
participate in the design of their play spaces a good thing, or might it
be harmful and should it be discouraged?

The question may seem a little retrospective, perhaps even irrelevant
to today's children's play lives, given that it was Roger Hart's introduction to his 'Ladder of Participation', in his now seminal UNICEF
Essay – *Children's Participation, From Tokenism to Citizenship*, published nearly twenty years ago, which began this debate for me. His
groundbreaking paper called on its readers to review their approach to
children's power relations and their struggle for equal rights, by
increasing their involvement in decisions that affected them, particularly through their greater participation in community projects.

However, there was something about this essay that troubled me, as I
wrote in my editorial in the *International Play Journal* at the time –
and got labelled a romantic for my troubles.

So what was my problem and why did it matter? My concern was not
that what Hart was suggesting in general terms was somehow inappropriate, far from it. Like him I also believed that children should have a
greater say in society as a whole *and* a greater role in community projects – I still do. However, whilst it made sense to me, for children to
work with adults to achieve common social and *community* goals, he

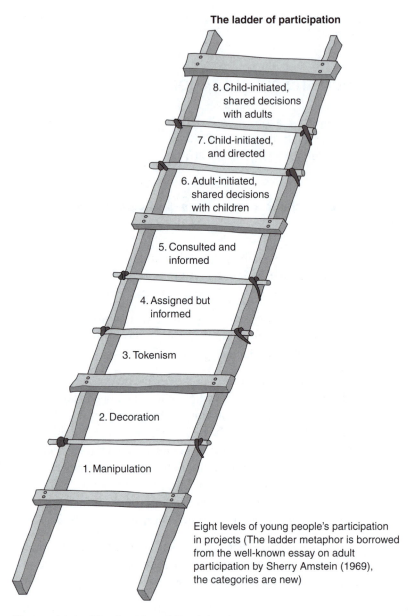

The ladder of participation

8. Child-initiated, shared decisions with adults

7. Child-initiated, and directed

6. Adult-initiated, shared decisions with children

5. Consulted and informed

4. Assigned but informed

3. Tokenism

2. Decoration

1. Manipulation

Eight levels of young people's participation in projects (The ladder metaphor is borrowed from the well-known essay on adult participation by Sherry Amstein (1969), the categories are new)

Figure 11.1 The Ladder of Participation.

314

was also proposing children's involvement in play space development as a way of doing that, something which didn't make the same sense, because it risked being appropriated by those who saw play primarily as a vehicle for community development and citizenship training, which could have resulted in the colonisation of the play space, *and* could also have had the effect of making children feel responsible if the play space under development failed.

In other words, at the time, I was worried that the process of consultation and participation he advocated could have the effect, in a play context at least, of hijacking children's play, and polluting it with what I saw as yet another adult agenda to accompany the oppressive health and safety legislation, equal opportunities, anti-bullying, anti-racism and anti-sexism agendas that were already being applied to play spaces in the UK by that time.

I held a particular view of play and provision for play, which was influenced by my own childhood play experiences and those of my friends, many aspects of which I discovered later also resonated through the literature and confirmed my belief that play was what children did when adults were not around, and that the only time space, particularly supervised space like an adventure playground, should be provided was when the built environment itself did not allow for children to range or to find good play experiences for themselves. It followed that when spaces and supervision were provided, any intervention in the play of the children attending should be both sensitive, minimal and in the children's best *play* interests. If, as Hart wished, children were able to create much of their play space, that was good, but if that involvement was conditional on them buying into an adult initiated and controlled process that required them to describe their fantasies and rationales and then see them subjected to the rigours of legislation and other adult agendas, then that was a breach of play's privacy and integrity and was not good.

Only two years prior to the publication of Hart's paper, I had already argued in Tokyo (Hughes 1990), that of all the rights children needed, other than those to food, drink and security, the right to play unhindered was most important, and certainly more important than the right to participate or be consulted. So that was where I was coming from.

So we differed. Hart advocated consultation and participation, and I perhaps neurotically worried about an adult colonisation of children's play, and if it hadn't have been for further developments, that would have been that.

But over the intervening years a number of things have happened that have demonstrated to me that I was right to be worried. First, over the eighteen years since the essay was published, in the UK there has been a wholesale adoption of consultation with children in play projects as a general practice. Children's consultation/participation is now a small industry there. It provides quite a few people with employment and involves a significant amount of money. This development is a direct result of Hart's paper and people cite that paper as their justification for doing what they do. More seriously, and also as a direct result of the same paper, children's consultation/participation have been made a condition for grant aid for the development of play spaces in the UK. Now most, if not all, local authorities, grant-aiding Quangos, and even Central Government itself, insist that children must be consulted about any play spaces that will affect them before any money is handed over, and many thousands of children have now been involved and are still being involved. However, what is interesting is that although these developments use Hart's paper as a justification for their intervention, at no time does Hart himself advocate involving children in the kind of formal consultations that are currently undertaken in the UK – he wanted children to be more involved, sure, but he never suggested this level or type of exploitation to achieve it – that came from individuals who appeared to hold the view that being politically correct was more important than being play correct – that participation in the development of play spaces was more important than playing on them.

In my opinion this was a hugely serious and retrograde development. Whatever its benefits, until recently play has always belonged to children. Asking them about play is like asking them about nutrition – how can they know? It is not something they consider consciously. Like eating, it is something they just do.

An additional concern is that asking children about play gives the asking adults a say in the child's play agenda. They can argue a case for certain behaviour, language, smoking, risky practices, or proto-sexual interaction to be curtailed or prohibited – in the interests of society or community, certainly not in the interests of the playing organism. A recent UK Central Government Strategic Document stated that from now on (because they were making funds available) children will be expected to treat one another with respect when they play. This is as biologically idiotic as it is politically attractive. Is this the same play, of which Bruner, Sylva, Gopnik, Neto, Johan Huizinga and so many others have written about so eloquently?

Second, the science has moved on significantly in the past eighteen years. Following Sutton-Smith, Beckoff, Byers and Burghardt's recent contributions I think it is fair to say that now there is a higher level of agreement than ever before, that it is authentic, (free) immersed, unconscious play behaviour which is responsible for a whole range of outcomes including good psychic health and neural growth and organisation. Now one can begin to speculate on whether the outcomes of consultation disturbing play patterns, memories, preferences, urges and perhaps the vital neural, psychic, cellular and muscular processes, that are the reported outcomes of playing, might be dissonance, or depression or what Grof (1975) calls 'an agonising metaphysical crisis', in the children involved. And what makes this outcome tolerable? That we adults can feel more secure that the piece of land we have chosen for a play space, or the piece of equipment we want to design and sell, is endorsed as appropriate by the children who are going to use it.

Whilst this is happening, everything I observe or read about play leads me to conclude something else: that play and its outcomes are the result of a conversation with the unconscious, or, as Sutton-Smith (2007) recently stated, 'a consultation with deep seated evolutionary

• brain plasticity/growth	(Byers 1998)
• neural organisation	(Brown 1998, Sutton-Smith 2007)
• muscular growth	(Byers 1998)
resilience and optimism	(Maston 2001, Rutter 2006, Lester and Russell 2008)
• flexible problem solving	(Bruner 1972, Sylva 1976 and Konner 2010)
• cortical maps and consciousness	(Damasio 2000, Brown 1998)
• ecological immersion and spatial navigation	(Orr 2002)
• the development of adaptive strategies	(Burghardt 2005)
• 'rolling with the punches' of life	(Siviy 1998)
• maintaining good relationships	(Pellis 1998)
• good physical and mental health	(Harlow 1971, Brown 1998, Sutton-Smith 1997, Stevens and Price 2000)

Figure 11.2 The bio-evolutionary benefits of play.

emotions'. Play is a fundamental part of our evolution, and this is what consultation is tapping into, but like the BP oil pipeline fracture in the Gulf of Mexico, these things are far harder to stop than to start. Whether we refer to play as games, den building, or swinging, or as Lorenz's non-specialisation, Huttenlocher's brain imaging, Gopnik's Theory Theory or the Brown/Damasio Cortical Maps, these are not the results of activity which is conscious, and can be consulted on – but rather the products of evolutionary currents, of quantum changes at sub atomic level and ancient archetypal influences on what Jung called the collective unconscious.

It is also possible that play material which is biologically sensitive and unconscious could be brought into the conscious realm, i.e., into a Winnicottian 'possibility space', where as well as reacting to its impulses, children may also be driven to attempt to encode it in language, or even to understand and control it. My worry is that by doing that, they will change it, and thus make it impossible to return it to its unconscious location – the effect being that these children will be so conscious of playing, self-conscious if you like, that they may be unable ever to play again.

My fear is that by engaging children in consultations about what they want from a play space, that will inevitably involve them in a conversation about play from an adult's perspective. This in a situation where children are experts and adults are novices, struggling to remember what play was like, whilst still applying adult-based play narratives to children, and creating their hideous Disneyesk attempts at both reconnecting with their own childhood and that of today's children, whilst the real beauty and power of play is avoided as too complex and therefore unsaleable.

We have to remember that although our knowledge of play has increased considerably in the past decade, we still know relatively little about what it is, what it does or how best to facilitate it.

Of course children *are* conscious of the game they are playing, or the den they're building or the tree they're climbing, but their awareness of what they are doing and their reasons for doing them are not adult in form. Rather, they are immersed in fantasy and imagination, and flooded with the emotions of new experience, not the language of legislation and quality criteria that we may rely on. The outcomes of calibration, flexibility and plasticity, so revered by the play scholar,

318

and the mechanisms of different types and intensities of play, that make those outcomes possible, are unconscious to the child. The child is neither aware, nor does she need to be aware, for them to occur. In fact it is my contention that the more the child *is* aware, the less these processes can happen, that awareness is an inhibiting rather than facilitating factor.

That playing is essential for children, that it builds their brains, that it makes them more flexible and adaptable, may be important for we adults to know, for any number of reasons, but for the child, all that matters is the act of climbing the tree, lighting the fire, moving to the music or telling the joke.

Children know intuitively how to play, and what the best play spaces feel like. To them, it's obvious, but it is not conscious. What engaging playing children in an adult process like consultation does is reduce play to behaviour, and their special spaces to provision, which might be fine for adults but could have the effect of rendering the involved children not only conscious of their play, and perhaps embarrassed by its transparency to adults, but could act as a spoiler, in the same way that someone who pre-empts the punch-line of a joke or reveals the plot of a film can spoil those experiences. And that may actually stop them wanting to play.

The possible theoretical dangers not only of disturbing, but of uprooting, aspects of the unconscious, through consultative probing, should not be minimised. Psychotherapists, play therapists and therapeutic playworkers train long and hard to avoid the kind of received information – where the interviewee says what she thinks the consultant wants to hear because an adult based-play narrative is being applied to her play (something I called a stereotypical play narrative (Hughes 2000)). And yet this might be precisely what the consultant elicits from the child.

So is consultation harmful? One colleague reminded me that since most children get this kind of input in education through most of their childhood, they are very capable of adapting to it. However, I am not so sure and I pose a couple of questions to bring this chapter to a close:

A sensitive period is defined by Byers (1998) as a window in development during which specific types of experience permanently alter the course of development. If, as is claimed, this is something play can do, is it also possible that the consultation process can do it too, and perhaps overlay play circuits with a more formalised neural hierarchy?

The different types of play have been described as archetypal. If the influence of those archetypes is inhibited by the impact of consultation, may we see the kind of frustration of archetypal intent to which evolutionary psychiatry refers, and which it suggests leads to different forms of psychopathology?

I think as children's play becomes an increasing focus for governments, academics and everyone else, as it will, we must be vigilant that we do not treat children as consumers of our play narratives as I think consultation/participation can. Not only is play their right, it belongs to them, they own it. We are merely bystanders trying to help, because we know that play is vital to them.

I think I want what most of us and most parents and families want for their children. The opportunity for them to have a diversity of good play experiences, and if that has to take place in environments that are operated by adults and created through a symbiosis between adults and children, that's fine by me. But I genuinely don't think that consultation is the way to achieve that. The success of such spaces will only be confirmed by the children returning to them by their own volition, not by inviting them to put all the right ticks in the right boxes of a consultation document.

MICK'S STORIES 6

The thirty years tug'o'war ...

The local pub that had hosted fundraising and celebration events for the playground (and the second leg of most management committee meetings) was facing closure as part of 'a rationalisation of the assets portfolio' according to the men in grey suits who visited one day. Together we organised a campaign to get as many signatures of support as possible, culminating in a 'Save the Rising Sun' play festival on the adjoining open space.

The final event was a tug'o'war between the playground children and the pub regulars. If the kids won, the adults had to donate £1 each to the playground. My co-worker Paul, who knew a thing or three about friction and engineering concepts, knew that if we had roughly the same total body weight on each side, the much larger number of children's feet would give them the extra traction that would ensure victory.

We ended up with about forty adults (most of them beefy builders and ex-dockers) agreeing to the deal and around a hundred mainly small children on the opposing team. Sure enough, the children inexorably hauled the adults towards the losing line. But suddenly the rope stopped moving in the children's favour, no matter how much they pulled. There was a loud crack as the fence rail to which the adults had tied their end of the rope disintegrated and everyone fell over.

I called foul, and we started again. Once again the children were winning and once again the rope stopped. 'Heave, heave!' we shouted. There was a different sort of creaking and straining noise as the twenty-foot tree behind the adult end started to tilt and come out of the ground.

Thirty-odd years later in my local pub in Islington, one of the regulars said to me 'You don't remember me, but I know you. You ran that playground in Bermondsey'. I didn't recognise him at first, but it was George, who had been in the print trade and had supplied us with vanloads of free paper – no adventure playground in Southwark had needed to buy any for years.

He eventually confessed it was him who had tied the tug'o'war rope to the fence and then the tree – George likes to keep his secrets to himself until the right time. He told me it was still the funniest thing he'd ever seen, and was delighted that I had thought Dennis the barman (and notorious bad loser) had been the culprit all along.

Ramps

George is a wheelchair user these days, and the pub has made a simple wooden ramp that can be moved as needed between the entrance step and an internal step to the beer garden so he can get in and out and around the pub. Carrying the ramp in one night I had another light bulb moment.

I suddenly remembered Charlie and his cousins in Devon spending days moving small ramps that had been made for other purposes around the back garden and the road in the neighbouring close to make bike and scooter jumps. Like the marble races of my childhood, most time and effort went into trying out and negotiating different configurations, though the highest jumps were also important. It dawned on me that staffed play areas could easily and cheaply do the same and have a supply of ramps of various sizes that children could move around as needed. In some cases they could double as disabled access ramps as well as loose parts play items.

South of the river

A few years after I left Bermondsey AP I called in when passing and got a couple of shocks. I recognised only a few of the children because they had grown up and changed much more than I imagined possible. What was even more thought-provoking was that the few of them who remembered me said something (only half-jokingly) along the lines of 'Oi, what are you doing back here, traitor?'

Leaving the playground was bad enough, but they knew I was working in Hackney, and moving north of the river was a heinous crime in their eyes, nearly as bad as grassing. My friend Robert was moving to Turin around then and a local asked him 'Where's that then?' 'North Italy.' 'Norf Italy? Norf Italy?! Could be worse I suppose, at least it's south of the river.'

Tears

It was Sue's last day at the playground after working there for nineteen years. I was waiting outside in the car to drive her and Charlie home. He came running out and said 'Sue's crying all her tears out!' Later she told me that one of the children had clung to her leg and begged her not to leave. But what had actually brought the tears was coming out of the toilet to find a crowd of children asking her to please stay, and suddenly realising how much she would miss them, and how much they would miss her.

322

The attachments that children might have to a playworker (and vice versa) are obviously different from the ones between children and their families and friends, but attachments nonetheless. Most play-workers I know share the experience of being told at some point or other 'It was far better when so-and-so used to work here'. I hope it was mostly said in a spirit of friendly ribbing, but of course you never really know.

Attachment to place as well as people is very important to children's well being. But there can be negative as well as positive aspects to these attachments, for example in the rise of the postcode gang culture. But could the dramatic reduction in younger children's ranging behaviour – down by 89 per cent from what it was only a generation ago – be a contributory factor?

When I was helping to develop a play policy for EC1 New Deal for Communities we held several consultation sessions with older children. Teenage boys consistently said that they moved around in gangs (their word) because that was the only way they felt safe outside their immediate home area. Girls said they moved around in a crowd (their word) for the same reason – and also because their parents would only let them out if they were with a group of mates.

CHAPTER 12

IS THE PLAY SETTING WORKING?

Obtaining the real data regarding whether the play setting is working or not – an increase in brain size and organisation, an increased ability to roll with the punches, improvements in resilience and optimism, greater mental flexibility in problem solving, the development of cortical maps, and an increase in successful adaptive strategies – is not possible in an ethical and rights based society, so we look for the next best thing. Assuming that these bio-outcomes are anticipated by the organism, the child should experience positive affects when they happen and these should be observable in a number of ways, including what I called mood descriptors in Hughes (2001, 2002) (see below).

However, to answer this question comprehensively, we also need to be clear about what it is the playground, playspace, play centre, after-school club, play environment, etc., actually exists to do. From the perspective of evolutionary playwork this is very clear. Play spaces exist to compensate the child either for the lack of freely accessible space per se, or for the lack of appropriate space. So our play settings exist as a compensation for adults' appropriation of playable space for other uses, for example, car park, roads, buildings, transport systems, agriculture, industry and so on, or because the spaces that are available are just unsuitable for children to play in – they are toxic, dangerous, at inappropriate interfaces like roads or residential accommodation, or maybe just plain boring. In other words, the only spaces available for play, in the absence of a designated play space, are spaces that inhibit, bias, adulterate and stop play and condemn the children affected to a type or intensity of play deprivation.

The playability of play spaces is often the last quality given consideration by those charged with providing them. All too often flat, treeless and featureless, they are about as useful to the playing child, as a blank book would be to an avid reader. And although not deliberate, it

324

is a symptom of the creative inertia, and lack of child-focus, that permeates many local authorities.

Can the play space work?

As I have implied throughout these pages, as well as being felt by the children to be secure and predator free, play spaces have to contain genuine stimulus diversity, malleability, elemental access, authentic risk and so on, for a space's effectiveness to even begin to be tested. A play space must satisfy these criteria first, for without that, it just cannot work.

If it does satisfy them, then the question about what the space exists to do morphs into another, 'what signs indicate that the space is working?' The answer to this is also straightforward – children are there in reasonable numbers, and they are playing. But how would we know they were playing? A knowledge of playtypes would help, but our own senses provide a more instantly useful diagnostic tool. Does it look and sound as if children are playing? Play is saturated with different kinds of movements and sounds. Running, crouching, hiding, chasing, climbing, what has been called 'gallumphing' – where the child's gait or facial expression is odd and exaggerated – in combination with, shrieking, laughing and calling out, including the movements and sounds generated by the excitement and fantasy of engaging in a game, a conversation, or a novel moment. If the children are immersed in their own world, where the adult world plays only a contextual or reference role, if their activity flows flawlessly from old focus to new focus and back again, if, in their heads they can change species, or fly, or become invisible, or Super Heroes, if there is continual, even if not obvious, evolution of what is happening, then play is taking play and the space is serving the purpose for which it is intended – it is a play space. If there is a game of 'football' taking place where the team numbers, genders, ages and abilities fluctuate, where the ball is huge and the obvious objective is to have fun, then that is play too. But if the activity is bounded by adult rules, if it is stiff, formalised and dominated by the need to score points and flatter one's ego, that is not play, it is something else.

In *The First Claim* (Hughes 2001, 2002) I devised a set of 'Mood Descriptors' (see later) as a way of making this kind of sensory analysis possible. Over the years, numerous criteria have been developed to evaluate the success or otherwise of play projects. Some people are understandably keen on the 'bums on seats' school of measurement, whilst others rely more on esoteric criteria, like 'it feels right', or 'the children had a good time'. So what is it that makes a setting like a supervised play space successful? There is no one criterion that can encapsulate or capture success. Play environments are notoriously fickle entities.

NUMBERS

Numbers are important, but should be seen rather as a barometer of successfully applied playwork than as a simple measure of success or failure. If the play space is sited in an area where there are few children, then however good it is, numerically it will struggle to be convincing. If, on the other hand, it is in an area in which there is a high birth rate and lots of young families, then however bad it is, it will still probably attract a lot of children, simply because for the children, it is somewhere to go.

Assuming that the size of the space and the staffing and resource levels was at an optimum, then I would expect that for half the time the space was open, it would be regarded by local children as an important enough life component to have a representation of the local child population of between 80 and 120 children. That is if we assume that the site is one-third of an acre, that it has three staff on duty at all times, and an intelligent budget, which caters for consumables, material replacements and environmental modification.

The other half of the time I would expect usage to be more of the 'drop-in' type, where children come to chat, to see their mates, to have a bit of quiet time – a slow period, a more conscious sensory and reflective period. (As a child I would often use the local outdoor swimming pool three times a day in the summer, because each session had a personality of its own. My favourite was the virtually empty morning sessions – when the water was clear and still undisturbed, the air was sharp and a few of us would relish the luxury of being able to dive for coins and just enjoy the glint of the sun on the water. The afternoon sessions were a more classic play period, with lots of other children, and involved games of tag, dive-bombing and water chase. Evenings

326

were more mythical. The water temperature had often risen through-out the day and the pool was now populated by lots of adults, who made big noises, big splashes and big waves. We all joined in, but it was their time more than ours. Needless to say, there were times when we were doing other things and did not go swimming, and there were other times when it was too cold or too wet to go.)

Like that swimming pool, play spaces should not by necessity be seen as spaces that have to have an intensive, round-the-clock usage. The whole process becomes too automated and stops the space being either useful or exciting if it does. I do appreciate the need felt to maximise a resource, but that is not always done successfully by filling it up all the time – benefits and numbers do not necessarily equate. As with the swimming pool example, children can get very different experi-ences from the same space at different times. Many factors – space, light, weather, seasons, time of day, noise levels – affect their percep-tions and the resulting value they put on an experience and the bene-fits they get from it. However, numbers do count. The play space must be being used or it will not survive.

ATMOSPHERE

Another criterion of success is the setting's prevailing atmosphere. If the atmosphere is simply changing from dread to anxiety to fear, obvi-ously something is seriously wrong. If, on the other hand, the space feels too well managed, too slick, too engineered, too predictable, then equally something is amiss. A good setting should be a good mix of the spontaneous, the random, and the planned, and feel fun, chaotic, and reliable as a consequence.

Playworkers have to be clear about what they are dealing with here and what a play space is intended for. Children are not generally dangerous *or* passive. Rather, they are lively, argumentative, inquiring, frustrating, micky-taking, scary, beautiful, compassionate, mind-bendingly funny and painfully scathing, and the atmosphere in the setting should be a flexible encapsulation of each of these and many other characteristics, like being supportive. When that is achieved, when the playworker knows that the children are more or less free to do what they want in the play space, then the setting is doing what it has been created for. However, the playworker does need to assess this over weeks, rather than days, as the swimming pool example illustrates. Keeping a diary is helpful; writing down how the place feels, assessing how you affect the space and the children, noting the weather, the play types that are in fashion, what might be on TV, will all help the playworker's awareness of what is positively affecting the space and what is not. The play space should always be a reflection of diversity and change. Individual playworker's environmental modification and the children's playful interaction with it should ensure that.

At Playgrounds A and C, the attendance shot up and down like dysfunctional blood pressure. There were manic days, frightening days and relaxed, beautiful days, which in totality were a good example of the ecstasy of variety playwork aims for; that no two days were ever the same. If it began to feel a bit flat, we would ask: Is it us, are we getting tired or bored? Is it the children, are they just coming here because it is easy? Is it the space, are we suffering from not being able to see the wood for the trees?

That interrogation would normally lead us to conclude that we had taken our eye off the ball a bit and that we needed to re-engage and refresh. It is worth pointing out, as any parent will confirm, that looking after lots of children is very tiring, especially over long school holidays, and all playworkers will occasionally lose the plot. The skill is in knowing this can happen and in realising when it is happening, so that something can be done about it. In my experience re-engagement is often accompanied by an exhilarating feeling of freshness.

THE FLOW OF MODIFICATION

Another useful indicator of success is an increase in the intensity and frequency of activity by the children during and after a bout of modification. Playworkers engage in environmental modification to increase the number and type of novel foci available to the children's play drive. Modification should result in an upswing in the level of activity as a result.

Environments engage children with increasing intensity. If we create a scale of engagement from, say, 0 to 5, with 0 equalling no engagement and 5 equalling total engagement, the hierarchy would look something like this:

328

Scale point	Level of engagement	Affect	Locomotion
0	None	Bored	None
1	Minimal	Attending	Extremities/static
2	Minor	Interested	Whole body/static
3	Significant	Enquiring	Moderate mobile
4	Interruptable	Happy/absorbed	Fast and free
5	Total	Invigorated/exhilarated	As necessary

Figure 12.1 The engagement hierarchy.

Earlier (see Chapter 4), I described play as a way of learning by absorption, where the play experience envelops the child and becomes the child's world, for as long as the experience is 'active'.

Note that it is not until scale point 4 that a child is sufficiently absorbed in a play experience, for any hitherto, unknown ingredients of that experience to be sensed and retained by the child. This means that a play environment has to have a high level of attraction and engagement before it is performing the function for which it is intended.

Although some children come to play spaces in total play mode, many others have things other than playing in the forefront of their minds, home and school problems for example. These more dominant topics, may interfere with the successful flow of their play drive, and distract them from fully immersing themselves in a game or other activity.

Although domestic and personal issues can have a diversionary impact, a child's drive to play is very powerful, and good modification, particularly that with a high novelty or excitement factor, can have the effect of overriding interfering problems and re-focusing children's attention on the activity and affect of playing instead.

Any good play environment will contain an infinite number of 'potential' play experiences, which lie hidden, in the same way different images are a part of the background in many children's puzzles. However, these potential experiences will not be 'activated' unless the child is able physically or psychologically to cross the environmental interface, which separates her from them. The action of modification provides a physical and psychological catalyst that stimulates engagement and triggers sensory and affective engagement. A high enough level of stimulation will enable the child to continue on her own, and

329

any interferers effectively neutralised and replaced by characteristics of the play drive instead; spontaneity or intrinsic motivation, for example.

The term 'the flow of modification' addresses that outcome. As modification and the children engage, so an activity transaction begins between them, which, as the child is absorbed, escalates in speed and intensity until the child is able to 'spin off' and engage in activity of his or her own choosing. In this sense, novelty and modification are the engines that drive the successful play space. However, the degree to which modification and novelty can overcome the blocking power of any interferer is still dependent on their potential to create sensory bridges between the child and themselves.

However, modification still has to be context specific. To undertake modification without assessing local need is nonsensical. The form modification takes, its scale, its location, its potential for novelty and perceived attraction, given children's current experience, is critical not only to its short-term success, but also to its longer-term impact.

THE PLAYWORKER

The final indicators of success are determined by what happens in the physical and psychological space that separates the playworker and the children. What playworkers transmit across that space, how they do it, and whether and how children reciprocate, provide critical indications of the health of the project and of its usefulness to children.

This space has been alluded to in a number of ways over the years. It has some resonance with Winnicott's 'potential space' (Ogden 1993: 223), and Heidegger referred to a similar idea as the clearing or 'lichtung' (Sturrock 1997). In reality, it is a *triple interface* where three different realities meet – the playworker's, the child's and the environment's – each one projecting its own characteristics onto the other two.

However, for the purposes of this text, I will restrict my discussion to the relationship between the playworker and the child. As with the scale of engagement, the relationship between these two individual entities is not linear; it is more cyclical, like the spirals. By this I mean

330

that, rather than having a scale of say 0–5, measuring from nothing to everything, on this cyclical scale, 0 and 5 are at the same point. Some likely playworker approaches are outlined below.

1 The perceived indifferent approach

I had been asked to meet with a number of adults who were working with children who had suffered indirectly from the Omagh bombing in August 1998. People were concerned about the most appropriate way to relate to these potentially 'damaged' children in a play context. The idea of good playwork as 'perceived indifference' developed from the notion of distance supervision as described in Hughes (1996b), and from conversations I had with a number of colleagues around that time.

Perceived indifference describes the hoped-for effect of appearing to be busy doing other things, whilst focused on a particular situation, i.e., that although the playworker wanted to give the impression of being otherwise engaged, her total concentration would be focused on the children and their 'state'. The rationale being that by using this approach, particularly in this type of context, affected children would feel able to go about their own business without feeling under surveillance, or that their privacy was being breached or that they would be interrupted, but if an intervention from a playworker was felt to be necessary, it would happen.

The playwork inference we can draw is that in a high-quality play project, unless conditions dictate otherwise, there is no need for a continual transaction between playworker/child and child/playworker, across the space between them. It is implicit from the atmosphere the playworkers have established, that they are there for the children, but

Level of child/playworker interaction	Perceived nature of interaction	Quality of child/playworker relationship
0	Indifferent	High
1	Repressive	Low
2	Nosy	Low
3	Functional	Moderate
4	Enthusiastic	High
5	Controlled authentic	High

Figure 12.2 The relationship between the playworker and the child.

that they want the children to feel free to play and not feel the need to continually refer back to them for approval, reassurance or any other form of adult-positive feedback. So the child's own input into the space is often of very high quality, although it is implicit – demonstrating trust, for example, rather than explicit. So the 'perceived indifferent' approach is an indicator of a high-quality child/playworker relationship.

2 The repressive approach

Adopting this approach probably means that the playworker is either frightened of the children, or of the context she is working in. I include it because I think that even the most capable of playworkers still find themselves in this mode from time to time – tiredness and feeling unsupported are probably the main causes.

For example, my employers on one of the projects I operated said that, if I was assaulted in the course of my work, they would not prosecute my attacker(s). It was not so much their refusal to prosecute that made me feel deflated. It was that by saying it, I felt valueless – that they just didn't care about my welfare even though I was an employee!

However, the playworker should be under no illusions. She must prepare for those times when it feels as if it is just the playwork team and the children – a stockade in a jungle – when nobody else wants to know. As well as looking after a large number of children, playworkers may have to deal with psychotic adults coming onto the project, drunks, people urinating in front of the children, boy racers driving at speed through or adjacent to the project, police with dogs charging in to chase a runaway, frightening everyone half to death, violent parents, older brothers, sisters or other relatives, even irate religious leaders, all without any meaningful support from any source. It can be madness, and when playworkers feel alone and unsupported, it is hardly surprising that they get grumpy from time to time, when it all gets a bit much.

My own experience of the repressive approach is that it is very transitory, it passes quickly and happens to most workers from time to time. And whilst various incidents like those I have mentioned do happen,

332

they are balanced, if not overwhelmed, by the positive nature of the work.

During the repressive approach, a playworker might catch herself in survival mode, saying 'don't' and 'no' far more than she would normally, simply because being there is not engaging or energising her. Then it is a bad space to be in. It feels bad for the playworker and is obviously not good for the children either. And the play space might be the only refuge they have, the only place they have a name other than 'Oy', the only place they can go without the fear of being hit or humiliated, so it is debilitating for everyone when it happens.

Even mildly repressive interaction manifests itself as low-quality child/playworker relationship. If children come to the play space to play and because the playworker feels insecure or vulnerable find their play being continually interrupted, or controlled by the playworker, it will be a disempowering and frustrating experience for the children, and they will probably react badly, and so the situation may get worse. So the repressive approach, although only temporary, will indicate a low-quality child/playworker relationship.

3 The nosy approach

Playworkers have fallen into the trap of the nosy approach – what is called 'infantile toxicity' by Else and Sturrock (1998) – when they identify with the children too much, and think they are one of them. For example, when they unwittingly force themselves into children's conversations, or into their spaces, and when the children are either too polite or compassionate to ask them to go away. Neither repression, in this context, or nosiness are particularly adulterative, because they are short lived, but nosiness is intrusive, can be dominating and should be resisted.

A lot of play space activity between children is intimate and private. This should not just be an illusion on the part of the children, it should be a reality, i.e., playworkers really should respect the child's space. Children do not want to be under surveillance when they are interacting and negotiating. If they want to do it in front of a playworker they will. If playworkers are just passing through, they will not mind that either, but to try to become a part of what is going on between children can be an embarrassing, cringe-filled distraction for them.

333

Ideally the relationship between the children and the playworker should reflect a recognition of the children's *and* the playworker's integrity. Because this category does not differentiate between a playworker being friends with the children, but not being one of them, I regard the nosy approach as an indicator of a low-quality child/playworker relationship.

4 The functional approach

The functional approach describes those occasions when the play-worker is working well, but is going through the motions, rather than allowing herself to become immersed into what is going on. Like the repressive approach this might also be a sign of tiredness or, worse still, of burn-out. Even the best playworkers get to this point. Probably the worst aspect of this mode is that modification slows down or drops out of the work programme. The children are fine and the playworker is fulfilling all of the legal obligations, etc., but the dynamism, which is normally the result of the dynamic between the playworker, the children, and the space, is lost to some extent.

This is a mode that needs monitoring. It can be short lived, but it can be a sign of losing interest or of needing support. This category describes a better quality relationship between the children and the playworker on a day-to-day basis than either the repressive or nosy modes. However, if the functional approach is being caused by tired-ness or worse still, lack of enthusiasm, it could decay into a low-quality relationship over time, But in general terms this will be an indicator of a moderate quality child/adult relationship.

5 The enthusiast approach

The enthusiast is born, not made. She is the animator. She cannot stand and watch, is neither nosy nor repressive, but does risk being overly interruptive. The enthusiast, like an inventor, has child-like characteristics that both children and adults find infectious. She is constantly making things happen, finding things that can be used, doing things and engaging in banter with the children. However, the enthusiast can also run the risk of presuming ownership of the space, in a way that no other playwork approach will.

334

In some circumstances this may deliver the ideal compensatory response, where a play space is provided, because of the implicit recognition of the need for novelty and activity. However, the enthusiast is often someone who reacts, rather than reflects, and she may not value analysis or reflection enough to step back and perhaps conclude that operating a play setting is less about what she wants, and her needs, and more about what the children are driven to do.

One veteran who springs to mind sees play in quite simple terms, seeing her function simply as a catalyst in the context of construction and other interactions. I understand the viewpoint, but as my IMEE acronym implies, there is more to playwork than what is reduced from our own personal intuition – what we did as children then never covers the whole spectrum of what can be done by children now, and we need to look to other sources to ensure a comprehensive approach. Like the rest of us, children operate on many different intellectual and psychic levels, and applying our own level alone, however resourceful it may be perceived initially, is limiting rather than liberating in the end.

Having said that, if every play project was operated by enthusiastic playworkers, then the children who attended those settings would always have access to very creative and inventive minds and high-quality playwork. And whilst play spaces operated by these individuals may not be as subtle as those operated by other kinds of playworkers, they often provide very visible examples of good playwork practice, particularly from the perspective of modification. So, even though the actual quality of their intervention may not be quite as high as some, the visible impact of their playwork is considerable.

6 The controlled authentic approach

Perhaps the major difference between this mode and others is in the outcome of their analysis of compensation. The perceived indifferent approach only works well in two situations – where children are confidently engaged with one another or their environment and only rarely need an intervention from the playworker, or where children are highly traumatised and may need a covert, i.e., indifferent, presence initially, rather than one that is interactive.

However, like the 'enthusiast', the playworker who is 'controlled authentic' is in the thick of things but the balance of input is always biased towards the children and their needs.

This mode is both facilitative and empowering. It is facilitative because it makes allowances for children who have lost some of their skill to interact playfully. That is, it recognises that some children are dysfunctional to a greater or lesser degree because freedom to play is very limited in some circumstances, and that some children may be losing interactive skill and physical motivation.

It is empowering, because the controlled authentic playworker will be looking for signs of improved confidence, or an increasing desire to retake the initiative and – perhaps, unlike the enthusiast – will unselfishly relinquish any control and pass it back to the child, by stepping back, or moving on from that interaction.

The difference in the quality of the space, between the perceived indifferent and the controlled authentic approaches, is dictated by differences in how they express their concern for the children. The former is implicit and the latter explicit. The concern expressed in the former is perhaps quieter and more reserved than the latter, who may be a more joyful and personally expressive person.

The children, in knowing they are cared about, either by the freedom they are given or by the quality of the interaction they share, are secure and able to engage in whatever play types the drive selects. This means that the play space is truly compensating for the absence or loss of wild, adult-free space.

CONCLUSION

Most playworkers are amalgams of several of these modes and manifest most of them at different times. Certainly I have been scared and repressive and I have felt out of my depth too, I have also been the nosy child and the tired functionalist. Part of me wishes that I had been the enthusiast but that would have required a level of ingenuity and creativity I don't have, although I have had the privilege of knowing numerous playworkers who did.

336

CHAPTER 13

SOME DEEPER CONSIDERATIONS

Because my thinking often outstrips the text, this chapter is given over to the full text of four papers presented at conferences to bring things up to speed. In some ways they represent my most up-to-date position on certain ideas.

TOWARDS A UNIFIED PLAYWORK THEORY FOR PROVISION FOR PLAY

Leeds Metropolitan University, 2010

Introduction

What is meant by good play provision, what does it do and what is it for? You might say 'To facilitate play, of course', but what's that, given that we all have such very different experiences of it.

In the past few years, the knowledge base about play has not only grown, it has been revolutionised by science, and one has to ask whether our thinking regarding what it is, and what we do with that knowledge, in terms of making provision for play, has kept pace with what we now understand play to be and do?

A review of play

As you know, play is not only what we see – for example children engaged in hide and seek, skipping and climbing trees – these are outward manifestations of a process that is also happening under the surface; while these activities are in motion, a complex multifaceted process that drives the playing child to engage in them is also underway.

For as well as being something which is visible, play is also invisible – a neurochemical phenomenon, a neurological phenomenon, a genetic phenomenon, and an evolutionary phenomenon too. That last category being perhaps the most profound. Konner (2010), quoting the great evolutionary geneticist Dobzanski, said, 'nothing in biology makes sense except in the light of evolution, we can now say that nothing in childhood does either'. 'And yet', said Konner, 'until very recently most of psychology, and here I would include playwork, care and early years too, was carried out as if evolution had never happened' (pp. 2–3).

And yet the games, the social interactions, the creativity that are intrinsic to play, are hugely important conduits that bring these deeper evolutionary processes into contact with the world around the child, and which through the child's senses and behaviour have the effect of informing both the child, and those deeper individual processes about the current state of the world and of its status in it.

It was Konrad Lorenz's work that originally brought the complexity and importance of play to my attention. In 1972 he wrote that natural selection would favour the most playful individuals 'for they will have acquired more useful information about the potential or otherwise of the environment *and* of their actions on it'. Since that initial pronouncement, that those who play will survive better and longer, our understanding of the relationship between playing and evolution, adaptation *and* our species capacity for avoiding the pressures of extinction, has gone through an incredible evolution itself.

For since the mid 1990s in particular, play has been shown to have an indispensable/intrinsic role in numerous processes vital to human survival and to human development, including:

I could go on.

So the science seems to be pretty categorical that play is the evolutionary engine, or at least one of them, that today drives every child on this planet, and that that has been the case for millennia, certainly since the Palaeolithic Age, up to forty thousand years ago, although Fagan (1981, 1987) places the origins of social and locomotor play nearer the dawn of mammals, 200 million years ago (Burghardt 2005).

So this list is not just impressive, its implication is that play feeds into almost every process on which our development and survival as a species depends, and always has.

338

• brain plasticity/growth	(Byers 1998)
• neural organisation	(Brown 1998, Sutton-Smith 2007)
• muscular growth	(Byers 1998)
• resilience and optimism	(Maston 2001, Rutter 2006, Lester and Russell 2008)
• flexible problem solving	(Bruner 1972, Sylva 1976 and Konner 2010)
• cortical maps and consciousness	(Damasio 2000, Brown 1998)
• ecological immersion and spatial navigation	(Orr 2002)
• the development of adaptive strategies	(Burghardt 2005)
• 'rolling with the punches' of life	(Siviy 1998)
• maintaining good relationships	(Pellis 1998)
• good physical and mental health	(Harlow 1971, Brown 1998, Sutton-Smith 1997, Stevens and Price 2000)

Figure 13.1 The bio-evolutionary benefits of play.

But what is play?

Burghardt (1998, 2005) suggests that the term encompasses several different behavioural repertoires, and this is in line with my own play types taxonomy, that lists sixteen different types of play. Burghardt says these different play types have different causal bases, functions and phylogenies, that is, they have evolved at different points in our evolutionary history, for different reasons and to do different things. Although we can only speculate on what those things might be, I suggest, simply because they have continued to be retained throughout millions of years of natural selection – and not be selected out – that they have a great deal to do with avoiding extinction, and the fact that as a species we are still here at all.

Most of the recent groundbreaking data about play are derived initially from ethological studies of species in the wild, or from species kept in stimulating spaces, where the beneficial outcomes of playing seem governed only by their natural drive to play and the nature of their conditions. This realisation is key to any meaningful re-evaluation of play provision. For it implies that the relationship between play and the outcomes listed earlier has to include a high degree of freedom and self-reliance, behaviour unfettered by cultural expectations, morality or human social hierarchy; life in a world of spontaneity, curiosity, and exploration if you like. Whilst this may not feel like a particularly conducive *social or societal* construct, given that we are talking about children's evolution, adaptation and particularly their survival, it does feel like a fitting biological one – it may not suit our modern preconceptions of how children should behave or be social-ised, but from a biological viewpoint it makes good sense.

Demonstrating just how potent is the impact of this free, wild, sponta-neous and repetitious behaviour, not withstanding the earlier list, Byers is quoted (Konner 2010) as saying 'The idea is that natural selec-tion designed play to shape brain development, and most likely they [the species he was observing at the time] are directing their own brain assembly'. This idea of brain self-modification is actually a well-recorded phenomenon. Many songbirds, for example, as young birds have to perform the *motor* act of singing (subsong), before the struc-ture of neurons that make audible song possible can even be created (Marler 1970, Kroodsma 1981).

This is what Byers is suggesting, i.e., that playing, perhaps drawing from what Panksepp (1998) identified as the thalamus area in the brain (perched on top of the brainstem), is designed by natural selection to construct and organise a human brain that 'fits' and 'anticipates', as Dennett (1997) says, the organism's evolutionary needs.

It makes great survival sense for any organism to have evolved a way of adapting its brain in line with contemporary changes in the environment.

But as well as orchestrating the deeper processes like brain self-modification, play is also a visible phenomenon, it can be seen. Recently this visual aspect was described in terms of a succession of different, almost 'magical' behaviours that when able to interact with certain kinds of environmental characteristics actually create these deep outcomes.

What are these so-called magical behaviours and what do they require from the environment? Well what do we see when we observe chil-dren playing? We don't see playtypes, that's for sure, they're an inter-pretation of what we do see and they have to be learnt. And, describing what we see in terms of games and creativity also falls short of reality. What I see is a continuously changing canvas of spon-taneous inter-reactions between the playing child and everything around it, a pattern of behaviour which I described almost as a dance, that incorporates assorted historical, cultural, behavioural and metaphysical elements of each child's life:

340

Activity	Translation
Paranormal Choreography of Playtypes	Second guessing other's behaviour
Animating the Inanimate	Creating relationships with everything
Invisibility and Flight	They can imagine disappearance and flight
Recapitulation	They revisit their evolutionary history
Shared Narratives	Children everywhere play the same games
Pre-proto and Post-proto Routines	Increasing complexity of behaviour
Synch of Game Intent and Structure	Game rules and outcomes change
Spontaneous and Free Expression	Independence/Children in their element
Sensory/Emotional Synthesis of Action	Whole body hyper-co-ordination/calibration
Cues and Meta Signalling	Instant fluency in non-verbal language
Journeys of Metaphysical Exploration	Consciousness of mortality/universality
Flow or Circulation = Navigation	Fluency of movement

Figure 13.2 The magic of play.

Making provision

I believe that it is these archetypal behaviours that generate the outcomes I listed earlier. However, the practical question for us is, what kind of environmental characteristics best activate these behaviours? We can get some clues from the ethological studies.

The biggest problem faced by play people and the children they work with is the disparity between what the ethological literature implies is needed – large, wild, free, autonomous, modifiable, novel, challenging spaces, and what society tends to be prepared to both tolerate, pay for and offer – normally cramped, restricted, boring, unchangeable and safe spaces.

Play is an evolved and evolving group of biological behaviours. I hope I have at least demonstrated that? That means that play cannot operate successfully according to inflexible social or community norms. Johan Huizinga recognised this when he stated 'Play is older than culture, for culture however inadequately defined, always presupposes human society, and animals (and children) have not waited for man to teach them how to play'.

The point is, we have to tailor our thinking about play, to what play is, and not what we want it to be. The square peg of play cannot fit into the round hole of society; society has to reorganise itself to 'fit' round play. After all, you can't make our lungs enjoy polluted air; it's nonsensical to expect that you can, so we introduced clean air legislation. We need that same focus with play. What the early part of this paper was describing was a biological process, in a biological context, and its biological outcomes. If we want the outcomes we have to facilitate the process that makes them possible by changing into a more bio-evolutionary society, and not expect play to adapt itself to a process of our choosing and convenience – biology doesn't work like that. So what are the general characteristics a play environment needs to have, to enable these magical behaviours, and facilitate the deeper outcomes?

Now this is where our decision-making process becomes more a function of intuitive, rather than objective, judgement. Where we draw less from everyday experience, and more from being members of a species and subject to collective experiences. In *Evolutionary Playwork*, I codified this process using the acronym IMEE, which stands for Intuition, childhood Memory, professional Experience and scientific Evidence. I suggested that by reflecting on our own childhood intuition and memory we could make valid judgements about what the play environment could look and feel like. What IMEE implies is that while evidence and experience are important, our individual and collective memories and experiences (unless adulterated) also give us vital insights. This is hardly surprising given that evolution, the play drive and playing are not only processes reported in the science, but processes we all experience first hand.

So whilst the science points us in the direction of *some* essential environmental features like:

- brain plasticity/growth
- neural organisation
- muscular growth
- resilience and optimism
- flexible problem solving $\implies$ **diversity, size, complexity, risk, EEA**
- cortical maps and consciousnesss **3D movement, other children/species**
- ecological immersion and spatial navigation
- the development of adaptive strategies
- 'rolling with the punches' of life
- maintaining good relationships
- good physical and mental health

Figure 13.3 Playwork indicators derived from bio-evolutionary benefits.

And descriptions of 'magical' play point us in the direction of some of the others:

342

Activity

Paranormal Choreography of PlayTypes
Animating the Inanimate
Invisibility and Flight
Recapitulation
Shared Narratives
Synch of Game Intent and Structure
  Spontaneous and Free Expression
Sensory/Emotional Synthesis of Action
Cues and Meta Signalling
Journeys of Metaphysical Exploration
Flow or Circulation = Navigation

$\Longrightarrow$ **freedom, self-reliance, flow spontaneity, curiosity and exploration**

Figure 13.4 Playwork indicators derived from magic.

It is only our childhood memories of play environments that take us to their essence. Because they are more about feelings and impressions, memories generate insights that are powerfully affective as well as rational, ancient as well as modern; more rooted in the dream-like nature of what a lot of play feels like to us as children, the limen or threshold of consciousness, where play experience morphs into biological process; where recollections are more akin to genetic echoes from a distant evolutionary past. It is only in this mental space that we can make the fundamental connections between what I'm calling the sub-play environment, and play behaviour and play's outcomes.

Some of my preferred sub-environmental indicators are:

Archetypal
Private
Liminal
Elemental
Languageable
Intuitively locomotor and imaginal

Let me briefly elaborate.

Archetypal – Jung says all children have an archetypal endowment for the development of characteristic patterns of personality and behaviour. Perhaps archetypes and playtypes are synonymous here. Archetypes need expression in the environment or children become ill. Making the conditions for the ancient and timeless just means that children need to know they have 'permission' to do this using dressing-up, ceremonies and rituals to express their archetypal drives. For example becoming mother, father, soldier, priest, magician, musician

343

and so on. Grof would even suggest that children should enter into the archetypes of other species too. Materials like heraldic, runic and astrological artefacts might help, but as with everything play orientated, children can normally work it out for themselves.

To be able to feel private and hidden is also a play necessity. Children need it whether creatively making camps, deep-playing war, or role-playing mothers and fathers. Being overlooked takes something valuable away from play and makes it difficult for children to engage in pretend routines like invisibility and flying, having lone conversations or games, or beginning the long journey of developing different relationships. Cover is vital for children's self-esteem and self-image simply because it lets them decide whether to be seen or not. I've often defined play as what children do, when adults can't see them.

Liminality is a dream-like quality where aspects of the play space are experienced as other-worldly, as a world through the looking glass. Liminality allows children to immerse themselves and exist on the boundary between the 'real' and the 'imaginal' world; between behaviour and biology. Liminality can be expressed through the judicious use of stained glass, mirrors, archways or doorways, by mazes and bridges or the offer of a serene/magical spaces. Talbot and Frost's 1996, *Magical Playscapes* has a number of good liminal examples.

Elemental/EEA – Children are driven to play with the elements of water, fire, air and earth. It is something human children have done for thousands of years. An elemental space will facilitate this interaction by offering access to water-play, mud, open-space, and fire. All experiences that will, as Lorenz pointed out, give children in-depth knowledge about the world around them.

Languageable – Good play spaces are describable by children, who give different parts of the ludic topography names – some that come to mind for me are: The Valley, The Caves, The Witches Garden, Snake River and the Tunnel. Naming gives a space a personal and symbolic meaning of belonging or of new territory. All too often with spaces, children are treated like zoo animals and have no sense of involvement with or ownership of them.

Intuitively locomotor and imaginal – obviously, adults will introduce some features into a play space. The skill is not to overwhelm it and make it adult rather than child. All too often – and this is frequently

344

the case with commercial providers – the work of the child's innate play drive is circumvented (hijacked) by a synthetic substitute, which takes control of play away from the child, and creates what I call a stereotypical play narrative – that's an adulterated play narrative – which reduces the experience the children have, to the play equivalent of fast food, convenience play, with all of what that implies.

Finally, establishing verifiable links between its biological outcomes, the behaviour that children manifest when playing and the environmental characteristics that generate that behaviour must represent an essential component of any meaningful re-evaluation of play provision. I hope this presentation has gone some way to providing those links?

PLAYTYPES AND ASSOCIATED CONSIDERATIONS

Play Scotland Conference, Ayr, 2008

Children are growing up in very difficult, perhaps unprecedented times. Every generation says that, but perhaps this time it is true.

In 2002, John Gray's controversial but hugely influential book *Straw Dogs* was published. In its devastating critique of human egocentric consciousness, it supports the Darwinian notion that far from being special, we humans are only assemblies of genes interacting at random with one another in a shifting environment. That for this and other reasons, humans can no more control their fate, or what happens in their habitat than can cats or parrots, and that the human species are not as they generally perceive, separate and special, but like all other species, all other animals, are locked into an inevitable cycle of birth, life and death, from which neither religion nor humanism nor politics can rescue them or offer them a metaphysical safety net. Life, death, the processes of evolution go on and the pressures of extinction take their toll irrespective of anything we can do.

In 2002, Jared Diamond told us that in the past few thousand years, the earth has lost getting on for 80 per cent of its species. There is no reason why we should not also meet a similar fate. And in some ways that would probably be a good thing, given as Gray states, 'The destruction of the natural world is not the result of global capitalism,

345

industrialisation, western civilisation or any flaw in human institutions or any cosmic catastrophe. It is [simply] a consequence of the evolutionary success of an exceptionally rapacious primate', a plague of people, as Lovelock has called it.

But even this rapacious primate is coming up against the realities of life, in particular life on a planet with finite resources. Paraphrasing the three laws of Thermodynamics, the physicist Stuart Kauffman describes modern life in the following terms: 'You can't win, you can't break even, and you can't get out of the game'. He adds 'But the game keeps getting more complicated and there are always more different ways to play' (2000).

And we may be reaching the limits of our own inventiveness and resilience too. The anthropologist Robin Fox (1989) likens our existence in this IT/technological age to a car which, having been built for a maximum speed of 85 miles per hour, is now continually expected to do 110, and increasingly risking falling to pieces as it struggles to keep up with the accelerating demands of life in the fast lane. It is no secret that technology and change are moving faster than any of us, scientist or child, can keep up with. And this pace of life, this race to keep up, has an impact that makes our situation even more precarious, if that is possible. Fox continues 'Force [the brain] to work outside of its range of adaptive responses and it will rebel. It will regress to those behaviours including the ... violent ones surrounding its primary functions, survival and reproduction'.

Gray (2002) offers another negative slant, 'The mass of humankind is ruled not by its intermittent moral sensations, still less by self-interest, but by the needs of the moment. It seems fated to wreck the balance of life on Earth, and thereby to be the agent of its own destruction'.

These Darwinian descriptions of the hopeless and almost kamikaze nature of human existence, without point or purpose, form an integral part of the backdrop into which children are born. A backdrop play evolved to help us to survive. But because play itself now seems under threat, children are increasingly manifesting problems with this depressing realisation, as they attempt to make sense of it through their increasingly impoverished play experiences.

In 2004, according to the National Statistics at least one in ten children in Great Britain suffered from a mental illness that could be

346

	5–10 year old		11–16 year olds		All 5–16 year olds
	Boys	Girls	Boys	Girls	
Emotional disorders	2.2	2.5	4.0	6.1	3.7
Conduct disorders	6.9	2.8	8.1	5.1	5.8
Hyperkinetic disorders	2.7	0.4	2.4	0.4	1.5
Less common disorders	2.2	0.4	1.6	1.1	1.3
Any disorder	10.2	5.1	12.6	10.3	9.6

Figure 13.5 Prevalence of children's mental health disorders, 2004, Great Britain (Source: National Statistics).

related to the stresses of modern life. This figure is undoubtedly higher now.

So one in ten children aged 5–16 had a clinically recognisable mental disorder, four per cent of them had an emotional disorder (anxiety or depression), six per cent had a conduct disorder, two per cent had a hyperkinetic disorder, and one per cent had a less common disorder. Two per cent of children had more than one type of disorder at the same time.

In 2007, more than 4000 under-14-year-olds tried to kill themselves in Great Britain. Rates of self-harm in the UK are amongst the highest in Europe (NICE 2002). There were 46000 Ritalin prescriptions given out in Scotland alone in 2005. In March 2008, Anthony Cole, a 15-year-old Milton Keynes schoolboy, was found hanged in his bedroom after his Ritalin prescription was increased.

One cannot fail to ask, as Fox does, whether children can sustain all the complexity that underpins their lives today? There is an assumption, he says, that human beings, the human brain, can in fact do anything, and thus our limitations do not need to be taken into account. But of course they do, and particularly if our species, especially the young, are starting to show increasing signs of strain as a consequence of the environment in which they live, which they do appear to be.

Yet there have always been wars and poverty and illness and they have always been difficult to come to terms with, particularly when images of these things are as omnipresent as they are in this media age. And yes, there are other issues too – global warming, AIDS, water shortages, child-on-child violence on the streets and in the playground, that children also feel powerless to do anything about.

But is it really any different for children now than for previous generations? Should these things be making children ill?

I want to explore theoretically if there is a link between modern life and anxiety and mental illness in children? To ask, are they being increasingly adversely affected by the pressures of modern life? Are they for some reason unable or unwilling to adjust, as previous generations seem to have done? Do they feel out of control, insignificant and anxious, and if so why, and more importantly why now?

Times were very different for children once. During our last recorded adaptation for example, during the late Palaeolithic period around 20,000 years ago, we humans lived in our ancestral environment, or what Bowlby terms the Environment of Evolutionary Adaptedness, or EEA – the last environment to which we ever adapted. As you can imagine this was an environment significantly different to the one we currently inhabit, not a paradise, but still one in which children would have not have felt anything like as powerless and insignificant as they may do now.

Certainly our ability to adapt to this, our local and global environment would have had important and positive physical and mental health implications for us all.

And that adaptive capability would have been significantly enhanced by the play Palaeolithic children engaged in – variations of the playtypes that children still manifest today, and that were afforded by the characteristics of the diverse natural environments they inhabited.

Burghardt (2005) tells us that throughout our evolutionary history, i.e., until the late Palaeolithic when we stopped evolving, new playtypes would have been a regular outcome of natural selection and I think that it's fairly safe to assume that each different type of play, each playtype, was selected because it helped the organism better to adapt and thus to survive. Burghardt himself supports this assertion by suggesting that different types of play not only appeared at different times in our evolutionary history, but appeared for different reasons and to address different deficits too.

What this suggests is that at least until the late Palaeolithic period we were a highly adapted species, that was totally in tune with the adaptive demands of the particular environments in which we found ourselves; that the different types of play that had evolved by then enabled children to respond flexibly to the demands of the whole planetary environment in which they found themselves, increasingly enhancing their ability to withstand the different 'ecological, physiological and behavioural pressures' (Burghardt 2005) that might have threatened them with extinction.

Palaeolithic humans seemed at one with their environment. As Gray says, 'for much of their history, and all of prehistory, humans did not see themselves as any different from the other animals among which they lived. The hunter gathers that peopled the Palaeolithic saw their prey as equals, if not superiors, and animals were worshiped as divinities in many traditional cultures.'

He says, 'the humanist sense of a gulf between ourselves and other animals, [and by inference the natural world] is an aberration. It is the animist feeling of belonging with the rest of nature that is normal.' He continues, 'Feeble as it may be today, the feeling of sharing a common destiny with other living things is embedded in the human psyche. Those who struggle to conserve what is left of the environment are moved by the love of living things, biophilia, the frail bond of feeling that ties humankind to the Earth.'

I feel this too, that humans are an amalgamation of all of our evolutionary stages, from the reptile, to the primate, the hunter-gatherer, and the modern human, and playing has acted as the amalgamating cement, integrating each new stage into the previous ones.

Many things changed in the 20,000 years that followed the Palaeolithic – along came agriculture, industry, mechanised warfare, and technology and now we find ourselves in very different circumstances. Still the same species, still at the same adaptive/evolutionary position we were at 20,000 years ago, children still with the same range of adaptive playtypes tools, but now in an environment which instead of being our predictable, sustaining and instructive version of the EEA, has changed out of all recognition and this change is continuing to happen at an exponential rate and is totally out of ours and our children's control.

For although we live in the modern built environment, with all of what that implies, we are still Palaeolithic creatures and only adapted to what the EEA was, not to this modern environment, and this mismatch has consequences for us all, especially modern children as I will elaborate further. For whilst we can do nothing to affect the march of progress, neither can we do anything to change our Palaeolithic characteristics. More recently, this situation has created an increasingly toxic interface between us and the world in which we live: between our modern habitat and our ancient evolutionary position/state. For if we are not adapting to the environment we are in, and we are not, then the stress created by the demands of modern life, will force change upon us, and some of that will be maladaptive, manifested in distortions in our neurology and resulting in psychopathology.

However, I believe that until as recently as forty years ago, even without biological adaptation, we had been reasonably successful at, at least, adjusting to the modern environment, because as children we played with it, and we became used to it, and were able to forecast and to some extent avoid its worst impacts, although we weren't immune to its general affects even then.

Until about forty years ago the environment was deemed relatively benign by parents, there were still large tracts of open accessible spaces that were not built on, TVs and cars were not as prevalent as they are now, and Huttenmoser and Degan-Zimmermann's battery children were a thing of science fiction. Plus, children were not under surveillance the whole time and were thus more likely to engage in the same kind of playtypes behaviour as their Palaeolithic peers.

However, in the last forty years all that seems to have gradually evaporated. Parents are now continually afraid and contaminating their children with their anxiety as a consequence. There is almost nowhere to range and play whether in urban or rural situations, cars are everywhere, children are pacified, babysat and exploited by TV, and the symptoms that plagued battery children – misery, dissatisfaction, hopelessness and aggression – are everywhere and increasing.

And on the playground health and safety legislation and the imposition of an 'adult agenda' addressing everything from what is perceived as bullying to racism and sexism have also played their part in impoverishing the play experience, and I suggest that each of these factors, symptomatic of the fracture to which Gray refers, the denial of our animal self and our construction of a false, non-natural self instead – an invincible, superior, dominating, consumer orientated self, overlaid as it has been onto the child's world, especially its play

350

– have gradually contributed to a psychic schism between who children sense they are as biological organisms and who they are told they should be, and this has resulted in many of their problems.

For as the statistics above demonstrate, children are increasingly manifesting a spectrum of conditions detrimental to their adaptive and survival potential. From simple clumsiness in coordination and relationship building, to inexplicable unhappiness and distress, through ADHD, depression and suicide, to dangerous psychotic conditions that seem rooted in the new disorder we describe as 'play deprivation'.

Today it is almost impossible for most children to play in ways in which their ancient forbears would have done, as biological organisms anticipating an unconditional adaptive interaction with the environment they inhabit. For example, although risk has always been everywhere – in the EEA there would have been hostile groups and wild animals to which children would have had to adapt – now risk is not seen as a fact of planetary life to which children *must* adapt or face injury, but as a choice they can avoid if only they are protected and watched enough. Of course the opposite is true. With protection and surveillance come an increasing inability to navigate the environment, a new and frightening disability for the young of our species, and a critical impediment to their capacity to adjust.

I find myself wondering if there is a link between this reduction in the frequency and diversity of play children are experiencing and their apparent increasing susceptibility to psychopathological conditions? However, addressing this question requires that I develop other strands to my argument. Forgive my rather primitive iteration of Jungian ideas.

Archetypes and playtypes

When he first developed his archetypal ideas, Jung described them as the 'primordial and universal images that through myth, symbol, religion and art underlie our personal understandings of the world, and which "evoke deep and sometimes unconscious responses"' (Jung 1953–1978).

During the fifty-plus million years of human evolution, our brain as it is currently structured has only gradually evolved. During this period,

Jung suggests that different but significant collections of our species evolutionary history, that he called archetypes, have become integrated into our brain's structure to form channels that act as the means through which individual human psychic and behavioural development have become routed and which guide much of what we need to think and do to achieve psychological stability.

And because 'every individual life is at the same time the eternal life of the species' (Jung 1953–78) and 'each person contains a minimum of everyone else' (Chawla 2002) we can see that these archetypes may represent mythological roles that are not only shared by all of us, but have always been a part of our species as it has evolved.

These archetypes, inherited, perhaps genetic, memories found in every society, for example, the mother, the father, the enemy, the joker, the healer, the player, could be described as our universal or transpersonal 'ways of being'.

Because the source of these archetypes is our individual and collective experience throughout our evolution, play archetypes, our play-types will have a pivotal role in our development. Burghardt proposes that types of play have evolved with some regularity over many tens of thousands of years and to date we have identified sixteen different types of play from the literature. Whilst this number may appear small given the time scale, if it is taken just as a representation, as a code for the many forms of playfully interacting within a changing environment, over thousands of years, it makes more sense.

For example, although we all have a good idea of what we mean by social play in a contemporary context, if we think about it in terms of the millions of years of our evolution, and in terms of the many different ways children across the globe might engage socially, we might well identify hundreds of significantly different but equally valid forms of what might also be termed social play too. In other words, the sixteen playtypes currently identified could be seen as representing sixteen play archetypes, behavioural standards around which we group the similarities that have prevailed in our own individual experiences of play.

352

An aside

We should also remind ourselves briefly whilst we are talking about play archetypes, that real authentic play, the play that children engage in when they are not under observation, the play that has evolved out of a biological process to enable survival and adaptation in all manner of circumstances, is not always going to be sweetness and light, nor should it be. The playtypes we can observe are a representation of a total evolutionary history, and they will not only reflect the lighter side of a child's human nature, there will inevitably be a dark side to them too, that will be cruel, violent, shadowy and primitive, for this is also an integral part of the child's nature – the part that Wilber was driving at when he said that all aspects of our evolution must become united, amalgamated or neuroses like those I have described earlier will result.

For if what children are experiencing when they play is going to be an authentic reflection of the physical and psychological reality – the vulnerability, the fear, the awe and the loneliness – experienced throughout their evolutionary history, from their earliest and most primitive ancestors, up to their own present day experiences, as they attempt to interpret a life unavoidably overlain with mythic values, fantasy and dreams, as they should (not to mention their own modern demons), then playtypes as manifested in today's children's play will unavoidably contain aspects that we may find challenging and which may require *us* (not the *children*), the professionals, to work out how best to facilitate them in our practice.

Now Stevens and Price say of this archetypal inheritance, that it is what prepares each of us for 'the natural life cycle of our species in the world in which we evolved' – the EEA. That as early humans went through life, these archetypes gave them insights into a whole variety of ancient roles that guided how they behaved towards children, mates, visitors, the powerful, animals, trees, mountains and so on, and by so doing, made it easier to adapt and survive. Jung's perspective was that it was imperative that they were able to behave in ways dictated by their archetypes and that meant that the environment, the culture they were a part of, had to be conducive to those ways too. If they weren't, and they failed to meet people's archetypal needs, then what Stevens calls the resulting 'frustration of archetypal intent' would result in [the] neuroses and psychopatholog[ies] I've described above. In other words, Palaeolithic humans would have become mentally ill if the environment had not allowed them to express their archetypal intentions, and that may well be the case today too.

Because of the living nature of the EEA and the relatively small number of people around at that time, it would have been easier for them to use both the environment and their evolving cultures to reflect their deeper psychological needs – their fears, beliefs, anxieties and myths. Nowadays that is almost impossible. Instead, the technical environment we live in is forging ahead irrespective of, even in spite of, our needs, and rather than nurturing biophilia in children, it is alienating them from it instead. The modern technical environment neither can nor does acknowledge that we are derived from ancient beings in its structures, and increasingly children may be suffering a form of dissociation as a consequence – becoming split off, separated psychologically, unable to connect with any part the world they inhabit, except perhaps its evolving virtual components, and that may also herald a mental health disaster.

Play archetypes, children's playful physical and psychic interactions with the world, are just as prone to this frustration as are other archetypes, and must also be regularly rehearsed if children are to avoid it, and its resultant psychopathologies. Or put another way, if the evolutionary rationales for playing are not being continually played out and reinforced, the neuronal pathways that support them may decay and children may become ill.

And this synapto-mortality may be the root of the symptoms of play deprivation. And if children are playing less, or playing less in some ways, perhaps it is a neurological collapse that is being experienced by an increasing number of children at the present time?

However, like the decline in play, play deprivation is a relatively recent phenomenon. Its first recorded appearance in the Stuart Brown studies was the late 1960s, about forty years ago (although even this only came to light in 1996 when they were published in *Animal Play*) and it may have been only slowly escalating since then as children have begun to experience both the contraction and adulteration of play that has resulted from the destruction of play habitats by builders and developers, increased levels of traffic, parental fears of predation on children, and perhaps even the growth in provision that has resulted recently, where because play has had to fit certain administrative parameters the quality of the experience has been overlooked.

And Frustration of Archetypal Intent may occur because these environments in which children are trying to play just aren't conducive to it, and that may be making them ill.

OK, that's one area. Now there's one other theoretical area that I want to look at today and that's looking at the idea of *A Hierarchy of Play*.

As stated earlier, in 1996 Burghardt postulated that 'different types of play may not only do different things, for different reasons, and appear at different times in a child's development, but importantly, that they may have appeared at different times in human evolutionary history too'. This suggests that some play experiences may be more fundamental to our early evolution than some others, and that primitive play may underpin later development. This may mean that there is a hierarchy of essential play experiences, and that children need to experience many aspects of each type of play in a particular order, or at specific periods in their lives, if the effectiveness, and perhaps the purpose or even existence of more recently evolved types of play, is not to be undermined?

In 2006 I alluded to this in *Speculations and Possibilities*. Drawing from Burghardt's work and the MacLean Triune Brain model of brain evolution, I suggested that different groupings of playtypes may have evolved at very different times to one another and that each may have formed the foundation for future groupings to evolve.

The groupings I arrived at were these in chronological order:

Grouping	MacLean's Equivalent		PlayTypes
1st Group	Reptilian Complex (Rc)	=	Deep, Exploratory, Locomotor, Object, Rough and Tumble
2nd Group	Limbic System	=	Creative, Dramatic, Fantasy, Imaginative, Socio-dramatic, Role
3rd Group	Neocortex	=	Communication, Recapitulative, Social, Mastery, Symbolic

Figure 13.6 Playtypes associated with MacLean's Triune Brain Model.

To me if viewed in the context of a developing child, these groupings suggest an experiential logic, which is totally integrated into the development of the human brain; a logic that says experience has to move from the primitive, through the cultural to the intellectual and beyond. That is, from playful interactions that facilitate the development of rudimentary abilities like basic survival, aggression, coping with death, gross and acute motor movements, feeding and the creation of basic shelter, to those that facilitate the development of culture and then technology.

The notion of a hierarchy can further be inferred from Burghardt and from Byers who both propose a relationship between playing and brain development, because for the brain to develop in the form MacLean's Triune model suggests, 'each part with a different phyloge-netic history, with its own special intelligence, its own special memory, and its own sense of time and space', would need, as a number of theories suggest, access to play that reflected each of the various stages of human evolution.

As I mentioned earlier, this is also implied by Wilber who suggests that development that was not joined up to previous evolutionary stages would result in neurosis. In other words, modern children 'playing out' the primitive experiences human beings had during the early stages of their evolution is essential and may act as a foundation, an anchor for later 'psychologically stable' development, whilst not playing them out, might undermine an individual's mental health.

Evolutionary psychiatry supports this idea, suggesting that should the environment fail to meet [the] specific demands of [different development stages] then different psychopatholog[ies], like the extremes of aggression and withdrawal referred to earlier, may result. Robbins (2002) also agrees, 'There is a window of vulnerability...in early childhood and early puberty', he says, '[when] the deprivation of social play, has a crucial effect in the development of schizophrenia'.

In other words, if primary forms of play are absent from a young child's play experiences, play deprivation could again result. And from that could result the forms of mental illness to which I alluded earlier.

The question is, what are these primary forms?

It is playwork's own professional definition that helped me to identify what I think these forms are. It states that play is behaviour that is spontaneous, goalless, freely chosen, personally directed and intrinsically motivated (PlayEducation 1984), and that implies that play has to be feral, wild and independent, as well as social, symbolic and sophisticated. And, like other species in the wild, which in a sense is what children in a play environment should be, children should be acting as if they are free to go wherever their play drive takes them, because at the root of everything they are biological organisms, not pieces of social plasticine to be moulded by political or social whim. And in the context of my analysis that means engaging in primitive experiences, playing at being the individual that is imprinted in their genes if you like, as the theory suggests.

And we all know what these primitive experiences are. Engaging in real risk, lighting fires, cooking, digging caves and constructing dens or tree houses, keeping other species, growing things, exploring, engaging in proto-sexual and 'family' behaviour, making tools and weapons and engaging in ritual, combat and war, etc.

Many of today's children don't even have a shadow of these primitive experiences that previous generations did, particularly prior to the last forty years.

So the notion I am putting forward to you is that the cause of a significant volume of children's poor mental health in the past forty or so years is the impact of three different forms of play deprivation resulting from impoverishment both in their play environment and their play experiences.

The first, 'archetypal play deprivation' is caused by the frustration of archetypal intent brought about by the impoverished nature of the modern environment – nobody's fault, it just turned out that way. In the modern environment children rarely get the opportunities they need to successfully actualise their archetypal 'intentions' because it is simply not as conducive in today's environment as it would have been in the EEA. I suspect that this may be something to do with the modern schism between the animism and the humanism to which Gray referred. There was a powerful story doing the rounds at Play-Wales a couple of years ago to do with this, where a group of children, having lost a friend, went through a spontaneous and complex ritual to bury him or to say goodbye. Most of us have one or two equivalent archetypal events in our personal or professional experiences, but they are rare these days.

The second, 'primitive play deprivation' is more our fault, or certainly the fault of inappropriate and poorly targeted Health and Safety legislation, the media and some parents. The primary component of primitive play is physical and psychological risk, it is the play form that trades death against freedom, takes chances, and makes possible new experiences and new developments, and provides the flexible and random experiences that undermine our compulsion for order and predictability. For example fire, which children throughout the ages have always played with, but which is now relegated to the Barbeque or to the adult domain. Children as the direct genetic descendants of the ancients will unconsciously know that there is something not right with this, but will be unable to do anything about it other than feel and experience powerlessness or loss of control, and that will damage them.

The third is the more 'general play deprivation' either of the type that Charles Whitman, the subject of Stuart Brown's research, experienced, resulting from chronic physical and psychological abuse, or the incessant bullying, sadism, extreme teasing or cruelty to which he also alluded or that inferred from Gray's writing, where play that make possible the creation of personally devised strategies for coping with life, or 'rolling with the punches' as Siviy put it, is actually replaced by adult interventions that diminish or divert the play experience.

I suppose now the question has to be, what practically can be done to avoid and allieviate these forms of play deprivation that appear to be so toxic to children?

I could talk here about the importance of persuasion and information, and they are important, but they are the long haul (as you've seen today) and humans as a species might have disappeared (or died of boredom) by the time everyone who needs to be convinced is. Like astronomy, play is more complicated than most people want it to be. Many people seem to prefer it simple, because that's how they remember childhood to be, me too, that the stars are metaphorically painted on the ceiling or there are holes in the roof that they shine through, and they want a considered analysis to be at about that level. But the constellations, quasars, dark energy and matter, and the quarks of astronomy, are hugely complex, so is play, and only by exploring it in terms of its atomic, molecular, quantum, neurochemical, psychiatric, neurological, evolutionary nature will we ever begin to explain and

358

understand it. The problem is that not everyone has had the revelatory play experiences that some of us have had. They aren't sold on play, they can't or won't intuit its value. Instead they will only rely on evidence and evidence in play is difficult ethically and experimentally to accrue. I've been trying to navigate ways of doing experiments that don't compromise my beliefs or children's privacy and ownership of what they're doing in my work with Islington Play Association, and I'm finding it incredibly difficult to do. In the meantime children are still engaging less and less in authentic playful experiences and that requires action on the ground now.

So what about action? Well, other than information, the other significant avenue would be to offer children access to environments other than the modern technological one they currently inhabit, but what kind of environment could conceivably overcome such malign effects as those we have discussed?

Look at this quote from Orr (1993): 'the human mind is a product of the Pleistocene Age, shaped by wildness that has all but disappeared. If we complete the destruction of nature, we will have succeeded in cutting ourselves off from the sources of sanity itself. So there's the warning again and a solution. The problem is we can't return to the EEA.'

Another clue from Fox, 'if we can't go back to the Palaeolithic, then perhaps we can…start thinking about how we can serve the stubborn human core within the context of the inhuman super society'.

Perhaps if children were able to engage with environments that re-evoked the EEA, that might have the therapeutic and neurological impact to which Fox alludes. They might re-establish psychological and physical links with the Earth and help to override the exploitative attitudes that have existed towards it since Palaeolithic times. They would certainly re-introduce children to the multitude of environmental components like novelty, diversity and malleability that perhaps still echo in their genes, *and* reactivate the playtypes, and engage children in mastery, locomotion, in ritual and the elements.

But that would require that we build versions of the EEA. And although I have been a fervent advocate of the idea of micro-national parks where children might go to play without adults other than specialist playworkers present, I am not as encouraged by the architectural attempts to produce natural play environments to date as others appear to be. For although unlike Disneyland they still feel more like an adult's stereotypical view of the child's chosen world than they do the child's.

Perhaps the most effective way of ensuring the diversity that children crave would be to create mini EEA's everywhere, with stone, tree trunks, water and undergrowth. In vacant lots, rough ground, at the bottom of gardens, in school playgrounds, and car parks, wherever there is space to allow for wilderness not overlooked by adults. That's the important bit for me – not overlooked by adults, so that children can once again immerse themselves in their archetypal narratives and primitive adventures, and re-gain control of the exploration and experimentation that is their play, especially if at the same time, like in the old Westerns, they choose to leave all that isolating, non-sensory technology, iPods, Game Boys, Guitar Heroes, Wiis, laptops, mobile phones, and TVs at the entrance.

'BUBBLE WRAPPED' CHILDREN, THE TECHNICAL AGE AND AN EXPERIMENT IN NOVELTY

(IPPA Conference, Dublin, 2008)

In their mid 1990s study of play-deprived children in Zurich, Huttenmoser and Degan-Zimmermann, described the children whose parents did not allow them out to play as 'battery children' and concluded that they were suffering from symptoms of 'Play Deprivation' as a result of their 'incarceration', citing unhappiness and aggression as two of its affects, and a lack of concentration and an inability to make friends as additional impacts.

The reasons given by parents for not allowing their children out to play were fear of predatory adults and traffic. Increasingly though many parents are prohibiting their children from playing out for far less rational reasons than potential abduction or death. They are simply afraid that they will hurt themselves. The potential impact of this phenomenon is a generation of children who are clumsy, unsocial, anxious and, if you'll forgive the term, potentially street stupid.

I am baffled, although I suspect this is caused, not by what might be construed as reasonable parental concerns about their children being

360

fatally injured or paralysed, but more to do with avoiding the blame and guilt, if anything should happen to them. It is as if some parents feel they have to construct a fantasy of immortality around their children, fearing that if they do not wrap them in non-experiential cotton wool they will be unable to avoid any potentially injurious interaction with the world and will not live forever. The sad thing is, of course, that it is a fantasy, their children will be injured or die sooner or later anyway, and like the rest of us, they will have to deal with that unpleasant reality. The real sadness though, is that by projecting their own fears of death and injury onto their children they are making these outcomes more, not less, likely. For in over protecting them they are making their children less competent to deal with life on a dangerous planet, by the unintended non-skilling that inevitably results from not encouraging them playfully to interface with the world and the Universe. It is after all through this very interaction that their children would have gained the skills to increase their flexible responses and thus their potential to survive the very experiences they most fear.

However, although this is undoubtedly an important issue, I would like to move our focus to a similar although potentially even more serious concern than children being bubble wrapped against physical injury – something that we can, after all, easily overcome. For whilst I agree that some, mainly middle-class children certainly are cosseted by parents and others against physical harm, almost all children, including the bubble wrapped, are left completely exposed to the psychological pressures of life in the modern world. And whilst children are at least well adapted to deal with risk and can expertly 'roll with the punches of [life] as Siviy (1998) puts it, as long as they get the chance to experience them, it is not possible for them to adapt to the modern technological high-speed world, and exposure without adaptation is very dangerous for them.

So in answering the conference question: Are today's children being over-protected? We find ourselves in the odd position that many children are being protected when they don't need to be, and aren't being protected when they ought to be. Here's why:

I understand that our last major evolutionary adaptation took place in the late Palaeolithic period (say 20,000 years ago) and most of what we are now evolved then. So although the world and the environment have moved on, we have stayed more or less the same. We have not adapted to the world we have created for ourselves.

However, although we are to all intents and purposes still Stone-Age, as a species we tend not to describe ourselves in terms of our Palaeolithic credentials, as you might expect, and this has inevitably fed the parental fantasy to which I allude. We prefer instead to perceive ourselves as sophisticated creatures with a much more recent cultural, technological, industrial and scientific heritage. Unfortunately because this view only narrates a tiny fragment of what we are, where we have come from, what we are capable of and most importantly what our needs are, it has had the effect of creating in us an almost schizophrenic schism – which is evident both in the phenomenon of bubble wrapping *and* the dissociated world we have created – between who we really are (modern Palaeolithic), and a fantasy of who we prefer to see ourselves as (only modern). And this gulf between our authentic selves and our preferred fantasy construct of a slim, rich, ageless, cosmetically perfect consumer, as opposed to a dangerous animal with a limited shelf-life, together with an increasing tendency to produce a world for our children which is more rooted in this fantasy, is increasingly causing them, our children, problems.

Far from the fantasy, the real modern world to which our children struggle to adapt is described neatly by the physicist Stuart Kauffman. In his book *Investigations*, he summarises the three Laws of Thermodynamics as follows: You can't win, you can't break even, and you can't get out of the game. He adds a fourth: 'But the game keeps getting more complicated and there are always more different ways to play'.

Although this is a great metaphor for life for today's children, it is frightening if compared to the kind of world to which they are actually adapted, what Bowlby called the ancestral environment, or environment of evolutionary adaptedness. Now, children are constantly running faster in an attempt to keep up with a game that is totally outside of either our or their control.

The anthropologist Robin Fox, like Kauffman, sees change as out of control, but perhaps unlike him, he is fearful of its effects. Fox likens our attempts to keep up with change, to a car which to have a cruising speed of say 85, has to be able to do 120. The point being that 120 is not its optimum speed, but its bolt shaking, cylinder over heating

362

maximum. Fox says, for years now human beings have been putting their feet on the cerebral gas thinking they can go faster and faster, and now we are all doing 110 most of the time, not the 85 we were built to do. How long can that last? He thinks, 'Not very long at all'.

Fox questions whether children can 'sustain all the complexity, the numbers, and the intricacy of organisation' that underpins their lives today? (p. 208). There is an assumption, he suggests, that human beings, the human brain, can in fact do anything, and thus our limitations do not need to be taken into account. But of course they do, and particularly if our species, especially the young, are starting to show increasing signs of strain, which they are. The other thing is that there is something essentially human missing from our technological world that existed in its Palaeolithic counterpart, and one might also ask if the young organism can live without that and the components that narrate it.

For at the same time as they are contorting their immature mind/ brains to adapt to what is to all intents and purposes the unadaptable, given the chance, children continue to be drawn to experiences that are more reflective of life in the EEA, exploring those things that give their lives purpose and meaning – love and attachment, things that interest them, beguile them, afford them privacy and intimacy, challenge and even frighten them, and cause them to stand in awe. For when they aren't being pressured to use Game boys and Wii's they are still manifesting ancient ideas and myth and ritual in their games, as human children have been doing for thousands of years.

It is as if they know they have been born into a context that is both alien and harmful, and although they are driven by their evolutionary heritage to attempt to adapt to it, when allowed they also seek other contexts in which they feel more comfortable, stable, more grounded and more at home – building fires, ranging, climbing, creating shelters, conversation and story telling, and being more engaged with nature.

In describing ourselves in these exclusively modern terms we effectively separate our ancient self, from what we have become, and that is a mistake. For as Wilber tells us, what we are now is an amalgamation of our current and our previous evolutionary stages, not a single separate discrete stage. Not only do we owe our ancient selves for everything we currently have – Fox says for example that modern society is only made possible by the grasping hand, binocular vision, and hand–eye co-ordination shaped by 70 million years in the trees (pp. 208–9), but to perceive ourselves as products of now in a deluded attempt to cast ourselves as only sophisticated and civilized, we run the risk of expecting more of ourselves than we can give, and separating ourselves from our true nature, whilst constructing modern criminal or medical explanations for, and reactions to, the crises our children are experiencing, which, when viewed through the lens of our Palaeolithic ancestors, are quite predictable.

My greatest fear is that because of the current tendency for their total immersion in technology from TV, to mobile phones, the internet and game consoles (given to them normally by the same parents who also 'bubble wrap' them) and an increasing detachment from planetary reality, children inevitably conclude that what is on offer is the only way the future can be constructed. This is new. I believe that as recently as 35–40 years ago most children accessed authentic comprehensive play experiences on a regular basis. And that meant that they encountered alternatives and choices to the worldview they were being moulded too. That is not the case now. The choices available through play to my and my children's generation are only accessed by my grandchildren's generation for a fraction of the time and all too often only then when their parents take them to them in a car.

We know that in interacting playfully with the environment, not only is neural matter created and organised; not only do children gain the skills of calibration and coordination; not only do they become increasingly flexible and adaptable in their responses; not only do they activate survival skills the organism has memorised from its ancient past; not only do they create and interpret cortical maps which may be the precursor to human consciousness, and not only do they use play as a therapeutic medium, but because the net outcome of children's interactions with one another and with the whole environment is randomness, creativity and unpredictability, new neural mechanisms and circuits can be formed, and new ways of organising, of communicating, of creating and problem-solving can come about. Without a comprehensive and uncensored play experience, the real risk is that children, and as an eventual consequence our whole species, end up in a stagnant cycle of repetition, rather than a random, creative, and dynamic development, which is underpinned by play in childhood. The drive to homogenise ourselves, to reduce our species to a one size fits all formula, where there is no 'there' any more, and

364

where every 'high street' is identical, is a catastrophe for our evolutionary and our survival need for diversity.

There is a price to pay if human children are unable to play, or to engage in play as a comprehensive experience to counteract the impact both of bubble wrapping and more effectively respond to the technological vice into which their heads are being forced. [Our brain], says Fox, 'is not an organ of cool rationality: it is a surging field of electrochemical activity replete with emotion and geared for a particular range of adaptive responses. Force it to try to work outside of that range for long enough [remember the car analogy], and it will act, it will rebel. It will regress to those pristine behaviours (including the very necessary aggressive ones) surrounding its primary functions, survival and reproduction' (p. 209).

In *Evolutionary Psychiatry*, Stevens and Price concur, citing suicide, depression, self-harming and a whole raft of what they call archetypal illnesses/disorders, as symptoms of children's inability to adapt to the world we are creating for them. In Russia, for example, 15 to 20 young people have committed suicide every month for years (*Pravda* 15/4/08). And in London and other big UK cities, knife and gun crimes between children and young people are at epidemic levels.

I have no doubt that particularly in highly urban environments, children are increasingly suffering psychiatric, archetypal and stress related illnesses, or alienation and dissociation, because they cannot adapt to the world they are in, and the world they are adapted to no longer exists (except perhaps in rare remote corners) and it is my belief that this has increasingly lethal consequences for them and for the rest of us. The play deprivation and trauma-control literature, although not huge, paints a very bleak picture. Increasingly children and young people are showing symptoms of a psychic bewilderment resulting from living in a reality where there is no longer any conducive space to be the creature they sense they are, and to playfully do battle with the physical and psychological universe, which in our 'real' history as a species is something as children we have always done.

However, as Kauffman suggests, we can neither stop the juggernaut of progress nor avoid it, but by creating authentic play spaces that reflect the EEA, that provide an oasis and sanctuary from the modern world, that do contain risk, as well as novelty, freedom, access to the elements *and* allow an evolutionary and emotional honesty which at the moment in a world of adult and technical surveillance is being increasingly repressed in children's lives, we may be able to help to equip current and future generations to more flexibly respond to the modern world and cope with it more effectively, and perhaps develop the skills to create social alternatives that better suit what we are.

Stevens and Price suggest that it is the potential of an environment to facilitate 'healthy development *and* prevent and treat mental disorders' which is paramount, and I agree with them. So it is an exploration of one particular aspect of such environmental potential on which I will focus now. That aspect is novelty. And to do this I would like to describe an experiment I've been running recently.

The experiment, which is work I am doing for the Islington Play Association in London, is centred on the impact of environmental changes on children's activity levels. The theory being that environmental modification, a common adventure playground practice, by providing what is called a neophilic focus and stimulating activity, has the effect of compensating for the children's lack of opportunity to range, and to access environmental variability. Today's children's Palaeolithic contemporaries would have played in an environment of great natural and experiential unpredictability, which would have contributed to their ability to adapt and to their feelings of place and significance. What I wanted to explore was if a similar reaction could be created using different modifications. So now I want to share with you a brief summary of the 'novel' changes that transpired during the experiment, and the effects they had.

The changes or modifications that were initiated during the experiment were intended to add excitement, fantasy and a varying degree of risk to each playground, but although the changes made on the first two playgrounds were interesting they were also predictable – for example one was a rope bridge, and the other involved runways and stepping stones, so although I will return to them, I want first to concentrate on what transpired on the three remaining playgrounds.

On the first of these, playworkers and children wanted something that would make it possible to access a graduated level of risk, a kind of puzzle that only the most competent players would be able to solve.

We decided on what I called a Mathematical Tower. It was a kind of large triangular structure, whose rungs not only rotated around the triangle but were increasingly further apart. So to scale the tower children had to climb around it, but as the rungs were further and further apart they also had to stretch and be increasingly competent climbers. When completed, the tower was topped by a small crow's nest.

On the next playground I collaborated with Zoe Akamiotaki, a PhD student who was researching playground design. We opted for an exploration of the impact of Nicholson's Theory of Loose Parts on the children's activity.

For those who are not familiar, Nicholson's Theory proposes that 'in any environment, both the degree of inventiveness and creativity, and the possibility of discovery, are directly proportional to the number and kind of variable (loose parts) in it'. What this meant was that our modification this time involved a selection of different loose parts.

During our five-hour experiment we gradually made a variety of different everyday objects – cloth, shells, boxes, string, washing-up bowls, inflated shapes, short canes, coloured balls and so on, randomly available to the children by placing them in a particular area of the playsite. Although uptake was initially slow, the materials gradually encouraged a complex and comprehensive, often high-level-locomotor narrative that took in at least thirty children over the whole play area.

On the final playground I had observed that some of the children who went there appeared depressed, even dissociated, and some twelve-year-olds were using strong drugs. Discussing this with playworkers and parents I wondered if we could create what Sturrock (2007), terms an 'iconic lure', which would address these children's deeper archetypal needs, and offer them a psychological door, a portal, through which they might see the playground in a different light.

Given that the children to which I refer were predominantly from the African continent they may have been looking intuitively for a particular cultural cue from the play environment that it was not offering, and I was concerned that the playground was acting more as a blockage than a facilitator to these children because of this.

It is well known, as Stevens and Price suggest, that environments that are perceived as rejecting, un-nurturing and alienating by children do badly at alleviating their archetypal problems and may assist in the creation of psychiatric illnesses instead.

The form this modification eventually took was informed by Sturrock's (2007) notion of a 'counter cue', something which is very different to what is already present in the environment, and so personal and powerful to the children that it will have the effect of unconsciously sacrilizing the play space for them and endowing it with sacred or at least some spiritual value. The intended affect being belonging rather than rejection.

The counter cues I initially considered included various 'western' religious icons, but I judged these as inappropriate. Eventually I found the cue I was looking for on the Internet. It was an image of an African Head, which had been discovered in Mexico and made around 3000 BC by the Olmecs. The hairs on the back of my neck stood up when this came on the screen.

As I speak the world-famous Nigerian sculptor and wood carver, Emmanuel Jegede, is actually engaged in creating his interpretation of that African Head, into a structure that will hopefully trigger feelings of worth and belonging in the children who attend this playground. It will be completed by the end of May 2008.

Findings

Each of these modifications has met with different reactions from the children. The permanent ones – the bridge, stepping-stones and tower – are used continually for a whole variety of fantasy and chase games. The bridge is very popular, as are the stepping-stones to a lesser degree – and this is two years on – but the tower is apparently a bit too tame, it is only seven metres high! On the day it was completed a boy of about seven or eight came in after school and asked if I'd like to see him climb it. I said OK, expecting him to get about half way up because of his diminutive size. Without batting an eyelid he flew up to the top of the structure and stood, not sat, stood on the crow's nest platform. It's a great view from up here he said. Apparently, so the playworkers told me later, the children had been all over the structure, from the very first day we'd started it.

If I have one criticism of the different modifications outlined above, it is that with the exception of the loose parts, and to some extent the HEAD project, they lacked the malleability, the potential for manipulation and

368

change by the children that is inherent in all aspects of a good play environment. The loose parts exercise, however, although not a permanent fixture, was totally the children's, and escalated over several hours into a wonderful chase/fight/prisoner sequence that attracted loads of children over the whole project and incorporated height, speed and social interaction throughout.

Each of these modifications triggered different reactions, which in turn resulted in a whole variety of risks, fantasies, social interactions, immersions and diversions, the latter being critical for children who often need to forget their stressful lives and just play.

This experiment shows how the problems resulting from bubble wrapping and technological over exposure can be approached playfully – by enabling more flexible responses to them and emotional holidays from them. But for many if not most children, play experiences of this diversity and challenge, incorporating the thrills of imagination, climbing, balance and coordination at height, and undertaking journeys of personal discovery, are never available to them. The huge benefits both from a physical and perhaps more important a psychological perspective are obvious. They should be available regularly and comprehensively to all children, not just the lucky few.

The big problem is not how to provide, but how to get parents to let their children engage in the authentic play experiences that good provision offers, and which carry huge biological benefits. I know that here and in the UK Government, providers, and particularly parents, do want children to have access to what they perceive as play, but I am concerned that they are confusing authentic biological play incorporating real risk and other issues which have yet to get this kind of public airing, with benign entertainment and that again is a manifestation of the gulf between our Palaeolithic needs and our modern interpretation of them. I know that many parents, who are striving for wealth, and for good education and life chances for their children, find the whole idea of viewing themselves and their children as animals, as Stone Age, repugnant and disgusting. But I think this has to be our starting point. We have to jettison our socio-cultural priorities and acknowledge the desperate need for a bio-evolutionary analysis instead.

To return to Fox for the last word, 'Where must we start in trying to re-understand ourselves? It will be a basic contention here that we must condemn as deficient any commentary on the human condition that fails to take into account the ancientness of the species and the more than five million years of natural selection that have moulded the questionable end product that includes the commentators and their commentaries. That is to say, anything but an evolutionary view of modern man is going to be insufficient if its purpose is to calculate the possibilities of human survival' (p. 207).

THE BEAUTY OF PLAY

(The 1st Beauty of Play Conference, The Hayes, Near Stone, Staffordshire, 2003.)

In the recent past a considerable amount has been written from a scientific perspective about play. Using evolutionary theory, the depth and other psychologies, the neurosciences, the behavioural sciences and a host of other perspectives, different playwork authors have tried to demonstrate the importance of play in getting us to where we are today, in fighting the pressures of extinction and in keeping ourselves sane, and I have been as guilty of this focus as anyone. And yet although I believe that play and playwork have benefited enormously from a scientific analysis, both have a significant creative and artistic component too. So at a time when playwork conversations are all too often liberally sprinkled with terms like neurochemical, evolutionary, plasticity, types, frames and cues, it is perhaps appropriate and timely that a gathering focussing on one of the more esoteric, softer but no less striking qualities of play, its beauty, has been organised. I thank Perry for that and for inviting me to give my views at it. However, typically, this invitation has faced me with a real challenge too.

Having accepted the invitation to do this and reflecting on what I might say, I began to realise that like other things in my life, I didn't have anything particularly tangible to say on the subject. I appreciate beauty – I know a beautiful sunset, a beautiful photograph or an area of outstanding natural beauty when I see it and I know a beautiful piece of music when I hear it, but neither my background – nor my education has provided me with the language to turn this emotional appreciation, what I *feel* about beauty, into a confident and accurate articulation which would do those feelings justice. So you will appreciate that the process

370

of developing this paper has been a revelation, a personal journey of enlightenment.

Beauty is defined as a combination of qualities that pleases the aesthetic, intellectual or moral senses. And beauty is only skin deep and in the eye of the beholder so the clichés tell us. Is it even appropriate to think of describing play as beautiful, if beauty is just subjectively all encompassing? But of course it isn't *just* anything. It is a complex concept and the phenomena we describe as beautiful encapsulate great aesthetic, emotional, even mystical capital that we trivialise at our peril.

So what is beauty and what does perceiving beauty mean? These are both hugely difficult and complex questions and to even begin to address them I need to construct some parameters for myself. If I say that defining the abstract notion of beauty *and* my active perception of it, both require a similar if not the same process, a process which culminates in the realisation of something nearing a perfect fit, a subjective congruence, then I can put a name to that process. It isn't a word commonly heard in playwork circles, but typically it is one I have heard Gordon Sturrock use, and if other instances of his adoption of terminology suited to playwork phenomena are anything to go by then it, like others, will be in common usage within a relatively short space of time. That word is epiphany. Epiphany for those unacquainted with the term was first used in a non-religious context by James Joyce in the book *Stephen Hero* written by Joyce in 1944. Hero is described as overhearing fragments of conversation between a young lady and a young gentleman, and he is so moved by what he hears, which he describes as a sudden spiritual manifestation, to contemplate the collection of such resultant 'epiphanies', which he seems to perceive as the moment when a number of what appear to be unrelated fragments come into focus to form an amalgamated reality of a higher order.

In the following passages Joyce describes first what beauty is, and then how it passes through its epiphany.

He takes as his starting point a definition of beauty devised by St Thomas Aquinas who in his *Summa Theologiae* gives three distinguishing characteristics of beauty: wholeness or integrity, proportion or harmony, and *claritas* which can be translated as splendour, radiance, light, brilliance. The chief characteristic (of beauty), he says, is *claritas*, 'radiance' ... beautiful things shine.

371

First Joyce's character Hero describes how he reaches his own definition, 'Consider the performance of your own mind when confronted
with any object hypothetically beautiful. Your mind, to apprehend,
that is, to understand, and, to capture that object divides the entire
universe into two parts, the object, and the void, which is not the
object. To apprehend it you must lift it away from everything else: and
then you perceive it is one integral thing, that is *a* thing. You recognise its integrity. That is the first quality of beauty: it is declared in a
sudden simple synthesis of the faculty which apprehends'.

'Then', he says, 'the mind considers the object in the whole and in
part, in relation to itself and to other objects, examines the balance of
its parts, contemplates the form of the object, traverses every cranny
of the structure. So the mind receives the impression of the symmetry of the object. The mind recognises that the object is, in the strict
sense of the word, a thing, a definitely constituted entity'. Symmetry
is Hero's second quality of beauty.

Hero now moves towards his interpretation of beauty's epiphany.
'Now for the third quality' he says. 'For a long time I couldn't make
out what Aquinas meant. He uses a figurative word (a very unusual
thing for him) but I have solved it. Claritas is quidditas (literally 'whatness'). After the analysis which discovers the second quality, the mind
makes the only logically possible synthesis and discovers the third
quality. This is the moment which I call epiphany'.

So beauty, as far as Joyce's Hero is concerned, can be defined by trans-
lating Aquinas's integrity, harmony, and radiance, into integrity, symmetry and epiphany, the last of which I understand as a kind of
Gestalt, or birth, a clarification or focus or even an amalgamated transcendence of all the parts, where the sum is far more than the total of
the components.

I love this process. As well as being a playworker I am a writer, in particular a songwriter, and I have long been a lover of such beautifully
put together language. However, although the construct of the words
feels beautiful, and although the definition which manifests itself feels
accurate, perhaps because of its subjective nature, or because of the
infinity of its sources, it also feels incomplete. Did Aquinas apply
beauty to too narrow a field, beautiful things, jewels or religious icons
perhaps? And did Joyce apply the reverse, seeing beauty in everything, in this example a street clock? The beauty I perceive may be

372

somewhere else, its field much wider than that perceived only by the rich, and yet narrower than the 'beauty is everything' perception, which reduces beauty to the mundane.

Reflecting on this I became interested to know when I used the word beautiful and to what it applied. I began to listen out for every time I said it and in which context I was saying it. Unsurprisingly, beautiful applied to a whole range of different situations, objects, feelings and vistas. What had they in common? What was their integrating pattern? Did they shine, or have symmetry, oneness or epiphany, I had no idea? I thought long and hard about this and found that the way I was perceiving beauty was not in terms of what it was, but in terms of what it did *to* me or, better still, *for* me. From this perspective, particularly in the context of play, I began to see beauty, in the sense that Joyce and Aquinas define it anyway, as a tool which may have evolved to provide us with a source of spiritual optimism, of strength and energy.

In John Steinbeck's *Log from the Sea of Cortez* there is a passage where he is writing about the marine biologist Ed Ricketts, Doc from Cannery Row and Sweet Thursday, in which Ed is quoted as saying, 'nearly everything that can happen to people not only does happen but has happened for a million years. Therefore, for everything that can happen there is a channel or mechanism in the human to take care of it, a channel worn down in prehistory and transmitted in the genes' (p. 20).

Indulge me for a moment. Life is not an easy process. And although we have no other home, the Earth is not an easy place to live it either. And as our species has evolved greater consciousness, so it has also become plagued by fears both real and imagined. How do we survive this onslaught of anxiety? How do we transcend the raw reality that once we are born the one remaining certainty is death? Of course, we can find any number of soporifics to blunt the sharp edges of this reality, and we all turn at different times to our drug of choice. But there is one characteristic of that same cruel reality, as real as death, disease and war itself, which instead of adding to the already mind numbingly frightening, enables us to still our racing hearts, transcend fear, and the production line of mortality and instead provides us with an axis, a counterpoint to, an opposite of the ugliness and horror of life. This characteristic is beauty.

What beauty does, however we individually perceive it, is tell us a whole other story, give us a whole new set of parameters about what life is, let us know that not only is it not all bad, but that on one level, it isn't bad at all. That if we sensitise ourselves to what is there, our view of life can be transformed by much of what surrounds us. We can transcend the shit. I don't mean that the shit goes away, of course it doesn't. But an appreciation of beauty provides a balancing mechanism, which says yes, it is like that too, but that is only a part of the story.

What this says to me is that natural selection may favour an appreciation of beauty and that the perception of something we call beauty has evolved so that we can draw inner strength from some of what we perceive, because with the realisation of beauty comes this powerful survival realisation, that however bad life becomes we know that that is not all there is. If we can hang on to that, if we can separate out the beauty from the rest, if we can apprehend it for the counterpoint it provides, then we can activate optimism from which we can draw strength both for ourselves and for others. The optimism we draw from beauty could be a significant factor in our survival as a species to date.

However, if an appreciation of beauty has facilitated survival, how might this vital quality have been passed onto each generation throughout our evolutionary history?

This brings me to one specific facet of the beauty of play, and it is one I have been alluding to over the past two/three years in material I've been writing. It is the beauty of what I see as a continuity and groundedness, which every one of us can perceive if we are enabled so to do. Notwithstanding its nasty eugenicists' interpretation, a very unbeautiful corruption, Stanley Hall's Recapitulation Theory holds within it what I perceive as a particularly beautiful idea, so integrated into the human psyche, so applicable to us all, so full of soul that it has its epiphany at the birth of every child.

In her book *Transformations*, Schwartzman says that Hall's (and Reaney's) thinking proposed 'that the various stages of childhood could be divided into "play periods", that corresponded with the various stages of human evolution'. Or as Garvey (1977) puts it, recapitulation 'reflects the course of evolution from prehistoric hominids to the present' (p. 9). What Hall proposed was that when children played they recapitulated or recapped the various stages of human evolutionary history. These stages were named the animal, savage, nomad, pastoral and the tribal, although I think there must have been many more of them. These recapitulated stages were identified in the following ways. The animal stage or period (birth to age 7) was reflected in swinging and climbing games; the savage stage (7–9) exhibited hunting and throwing games; the nomad stage (9–12) was reflected in skill and adventure games and 'an interest in keeping pets', and the pastoral and tribal stages (12–17) were characterised by doll play, gardening and finally team games (p. 47).

What Hall and later Ken Wilber seem to be suggesting is that not only do children reflect the past in their play patterns but that there is a reason for this. That our evolution dictates that past evolutionary stages have to be passed on to each new generation during procreation, genetically I assume. That part of our evolution is that our evolutionary history is always a part of what we are, our evolutionary present. Wilber in particular suggests the notion that human beings are composites, amalgamations, both of the present and of their evolutionary past. What I infer from this is that as our evolution has progressed, rather than shedding our past forms like snakes shedding their skin, human evolution has devised a way of incorporating all past stages into each new one (together with all of the physiological and psychological survival lessons each stage has accrued, including, in this context, an appreciation of beauty). How does it do this? I would like to hazard a guess. Although this additional genetic material has been passed on, for it to be usable, it needs to be integrated into the child's current consciousness, actualised into its contemporary behaviour. To do this each child in each new generation needs to be rebooted in order to transform latent genetic material into an integral part of that child's being. And for this to happen, and of course I am guessing, each new child, together with its past evolutionary stages encoded in its genes, undergoes a complete revamp during the first eight years of its life, i.e., during what is known as the 'sensitive period', by gradually 'playing itself up to contemporary evolutionary speed' via a kind of actualising recap. This is the 'rebooting' process I mentioned earlier. This systems update, which is evident in other species including songbirds, where all past stages become integrated into the current one, was what I believe Hall saw taking place when he observed children engaging in recapitulative play.

Wilber suggests that the integration of evolutionary stages is vitally important and that if for any reason it doesn't happen we become ill, which gives us an indication of how important recapitulative play might be to us. ' … each stage of evolution transcends but includes its predecessor', Wilber says, 'each stage of human evolution, although it transcends its predecessor, must include and integrate [it]. Failure to integrate each stage', he says, 'will result in neurosis'.

What Hall and Wilber seem to suggest is that engaging in recapitulation should not be viewed as a choice but as a survival and developmental imperative. That if human beings are not able to engage in recapitulative activity, including for example taking risks, then a vital part of the adaptive process which is essential for their survival will falter and the symptomology of this happening will be the development of neuroses. For not only will a lack of recapitulation give children a dangerously incomplete account of who and what they are (p. 10), it will take away millions of years of groundedness, and leave them floating unanchored in psychic space, without reference points – a powerful breeding ground for anxiety. In short not recapitulating will malform the child, rendering a beautiful and symmetrical process, including the mechanism for an appreciation of beauty, into an unsymmetrical and uncontextualised product, in which that mechanism and others are absent.

Although that is a very unbeautiful prospect, that evolution has created this complex recapitulative mechanism in the first place is in itself an incredibly beautiful notion.

This is part of the beauty I perceive when I observe children playing. The living manifestation of the powerful relationship between our survival as a species, our evolution and playing. And to some extent this relationship does satisfy both Joyce's and Aquinas's criteria, although I don't want to get too bogged down with them. Certainly recapitulation has its own integrity by displaying a completeness, which can be separated by the intellect from other play phenomena. It has symmetry in the sense that it displays both a generational enclosure and the same overall replay/recap narrative for us all, irrespective of culture, geography, gender or socio-economic status, and it culminates in incandescent epiphany at the rebirth of its own whatness, its soul, every time a child is born and is transformed during its early childhood by its engagement in recapitulative play.

Needless to say, the problem about attempting to define beauty, let alone play, is that beauty has so many faces. Here I have attempted to explore the beauty of play from a Western literary/religious perspective. However, the beauty of play as an abstract evolutionary idea, and the somewhat heavy handedness of the definitions I have used to provide an analysis of it, although useful, only go so far in helping me to understand the beauty of play the behaviour. For a more precise focus I need another set of parameters.

What has always struck me about play is that its external manifestations are always so simple. No wonder those less familiar with the awesome ideas contained within the play literature opt for words like fun to describe play. Perhaps because of the flamboyance and exclusivity of the Joyce/Aquinas definition I feel happier describing the beauty of play as external simplicity and internal complexity. What you see in play is definitely not all you get. There is a term in Zen Buddhism, which means 'aloofness in the midst of multiplicities' (p. 217). That term is 'wabi' and to a limited extent alludes to 'Joyce's quidditas or whatness'. 'Wabi' refers to 'simplicity in all things and the absence of visible skill' (p. 217), where one is seduced by 'aesthetic refinement', rather than the gilded definition offered by Joyce and Aquinas. To me this simplicity, this essence, is closer to the beautiful play I perceive, than the ornate western literary view. I would like to allude to this idea of essence, of simplicity and complexity in my final piece, the true face of the beauty of play, the playing child.

I've always said that you only need an hour walking with a child to be provided with a visual presentation of everything you need to know to be a good playworker. Young children especially will just play as you walk and any observant playworker will begin to see how the play process operates as it unfolds before their very eyes.

Over this summer I've had the privilege of spending some long periods playing with and observing the play of a two–and-a-half-year-old. During one play bout in which I was marginally included he spent considerable tracts of time involved in the following episodes.

The first episode was called Ahhhhh magic and it was a communication/locomotor game that he spontaneously created, a bit like snap. With snap you alternately lay cards, anticipating similar cards being laid and then, when they are, you say/shout snap. For the adult and young child none of the fun is in the cards, all the fun is in how and how quickly you say snap! It's all the fun and security of repetition, spiced up with minor tonal variation. Ahhhhh magic feels similar. The Ahhhh part is the equivalent of laying the cards in snap, it is the prelude, the foreplay, the build-up to the really exciting bit – MAAAAAAAGIC, which he/we shouted, elongated and laughed through. He developed a number of variations of Ahhhhhh magic, including chasing round a tree saying Ahhh, and saying magic when one of us was caught by the other, chasing round a tree with a stick (wand), each saying Ahhh and magic when one of us was caught in a spell by the other, jumping onto a manhole cover and saying Ahhh as we jumped and magic as we landed, and throwing a stick at each other, saying Ahhh before we threw, and magic as we threw. His repetition was punctuated by joyful laughter, he appeared totally at ease with what he was doing, although to undertake each episode required a vast range of different developing physical and psychological skills and awarenesses. In total these 'simple' moments were just so beautifully complex and astounding. Minutes after finishing Ahhh-hhhhhhh magic, he sat in an indentation in the grass, smiled at me and said 'I'm a flower'. Fwouwer. (as in cower). Incredible.

What I was watching, and what was to me so reflective of the Zen notion of external simplicity born of internal complexity, was a young human organism, spontaneously engaging in a diverse range of vocal, locomotor, imaginative, repetitive, competitive, coordinational, deep, calibrational, social and immersed activity. Often apparently at the same time, although I think the separation between each one was just too fast for me to see. What drove him to do what he did? Given his range of vocalisation and movements, I would say that he was experiencing a lot of pleasure and a tiny, tiny measure of terror simultaneously. The pleasure was derived from the doing, the action and interaction, I imagine. The terror, if that is the correct term, perhaps came from an instinctive assessment that some of what was happening was out of his control. What he was doing was taking a risk, which clearly he wanted to do, but he felt a little fear in so doing. He was the initiator and the controller, but he was driven to go marginally outside of what he knew to broaden his experience on each play occasion.

After this, I sat on a park bench and just watched him on the periphery of my vision. He began to collect the flotsam and jetsam surrounding the bench. There were beer bottle tops which he dug out of the ground with his fingers and then with a lolly stick, arranging them in patterns. There were used matches and drinking straws, which he poked in the slats of the bench. Then getting behind the bench he invited me to join him in what appeared to be an imaginary shelter or hide away – he wanted me to sit on the ground behind the bench with him. He was very insistent, almost urgent that I did it in the right way. It wasn't good enough that I pretended, I had to be. And he appeared relieved when it seemed real enough to him. After a few moments of that he moved on again.

For him his imagined scenario had to be authentic, a kind of reality, I couldn't pretend, he'd know instantly that that was what I was doing. He had an inbuilt fraud detector that would know when the fit was right and more importantly when it was not. The idea of fit, although perhaps reminiscent of integrity and symmetry too, also brings us back to the Zen notion of Wabi. Fit is a very simple term to visualise – imagine keys into locks, for example – but fit is incredibly complex to imagine as a biological mechanism, being challenged as it is by the neuroscientific explanation of how synapses function and how neurochemicals might move across them. My guess is that what he was feeling was not an emotion when he was being urgently insistent. As I have said several times recently, I think it was from an even deeper source than that. It was to do with this idea of fit. It was as if he already knew the answer in his whole body but needed it actualised to enable him to make the connection between his internal world and the external world he was learning to navigate. It had to *be* right. Not feel right. *Be* right. He knew the answer already, but had to recap it, perhaps because he could only complete a neural circuit, and that part of his systems update, by so doing.

Research is beginning to tell us that playing species have complete neural circuits developed that enable them to recognise authentic play cues and play patterns in others. It also states that enacting certain motor patterns is an essential precursor to being able to perform certain behaviours – a kind of sub-play – and I think that what he might have been doing was trying to help me to fit a pattern that he sensed from his own neural structure. It is that 'fitness' that I think moves us near to one of my earliest descriptions of beauty. That is, it is in the eye of the beholder. We *know* when something is beautiful to us, perhaps because it closely 'fits' one of these preset neural templates.

And it is this 'fit' that I think the drinking straws and matches episode was about too. It reminded me of 'a dolls and chainlink fence' scenario Gordon Sturrock had talked to me about a couple of years ago. Then we had talked about symbolic interpretations to explain it, and that may still be the case here, he may have been looking for security by creating order – order with the straws and matchsticks, *and* in the patterns he was creating with the bottle tops (at one point I said 'That's a pattern', and he re-arranged them (he's 2.5) and said, 'There's another pattern').

Alternatively it may have been an exercise in mastery – that he wanted to have control of the shape of the bench and was using the available props, in this case matches and straws, to change it. But my guess was that he was probably engaging in a calibration experiment with the gaps between the slats simply to see if the straws and matches would fit and if they would stay where he put them, thus confirming another piece of his genetically projected neural jigsaw. Perhaps he instinctively knew that the gap was bigger than the objects he was inserting. Perhaps he had already calibrated the activity visually, but needed to do it physically, just to confirm it and thus remove any potential for anxiety and frustration. Whatever.

Certainly what I perceived were hypotheses being tested and confirmed or discarded. I saw unconscious contextualisation too. When left to play with what was there, he naturally gravitated to the available props. He didn't ask for anything, he simply went and found things and used them to test out their potency in providing him with what he needed. These props told him about where he was. If he had been in India, Russia or Australia they would have been different props, providing him with information about that location. There is a beauty in this that I feel genuinely overawed by. Aquinas says beautiful things shine. And when I observe this interlocking complexity where so many different biological processes, so dependent one upon the other, feedback in unison like a mad interconnected process of maelstroms or vortexes, it feels to me that I am witnessing a universe of which I have little comprehension except the beauty of the reality I observe. And there is a radiance about that which I can only describe as cosmic.

Is play beautiful? Clearly it has many beautiful aspects but what I find overarchingly beautiful about play is that given the functions

380

attributed to it by science, primarily its role as the enabler of our individual and species adaptation and survival, it manifests itself as such a spiritual and quirky process. Its 'whatness', its quidditas, its essence is that it is of children. And because of that, play is lairy, mad, bonkers and hilarious, it has to be because that's what children have to be, without it they would have no antidote to the 'shadow' and we would not survive as a species.

This is play's beautiful secret. It has evolved as an evolutionary tool to be activated when the need arises, and because we are a diverse species, found in a diversity of contexts, evolving through time, for play to be, and to have been of value to us all, irrespective of location or circumstances or culture, or historical period, it has had to be able to operate usefully within that diversity, that means that the rules that govern play, determine its simple manifestations and ensure that children return to it again and again, must have their source at the very molecular/atomic autopoietic core of the child.

Albert Camus said, 'Beauty is unbearable, [it] drives us to despair, offering us for a minute the glimpse of an eternity that we should like to stretch out over the whole of time', and there is something inescapably and unbearably timeless and yearning about play too. And there are inevitable traps in writing about either of these subjects, traps of subjectivity, lost youth, sentiment and edited or embellished experience.

However, having said that and irrespective of which definition I use, play is still the most beautiful phenomenon I know. I say this for the following reasons. This outwardly simple process has guaranteed our continuation for millions of years during which countless numbers of non-playing species have disappeared. It has enabled us to continually develop and evolve skills and perceptions which both enrich our lives and help us to cope with our frightening planetary predicament. And most importantly it is our life giver, enabling our children, and theirs, and the generations that hopefully follow, to respond flexibly to change, to adapt, and through that process to continue to transcend their current humanness and humanity. That such simple actions could result in such awesome and complex consequences is truly beautiful.

MICK'S STORIES 7

The door

One of the most interesting play structures I've ever seen on an adventure playground is a door. That's it – just a doorframe with a perfectly normal domestic door. But the children have invented dozens of games with and without rules about 'the door to nowhere' – who can use it when and in which direction in chasing games; fantasies about what might be on the other sides; elaborate rituals of politely visiting and receiving visitors or less polite games of 'Police! Open up!' Knock Down Ginger made a re-appearance on the playground after decades of absence in the surrounding area.

At the same playground the playworkers have thought carefully about the entrance to the playground. Some of the younger children in the neighbourhood were not using the playground, so they visited local primary schools, family and community centres to try to find out why. They discovered that it was because children and parents were unsure about their welcome – partly because they felt the entrance was intimidating and didn't give sufficiently welcoming visual signals.

They spent several weeks experimenting with 'dressing' the entrance with art activities outside the gate. As well as ending up with an entrance that was more inviting in the child's eye view, the presence of a playworker doing interesting things at the gate created an inviting threshold.

I have come to believe that we should put at least as much thought into what messages playground thresholds and boundaries send to children as we do to the structures, features and 'implicit permissions' inside. Doors, gates and fences on adventure playgrounds have more subtle and complex roles and functions than in most other places – they are not just physical entrances and boundaries.

If they don't send clear signals that 'this is a place for children' and imply a welcome, then it is hardly surprising if some children are wary about coming in.

Puddles and rainbows

From when I was a small child to this day I have been fascinated by puddles. Back then I loved the upside-down world in their reflections, but became a little bit wary of them after a cousin told me that if you saw a rainbow in one you would fall into fairyland and never be able to get back. Fifty-odd years later a little niece warned me that something similar could happen: 'You might fall upside-down into the sky and never, ever fly back up'.

It had been pouring rain during a morning finance meeting at the playground, and four-year-old Martin, the son of our committee chair, was bored with painting. The sun came out, and his mum said he could go out to play. Just as the meeting ended he came running in shouting 'Rainbow! Rainbow!'

Out we went and looked up – no sign of a rainbow. With a grin Martin pointed to the puddle-strewn pathway to the playground structures – every puddle was a different colour of the rainbow, with around half a tin of our precious powder paints carefully stirred into each.

Astronomy

The playground was part of a consortium that had successfully fund-raised to run camping holidays in the summer for many years. They bought a proper reflecting telescope to stargaze on clear nights in the countryside. During a sleepover back in London they borrowed it as the forecast was a clear night with a full moon.

The playworkers suddenly noticed that all the boys had disappeared outside, but thought no more of it. When they were called back in for supper, they were in hysterics, and a playworker decided to go out and investigate why. The telescope was focussed, not on the skies, but on the window of an eleventh floor flat in a tower block, where a young woman had no idea that anyone would be able to see her with no clothes on.

A partially blocked drain meant that on many days there was a large puddle that the playworkers left alone because children endlessly played with and in it – in all sorts of ways. They floated self-made paper or other boats on it; put bricks in as stepping stones for varieties of chase games; or just exuberantly jumped in it to splash other children.

A playworker had been thinking about how the children could observe the 1999 solar eclipse without the palaver of special glasses or indirect viewers to protect their eyes. She suddenly realised that the slightly muddy puddle would be the perfect viewer in which to safely see the sun disappear and reappear and would provide a grandstand view of the eclipse for everyone.

CHAPTER 14

CONCLUSION

In his book *The Wild Places*, MacFarlane (2010) explores the etymology of the term 'wildness'. 'Rooted...in a descriptive meaning of wilful, or uncontrollable, wildness', he says, 'is an expression of independence from human direction', and can be said to be 'self-willed'. He is talking about wild spaces, or wilderness, but the description applies equally well to my own perception of the child at play. In the preceding text, I have used the term feral to describe this quality, but feral does not really provide an adequate linguistic fit, or visual representation of the player. MacFarlane also writes of wildness, '[It] proceeds according to its own laws and principles whose habits are of its own devising and own execution. [It] acts or moves freely without restraint; is unconfined, unrestricted' (p. 30).

So my wild playing child, as a representation of everything human that has gone before, is as ancient and ageless as the land; the wise sage and the awestruck newcomer; the timeless survivor and the passionate explorer.

This view of the nature of the player, amalgamated as it is with the findings of the more recent science, underpin a powerful argument in favour of some kind of 'playwork' intervention, when children are either not able to play, or where play opportunities are biased, impoverished, or their range incomplete. The material provided by Beckoff and Byers (1998) and Burghardt (2005) in particular demonstrates that play – as an adult-free, independent set of timeless behavioural routines – provides a crucial underpinning for the continuing survival, adaptation and evolution of a mentally-fit human-kind.

In short, human children have to play, and whether they range freely or visit play settings, it is crucial we describe that play as MacFarlane's wildness does, rather than the more convenient, but ultimately toxic description used in education, socialisation and domestication. Children, and all human beings, must retain their relationship to their primeval evolutionary past, and I am deeply concerned that the links are decaying, simply as a result of a general decrease in the frequency with which modern children are accessing those 'authentic' play experiences that include risk, independence, sex, the elements, mastery, other children, and other species.

The best outcome we can hope for, if this transition from player to non-player is completed, will be anxious humans, who are totally dependent on a perception of life that is virtual; that is generated by the kind of 'convenient partiality' of which Orwell wrote. The worst will be that we do not survive it.

The survival of our optimism in particular depends as much on our voracity as it does our creativity; as much on our collective independence, as our gregariousness. But a playless childhood, or worse still the manufactured, artificial, programmed, pre-determined, unsurprising, predictable 'playful' childhood towards which we are drifting, will create an unchallenging and uniform experience for children, that will produce not Palmer's 'ecstasy of variety', but Hughes and King's (1985) 'depression of expectation'.

This year, the UN will revisit Article 31 and attempt to bring it up to date. It is crucial that the result is unambiguously pro-free play, for one reason more than any other. For the past three decades, the UN Convention on the Rights of the Child has been distorted and re-interpreted to legitimise the deliberate adulteration of children's play by all manner of well-meaning, but in my view reckless and short-sighted individuals. It is essential, following this timely revision, that play is returned to the children we serve, and protected against this dangerous corruption.

For if authentic children's play continues to be marginalised and squeezed, then like the Native Americans and other indigenous peoples, more and more of future generations of children will be forced into less and less enriching spaces, and will share a similar fate.

It is vital that we understand that our children are our future, that without them we do not have one, and without 'wild' play neither do they. To play they need freedom and space, and both should be

386

awarded freely and ungrudgingly, as a demonstration of our civilisation.

Finally, out of the recent science, which has been such a dominant feature of this text, I would draw these conclusions:

- In the final analysis there is no substitute for free ranging play. Every child freely 'playing out' should be both anticipated and encouraged.
- When provision is made, we should value it highly. This would be demonstrated through its quality, quantity and appropriateness.
- All provision for play should tend towards the nature of the Environment of Evolutionary Adaptedness.
- Schools are redundant. Play provision should offer education as a supplement to play.
- Space and spaces – reflective of the proportion children represent of the population – should be dedicated to children, so that they can escape technology, overcrowding, and most importantly, the pernicious influences of adult society.
- That the right of all children to interact as normal children, with their peers, the environment and the elements is seen as essential and is acknowledged as an obvious and essential part of their healthy development.
- That the rules of engagement between professionals and children in play settings ensure that neither the playworkers' nor society's needs override those of the playing child.
- That an essential component of the play experience is that children have control over the content and intent of what they do.
- That any commercial content of, or modifications to, a play setting should only be considered if it demonstrably and significantly furthers play's bio-evolutionary outcomes.
- That settings provided for play should reflect a proper valuation of, and trust in, our children, and that as a consequence they are properly funded and staffed, and suitably located.
- That legal judgements on playground accidents only be made after due consideration of the bio-evolutionary modes and purposes of play.

Although all societies must recognise the needs of our current and future generations of children to be able to regularly play, for at least two hours every day, this appeal has to be directed primarily at the richer, so called developed nations. Why? Because it is they who are deliberately and consciously forcing play off the agenda, and out of children's lives, replacing it with hobbies and homework. Parents who allow their children to 'play out' these days are often labelled as 'bad' parents.

To finish, I return to a paraphrased and timely warning from Robin Fox, 'Where must we start in trying to re-understand ourselves? It will be a basic contention here that we must condemn as deficient any commentary on the human condition that fails to take into account the ancientness of the species and the more than five million years of natural selection that have moulded the questionable end-product. That is to say, anything but an evolutionary view of modern man is going to be insufficient if its purpose is to calculate the possibilities of human survival' (1989, p. 207).

Bob Hughes
March 2011

AFTERWORD

I wish I had been able to write a better book. The subject deserves it, but playwork is littered with characters, events and phenomena that defy my description! This book is dedicated to playworkers past and present – real, creative and civilised human beings who only care/cared about the child's right to life-affirming play experiences. This text is just what eventually transpired out of my inadequate attempts to give voice to them.

However, I've said most of what I meant to say, and probably several things that I didn't. I certainly would have liked to have said all of them better, but that's the way it goes. What really matters is that you have found it useful.

388

BIBLIOGRAPHY

Abernethy, W. D. (1977) *Playleadership*. London: NPFA.

Abernethy, W. D. (1984) in *Playwork: Bases, Methods and Objectives. Proceedings of PlayEd '84*. Bolton: PlayEducation/Bolton MBC.

Allport, G. W. (1954) *The Nature of Prejudice*. Cambridge, MA: Addison-Wesley.

Amir, Y. (1969) 'Contact Hypothesis in Ethnic Relations', *Psychological Bulletin*, 71, 319–42.

Arendt, H. (1958) *The Human Condition*. Chicago: University of Chicago Press.

Austin, R. (1986) 'Playground Culture in Northern Ireland', *Junior Education*, November.

Balbernie, R. (1999) 'Infant Mental Health', *Young Minds Magazine*, 39.

Baldwin, J. D. (1982) 'The Nature–Nurture Error Again', *The Behaviour and Brain Sciences*, 5, 155–56.

Ball, D. J. and King, K. L. (1991) 'Playground Injuries: A Scientific Appraisal of Popular Concerns', *J. Roy. Soc. Health*, August, 134–37.

Bar-On, D. (1993) 'Children as Unintentional Transmitters of Undisclosable Life Events', in Stiftung für Kinder (ed.), *Children, War and Prosecution*. Osnabrück: Stiftung für Kinder, UNICEF.

Bateson, G. (1955) 'A Theory of Play and Fantasy', *Psychiatric Research Reports*, 2, 39–51.

Bateson, P. P. G. and Hinde, R. A. (1976) *Growing Points in Ethology*. Cambridge: Cambridge University Press.

Bateson, P. and Martin, P. (1999) *Design for Life*. London: Cape.

Battram, A. (1997) 'Designing Possibility Space', *PlayEd '97*, Ely: PlayEducation.

BBC (1998) 'Beyond a Joke'. *Horizon*.

Bekoff, M. (1997) 'Social Communication in Canids. Evidence for the Evolution of a Stereotyped Mammalian Display'. *Science*, 197, 1097–99

Bekoff, M. and Allen, C. (1998) Intentional Communication and Social Play: How and Why Animals Negotiate and Agree to Play, in Bekoff, M. and Byers, J. A. (1998) (eds.) *Animal Play: Evolutionary, Comparative, and Ecological Perspectives*. Cambridge: Cambridge University Press.

Belfrage, S. (1987) *The Crack*. London: Grafton Books.

Bennett, E. L., Diamond, M. C., Krech, D. and Rosenzweig, M. R. (1964) 'Chemical and Anatomical Plasticity of Brain', *Science*, 146, Oct.

389

Bexton, W. H., Heron, W. and Scott, T. H. (1954) 'Effects of Decreasing Variation in the Sensory Environment', *Canadian Journal of Psychology*, 8, 2.

Bingham, C. (2010) 'Hermeneutics', in Peterson, P., Baker, E. and McGaw, B. (eds.) *The International Encyclopedia of Education*. Volume 6. Oxford: Elsevier.

Boden, M. A. (1979) *Piaget*. Brighton: The Harvester Press Ltd.

Bonel, P. and Lindon, J. (1996) *Good Practice in Playwork*. Cheltenham: Stanley Thornes.

Bowlby, J. (1958) 'The nature of the child's tie to his mother', *International Journal of Psych-Analysis*, 39, pp. 350–373.

Brown, S. L., (1998) 'Play as an organising principle:clinical evidence and personal observations', in Marc Bekoff and John A. Byers (eds.) *Animal Play. Evolutionary, Comparative and Ethological Perspectives*. Cambridge: Cambridge University Press.

Brown, S. (2009) *Play*. New York: Avery.

Brown, S. L., and Lomax, J. (1969) 'A pilot study of young murderers'. *Hogg Foundation Annual Report*, Austin, Texas.

Bruce, T. (1994) 'Play, the Universe and Everything', in Moyles, J. R. (ed.), *The Excellence of Play*. Buckingham; Philadelphia: Open University Press.

Bruner, J. S. (1972) 'Nature and Uses of Immaturity', *American Psychologist*, 27(8).

Bruner, J. S. (1974) 'Child's Play', *New Scientist*, 62, 126.

Bruner, J. S. (1976) 'Introduction', *Play: Its Role in Development and Evolution*. New York: Penguin.

Bruner, J. S., Jolly, A. and Sylva, K. (1976) *Play: Its Role in Development and Evolution*. New York: Penguin.

Burghardt, G. (2005) *The Genesis of Animal Play*. Cambridge: The MIT Press.

Burman, S. (1986) 'The Context of Childhood in South Africa: An Introduction', in Burman, S. and Reynolds, P. (eds.), *Growing Up in a Divided Society*. Johannesburg: Ravan Press.

Byers, J. A. (1998) 'Biological effects of locomotor play; getting into shape, or something more specific?' in Bekoff, M. and Byers, J. A. (eds.) *Animal Play: Evolutionary, Comparative, and Ecological Perspectives*. Cambridge: Cambridge University Press.

Cairns, E. (1987) 'Society as Child Abuser: Northern Ireland', in Rogers, W. S., Hervey, D. and Ash, E. (eds.), *Child Abuse and Neglect. Facing the Challenge*. Milton Keynes: The Open University.

Chawla, L. (2002) 'Spots of Time', in Kahn, P. H. and Kellert, S. R. (eds.) *Children and Nature*. Cambridge: The MIT Press.

Children Act (1989) *Guidance and Regulations*. Vol. 2, Chapter 6.

Chilton-Pearce, J. (1980) *Magical Child*. New York: Bantam Books.

Chugani, H. (1998) *BBC News*, 20 April.

Cobb, E. (1993) *The Ecology of Imagination in Childhood*. Dallas: Spring Publications.

Connolly, K. (1973) 'Factors Influencing the Learning of Manual Skills by Young Children', in Hinde, R. A. and Stevenson-Hinde, J. G. (eds.), *Constraints on Learning: Limitations and Predispositions*. London: Academic Press.

390

Convention on the Rights of the Child, United Nations, September 1990.

Conway, H. and Farley, T. (1999) *Quality in Play*. London: Hackney Play Association

Conway, M. (1996) 'Puddles – a workshop', *PlayEd '96*. Ely: PlayEducation.

Cooper, R. (1996) *The Evolving Mind*. Birmingham: Windhorse Publications.

Cosco, N. (1999) Personal communication.

Damasio, A. R. (1994) *Descartes' Error*. New York: Quill.

Darwin, C. (1859) *On the Origin of the Species*. Oxford: Oxford University Press.

Dawkins, R. (1989) *The Selfish Gene*. Oxford: Oxford University Press.

Dennett, D. C. (1997) *Kinds of Minds: Towards an Understanding of Consciousness*. London: Phoenix.

Duncan, M. R. (1977) 'The Cultural Ramifications of Recreation in Belfast, North Ireland', in Stevens, P. (ed.), *Studies in the Anthropology of Play*. West Point, N.Y.: Leisure Press.

Eaton, S. B., Konner, M. and Shostak, M. (1988) 'Stone agers in the fast lane: chronic degenerative diseases in evolutionary perspective', *American Journal of Medicine*, April 84(4): 739–49.

Edelman, G. (1992) *Bright Air, Brilliant Fire*. London: Penguin Books.

Eibl-Eibesfeldt, I. (1967) 'Concepts of Ethology and their Significance in the Study of Human Behaviour', in Stevenson, W. W. and Rheingold, H. L. (eds.), *Early Behaviour: Comparative and Developmental Approaches*. New York: Wiley.

Eibl-Eibesfeldt, I. (1970) *Ethology: The Biology of Behaviour*. New York: Holt, Rinehart and Winston.

Einon, D. (1985) *Creative Play*. Harmondsworth: Penguin.

Einon, D. F., Morgan, M. J. and Kibbler, C. C. (1978) 'Brief Period of Socialisation and Later Behaviour in the Rat', *Developmental Psychobiology*, 11(3).333.

Else, P. (2009) *The Value of Play*. London: Continuum.

Else, P. and Sturrock, G. (1998) 'The Playground as Therapeutic Space: Playwork as Healing', in *Play in a Changing Society: Research, Design, Application*, the Proceedings of the IPA/USA Triennial National Conference. Longmont, CO: IPA.

Erikson, E. H. (1963) *Childhood and Society*. New York: W.W. Norton.

Evans, D. and Zarate, O. (1999) *Introducing Evolutionary Psychology*. Cambridge: Icon.

Fagan, R. (1974) 'Modelling How and Why Play Works', in Bruner, J. S., Jolly, A. and Sylva, K. (eds.), *Play, Its Role in Development and Evolution*. London: Penguin Books.

Fagan, R. M. (1978) 'Evolutionary Biological Models of Animal Play Behaviour', in Burghardt, G. M. and Bekoff, M. (eds.), *Development of Behaviour*. New York: Garland Press.

Feitelson, D. (1977) 'Cross-Cultural Studies of Representational Play', in Tizard, B. and Harvey, D. (eds.), *Biology of Play*. London: William Heinemann Medical Books Ltd.

Ferchmin, P. A. and Eterovic, V. A. (1979) 'Mechanisms of Brain Growth by Environmental Stimulation', *Science*, 205, 3.

391

Fox, R. (1989) *The Search for Society. Quest for a Biosocial Science and Morality*. London: Rutgers University Press.

Fraser, M. (1974) *Children in Conflict*. Harmondsworth: Penguin.

Freud, S. (1918) *Totems and Taboo*. New York: New Republic.

Frost, J. L. and Jacobs, P. J. (1995) 'Play-deprivation: A Factor in Juvenile Violence', *Dimensions*, 3, 3.

Furedi, F. (1999) 'Why Are We Afraid For Our Children?', in *Proceedings of PLAYLINK/Portsmouth City Council Conference*. Portsmouth: PLAYLINK.

Garbarino, J. (1993) 'Challenges We Face in Understanding Children and War: A Personal Essay', *Child Abuse and Neglect*, 17, 787–93.

Garbarino, J. and Kostelny, K. (1997) 'What Children Can Tell Us From Living in a War Zone', in Osofsky, J. D. (ed.), *Children in a Violent Society*. New York: The Guilford Press.

Garvey, C. (1977) *Play*. London: Fontana/Open Books Original.

Geertz, C. (1972) 'Deep Play: a Description of a Balinese Cockfight', *Daedalus*, 101.

Geertz, C. (1973) *The Interpretation of Cultures*. New York: Basic Books.

Goleman, D. (1995) *Emotional Intelligence*. London: Bloomsbury Publishing Plc.

Gopnik, A. (2002) 'The theory theory as an alternative to the innateness hypothesis', in Anthony, L. and Hornsteir, N. (2003) *Chomsky and his Critics*. New York: Basil Blackwell.

Gopnik, A., Meltzoff, A. and Kuhl, P. (1999) *The Scientist in the Crib*. New York: William Morrow.

Gordon, C. (1999) 'Riskogenics: An Exploration of Risk', *PlayEd '99*. Ely: PlayEducation.

Gould, S. J. (1996) *Full House: The Spread of Excellence from Plato to Darwin*. New York: Harmony Books.

Grandy, D. A., (2008) 'Quantum Uncertainty, Quantum Play, Quantum Sorrow'. *The Journal of Natural and Social Philosophy*, Vol. 4, No 1–2.

Gray, J. (2002) *Straw Dogs: Thought on Humans and Other Animals*. London: Granta Books.

Grof, S. (1975) *Realms of the Human Unconscious*. New York: The Viking Press.

Groos, K. (1898) *The Play of Animals*. New York: Appleton.

Gruber, H. E. (1974) *Darwin on Man*. New York: Dutton.

Gunner, M. (1998) 'Stress and Brain Development'. Talk delivered to Michigan Association of Infant Mental Health. 22nd Annual Conference.

Hall, G. S. (1904) *Adolescence: its Psychology and its Relations to Physiology, Anthropology, Sociology, Sex, Crime, Religion and Education*. Vol. 1. New York: Appleton.

Handscomb, B. (1999) 'Who is Judging Who? Part One', *PlayEd '99*. Ely: PlayEducation.

Hardin, R. (1995) *One for All*. Princeton, New Jersey: Princeton University Press.

Harlow, H. F. and Harlow, M. K. (1962) 'The Effect of Rearing Conditions on Behaviour', *Bulletin of the Menninger Clinic*, 26, 213–24.

Harlow, H. F. and Suomi, S. J. (1971) 'Social Recovery by Isolation-Reared Monkeys', *Proc. Nat. Acad. Sci. USA*, 68(7), 1534–38.

Hart, R. (1979) *Children's Experience of Place*. New York: Irvington.

Hart, R. (1999) Personal Communication. 24 September.

Heron, W. (1957) 'The Pathology of Boredom', *Scientific American*, 196.

Hickey, E. W. (1991) *Serial Murderers and their Victims*. Pacific Grove, CA: Brooks/Publishing Co.

Hodgkin, R. A. (1985) *Play and Exploring*. London: Methuen.

Hughes, B. (1984) 'Play a Definition by Synthesis', in *Play Provision and Play Needs*. Lancaster: PlayEducation.

Hughes, B. (1988) 'Play and the Environment', *Leisure Manager*, 6, 1.

Hughes, B. (1993) 'A Child's World: Risk, Reality and Learning', *PlayLinks*, Feb.

Hughes, B. (1995) 'Editorial', *International Play Journal*, 3, 2.

Hughes, B. (1996a) *A Playworker's Taxonomy of Play Types*. London: PLAY-LINK.

Hughes, B. (1996b) *Play Environments: A Question of Quality*. London: PLAY-LINK.

Hughes, B. (1997a) 'Playwork in Extremis: One of Many Applications of Playwork's Values, Methods and Worth', in *Proceedings of The World of Play, The Changing Nature of Children's Play and Playwork*, San Antonio, TX: University of the Incarnate Word.

Hughes, B. (1997b) 'Towards a Technology of Playwork', in *Proceedings of PLAYLINK/Portsmouth City Council Conference*. Portsmouth: PLAYLINK.

Hughes, B. (1998) 'Playwork in Extremis – The RAP Approach', in *Proceedings of Childhood and Youth Studies: Towards an Interdisciplinary Framework*. Cambridge: Anglia Polytechnic University and DfEE.

Hughes, B. (1999a) 'Does Playwork Have a Neurological Rationale?', in *The Proceedings of PlayEducation '99 Part One*. Ely: PlayEducation.

Hughes, B. (1999b) *Games Not Names*. Belfast: PlayBoard.

Hughes, B. (1999c) 'Uncensoring Play – Towards an Evolutionary Perspective for Facilitating Recapitulation', in the *Proceedings of the 14th IPA World Conference, Lisbon, Portugal*. IPA: Lisbon.

Hughes, B. (2000) 'A Dark and Evil Cul-De-Sac: Has Children's Play in Urban Belfast Been Adulterated by the Troubles?' MA Dissertation. Cambridge: Anglia Polytechnic University.

Hughes, B. (2001) *The First Claim, A Framework for Playwork Quality Assessment*. Cardiff: PlayWales.

Hughes, B. (2002) *The First Claim, Desirable Processes. A Framework for Advanced Playwork Quality Assessment*. Cardiff: PlayWales.

Hughes, B. (2003a) 'The Journey', Cornwall Play Conference.

Hughes, B. (2005) 'The Consequences of Play Deprivation'. PlayBoard AGM.

Hughes, B. (2006) 'PlayTypes Speculations and Possibilities'. London: LNCPET.

Hughes, B. and King, F. M. (1985) Merseyside Playwork Training Project.

Hughes, B. and Williams, H. (1982) 'Talking About Play 1–5', *Play Times*, London: N.P.F.A.

Hutt, C. (1979) 'Exploration and Play', in Sutton-Smith, B. (ed.), *Play and Learning*. New York: Gardener Press.

393

Hutt, S. J., Tyler, S., Hutt, C. and Christopherson, H. (1989) *Play, Exploration and Learning*. London: Routledge.

Huttenlocher, P. R. (1990) 'Morphometric Study of Human Cerebral Cortex Development', *Neuropsychologia*, 28, 6.

Huttenlocher, P. R. (1992) 'Neural Plasticity', in Asbury, McKhann and McDonald (eds.), *Diseases of the Nervous System*, 1, 63–71.

Huttenmoser, M. and Degan-Zimmermann, D. (1995) *Lebenstraume für Kinder*. Zurich: Swiss Science Foundation.

International Play Journal (1996) Vol. 4 Number 3 IP-DiP, (2007 –).

Jennings, S. (1995) 'Playing for Real', *International Play Journal*, 3, 2, 132–41.

Jones, S. (1993) *The Language of the Genes*. London: Flamingo.

Jung, C. G. (1953–1978) *Collected Works*. (eds.) Read, H., Fordham, M., and Adler, G. London: Routledge.

Kauffman, S. (2000) *Investigations*. New York: Oxford University Press.

King, F. M. (1987) 'Play Environment's Criteria', Paper, Merseyside Playwork Training Project.

King, F. M. (1988) 'Informed Choices'. Liverpool: PlayEducation Meeting.

King, F. M. (1988) *Bristol Play Policy*. Bristol City Council: Leisure Services.

Kobayashi, M., Kikuchi, D. and Okamura, H. (2009) 'Imagining of Ultraweak Spontaneous Photon Emmission for Human Body Displaying Diurnal Rhythm'. PloS ONE 4(7): e 6256. doi: 10. 1371/journal.pone.0006256.

Koestler, A. (1967) *The Ghost in the Machine*. London: Hutchinson.

Konner, M. (2010) *The Evolution of Childhood*. Cambridge: The Belknap Press of Harvard University.

Kotulak, R. (1996) *Inside the Brain*. Kansas City: Andrews and McNeel.

Kroodsma, D. E. (1981) 'Ontogeny of birdsong'. In *Behavioural Development*. The Bielefeld Interdisciplinary Project, K. Immelmann, G. W. Barlow, L. Petrinovich and M. Main (eds.), pp. 518–532. Cambridge: Cambridge University Press.

Lester, S. and Russell, W. (2008) *Play for a Change*. London: Play England.

Loizos, C. (1967) 'Play Behaviour in Higher Primates: a Review', in Morris, D. (ed.), *Primate Ethology*. Chicago: Aldine Press.

Lorenz, K. (1972) 'Psychology and Phylogeny', in *Studies in Animal and Human Behaviour*. Cambridge, MA: Harvard University Press.

Lyons, H. A. (1974) 'Terrorist Bombing and the Psychological Sequelae', *Journal of the Irish Medical Association*, 67, 15.

Machel, Grac'a (1996) *Impact of Armed Conflict on Children*. United Nations Department for Policy Co-ordination and Sustainable Development (DPCSD), August 1996.

MacFarlane, R. (2010) *The Wild Places*. London: Granta Books.

MacLean, P. D. (1973) *A Triune Concept of the Brain and Behaviour*, University of Toronto Press, Toronto.

MacLean, P. D. (1976) 'Sensory and Perceptive Factors in Emotional Function of the Triune Brain', in R. G. Grennell and S. Gabay (eds.) *Biological Foundations of Psychiatry*, Vol. 1., pp. 177–198.

McEwen, B. S. (1999) 'Stress and Hippocampal Plasticity', *Annual Review of the Neurosciences*, 22, 105–22.

394

McFadden, J. (2000) *Quantum Evolution*. London: HarperCollins.

McFarland, D. J. (1973) Discussion of Connolly's (1973) contribution.

McGrath, A. and Wilson, R. (1985) 'Factors Which Influence the Prevalence and Variation of Psychological Problems in Children in Northern Ireland'. Unpublished paper: Annual Conference, The Development Society, Belfast.

McKee, M. (1986) 'Playwork', *PlayEd '86*. Ely: PlayEducation.

McKinney, W. T., Young, L. D., Suomi, S. J. and Davis, J. M. (1973) 'Chlorpromazine Treatment of Disturbed Monkeys', *Arch. Gen. Psychiatry*, 29, Oct.

Meares, R. (1993) *The Metaphor of Play*. London: Jason Aronson Inc.

Meeker, J. W. (1997) *The Comedy of Survival*. New York: Charles Scibners and Sons.

Melville, S. (1996) Personal Communication.

Melville, S. (2000) Personal Communication.

Miller, S. (1973) 'Ends, Means and Galumphing: Some Leitmotifs of Play', *American Anthropologist*, 75, 87–98.

Milne, J. (1997) 'Play Structures', *PlayEd '97*. Ely: PlayEducation.

Moore, R. C. (1986) *Childhood's Domain*. London: Croom Helm.

Morris, D. (1964) 'The Response of Animals to a Restricted Environment', *Symposium of the Zoological Society of London*, 13, 99.

Morris, D. (ed.) (1967) *Primate Ethology*. Weidenfeld & Nicolson.

Murphy, D. (1978) *A Place Apart*. London: Penguin Books.

National Centres for Playwork Education and Training (1995) Values Guide – National Vocational Qualifications in Playwork.

Neumann, E. A. (1971) The elements of play. Unpublished doctoral dissertation. University of Illinois.

Nicholson, S. (1971) 'How Not to Cheat Children: The Theory of Loose Parts', *Landscape Architecture*, Oct.

Novak, M. A. and Harlow, H. F. (1975) 'Social Recovery of Monkeys Isolated for the First Year of Life: 1. Rehabilitation and Therapy', *Developmental Psychology*, 11, 4.

NPFA (1980) *Towards A Safer Adventure Playground*. London: NPFA.

Ogden, T. (1993) *In One's Bones – The Clinical Genius of Winnicott*, Goldman, D. (ed.), New York: Aronson.

Orr, D. W. (1993) 'Love It or Lose It: The Coming Biophilia Revolution', in Kellert, S. R. and Wilson, E. O. (eds.), *The Biophilia Hypothesis*. Washington, DC: Island Press.

Palmer, K. (1994a) http://dialog.net:85/homepage

Palmer, K. (1994b) *Steps to the Threshold of the Social. Part 3: Anti-Category Theory*. Copyright 1994 Kent D. Palmer.

Palmer, S. and Major, B. (1987) 'Adventure Playgrounds – Survive and Thrive', *PlayEd '87*. Ely: PlayEducation.

Panksepp, J. (1998) *Affective Neuroscience*. Oxford: Oxford University Press.

Panksepp, J. (2007) 'Can PLAY Diminish ADHD and Facilitate the Construction of the Social Brain?', *Journal of the Canadian Academy of Child and Adolescent Psychiatry*, 16:2 May 2007.

Parkinson, C. (1987) *Children's Range Behaviour*. Birmingham: PlayBoard.

Patrick, G. T. W. (1914) 'The Psychology of Play', *Journal of Genetic Psychology*, 21, 469–84.

Pearce, J. C. (1977) *Magical Child*. New York: Bantam.

Pellis, S. M. and Pellis, V. C. (1998) 'Structure-function interface in the analysis of play fighting,' in Beckoff, M., and Byers, J. A. (eds.) *Animal Play: Evolutionary, Comparative and Ecological Perspectives*. Cambridge: Cambridge University Press.

Pellis, S. and Pellis, V. (2009) *The Playful Brain*. Oxford: One World.

Perry, B. D. (1994) 'Neurobiological Sequelae of Childhood Trauma: Post Traumatic Stress Disorders in Children', in Murberg, M. (ed.), *Catecholamines in Post-Traumatic Stress Disorder: Emerging Concepts*. Washington, DC: American Psychiatric Association.

Perry, B. D. (1995) 'Childhood Trauma. The Neurobiology of Adaptation and Use-Dependent Development of the Brain. How States Become Traits', *Infant Mental Health Journal*, 16, 4.

Perry, B. D. (2001) 'The neurodevelopmental impact of violence in childhood', in *Textbook of Child and Adolescent Forensic Psychiatry*. (D. Schetky and E. P. Benedek (eds.)) Washington D.C.: American Psychiatric Press Inc.

Perry, B. D., Arvinte, A., Marcellus, J. and Pollard, R. (1996) 'Syncope, Bradycardia, Cataplexy and Paralysis: Sensitisation of an Opiod-Mediated Dissociative Response Following Childhood Trauma', *Journal of the American Academy of Child and Adolescent Psychiatry*.

Petrie, P. (1996) Personal Communication.

Piaget, J. (1951) *Play, Dreams and Imitation in Childhood*. New York: W.W. Norton.

Pinker, S. (1998) *How the Mind Works*. Harmondsworth: Penguin.

PlayBoard (1990) *Play Without Frontiers*. Belfast: PlayBoard (NI).

PLAYLINK (1992) *Open Access Play and the Children Act*. London: PLAYLINK.

PLAYLINK (1997) *Risk and Safety in Play: the Law and Practice for Adventure Playgrounds*. London: Routledge.

Rankin, D. J., and Lopez-Sepulcre, A. (2005) *Can Adaptation Lead to Extinction?* IOKOS 111: 3.

Reaney, M. J. (1916) *The Psychology of the Organized Game*. Cambridge: Cambridge University Press.

Rennie, S. (1997) *The Roots of Consensus*. M.A. Dissertation, Leeds Metropolitan University.

Rennie, S. (1999) 'The Isms of Playwork', *PlayEd '99*. Ely: PlayEducation.

Robbins, Jones and Wilkinson, S. (1996) 'Behavioural and neurochemical effects of early social deprivation in the rat'. *J. Psychpharmacology*, Vol 10, No 1, 39–47 January.

Robbins, T. W. (2002) 'Modelling the Schizophrenic Brain', *Novartis Foundation Bulletin*, Issue 11.

Rosenzweig, M. R. (1971) 'Effects of Environments on Development of Brain and of Behaviour', in Tobach, E., Aronson, L. R. and Shaw, E. (eds.), *The Bio-Psychology of Development*. New York: Academic Press.

Rosenzweig, M. R., Krech, D., Bennett, E. L. and Diamond, M. C. (1962) 'Effects of Environmental Complexity and Training on Brain Chemistry and

Anatomy', *Journal of Comparative and Physiological Psychology*, 55(4), 429–37.

Rosenzweig, M. R., Bennett, E. L. and Diamond, M. C. (1972) 'Brain Changes in Response to Experience', *Scientific American*, Feb.

Rowe, J. (1986) 'The Green Play Concept', *PlayEd '86*. Ely: PlayEducation.

Ruse, M. (1979) *Sociobiology – Sense or Nonsense*. Boston: Reidel.

Schlosberg, H. (1947) 'The Concept of Play', *Psych. Rev.*, 54, 229–31.

Schwartzman, H. B. (1978) *Transformations – The Anthropology of Children's Play*. London: Plenum Press.

Shepard, P. (1982) *Nature and Madness*. San Francisco: Sierra Club.

Simpson, M. J. A. (1976) 'The Study of Animal Play', in Bateson, P. P. G. and Hinde, R. A. (eds.), *Growing Points in Ethology*. Cambridge: Cambridge University Press.

Singer, J. L. (1973) *The Child's World of Make-Believe*. New York: Academic Press.

Siviy, S. M. (1998) 'Neurobiological substrates of play behaviour: glimpses into the structure and function of mammalian playfulness', in Bekoff, M. and Byers, J. A. (eds), *Animal Play: Evolutionary, Comparative, and Ecological Perspectives*. Cambridge: Cambridge University Press.

Smith, P. K. (1978) 'Play is Only One Way to Learn', *New Society*, July.

Smith, P. K. (1982) 'Does Play Matter? Functional and Evolutionary Aspects of Animal and Human Play', *The Behavioural and Brain Sciences*, 5.

Smith, P. K. (1994) 'Play Training: An Overview', in Hellendoorn, J., van der Kooij, R. and Sutton-Smith, B. (eds.), *Play and Intervention*. Albany: State University of New York Press.

Smith, P. K., Cowie, H. and Blades, M. (1998) *Understanding Children's Development*. Oxford: Blackwell Publishers.

Smyth, M. (1998) *Half the Battle*. Derry Londonderry: INCORE.

Snyder, G. (1977) *The Old Ways*. San Francisco, CA: City Lights Books.

Sobel, D. (1993) *Children's Special Places: Exploring the Role of Forts, Dens and Bush Houses in Middle-childhood*. Tucson: Zephyr Press.

Sokolov, E. N., and Nezlina, N. I. (2004) 'Long-term memory, Neurogenesis, and Signal Novelty', *Neuroscience and Behavioural Psychology*, 34(8) 847–57 October.

Spencer, H. (1896) *Principles of Psychology*. Vol. 2, Part 2 (3rd edn). New York: Appleton.

Steinbeck, J. (1935) *To A God Unknown*. London: Heinemann.

Steinbeck, J. (1958) *Log from the Sea of Cortez*. London: Heinemann.

Stevens, A. (1982) *Archetype: A Natural History of the Self*. London: Routledge, Paul and Kegan.

Stevens, A. and Price, J. (1996) *Evolutionary Psychiatry. A new beginning*. London: Routledge.

Sturrock, G. (1989) 'Shamanism', *PlayEd '89*. Ely: PlayEducation.

Sturrock, G. (1997) Personal Communication.

Sturrock, G. (1999) Personal Communication.

Sturrock, G. and Hughes, B. (1998) 'Definition of Sectarianism', in Hughes, B. *Games Not Names*. Belfast: PlayBoard.

Suomi, S. J. and Harlow, H. F. (1971) 'Monkeys Without Play', in *Play*, a *Natural History Magazine Special Supplement*, December.

Sutton-Smith, B. (ed.) (1979) *Play and Learning*. New York: Gardener Press, Inc.

Sutton-Smith, B. (1997) *The Ambiguity of Play*. Cambridge, MA: Harvard University Press.

Sutton-Smith, B. (2007) 'Play as Emotional Survival' In Hendricks, T. S. (2009) *Orderly and Disorderly Play. American Journal of Play*, 2(1).

Sylva, K. (1977) 'Play and Learning', in Tizard, B. and Harvey, D. (eds.), *Biology of Play*. London: Heinemann.

Talbot, J. and Frost, V. L. (1989) 'Magical Playscapes', *Childhood Education*, 66(1) 11–19.

Taylor, C., Bonel, P. and Bagnall-Oakley, R. (1999) 'The Good Enough Playworker and the Facilitating Environment', in *The Proceedings of PlayEducation '99 Part One*. Ely: PlayEducation.

The Children Act (1989) *Guidance and Regulations*, Vol. 2, Chapter 6. Section A.

Thomashow, M. (1995) *Ecological Identity*. Cambridge, MA: MIT Press.

Tobin, J. (1997) 'A Second Chance for Christian', *The Detroit News*, 9th February.

Tsukamoto, I. (1997) 'Playing, Praying and Painting', *PlayEd '97*. Ely: PlayEducation.

Vachss, A. H. and Bakal, Y. (1979) *The Lifestyle Violent Juvenile: The Secure Treatment Approach*. Lexington, MA: Lexington Books/D.C. Heath.

Vandenberg, B. (1978) 'Play and Development from an Ethological Perspective', *American Psychologist*, 724–36.

van Hooff, J. A. R. A. M. (1972) 'A Comparative Approach to the Phylogeny of Laughter and Smiling', in Hinde, R. A. (ed.), *Non-verbal Communication*. Cambridge: Cambridge University Press.

Vygotsky, L. S. (1978) *Mind in Society*. Cole, M., John-Steiner, V., Scribner, S. and Souberman, E. (eds.) Cambridge: Harvard University Press.

Wilber, K. (1996) *Up from Eden*. Wheaton, IL: Quest Books.

Wilcox, B. L. and Naimark, H. (1991) 'The Rights of the Child, Progress Towards Human Dignity', *American Psychologist*, 46, 1, 49.

Wilson, E. O. (1975) *Sociobiology*. Cambridge: Harvard University Press.

Wilson, E. O. (1992) *The Diversity of Life*. London: Penguin Books.

Winnicott, D. W. (1992) *Playing and Reality*. London: Routledge.

Wood, D. J., Bruner, J. S. and Ross, G. (1976) 'The Role of Tutoring in Problem Solving', *Journal of Child Psychology and Psychiatry*, 17, 89–100.

Woolcott, J. (1987) 'Activity – Exploration or Entertainment?' *PlayEd '87*. Ely: PlayEducation.

Zuckerman, M. (1969) 'Theoretical Formulations: 1', in Zubek, J. P. (ed.), *Sensory Deprivation: Fifteen Years of Research*. New York: Appleton-Century-Crofts.

Zuckerman, M. (1984) 'Sensation Seeking: A Comparative Approach to a Human Trait', *The Behaviour and Brain Sciences*, 7.

INDEX

401

407

Internationalization and Diversity in Higher Education

Implications for Teaching, Learning and Assessment

David Killick

 macmillan education   palgrave

First published 2017 by
PALGRAVE

Palgrave in the UK is an imprint of Macmillan Publishers Limited, registered in England, company number 785998, of 4 Crinan Street, London, N1 9XW.

Palgrave Macmillan in the US is a division of St Martin's Press LLC, 175 Fifth Avenue, New York, NY 10010.

Palgrave is a global imprint of the above companies and is represented throughout the world.

Palgrave® and Macmillan® are registered trademarks in the United States, the United Kingdom, Europe and other countries.

ISBN 978–1–137–52616–8 paperback

This book is printed on paper suitable for recycling and made from fully managed and sustained forest sources. Logging, pulping and manufacturing processes are expected to conform to the environmental regulations of the country of origin.

A catalogue record for this book is available from the British Library.

A catalog record for this book is available from the Library of Congress.

Printed and bound by CPI Group (UK) Ltd, Croydon, CR0 4YY

Contents

List of tables and figures

Series editor's preface

It is with great pleasure that I include within the Palgrave Teaching and Learning series this volume by my colleague and friend, David Killick. The series has the express aim of providing useful, relevant, current and helpful guidance on key issues in learning and teaching in the tertiary/post-compulsory education sector, and few can be more compelling and highly readable than this volume. Texts in this series address a range of essential teaching and learning imperatives, with a deliberately international focus, and at a time when all universities are looking to be truly globally-orientated, this book makes a particularly valuable contribution.

David is a UK National Teaching Fellow, recognised for his innovative and reflective excellent teaching, and like the rest of the NTF community, is committed to sharing good practice with others. He has made a particularly strong contribution in the area of cross-cultural capability, and his lead in encouraging universities to consider how they can offer all their students opportunities to benefit from internationalized higher education learning communities through co-working and mutual support is widely recognised.

David has drawn on decades of his own and others' research to produce this evidence-informed and highly practical examination of how best to internationalize our universities and produce graduates who are culturally aware and well prepared to become global good citizens. This is a very welcome contribution to the series: having learned much from David over recent years and in particular from this book, I commend it to readers wholeheartedly.

Sally Brown
August 2016

Introduction

As we approach the third decade of the twenty-first century, a rapidly expanding and transforming global higher education sector is adding significantly to the engagement of increasingly diverse students in increasingly diverse contexts. At the same time, other processes of globalization are bringing together diverse peoples and cultures in unprecedented ways, requiring that our university learning experiences prepare our students to make their ways within a multicultural milieu locally and globally. There are other complex, contested, and in-progress interrelationships between diverse higher education and the movements within globalization (Dodds, 2008; Lindsay & Blanchett, 2011). But it is the two, related, changes – increasingly diverse higher education students in increasingly diverse higher education contexts, and the increasingly diverse world in which those students will engage as graduates, which have prompted this book.

Small numbers of our students will become global leaders, high-powered executives, highly influential cultural or sporting icons, but all our students will find themselves interacting with others who are different, perhaps different in their values, perhaps in the simple ways in which they prefer to enact their lives, perhaps in the choices and freedoms they have. Those who are different to ourselves can be interpreted as odd, inferior, and threatening, or as interesting, equal, and valuable. The world in which our students will make their lives, and the world they will make through the living of those lives, will in large part depend upon which of those polarized positions dominate individual social, professional, and political standpoints. We are now witness, on a daily basis, to the outrageous consequences which can follow when people are defined by others solely on the basis of their cultures or their ethnicities or their religions, rather than being seen as individual human beings.

As the human diversity represented within higher education moves (albeit in some areas somewhat glacially) to better reflect that of the multicultural and globalizing world in which it is situated, there are significant implications for students and faculty. This book explores a number of these, with the hope that in doing so, we might take steps towards shaping learning environments and practices which offer more equitable learning experiences and more appropriate learning outcomes across the full range of student and faculty diversity. The book focusses principally on cultural diversities, be they within domestic and international student communities, or between them;

be they in our physical or our virtual learning spaces. The issues explored, though, are relevant also for other dimensions of diversity, including socio-economic status, disability, age, gender, sexuality, and religion, and the intersectional (Crenshaw, 1991) interplay between all of these in the individual student and her learning environment. I am sure that these links are apparent to readers, but I do, occasionally, remind us within the text.

The book does not rehearse the now well-explored, and among academics largely much-deplored, 'neo-liberal agenda' within higher education, in 'Western' anglophone nations, at least. The emerging global higher education landscape which is the backdrop for the discussions throughout the book can be deconstructed as an expansion of the neo-liberal project. My concern here is with the students and the faculty who are dedicated to advancing learning within these global spaces. That their lives in those spaces are impacted by an underpinning philosophy of market liberalization, manifested in policies focussed around efficiency, commodification, growth, employability outcomes, performativity, and the like is, I think, beyond question. That higher education, through its academic community of faculty and students, can still offer much more, continue to be transformative and enable students to be critical, self-aware, other-aware *individuals,* informed by global perspectives and committed to global social justice is not beyond question, but nor is it beyond hope.

Intercultural dialogue is given significant prominence throughout the book. As well as being a prerequisite for democratic life in culturally diverse societies (Council of Europe, 2016), intercultural dialogue is also a fundamental constituent of inclusive education in diverse learning spaces. The book is written from a belief that, in our times, higher education which successfully embraces diverse cultures in its values, its aspirations, its pedagogies, and its services is the only type deserving to call itself *higher* education. It is, after all, through respectful dialogue with diverse ideas and individuals that informed critical perspectives on self and other, our ways and their ways, are developed. It is through experiencing each Other under the 'right' conditions that we come to understand, and perhaps to reframe the 'Other' as 'other', or even as 'we'. Global and local social justice is advanced by people who see global and local others as equally human. Through engaging in *conversation* (real and virtual) with diverse and differently situated others, our students might come to see how their own lives are impacted by and implicated in global inequalities and injustices. It is also through equitably designed and experienced conversations with others, framed within a curriculum which respects and expects critical engagement with own and others' perspectives, that higher education can become a much more inclusive, and so more equitable, experience for all students, and a greater force for good *in the world.*

In much literature and within many university mission statements and web sites, these aspirations are related to a number of debated, but essentially related, objectives for students and graduates, such as global citizenship, or multicultural personhood, or cosmopolitanism, or global heart-set. My preferred term is 'global-self', and my personal take on the development of students as global-selves is outlined in Chapter Two as one model with which to explore the central points concerning equitable development for all our students – the predominantly young people who entrust their learning to the rapidly changing world of higher education. Readers wanting more detailed discussion on the shape of global gradu-ates will find a number of publications dealing with both aspirations and mechanisms from a variety of perspectives (for example, see Alred et al., 2006; Clifford & Montgomery, 2011; Council of Europe, 2016; Deardorff, 2006; Killick, 2014b; Lilley et al., 2015; Richardson, 2016; Spencer-Oatey & Stadler, 2009).

Synergies between internationalization and equality and diversity/multi-cultural education have been recognized before, but only in a few publica-tions and initiatives (for example, Berry & Loke, 2011; Charles et al., 2013; Olson et al., 2007). In the UK, the Higher Education Academy's Framework for Internationalising Higher Education (HEA, 2014a) makes specific refer-ence to 'fostering an inclusive ethos', 'respect', 'equity', 'reciprocity', and 'diverse cultures and practices' – all of which are live concerns within mul-ticultural education. However, little progress has been made in co-joining what Caruana and Ploner's review of the fields identified as two 'separate and unrelated discourses' (2010, p. 9). In the USA, it has been argued that a significant distinguishing feature of multicultural education over interna-tionalization has been its focus on social critique and social justice, yet an 'integrated approach to global learning and multicultural education captures the greatest potential for student development' (Charles et al., 2013, p. 49). Some of us in the internationalization field would assert that we have been arguing for a global social justice focus from the outset. But most of us would probably concur with De Vita and Case (2003, p. 385), that while 'the development of global citizenship and commensurate responsibility should be the principal aim of the internationalisation agenda in education', most institutions have failed to make it so. On the other hand, multicultural education work may have been focussed on the local rather than the global, but this too is changing. In the preface to the third edition of their volume on teaching for diversity and social justice, Adams et al. (2016, p. xi) advise readers that '[i]t no longer makes sense, if it ever did, to think of U.S.-based issues as separate from their transnational roots or repercussions', and so they offer examples and analysis which seek to show 'global implications and interconnections'. In their review of domestic and global engagement in Historically Black Colleges and Universities (HBCUs), Lindsay and Scales Williams (2011, p. 120) show forceful examples of missions in institutions in post-Hurricane Katrina New Orleans which encompass international and global vision, concluding that in HBCUs, 'attuning to global geopolitical phenomena must be meshed with the local'.

It is timely, then, that the American Council on Education has called for 'visible leadership and collaborative strategies' to 'transcend the historical divide between internationalization and multicultural education' (Olson et al., 2007, p. v). In line with the underpinning tenets of this book, what they believe is needed are *spaces* in which expertise can be shared, and *a common will* for collaborative conversations to take place. This volume seeks to take some of that work forward by illustrating links and opportunities for mutual learning between these two fields, and holds *global* and *local* social critique and justice to be legitimate areas of focus within an internationalized curriculum, especially, but not exclusively, where that curriculum is transposed to diverse transnational education (TNE) contexts or 'delivered' to multicultural student bodies at home or online.

Emerging global higher education spaces raise quite specific equity issues, some of which tread familiar ground, and others of which show similar vistas but among different communities. To take some of the more obvious critical diversity issues raised by the international contexts in which many anglophone institutions are now working:

▶ How is a 'Western' university, committed to equality and diversity, and with those values embedded in its academic practice, including its learning, teaching, and assessment activities, to effectively and equitably manage the student experience in a context where male and female students are physically segregated on campus, or where LGBT students cannot express their perspectives gained from a life lived illegally and illicitly, or where students of secular or minority religious beliefs are not admitted to the university at all?

▶ How are students from diverse groups within these spaces to gain access, find voice, and experience equitable learning?

▶ How do Western anglophone institutions and faculty, traditionally positioned as 'expert', ensure they do not dominate TNE partnerships and impose academic cultures and practices which create inappropriate, and thereby inequitable, learning experiences?

▶ How do faculty working across diverse cultures or among diverse students protect their own values and identities while seeking out ways of working which best serve each of their students?

▶ How can we connect diverse students in diverse contexts in ways which will enhance their capabilities for living within a multicultural and globalizing world without risking undermining their own cultural heritage?

The American Council on Education (ACE) refers to some of these areas as 'negotiated space', requiring explicit consideration as part of the due diligence process when partnerships are in development. Within this, 'individual institutions must determine where they need to draw the line on controversial issues, and what compromises they are willing (and unwilling) to make in order to move a relationship forward' (ACE, 2015, p. 32). Like ACE, this book does not have clear answers to these questions, but in offering perspectives on students, academics, learning environments, and practice in subsequent chapters, it emphasizes the need for institutions and, in particular, for academic staff (faculty) to be engaging with such questions.

The educational consequences of the increasing diversity within and surrounding global higher education should be enriching. Some consequences, however, risk being tragic for certain individuals and communities who entrust their education to us. Tragic consequences arise where we fail to critically interrogate our practice for its potential to marginalize, to disenfranchise, and to disempower. Of course, such has always been the experience of some students, but in the emerging world of universities who *trade* beyond their home cultures and countries, the dangers expand significantly, as some of the questions above illustrate. It is through the diligence of faculty in ensuring that learning, teaching, and assessment strategies are as equitable as they can be for all students, in all their contexts, that higher education will be empowering, liberating, and transformational in ways which will serve the individual student and our global societies well. Chun and Evans (2009, p. 9) propose that '[g]lobalization may indeed represent the unbalancing force that will overcome barriers to inclusion in the university'. I argue that to fulfil such a hope, faculty and students need to collaborate in order to create equitable and meaningful learning experiences and outcomes.

In its position paper on higher education in a globalized society, UNESCO sets out the principle that 'equity and equality of opportunities in higher education should guide the development of policy frameworks as a response to higher education in a global society' (2004, p. 16). This should not seem very controversial to academics in most contexts. Those same academics will also immediately recognize that the principle is easier to set down than it is to realize, and that 'policy frameworks', while necessary, do not translate into academic practice or student experience without both the will and the work of faculty. This book is concerned with learning and teaching practice, but to explore these we review theoretical frameworks, lived experiences of faculty and students, and 'good practice' principles. I hope elements will offer insights from less familiar areas of practice, 'food for thought', sources for reflection, reflexion, and development. However, this book is not intended as a set of tips and tricks. I am not the expert in your classroom. If you find ideas within the book which prompt changes, I am afraid you will need to do the really hard work.

The book is divided into six chapters:

Chapter One – *Global Higher Education* presents an overview of the ongoing globalization of higher education, and the emergence therein of the 'post-national' university. This context frames all the discussions which follow.

Chapter Two – *Global Graduates* illustrates how making their ways among complex human diversity will significantly shape the personal, social, and professional experiences of our graduates, along with perspectives on why they might resist, and one model of the capabilities they might develop as students to help them succeed.

Chapter Three – *Global Academics* discusses the (re)formulation of academic identities and academic knowing for working with diverse students in diverse contexts, with a particular focus on intercultural issues and their relationships to learning.

Chapter Four – *Global Learning Spaces* looks at the lived experience of diverse students and diverse faculty within university learning spaces, considering in particular stereotyping and deficit models, but also positive learning gain generated through working with diverse others, and how attention to communication within these spaces facilitates reciprocal learning.

Chapter Five – *Global Good Practice* examines the underpinning conditions which might facilitate successful intercultural encounters within any learning activity, and takes these through to a formulation of principles for good practice in curriculum design, pedagogy, and faculty development within the post-national university.

Chapter Six – *Global Grounded Practice* provides illustrations of good practice extracted from practitioner research, guidelines documentation, reported examples, and five case studies, kindly submitted for inclusion in this book. Readers are invited to engage with a series of related reflective questions.

It may be surprising that a book produced in the current era does not have a chapter devoted to learning technologies. This is not because learning technologies are not in themselves transforming elements of practice in higher education. They are essential and exciting tools of the trade, but they are not the trade. That is to say, any learning technology, used well, can facilitate great learning; used badly it can inhibit learning. As illustrated in some of the case studies in Chapter Six, unequal access to learning technologies is very relevant to a globalizing higher education; utilizing learning technologies to facilitate intercultural contacts is very relevant; and ensuring that when learning technologies are used, their design does not create inequitable experiences is very relevant. These are referenced in the book, but all the themes explored apply across physical and virtual learning environments, at home and overseas, with regard to any of the technologies used within them – from physical blackboards to virtual worlds.

▶ Notes on Terminology

There are references throughout the book to 'equitable' practice and academic 'equity'. As used here, equity refers to providing students with *what they need* in order to have an equal chance of:

- ▶ learning what is intended;
- ▶ demonstrating that they have done so; and
- ▶ having that demonstration evaluated with equal recognition.

Equity is about student need, and recognizes that students' needs are oft times different. Equitable, then, will often mean *different*. However, there is also a sense that many actions and attitudes we adopt for a particular student or group of students contributes to learning spaces which are more equitable for all students. Adopting inclusive actions and attitudes is important among faculty, but also among students, each of whom influences the learning environments and experiences of her peers.

I am aware that terminological differences can be jarring and confusing to readers from different national and/or linguistic backgrounds. A few of these are dealt with by switching between preferred terms, such as 'faculty' and 'academic staff' throughout the book, others need a little more explanation, and I have picked up on these as they are introduced. Spelling conventions also differ, and the book has adopted American conventions of 'z' in verbs and their associated nouns such as 'globalize' and 'globalization', but otherwise uses British English spellings, except within phrases which occur almost exclusively in US contexts, such as 'students of color'.

More significantly, I am very aware that the use of some of terminology, such as 'Other', 'Western', 'minority' and 'majority', 'Black', 'White', 'BME'

(Black and Minority Ethnic – a categorization used in official statistics in the UK), 'LGBT' (Lesbian, Gay, Bisexual and Transgender – sometimes with additional sexualities such as Queer and Questioning), carry contestations and are open to accusations of over-generalization. On occasions, where I feel clarity is particularly important, I employ quotation marks to remind myself and readers of the need for care, but to mention these sensitivities repeatedly in the text would become tedious.

Although I aim to demonstrate the synergies between them, I have struggled to find a transparent single term to express the processes of both the internationalization and the equalization of diverse student learning experiences as they pertain to international students and multicultural and otherwise diverse students on 'home' campuses and in 'overseas' and virtual study locations. It is within emerging international contexts that rehearsed, though not resolved, equality and diversity issues are taking on new immediacies; equity questions which we continue to struggle with on our domestic campuses are given added significance when we draw increasingly diverse international students into home campuses, while simultaneously opening up new international and virtual learning spaces. I tend, therefore, towards referring most frequently to 'internationalization', but also use 'internationalization and equalization' at points where re-emphasizing the connections seems timely. In referring to 'internationalization', I am aware that much of the work in the book is drawn from furrows already arduously ploughed by colleagues in the equality and diversity or multicultural education field. This is not an attempt to appropriate that work, but recognition of a deficiency in internationalization discourse to date, and a deficiency which the reshaping of global higher education requires us to address.

I draw upon Langer's (1989) work on *mindfulness* at several points in the book. As I do so, I indicate its relevance through direct reference to the original construct where appropriate, but note here that some currently popular interpretations of mindfulness may not contain the depth or breadth of thought captured in Langer's work, and the concept as employed in this book should not be confused with some of those interpretations.

University education is generally seen as adult education, and where it has strong tendencies towards independent learning, at least, often refers to 'andragogy' (Knowles, 1980), and more recently 'heutagogy' (Hase & Kenyon, 2013) when discussing the processes and drivers which stimulate adult and self-determined learning. While possibly irritating for readers familiar with those paradigms, I use the more generally familiar 'pedagogy' as a catch-all term throughout.

Students and faculty are individuals. I have, therefore, sought to avoid third person plural, gender-neutral pronouns, instead alternating broadly between 'he' and 'she' as the narrative allows.

I also use my own voice frequently, and hope this captures something of the conversational ethos of a book, which seeks to suggest ways forward but also to acknowledge limitations regarding their applicability to contexts in which you, the reader, has greater experience.

▶ Thin Lines

In exploring educational responses to locally and globally diverse peoples, the lines between support, condescension and complicity in repression are challenging to negotiate, as are those surrounding cultural relativism and essentialism, common cause and hegemony. In case I have failed to tread these lines with appropriate balance at times, I preface all which follows with a quote which reflects its underpinning views and the values:

> It is our hope that there will always be ambiguity and nuance in understanding ourselves and others as cultural beings, learners, community members, and world citizens. However, being aware of and responsive to cultural variation is an essential aspect of equitable instruction.
>
> (Ginsberg & Wlodkowski, 2009, p. 8)

I hope you enjoy the book.

1 Global Higher Education

▶ **1.1 Chapter Introduction**

The sweeping forces of globalization have heightened the importance and priority of diversity in higher education.

(Chun & Evans, 2009, p. 3)

This chapter reviews emerging local and international contexts of twenty-first-century higher education, and suggests links between internationalization of the student learning experience and multicultural/diversity education agendas to equalize those experiences for domestic students. To develop a current perspective, this opening chapter draws upon economic and demographic data, and also illustrates something of how diversity perspectives and priorities can be differently framed in different contexts. Indeed, these differences are a significant part of the backstory to this volume. There is an impressive amount of such data available, but also significant gaps, some contradictions, and substantial questions concerning its validity. Furthermore, the arena is, like much within globalizing education, advancing rapidly, and details of numbers and players will soon be outdated. However, the trends will not, and we need to develop practice from an informed vantage point, even when the image which reaches us is blurred, represents only part of the game, and may not always be one we welcome. A recurrent theme, illustrated in this chapter, is that the shifting drivers and environments in which we enable learning demand dynamic and mutable approaches. So that, as higher education is reformulating itself into a globally connected and engaged entity, faculty need to adopt a *mindful* (Langer, 1989) approach to the development and implementation of policy and practice. To set the scene, this chapter explores three themes:

▶ current and emerging higher education directions relating to internationalization and equalization, with attention to transnational education (TNE) and to international and domestic student diversity at home and overseas;

▶ the emergence of the 'post-national' university within this milieu, modelled on the basis of balances in institutional risk, stakeholder impact, and embedded intercultural learning; and

▶ ways in which these shifts are impacting upon our students, our faculty, and our learning spaces.

▶ 1.2 Internationalization, Equality, and Diversity

Internationalization of higher education is no longer a new phenomenon. At the beginning of the millennium, it was recognized to be 'among the "success stories" of innovation in 20th Century education' (Altbach & Teichler, 2001, p. 10), Hans de Wit asserted it to be 'high on the agendas of national governments, international bodies, and institutions of higher education' (de Wit, 2000, p. 9), and Taylor identified it as one of the 'most significant drivers of change facing the modern university' (Taylor, 2004, p. 168). Its place in university strategies since then has grown significantly. For example, 95 per cent of Canadian universities recently identified internationalization as part of their strategic planning, with 89 per cent saying the 'pace of internationalization on their campuses has accelerated (greatly or somewhat) during the past three years'; in 2006, 41 per cent of institutions reported that internationalization of the curriculum (IOC) was in development, and eight years later 72 per cent reported being engaged in IOC initiatives (AUCC, 2014, pp. 4 & 29). The American Council on Education asserts that today, increasingly, for all types of university and college **'the question is not whether to engage globally, but how'** (ACE, 2015, p. 5, emphasis in original).

There is now a more significant dimension to the spread of internationalization; what was principally a process within Western institutions in the twentieth century is advancing as a global phenomenon, with reach into the lives of millions of students, and the families, communities, and societies among whom they go on to make their lives. Western commentators are often quick to identify problems within the educational values or practices of emerging global players (see for example, Altbach, 2013), and such deficit modelling can deflect Western institutions, and academics, from a critical stance towards the suitability of their own practice norms for a multicultural and globalizing world.

Within the global expansion of higher education, institutional motivations for embarking upon internationalization processes are highly variable, and so the activities which fall under its umbrella are also diverse. Indeed, in some cases rationale, strategy, and activities across institutions are so varied as to make 'internationalization' an empty signifier – highly visible in strategies and reports, but meaning so many different things across them as to mean nothing. It is important, therefore, to review what the term might refer to when being discussed by a particular institution, and how it is used within this book. Internationalization rationales are set by a range of intersecting and diverging priorities, including:

▶ following national/governmental policies (e.g. national security or national global reputation);
▶ building institutional reputation (including global rankings);
▶ generating income;
▶ developing research capacity/reach;
▶ realizing educational objectives; or
▶ pursuing ethical missions – such as (global) social justice or sustainability.

Arguably, in most anglophone contexts at least, income generation and institutional reputation have accounted for most institutional strategic activity. Within Europe, largely stemming from Bengt Nilsson's original work in Malmö, Sweden (Beelen, 2011, 2007; Nilsson, 2003), some institutions have embraced a wider focus through Internationalization at Home (IAH). Although there is no direct reference to the IAH paradigm in the following chapters, the perspectives raised concerning the student, the academic, and the learning spaces of emerging university contexts are relevant also to the framing of IAH. Since our universities increasingly conduct a substantive amount of their learning and teaching practice *away from* their own homes (and within somebody else's), internationalization, multicultural and diversity educational paradigms, and IAH are all in need of some reconstruction.

Europe is engaged in a long-running process of 'Europeanization', in higher education this largely concerns homogenization of academic regulations and structures, and building institutional partnerships and student exchanges, occasionally accompanying broader internationalization work. The political agenda of forging a stronger *European* identity might be interpreted as working against a broader global citizenship identity, and to be of limited value within a multicultural education philosophy. In other international contexts, the dominant foci of internationalization are seen as inappropriate for local priorities, perhaps even as neocolonialism. In South Africa, for example, internationalization has been interpreted to entail both the rejection of Western models and a process of 'relocalisation and Africanisation, which includes the pursuit of African identities and epistemologies', a move which resonates with the missions of many Historically Black and Indigenous institutions in the USA but also with a view to 'enriching the educational experience and knowledge base by engaging across cultures' (Backhouse & Adam, 2013, pp. 242 & 243). While the South African focus is strongly upon engaging across the cultures which apartheid segregated, cross-cultural engagement more generically is argued here to be a necessary target for all higher education in a multicultural and globalizing world.

Depending upon the balance of their priorities, and a range of local circumstances (capacity for growth, English-language capability, visas/mobility restrictions, social mobility aspirations, local social and political agendas), institutions will engage in different internationalization-related activities to greater or lesser extents. Most prominent among these activities are (in no order of priority):

- international student recruitment;
- international mobility for domestic students (study abroad, international internships, etc.);
- international (or more regional) collaborative partnerships;
- internationalization of the curriculum;
- dual degrees and/or franchised delivery; and
- international faculty exchange and/or recruitment.

Each of those priorities and activities can be fully aligned to constitute a 'comprehensive internationalization' strategy (Hudzik, 2014). In my experience, they rarely are, and where they are introduced ad hoc, often under the responsibility of separate departments and spread between different senior administrators, they can, indeed, create conflicting practices. Tendencies to 'top-down' approaches to institutional change also predominate in much of the internationalization field. Although faculty may see disconnects between institutional internationalization objectives and policies and their own work to design and deliver appropriate learning experiences for their students, their roles are often significantly impacted by those objectives and policies. Failure to engage can lead to academics being faced with radical shifts in their professional contexts, for which they are ill-prepared in terms of their own practice.

There are also concerns about the relationship between internationalization and the homogenization or denationalization of the university qua university (university as 'victim' of supranational policies, globalization, neo-liberal agendas, and curricula priorities shifted to generic 'employability skills') – a geographical expansion, through Western higher education influence, of the 'hollowed-out university' (Cribb & Gewirtz, 2013), in which learner needs are sacrificed to sociopolitical agendas. While recognizing that internationalization has brought some 'much needed change and adaptation to new world realities', Vinther and Slethaug (2013, p. 805) caution against loss of autonomy, converging goals, teaching and assessment methodologies, and institutional value being measured by decontextualized metrics.

They assert that recognizing higher education's international perspective 'must go hand in hand with an affirmation of underlying local values and beliefs' (op. cit., p. 805). Disconnects between higher education and student cultures are not only a matter of concern in international contexts; locally, also, we need to interrogate how prevailing academic values and beliefs are enacted, and be willing to respond with urgency when we see that aspects of our practice impinge upon the equity of any of our students' learning experiences. For diverse students at home and overseas, in virtual or physical learning spaces, socioculturally *appropriate* and *relevant* learning, teaching, and assessment practices are the roots of equitable learning experiences. This means, above all else, attending to the voices of *all* our students, and of *all* the faculty who shape and deliver their experiences. In some contexts, the discourse of equality and diversity risks implying that equitable academic practice needs to be interrogated only with regard to 'students of color', while internationalization discourse risks suggesting that our focus should be exclusively on the international student. While local circumstances may force attention to specific disadvantaged groups, equitable practice per se is not about any particular type of student. This has become more visibly the case as Western universities extend their activities and influence into diverse international contexts, in some of which the parameters of disadvantage are differently drawn.

As this book is concerned principally with the *educational* dimensions to internationalization and equalization, our focus is on actions and processes which can:

▶ inhibit or develop inclusive learning, teaching, and assessment practices; and
▶ better prepare our students to make their way in the multicultural and globalizing world of their futures.

In subsequent chapters, therefore, institutional internationalization activities associated principally with income generation and/or institutional reputation are put to one side. However, it is because these are, in many cases, now reaching such significant proportions that we need to critique the ways in which they impact academic equity for the expanding, diversifying, and diversely situated student body they are responsible for creating.

Transnational Education

A significant development in internationalization since the start of this millennium has been the 'exponential' expansion in TNE, which has emerged as a new 'thematic field' within higher education research (Kosmützky & Putty, 2016).

There are few countries which are not now engaging with some form of TNE activity, either through their own higher education institutions (HEIs) acting as the local provider of programmes/parts of programmes owned by an overseas institution, or as programme-owning institutions, or as both. TNE is so significant as to have become implicated in the very globalization to which higher education is seeking to respond (Leask, 2008a).

As with internationalization more broadly, what constitutes TNE is not fully agreed. Several authors and authorities offer their own definitions, some for example explicitly require the involvement of face-to-face learning (DEST, 2005), where others explicitly include distance learning (UNESCO/COUNCIL OF EUROPE, 2002). There is even a 'particularly pressing need' to achieve a better definition of the seemingly straightforward concept of what constitutes an international branch campus (BIS, 2014, p. 8). This vagueness can make an institution's TNE activity almost invisible to faculty and students who are not directly engaged within one initiative or another. This is enabling a kind of internationalization-by-stealth, a result of which is potentially weak institutional oversight, particularly on the part of the academic community and with regard to the implications for/impacts upon faculty and students.

Of eleven aims for establishing TNE partnerships identified in a UK government study, only one relates to enhancing the learning experience (BIS, 2014, p. 59). The literature on TNE is dominated by themes relating to 'globalisation, trade, quality and regulation; teaching and learning have a lower priority' (O'Mahony, 2014, p. 4). So, as here, the definition commonly focusses on the programme and the providers: 'TNE involves the mobility of academic programme and providers/institutions across jurisdictional borders to offer education and training opportunities' (British Council, 2014, p. 4). However, as we are concerned with the *student* experience of learning, teaching, and assessment, I use 'TNE' to refer to:

Higher education in which students undertake some or all of their programme of study while residing outside the country in which the programme-owning institution is based.

This includes forms of study which do occur regularly within some definitions:

▶ articulation arrangements (top-up awards), typically with early year(s) undertaken in the student's home country;
▶ joint and dual awards, with study undertaken in institutions based in each partner country;
▶ franchised awards, with study undertaken wholly in an institution based in the student's home country;

▶ overseas campus awards, with study undertaken wholly in the student's home country at a campus of the programme-owning institution;

▶ distance learning awards, with study undertaken by students resident in countries other than that of the programme-owning institution;

▶ blended learning awards, with distance elements undertaken by students resident in countries other than that of the programme-owning institution;

But it also includes

▶ a student undertaking credit-bearing activity outside her home country, including study abroad and international exchanges, work placements (internships), service learning, and volunteering.

These neat categories are often much more complex and overlapping, for example:

A 'distance learning' MBA that is delivered with online material from the UK but supported by face-to-face teaching by staff from a local provider and by flying faculty, together with attendance at short residential programmes in the UK. (BIS, 2014, p. 16)

Other definitions may also include less direct 'educational' activities from which a HEI in one country gains income through activities in other countries, such as:

▶ consultancy services;

▶ sales of learning materials;

▶ collaborative research projects;

▶ international visiting scholar programmes; or

▶ staff development and/or accreditation services.

Such differences, coupled with the rapid growth in TNE activities globally, make it currently impossible to offer any definitive data on its value, the number of institutions involved, or the number of students participating. However, it is clear that TNE is growing, is impactful, and is recognized by both governments and institutions as an increasingly important part of internationalization portfolios. Despite a lack of published selection criteria, China is opening to greater TNE collaboration, with 64 government-approved transnational institutions and more than 1,000 TNE programmes reported by June 2015 (He, 2016), and the branch campuses of the Universities of

Liverpool and Nottingham in China collectively have around 14,000 students (Wilikins, 2016). In the UK, currently the 'largest provider of TNE in the world' (Lawton & Jensen, 2015, p. 4) (others claim this accolade belongs to Australia (Kosmützky & Putty, 2016, p. 10), itself illustrating the confusion within the field), the government department responsible for universities (notably, the Department of Business, Innovation and Skills, not the Department of Education) identifies TNE as 'an important element in … the UK's educational export portfolio', with an estimated value to the economy of almost 500 million GB pounds, about 11 per cent of international fee revenues (BIS, 2014, pp. 1 & 3). An analysis of one aspect of UK TNE activity identified that in 2010/11 over 571,000 students were studying 'wholly overseas' for a UK HEI award, with over 86 per cent located *outside* the EU (Baskerville, 2013, p. 10). The 2014 BIS report (op. cit.), based on a census which included only 69 UK institutions, identified 253,695 active enrolments across 2,875 TNE programmes, with a mean across participating institutions of 24 programmes each. The top countries partnering the UK in the same report were spread across South East Asia, the Middle East, the Indian subcontinent, and Europe, and while Business and Management was the dominant subject area, Arts and Humanities, Engineering, Technology & Architecture, and Maths and Computing each were engaged in at least 300 programmes. It is not surprising that relevant UK government bodies are engaged in discussions with partner countries to achieve 'mutual recognition of qualifications' (BIS, 2013, p. 8), to further ease international mobility. While a significant amount of this development is located in public universities, in most cases, 'as soon as they cross a border they functionally become a private entity in terms of legislation in the receiving country' (UNESCO, 2004, p. 12). There is a simultaneous growth within fully private international providers of education services (Pearson alone had 7 billion US$ in education revenues in 2011, a four-year growth of over 40 per cent (BIS, 2013, p. 29)), and increasingly complex public–private international education partnerships. With the blurring of the boundaries across complex TNE provision, home governments may also soon be reviewing the governance and fiscal implications of the private operations of their public institutions. The current lack of clarity on TNE and its various constituent parts makes for an unhealthy confusion and absence of international oversight or regulation. At the very least, global higher education needs to achieve agreed definitions to enable meaningful data compilation and analysis (see Knight, 2016 for proposals on this).

TNE, then, is a vibrant arena of significant, and complex, developments. Where developments draw public universities into international private business operations, they may fundamentally change the nature of the institution. All TNE developments influence learning and teaching practice – at levels of policy, regulation, and assessment structures, through to mundane pressures such as requirements on faculty and students to work across global time zones. TNE activities add new dimensions to the ways in which academics must think, and act, to ensure equitable learning experiences for all students. Diversity issues still being fought for among domestic student populations become no less urgent and significantly more complex and difficult to identify in overseas and online cohorts.

Diversity and the Home Campus

The general expansion in global higher education is reflected in an increase in international student mobility, and to a degree paralleled by more long-standing moves to widen access to higher education among the domestic population, with over 70 per cent of college students in the USA identified as 'non-traditional learners', for example (Ginsberg & Wlodkowski, 2009, p. 5). Though, as with TNE, definitions of international mobility and of 'non-traditional' can make it difficult to reconcile reported numbers.

From World Bank data, the British Council estimates a 21 million increase in the total number of higher education students worldwide between 2011 and 2020 (from 178 to 199 million), with 450,000 expected to be internationally mobile (cited in BIS, 2013, p. 15). UNESCO (2015), however, reported that between 2000 and 2012, the global number of internationally mobile students rose by 100 per cent, from 2 to 4 million. Although the major sending and receiving countries have remained the same for several years, their dominance is steadily declining, with complex changes as other players come onto the field. For example, the number of African students studying in China in 2005 was fewer than 3,000, but nearly 12,500 by 2009 (Ngalomba, 2015). Of the approximately 500 Chinese Confucius Institutes established worldwide since 2004, the 46 currently housed within African public universities have all been established since 2012. The major international student recruiting countries remain ambitious about growth. For example, Australia aims for 520,000 students by 2020, Canada for 478,000 by 2022, and the UK anticipates growth of 15–20 per cent between 2013 and 2018 (BIS, 2013, p. 32). Significant for this book is the number of international students in-country per national student studying abroad, with Australia (21:1), the UK (14:1), and the USA (12:1) far outstripping all others (OECD, 2015a, p. 369). At the same time, several countries where English is not the first language are building their existing capabilities to receive international students through the expansion of academic programmes delivered in English. Germany and the Netherlands claim over 1,770 and over 1,300 such courses, respectively (DAAD, 2016; Study in Holland, 2015), over 730 courses are available in Taiwan (National Taiwan University Course

Information System, 2015), in Malaysia 'all courses' at private universities and 'most' postgraduate courses in public universities are now delivered in English (TARGET, 2014), while English is the official language of instruction at all universities in Singapore. The move to instruction in English as a lingua franca (ELF) or English-medium instruction (EMI) raises its own equity questions, as it demands high levels of English-language proficiency from domestic students and faculty (including, of course, those for whom the dominant national language may, itself, not be their first language), may require academics skilled in meeting the needs of students with varying degrees of ability in English (Ghazarian & Youhne, 2015), and may restrict or delocalize the curriculum through reliance upon resources available in English (Preisler et al., 2011). Increases and shifts in international student mobility can open spaces for exciting developments in our learning and teaching practice, and in the richness of potential intercultural experiences for all our students. However, they also make the tasks associated with providing equitable academic experience for everybody more challenging, especially, but not only, when 'delivering', on campuses or online, to students in a range of countries.

There is a dearth of reliable data for most dimensions of diversity among international students and across domestic university populations globally (Harrison & Peacock, 2010; James, 2012). Nonetheless, predicted trends point to increasing diversity across the higher education student population globally, with participation by women anticipated to 'substantially expand' everywhere, along with older, part-time, and international students, while the social base 'will continue to broaden' (OECD, 2008, cited in Altbach et al., 2009, p. xix).

As a matter of significant principle, I see these as moves in the right direction. However, cumulatively, they indicate a more complex higher education student community, whose expectations, experiences, and aspirations are also more complex.

Across countries where race and ethnicity are recognized as significant demographic variables among the domestic population, there remain strong indicators that access to and success within and beyond higher education is inequitably distributed between minority and majority groups. In South Africa in 2007, 60 per cent of the 20- to 14-year-old cohort within the White population were enrolled in higher education, compared to 12 per cent of their Black peers (Scott et al., 2007, cited in Smit, 2012); in the USA in 2008, 44 per cent of White 18- to 24-year-olds were enrolled in colleges and universities, compared to 32 per cent of Black 18- to 24-year-olds, and 26 per cent of Hispanic 18- to 24-year-olds. In the same year, around 33 per cent of the White population of the USA held bachelor's degrees, compared to 17 per cent of the Black population and 11 per cent of the Hispanic population. By contrast, 60 per cent of the Asian population, contrary to the minority:majority trend, held a bachelor degree. These headline figures, of course, hide deeper complexities, for example variability across the Hispanic population ranged from 7.8 per cent among Salvadorians to 30 per cent for Cubans. Or, when gender is factored in among the same group, only 34 per cent of the bachelor's degrees awarded to Black students went to Black males, compared to 44 per cent among the White student population (all USA data from NCES, 2010). In the UK, national statistics consistently point to lower participation and final degree achievement by domestic Black and Minority Ethnic (BME) students (Berry & Loke, 2011; ECU, 2014b). Furthermore, BME representation is not evenly spread, with, for example, more Black students at *one* London university than in the 'top' 20 UK universities combined (Elevations Networks Trust, 2012, cited in Stevenson, 2012). At the graduate level, recent UK research has demonstrated that both Black Caribbean students and students from disadvantaged backgrounds are significantly underrepresented in professional employment immediately following and at 40 weeks following graduation (HEFCE, 2015). While great care is needed in the collection and analysis of data pertaining to such generalized categories, since 'students of similar racial backgrounds do not necessarily share the same beliefs, values or attitudes towards education' (Singh, 2011, p. 4), and intersectional complexities are masked, the repeated trends do indicate that higher education has not yet learned how to provide equitable access and learning opportunities.

In their review of internationalization and diversity literature, Caruana and Ploner (2010, p. 11) identify three levels of diversity in higher education, in summary:

- ▶ **structural diversity** – 'the changing demographic mix and level of racial/ ethnic diversity in the student body at any one university'
- ▶ **classroom diversity** – 'its representation in the curriculum, learning about diverse people and gaining experience with diverse peers in class'
- ▶ **informal interactional diversity** – 'the frequency and quality of inter-group interaction, the majority of which will take place outside the classroom and will be central to meaningful diversity experiences'.

They go on to note that the greatest damage potentially occurs where institutional values most reflect those of the dominant social group, 'reproducing existing patterns of privilege' (op. cit.).

For our students, institutional values and patterns of privilege are most directly encountered within the learning experiences which faculty design and deliver. This is not to say that other areas of the university can neglect to focus on the values reflected within their work, but to emphasize the need for faculty to interrogate learning, teaching, and assessment practices. Even if we cannot impact directly upon structural diversity, we can change classroom and informal interactional diversity, and it is 'both an ethical and a practical matter to consider what is happening and what can be done on campus, in the present' (Caplan & Ford, 2014, p. 31).

While issues across diverse ethnicities and nationalities are important, they are not the only dimensions of diversity to remain problematic in higher education, and some may demand particular consideration precisely because our home campuses are becoming more diverse. In supporting guidance relating to the higher education LGBT community in the UK, one vice-chancellor noted that 'for too long, untested assumptions about the liberal culture of our universities and colleges being wholly supportive of diversity have been allowed to mask certain failings' (Dianne Willcocks, Foreword to Hall, 2010). Such failings are, rightly, considered with regard to institutional practice. However, we must also become more mindful of how our diverse students themselves may be *equipped* to respond to some of the dimensions of diversity they find around them in their learning spaces. Not all of our students have reached our campuses from communities or countries where 'liberal culture' extends to LGBT citizens, women, the disabled, or specific ethnicities, religions, or races. In many cases, developing learning experiences and spaces to serve the needs of the diverse students on home campuses entails supporting them across difficult terrain to find ways of working with their peers which are appropriate for a multicultural and globalizing world.

Diversity Within Transnational Provision

TNE, as defined earlier, spans student experience in public and private providers across six continents, and involving most countries. There is a paucity of demographic data such as that presented above pertaining to student cohorts in many TNE contexts. However, invisibility does not mean absence, and while it is true on our home campuses that we need to monitor differential outcomes, because 'equal participation is not simply about gaining access to higher education, but also about achieving parity in terms of educational outcomes' (Richardson, 2008, p. 46), this is arguably even more critical with regard to the less-visible minority students accessing our TNE provision.

The challenges for an academic delivering learning in diverse TNE cultural contexts include his own capabilities to work effectively across cultures, appropriateness of the curriculum, expectations and standards relating to quality assurance, and students' familiarity with required approaches to communications or assessments (Djerasimovic, 2014, p. 205). These will be discussed at length through various chapters, but a brief comment here on just one aspect helpfully illustrates the contested territory which faculty must negotiate. Theories concerning different student learning styles, although contested (Coffield et al., 2004), often feature strongly in work to equalize learning experiences. A specific area of learning style theory relates to cultural variations in learning styles, with particular nationalities (or even continents) sometimes characterized as being restricted by preferred learning styles which do not correspond to those of the provider institution. Such characterizations have contributed to a 'deficit model' of international students, historically familiar to multicultural educators (Schmeichel, 2012), and now emerging with regard to cohorts within TNE contexts (see for example, O'Mahony, 2014, pp. 15–16). This is not the place to weigh the validity of learning styles theory per se, but, rather, to raise the problem of ascribing a learning style to a nationality or to any 'type' of student, when even an individual student, 'may have different preferred thinking and learning styles in different social situations and even for different tasks' (Jarvis, 2006, p. 108). As TNE contexts become more diverse, international student mobility expands, and participation widens across domestic students, academics designing and delivering learning need to be cautious not to overgeneralize the learning styles of the students they are working with. This example serves to illustrate a wider point. From the programme-owning institution's perspective, and from the perspective of that institution's academic community, all TNE students may be considered to be 'international' students, since many of their collective characteristics conform to those which have come to be associated by many with international students, and some identified minority students, on domestic campuses (low English-language proficiency, lack of familiarity with common cultural references, not able to negotiate academic expectations or regulations, source of additional income). Clearly, though, the spectrum of student diversity *within and across* many of the TNE recipient/hosting countries and many online cohorts varies considerably, perhaps in dimensions which faculty may be unfamiliar with. Obvious examples would relate to the absence of gender diversity in those countries where higher education is a segregated practice, to ethnic diversity in those countries where the indigenous population is highly ethnically heterogeneous or where access to higher education is restricted to a dominant ethnic group. The unhappy higher education situations concerning race and ethnicity outlined in the previous section pertain (similarly or differently) across genders, sexualities, socio-economic groups, and disabilities in countries where institutions are forging international partnerships. As universities develop TNE collaborations in diverse countries and cultures, they need to raise questions concerning how female, LGBT, and specific ethnicities, religions, or races among faculty and students might be framed within partner universities and their communities. How academics are equipped to respond to experiences of prejudice and discrimination when working in diverse international contexts seems to have gained scant attention to date.

Values such as equality and respectful dialogue permeate the design and delivery of curricula created within 'liberal democracies' and being delivered elsewhere. Achieving academic equity and delivering an inclusive curriculum in those contexts where some group and individual characteristics are absent from the cohort, or undisclosed within the cohort, is no less an imperative for faculty working overseas than it is at home. This is substantively more complex in the context of those TNE classrooms where the programme-owning institution and the underpinnings of its courses may be at some variance with the values within the local society. This might be particularly salient with regard to specific ethnicities, genders, or to other identities which may be unrecorded, unrecognized, and unwelcome (or even illegal).

▶ 1.3 The Emergence of the Post-National University

Most universities in the USA have an Office, Centre, or similar, of Multicultural Affairs, Programmes, or similar. From outside, this can be a little perplexing. Why should universities situated in one of the most culturally diverse nations in the world, institutions dedicated to knowledge and the advancement of learning, need a *separate* unit to deal with multicultural matters? I extract rationales from a few of these, anonymously, below:

> *The primary mission of the Multicultural Centre is to develop a sense of community between students, staff, and faculty of color on the ... campus.*
>
> *The Multicultural Resource Centre ... provides individual counselling and educational services for undergraduate multicultural students at...*
>
> *The Mission of the Office for Multicultural Learning is to coordinate, collaborate and promote cross-campus educational co-curricular programs that further integrate multicultural learning into the university's core curriculum, overall undergraduate curriculum and student life.*
>
> *The Centre for Multicultural and Diversity Education provides academic, cultural and social programmes intended to promote inclusiveness, foster achievement and assist in the development and advancement of a diverse student body.*

These are important objectives, but they are objectives demanding ownership by all members of a university, including its academics, rather than being delegated to a separate unit, however high-profile and well-resourced it might be (or might not be). They are also objectives which cannot be limited to 'faculty of color', or 'undergraduate multicultural students' (in fairness, many units are much more inclusive in their representation of diversity than those two examples might suggest). I do not live in the USA, and I am not a person of color, so my perspective does not derive from any lived experience of the impacts of the structural inequalities and discriminatory practices which pertain there (or here, in the UK, for that matter). However, when any aspect of university life is detached from the mainstream academic experience of every student, its impact is limited, or its impact is perhaps profound, but only for the limited number of students who participate. This is true, also, of 'Study Abroad' units, staffed by committed and enthusiastic 'international educators', and those units dedicated to supporting international students on campus; in a global age, why are all educators not 'international educators' equipped to work effectively with multicultural cohorts? And, as importantly, the kind of learning being advanced by multicultural and international educators for a minority of students is the kind of learning which all students require as graduates who will *unavoidably* need to make their way in the multicultural and globalizing worlds of their futures (see Chapter Two).

Multicultural education work has identified factors which inhibit or contribute towards greater equality in learning and teaching, and these need to inform our emerging international university activities in their international as well as their domestic work. A tenet of multicultural education is that 'the structural organization of the school system is designed to advantage the dominant group' and that therefore, 'systematic changes are needed ... to establish equity and equal opportunity for all to participate and gain ownership in the learning and teaching environment' (Saint-Hilaire, 2014, p. 595). In the current global higher education context, this perspective needs to be extended from higher education's domestic work to its international work, given the structural equalities in the various contexts of the emerging global higher education landscape, touched on in previous sections. Where once it was possible to focus exclusively upon disparities among, for example, the learning experiences of Black and White students, the parameters of inequality in global higher education are more complex. Universities, like many communities worldwide, are becoming *multi*cultural spaces in ways which they have never been before. The term 'multicultural university' was appealing for this book, but it is their emerging geographical, cross-national, spread which particularly prompts the need to find synergies between *internationalized and equalized* learning. The discussion which follows sets out the idea of the 'post-national' university as a generalized model for the rest of the book. Within that model, equality and diversity, and multicultural education work, are seen as fundamental for learning and teaching at home, overseas, and online. Furthermore, the bedrock of that work is argued to be located within the *mainstream* learning spaces and activities of all students.

Hitherto, universities have been essentially national entities (or even subnational, such as state/regional institutions or religious/denominational institutions, for example). As they engage increasingly within new international contexts, serving globally diverse students through physical or virtual learning activities, Marginson (2007, p. 39) speaks of universities becoming 'disembedded' from their national contexts, especially concerning their relationships to government – as mentioned above, effectively becoming private enterprises in overseas contexts. Some universities now proudly claim to be 'international' institutions, some even claim to be 'global' institutions. But, notwithstanding data explored above, I suggest these claims are, possibly with a handful of exceptions, still aspirational by any tangible measures. Seeking to bring some clarity to the 'international' ascription, Jane Knight has proposed a three-level 'typology' of international universities:

▶ the *classic* model – 'an institution that has developed multiple activities and partners, both at home and abroad, and involves a broad spectrum of intercultural and international academic, research, service, and management initiatives';
▶ the *satellite model* – 'institutions that have concentrated on developing off-campus research centers, international branch campuses..., and offices for alumni relations, student recruitment, or consultancy purposes';
▶ the international *co-founded model* – 'new stand-alone independent institutions that have been co-founded or co-developed by two or more international partners' (summarized from Knight, 2015, p. 109).

While helpful in foregrounding the range and variety of transactional activities which may contribute to the mix, the typology does not set out measures by which we might begin to determine whether a particular institution has become international. More significantly, the typology does not refer to any international dimension within curricula, assessment requirements, or graduate attributes. In this section I model factors which might be brought into a calculation to justify a claim to be 'international'. I suggest that several institutions are currently, or will shortly become, sufficiently engaged in activities beyond the boundaries of their home nation and culture(s) to be considered 'post-national', if not yet 'international'. The boundary lines are complex and fuzzy, but as a heuristic, I offer a simple continuum, as in Figure 1.1.

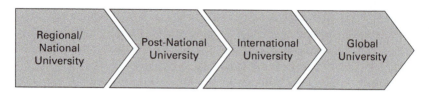

Figure 1.1 Illustration of Continuum of University Types

The boundaries are complex and fuzzy because it is a complex balance across a wide range of university activities which need to be considered – represented in the sections below as balances between *domestic and international institutional risk, stakeholder impact, and learning culture*. Prominent among the factors which need weighing within the equation are suggested in Table 1.1.

This discussion may be seen as lacking relevance to the equality and diversity (or multicultural education) agenda, hitherto largely focussed on domestic students in domestic contexts. However, a review of Table 1.1 from an equality and diversity perspective reveals synergies, as alluded to earlier; international students whether situated on home campuses, overseas campuses, or as distance learners are also diverse as they arrive in our learning spaces; in doing so, they carry with them whatever structural inequalities, stereotypes, prejudices, discriminations, and identity mismatches which have framed their lives within their local contexts *and* through their globally situated sociocultural/geopolitical contexts – international faculty, similarly so. Diverse students' representations in the curriculum, their voices in learning spaces, their impacts upon differentially positioned peers, their claim to resources, their relationships with other agencies – all demand equitable attention. In setting up the post-national university as the focus of this book, it is precisely this which I am suggesting brings new synergies and necessitates the expertise of both internationalization and multicultural educator communities if we are to serve our students, and other stakeholders, as they deserve.

The Times Higher Education Supplement produces an annual ranking of the 100 most international universities based upon their 'international outlook' indicator (THES, 2015). This list and other rankings are significant drivers for many HEIs globally, and data for calculating outcomes need to be reliable (and available). This restricts the kind of data which is utilized, and, therefore, impacts upon the capability of rankings to capture more qualitative pictures. As available data become more nuanced, it may be that a fair and transparent algorithm could be devised to appropriately calculate the factors identified in Table 1.1, and doubtless others not listed, to produce a single index number for such a ranking. However, we are not yet at that

Table 1.1 Indicative Factors to Weigh in the Domestic:International Balance of Institutional Activities

The balance between

Domestic		International
	FINANCE	
	Income	
	Expenditure	
	Debt	
	Investments	
	STUDENT BODY	
	Students studying on home campus	
	Students studying on home institution campuses (branch campuses) overseas	
	Students studying on campuses of overseas partners	
	Students studying on distance learning programmes	
	The sum of all the above in any specific discipline or level of study	
	The sum of all the above across the institution's programmes	
	PARTNERS & AGENCIES	
	Number and types of academic partner institutions	
	Number and types of engagement with national quality assurance agencies, ministries, and/or NGOs	
	Number and types of relationships with Professional, Statutory and Regulatory Bodies (PSRBs)	
	ACADEMIC PROGRAMMES	
	The number and range of programmes delivered	
	The number, range, and participation of students in overseas study, work, or other experience as part of their course	
	The number, range, and participation of students in virtual learning with other students overseas as part of their course	
	The sources of content, range of learning activities, etc. embedded within the curricula	
	STAFF	
	The number and diversity of staff of all types and at all levels	
	The number and range of staff spending part or all of their professional lives working overseas	
	Staff development activity	
	MISCELLANEOUS – FOR EXAMPLE	
	The number and location of overseas banks, debt collection agencies, educational agents, consultants, and/or legal representatives engaged within business processes required for the above;	
	The tax authorities which may have an interest in income generated within these activities;	
	The cultural, religious, and ethical mores which may be challenged, and the consequences of such challenges;	
	The number of active alumni in prestige/influential positions overseas.	

point. Notwithstanding these limitations, I propose calculations of an institution's 'internationalism' be based on three dimensions, the balance between:

▶ international and domestic *institutional risk*;
▶ international and domestic *stakeholder impact*; and
▶ international/multicultural *learning* and national/dominant culture *learning embedded across curricula*.

The three dimensions are outlined briefly below, but this book is most concerned with the third, and explores it in detail throughout subsequent chapters.

Institutional Risk

In several countries, many institutions have been moving towards a greater portion of their risk being associated with international activity in areas listed in Table 1.1 for many years, and this movement has accelerated and extended in reach considerably in recent years. In Figure 1.2, I extend the original heuristic with an illustrative formula to classify an institution on a 'regional/national' to 'global' university continuum base on the balance of *risk*.

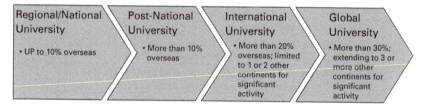

Figure 1.2 Illustration of Continuum of University Types According to Balance Between Risk Exposure Through Domestic and International Activities

The percentages given are meant only to be illustrative, but let us say that when activity generating more than around 10 per cent of an institution's *total risk* lies outside its national home, that institution can probably no longer be regarded as simply a regional or national entity, nor a public one. By the measures proposed in Figure 1.2, a few universities would probably currently qualify as international, and probably none could claim to be global, but recent developments in international higher education outlined in previous sections mean that many now fit, and more will soon fit, the *post-national* category.

Each of the factors listed above, along with variations in the 'values, norms, and assumptions of governing a higher education institution' (Knight, 2015, p. 117) which impact across them, has consequences for academic staff, their practice, and their students, but I suggest that some are particularly relevant to equitable learning, teaching, and assessment. Some key factors impacting on practice and practitioners are listed in Section 1.4, and are covered in more depth in ensuing chapters.

Stakeholder Impact

The second dimension to the measurement of an institution's international engagement concerns the balance of stakeholder impact. A local university, with students largely from its own region, who tend to stay and take up employment locally, and whose civic engagement is focussed mostly on community issues, principally impacts on stakeholders within its immediate region. Such institutions are now probably more common outside the Western, anglophone world. However, when an institution includes more international activity in areas such as those as set down in Table 1.1, it is not only the balance in its own exposure to risk which begins to shift but also the balance in the locus of stakeholder impact. By way of example, when a university builds an overseas branch campus it may employ local faculty – its stakeholders, then, extend not only to directly employed local academics but also to their dependents, and also to other universities in the region who might find their own faculty taking up employment opportunities with the new university, or seeking changes to their own employment terms and conditions to reflect those of the new institution. Through leasing buildings, utilizing local tradespeople, and employing service staff, stakeholders extend to other areas of the local economy. The new branch campus offers local students more choice, and may become a prestige institution of the region – again impacting upon other institutions by competing for the 'brightest and the best', and also perhaps through the introduction of new technologies, pedagogies, quality 'standards', or employment terms and conditions. While these impacts might be associated with raising quality, they may also represent a threat to local academic traditions and identities. Through their students-as-graduates taking up local employment, the branch campus impact extends to business stakeholders, possibly coming to challenge their sustainable business models or HR equality agendas. So, while the most immediate stakeholders with regard to learning and teaching are the students, stakeholder impact extends much further. Although universities 'trading' outside their own countries may always be de facto private entities, this does not mean they can abandon their responsibilities to these stakeholders.

The ethical considerations of doing business only increase when we do it in somebody else's country. For the academic community, this raises as many questions as it might for senior administrators. We need to be confident that the programmes we create, and the learning experiences we deliver, are relevant and meaningful to our immediate stakeholders, our students, and also that they do not unintentionally disrupt or devalue local competitors, local values, or faculty in local institutions. At their best, TNE activities should add value to all of these.

So, alongside our continuum of institutional risk, we need to add a continuum of stakeholder impact, as illustrated in Figure 1.3.

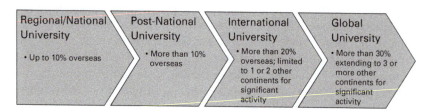

Figure 1.3 Illustration of Continuum of University Types According to Balance Between Stakeholder Impact Through Domestic and International Activities

International/Multicultural Learning

This third dimension is explored throughout this book, and includes the equalization of learning opportunity (through objectives, activities, assessments, environments) for diverse students in diverse contexts, and, closely related but not the same, building learning gain (through objectives, activities, assessments, environments) which prepares students for intercultural living in a multicultural and globalizing world. Something of this is captured in emerging programme-level accreditation of internationalization quality (the only operational framework which actually leads to accreditation which I am aware of can be found at ECA, 2013). I have used the awkward 'international/multicultural' descriptor for this dimension because both are necessary, and as noted, currently not all international learning incorporates multicultural perspectives and not all multicultural learning incorporates global perspectives. For most of the book, I use the terms *intercultural learning* and *global-self* to refer, respectively, to the process of learning among diverse international and multicultural others, and to the aspirational learning gain of that process. 'Global-self' is explored in detail in Chapter Two.

Institutional risk and stakeholder impact are related, but not necessarily proportionately so, in any given institution; the learning dimension is potentially enhanced through increased international activity, but may also remain neglected, and it may be strongly present even in the absence of significant international activity. If represented as a three-dimensional matrix as in Figure 1.4, movement on any axis towards the international end pulls the university closer to becoming post-national, international, or global – and has potential to push the other axes also towards the international end to some degree or other. I propose that all three dimensions need to be present, but the absence of *significant* international/multicultural activity on the learning axis would void a claim to being an international institution, no matter how great its international risk and stakeholder impact.

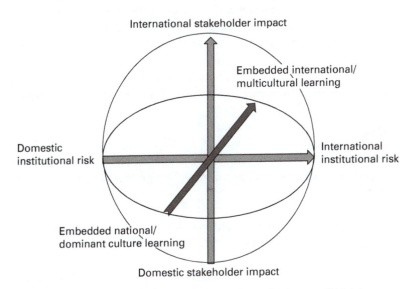

Figure 1.4 Three Dimensions of Domestic:International Balance to Weigh in Considerations of an Institution's 'International' Ascription

It will be noted that I have not included a dimension specifically related to the research activities of a university. As modelled here, domestic:international research *activity* contributes to the risk dimension, research *output* and research *students* are part of the stakeholder impact dimension, and *research-informed teaching* is part of the learning dimension.

Many international businesses, through 'integrated' or 'triple-bottom line' (Elkington, 1997) corporate social responsibility (CSR) accounting practices, report on stakeholder as well as shareholder interests and impacts. Adopting a CSR accounting approach seems a suitable approach for a university as it moves towards international and private company trading. An examination of stakeholder impact, including current domestic students and faculty stakeholders, should at least inform the business case and business development processes for new overseas ventures.

▶ 1.4 Aspects of the Post-National University Impacting on Academic Practice and Practitioners

This section illustrates the kinds of implications which contexts of global higher education and the emerging post-national university may have for learning and teaching practice and the role of the global academic practitioner. These illustrations provide an introduction to themes explored in more depth in the chapters to follow. As elsewhere, in line with the primary focus of the book, the examples given below reference students of different nationalities and ethnicities, but points made apply also, if variably in some cases, to students of different genders, sexualities, (dis)abilities, or religions.

Students

The demographics and location of the student body, as an institution's international activities expand and diversify, are perhaps the most significant single factor, including:

- ▶ the number and variety of **nationalities and ethnicities of students studying on programmes** which an academic is designing and/or delivering;
- ▶ the percentage of **diverse nationalities and ethnicities** within any given discipline area, programme of study, or level of award; and
- ▶ the demographic and educational characteristics of **students studying in partner institutions** overseas.

Differences in such areas have the potential to disrupt equitable academic practice in a number of ways. Small percentages of international students or a limited history of a multicultural student body can mean a lack of awareness of the diverse experiences and perspectives being brought to a course, including students' own experiences of being a member of a minority group or of working with diverse others. By contrast, larger numbers (even if still a minority group) of students of a particular ethnicity or nationality can result in stereotyping, loss of focus on the individual student, and factionalism within classes/on campus. Where a single nationality or ethnicity constitute a majority on a particular course, they have the potential to skew the curriculum and/or its delivery to favour their own experience and academic strengths. For an established student cohort, an increase in international students or an expansion in student diversity on campus can activate resistance and intolerance. Our on-campus diversities offer 'ideal social forums for promoting cultural understanding; fostering tolerance of diversity; discovering alternative ways of thinking; and developing intercultural skills' (Volet & Ang, 2012, p. 22), invaluable opportunities for all students to gain capabilities for multicultural global living. Such opportunities now extend to virtual learning spaces, perhaps across online cohorts, perhaps between cohorts on home and international campuses. However, such opportunities require deliberately constructed learning experiences and environments to support intercultural learning. These and other challenges are considered in detail in Chapter Two.

Academic Staff

The make-up and deployment of academic staff as an institution's international activities expand and diversify are a second key factor, including:

▶ the number of **domestic faculty spending part of their time overseas**, the range of countries and cultures involved, and the types of activities they are engaged in;
▶ the number and diversity of **non-domestic faculty** employed by or delivering learning on behalf of an institution, and differences which might pertain in different national contexts; and
▶ the mix of **ethnicities and nationalities across all faculty**, and the nature of their status/roles, and range of activities they are engaged in.

Working across cultural and other diversity boundaries and in diverse contexts requires additional professional responsibilities and capabilities from faculty. This might apply most strongly to those from majority groups who have had few cross-cultural professional experiences, or to those faculty required, often quite suddenly, to deliver in new physical locations or within new academic cultures.

An academic working overseas needs resilience when working without the immediate support of her home institution. Apart from the physical and emotional drain of international travel and distance from personal and professional domestic roles, this may include a capacity to deal with unforeseen extensions to her normal range of responsibility, perhaps 'acting up' to a more senior role with respect to on-the-ground decision-making, or assuming the role of institutional representative/ambassador (possibly even national representative) when working within an overseas community. An international faculty member may face the challenge of ensuring his voice is heard among more powerfully situated local faculty; members of the dominant local group face the concomitant challenge of ensuring they give voice to colleagues from minority groups. Both face the key challenge of recognizing inequitable practice and establishing equal status among students, including, crucially, in the ways students respond to each other.

In all of these, most importantly, faculty need to develop practice based upon transferrable learning paradigms, and to exhibit effective cross-cultural capabilities for working with diverse students and colleagues in diverse contexts. Such capabilities, as presented in this book, resonate strongly with those explored by multicultural educators. These and related challenges are considered in detail in Chapter Three.

Learning Spaces

The physical and virtual spaces in which learning takes place can support or contest with the equality aspirations of the faculty and students who populate those spaces. As the examples below illustrate, aspects of international developments impacting on learning spaces are varied, and far-reaching:

▶ the number and range of **programmes delivered** at international campuses, whether as branch campuses or under international collaboration/franchise agreements;

▶ the number and range of **programmes delivered online** to students in international contexts;

▶ the number of **students undertaking part of their course overseas**, the range of countries involved, and the types of activities they are engaged in;

▶ the number of **students spending part of their course engaging virtually with students overseas**, the range of countries involved, and the types of activities they are engaged in;

▶ the extent to which **institutional values extend** across the diverse locations in which they operate and the diverse peoples they employ and teach; and

▶ the **changing global context** our students are preparing for, and for which faculty must devise curriculum and associated learning experiences.

Such differences have the potential to impact on faculty and disrupt equitable practice in a number of ways. Where international collaborations, franchises, or branch campuses exist as significant entities, programmes need to be developed and adapted to meet the needs of more diverse students in more diverse contexts. Academic staff may be responsible for such developments, but not be regional or cultural experts; regional and cultural expertise among other faculty and students needs to be recognized, valued, and drawn into collaborative working practices. Faculty need to research sources beyond their established canon, and establish case studies based upon scenarios they are unfamiliar with from their own cultural contexts. Faculty from provider institutions may be called upon to support, mentor, monitor, or develop academics in partner institutions engaged in delivering and assessing student work. This involves sensitive cross-cultural working, and being mindful of own attitudes and behaviours towards diverse others. In addition to being required to cross-moderate or double-mark assessments from an expanded diversity of students, faculty may also be required to engage in, navigate, or manage engagement with diverse sets of academic regulations and legal requirements – while ensuring consistency across delivery contexts. Devising and delivering equitable learning experiences and spaces require additional skills, knowledge, and resilience from academics and students alike. These and other challenges are considered in detail in Chapter Four.

Good Practice Principles for Learning & Teaching

Each of these aspects of internationalization and equalization raises questions concerning how faculty transform practice to enable students to make their ways positively and appropriately as co-constructors of their learning and of their multicultural and globalizing world. This cannot be the job of academics alone, but insofar as it is faculty who shape the learning, teaching, and assessment experiences, and the learning spaces of those students – locally and globally – it is the academic community which must take on the challenges and pick up the opportunities. Principles for good practice, hitherto principally evolved for domestic campuses, need to be developed in ways which are appropriate to the diversities of the post-national university. These ideas are the focus of Chapter Five.

Practice in Action

The academic community is already responding to the challenge of building learning spaces and activities, internationally and locally, online and physically, which are more equitable and more directed to creating learning gain appropriate to a multicultural and globalizing world. Such work is often situated in small-scale projects, for which there has been limited institutional support, though examples of more strategic initiatives also exist. While all such initiatives are grounded in specific contexts, they offer real-world examples for others to reflect upon, to transfer, or to adapt. Sharing these examples is a step to building a global community of academic practice, and the contributors of case studies for this book are especially thanked for their willingness to join these professional conversations. Examples of ongoing developments to practice in emerging post-national university spaces are the subject of Chapter Six.

▶ 1.5 Chapter Summary

This chapter has presented some emerging higher education contexts within which the further discussions in this book are situated, suggesting they relate to both internationalization and multicultural education. Internationalization itself includes a variety of activities and may be underpinned by one or more rationales, including some associated with income generation or institutional reputation. TNE and continuing international student recruitment have been highlighted as particular arenas which are shifting the constitution of increasing numbers of institutions towards that of *post-national university*. I have proposed we model this on the basis of the domestic:international balance in institutional risk, stakeholder impact, and the embedding of international/multicultural learning. The shift in institutional engagement to more international arenas multiplies and adds nuance to the diversity of students and faculty, adding complexity to ongoing work to enhance access and success for diverse students at home. This is the context in which we go on to consider how faculty, and the wider academic community of our students, can respond to the changes which are gaining pace, in particular with regard to designing, delivering, and participating in learning spaces and learning experiences which are:

- ▶ equitable across the increasing diversity in students and locations; and
- ▶ appropriate for the multicultural and globalizing worlds into which they will graduate.

2 Global Graduates

▶ **2.1 Chapter Introduction**

Globalization is interpreted here as a complex of processes shaped and driven by *human* agents; 'their value systems and the means they employ to achieve their goals' are the 'primary creators' of the world (Group of Lisbon, 1995, p. 14, cited in Strijbos, 2002, p. 230). Among these people are our students and graduates. How the world impacts upon them and how they go on to impact upon the world are related matters. How they experience their university will influence both – for good or for ill. Living with, working with, shaping futures with diverse others *locally and globally* is fundamental to the well-being of our students *and* to the well-being of the global and local communities to which they will contribute. Enabling our students to participate positively is the key driver for the internationalization and equalization of the student learning experience. This chapter explores how daily encounters with increasingly complex human diversity are framing the multicultural and globalizing world for our students and our graduates. Enabling students to respond positively to this is not a small matter. It requires more than skills acquisition. It is about shifting their identities: developing a 'new paradigm' (Fantini, 2003, p. 15) for how they view themselves in the world, and moving beyond established ethnic or national identifications of self and others.

As real and virtual flows connect our students with like-minded and differently minded, like-experienced and differently experienced, like-privileged and differently privileged peoples locally and globally, they *learn* how they feel about, think about, and behave towards those others. This learning tends to be unintentional and even unnoticed because, in large part, participants tend not to be *mindful* (Langer, 1989) within their encounters. It is 'learning' nonetheless, and its impacts can have monumental consequences if students are unsupported in developing themselves to become more effective intercultural beings. In this chapter we look at three connected dimensions to living as a global student and a global graduate:

(i) arenas which regularly bring increased encounters with human diversity into the lives of our students and graduates;

(ii) aspects of our students' resistance to engaging with those challenges which need to be overcome through their university experience; and

(iii) capabilities they need to make their way in the increasingly diverse multicultural and globalizing worlds of their futures.

▶ 2.2 Diverse Others in Uncertain Spaces

Globalization is accused of destroying human and cultural diversity by spreading a homogenizing culture of Western consumerism and its associated 'nothing' brands (Ritzer, 2002, 2004) into contexts where they have no local historical or cultural salience. Higher education, particularly through the export of particular forms of academic culture in the development of postnational universities, may itself be becoming one of those homogenizing 'nothing' brands – a foreign presence which strips value from the local and traditional. There are concerns that transnational education (TNE) is intellectually, and practically, a colonizing activity, and multicultural educators have taught us that there is little incentive for any student to participate in a higher education whose norms, values, and aspirations hold little relevance for him or his communities. Wherever higher education is experienced, it has the potential to impose its own norms and values onto the students who access it. It does so through the demands it makes for compliance with its own academic rituals and rules. It also does so, if great care is not taken, through *creating* learning spaces where alternative voices have limited legitimacy and curricula in which alternative cultures are invisible. Working in 'our' established ways may ill-serve the global graduate or her communities. In a global perspective, we, too, are 'others', and the extension of 'our' academic institutions, programmes, and values into diverse geographical and cultural spaces is not without its consequences.

While we see ample evidence of cultural homogenization, we simultaneously see significant growth in human and cultural diversity *as experienced* by increasing numbers of our students in the course of their daily lives. These mundane encounters may seem rather insignificant set beside other ways in which diverse others frame current global realities – fundamentalist terrorism, massive forced migrations, the suppression of human rights, people trafficking, rampant racism, and a multitude of other ills; or, more positively, institutions and actions such as the European Court of Human Rights, the Geneva Convention, the United Nations, the Red Cross and Red Crescent, and the charitable donations and volunteerism of millions of individuals. However, each of these, the goods and the ills, are driven forward or held back by the ways in which individuals identify themselves and their relationships with and responsibilities towards others. The essence of these identities are forged, for most of our students, in the mundane, and in how their societies and their educations frame those who are different. This section explores arenas for these mundane encounters at some length to illustrate how cultural 'others' increasingly frame the lives of our students and graduates:

▶ *physically* as they tour or as they are toured; work in multicultural or multi-national teams, or under a manager of a different ethnicity, gender, or sexual orientation; encounter or become economic or 'lifestyle' migrants, or perhaps even life-need migrants; or are faced with the ethical dilemmas of how to respond to these most desperate of travellers;

▶ *virtually* through news media, cultural showcases and publications, social media and gaming; and

▶ *transactionally*, as they exchange capital for goods produced in other places by people whose lives they may never witness, or which may sometimes be glimpsed through a media exposé on their conditions of employment.

The cumulative impact of such encounters on our students, locally and globally, is the most pressing reason for the kinds of approaches to higher education being argued for here. As already suggested, one dimension to the impacts may be an erosion of personal security and sense of belonging arising as ethnic or national identities are diminished (Appadurai, 1997, p. 4; Scholte, 2000). Our daily encounters with complex human diversity are at odds with established, simplistic, ethnocentric representations of world, so, '[e]veryday life has become cosmopolitan in banal ways' and yet 'our habits of thought and consciousness... disguise the growing unreality of the world of nation states' (Beck, 2006, pp. 19 & 21).

For many of our students, their nation state is an important source of identity, but evidence supports the view that it is losing its place on the world stage. Perhaps by as soon as 2025 the international system 'will have morphed to accommodate [this] new reality', national power and relevance being replaced by 'various non-state actors – including businesses, tribes, religious organizations, and even criminal networks' (National Intelligence Council, 2008, p. 81). Our students-as-graduates will, we hope, live out 70 or more years responding on a daily basis to the almost certainly increasingly complex human diversity. Surrounding those experiences will be the challenges of the dissolution of cherished identities such as nationhood, and the distressing allure, for some, of various fundamentalisms. In such a context, higher education has an important role to play in enabling students and graduates to shape their identities in more inclusive and expansive ways;

the question is not 'whether to impart appropriate global preparedness', but about how we can best do so for all our students (Richardson, 2016, p. 9). The following sections review illustrative trends within five mundane arenas of intercultural encounter, collectively giving significant shape to the global stage upon which our students and graduates need to locate themselves and make their ways.

Arena One – Human Migration

The highly controversial issue of human migration often engenders emotionally charged reactions. Although we have, not entirely accurate, statistics which indicate, for example, that in 2013 there were estimated to be over 230 million international migrants in the world (3.2 per cent of the world population), 60 per cent of whom 'reside in the developed regions', with global migration between 2000 and 2010 growing twice as fast as in the previous decade (UN-DESA & OECD, 2013, p. 36), *perceptions* of migration and its impacts often outstrip the figures.

About half of global migrants live in just ten countries, and national policies often locate migrant populations in particular areas, so depending upon their country, state, and even city, of residence, individual students will have had differential direct contact with migrating others. Some will have migrated themselves, or have living family members who did so, others will have formed their images and attitudes towards migrants through media they have seen little need to interrogate. As our universities engage in more international work, physically or virtually, the range of experience of migrations among students and academics also widens. The ways in which a student's nation, her media, and her particular community and family and peers within that community portray migrants will have impacted upon how she envisions others, herself, and the relationships between them before she arrives at university. Her learning experiences among diverse peers while at university will impact upon how she formulates those relationships when she graduates.

How migration is construed is important for each of our students-as-graduates because of the salience of migration to identity construction. For the graduate migrant, because, '[w]hen people move they usually experience new interpersonal relations that will impact their understandings of their own identities' (Easthope, 2009, p. 69, citing Goffman, 1959). And for graduate as host, since we know from the many instances of race hatred which are reported in Western media that those who are migrated to are not always willing or able to interrogate their understandings of their own identities against the (real or imagined) reshaping of their communities.

The settled can feel disempowered and fear becoming themselves dispossessed, of resources, spaces, traditions, norms, and values.

Focussing on the complex diversity *among* immigration populations, their circumstances, and their new locale, in Britain (and citing similar perspectives by Fong and Shibuya (2005) in the USA), Vertovec (2007) proposes that social policy and theory has failed to keep pace with the new 'super-diversity' to have emerged in recent decades. The construct of super-diversity has found strong resonance, by 2015 appearing as the most cited article in the Journal of Ethical and Racial Studies' history, and bringing forth a collation of sympathetic studies across cities in eight countries on four continents (see Meissner & Vertovec, 2015).

There seems no reason to believe that the multicultural and globalizing world in which our graduates will live out the rest of their lives will present them with easier migration issues. Among, or as, migrants, our graduates will need to take personal responsibility for adopting nuanced understandings of their new neighbours. Super-diversity is proposed to hold 'the potential for novel insights', in ways which resonate well with the generic construct of critical thinking which higher education values so highly:

> *rethinking patterns* of inequality, prejudice and segregation; *gaining a more nuanced understanding* of social interactions, cosmopolitanism and creolization; *elaborating theories* of mobility; and *obfuscating the spurious dualism* of transnationalism versus integration.
>
> (Meissner & Vertovec, 2015, p. 543, emphasis added)

Alongside such skills for interpreting super-complex migration, our students also need the will, the confidence, and the competencies to challenge where it is misrepresented, and a sense of a common humanity which will take them beyond calculating their own attitudes upon simple metrics such as 'value to the economy', and beyond blanket categorizations of diverse migrating others. Capabilities to see current human migration in human terms, to recognize the diversity within and across immigrant 'types', to be critically engaged in the process of decision-making, to be able to resist the myths and easy solutions of popular media, and so forth, might be the difference between fundamentalism, curfews, and geopolitical disintegration – and the hopes of a negotiated, sustainable, and global multiculturalism. In the face of such potent dilemma, I find it difficult to understand those who assert that educational practice which helps our students-as-graduates negotiate this space is not relevant for engineers, theoretical physicists, or computer programmers. If the curriculum is too crowded, perhaps there is a need to critique disciplinary priorities for higher education in the current milieu.

Arena Two – Tourism

Between 2013 and 2014 the number of international tourists globally increased by 51 million to 1,138,000,000, a growth trend almost uninterrupted since 1995 (UNWTO, 2015). Whether a student experiences these flows principally as tourist or as toured will, again, depend upon her country of residence and, indeed, upon her city or region and social status within that country. It will also change in significant ways over her lifetime. Travel brings us into different places, into contact with different people, and 'thrusts the new into the middle of life, it opens up life to contingency and creates 'exotica' (matter out of place)' (Featherstone, 1995, p. 152). 'Matter out of place' can be puzzling, encouraging curiosity and exploration, or troublesome – promoting defensiveness and hostility.

How people tour can have very differential impacts on the lives of the toured, and upon the nature of what the tourist derives from the experience, and subsequently shares vicariously with his peers and home communities. How people *are toured* has significant impacts upon their lives; while the individual tourist may stay only a matter of days, or even hours, the inbound tourist flow may last all season or all year, every year. Some of our students will have experienced life more as a tourist, and some more as someone whose communities are toured; some will have limited experience of either, but will be very aware that others tour while they cannot afford to do so. Typically, the wealth, the power, and the role relationship between toured and tourist is asymmetrical, and our students, therefore, carry different experiences of power and wealth between themselves and others within the tourist world. These differentials are becoming more pronounced as our learning spaces comprise more diverse cultures and communities, each differently placed on the tourist: toured continuum. In such a milieu, there are 'clearly problems involved in creating the conditions for dialogue that are founded upon equity and inclusion, and which is transformational' (Robinson & Picard, 2006).

Within individual experiences of the tourism milieu, each of our students has constructed his representations of the toured or the tourist. Under the 'tourist gaze' (Urry, 2002, 2003), the toured may be cast as curio, as the quaint representation of a simpler lifestyle, as the ignorant waiter, as the marvellous creator of a local artefact; and the tourist cast as insensitive buffoon, immodest libertine, arrogant oaf. Any such one-dimensional avatar, which can emerge through the tourist industry and imagination, seems unlikely to encourage critical, reflective engagement with the encountered other. Tourism, of course, can open the mind, bring new perspectives, or show our students how the world can work in different ways, but it is often experienced in ways which are more likely to perpetuate unreflective cultural 'chauvinism' (*how we do it is better*) or 'romanticism' (*it must be so idyllic to live so simply*)

(Nussbaum, 1998). Neither response will serve students well in interactions with their peers, or serve graduates well in the task of living in a multicultural globalizing world. Through doing deliberate work in developing generic capabilities for encounter with the other, university life can play a significant role in enabling a student to challenge images of others brought through her tourism experiences. Among wider benefits, this may also enable her to become a positive component in the global tourism matrix, and thereby to help the tourism process itself become more positively transformational for other individuals and societies. The underpinning attitudes and skills are relevant for, and transferrable to/from, critical and reflective work around how any international and intercultural disciplinary and professional engagement ought to be approached.

Arena Three – Employment

Graduate employability is increasingly situated within an international and cross-cultural arena. According to a survey of UK employers responsible for over 3,500 graduate recruits, they are seeking employees able to 'work across national borders, manage complex international and intercultural relationships, and understand global aspects of the world of work' (Diamond et al., n.d., p. 5). The same report found the top competency sought in global graduates to be an 'ability to work collaboratively with teams of people from a range of backgrounds and companies' (op. cit., p. 6). Within the report are quotes from employers, which include:

> You need the mindset that says, 'The person I'm talking to isn't like me and I need to understand what they are like and then work with them.' It isn't only about having the technical knowledge, it's also necessary to understand the values, customs, cultures and behaviours that are significant to them.
>
> (National Grid)

> I think cultural dexterity is important: an ability not to impose one's own culture on another one, to be sensitive to other cultures and how to do business in different environments.
>
> (PWC)

These aspirations are not based in cosmopolitan idealism. Rather, they flow from the hard arenas of global competitiveness and human resource management. Multinational companies are growing globally, moving into some and out of other countries, and are very differently impactful in areas such as the percentage of national labour forces they employ directly (OECD, 2015b). While the OECD data does not show how the globally and culturally diverse individuals within multinational companies come into contact with each other, in many countries, company policies, working practices, management styles, and managers are 'foreign imports', each contributing to the ways in which individuals locally might come to regard the global other. In many cases, these will have influence beyond the company's immediate employees through impacts on local communities, their cultures and their environments – similar to that outlined for university stakeholders in Chapter One. In some cases, globalization will be perceived as a threat to local employment opportunities, with the movement of the business offshore, 'dumping' of cheaper products on local markets, or jobs being outsourced overseas, contributing to local unemployment, potentially engendering a polarized view of the 'others' who have stolen livelihoods, and concomitant limitations to global perspectives regarding the lives and life-chances of those others. At the same time, foreign employees and employers are cultural others who may exhibit behaviours, norms, and values which are not in accord with the local population. With the expansion of international corporations and the more local spread of Western management styles (partly because of international students returning from Business degrees), some or other of these processes will be taking place in the community, the society, and the nation which are homes to our students, and so contributing to their interpretations of these others and their communities, societies, and nations.

The global employment arena, then, brings other peoples and other practices into the everyday lives of some students, and at the same time may be stripping established life-chances from the communities of others. Each is a troublesome reality, potentially impacting on how our students perceive each other. University education holds a responsibility to equip our students for work within multinational and multicultural employment spaces as a matter of their own employability. Such preparation, though, should not disable them from successfully working within local employment cultures. Furthermore, focussing only on what '**employers expect** of graduates in order to succeed in the global **economy**' (Diamond et al., n.d., p. 7, emphasis added) are not adequate goals for the global graduate. As global graduates, their relationships with their co-workers globally, and their critical engagement with the employment policies and stakeholder cultures of the organizations they work within, are part of their 'employability', and their success is about more than their positioning within the economy. The kinds of capabilities which will enable our students to be effective employees and colleagues on these terms need to be explicit within their curricula, learning experiences, and assessments.

Arena Four – International Education

Student mobility contributes to global flows of people and capital. UNESCO publish online interactive data sets which enable us to explore the numbers involved. At the time of writing, for example, figures indicated that:

- over 210,000 students flowed out of China to study annually in the USA, and just short of 8,000 students flowed out of the USA to study annually in China or Hong Kong;
- nearly 77,000 Chinese students were studying in the UK, and 34 [*sic*] UK students were studying in China or Hong Kong;
- almost 700,000 Chinese students were studying abroad, while China hosted around 89,000 international students;
- almost 190,000 Indian students were studying abroad, while India hosted around 28,000 international students;
- almost 50,000 Nigerian students studying abroad, while Nigeria hosted 0 international students.

And the numbers of students studying overseas 'continues to surge'.

(UNESCO, 2015)

The monetary flows associated with student mobility, mentioned in Chapter One, are starkly illustrated in these sample figures. But here we are concerned with the contribution which student mobility makes to the ways in which each of our students may encounter the global other. Again by way of example, Australia receives around 20 times more international students annually (c250,000) than it sends overseas (c11,000) (UNESCO, op. cit.), and (after 60 years of international education) it lays claim to international alumni of around 2.5 million (Australian Government, 2016). While international students make up around 23 per cent of Australia's higher education student population, its indigenous (Aboriginal and Torres Strait Islander cultures) population accounts for only around 1.1 per cent, and students of low socio-economic status only around 17 per cent (Australian Government, 2014). Although Australia's non-indigenous population includes generations of migrants from a great variety of cultures and nationalities, it is clear that international students represent a potentially significant source of additional cross-cultural contact. For the international students themselves, their international and domestic peers also significantly impact upon their own experiences of global others. This holds true also, of course, across the diversities which present themselves *within* international and domestic student populations. It should be noted that this may be particularly so for those students, domestic or international, whose previous exposure to sociocultural diversity has been limited within their local communities and socialization spaces. The rich human diversity enjoyed on many post-national anglophone or 'first-world' university campuses, though not in all subject areas, often does not pertain on the campuses of TNE partners in other regions. Also, TNE partnerships and branch campuses are adding to the imbalance in the directions of student flow.

Higher education is, through policies of internationalization and widening participation, creating learning environments which are deliberately diverse. To anticipate that our students can and will undertake the learning and development required to effectively, respectfully, critically, reflectively, and enjoyably live and learn among their diverse peers is, at best, optimistic. As explored in Chapter Four, encounters with peers from different cultures within our university learning spaces are often perfunctory, and can add to rather than diminish existing stereotypes and prejudices, and demonstrate in some depth how international students are often characterized by domestic students, and sometimes by faculty. As we create these diverse environments, it behoves us also to scaffold students through successful learning encounters. Where we are successful in creating inclusive intercultural interactions on campuses or within online courses with a diverse student body, we need also to think how we similarly create intercultural learning opportunities for students who may be studying with us within more mono-cultural campuses or cohorts, perhaps with a single dominant ethnicity or gender presence.

We should not leave the discussion on international education as an arena for student encounters with human diversity without also mentioning the internationally mobile academic. Chapter Three looks at this group in more detail, but it is relevant to note that for our students, the value of encounters with academic staff from other nations, cultures, and first-language backgrounds can be rich or impoverished dependent upon a range of factors, including the frequency ('normality') of encounters, the esteem in which such colleagues are *seen to be* held by their peers and by the institution more broadly, and the ways students perceive their competence and performance as academics. How a student characterizes diverse faculty will influence his general interpretation of others and his relationships with them – for better or for worse.

Arena Five – Media & Social Media

Until relatively recently, many of our students' exposure to broadcast media was limited to nationally produced sources and, perhaps, a dominant 'international' media such as American Forces Radio, the BBC World Service or CNN. Today we see the emergence of alternatives, such as Al Jazeera, whose audience of over 160,000,000 is 96 per cent Muslim across more than 50 per cent of the Islamic world (Al Jazeera, 2015). While these figures do not suggest Al Jazeera is a significant window into the lives, cultures, or concerns of diverse others beyond the Muslim world, its existence as a significant alternative media voice is indicative of greater diversity within media interpretations of events. Within all broadcast media, global telecoms and satellite connectivity have brought a real-time immediacy to international reporting. Additionally, increasing access to locally produced, and private citizen-captured, video often leads to surprise encounters with radically different, unedited worldviews within our own living rooms. Again, our diverse students will have experienced rather varied media windows on the world, with levels of censorship, areas of cultural sensitivity, variations in local priorities, and other factors offering different vistas within which global others are presented and interpreted. As with the discussion on other arenas above, these diverse media experiences and the worldviews they contribute to have the potential to bring richer critiques into our learning spaces, but they can also prompt dialogues to become acrimonious or prematurely closed down where students are not supported in developing openness to engaging with alternative perspectives.

Social media enables anybody to create spaces for specific groups to share their own priorities and perspectives on the significant and the insignificant. Facebook alone has 1.2 billion users worldwide, and 58 per cent of the adult population of the USA regularly uses the platform (Duggan et al., 2015). Many of our students have already grown up ignoring Facebook in favour of alternatives which appeal because older generations are largely absent. In providing perspectives which speak to local priorities, locally produced media and social media are valuable community assets, but the global reach of social media also allows communities of the like-minded to form across geographical distances, unimaginable only 20 years ago. Even the most esoteric of worldviews can now build a community in which its values and rituals are normalized by adherents who may be globally spread, but ideologically linked. New platforms, able to offer more secure communications spaces, are increasingly being favoured by more fundamentalist groups.

The purpose of this section is not to demonize or to valorize any media, but to illustrate how it is now a much more complex and pervasive arena. On the one hand, it brings interesting and potentially threatening alternative worlds very vividly into our students' consciousness; on the other hand, a student can harness it to reinforce his established perspectives. Diverse students in diverse locations will have different attitudes towards the trustworthiness and the validity of media, but all will have views about themselves and others which have been influenced by the media which surrounds them. Access to multiple windows on the world has the potential to open new vistas through which wider understandings might emerge. However, these windows require students who are willing and capable to look beyond the familiar and comfortable views they are accustomed to; to critically engage with the various perspectives on offer; and to be alert to the risks of building their own worlds enclosed within narrow and potentially dangerous communities. Higher education has always espoused the intention to build critical thinking skills; to do so in today's media-drenched world requires a curriculum which encompasses and critiques diverse perspectives from diverse sources among which those skills may be built and exercised. In global higher education, how we build media literacy, particularly critical engagement across a range of media, is necessary work in equalizing the educational landscape. Used well, social media platforms can be of significant value across the global learning spaces of the post-national university, as illustrated in Case Studies 1 and 2 in Chapter Six.

The Global Stage – Ethnoscapes

The globally interconnected social arenas outlined above illustrate that claims concerning the diversity of peoples, with their values, behaviours, life experiences, and life expectancies, flowing around the lives of our students are not hollow or exaggerated. For better or worse (I believe 'better'), living among difference is becoming the norm. However, this is complex territory, with contested and incomplete understandings, where anxiety and uncertainty mixes with established ethnocentrisms to impede even the willingness to enter intercultural interactions (Logan et al., 2015). The role universities play in enabling students to accommodate to this reality is a matter for more urgent attention than we seem to be currently giving. As already noted, this is not a question, only, of the numbers and direction of the flows of ideas, images, information, and people – but of the impact of the *manner* in which they are experienced on the identity formation of our students.

How each of our students *imagines* or *constitutes* diverse others shapes how she will treat with them. American anthropologist Ajun Appadurai refers to the cumulative representations of these others within and on the peripheries of our lives as our 'ethnoscapes' (one of five 'scapes', the others being mediascapes, technoscapes, ideoscapes, and financescapes). Appadurai suggests 'scapes' is a helpful construct because it alerts us to the fact that these others and our relations with them do not 'look the same from every angle of vision', but are perspectives, 'inflected by the historical, linguistic, and political situatedness' of the people within them, from the level of the state through to the local community, neighbours and family (Appadurai, 2006/1966, p. 181), and, we might add, 'universities' and 'fellow students'.

What 'ethnoscape' helps encapsulate is that the individual responses of students and faculty to the others encountered in the arenas of migration, tourism, employment, education, and the media have been *created,* and how those creations are shaped for and by each student arises from the accidents of her experience – the unique accumulation of her biography. Biographies lived among single cultures or narrowly constrained perspectives on others have little opportunity to move beyond dominant categorizations. Each student arrives on our campuses, among our distance learning cohorts, in our virtual environments, and into the classrooms of our TNE partners and our branch campuses, with her biography in place, and her identifications of others pre-formed, *but not hard-wired.* As educators we have to believe that learning continues to take shape as biographies continue to evolve, 'works-in-progress, meshing the positions and resources on offer in dialogue with the biographical solutions of the individual' (Singh & Doherty, 2008, p. 120). Entangled with each student's representations of herself among others are affective qualities, such as how 'comfortable' and 'willing to engage in discussion' with these others she feels. Higher education for a multicultural and globalizing world needs to ensure that her university experiences contribute to rather than detract from such qualities, while responding to her unique prior experience of others in the arenas of migration or tourism, employment or education, the media or her own communities. This links intercultural learning spaces to constructs of multiculturalism as something beyond an ideology about 'living respectfully at a distance from cultural others', by virtue of being *experienced* 'as a lived practice of embodied and felt encounter' among pre-established power relations (Harris, 2009, p. 191). The spaces of the post-national university add significant and nuanced dimensions to those power relations and their experiencing among both students and faculty. The ethnoscapes of the global stage flow into our learning spaces, and learning experiences contribute to their ongoing stasis or development. Academics need to take account of the fact that, whatever a student's prior experiences, she may be unable to take evidence-informed critical stances towards her own social or disciplinary beliefs, norms, and values unless her learning environments give her opportunities to engage with those of others as an equal.

▶ 2.3 Tendencies to Resist – Social Identity, Habitus, and Cultural Capital

The majority of full-time undergraduate students are at a stage of 'self-authorship' (Baxter Magolda, 2001, 2009) as they transition from adolescence to adulthood. This is a time at which they are focussed upon developing their sense of self and their relationship to/with/for others in and around their lives, a time when individuals 'begin to explore where they see themselves fitting into society and the political discourse' (Sorensen et al., 2009, p. 4). In other words, a significant stage in their identity formation.

Much identity groundwork has already been laid through the socialization of family, community, school, and other significant features of their pre-university biographies, including the ethnoscapes explored above, and so their 'exploration' is not unfettered or unproblematic. However, in social constructivist and social psychologist perspectives, we are each 'conscious of myself and become myself only while revealing myself for another, through another, and with the help of another' (Bakhtin, 1984, p. 287) – hence, the importance of students conducting their self-exploration among *different* others. Here we look at some *theoretical perspectives* on why it may not be sufficient to simply collect students from different ethnicities or nationalities into common learning spaces, and this will be further explored in Chapter Four through *student perspectives* on their lived experience of their diverse peers.

Theories of social identity development (Erikson, 1959) and associated Identity Threat (Tajfel, 1981; Tajfel & Turner, 1986) posit that as human beings we forge our sense of who we are in the crucible of our experiencing of others in the world. We find identity support among those who surround us by becoming as them, enabling their values and behaviours, likes and dislikes, beliefs, and norms to reflect back in ways which show us to ourselves in a positive light. In adolescence, intolerance and exclusion of others tends to be particularly strong, and, importantly for some of our post-adolescent undergraduate students, failure to find satisfactory resolution to questions of self-identity at this stage results in *distantiation,* whereby adults remain ready to 'repudiate, to isolate, and, if necessary, to destroy those forces and people whose essence seems dangerous' to their own (Erikson, 1959, p. 101). While my representation here is a simplistic framing of a complex interplay of processes, it illustrates how we come to feel at ease among our in-groups, our communities of similitude. A fundamental characteristic of being within an in-group is defining ourselves *against* members of our out-groups. This will not be unfamiliar to most readers, but it is valuable to reflect how influential this can be as our students forge and defend emerging identities. Actions, events, ideas and individuals who may come to weaken a student's in-groups pose a threat to her sense of self.

Few individuals are restricted to a single in-group, and as a student flows between his in-groups, aspects of his identity, who he is and how he acts, change also. When among his family, the strongest of his identity features may relate to familial roles as younger brother, troublesome son, or carer to an ill mother. When at university, his student identities come to the fore. When at leisure, it may be as a fan of a specific football team or as a member of a particular climbing club that he 'performs' himself among others. It is not unusual, then, for any of us to inhabit different identities at different times, in different spaces, and among different people. While it is still in many ways 'I-David' who moves among my various in-groups, I do so according to different rules, and within varying systems of values. Had I grown up and not experienced being successfully integrated to a group of football fans, they would not be one of my in-groups, and to join them would require the confidence to risk performing incorrectly, being rejected, making a fool of myself, or giving offence. Similarly, within the identity 'turmoil' of intercultural encounters, '[e]motional vulnerability is part of an inevitable identity change process' (Ting-Toomey, 1999, p. vii). And yet, it is precisely within such challenging novelty that personal transformation is most likely to occur; the *direction* of such transformation, though, is dependent upon a number of personal and situational factors. While 'emotional vulnerability' may seem a highly charged description, we should not underestimate the significance of the risks and vulnerabilities which students are exposed to as they seek to find their place at university, and then within their class, tutor, and peer groups. How we construct the learning environments and experiences within which students evolve identities which *incline* them towards learning with and from their diverse peers does not tend to receive the attention it deserves within good practice literature on learning and teaching in higher education.

The fact that, as a species, we have progressively developed our ways of living towards the social complexities of modern society appears to be at odds with heuristic systems such as the simple 'us' versus 'them' categorization referred to above. Arguably, we have had to be capable of evolving more appropriate heuristics, because otherwise each new encounter would play out in the same way as the previous one. In other words, living with diverse others may lead to a re-organization of existing cognitive *structures*. Reformulating the social dichotomies which may have served the survival of distant ancestors well, some evolutionary psychologists claim, 'may be the key to understanding how humans successfully adapt to social diversity' (Crisp & Meleady, 2012, p. 854). From experimental research, the same authors (op. cit., p. 854) propose two cognitive systems are engaged during intercultural contact:

> while humans are evolutionarily disposed to think heuristically about category boundaries (System 1), they also possess the computational mechanics that allow a bypassing of this system when it is necessary to update and revise these representations (System 2).

As in general learning theory, when faced with something (or in this case somebody) at odds with our established categories for the world, we are faced with a dilemma from which we may learn. As proposed, the second system is both second in the processing journey, and second in so far as it requires cognitive work to override (my terminology) the work of the initial categorization. The authors postulate the existence of a 'diversity tipping point' whereby daily intercultural experience becomes so much the norm that System 2 is regularly and automatically activated.

This model of cognitive processing continues to predict that simply bringing diverse students together, particularly where such diversity experience is relatively novel for an individual, is unlikely to result in much development, as it may do 'little other than initiate System 1' (op. cit.). The model strengthens the case for providing intercultural and multicultural learning experiences in which students engage *successfully* with others, since it is through these that the second, 'coalition', system may evolve. The requirement for students to engage in more cognitive work to extend their in-group categorizations suggests benefits in facilitating critical reflection on their experiences, and demonstrating support for what may yet be tentative extensions of a student's sociocultural identity.

Intercultural encounters do not only present cognitive challenge, they also have emotional impact. Research in the USA (for a brief review of this research, see Sorensen et al., 2009) indicates that engagement in interracial interactions invokes anxiety, threat, and uncertainty, resulting in nervous behaviour such as fidgeting, averting eye-gaze, and increasing personal distance. This has been shown to be true of both minority and majority group members, with some cited research indicating that the experience may be more stressful for Whites than for African Americans. It would not be surprising for students of either group to seek to minimize contact which evoked such stress. For domestic students, 'intergroup anxiety' experienced when anticipating interactions with international students 'may include feelings of uncertainty about how to interact, doubts about cross-cultural competency and anxiety about acting in a discriminatory or offensive manner' (Mak et al., 2014, p. 493). The same authors report how first-language differences, which are most common between international and domestic students, add a particular type of threat, and associated anxiety, to intercultural contact for domestic students – and to their evaluation of the contact experience. When we consider the varied TNE contexts in which the post-national university may be working, the visiting academic may herself represent to her students an 'alien' culture, and encounters with her may then evoke a range of emotional stresses. Where more emotional work is involved for a student encountering peers or faculty who are perceived as 'different', being *mindful* (as student or faculty) of the affective impacts offers a coping and a learning strategy. A student's emotions shape how he learns, what he learns, how he sees others, and how he comes to regard his own capabilities to make his way among the diverse milieu of university and society.

Whether enabling students to cross in-/out-group boundaries is best achieved by minimizing reference to those boundaries or by bringing them to the fore is a contested point, resting in part on the salience of structural inequalities between the groups concerned. For example, some may take a 'colour-blind' stance in order to diminish the boundaries between Black and White students and thereby promote greater collaboration, but this approach obscures how societal and institutional racial discriminations continue to impact differentially on life experiences, aspirations, and chances of students from each race. Structural inequalities exist across other diversity dimensions, gender being one example, and of relevance to those designing learning spaces in the post-national university, these are differently salient in different nations and communities. Consciousness of and experience of these structural inequalities also differs among members of those nations and communities, adding further complexity to the educator's task when working with diverse students in diverse contexts. The general position taken in this book is that it is necessary to include an explicit focus on where and how others may be (dis)advantaged, and to acknowledge openly that some boundary crossings require more courage, work, and time than others. Apart from being important for facilitating meaningful intercultural interactions on campus, exposing and critiquing the structural inequalities within *local and global* contexts is likely to make an important contribution to any future will to dismantle them.

Inequalities within the educational value deriving from the sociocultural experiences of students as they enter university from different ethnicities, nationalities, genders, etc., their diverse 'cultural capital' (Bourdieu, 2006/1986), establish a further inhibitor to equalized learning. Cultural capital is carried by an individual 'in the form of long-lasting dispositions of the mind and body' (op. cit., p. 106), it shapes a 'habitus', subconsciously enacted as each student performs herself in her learning spaces. Those whose habitus broadly reflects our own will more readily find acceptance and comfort among us and the environments we inhabit. Unlike economic capital, which may be transferred easily by one individual to another, or even earned by one individual for another, cultural capital always requires time, effort, and personal investment to acquire – though much of this is unthinkingly given, and much cultural capital is unconsciously present. Bourdieu thought cultural capital to be undoubtedly 'the best hidden form of hereditary transmission of capital' (op. cit., p. 108), and most responsible for the inequitable outcomes of education. Devlin (2011, p. 940) suggests cultural capital to be 'critical' to our understanding of the experiences of students from low socio-economic backgrounds. An individual student's class culture translates into valuable cultural capital 'to the extent that [her] knowledge, familiarity and comfort...affords [her] material advantage' (Adams et al., 2015, p. 217) within the university culture. Although commonly associated with social class, mismatched cultural capital may be found between a university and many other iterations of diversity, and this is critical for understanding why we need to equalize learning experiences for a wide range of 'non-traditional' students locally and internationally. The post-national university is extending that range, and hence the greater urgency for faculty to focus on equitable learning and teaching practices. One significant outcome of success in education is in providing a 'crucial gateway' (Brighouse & Swift, 2014, p. 15) to social and economic capital, and hence to building further cultural capital. Since these 'goods' are not distributed equally either locally or globally, equitable learning and teaching is in itself a tool for advancing global social justice.

A student's cultural capital has most value, is most readily realized, then, when it is attuned to the valued cultural capital of the society, or institution, or group in which she finds herself. In Case Study 1 in Chapter Six, we see one example of work which explicitly sought to 'validate' the cultural capital of non-UK students in a virtual collaboration with students in Hong Kong and Singapore. For our diverse students, a habitus embodied through each unique biography within another culture, social class or underrepresented group, which may have imbued a student with significant cultural capital in those social and academic contexts, may translate into cultural deficit in the context of his new university. We can either put responsibility for acquiring a habitus which will enable him to assimilate quickly upon the student, and attribute failure to his deficiencies, or blame the institution for being inappropriately responsive; thinking which equates failure to succeed at university with a lack of 'skill or will' on the part of the student is 'highly problematic' (Devlin, 2011, p. 944).

Knowing that a habitus requires prolonged periods of time to become 'embodied' prompts us to recognize that it is not simple or quick work for students, or faculty, to become at ease with new ideas and practices. We may hear (and perhaps voice) complaints about students not coming to behave in ways which we expect (see further discussion on this with regard to stereotyping and deficit models in Chapter Four). It may be, for example, that an international student does not ask questions in a lecture, preferring to speak to her tutor individually later, or that she fails to perform within the parameters of academic integrity set down in university regulations. While requiring conformity to our norms *may* be appropriate, habitus and cultural capital suggest the need for a student to be supported *over time* if she is to be enabled to own the behaviours we value. Also, though, in the era of the post-national university, a principle of academic equity requires institutions to examine how they may unwittingly and unnecessarily bias some forms of cultural capital within their learning, teaching, and assessment practice.

In TNE contexts, students may find themselves in a physical institution which exhibits and values the cultural capital they have acquired 'locally', while simultaneously needing to exhibit academic performance within the curricular expectations of a very different programme-owning institution. An example of this is illustrated in Case Study 3 in Chapter Six. Perhaps also, in this situation, students are being taught or assessed by faculty whose personal recognition and valuing of their students' cultural capital may be based upon their own, different, cultural and academic backgrounds.

A student's *intercultural capital* (Pöllmann, 2013) may include capabilities to perform within her new university's expectations. Djerasimovic proposes that if we conceptualize our TNE students as holding the requisite capital and agency to employ it 'in re-working the encountered values and ideologies', we can re-examine 'the academic discourse of imposition of values, or, indeed, ideologies, onto the powerless host universities and off-shore students' (Djerasimovic, 2014, p. 210). Pöllmann (op. cit., p. 5), however, cites several authors to support the view that the greatest beneficiaries of opportunities to employ and extend their intercultural capital are those with 'higher levels of socio-economic status and majority ethno-racial backgrounds', and because 'those who have already realized comparatively high levels of highly valued and widely convertible (officially recognizable) intercultural capital are likely to realize even more of it with more ease, such systematic inequalities may well exacerbate rather than diminish over time'.

We do not have data to ascertain whether or not differently experienced and privileged TNE students are successfully reworking their intercultural capital in the light of any valued alternatives which they encounter in their new academic spaces. Whether Djerasimovic or Pöllmann, or both, are correct, however, we need to pay attention to the development of intercultural capital among majority and minority domestic students in TNE contexts, any of whose biographies, including their education experiences, may have afforded at least as wide a difference in the development of intercultural capital as may be found among domestic student populations. In both internationalization and multicultural education, the creation of equitable group learning spaces in which all voices and ways of voicing are enabled and respected is an important issue. The cultural capital carried by *majority* students in the specific form of academic capital, manifested in a habitus which reflects and is reflected in the norms, expectations, and rewards of the academic culture of the university may significantly advantage them. Failure to create the need to engage with alternatives, given the resistances already noted, may also limit their experience of the disequilibrium necessary for transformative learning.

A specific dimension of intercultural capital is linguistic capital. A student's competency in the language of his university may be a significant determiner of the interpretation of his performance by his peers and his tutors. Linguistic competency may be a matter of whether or not a student speaks the institutional language as her first language (or proficiently as a second or foreign language). However, for native speakers of the institutional language it may, alternatively, be a matter of the *variety* of language she speaks. As with other forms of cultural capital, the *impact* of a student being a 'non-native' speaker, or a speaker of a less accepted variety of the institutional language, will, in large part, be determined by its value-recognition within the contexts of her learning. In many post-national universities, a standard variety of English is the first language of majority students on its home campuses, and has become the language of instruction in TNE contexts where it is a second or a foreign language for all students. 'Well-spoken', anglophone students, and faculty, carry their linguistic capital into learning spaces where it has the potential to imbue significant disadvantage on others unless there is deliberate work done to dismantle its power. Case Study 4 in Chapter Six shows an example of an anglophone university seeking greater academic equity by enabling its curriculum in one programme to be taught and examined in Greek, the language native to its partner college students, and Chapter Four explores the importance language in some detail.

▶ 2.4 Global Graduates

This chapter has portrayed the increasing salience of diverse intercultural encounters for graduates who will make their way in our multicultural and globalizing world, some perspectives on why our students may be resistant to engaging in and learning from such encounters, and how individual students carry with them forms of capital which may ease or inhibit their success within the new sociocultural spaces of our universities. This section asks what attributes our global graduates need in order to make their way among diverse others, and presents one model of objectives for the outcomes of a higher education designed for a multicultural and globalizing world.

Graduate Attributes

Internationalization and equalization, framed as a process through which we seek to develop learning experiences which will enable all our students to make their way in a multicultural and globalizing world, requires decisions concerning the capabilities which our students-as-graduates will need. The way those capabilities are framed needs to be applicable to all our students, regardless of their chosen discipline. Such capabilities have come to be described in some contexts as *graduate attributes*, and their introduction has often been associated with performative, normative, and neo-liberal agendas for higher education. Rather than deter academics, this argues for rather robust engagement to ensure that a student develops her graduate attributes in ways which contribute to, rather than compete with, disciplinary goals and perspectives. A social justice agenda requires graduates whose attributes include 'a sense of their own agency as well as a sense of social responsibility' (Bell, 2016, p. 3), as people who can 'take charge of what corresponds directly to them and of what is in hand' in the wider world (Amaluisa Fiallos, 2006, p. 26).

Australia undertook a significant national policy project to articulate institutional graduate attributes at all its universities. Overall, critiques of the process and its outcomes are not enthusiastic concerning impact (Barrie, 2004, 2006). There is much to be learned from the research into the Australia project, but its limitations should not lead institutions to abandon graduate attributes. Indeed, higher education has always held notions of what it means to be a graduate – commonly referred to in several countries, for example, would be a capacity for critical thinking. Many of the attributes set out in various publications on the internationalization of the curriculum (IOC) closely reflect long-held notions of graduateness. The most significant difference is the geopolitical and sociocultural contexts in which advocates of internationalization believe those graduate attributes are to be formulated and applied. Within multicultural education, one area of focus has been upon the academic attributes which might be derived by engaging with racial or ethnic others, as explored in Chapter Four. In my own work, I have referred to attributes associated with *cross-cultural capability* and *global perspectives* (Jones & Killick, 2007; Killick, 2006), and to the development of graduates as *global-selves* (Killick, 2012a, 2014b). The term 'global-self' highlights a holistic view of graduates, and because living successfully in a diverse global world requires more than knowledge and skills, their education needs to encompass also the development of affective capabilities. This presents a not insignificant problem for those, actually quite recent, higher education 'traditions' in which measurable outcomes are the sole architect of the curriculum and its assessment. I put significant emphasis in Chapter Five on the role of learning outcomes and associated processes of constructive alignment in curriculum internationalization and equalization, but I recognize also that this is problematic, and that the inherent conflict between holistic learning and predetermined, measurable outcomes is not something anyone has come close to resolving.

The majority of students attend universities principally to study a discipline, and the greater proportion of their learning experience lies within their selected programme. In some systems this means studying with a consistent cohort of their peers for three or four years; in other systems, students attend modules in classes with multiple sets of peers, perhaps even across different levels of study at the same time. Whatever *structure* applies, a student is studying 'biology' or 'computer science', and not (unless of course it is their chosen discipline) 'intercultural communication', 'global ethics', or 'diversity'. For most students, additional courses or general credit courses (in institutions which allow these) are taken less seriously that those which relate directly to their major. Therefore, impactful work to develop graduate attributes needs to be *embedded* within a student's primary disciplinary curriculum and learning experiences, as explored in Chapter Five. To achieve this, defining institutional graduate attributes requires development processes in which disciplinary experts are fully engaged. The next section sets out my own proposals for appropriate capabilities, but not with the intention that they be adopted into a programme without critical attention to the specific ways in which they might apply to your students, in your contexts, and your disciplines.

Cross-Cultural Capability, Global Perspectives, and the Global-self

The complementary constructs of cross-cultural capability and global perspectives were originally developed as guidance for a cross-disciplinary curriculum review process (Killick, 2006):

▶ **Cross-cultural capability** refers to the affective, behavioural and cognitive capabilities which will enable a [biology] student to make her way in a culturally diverse world – as [biologist] and as a culturally- and socially-situated human being.

▶ **Global perspectives** refers to the affective, behavioural and cognitive capabilities which will enable a [biology] student to make his way in a socially and economically diverse world – as [biologist] and as a socio-economically and geo-politically situated human being.

These collectively constitute what I have come to refer to as the *global-self,* and which I now describe as one who has 'the capabilities to lead a life s/he has reason to value in a multicultural, globalizing world'. Some readers will recognize that I have derived this formulation from the development economics work of Nobel Laureate Amartya Sen (1993, 1999, 2003). Sen refers to the 'freedoms' accorded to individuals by the socio-economic and geopolitical contexts in which they enact their lives. I characterize these freedoms as comprising the *objective* and *subjective* capabilities which, daily, give shape to their lived experience. Among objective capabilities I include, for example, the individual's access to education, clean drinking water, health care, and a life lived free from political or sexual persecution, war, and domestic violence. Global higher education may come to enhance some of these objective capabilities for many peoples over time. However, its more immediate remit lies in the development of the subjective capabilities of its students-as-graduates, which I divide into:

▶ *act-in-the-world* capabilities – a student's knowledge and skills for interacting in/with the world, for example being able to read and write, to speak in a public forum, to access and evaluate information, to cook nutritious food, to see an issue from other perspectives; and

▶ *self-in-the-world* capabilities – a student's view of herself and her place in the world; that is, how she envisions herself in relation to 'others', for example 'I am someone – who treads lightly in the lives of others; who is curious among other people/in other places; who has communicated successfully across cultures; who is *willing* to see an issue from another perspective'.

By way of illustration, examples of the kinds of subjective capability which I think would be associated with each of these for any graduate are set out in Table 2.1. Linking these to the earlier reference to holistic learning and outcomes-based curricula, it is in the arena of the affective qualities reflected in *self-in-the-world* capabilities that higher education struggles.

Rather than capabilities, recent education guidelines (Council of Europe, 2016) refer, instead, to 'competences' which will enable citizens to 'live together as equals in culturally diverse democratic societies'. However, their framework of 20 competences is similarly holistic, including three 'values' and six 'attitudes' alongside behavioural 'skills' and cognitive 'knowledge and critical understanding' dimensions. As with my capabilities model, 'competence' itself is not limited to *holding* competences, but requires their 'selection, activation, organization' and thence, their *application* 'in a co-ordinated, adaptive and dynamic manner' (op. cit., p. 10).

Table 2.1 Illustrative Global-Self Capabilities Associated with Cross-Cultural Capability and Global Perspectives

	Act-in-the-world capability Being the kind of person who *is able* to:	*Self-in-the-world* capability Being the kind of person who *is willing* to:
Cross-cultural capability	▷ reflect upon one's own cognitive, affective, and behavioural responses to the ideas, behaviours, and values of others; ▷ modify one's own communication in order to ensure others understand and are understood; ▷ take a mindful stance when engaging with others; ▷ accept that all cultural norms, including one's own, are arbitrary and susceptible to critique; and ▷ critique cultural norms from a respectful and informed position.	
Global perspectives	▷ evaluate how an action might impact upon the lives of others; ▷ critique a policy or practice from the perspectives of peoples in diverse contexts; ▷ locate and draw upon alternative data sources to gain a more complete understanding of an issue; and ▷ reflect upon how one's own choices make differences to the capabilities of others to lead lives they have reason to value.	

▷ 2.5 Chapter Summary

The chapter began by outlining contexts in which our multicultural and globalizing world is drawing diverse others into the lives of our students and our graduates. These emerging and shifting ethnoscapes are a highly significant feature of the worlds in which our graduates will live, and a major driver for the focus on internationalization and equalization is to develop the capabilities which will enable them to make their way among diverse others – personally and professionally, locally and globally. A number of psychological and sociological perspectives suggest, however, that successful cross-cultural interactions are difficult on a number of levels, and these difficulties are often differentially experienced by our students on the basis of (mis)matches between their own cultural capital and habitus and those which dominate an institution. Therefore, while our learning spaces in the emerging post-national university are increasingly reflective of the multicultural globalizing world, successful intercultural learning is unlikely to prevail unless we design and deliver learning experiences to scaffold the holistic development of all our learners. This begs the question of the kind of attributes we should be seeking to develop in our students to enable them to be 'global graduates'. Notwithstanding some misgivings and contestations, envisioning generic graduate attributes for all students, and embedding these in disciplinary curricula was proposed to be the most appropriate way forward. By way of example, the chapter concluded with my framing of the graduate as *global-self*. As global-selves, our graduates need to emerge from their university education with the *act-* and *self-* in the world capabilities associated with cross-cultural being, founded within global perspectives on self and others. Other models exist, and others should be developed to suit contexts and times. However, this model of the global graduate informs the discussions in this book on the internationalization and equalization of academic practice. More detail on a project in one UK university to fuse internationalization and inclusivity in a single graduate attribute has been published in a case study and related guidance documentation (Jones & Killick, 2013; Killick, 2014a, 2014c, 2014d).

3 Global Academics

▶ **3.1 Chapter Introduction**

The three sections of this chapter explore two major themes: academic identity and transnational working, and knowledge underpinnings for learning and teaching practices with diverse students in diverse contexts, specifically with regard to theories of culture and of learning and teaching.

In the reshaping of global higher education, part of which is the emergence of the post-national university and the associated expansion in learner diversity, new academic spaces, practices, and relationships are being formed and dissolved. As with other impacts of globalization, inequalities and contestations emerge for the academic community, raising in particular questions concerning who has access to these new spaces, on whose terms, with regard to whose worldviews, embedded in whose academic cultures, and performed in whose language. As has long been experienced by faculty identified as members of minority groups, there is significant danger, and some evidence, that majority voices are loudest and ears least open.

Even within their established university working environments, BME faculty, 'regardless of location or the staff and student demographic' continue to encounter racial discrimination and prejudice (Professor Mark Clearly, Foreword to ECU, 2015); women, LGBT colleagues, and those with disabilities, likewise. In the contexts of the post-national university, all faculty find themselves required to respond to students who may be 'heterogeneous in culture, history and lingua franca, religion and regional, social class and community affiliations, credentials and training histories, background knowledge, schemata and motivational structures' (Luke, 2010, p. 48). Where the experiences of diverse faculty as employees, as colleagues, and as tutors remain ones of unequal respect and inclusion, how are they to develop equitable learning spaces and appropriate learning outcomes across the complexities of the seen and hidden intersecting diversities of new student populations?

In this light, this chapter will explore:

▶ the changing nature of the global academic's professional positioning and environments;

▶ dimensions of culture and cultures which may manifest in those evolving spaces; and

▶ the relationship between these and theoretical and good practice perspectives on learning and teaching.

▶ 3.2 Global Academic Being

This section surfaces a range of challenges for faculty generated by intercultural and transnational working. These need to be recognized and addressed. However, as we do so, we must not lose sight of the joys, large and small, which new locations of practice also offer the global academic – friendships, cultural enrichment, professional satisfaction, expanded horizons, refreshed commitment, alternative perspectives, new competencies, greater empathy, personalized global perspectives, and more.

Academic Identities

Academic identity, like all others, is rooted in values and enacted in behaviours. It remains a moot question whether or not there may be such things as 'universal' academic values. Even if global academia does share a system of values, academics hold to different *practices* when it comes to learning, teaching, and assessing, and those practices are based upon different *beliefs* concerning:

▶ the nature of learning;
▶ the nature of the relationships between academic, student, and institution; and
▶ the nature and purpose of higher education.

Adopting a *mindful* approach when faculty encounter diverse practices and beliefs offers opportunities to learn (as explored in Section 3.4), whereas mindlessness 'limits our control by preventing us from making intelligent choices' (Langer, 1989, p. 50). Given the growth of the post-national university, the ongoing expansion in the international mobility of students, and the increasingly diverse nature of domestic student populations, questions of academic practices and beliefs become increasingly relevant for faculty whose professional lives are located, permanently or temporarily, within new spaces and communities of practice, for which they may have been ill-prepared (Hoare, 2013), and within which it may be 'very difficult for an instructor to satisfy the cultural expectations of [his] students' (Ghazarian & Youhne, 2015, p. 477).

As post-national universities engage with academic staff in new international and cultural arenas, and as they recruit more diverse faculty at home, how an individual colleague shapes her academic identity grows in significance. We may hope to have escaped the tokenism of hiring diverse faculty 'for show, with arms and legs arranged so as to depict a certain pose and used to appease racial and ethnic communities' (Chun & Evans, 2009, p. 22, citing Valverde, 2003), but a tokenistic presence or complete absence of diverse colleagues in newly developing cross-border educational collaborations bring new identity issues.

The ECU report referred to in the Introduction to this chapter examines the experiences of BME staff in academic, professional, and support roles in a selection of British universities. The reported experiences of these colleagues may be surprising to many non-BME academics in the UK, and possibly elsewhere. Gaps are shown between policy and the experiences of BME staff which indicated 'ongoing institutional barriers and discriminatory practices in the higher education sector' (ECU, 2015, p. 4). In addition to the kind of structural inequalities recognized in the UK and other majority-White nations, such as the lack of BME staff in senior roles (an earlier ECU report, for example, found only 2.6 per cent of deputy/pro vice-chancellors and none of the 140 heads of UK institutions involved were BME (ECU, 2014a)), this report highlights a number of less easily quantifiable experiences of discrimination. Among the specific findings are that UK BME staff in the study experienced:

▶ having less personal influence than others, at departmental, faculty, and institutional levels;
▶ the inconsistent implementation of centrally devised equality policies (often created with limited BME staff involvement);
▶ a disconnect between policy and practice with regard to staff recruitment, workload allocation, and promotion;
▶ 'being treated in a subordinating or excluding way because of … race';
▶ casual racism in management behaviours; and
▶ no action being taken in response to overt racism.

The report also noted that many BME staff across roles and genders:

> experienced exclusion or discomfort about being asked to socialise in forms and spaces that took no account of cultural preferences and patterns … This could cut them off from establishing social relationships with colleagues and also, in some instances, from receiving important information.
>
> (ECU, op. cit., p. 24)

This last experience is significant and lies beyond policy and the reach of legislation, but also lies very much within the hands of individual colleagues to address. BME faculty are, of course, only one diversity category, and others also experience university life as similarly (or differently) unsupportive and discriminatory. International faculty are much less researched as a group, and do, of course, include Black colleagues, female colleagues, LGBT colleagues, and all other dimensions of diversity in their number. The fact that they may be primarily *identified* as 'international' or 'Chinese' by their colleagues, their institutions, their students, and the wider society they have joined situates them somewhat similarly to their international students.

There is little reason to believe that the experience of faculty from minority groups is significantly better in other countries. Indeed, we may suppose it to be worse in some contexts in which faculty of post-national universities are becoming engaged. Issues, such as parity of esteem, emerge as institutions create academic collaborations with faculty employed by international partners, or even third-party agents (as alluded to in Case Study 2 in Chapter Six), to work on their overseas programmes. In the post-national university, faculty working in diverse locations may be predominantly from within a single BME category, or may not include BME colleagues at all; some will comprise only either male or female colleagues; some will not include any staff with physical disabilities; but all will encompass some dimensions of diversity. Given the continuation of discriminatory and excluding experiences within UK institutions (for example) *with* equality policies and subject to quite extensive equality legislation, we may suppose that faculty experiences of discrimination may be heightened and include requirements to hide some types of diversity, such as sexuality in contexts where neither policy nor legislation exist. The implications for an individual academic might be profound, whether she is living permanently or working temporarily with colleagues and students within such contexts. Any faculty may experience culture shock and other psychological and emotional difficulties adapting to new learning environments, but some may be particularly challenged in contexts where discrimination or exclusion are more overtly present within the institution and wider community. How minority groups are identified and treated locally needs to be explored in depth during the development of new partnerships.

Whatever the physical location of their work, establishing and performing a 'cosmopolitan identity' may need to become a significant part of the work of all faculty in the post-national university. Sanderson (2008, cited in Tran & Ngyuen 2015) proposes that the development of cosmopolitan identity results from:

(i)   instrumental motivations relating to the requirements placed upon academics by a marketized, neoliberal higher education paradigm; and
(ii) more humanistic perspectives concerning the development of mutual respect, openness, and reciprocity in relationships with global others.

Given that *why* I am the person I am is fundamental to my self-identity, the inherent tensions in these two drivers in the post-national university add to the already 'dislocated' (Di Napoli & Barnett, 2008) nature of modern academic identity.

A further element in this dislocation arises from the pace at which much current knowledge is being displaced or challenged. This also presents a threat to academic identity, since the academic as 'expert knower' continues to be increasingly irrelevant in a world where 'the useful life of knowledge is diminishing as its value and currency degrade more rapidly than ever before' (Chun & Evans, 2009, p. 14). How increased international and intercultural working impacts on this particular aspect of academic identity is not yet researched. However, participants in Tran and Ngyuen's (op. cit.) study with Australian vocational education teachers revealed the emergence of two major identity positions, teacher as:

(i) intercultural learner; and
(ii) adaptive agent.

As *intercultural learner*, excerpts from participant interviews illustrate, for example, how faculty 'deliberately take on the stance as an intercultural learner, and throughout their learning journey ... search for a more culturally responsive teaching pedagogy', and 'redefine their professional roles ... to becoming active intercultural learners' (op. cit. p. 8). Such a professional identity echoes that advocated for teachers in a culturally relevant pedagogy approach (Ladson-Billings, 1995a), discussed in Chapter Five. Faculty working in new international contexts and with new dimensions of student diversity must, necessarily, be open to learning from and with their new colleagues and students. However, institutions and faculty developers need to recognize that the learning involved can be challenging to established academic identities. Such transformational learning requires space and time, and is unlikely to be addressed by short intercultural training courses.

With regard to emerging *adaptive agent* identity, the study found examples of teachers making transformative changes to their own practice as a result of recognizing themselves as intercultural learners and their students as agents in their learning. While these participants related how this had occurred in their practice, others (perhaps unheard BME staff or marginalized female academics) may find their opportunities to change established practice continue to be limited by how they are positioned.

Fanghanel (2012, p. 100) suggests that being a global academic 'is about being connected with colleagues and students across the world'. However, some academics in her study were found to be 'so overwhelmed in their own struggle to get on with the job, or engaged with professional aspects of their discipline, that they displayed little inclination to look elsewhere and engage globally' (op. cit., p. 103). The development of an academic identity as intercultural learner and adaptive agent fits with emerging post-national university learning and teaching environments. For academics, in the main, self-identification as 'learner' is probably common, but the 'intercultural' dimension may be a new identity marker. Identification as 'adaptive agent' is possibly more problematic – and perhaps most so for colleagues whose academic spaces have hitherto given them little voice or escape from the daily struggle, and so allowed limited agency.

Academic Locations

Global academic locations are characterized as a 'paradox', with an increasingly diverse student body set aside drives towards 'more international standardisation, unification and convergence in goals, teaching methodology, evaluation, testing and assessment' (Vinther & Slethaug, 2013, p. 799). At the time of their study, half of newly hired staff and one-third of students at Oxford University were international. The degree to which that university was interrogating its approaches to learning, teaching, and assessment in light of this diversity are not explored in the article, but the authors do question the homogenization of approaches across Europe and more globally, citing examples which suggest 'systemic differences in educational philosophy' (op. cit. p. 801), even within the relatively small geographical region of northern Europe and Scandinavia. As institutions recruit more international students, and fail to engage with them as diverse learners, and as international educational policies impose common policy frameworks which pull practice 'away from nationally or regionally based pedagogy', 'it makes lecturers hostage in a no-man's land between ideals and reality' (op. cit., pp. 804 & 806).

In a position paper, UNESCO (2004, p. 14) identifies 'preserving national cultural identity' as one of the four most important challenges arising from the globalization of higher education. Extending the dilemmas which apply when working locally with students of different religious or ethnic identities, transnational education forces questions concerning an academic's responsibilities towards national and cultural identities and the learning she facilitates. Within multicultural education, there is a fundamental principle of not undermining students' cultural identities, but to what extent can a global academic apply this when working, for example:

▶ in an overseas university on their programmes;
▶ in an overseas university on programmes from his own university;

▶ in an offshore campus of his own university;
▶ online with students who may be spread across a wide range of nations; or
▶ as a visiting international scholar, invited on the basis of specific expertise.

In such contexts, the global academic is often positioned at the nexus of national or more local dilemmas, which extend beyond his classroom or his discipline, but which he has to negotiate to the best effect he can for his students, and himself, as illustrated in Case Study 3 in Chapter Six. However, there is much negotiation which should be done at institutional level during the process of partnership development to minimize the demands on the academic, and ensure safe and appropriate locations for her work. As cited in the Introduction to this book, the American Council on Education (ACE) also references 'negotiation', and it is worth quoting at length how they illustrate some of the dilemmas in the 'negotiated spaces' of international higher education:

> Along with issues of resource imbalances and academic freedom, a wide variety of other cultural and practical conflicts are possible. If one partner believes that women should not be admitted to a joint program, or that certain ethnic groups should not have access, should local customs be honored? In contexts where personal relationships are typically taken into account in decisions about student admissions, hiring, vendor selection, and other areas of program operation, what are the potential implications for equity and transparency? Should a faculty member involved in an international research collaboration be expected to adhere to the intellectual property laws of the partner country, if such regulations are less stringent (by law or in practice) in her or his home country? Such questions abound.
>
> (ACE, 2015, p. 32)

ACE are clear that, while these dilemmas offer 'no easy answers', institutions need to scrutinize the ethical and political issues appertaining to any potential partnerships within initial due diligence work. The UK government Department for Business Innovation and Skills, even when focussing exclusively on value and business effectiveness in transnational education (TNE) (BIS, 2014), neglects to make *any* recommendations on due diligence, and the UK Quality Assurance Agency (QAA) (effectively the national regulatory body for higher education), propose that due diligence enquiries will need to be 'tailored and proportionate', and limit suggestions for what to assess to 'financial, legal, academic and reputational risks' (QAA, 2011, p. 7) – a somewhat abstract list in the context of the ethical dilemmas under discussion. In Australia, a guide issued by the Australian Department of Education, Employment and Workplace Relations includes a more detailed due diligence 'checklist'. Its 23 items include two of relevance (IEAA, 2008, p. 55): the 'safety of the social/cultural context for Australian provider staff', and a prospective partner's 'experience of "western" education'. The guide goes on to note that 'applying this full array of requirements in different social/cultural contexts is not straightforward', but does not advise at what point any difficulties might cause an institution not to proceed. Regardless of national guidelines, and however good an institution's own regulations might be, due diligence work in reality may be based on a single institutional template which leaves little opportunity to tailor it to the specifics of each international context. A further limitation can be a lack of international and cross-cultural experience among those managing and conducting due diligence work. Institutions failing to perform full due diligence on prospective partnerships are acting negligently, and regulation and monitoring processes need to be sufficiently robust to ensure this does not happen. Current limited experience in international academic working means that these processes remain unfit for purpose in many institutions.

Once a partnership is established, faculty become de facto front-line negotiators on the ground, on a daily basis. Global academics in TNE contexts, in common with minority faculty at home, are frequently faced with negotiating respect and power differentials between each other, as well as between themselves, their students, and their institutions. Such differentials have been well rehearsed, though not resolved, within multicultural education, perhaps most directly in critical race theory, where an emphasis on deliberate, conscious work to bring in the knowledge and the lived experience of racial minorities is stressed. In TNE contexts, it may not be race per se which is the primary producer of 'an "apartheid" of knowledge that marginalizes and devalues the scholarship of minority faculty' (Bernal & Villalpando, 2002, cited in Chun & Evans, 2009, p. 6). It is as likely to be a local *majority* whose scholarship and practice are suddenly marginalized and devalued by a Western programme-owning institution's paradigms of 'best practice' – perhaps embodied in the habitus of a visiting academic, regardless of her race or gender. Individual faculty, whatever their institutional home, have the right to conduct their professional lives within environments where they are afforded equal opportunity, and where their knowledge and experience are equally valued. We know that there is still much work to be done in the working contexts with which we are familiar, and as rehearsed above, post-national universities, in opening new working environments in diverse contexts, need to take such matters seriously when establishing partnerships and offshore campuses, and when deploying faculty to work in them. However, individual faculty also need to be mindful of their own responses to diverse peers, remembering that culturally bound behaviours can easily convey unintentional messages and disrupt communications and relationship-building. A global graduate requires cultural fluidity and individual agency in her relationship to her own cultural roots as well as those of others, and the same is appropriate for academics in transnational and multicultural working. But this principle does not much help an academic who finds aspects of a local or a foreign culture, with their learning expectations, and teaching traditions at odds with the underpinning philosophy of the programme being delivered or the learners they are engaging with. Such situations are increasingly real, as the following examples illustrate.

Having concluded that foreign academics, even with many years' experience in the region, made few adjustments to their established approaches to teaching when working in a Saudi university, Alghamdi (2014, p. 221) recommends that institutions needed to consider the principles of culturally relevant pedagogy when *selecting* foreign faculty. The article offers a rare 'insider' perspective, and prompts a number of wider questions of relevance to this book. For example:

▶ What are reasonable expectations for/of faculty who cross national borders or cultural boundaries, physically or virtually, in order to teach local students?
▶ Are those expectations the same for English-speaking academics moving into non-English-speaking contexts, such as Saudi Arabia, as they are for non-English-speaking colleagues moving into English-speaking contexts?
▶ What impact do/should 'foreign' and 'minority' faculty have on their peers in their host institution?
▶ Who among the academy is/should be doing 'cosmopolitan work' (Tran & Nguyen, 2015)?

Within the study, Alghamdi (op. cit.) argues that critical thinking among young Saudis is 'discouraged in schools' whose ontological stance is that 'all knowledge is fixed'. This leads to a university education which is 'based on the transmission of uncontested knowledge from professors to students', heavily dependent upon rote learning, and which 'generally fails to impart critical – and analytical – thinking skills' (op. cit., p. 204). Alghamdi believes the development of critical thinking to be fundamental to the development of a knowledge economy in the Saudi context, but he is concerned that many foreign teachers do not apply pedagogies which are appropriate to student needs. At the heart of Alghamdi's concern is that the 'modernist view of knowledge' among foreign teachers differs from students' 'traditional absolutist view of knowledge' and that, despite the individual efforts of some teachers, the gap is not being successfully bridged (op. cit., p. 216). He proposes that there needs to be greater focus on helping students develop key academic skills such as critical thinking, but more importantly, proposes that institutions must ensure that foreign teachers carry with them capabilities such as those advocated for within a culturally relevant pedagogy paradigm, including, specifically (my summary):

- respecting their students and their students' cultural identities;
- believing that their students can/will learn;
- drawing on diverse conceptions of self and others as a resource rather than as a source of conflict;
- enabling students to be comfortable with their own culture while adopting new learning approaches; and
- scaffolding students from where they are rather than presuppositions about where they should be.

Alghamdi implies that Saudi higher education is struggling to balance local ontologies of knowledge and epistemologies of learning with new educational aspirations. Foreign faculty are caught in the middle.

A study in South Korea (Ghazarian & Youhne, 2015, p. 486), by contrast, noting a significant increase in international faculty in recent years, found that recently arrived foreign academics were more likely to employ 'formal authority' and 'expert teaching style' in line with the prevailing national approach than those who had been teaching there for longer periods. They suggest this may, in part, be attributable to those experienced faculty developing an 'intercultural identity' within which they could employ their personal teaching styles while taking 'steps to ease the transition for their students' and 'make use of their knowledge of learners to help them grow accustomed to new and unfamiliar teaching styles'. It may also, they recognize, be a result of misperceptions of the distinctiveness of their teaching styles among those experienced faculty within the self-reported research survey. In either case, individual faculty are again responsible for negotiating the cultural borderlands between their own and local epistemologies of learning.

A related dilemma has been identified for local Chinese university teachers required to respond to national-level policy decisions to adopt Western good practice. Respondents 'did not think a radical change from teacher-centred to student-centred teaching approaches was appropriate' and the authors note that both 'the capabilities of frontline teachers and the habits of students are very difficult to change in the short term' (extracted from Liu, 2013, pp. 203 & 204).

McNaught (2012) identified that in one university in Hong Kong at least, while change does require time to become embedded, more interactive approaches could be successfully introduced. The success of such approaches is, again, based upon faculty being willing and able to scaffold students through new learning experiences over quite significant time, and to *adapt* existing approaches to respond to local educational and social traditions such as maintaining face (see Section 4.4), rather than importing them wholesale.

These examples have briefly illustrated international contexts where faculty may be quite alert to cultural differences in learning and teaching approaches because they are themselves experiencing life in a different culture or having alien practice imposed upon them. However, mismatches found in those contexts may be less visibly present within culturally diverse home campuses in distance learning contexts, where it may be much harder for academics to become aware of difficulties being experienced by some students (Ho et al., 2004). For example, a small-scale study of culturally and linguistically diverse students on an undergraduate programme in Australia found those students to be 'further disadvantaged' by 'individualistic teaching and learning pedagogy taught exclusively through the lens of a Western paradigm' (Testa & Egan, 2014, p. 240). Post-national universities are extending the likelihood that an academic will find herself working in contexts where educational values and practices are in some ways at odds with those with which she is familiar, or find established practices suddenly challenged by imported programmes and faculty, or find newly diverse students for whom her established modes of practice do not work. Whether working at home, online, or overseas, mismatches between learning and teaching approaches need to be interpreted and responded to by faculty.

Such responses require sensitivity, flexibility, and a willingness from both parties to critique their own practice. All the examples above illustrate in some way how approaches to teaching which dominate practice in Western universities are challenging established practice elsewhere. There are implicit and explicit assumptions and assertions concerning the capabilities of students within these traditions to think critically. These need to be challenged, and global academics are well positioned to collaborate with peers and students to observe, investigate, and test them. As explored in Section 3.4, learning *theory* should be open to critique, as should notions of how teaching needs to be shaped to best enable diverse students to engage and benefit.

As with due diligence, requirements on institutions to ensure that faculty in both partners are given appropriate development for their intercultural working are variable. In the UK, the QAA Code in collaborative provision includes a clear statement in Indicator 17 (QAA, 2011, p. 22) that:

> The awarding institution should be able to satisfy itself that staff engaged in delivering or supporting a collaborative programme are appropriately qualified for their role, and that a partner organisation has effective measures to monitor and assure the proficiency of such staff.

However, there is no reference in the accompanying narrative to any responsibilities for supporting or assuring the UK institution's own academic staff in their international working. Australian guidelines on offshore delivery (IEAA, 2008, p. 74) do have a detailed section dedicated to 'provider staff selection, induction and training', with minimum standards including 'cultural sensitivity and empathy', 'effective communication skills that cross language barriers', 'sound moral values' (by whose standards, and how judged is not elaborated), 'adaptability and flexibility in thinking and action', and 'patience and forbearance to cope with factors beyond personal control in an unfamiliar environment'. I am not aware how Australian institutional educational development programmes approach their responsibilities with regard to these capabilities, but I can say that any successes have not been extensively reported.

In their Guidelines for Quality provision in Cross-border Higher Education, the OECD make specific reference to the importance, not only of the quality of academic staff per se, but also to recognizing that the *conditions under which they work*, should be such as to 'foster independent and critical enquiry' (OECD, 2005, p. 14). This can be problematic when faculty are teaching for most of their contracted hours, or where there is a heavy reliance on third-party agency staff (see Case Study 2 in Chapter Six). Limited opportunities to participate in the global research community, and underprivilege relating to resources are two further restrictions on academic working conditions for many TNE–based colleagues, with the 'supremacy of English as the language of research' compounding the problem (Fanghanel, 2012, p. 104).

How faculty relate to each other, their mutual esteem and sense of collegiality, is an important dimension to academic working conditions. Exchanging good practice and building international academic networks between local and international faculty is proclaimed as one of the significant benefits of TNE. The reality, though, often seems to fall short of the aspiration. O'Mahony's study for the HEA (2014, p. 21) noted how it could be 'a major challenge' even to simply find people within a university who were actually aware that the institution was participating in TNE work. Research among faculty involved in Australian:Malaysian TNE collaborations found 'contacts between teaching team members were largely confined to email and for over 50 per cent of participants this communication occurred only twice per session', with the overall communications picture leading to the conclusion that it did 'not encourage dialogic interaction' and was 'unlikely to render a sense of belonging and connectedness' (Keevers et al., 2014, pp. 239 & 240).

Even where communications around delivery of the curriculum are well-established, transnational partner faculty have tended not to be involved in its creation (Djerasimovic, 2014). Being seen to be 'on an equal footing' was identified as important to faculty relationships, but the study found frustration at the limited support for collaborative work: 'we weren't encouraged to do research with them, which is just bizarre' (participant quoted in a study by Smith, 2014, p. 128). Several case studies in Chapter Six highlight the effectiveness of collaborative working between faculty in TNE partner institutions, but in all cases, initiating that work seems to be have been dependent upon the individuals involved, and in several examples, occurred post hoc, after agreements had been signed and students recruited. Among other observations, leading Pon and Richie (2014, p. 114) to a general conclusion that the commonly reported franchise 'parent and child' model should be changed to reflect the 'more evenly balanced model where both partners are benefitting from mutual cooperation', was the 'unexpected benefit' (!) of enhancing faculty understandings of student learning through contact with their international peers and students, thereby 'enhancing both academic staff development and the student experience in their home institution'. These authors also note that a key factor in the success of these franchises is 'the readiness of the HEI to support academic staff'. Opportunities for faculty to benefit from emerging international spaces and communities are unrealized because such considerations are absent from institutional learning and teaching strategies. Lack of strategic direction limits the potential for cross-institutional learning by derogating responsibility for developing global academic capabilities to those faculty who choose to become engaged, cosmopolitan learners, and by lack of resources to support either the development or the dissemination of their learning. Faculty need opportunities, including some liberation from the daily 'struggle', to develop their global capabilities, and universities, as learning organizations, need spaces where those capabilities can be shared.

This section has set out some of the features of the 'negotiated' TNE spaces within which global academics are increasingly practising, including limitations to current regulations, guidelines, and support. These spaces each perform their own range of structural inequalities, and shifts within power relations brought by new international partnerships are embodied within the academics who find themselves working together. Positive reciprocal learning is occurring within these new academic spaces, as illustrated in several case studies in Chapter Six. However, aspects of TNE locations, such as those briefly explored above, can militate against reciprocity and respect-ful dialogue. With a few exceptions, institutions building TNE partnerships do not adequately plan for, or support faculty in, researching or sharing practice. As Hoare (2013, p. 1) argues, the 'preparedness' of faculty to learn 'should not be left to chance lest it does not eventuate', and for this to hap-pen universities 'must formally recognize the need to provide time, resources and quality, ethical learning interventions'. This theme is further elaborated in Chapter Five.

> ### 3.3 Global Academic Knowing: Culture, Cultures, and Individuals

What Do We Mean by 'Culture'?

Because we live inside our own culture, it seems 'basic and natural', yet it profoundly affects the way we 'think, feel, and behave' (Kim, 2001, p. 58). Because it 'shapes and colors our experiences, behaviours, attitudes and feel-ings' (Matsumoto & Juang, 2004, p. 319), it determines how we think and feel about, and how we behave towards, those whose cultures are different to our own. Our students and our colleagues come from and are located within increasing diverse cultures – each of which seems basic and natural to them, while also affecting how they think, feel, and behave. This book makes significant reference to 'culture' and to cross-cultural/intercultural commu-nication, encounter, and capability. How we understand 'culture' is of great importance to those discussions, and to academic practice in a multicultural, globalizing world.

In this book, culture is conceived of as a way of *interpreting* and *being in* the world, which is shared by and transmitted by an identifiable group of people. Thus, there are national cultures (e.g. *Australian),* supra-national cultures (e.g. *Islamic*), and sub-national cultures (e.g. *Hispanic-American*). Notwithstanding impact of deterritorialization mentioned in Chapter Two, *national* cultures possibly hold the least salience for the largest number of our students (at least until they find themselves removed from their national homes), and a vast array of sub-national cultures and local groupings prob-ably hold the greatest salience. Thus, for example, a student may hold being a member of the Nigerian Church of England as more important to her than being Nigerian or Christian per se; and the specific Lagos congregation to which she *belongs,* even more so. Holliday has characterized such 'small social groupings or activities' with their particular 'cohesive behaviours' (Holliday, 1999, p. 237) as a type of 'small culture' – a concept intended to 'liberate "culture" from the notions of ethnicity and nation', and any associated 'reductionist overgeneralizations'. This alerts us to the caution needed when labelling our students according to any large cultural systems, and thereby ignoring 'the considerable differences within cultures as well as between them' (Ryan, 2013, p. 279).

Holliday characterizes the small culture paradigm as being 'non-essentialist' and focussed on 'emerging social processes'. Group members influence the development of the emerging small culture, in part based upon the 'culture residues' they bring to the table. The unit of analysis is what the emerging group *does,* its behaviours and activities, rather than who the group might be in terms of, say, their ethnicities. This, essentially ethnographic, approach to cultural interpretation provides us with a valuable lens through which to see our students, that is to say, by looking more closely at how they actually act (engage with their learning, in our case) within their cohort, seminar group, tutorial, and so forth, rather than at their large culture backgrounds, with all our attenuated preconceptions. However, we cannot ignore the fact that each of our students does also exist in relation to larger cultures as insider and as outsider. Nor can we forget that individual students are not each equally placed to have their 'culture residues' valued. Additionally, the dominant cultural norms of university wider learning spaces, large and small, impact significantly on the shaping of a small culture's emerging social processes. Once formulated, those processes become as 'basic and natural', valued and resistant to change, as in any other culture. Therefore, exclusion and inequitable treatment can also come to characterize the small cultures which emerge as students come together (or not) in their university spaces. For most of us most of the time, the values, norms, and practices of our own cultures, *large or small,* remain unexamined, subconscious even – surfacing only when faced with a contending value, norm, or practice. Such 'clashes' are challenging (as in the discussion on Identity Threat in Chapter Two), and may lead to conflict, to prejudice, and to heightened ethnocentrisms.

The communities of practice (Lave & Wenger, 1998) of academia have been interpreted as small cultures (Montgomery, 2010), and a question for the global academic in the post-national university is becoming the degree to which her disciplinary communities of practice share values and norms and the kinds of 'cohesive behaviours' across international spaces which would constitute them as small cultures across large frontiers. This associates with previous discussions concerning the portability of an academic's cultural capital into new transnational collegiate communities and learning spaces.

Small differences in how his cultural capital is displayed (habitus) can have significant impact on how he is interpreted and valued – the seemingly simple variation in 'Call me "Professor"' or 'Call me "David"' springs to mind.

An individual student will, almost certainly, belong to a number of small cultures (what Holliday refers to as a 'melange'), based on a wide variety of identifiable features, including ethnicity, sport-affiliation, historical movements, economic status, physical attributes, and one or another, may be strongly or weakly present for any given student at different times. She will also belong to different combinations and configurations of such cultures – and so our students, our colleagues, and ourselves are each culturally unique. The salience of each element within a student's unique set of cultural identity-makers will depend upon the contexts in which she has built her biography. Somewhat simplistically, if a student has experienced her gendered-self in a culture and society in which females are overtly excluded, her self-identification as a woman may be more salient to her experience of university than it is for another student – for whom ethnicity has been a stronger excluding identity. A student will always carry gender, ethnicity, sexuality, and other identity markers and makers, but how they come together to form and influence the individual, and the reactions of others to that individual, is variable. This 'intersectionality' (Crenshaw, 1991) is explored in literature on multicultural and feminist education and in work on culturally relevant pedagogies. It is lost in a simplistic ascription of identity to national and larger cultural groupings. Arguably, higher education has largely managed to ignore these complexities in the ways in which it identifies *the* international student or students of color on home campuses, and is in danger of doing so in the global learning environments of the post-national university. Academics responsible for the learning of diverse students in diverse locations need to acknowledge their learners through an intersectional lens. Additionally, academics need to see that their uniquely diverse learners also come to 'intersection' with the particular context and small cultures in which they come to enact their learning, which may be, for example, in a country where structural inequalities pertaining to race, gender, or religion have strong historical and current relevance, or in a student group dominated by members of a majority culture. Playing among such intersections, the *ascription* of 'international student' cannot be entirely dismissed. What being an international student means in the contexts of a student's prior experience, and what it means in her current learning context and among her peers, can impact on her identity and on the ways in which she performs herself and her learning. Intersectionality points us to the imperative of not believing we know what it is to be student 'x' just because that's what being Black (female, gay, disabled, Chinese, or 'international') means or would mean to me, or because it is what it has meant to other Black students I have known.

Setting the context for a mindful rather than a mindless approach to the world, Langer (Langer, 1989, p. 43) notes that through the ordinary process of mindless living, we come to 'know our scripts by heart. In the routine of daily life we do not notice what we are doing unless there is a problem'. Welikala (2013, p. 27) identifies the unique individual student as carrying with him 'cultural scripts', influenced but not determined by his nationality. Such scripts provide readily available roles for the student to adopt within his new educational setting. Potentially, the more extensive and varied the intersecting cultural networks within which a student or a faculty member has enacted his role, the more scripts he has available, and the greater the ease which he might experience when engaging with new small cultures.

Culture is something we 'do' mostly without thought until we encounter a different way. The daily goings on of our small cultures may be more salient than larger cultural systems to which we are seen to belong, and each of us has evolved a unique identity through the intersections of large and small cultural markers and makers within our life course. The cultural scripts which an academic and a student has available carry capital which may, or may not, be valued as she moves into new cultural spaces, and a greater repertoire of scripts may help her negotiate a new cultural milieu.

Dimensions of Cultural Difference

Intercultural research has suggested that there are high-level human value dimensions, and that different large cultures might be mapped to relative positions along these dimensions. Such large culture differences are often cited as being responsible for both the psychological and the sociocultural difficulties experienced when encountering or working among different nationalities. Of these dimensions, the most cited stems from early work by Hofstede (1991) among IBM employees in a range of locations worldwide. Further work has been undertaken since Hofstede's influential models, with different dimensions or groupings of dimensions being developed by different researchers and intercultural trainers (Lewis, 2012; Schwartz, 1994). The division of the world into predominantly 'collectivist' and predominantly 'individualist' cultures has been taken up by a number of writers concerned with academic cultures, and is discussed in particular with reference to Chinese or (moving to a VERY large culture) 'Asian' students. Given the attractiveness of this particular dimension, it is worth noting that a survey of 'world views' (Saucier et al., 2015) involving 8,883 higher education students across 33 countries identified larger salience was attributed to religion, regularity-norms, ethno-nationalism, and hierarchy of family values than to individualism and collectivism. Training in how to teach (or, indeed, how to do business with) 'the' Chinese on the basis of large culture traits is appealing because it offers simple models. It is, though, far from helpful when it comes to teaching 'a' Chinese student. The unacceptability of casting our Chinese (Black, female, LBGT, White) students according to theoretical macro-characteristics is picked up again in Chapter Four when we look at stereotyping and deficit models, but suffice to say at this point that it is not an approach advocated in this book. This said, a general appreciation of ways in which practices of large cultures and small cultures may be differently enacted and experienced, and how such differences may be related to differences in values is helpful to faculty and students – perhaps especially when it comes to identifying own values and the ways in which they are expressed and interpreted through practice. Any application of such generalized models needs, always, to be tempered by a will to see each of our students and our colleagues as more than the sum of the ways in which their (assumed) cultural backgrounds have been interpreted for them. Furthermore, riding the waves of our more intimate, daily social groupings (our small cultures and communities of practice) is likely to be of more consequence to most of us most of the time. This is not to diminish the significant impacts which can ensue when the cultural norms and practices, and perhaps occasionally values, of student, faculty, and institution collide. It is, though, to say that we should never interpret an individual student on the basis of a large or very large cultural ascription which may hold little or no significance for him personally. Chapter Four explores this in more detail, but by way of just one example of how such ascriptions do happen, Ryan illustrates the 'binary' stance adopted in much of the literature concerning cultures of learning in Chinese and British contexts. She is careful to raise the dangers of stereotyping which attach to this approach, but notes that 'educational cultures derive from different historical and cultural circumstances and teaching and learning traditions within them can place emphasis on different academic values' (Ryan, 2013, p. 282). She illustrates some current polarized perspectives as summarized below:

Chinese academic values focus on:	UK academic values focus on:
▶ Level of knowledge	▶ Type of thinking (critical thinking)
▶ Learning from the teacher	▶ Independent learning
▶ Respect for teachers and texts	▶ Questioning teachers and texts
▶ Harmony of the group	▶ Student-centred learning
▶ Consensus & conflict avoidance	▶ Argumentation or assertiveness
▶ 'Reflective' learning	▶ 'Deep' learning – learners seeking meaning
▶ Critique of the 'self'	▶ Critique of the 'other'

To reiterate, even if such a set of dichotomous values were to be typical of these two national academic cultures, the degree to which an individual faculty member or student of either nationality may subscribe to them will be highly variable. If any Australian, British, or American academic were to critically interrogate the right hand column, it is likely that there would be some serious questioning as to how strongly some of those academic values permeated the academy or their domestic students as a whole. It may also be argued that greater value for 'critique of the self' would significantly enhance the critical thinking skills of the 'Western' student. However, we will each be more familiar with, more at home with, more easily able to work with whichever academic cultural values and practices have featured prominently within our experience. As shown in the brief illustrations in Section 3.2, and in Case Study 3 in Chapter Six, students and faculty accustomed to a dominant educational paradigm will find transitioning to a different paradigm requires developmental scaffolding. One individual Chinese student's preferred ways of working academically may be delineated within a strongly Confucian-heritage and collectivist model, for his Chinese peer they may not; for a particular Hispanic student, they may have been delineated within a strongly South American Catholic-heritage collectivist model, for another Hispanic student they may not. A study of exchange students from a range of European countries attending a UK university (Sutherland et al., 2015) found that they, also, struggled with the academic expectations of their new institution. These countries would not be identified as highly collectivist, and the difficulties arose from experience of different educational *practices* rather than divergent macro-culture *values*. The global academic will not know her student until she meets him; recognizing features of alternative academic approaches might help her to scaffold his learning, but should not be presupposed on the basis of his nationality, ethnicity, race, or any theoretical supra-national ascription.

As an associated point, for many students, international and domestic, the academic culture(s) through which they have travelled may always have been closely attuned to their own habitus and cultural capital, and for many others they may always have been at odds. These experiences of fit or misfit, across the values, attitudes, and behaviours of schooling, can formulate a self-identification as 'someone for whom *any* education is, or is not, an experience from which I will benefit, within which I will thrive'. The shape of this self-identification may be the most significant barrier to accessing or succeeding within higher education for a number of socially excluded individuals and groups – wherever in the world they are situated.

Typically, what we experience in encounters with people from different cultures will be differences in behaviour rather than actual values. It appears common, however, to extrapolate from behaviours and *misattribute* to them the attitudes or values which such a behaviour would signify if exhibited by someone in one's own culture. This will be dealt with at greater length through illustrations relating to intercultural communication behaviours in Chapter Four, but it is relevant here to reflect upon some of the commonly cited academic culture behaviours and potential misattributed interpretations set out in Table 3.1.

Table 3.1 Illustrative Examples of Misattributed Interpretations of Student and Faculty Behaviours Deriving from Different Academic Cultures

Student is familiar with academic cultural behaviour	University academic culture expects that	Potential interpretations ascribed by faculty to student	Potential interpretations ascribed by student to faculty
Students remain silent in class unless directly asked a question	Students volunteer ideas in an open class discussion	She is unprepared for this class; she is *undeserving* of my time	He does not think he should give everyone an opportunity; he does not *care* who speaks
Students must develop a deep understanding of an idea/author before they challenge it	Through challenging ideas/authors, students gain a deep understanding	He is incapable of critical thinking; he should not be in this course/institution	She encourages shallow thinking; she is not authoritative herself regarding this idea/author
Good students always take a strong leadership role in group work	Students work cooperatively and democratically in group work	She is a poor team worker; she is arrogant and self-centred	He is incapable of recognising my value; he dislikes me
Students ask questions if they do not follow something in a class	Students who do not follow something in a class must take responsibility to learn about it later	He wastes the time of other students; he is rude and lazy	She is not interested in her students' learning; her classes are ill-prepared
Students cite authoritative sources beyond those given during the course	Students cite only the authoritative sources selected for the course	She does not trust my judgement; she is arrogant	He does not value my ideas; he only recognises the limited sources he already knows
Students and teachers use first names when addressing each other	Students and teachers use surnames & titles when addressing each other	He is unfriendly; he is conceited and thinks his title should impress me	She is disrespectful and arrogant

Academics whose students have come through diverse educational traditions may well identify with some of the conflicting perspectives illustrated in Table 3.1. However, pre-determining that 'this is how those students will behave *and* this is the reason why' needs to be more carefully interrogated than might commonly be the case. Cousin situates the 'west/non-west dualism' as having 'congealed into a grand narrative that inhibits our explorations' and 'limits our thinking' (Cousin, 2011, p. 585) when it comes to curriculum internationalization. She argues that 'pedagogic preferences and approaches travel the world, adapting to local contexts' and that to see them as hermetically sealed is to 'yield' to 'simplicity and to cultural relativist readings of the world' (op. cit., p. 592). However, while we hope and work so that our understandings of good practice might travel and adapt, and TNE potentially enhances the chance that they might do so in more than one direction, this does not mean that we should, either, expect all learners to be equally experienced with or comfortable in the pedagogic preferences we may currently hold and unpack as we fly into distant learning spaces or when among students locally and online whose social and educational backgrounds have rewarded alternative behaviours. Nor should we assume that it is necessarily, or only, the job of the student to undertake the task of assimilating to our model (we will return to this with specific regard to student-centred learning in the next section). That international students in TNE contexts are beginning to be represented in some literature as carrying the capital/capabilities/agency to themselves rework the values and the practices they encounter (Djerasimovic, 2014) should not surprise us since all our students have to do this to some extent, and this is not under dispute here. However, ways of doing 'good' academic work are as culturally bound as any other practice, and any student in any location may be faced with the additional hurdle of being required to work within practices and expectations which conflict with his own. Whether these are grounded in his large culture, or in his various experiences of small cultures, or both, 'underperformance' may ensue through the difficulties he encounters in the pedagogical approach being taken, and also through the difficulties academic staff have in seeing value in the particular ways in which he engages with them. Cultural *behaviours* among our students should not be confused with cultural *values*; differences in academic *performance* do not necessarily signify that critical thinking or academic integrity is absent.

Acculturation and Adaptation

Acculturation and intercultural adaptation/adjustment theories (see for example, Berry, 2005; Ward, 2001) are based in investigations into psychological impacts when 'sojourners' encounter the cultural milieu of a new home.

They have been applied to the experience of international students seeking to adapt to their new university. The related and contested theory of 'culture shock' (Oberg, 1954) has been commonly cited with regard to international students and to domestic students engaging in international study or work placements (internships) abroad. A number of propositions from the field offer insights for the global academic working with students for whom the learning environment of their university, physical or virtual, presents a new cultural milieu.

Crossing cultures presents the travelling academic, as much as the sojourning student, with new behaviours, attitudes, and possibly at times, values. She is less free than the tourist to view these as 'curious', 'exotic', or 'weird', or as something she can choose to not engage with. As suggested in sections above, she may be confronted with different experiences and expectations, challenging not only her comforts and capabilities, but also dearly held beliefs. Since 'acculturative stress' is compounded when the sojourner encounters discrimination from majority population members, anything which easily identifies student or academic as different from her peers – be it race, ethnicity, displayed language competence, gender, sexuality, wearing a hijab, etc. – has the potential to add to the difficulties of moving into new academic cultural spaces. Less frequently mentioned, members of a majority group may also feel acculturative stress as they encounter (or *perceive* themselves to be 'surrounded' by) these Others, and the tendency may then be to engage in discrimination in order to protect their dominant group identity (see cited research in Crisp & Turner, 2011, p. 246).

Ease of adjustment to a new cultural milieu is influenced by psychological factors and by factors deriving from the new cultural environment. Across several studies, Ward and colleagues (for an overview, see Ward, 2001) have identified psychological factors relevant to intercultural adjustment to include *perceived* discrimination and individual coping styles. Matsumoto and colleagues (Matsumoto et al., 2004; Matsumoto et al., 2007) have identified openness, flexibility, critical thinking, and emotional intelligence as being primary predictors of intercultural adjustment. Of these, emotional intelligence is the most important, as it enables individuals to 'manage their emotional reactions' while engaging in intercultural conflicts, which in turn allows them to build new cognitive structures 'that reduce conflict and build interpersonal and intercultural relations' (Matsumoto et al., 2007, p. 748). They conclude (op. cit., p. 757) that this is 'good news', because unlike general intelligence and personality factors, these skills 'can be trained'. Mindfulness, which we will look at in more detail in subsequent chapters, is seen to be a key process for emotion recognition and regulation.

Gudykunst and others (see for example, Gudykunst, 1995, 2002) developed the Anxiety/Uncertainty Management Theory (AUM) to account for significant psychological factors. In this model, anxiety management and uncertainty management are identified as 'basic causes', influencing intercultural adjustment generally, intercultural communication effectiveness, and a participant's perception of her effectiveness. The theory also identifies a number of 'superficial causes' which contribute to these basic capabilities. Among these, psychological factors include:

- self-concept, self-esteem;
- motivation to interact with strangers, need for group inclusion;
- ability to tolerate ambiguity, ability to empathize with strangers; and
- positive expectations for strangers, ability to understand group differences/similarities.

These impact upon the effectiveness of individual students and faculty to work effectively and comfortably among diverse cultural others. The ways in which intercultural encounters are *experienced* will have significant impact on these largely affective factors. Reflection on those experiences can help gain both self-awareness and greater self-efficacy in similar situations, and mindfulness *within* the encounter can diminish anxiety and uncertainty. In setting up learning activities in which intercultural encounter features, explicitly developing each student's capabilities in these could facilitate acculturation, and so enhance how she comes to see herself and to enact her life as a global-self.

AUM also identifies what are more *situational* 'superficial causes', including:

- rigidity of intergroup attitudes towards strangers;
- cooperative structure of tasks;
- informality of the interaction situation;
- normative support for interacting with strangers; and
- quality and quantity of contact with strangers.

Other researchers have identified a relationship between ease of adjustment and the degree or type of difference (real or perceived) between a sojourner's own culture and that of her new environment, with specific foci on the collectivism and individualism dimension cited earlier (e.g. Triandis, 1994, and subsequent), or on the degree to which the sojourner's group is (is perceived to be) in a minority position or to be a threat to local identities by the host, or on the development of 'close interpersonal relationships with host nationals'

(Shupe, 2007, p. 762, citing various previous research). Where a student or an academic is situated amidst cultural diversity, perhaps with limited experience, and with limited confidence in his own capabilities for successful intercultural interaction or limited motivation to risk the vulnerabilities of engagement, he may 'simply choose to ignore one of the conflicting culture frames and withdraw entirely from the host culture' (Crisp & Turner, 2011, p. 245). To ignore and withdraw will not only impact negatively on his well-being and performance while at university, but will also significantly limit any ongoing development. Although Crisp and Turner present this as an issue for the sojourner and his relationship with the host culture, it is also relevant to host culture members and their relationships with inbound sojourners, and to majority culture members' relationships with minority group peers.

Berry (1990) claims individual *attitude* to be key to intercultural adjustment, with a model proposing that adapting to a new culture requires that the sojourner considers it of value to maintain *both* her own cultural identity and characteristics, *and* relationships with others within a new culture. Enabling a student to develop affirming attitudes towards both her own and others' cultures, along the lines suggested in Berry's model, are part of an intercultural education process. A student's attitudes towards others and towards his own relationships with others, along with the attitudes he perceives to pertain among faculty and within his wider learning communities play a significant role in determining if/how he will seek to engage with and learn from diverse peers, a causal relationship identified for other minority groups, including recent immigrants (Berry & Sabatier, 2010).

Berry's model focusses attention on the attitudinal stance of the individual, but the institution in which a student is situated and the small cultures in which she participates need to similarly see value in assuring she can maintain her own cultural identity, if she is not to be subjected to an assimilationist process. Universities send their strongest signals concerning what they value academically through the ways in which students are recognized and rewarded in their assessments. Faculty can help signal the importance of valuing both own cultural identity and that of others by formative and summative assessments which include this in their success criteria.

Adjustment itself manifests in 'psychological' and 'sociological' dimensions; psychologically 'reflecting the sojourner's satisfaction and psychological well-being' regarding the intercultural experience, and developing sociocultural behaviours 'characterized by the ability to "fit in" the host culture' and linked to 'effective communication and other social skills' (Shupe, 2007, p. 715). While the two are related, a student may exhibit behaviours which seem to evidence feeling at ease within her new cultural learning environment while remaining psychologically conflicted, and therefore academically

disadvantaged. Universities tend to be very concerned that students and faculty should adapt their behaviours to conform with established academic norms, and often offer comprehensive guidance on how to do so. Students and faculty who behave according to the rules, explicit and tacit, of the learning spaces they join are likely to find that they are more easily accepted by their peers, and their academic work is more readily rewarded. However, behavioural change may not be a good indicator of psychological acceptance; indeed, acting outside her own academic and social norms may lead a student or a faculty member into further stress. Furthermore, such conformity risks undermining the diversity created by our international and multicultural students. Questioning the validity of established norms, learning about, and even learning from, the ways in which others frame their academic practices would be to embark upon more equalized partnerships – adapting Berry's two dimensional model of valuing both own and others' cultures – a mark of a post-national university with truly international ambitions and multicultural values.

Global academics, wherever situated, need to reflect upon the role they play in opening equitable spaces for intercultural learning, and the capabilities they need to develop to achieve this for themselves and in order to enable majority and minority group students to do the same. This section has presented perspectives on culture and on factors pertaining to intercultural adaptation/adjustment. These are proposed to be important areas of knowledge to underpin the practice of the global academic, working in multicultural and internationally complex contexts. We will explore how these relate to concrete practice in Chapter Five.

▶ 3.4 Global Academic Knowing: Learning Processes

Relating Teaching and Learning

How faculty set out to 'teach' their students impacts upon how those students learn, and for students to learn effectively, and for academics to teach effectively, the work they do needs to be consonant with their beliefs about what good teaching and good learning look like. In many contexts, though not all, faculty have significant freedom in how they design and deliver their teaching, but such freedom comes with 'responsibility to design appropriate spaces for learning', not least because students enter those spaces 'on trust because they are seldom sure what they are letting themselves in for' (Harland & Pickering, 2011, p. 44). International students, students from groups who participate less in higher education, and students in TNE contexts are significantly less 'sure' than their majority group peers.

Among even a small sample of faculty in just two science subjects (physics and chemistry) in just two Australian universities, Prosser et al. (1994) identified five 'qualitatively different categories' in conceptions of undergraduate learning. In summary (my emphasis):

A: accumulating more **information** to satisfy **external** demands
B: acquiring **concepts** to satisfy **external** demands
C: acquiring **concepts** to satisfy **internal** demands
D: **conceptual development** to satisfy **internal** demands
E: **conceptual change** to satisfy **internal** demands

This can be presented as two axes for conceptualizing learning. The first being views on *who is the driver* – the individual learner or someone external to the learner (e.g. parent, exam body, employer, faculty) – and the second being the nature of what is to be learned – information, concepts as fixed entities, concepts as growing entities within an established broader worldview, concepts as dynamic entities, with change 'involving the adoption of a new world view rather than the development of meaning within a world view' (op. cit. p. 222). This final process is similar to perspective transformation as set out in Mezirow's (1991, 2000) model of transformative learning discussed below.

As Prosser et al. go on to identify, there is a relationship between an individual academic's conceptualization of the learning process and his understanding of the teaching process, as illustrated in Figure 3.1.

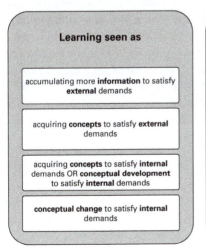
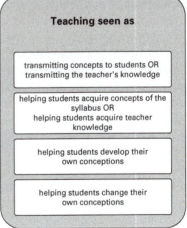

Figure 3.1 Relationships between Faculty Conceptualization of Learning and Understandings of the Teaching Process (based on Prosser et al., 1994)

This research contributed to a meta-analysis of the field, which concluded that conceptualizations of learning influence 'teaching approaches which in turn effect student learning approaches and subsequently learning outcomes' (Kember, 1997, p. 273). In essence, what it is to learn is broadly characterized either as knowledge *construction* or as knowledge *transmission*, following from which student-centred or teacher-centred paradigms will dominate, and which of these shape the student experience will make a significant difference to what they actually learn. As in other areas, much of this research has been conducted by Western academics. However, a recent Chinese study among school teachers similarly found that epistemological beliefs affect their conceptions of teaching and learning, and so 'impact teachers' instructional practices' (Lee et al., 2013, p. 141).

The same relationship exists between a student's conceptions of knowledge and her conceptions of what constitutes 'good' learning (see Entwistle & Peterson, 2004 for examples and a synthesis of perspectives). The emerging contexts of the post-national university bring together diverse epistemologies of learning across both academics and students. For an academic, it is not only that her students are 'heterogeneous in culture, history and lingua franca, religion and regional, social class and community affiliations, credentials and training histories, background knowledge', as previously explored, but these differences impact also on their 'schemata and motivational structures' (Luke, 2010, p. 48), meaning that diverse students *learn* in diverse ways.

Although theories concerning the internal processes which constitute human learning have long been explored among educationalists, they have historically, perhaps, had little influence on university teaching. However, the emergence of 'educational developers' in Western universities in recent decades has led to a burgeoning 'good practice' literature, some tenets of which are critiqued in Chapter Five. Good practice in higher education curriculum design, the organization and management of learning experiences, the structuring of assessments, and the ways in which students are generally supported in their learning has developed into a sub-discipline in its own right. In some countries, good practice precepts have now assumed such a dominant orthodoxy as to form the underpinnings for national professional recognition schemes. In the UK, thousands of faculty have achieved or are undergoing 'recognition' against one such national framework (HEA, 2011), and the government is currently shaping a Teaching Excellence Framework to be used in assessing teaching quality across universities nationally, with the proposal that performance in this will bear directly upon the student fees which an individual university is allowed to levy.

The largest contributors to good practice 'knowledge' in recent times have been Western faculty developers and their professional organizations, with a concentration, again, within the anglophone world. As already noted, there has been some tendency to export or import rather than critique these established orthodoxies, not always successfully where they do not fit with existing epistemologies. Within macro-cultural values dimensions, such as those explored in Section 3.3, Chinese education is presented as fitting with a hierarchical (large 'power-distance') social model, and is characterized by knowledge transmission and teacher-centredness. However, Lee et al. (2013) identify a rather different picture emerging, with constructivist models impacting on current practice. Liu's study (2013), cited earlier in this chapter, suggests that the conflicts between government and university policy and faculty perspectives might be overcome by a dualistic approach, whereby Chinese universities develop and make available 'two different academic norms simultaneously' and leave students the option 'to choose the way they prefer' (Liu, 2013, p. 208). The complexities of such an approach are clear, but the suggestion does illustrate the difficulties which arise when learning and teaching practices compete with established epistemologies. Given the connections between how faculty and students frame the relationships between knowledge, learning processes, and teaching processes, it is necessary to question whether there is sufficient reflection during partnership building on the degree of fit between exported good practice and the diverse faculty and diverse students among whom it is meant to apply. The relationship between beliefs concerning knowledge, learning, and approaches to teaching indicates that being encouraged, and perhaps even 'developed', to engage in pedagogy or in learning activities which do not correspond with the existing epistemological beliefs of either faculty or students is unlikely to lead to significant change. Similar experience underpins the concerns of multicultural educators and the development of universities for indigenous peoples and the Historically Black Colleges and Universities. Global academics and students, whatever their location, need to adopt a critically reflective stance towards their *beliefs* about learning processes, and policymakers and institutions also need to be aware that *approaches* to teaching and learning are not simply transferrable when practitioners or students do not find resonance or relevance in the tenets they are founded upon.

Learning

This section presents an overview of relevant aspects of learning theory (see Jarvis, 2006 and subsequent volumes for an excellent, detailed review). It is important at the outset that we differentiate between *theories* concerning:

- the internal processes which constitute learning;
- the external processes which stimulate (or inhibit) learning; and
- the outcome of these (which we also referring as 'learning').

Aspirations for outcomes have been explored in previous chapters. This section focusses on internal and external processes. Learning and teaching practice principles which have been established within dominant Western understandings of these two dimensions to learning are discussed in Chapter Five.

We can define learning as a process through which cognitive, behavioural, and affective change takes place. Having learned means having changed; it need not mean that the change has brought a student to *better* understandings or ways of acting in the world, just *different* ones. Learning to be more prejudiced is still learning, and is influenced by the same factors as change in the other direction. There is a tendency not to classify 'bad' learning as learning at all, but this is unhelpful when designing learning environments and activities. The learning process is always active, and any experience can engender unintended, and perhaps unwanted learning. An ill-executed piece of intercultural group work may lead to a student learning that her Black or Chinese or English-language-speaking peers are, indeed, as arrogant as she had always believed. Recognizing that such learning is an outcome of the way in which the learning activity has been designed or delivered highlights how faculty responsibilities must extend beyond building only disciplinary expertise. Even faculty who do not believe they hold responsibilities to *enable* intercultural learning should recognize their responsibilities not to *disable* it.

Human learning is a continuous process, not restricted to formal learning environments or activities. When a student encounters something which is at odds with what he currently 'knows' of the world, he is faced with the choice of changing that which he knows so it better fits a world in which the newly encountered has a place, or of seeking to fit the newly encountered into the view of the world he has already established. The latter is often much easier, and less threatening if there are matters of personal significance involved. In the terminology of cognitive psychology, the former involves changes to established schema, the student's categorized packages of understandings about how the world is. This process requires more cognitive work, and if his representation of the world is changed, it may also be that his place within it, his identity, must also change, and this is affectively as well as cognitively challenging. Being 'mindful' means being 'alert', attentive and *open* to the possibilities for new knowledge and perspectives to enrich our learning, as explored further in Chapter Four, but 'the grooves of mindlessness run deep' (Langer, 1989, p. 43). Major changes in perspective and/or self are often referred to as transformative (Mezirow, 1991, 2000) or significant (Rogers, 1969) learning. In the transformative process, we change 'our taken-for-granted frames of reference (meaning perspectives, habits of mind, mind-sets) to make them more inclusive, discriminating, open, emotionally capable of change, and reflective' (Mezirow, 2000, pp. 7–8). Significant learning leads to differences in behaviour, in future action choices, in attitudes, and in personality; it is 'pervasive learning which is not just an accretion of knowledge, but which interpenetrates with every portion of his existence' (Rogers, 1961, p. 280).

Although Mezirow acknowledges there are emotional dimensions to transformative learning, Rogers' significant learning model is more holistic at its core, and for a student to undertake the process of becoming a global-self, her learning needs to be holistic, that is to say, to involve not only cognitive knowledge building and behavioural development but, crucially, developments also within her affective domain and self-identity (for more detailed discussion on this specifically, see Killick, 2014b). Examples of appropriate affective learning for her would be: coming to *feel* more at ease among those who are different; being better at regulating *emotions* when involved in discomforting cross-cultural contact situations; or being more *confident* and *resilient* when intercultural contact produces uncertainty or ambiguity. As noted, how universities currently set out and reward student learning neglects affective development. When a university student does experience learning in this domain, therefore, she currently does so *beyond* what is prescribed in her curriculum or recognized and valued in her assessments.

In both transformative and significant models of learning, change within an individual is stimulated *only* when something new (hitherto outside or at odds with the learner's established knowing of the world) is encountered. A form of 'dilemma' is created which is resolved through the learning process; significant learning is stimulated by the dilemma, and always 'to some degree painful and involves turbulence' (Rogers, 1969, p. 339). When the new is too disturbing, the dilemma too great; the learner has the alternative process to resort to, denying what appears at odds and making *it conform* to his established knowing. This type of process is commonly cited in discussions on stereotyping, where non-conforming behaviours by the stereotyped are either ignored, not remembered, or classified as anomalies which, therefore, need not impact the stereotype. This process is not limited to stereotyping, but is available with regard to any phenomenon. Therefore, it is important that the learning experiences which faculty deliberately create offer *appropriate* levels of challenge if students are to derive new knowledge from them; this includes appropriate levels of affective challenge.

When a student is studying with peers or with faculty whose cultural values or behaviours do not match her own, she may be faced with affective challenges which are too significant to be accommodated, leading to discomfort, confusion, defensiveness, and the loss of potentially significant learning. Planned intercultural learning activities, therefore, need to be built with care, allowing for small steps to be taken on what may be a long journey. 'Simply' learning to *feel at ease* among others is a prerequisite for effectively engaging with their perspectives.

Transformative learning 'involves participation in discourse to use the experience of others to assess reasons justifying [one's] assumptions, and making an action decision based upon the resulting insight' (Mezirow, 2000, p. 8). In experiential learning theory, rooted in John Dewey's work (1916/2012), '[d]iscoursing is not merely a communication process which supports learning. Rather the process of engaging with the minds of others through discourse is the learning process' (Northedge & McArthur, 2009, p. 111). Social constructivist models (Vygotsky, 1978) characterize all learning as a fundamentally social act, with others in the learning arena acting as 'more knowledgeable others' and as knowledge 'co-constructors', and the learner *actively constructing* his knowledge in and through the dialogic space he co-inhabits and co-creates. Social actors in the learning spaces and experiences of a university include the student, her peers, her academics, and others introduced 'virtually' through their ideas and experiences, in print, on video, or by podcast. These conceptions of the learning process and associated roles in that process contrasts starkly with a knowledge-transmission model of learning, in which a guru speaks or writes (a professor professes), and a learner absorbs through passive engagement.

Constructivist models of learning have gained dominance among Western educational developers (including myself), and they are provoking receptive, unreceptive, and 'nuanced' responses among teachers in China, as mentioned in the studies already cited by Lee et al. (2013) and Liu (2013), and explored in studies by McNaught in Hong Kong (for an overview, see McNaught, 2012). Similar ambiguities are likely to be found elsewhere, including, actually, among faculty across disciplines within Western universities. It is not appropriate, either, to assume that 'Non-Western' students are resistant or Western students are comfortable with constructivist *teaching* methods.

Within the social constructivist perspective, the *manner* in which social interactions take place within learning environments is fundamental to how learning progresses. We cannot establish equitable learning outcomes unless we equalize the ways in which diverse students in diverse contexts *experience* and *are experienced by* the others within their learning environments. As these social actors are fundamental to each student's learning *process*, issues of differential power and recognition, voice, and identification necessarily become entangled with the ways in which faculty design learning *experiences*. Much that is said in dominant best practice literature concerning the value of group work and other forms of student-student interaction is founded upon principles within the constructivist paradigm. Global academics working with diverse, multicultural students need approaches to group work which help all their students to recognize value in the interactions they are asked to undertake *and* value in the peers with whom those interactions take place. De Vita proposes that no teaching based on student participation can be successful in a multicultural classroom unless the tutor, from the very beginning 'sends an unambiguous message of equality to students, a message that promotes an environment which embraces cultural diversity and within which all students feel they have something significant to contribute' (De Vita, 2000, p. 175). This is not only about being inclusive on ethical grounds; the social constructivist model means that inclusivity is also about facilitating learning.

Much of the discourse concerning weak critical thinking among Chinese or Arabic students alluded to above arises because of confusion between these theoretical models of:

▶ the internal processes which constitute learning; and
▶ the external processes which stimulate (or inhibit) learning.

Relationships between these two are not proven, and constructivist paradigms, like any other, should be open to scrutiny. It is clearly empirically absurd (and racist) to assert that Chinese or Arabic learners are less capable of critical thinking than their Western peers. It *may be* that the external processes experienced within their education systems are less effective at stimulating the internal process to develop critical thinking capacities. It also may be that they are equally or more effective, and any weakness lies in how that learning is currently recognized. Teaching across learning cultures, in the spaces emerging in the post-national university, offers opportunities to explore both possibilities, and for global academics to *learn* what works best for diverse learners in diverse contexts. There is need to be circumspect, mindful, and reflective when seeking to transpose or impose methodologies based within particular models of learning processes.

▶ 3.5 Chapter Summary

This chapter has explored rather wide-ranging dimensions to being a global academic working with diverse students in the emerging contexts of the post-national university. It has done so through two lenses. The first has explored emerging academic identities, identifications, relationships, and communities – noting their potential richness, but mostly problematizing uncertainties, negotiations, and levels of support. Issues of power, recognition, and voice for faculty, long recognized with regard to race and gender, re-emerge and perhaps re-configure in these spaces. The second lens has focussed on aspects of knowing, beyond disciplinary knowledge, which need to underpin the work of the global academic as he engages with culturally diverse students and colleagues, and builds curricula and learning experiences which are appropriate to diverse ontologies and epistemologies. In both of these areas, the global academic is faced with the choice of restricting himself within his established categories of who he is and how he enacts his practice in this globalizing world, or of 'liberating' himself through openness to different perspectives and becoming 'mindfully aware of views' which differ from his own (Langer, 1989, p. 68). Taking a reciprocal learning approach to their practice, faculty and students can explore and develop inclusive and effective learning experiences which build from and build on learning theory.

4 Global Learning Spaces

▶ 4.1 Chapter Introduction

Unlike the ethnoscapes arising within the connecting processes of globalization explored in Chapter Two, education is a planned and deliberate intervention *intended* and *designed* to provide experiences to enable learning in particular ways. This is the space of the formal curriculum. University learning is also enacted in spaces where unplanned, non-deliberate, unintended experience unfolds – experience framed by the unspoken, implied, tacit norms and rituals permeating those spaces. These are the spaces of the hidden curriculum. Those spaces are populated by students, and each individual student and her students-as-peers have a significant impact upon the ways she and they experience their learning. As the composition of faculty and students become increasingly diverse, so do the responsibilities of all to all within the learning spaces they occupy. Clearly, *being diverse* and *doing diversity* are hugely different (Ahmed, 2006, cited in ECU, 2015, p. 4), and '[h]istory teaches us that left alone, diversity may exist, but inclusion may not' (Winkle-Wagner & Locks, 2014, p. 4). Whatever the nature of a learning activity, the people within the learning space significantly influence how everybody is enabled or disabled from participation and learning.

University policies and processes are necessary for 'the consistent uptake of inclusive practices', but these only work when the individuals within an institution are willing and able to exhibit and promote inclusive behaviours and beliefs (May & Bridger, 2010, p. 6). How individual students are identified and treated, both by their peers and their faculty, shapes learning spaces and the learning which they promote. The ways of *doing things* in higher education, like elsewhere, are shaped by the majority group, and come to be understood as 'part of the natural order, even by those who are disempowered or marginalized by it' (Ginsberg & Wlodkowski, 2009, p. 6). What is required in our post-national universities, by way of contrast, are learning spaces which establish everybody's 'sense of worth and self-expression without fear of threat or blame', where all students 'feel respected because their perspective matters' (op. cit., p. 75).

Marginson (2007, pp. 32 & 33) proposes that the 'idea of a university' encompasses:

> the right to speak; to conduct dialogues on the basis of honesty and mutual respect; and intra-institutional and inter-institutional relationships grounded in justice, solidarity, compassion, cosmopolitan tolerance and empathy for the other.

Some of the evidence presented in this chapter indicates that these rights and relationships are absent from the experiences of many of our students. The learning spaces of the emerging post-national university, with their newly diverse learners and academic communities, offer the potential for dialogue and inclusive, cosmopolitan communities. For these to emerge requires renewed attention to the ways in which we and our students conduct dialogue and enable positive reciprocal learning. The three sections in this chapter focus specifically on learning spaces by exploring:

▶ how cultures and their boundaries within university learning spaces are shaped and experienced by students and faculty;
▶ how human diversity in learning spaces can promote learning; and
▶ how diverse students and faculty can approach their cross-cultural communications to create mutually inclusive learning spaces.

The attitudes and behaviours explored in all three sections apply to virtual as well as face-to-face learning spaces, particularly when direct interactions by audio or video links play a part.

▶ 4.2 Situating and Situated Students

Chapter Two focussed on *theoretical* perspectives on tendencies among students, academics, and institutions to resist meaningful integration and inclusive responses to other-ness. In this section, we explore evidence which suggests that this is, for many students, reflected in their *lived experience* of university learning spaces.

Minority students in the USA may be labelled as 'Native Americans, African Americans or Blacks, Asian Americans, Latino', and Chinese, Vietnamese and Indians as 'Asian'. Self-identified 'Black educator' Saint-Hilaire (2014, p. 599) notes that these racial categorizations, based on physical appearance, in reality represent diverse cultures which have 'different ancestral cultures' and 'do not share cultural practices, beliefs and attitudes'. A similarly broad categorization 'encourages an inappropriate view that [domestic] students are homogeneous, and different from "international students"' (Scudamore, 2013, p. 3). The various minority groups who are identified as 'contributing to' the diversity of our universities are themselves highly diverse, as indeed are those often identified simply as 'majority' group students.

The dualistic discourse surrounding domestic and international students in much writing on 'the' international student experience and that surrounding majority and minority students in multicultural education contributes to 'deficit modelling' and to related institutional and faculty responses built around 'support for international [minority] students to catch up with home [majority] students' (Welikala, 2013, p. 28, with my words in brackets). There are identified differentials in representations and attainments across 'types' of BME students (Berry & Loke, 2011, p. 18). Recognizing the range of 'difference within difference' (Luke, 2010, p. 61), poses challenges for students and faculty alike, which are further complicated in the post-national university where physical and virtual learning environments are dispersed in terms of geographical and cultural location, and in which both faculty and students are likely to encounter new and variable demographics and cultures among peers and colleagues. The challenge in all locations is in part created by the tendencies to resist cultural, social, racial, linguistic, and other boundary crossings, as explored in previous chapters. However, the lived experience of diversity in university spaces also offers opportunity for students to outperform these restrictions, to engage in what Harris (2009, p. 189) refers to as 'more dynamic practices, agentic expressions and negotiations'. In the focus below on the 'everyday', we see students, and faculty, *producing* 'both racism and openness in unspectacular ways, rather than seeing these practices as the exceptional acts of exceptional people' (op. cit.).

Lived Experiences of Others and Othering

Taking as her reference point a landmark Australian study from a decade earlier (Volet & Ang, 1998), Montgomery (2009) investigated UK student experiences of intercultural interactions. The negative stereotyping and ethnocentricity which the earlier study had identified as significant barriers seemed less prevalent a decade later (and a geographical world apart). While there were disagreements between students, Montgomery identified these as being more disciplinary-based than nationality-based, and she reported 'a noticeable informality in the relationships between international and home students that was not mentioned in the 1998 study' (op. cit., p. 226). Despite Montgomery's optimistic conclusion that experiences and attitudes among students in cross-cultural groups may be changing, much research continues to find that students fail to voluntarily interact with peers who are 'demographically or racially/ethnically different from themselves' (Ross, 2014, p. 871). Adopting 'polarised positions' (Spiro, 2014) 'reflects worldwide trends' and is a 'recurrent finding' in the USA, England, and New Zealand (Mak et al., 2014, p. 492). Despite best intentions, Strauss et al. (2014, p. 230) found 'much evidence' that their own university in New Zealand was 'having indifferent success in creating an environment where students from different backgrounds work together harmoniously'. International students in the USA have been shown to perceive discrimination and lack of understanding from domestic peers (Lee & Rice, 2007; Sherry et al., 2010). UK students report that where campus events include 'international' or 'diversity', they perceive them as being for their overseas peers and do not participate (Sheil, 2006), whereas some minority students feel that established societies and clubs are oriented towards White students and built around an unattractive culture of alcohol consumption (Stevenson, 2012).

The low interest exhibited by many domestic students for socializing with their international peers may be founded more in indifference than prejudice or psychological vulnerability, since domestic students often have established friendship groups, and may feel little incentive to develop relationships with students perceived to be just 'passing through'. Indifference, however, is replaced by stronger feelings when it comes to intercultural learning activities. Spencer-Rodgers and McGovern (2002) found that domestic students, whether identifying as European American or as Asian American, 'felt impatient, uncomfortable and frustrated when interacting with foreign students' (cited by Mak et al., 2014, p. 494). There is a 'great deal' of evidence that domestic students are often hostile towards intercultural groups, with concern that international peers will reduce group grades, take the domestic students so far outside their comfort zones that it negatively impacts their learning, and, even when there are no first language differences, they still prefer to work in non-diverse groups (Strauss et al., 2014). This last point is further illustrated by research among English-language-speaking UK students on study abroad in Australia (Killick, Forthcoming) which found that even with a common language and strong cultural and historical ties, these White UK students also felt their Australian peers were largely disinterested in them, and eventually (initially to their disappointment) their university socializing was mostly with other international students, with whom they did not share a common first language.

Frequently, then, international students report low levels of interaction with their domestic student peers. They commonly attribute this to a lack of interest among domestic students or to perceptions concerning their English-language skills – which, we should remember, are advanced enough in most cases to enable them to live, work, and study in their host country (see for example Australian Government, 2015, p. 13). Minority group students, international or domestic, may themselves choose not to integrate closely with majority peers. International students report finding the cultural familiarity and linguistic ease afforded by their co-nationals encourages them to seek their company (Eisenchlas & Trevaskes, 2007). In some cases, the common identity of being an international student, and employing the *lingua franca* of English as a *foreign language* (see further discussion on this in the section on intercultural communication in this chapter) might of itself encourage socialization with each other rather than with domestic students. Students of color and LGBT students may find shared prior or current experiences of prejudice makes community with similarly situated others more meaningful and supportive.

The words chosen by this student show how the lived experience of campus segregation and the prejudice of peers can have significant emotional impacts and erode the will to integrate:

> Sometimes it hurts because when you're in this country, they want you to connect or you to have [to] like, become them. That's why I would say. If you don't do that, they just left you out. They will not come to try to join you or understand. So, sometimes it hurts, but sometimes I'm just like, well I'm here to study. If I don't make people, friends on campus, I can make friends outside of campus without an attitude.
>
> (Undergraduate female student from Africa quoted in Glass et al., 2014, p. 24)

The following brief examples further illustrate the impacts on students' well-being, sense of worth, confidence, and willingness to participate. Chinese students on undergraduate and postgraduate programmes in a UK university experienced 'disappointment and disillusionment' and 'a sense of isolation, "otherization" and an enhanced sense of cultural distinction' (Tian & Lowe, 2010, p. 301). A study on four American campuses revealed domestic student experiences of racism and sexism, caused 'confusion, sadness, self-doubt, anxiety, and frustration and constituting drains on their energy and attention' (Caplan & Ford, 2014, p. 40). BME students in the UK 'reported being unwilling to ask questions in class for fear of reinforcing prejudiced expectations about lack of ability' (Cotton et al., 2013, p. 3).

The lived experience reported by many minority and international students, as predicted by theories explored in Chapter Two, illustrates that simply bringing together culturally diverse students does not create learning spaces which foster successful interactions or enhance how students' envisage their diverse peers. Some research even suggests that students' attitudes towards intercultural mixing may worsen during their time at university (Nesdale & Todd, 1993, cited in Volet and Ang, op. cit.) and, perhaps, notwithstanding contrary indications (see several chapters, for example, in Savicki, 2008), even during extensive periods on study abroad (Coleman, 1998, 1999). One study (Ramos et al., 2016) has indicated that when international students *perceive* discrimination among their domestic peers, they come to feel that the majority population group is 'impermeable', leading them to avoid the host and endorse their own cultural backgrounds.

Minority and majority group students, then, are frequently situated, or situate themselves, as separate from their peers, contributing to the creation of segregated learning spaces. Some are unhappy with this, but many find culturally homogeneous spaces more comfortable, easier, and possibly more conducive to the learning tasks confronting them. While some of the responsibility for proactively seeking to work across cultures might be laid upon the individual students, 'the responsibility of institutions and academics should not be minimised' (Volet & Ang, 1998, p. 6). In terms of both internationalization and equalization, low levels of integration, and the continuing othering of diverse students by diverse students, pose a significant challenge to university educators. Stereotypes within the university community are a significant factor, and contribute to a student's self-identity and her will to conduct her life apart. Conducting a life apart minimizes opportunities for stereotypes to be challenged.

Stereotyping

Stereotyping is a cognitive process, an example of categorization (or schema development, as discussed in Chapter Three (Piaget, 1954)). It provides a mechanism 'to manage our chaotic environment in a predictable and efficient fashion' (Ting-Toomey, 1999, p. 149), enabling rapid cognitive recognition, retrieval, and linking. It is unlikely that anyone does not at some level on some occasions stereotype other human beings. If we are to challenge ourselves and our students to recognize and reform our established representations of others, we need first to acknowledge that we have them. The approach we and our students might take to stereotyping is not that we should cease to categorize people since 'attempting to eliminate the perception of differences may be doomed to fail. We will not surrender our categories easily' (Langer, 1989, p. 154). Rather, it is, in line with Langer's mindfulness construct, that we should *extend* and then further extend the range of categories to which people we encounter belong – resulting in a process of individualization which comes about, essentially, through coming to categorize someone *more complexly*:

> A mindful outlook recognizes that we are all deviant from the majority with respect to some of our attributes, and also that each attribute or skill lies on a continuum. Such an awareness leads to more categorizing and consequently fewer global stereotypes.
>
> (Langer, 1989, p. 167)

Research among students in a number of contexts points to stereotyping of and by minority and majority groups. Teachers are advised that 'students who are racial or ethnic minorities see, view, and perceive themselves and others differently than those who are of the majority group' (Brown-Jeffy & Cooper, 2011, p. 73). Studies on the experiences of Black students in American universities have found stereotyping by their White peers to be common. For example, participants in focus groups of Black students at a predominantly White southern state university (Bourke, 2010) cited examples of a prevalent stereotype concerning their high sporting capabilities. This might, on first reading, appear a positive image to extend, but as Bourke (op. cit., p. 128) points out, the underlying assumption is that White students 'seem to believe that Black students cannot be at [the university] based on academic achievement'. The same study (op. cit., p. 129) noted the common experience of Black students to be called upon to 'play the educator' by either acting as the spokesperson for their race, or by being asked 'to explain the myriad ways in which they are different from the norms of Whiteness'. International students can be expected, sometimes by domestic peers and sometimes by faculty, to do similarly for their nation (or, even, for the whole of the 'Asian' population (!)), as can international faculty on home campuses or when working in transnational education (TNE) contexts. An Australian study found that monolingual (English), mono-cultural domestic students based their linguistic stereotyping of international students in part on visible racial characteristics, so that 'Anglo-looking [international] students were assumed to be more proficient in English than students from visibly different cultural backgrounds' (Colvin et al., 2015, cited as 2013 in Strauss et al., 2014, p. 231). Challenging students to recognize their own tendencies to stereotype, and to see them as contributing to inequitable learning experiences for their peers, is a necessary part of creating effective multicultural and intercultural learning spaces. A significant part of this work can be achieved through setting the wider culture of the learning space by shaping learning activities which expect and *value* diverse contributions.

The ways in which academics themselves exhibit their views on others are also fundamental to the shaping of equitable learning spaces. Unfortunately, research shows that academics can also be culpable of stereotyping their students. Surveys have shown, variously (for examples, see citations in Barron et al., 2010; Griffiths, 2010), that significant percentages of academic staff will state or align themselves with statements which cast international students as 'more dependant', 'less willing to participate in discussion', 'poor speakers of English', 'inability to be "critical thinkers"', 'the prevalence of plagiarism', and 'increased workload for staff' – and on the positive side, 'good attenders', 'diligent note takers', 'hard working', or 'respectful'. The first set of these contribute to the 'deficit model' discussed below. In another study, even faculty and students who 'overtly' maintained that they 'did not "see" gender or ethnicity' were found to be 'influenced by widespread stereotypes about different types of student' (Cotton et al., 2013, p. 5). 'Many' respondents in Barron et al.'s study did recognize 'a need to treat people as individuals irrespective of their background' (Barron et al., 2010, pp. 483–484). Those faculty who were not part of the 'many', in common with colleagues I have spoken to in corridors, at conferences, and on academic development programmes, may well have encountered international students who display some, perhaps even all, of the reported characteristics. However, as with all stereotypes:

▶ it is not only international students who present such difficulties;
▶ it is not all international students who present such difficulties; and
▶ these are not the only 'difficulties' which some international students may be experiencing.

As with domestic students, some international students may have learning disabilities, may be coming to terms with their sexuality, may be struggling with a mental health issue, may be in serious financial difficulties, may have caring responsibilities, or may be homesick. When faculty do not differentiate *within* diverse student groups, 'they truly do not see their students at all' (Brown-Jeffy & Cooper, 2011, p. 74). Furthermore, by promulgating stereotypical accounts of any student group, they may inhibit the abilities of colleagues and other students to see them, too.

The ways in which diverse students studying in many TNE contexts are framed within their local communities, or by their peers and the academics they encounter, and how they come to frame themselves is unresearched. Stereotypical ascriptions may be based upon wider social castings, of which a visiting academic or student is unaware, making them less visible, more difficult to interpret, and unlikely to be challenged.

Stereotypes, then, undermine the ways in which a student experiences his learning environments, and the ways in which his peers (re)formulate their own impressions and attitudes towards studying and socializing with him. Stereotyping has also been shown to impact negatively on the performance of some groups. Stereotype Threat Theory (Steele et al., 2002) proposes that 'contingencies' can arise as a result of negative stereotyping of a social or cultural group. When such contingencies are internalized, they may lead the individual to act in accordance with the stereotype. In simplified form, Steele has demonstrated, in a number of empirical tests, that an individual may come to identify with a stereotype held by others of her group in such a way that her performance is diminished when the self-held stereotype becomes salient through the test conditions. Since, as Steele et al. (op. cit., p. 422) posit, 'this threat can be aroused by relatively small, seemingly innocuous cues', students who have already been caste as 'disadvantaged', 'non-traditional', etc., may underperform in ways which reflect the stereotypes held by wider society, and by students and academics in their new university, particularly when performing in learning spaces where those views are salient. For example, if international students are aware that their lecturers and their peers regard them as taciturn, unwilling to speak out or deficient in language skills, this may inhibit maximal performance in group work situations or assessments requiring participation and clear communication. However, being successful in 'counterstereotypical domains' [*sic*] can lead individuals to 'develop the psychological means to deflect stereotype threat' (Crisp & Turner, 2011, p. 255, citing work by Crisp et al., 2009). For minority students, learning spaces which validate their own cultures and world views could be important domains in which to shed the limitations imposed by stereotypes, as could the experience of successful participation in intercultural group work for some international students.

Deficit Modelling and Unconscious Bias

The convergence of a range of negative stereotypes about a group leads to their representation through a 'deficit model'. Deficit modelling in the internationalization context positions 'international students as interculturally deficient and home students as interculturally efficient' (Leask, 2009, p. 218). Similarly, in the context of widening participation, 'dominant thinking' frames 'students and their families of origin as lacking the academic, cultural and moral resources necessary to succeed' (Smit, 2012, p. 270). Even the language commonly used to categorize students 'in terms of what they are not: *not* prepared for higher education, *not* in a position of privilege or advantage' contributes to the deficit, and 'defers responsibility for any critical examination of practices in higher education itself' (Smit, 2012, p. 310, original italics). Although long recognized within multicultural education, recent work on the international student experience is identifying an 'ethnocentric' characteristic in much previous literature, and a focus on the learning behaviours and performance of international students which is 'almost totally based on a deficit model' (Volet & Ang, 1998, p. 8). Through deficit modelling, it is the international student or the minority student and her background which deem her unsuitable, rather than features with the learning spaces she encounters, and so the objectives for an international or a minority student in terms of her relationship with higher education are cast in an assimilationist frame (Ippolito, 2007); she must become like us.

Which students are victims of deficit modelling varies by context – Blacks and Hispanics in the USA; students regardless of race who come from 'non-traditional' backgrounds (i.e. outside the dominant socio-economic middle classes, and likely first-generation in family to study at university) gain more attention in the 'widening participation' work of UK; indigenous peoples feature in Australasia and, again, the USA. In many contexts there is significant focus given to providing environments to *support* students with disabilities; others focus on recent immigrant populations (e.g. Somali refugees) or traditional minority groups (e.g. Romani peoples). Deficit modelling can apply to any minority, and who may or may not be the object of deficit modelling changes by national and social context, and by current events and reporting. Students and faculty from diverse global contexts may carry with them deficit models of others derived from their own communities, or may have been the object of deficit models which faculty and peers in their new learning spaces know nothing about.

As with stereotypes, deficit models have been shown to diminish student learning and performance. Deficit modelling of low socio-economic groups and students of color has been linked to higher than average high school dropout rates and over-representation in special education, leading to schooling actually becoming a 'subtractive' experience (Valenzuela, 1999, cited in Irizzary, 2009) for those students – i.e. they leave with *less* than they entered with, for example in terms of self-efficacy, pride, confidence, or learning aspirations. Smit (2012, pp. 372–373) summarizes at length early work in South Africa (Tema, 1985) which highlighted how deficit modelling can destroy dreams and alienate its victims:

> The effect of the deficit thinking model on students can be devastating. Tema (1985) points out that the students from disadvantaged backgrounds who get to university see themselves as survivors of an inferior schooling system, as strong, successful individuals who have beaten the

system and who, in many cases, carry with them the hopes and dreams of families they leave behind. These students arrive at higher education institutions and are told, in effect, that they stand very little chance of succeeding, that they are lacking in a number of aspects and that they have to 'catch up'. They are marked and separated from the 'mainstream' by virtue of their deficiency, and their 'other-ness' is reinforced. In these ways students are in effect alienated from the very system they have worked hard to be part of.

Some of our minority, international, and TNE students have also struggled, though perhaps only exceptionally in contexts as challenging of those in South Africa, only to find themselves othered, alienated, and failed by the deficit modelling of peers and faculty. Some of these students may purposefully elect not to engage in intercultural learning spaces and activities, exercising 'agency' in their choices (Marginson & Sawir, 2011), and others may identify themselves as 'active co-contributors to the process of cross-cultural learning, not as simply receptive beneficiaries' (Shannon-Little, 2013, p. 272). However, we see in stereotype threat and deficit modelling that when others in their learning spaces do not recognize them as peers or as individuals, diverse learners can be stripped of agency and the will to be active co-contributors.

Just as deficit modelling can impede learning and performance among those who are its object, it can also create *unconscious bias* on the part of their peers and faculty. Viewing others 'through the lens of the dominant culture' (Chun & Evans, 2009) can lead academics and students to *expect* particular characteristics among minority students, and to read such characteristics within them, even if actual behaviour or performance is at odds with the expectation. Unconscious bias can operate in two directions – discriminating *against* students identified by one characteristic and *in favour of* students identified by another. The interpretation of diverse others, by students and academics, can lead to classroom and campus interactions which result in either 'positive outcomes, such as mutual enrichment or negative outcomes such as fear and conflict' (Ross, 2014, p. 870, citing Salzman & D'Andrea, 2001).

Unconscious bias has been shown to influence human judgement actions in a range of fields, from employment and promotion decisions to choice of lifelong partners. In the context of learning spaces, unconscious bias in university admissions and in the grading of student work has led some institutions to introduce systems for anonymous selection and marking. In terms of building equitable learning environments in which multicultural learning communities can encounter and learn from each other, developing *student* awareness of unconscious bias is equally important. Unconscious bias research has largely focussed upon students of color, women, and those with disabilities, but its implications encompass international students and other minorities within the physical and virtual learning communities of the post-national university.

As knowledge of unconscious bias is now quite widespread in education, the term 'implicit bias' has been introduced to question the degree to which it can still be considered unconscious. When 'we know that biases are not always explicit, we are responsible for them' (ECU, 2013c, p. 11). The ECU position is clear: faculty and students have a responsibility to resist acting under the influence of implicit biases, whether they concern gender, race, religion, sexuality, disability, age or nationality. However, it must be acknowledged that this is difficult work, and requires deliberate and sustained attention within learning and teaching activities. Harvard University (Harvard University, n.d.) offer an online test of implicit attitudes for anyone interested in exploring their own.

Unconscious bias and deficit modelling can promulgate well-intentioned but flawed responses, and the impacts on the ways in which the academic community frames the players in its learning spaces needs continuous examination. In a practical guide to inclusive teaching in universities, Griffiths (2010, p. 4) observes that '[m]any commentators agree that since widening participation brings in more students from under-represented groups more support is needed to assist them to complete their course'. However, seeking to ensure academic equity is not a matter of supporting minority groups who are somehow homogeneously 'deficient', so much as building learning spaces and practices which support *all* students to develop their capabilities to make their own way among the complexities of their diverse worlds, the most immediate of which may, indeed, be the world of their current studies. Individual students may need specific forms of interventions to equalize the learning spaces they join. Where individual weaknesses impede successful engagement with learning, an educational response is called for – whatever the national, ethnic, or other sociocultural characteristics of the individual student concerned. Stereotyping, deficit modelling, and unconscious bias can all lead to academic 'support' interventions which actually serve to reinforce the stereotypes, and target resources at students who may not need them, while simultaneously denying other individuals needed support which has been masked by the ways in which they are categorized by their most visible 'type'.

Rather than through 'support' interventions, unconscious bias in our learning spaces may be reduced through increased contact or close friendships, or even *imagined* positive encounters, with diverse others (see ECU,

2013b for a review of literature in this area). This, and other learning gains explored in the next section, further attest to the importance of building learning spaces in which successful intercultural encounters are the norm rather than the exception. Relevant to the section on mindfulness later in this chapter, unconscious bias reduction has been linked to deliberately raising its potential to consciousness within the context of an encounter (Mendez Garcia, 2006).

▶ 4.3 Learning Gain in Diverse Learning Spaces

This chapter has focussed on unhappy experiences and unhelpful learning outcomes deriving from how students and faculty in diverse learning spaces relate to each other. However, research has identified outcomes which attest to the value which can derive from sharing learning spaces with diverse others or explicitly studying about diversity and interculturality. Indeed, in the USA following several legal judgements concerning affirmative action with regard to race, the *educational value* brought by studying among diverse others has become the recognized *legal* rationale for actions to promote greater campus diversity.

The most direct positive impact of learning experiences among diverse others is enhanced effectiveness when an individual works within diverse groups on future occasions. This has been indicated to increase 'instrumentally with the number of international or intercultural experiences that person engages in' (Higson & Liu, 2013, p. 111, citing work by Herdzfeldt, 2007). Mak et al. (2014, p. 492) identify various researchers to have shown that positive interactions among domestic and international students benefit both 'the psychological and educational outcomes of international students from culturally diverse backgrounds'. Although they also note that the effects of this contact on domestic students 'has received little attention worldwide', learning gains have similarly been identified across minority and majority domestic students within multicultural education. That interactions with diverse others should stimulate learning gain outcomes is consistent with learning theory outlined in Chapter Three, specifically that learning derives from situations in which the learner finds herself faced with the dilemma of resolving differences between her established schema and conflicting or contrasting information presented in her interactions with the world. Established schema may relate to what she 'knows' about issues, and also what she 'knows' about those raising the issue – hence the importance of deconstructing stereotypes and deficit models. Although, when they set out the categorization conditions for their model of Categorization-Processing-Adaptation-Generalization (CPAG) (discussed in more detail later in this section), Crisp and Turner (2011, pp. 247–248) suggest that research into minority influences on cognition identifies that the categories a student may hold towards minorities are themselves a stimulus to learning because they present others 'as inconsistent with the norm of the superordinate category'.

Several studies in the USA have pointed to the potential for diversity experiences to bring a range of educational gains (for details of their own research and discussion of previous studies, see Gurin et al., 2002; Hurtado, 2001; Loes et al., 2012; Pascarella et al., 2014). Across these studies, results have included significant indications that formal or informal exposure to diversity at university has the potential to develop students 'for a global society' (Denson & Bowman, 2013, p. 565) and enhances learning in the cognitive domain (for a meta-analysis of literature in this specific area, see Bowman, 2010 from whom the terms 'cognitive skills' and 'cognitive tendencies' below are borrowed). Cognitive 'skills' are specific thinking abilities, while cognitive 'tendencies' indicate an inclination towards more generic thinking styles. A summary of cognitive learning gain identified across the research indicated above is set out below:

- ▶ Cognitive Skills – Enhanced:
  - ▶ outcomes of post-secondary education
  - ▶ general cognitive development
  - ▶ critical thinking and problem solving
  - ▶ creativity

- ▶ Cognitive Tendencies – Enhanced tendencies for:
  - ▶ effortful thinking
  - ▶ seeking complex explanations for human behaviours

Beyond cognitive skills and tendencies, links have been found between diversity engagement and learning gain concerning *attitudes* towards self and others. These include elements such as enhanced:

- ▶ stereotype and/or prejudice reduction;
- ▶ civic mindedness;
- ▶ open-mindedness;
- ▶ willingness to initiate social interaction;
- ▶ racial understanding;
- ▶ importance attached to social justice; and
- ▶ support towards affirmative action.

In addition to academic and self-concept learning gains, Tienda (2013, p. 470) also claims that 'students who interact with peers from different ethnic and racial backgrounds...graduate at higher rates, achieve superior leadership skills, have higher levels of civic involvement, and importantly, exhibit lower levels of prejudice after graduation'.

While recognizing potential learning gain for all students engaging in intercultural encounters, some research in multicultural education also points to differential gains across different groups, in particular suggesting that the most significant learning may accrue to White students or to students admitted to college with lower high school attainment and from lower socio-economic backgrounds. Pascarella et al. (op. cit., p. 91), for example, found that over the full four years of college education there was significant development in critical thinking skills among students who were more actively engaged in diversity activities, and that the development was greatest in those with lower college entry scores, suggesting that:

> interactional diversity may act in a compensatory manner for those students who are relatively less prepared to acquire critical thinking skills from undergraduate academic experiences when they enter college.

Where gains appear strongest for White students, the experience of being a majority group at high school, with the consequence of having had limited opportunity or need to engage in meaningful and positive diversity interactions, may be a significant contributor. Loes et al. (2012, p. 18) note, for example, that in their study on gains in critical thinking, about 80 per cent of the White student participants had attended secondary schools composed 'totally' or 'mostly' of other White students, in contrast with participants of color, of whom only 30 per cent had attended schools with similar profiles of students of color, with 42 per cent having attended predominantly White schools.

Many of the generic and intercultural learning gains noted across the multicultural education research cited above have for many years also been cited as outcomes from study abroad (SA) experiences of all types. A review of 24 studies at the time, spanning a ten-year period (Killick, 2012b, p. 105), identified twenty repeated specific areas of learning gain, with the following cited most frequently (parenthesis indicates number of studies):

- knowledge/awareness of other cultures (16);
- self-confidence (13);
- awareness of own culture (including multiculturalism) (10); and
- flexibility & adaptability/open-mindedness (9).

Subsequent research not included in the above analysis continues to identify these and other dimensions of learning gain (for some particularly rich examples, see Savicki, 2008). Leask (2010, p. 10) proposes three learning gain themes which, notably, reflect cognitive, affective, and behavioural learning dimensions:

- understanding the world out there;
- respect for cultural difference; and
- ability to work across cultures.

Reported gains in each dimension are highly relevant to students as global-selves, though very little research has identified how embedded or lifelong this learning is. Despite significant national and pan-national (European) initiatives to boost participation in SA, it remains a minority pursuit, and the demographics of that minority remain predominantly White students whose cultural capital is already relatively high. Nonetheless, the 'life-changing' learning gain value of SA suggests that we should seek to identify those features of the experience which might be replicated within the learning environments of those who stay at home or study predominantly online. This is particularly needed for emerging post-national university education, as TNE students situated in poorer nations have highly limited, if any, access to SA. Current SA programmes, in this context, can be seen as a contributor to inequitable learning. In the USA, in particular, SA experiences are often run by commercial enterprises, and prompt criticisms concerning their pursuit of exotic rather than educational experiences. Learning gains associated with students who may experience SA as a commodity, with limited concern for the impact on hosting communities, also need to be investigated. To my knowledge, no research has investigated *differential* learning gains across diverse SA participants, though the predominantly White and relatively wealthy demographic makes such research difficult. Emerging research also indicates that rich learning gain might be generated through virtual, online, and blended student collaborations across cultures (Ellenwood & Snyders, 2010).

Several specific features of learning spaces and experiences have been identified to influence learning gain accruing from intercultural and diversity experiences. Bowman's meta-analysis (2010, p. 20) found that while a variety of diversity experience types could be beneficial, those involving *interpersonal interaction* with *racial* diversity, rather than exposure to diversity *knowledge*, to have the strongest impact of cognitive development. A 'positive' campus climate in which there is a 'conscious use of "difference" in the curriculum' and 'structured opportunities for interaction in and out of formal learning environments' (Caruana & Ploner, 2010, p. 11) seems to be crucial to a variety of specific approaches. Ross (2014, p. 871) suggests that diversity education courses in which classrooms 'facilitate interactions among diverse students' through a social justice approach represent 'optimal sites'. In her example, Ross brought together students from two courses – Women's and Gender Studies (a majority of the group self-identified as White female) and African American Studies (a majority of the group self-identified as African American or Black). The course was delivered to two cohorts, one of which experienced conflict between Christian and LGBT students, the other did not. Student comments suggest many in the conflicted group 'revealed tremendous growth' (op. cit., p. 875), with a higher percentage reporting that 'coalition building' was possible than in the second group. Ross echoes the observation above that this is consonant with learning theory.

Cole and Zhou (2014) identified development of civic mindedness with engagement in a range of diversity experiences, including service learning, multicultural courses, interracial interactions, racial awareness workshops, student-faculty interactions, and racial harmony on campus, with the *intense and extended* experience of service learning having the largest association. In line with other cited research, of the variables tested in an Australian study of domestic undergraduates, the *quality* of intercultural contact was the strongest predictor of positive attitudes among participants, with contact quantity being not significant (Mak et al., 2014). In another Australian study, not only were structured curricular diversity activities and *positive, daily* interactions with diverse peers shown to be associated with civic engagement and improved intergroup activities, but poor quality engagement with diverse others was shown to be detrimental to such gains (Denson & Bowman, 2013).

Crisp and Turner (2011) argue the need for experiencing diversity in ways which *challenge existing stereotypical expectations*, but caution that such experiences may have detrimental outcomes if individuals are not first motivated to engage cognitively with the encountered stereotype challenges, or if the challenging encounter is an isolated event. For these authors, requirements for effectively reforming stereotypes require 'repeated exposure to stereotype-challenging diversity, in varied settings' (op. cit., p. 254), and students willing and able to engage in the associated cognitive work. They further argue that, given the right conditions, impacts become generalized towards other contexts and tasks in which there is need for the resolution of inconsistencies, because participants have 'cognitively adapted' and their experience of the mental work involved has enabled them to automatically and 'effortlessly inhibit the influence of stereotypical information on their thought processes'.

In addition to group and situational factors noted above, individual personality traits and existing attitudes have also been found to influence the learning gain of diversity learning experiences. Ross (2014) found differences in the *perceptions* of students concerning the *possibilities* of coalition building across diversity divides to be significant. While 'race' was cited as the biggest barrier to coalition building by between 50 per cent and 78 per cent of Black students across her cohorts, it was similarly ranked by only 14–29 per cent of White students. Gerson and Neilson (2014) found empathy and stage of identity development, in particular, to be strong indicators of students' openness to diversity in the first place. Other research (Lewis et al., 2012) has linked a student's color-blind race ideology (CBRI) to learning gain. CBRI is described as 'the commonly held set of beliefs that serve to deny, distort, and/or minimize racism and racial issues' (op. cit., p. 120); others claim it 'actually reproduces racism' (Bell, et al., 2015, p. 170). In Bell et al.'s study, CBRI among students entering college was the 'strongest predictor of their interest in social justice at the end of the year', and those who participated in more campus diversity experience had lower CBRI scores at the end of the year, indicating the development of 'a critical awareness of racism' (Lewis et al., 2012, p. 131). This study also found some differential learning gain, with greater variation in the CBRI scores of White students at entry and at end of first year.

One rarely noted area of learning gain from the recruitment of international students relates to impacts upon a university's wider stakeholders in the local community. A Canadian report refers to benefits accruing from international students who are accommodated in local 'homestays'; the report offers case study examples of work in this area, and suggests that stakeholder learning gain could be enhanced, with institutions doing more to develop activities that 'actively engage the campus and the community' (BCCIE, 2003, p. 7). Although referring to international students, the potential for other dimensions of student diversity to contribute to community learning is clear.

Learning gain from engaging with diverse peers in learning spaces has been indicated to include behavioural, cognitive, and affective dimensions. The importance of the design of learning activities and environment for learning gain has been indicated by research in diversity education. This research points to sustained, meaningful, and challenging learning activities, with well-framed *interaction spaces* holding the greatest learning gain potential. The importance of communication within those interaction spaces is explored below, and criteria for what constitutes a 'well-framed' interaction space are further explored in Chapter Five.

▶ 4.4 Communication in Diverse Learning Spaces

Formal Language

An institution's official language of instruction imbues differential power upon those for whom it is their first language and those for whom it is not. Commonly in TNE partnerships, students and faculty studying for an award of a foreign partner are required to do their academic work in the language of the award-owning institution, establishing inequalities immediately between students in the various locations of delivery. Case Study 4 in Chapter Six offers a rare example where work was done to ensure this was not the case. On most anglophone campuses, within anglophone online programmes, and in some non-anglophone contexts, students and faculty who do not speak English as their first language are also unequally positioned.

Literature on international students regularly cites English-language proficiency as a specific inhibitor to intercultural working (Shupe, 2007, p. 762). Indeed, where international students are most regularly held to be 'deficient' by their peers and their faculty is in their level of English. Many international students, of course, speak English as their first language, many as their second language (that is to say, as the language they have been educated in and conducted official business in since infancy), and many more have attested capability as highly proficient speakers of English as a foreign language. Some, and this is largely dependent upon the institution's own admissions policy, do find studying and performing in English a significant challenge. In many countries, similarly, the domestic student population may well include students for whom English, as their second or a foreign language, also presents considerable levels of challenge. To identify *all* international students *specifically* as having poor English-language skills is clearly inappropriate.

Differences in a student's first languages may lead to misunderstandings based, simply, on the use of unknown words, idiomatic expressions, complex sentence structures, strong regional accents, and so forth by members of the dominant language group (typically 'native' English-language speakers). In work by Spencer-Oatey (2013), one postgraduate student commented with regard to his/her international peers' perceived low language proficiency: 'This is infuriating for all English-speaking students and systems should be in place to prevent it!' However, the paper also presents examples of a much more collaborative approach between host country nationals (Belgian) and their international peers, where English was the language of instruction but not the local native language. By way of just one example of a student comment:

> I had some difficulties with communicating with a Chinese student in my lab group. We had difficulties with understanding each other, because I spoke too fast and he mumbled sometimes. But if we spoke slowly and articulated well, it was much easier to communicate with each other.
>
> (op. cit., n.p.)

This is a small but powerful illustration of how what are identified by some students as English-language 'deficits' among their international peers can be redefined as communication and attitudinal deficits among the dominant student population. In the example above, the more proficient Belgians showed self-awareness and willingness to play their part in the communication game. Dominant language group members' linguistic behaviours can be responsible for creating or ameliorating inequalities in learning spaces. This point has wider implications in a globalizing world in which English has become a *world language* – meaning that it is now spoken *most frequently* by peoples for whom it is not their first language and most commonly in communication with others for whom it is also not their first language. Our anglophone students-as-graduates will continue to find themselves in communication spaces where English is being used as a *lingua franca*, and where their skills in communicating in English with international peers are deficient. Unless university learning experiences enable them to develop appropriate communication attitudes, and competencies in *English as a world language*, this dimension of global-selfhood will be absent for members of this, global minority, group.

More complex than linguistic features such as vocabulary, sentence structure, and accent are the cultural conventions concerning the appropriate turn of phrase or nuance of expression. A student's own cultural linguistic conventions for politeness, for example, may require 'being indirect, suggesting rather than telling, impersonalising a discussion', leading her to come across to others as 'overly vague, weak or deferential', while another student's politeness conventions prompt him to overtly exhibit attention, actively agree, and promise action, causing others to regard him as 'uncritical or even sycophantic', and so forth (Scudamore, 2013).

Beyond these, are the rules which frame the sequencing and turn-taking within an interaction. As with other aspects of big culture behaviours discussed in Chapter Two, care needs to exercised when we attribute communication behaviours to cultures, but with that caveat, an example is useful to consider. In guidance on culturally responsive pedagogy, Gray (2000, p. 91) illustrates how educational communication styles may not match those of minority groups. Within the *participatory-interactive* style observed among African Americans, Latinos, and Native Hawaiians, '[s]peakers expect listeners to engage them actively through vocalized, motion, and movement responses *as they are speaking*'. Gray continues to outline a number of aspects of discourse structuring which can manifest differently across cultures, included under headings such as 'organizing ideas in discourse', 'storytelling as topic-chaining discourse', 'taking position and presenting self', 'personalizing or objectifying communications', '"playing with and on" words', 'ambivalence and distancing in communication', and 'gender variations in discourse styles'. These, and any other discourse style, may manifest more strongly among individuals who identify most strongly with a particular culture, and among those who have had 'fewer opportunities to interact with people different from themselves' (op. cit., p. 91). Gray cites lower-income families as an example, but this applies also to many White middle-class students, among whom will be individuals who have not experienced multicultural living or any need to bring their own communication styles to consciousness, let alone to seek to modify them. In the context of international and multicultural learning spaces, those with least experience of, or inclination towards, or strategies for, adapting their own communication are likely to be found in the anglophone majority speaking, socially-valued variety of English.

Paralinguistics

In addition to formal linguistic dimensions to effective and satisfactory intercultural communication are the miscommunications which arise because of *paralinguistic* features within the communication process. Messages may be conveyed by our use of intonation, and also through eye contact, body language, facial expressions, how close we stand, if and where we touch, and so forth. In early work, Mehrabian (1971) suggests we can attribute only 7 per cent of the social import of a message to the actual words used, with 38 per cent being communicated through tone of voice and 55 per cent through body uses such as those noted above; in intercultural interactions, 'culturally congruent non-verbal behaviours' have been shown to be stronger predictors of personal attraction than ethnicity (Ward, 2001, p. 422).

In Chapter Three we looked at the role which schema play in the learning process and in student engagement with academic cultures and practices. Schema also frame communication acts, and as with verbal languages, culture 'exerts considerable influence over our nonverbal languages'

(Matsumoto & Yoo, 2005, p. 260). As mentioned in Chapter Three, mismatched behaviours can lead to the misattribution of values.

Politeness is only one small example of the messages carried in the paralinguistic system (honesty, threat, and love are but a few others), but politeness conventions can again provide an example. Communication between those whose schema for 'how to be polite' are very similar will find interactors subconsciously displaying a range of linguistic and non-verbal communication behaviours which are mutually interpreted to mean 'in this conversation I am (she is) being polite' OR 'I am (she is) not being polite'.

Politeness is also conveyed by more complex social rituals such as whether or not we stand in line (queue), buy a round of drinks, proffer or accept a gift, or invite a colleague into our home; and by how we dress, wear our hair, or expose our bodies. In all of these examples, and more, the particular ways in which culture *a* uses these various communication acts may differ from culture *b*. This does not make culture *a* or *b* more, or less, polite, but the *interpretation* of behaviours may be such that during intercultural encounters members of both cultures feel the other terribly impolite, or overly polite, dishonest, threatening, intimate, or diffident. To a large extent, such responses are triggered because the participants are caught up entirely in the social communication act, lacking focussed attention or 'mindfulness' and not 'being aware of our own and others' behaviour in the situation', because we are not paying attention to 'the *process* of communication taking place between us and dissimilar others' (Ting-Toomey, 1999, p. 16).

A further aspect of communication is the work we do to maintain 'face'. Erving Goffman's (1967) pioneering work on face identified that when people are, ordinarily, engaged in a social interaction (students and faculty, for example, participating in group work, a seminar, or a lecture), all participants have a will to ensure that nobody loses face. The possibilities for face loss cut both ways – participants are 'mutually susceptible' (Barnes, 2000) – and losing face by one participant creates negative emotional reactions for all concerned. There are complex, and again subconsciously enacted, routines for maintaining face throughout an interaction. These are not universal, and what actually constitutes a loss of face in one culture may have no salience at all in another. For some students, for example, asking a question might imply stupidity or arrogance and lead to loss of personal face, but for others it might be interpreted to imply something negative about the lecturer's competence – 'he didn't explain it well', leading to loss of face for him.

As mentioned, when students or academics encounter mismatched communication behaviours in intercultural interactions, with or without loss of face, their responses will often be emotional, and not brought to conscious attention. When cognitive processing is applied, it can lead to *misattribution* of a value position to the observed behaviour. Going back to our example of politeness, if someone fails to stand in line in a culture where the particular social situation would expect it (a British bus stop is a good example), others may simply get annoyed. However, they may also misattribute the action along the lines of, 'She didn't stand in line. If I didn't stand in line, I would be impolite. She is impolite.' Not, you notice, 'She acted impolitely' but 'She *is* impolite.' Where she is of another culture, race, sexuality, or age, the temptation to a further move along the lines of 'She is impolite. She is Spanish. Spaniards (or foreigners) are impolite' constitutes the consolidation or the birth of a stereotype. The offending queue-jumper, oblivious to the impact of her own 'normal' behaviour sees the behaviours of others at the bus stop as confirming her experience that the British are ill-tempered and unfriendly to foreigners.

When we create learning spaces in which our students are encountering diverse others whose paralinguistic, face-maintaining, or social etiquette norms differ from one another, emotional and cognitive reactions risk strengthening their stereotypes and prejudices. Building awareness of features of intercultural communication and opportunities for students to explicitly reflect upon their personal responses to their peers should be deliberately designed into multicultural group work. Academics concerned with equitable and culturally responsive teaching also need to raise their own awareness, willingness, and capabilities to communicate in ways which are accessible to students of diverse cultural and linguistic backgrounds (Gray, 2000, p. 110).

Mindfulness

Mindfulness, cited for various contexts in this book, refers to an attitude towards the world which is typified by a conscious effort to be aware of what is going on, to recognize and welcome alternative truths as they emerge, to learn with openness. These stances are liberating and 'joyful' because they present and develop acceptance that there is more than one set of rules available, and therefore more opportunity to make intelligent choices concerning our own lives:

> The consequences of trying different perspectives are important. First, we gain more choices in how to respond. A single-minded label produces an automatic reactions, which reduces our options. Also, to understand that other people might not be so different allows us empathy and enlarges our range of responses. We are less likely to feel locked into a polarized struggle.

Second, when we apply this open-minded attitude to our own behavior, changes become possible.

(Langer, 1989, p. 71)

Being aware of 'what is going on' means, in Langer's terms, an attention to the *process* in which one is involved. Specifically, for our multicultural learning spaces and activities, this can mean attentiveness with regard to self and other *within* an intercultural encounter in order that we might avoid making 'instant' judgements based upon our existing schema. It is akin to the idea of reflection-in-action (Schön, 1983), specifically focussed on the reciprocal impacts of interaction behaviours on self and others. Communication, we have seen, goes far beyond words and sentence structures, and the impacts of engaging with others operating to different rules for social interaction can be emotionally challenging, *to the extent* that the intended content of the message and intent of the speaker is not only obscured, but possibly dismissed or metamorphosed in the process. Mindfulness, our orientation towards the *processes* in play within the interaction, is necessary if we are to mitigate this potential.

Within intercultural interactions, specifically, there is a need to seek to become intentionally 'attuned to others' salient identity issues' (Ting-Toomey, 2005, p. 217). Such tuning, in addition to the *inclination* to 'meet cultural difference on its own terms' and 'search for multiple interpretations of a situation at hand' (Yershova et al., 2000, p. 47), and the *capacity* to act while observing oneself in action, depends upon abilities to both recognize and regulate one's own emotions (Y.S et al., 2006) and 'predict and explain one's own behaviours and that of others during interactions' (Zhou et al., 2008, p. 67), and it is for this reason that the global student and the global academic, if he and his co-participants are to find intercultural encounter meets its potential for positive learning gain, need an understanding of the ways in which subconscious communication is carried by subconscious activity, and to recognize that the impacts of this can be emotional and cognitive. Mindful thinking creates a space for a student to reflect upon what she knows and believes in light of what is happening, and to use that to change her established ways of acting, of interpreting, and, perhaps, of feeling. Such mindful *reflexion* in action not only has the potential to help the student negotiate the encounter, but also, through changes she makes in her behaviour, to help the other(s). Being mindful *throughout* an interaction can lead to repair and retrieval of the ongoing situation, and a 'successful' outcome upon which future encounters might be built. Mindfulness can be applied to activities and situations far beyond intercultural encounter, and helping students apply its precepts within intercultural encounters may build the capacity more generally, and aid reflexivity in all aspects of student engagement and graduate performance.

▶ 4.5 Chapter Summary

In this chapter, we have looked at the spaces in which learning might be enacted, with particular reference to how those spaces may be experienced by 'minority' students, 'international students', and 'majority' students, arguing that a student's learning is not only influenced by her learning spaces but that she also contributes significantly to how others experience those spaces. The first theme of the chapter explored how the lived experience of her learning spaces can be negatively impacted by other students and, on occasions, by faculty also. Caplan and Ford (2014, pp. 40–41) conclude that '[t]oo many' of the participants in their US study, 'at a vulnerable time in their lives', feel 'they do not have a sense of belonging or fitting in in either the academic or the social realm', and we see from this chapter that a student's sense of belonging is largely shaped by the construction of his learning spaces and how he is categorized and responded to by his peers and his faculty. The existence and some of the impacts of stereotyping, unconscious bias, and stereotype threat have been explored, and set in the context of deficit modelling of both international students and minority students. By contrast, participating in some learning spaces among diverse others has been demonstrated to facilitate learning gain in areas which are relevant to the development of the global-self, across cognitive, behavioural, and affective domains. Factors in the learning environment, along with a student's prior experience and dispositions regarding diversity, can impact upon the quality and the direction of his learning.

The second major theme of this chapter illustrated that the ways in which students and faculty communicate within intercultural encounters, particularly where first languages may be different, can have a significant impact on how a student experiences learning spaces and learning activities. Students from diverse backgrounds employing differing linguistic and paralinguistic rules impact on emotions, attitudes, and cognitive framings of others and on the act of engaging in intercultural encounter per se. Achieving a mindful state within intercultural learning encounters is a stance which may militate against communication breakdowns, and bring maximal intercultural learning potential to fruition.

5 Global Good Practice

▶ 5.1 Chapter Introduction

In the preceding chapters we have explored features of the emerging global higher education landscape, with the post-national university presented as a complexly diverse space within which faculty and students conduct their academic lives. Through forays into work in the complementary, but hitherto largely separate, fields of internationalization and multicultural education, those chapters have explored theoretical and experiential perspectives on the global student, the global graduate, the global academic, and global learning spaces in order to illustrate *why* the practice of learning and teaching needs to be reviewed to meet the needs of diverse students in diverse contexts. To summarize, we have looked specifically at:

- ▶ the emergence of a global higher education 'industry', caught in and contributing to international/intercultural human flows, and other dimensions of globalization, arguing this to be reshaping the hitherto principally national/local university into a post-national one, with consequences on its impacts, practices, and responsibilities;
- ▶ the impacts of increasing human diversity within lives lived in a multicultural and globalizing world, arguing that these elevate the imperative for higher education learning to enable all our students-as-graduates to be able to make their way as global-selves;
- ▶ psychological and cultural perspectives on why crossing into new cultural encounters is complex, and cognitively and affectively challenging for our students in their learning spaces, our graduates in their living spaces, and faculty in their teaching spaces;
- ▶ the implications and impacts of the post-national university regarding the ways in which faculty identify themselves, are identified by others, and can/should conduct their practice;
- ▶ learning spaces within the post-national university, and how diversity experiences and attributions by students and faculty frame them, both as inequitable spaces and as spaces within which learning gain might occur which is consistent with developing the global-self; and

▶ processes and approaches which may facilitate intercultural being and learning, and the communication flows within intercultural encounter.

This chapter builds from these theoretical and experiential perspectives to provide a critical overview of *how* we might approach the internationalization and equalization of learning and teaching practice for diverse students in diverse contexts. It does so through an initial exploration of design features underpinning successful intercultural activities, and thence, through a focus on principles for design and delivery of the formal curriculum and a brief exploration of the hidden and extended curricula. The chapter concludes with a discussion on implications regarding development for faculty facing the demands of their roles in the post-national university. The four substantive sections of the chapter explore internationalization and equalization of practice with regard to:

▶ conditions for successful intercultural learning;
▶ designing the formal curriculum;
▶ pedagogy; and
▶ faculty development.

▶ 5.2 Conditions for Successful Intercultural Learning

We have seen that when intercultural contact, whether involving international students or minority students, does occur in university learning spaces the experience can be highly unsatisfactory, and also that in some circumstances successful learning happens. Global-selfhood, outlined in Chapter Two, requires affective, cognitive, and behavioural capabilities for engaging in intercultural encounters, seen as *fundamental* to successful social engagement, employability, and advancing social justice in the milieu of a multicultural and globalizing world. This section explores what might be required with regard to the ways in which intercultural encounters are framed within physical and virtual university learning environments in order to maximize their potential to (i) engender successful intercultural learning, and (ii) encourage students to become interested in and confident about pursuing further contact with diverse others – globally and/or locally.

Seminal work in this area (Allport, 1979/1954) proposes that intercultural contact has the possibility to reduce prejudice, and is most likely to do so when a set of conditions pertain within the contact situation; chief among these are:

- ▶ equality of status among all participants;
- ▶ sustained engagement in *cooperative* tasks;
- ▶ working towards a common goal; and
- ▶ the support of relevant authorities;

Since its publication, Allport's Intergroup Contact Hypothesis has been utilized and scrutinized in both multicultural and international education contexts, some of which are noted below, and has influenced policy at the state level and the national level in the USA, including the eventual desegregation of schooling.

When we consider each of those four primary conditions from Allport's original theory in the context of learning spaces and activities in the post-national university, a number of questions for practice emerge, as illustrated in Table 5.1. These questions apply to any learning activity, from lecture theatre to online seminar group, to field trip, and with any cohort, however constituted. The questions are framed around 'my students in this context' because different elements and responses will apply according to student mix and each person's historical and current social and educational positioning (intersectionality, as discussed in Chapter Three), and do therefore require a focus on the *individuals* who make up a particular learning group. This is also the approach advocated for culturally aware teaching, which is about 'observing and understanding students as individuals' and 'exploring their responses rather than judging them by ethnocentric standards' (MacLean & Ransom, 2006, p. 61).

Table 5.1 Questions Concerning the Structuring of University Learning Activities Arising from the Primary Conditions for Successful Intercultural Contact within the Intergroup Contact Hypothesis (Allport, 1979/1954)

Contact Hypothesis Condition	Questions pertaining to the structuring of university learning activities
equality of status among all participants	How can a university learning activity *with my students in this context* be structured in order to equalize the inequalities between participants arising from: ▶ unequally regarded (academic) cultural capital? ▶ unequally regarded linguistic competencies? ▶ differential power/status afforded by broader societal structural inequalities? ▶ existing stereotypes and prejudices among participating students?

(Continued)

Table 5.1 (Continued)

Contact Hypothesis Condition	Questions pertaining to the structuring of university learning activities
	▶ the requirement that *all* participants regard each other as equal? ▶ curriculum content predominantly presented from and illustrated through a single social or cultural or national perspective?
sustained engagement in *cooperative* tasks	How can a university learning activity *with my students in this context* be structured in order to create cooperative working over a sustained period, given: ▶ the pressures of assessment on students' perception of the worth of a given task? ▶ the scheduling of learning activities within a single module, term, or semester? ▶ the potential for communication breakdowns to militate against continued cooperation? ▶ an established ethos of competition, need to be 'the best', among some students?
working towards a common goal	How can a university learning activity *with my students in this context* be structured in order that *all* members of the group identify themselves and others as contributing to a common goal, given: ▶ differences in participation 'style' (regard for 'face', extroversion, need to lead, etc.)? ▶ students from different cultures/social groups may have different levels of interest in a topic and/or in the completion of a given task? ▶ a norm among some of individual working towards a group assignment/assessment?
the support of relevant authorities	How can a university learning activity *with my students in this context* be structured in order to convey to all participants that engaging in the task with an equitable regard for other participants is an expectation held by faculty and the wider authorities of the university, given: ▶ formal assessments are incapable of assessing affective and attitudinal dimensions in performance? ▶ students from diverse backgrounds may not recognize that the authorities in *this* context implicitly value equitable regard and reciprocal learning? ▶ students from diverse backgrounds may not themselves recognize value in this particular type of learning activity (e.g. student-centered learning with an emphasis on students as co-constructors of learning rather than faculty as 'sage-on-the-stage')? ▶ assessment criteria typically focus on learning product rather than on learning process?

In an early work, Pettigrew (1998) undertook a 'reformulation' of Allport's original hypothesis, which included a heuristic model for the reduction of prejudice through development *over time* as processes of *decategorization, salient categorization*, and *recategorization* of other(s).

Implicated in successful progress through these stages are:

- ▶ the prior experience and characteristics of the participants;
- ▶ situational factors which facilitate the process at the onset; and
- ▶ societal and institutional contexts surrounding the process.

At initial contact, amidst some anxiety, optimal situations will lead to *decategorization* – 'liking without generalization'; once contact has been established, optimal situations will lead to *salient categorization* – 'reduced prejudice with generalization'; once within a unified group, optimal situations will lead to *recategorization* – 'maximum reduction in prejudice'. The propositions that:

(i) the characteristics of participants, of facilitating situation factors, and of the wider context bear upon the conditions within the contact situation, and

(ii) even where all those are optimal, a transformative learning process of this kind in itself requires time – and progressive development through stages to effect schema change

have lessons for faculty when creating intercultural learning activities, for example:

- ▶ an activity which 'works well' with one group of students may not do so with another; individual students will influence a cohort through their unique prior experience, characteristics, and 'intersectional' identities;
- ▶ unless situations are deliberately created with a view to building effective intercultural contact, essential factors are likely to be absent;
- ▶ early intercultural contact learning activities need to recognize the likelihood that they will be anxiety-inducing, and so be designed to build from less challenging beginnings; and
- ▶ even when all factors are optimally aligned, progress towards prejudice reduction will take time; expecting, recognizing, and rewarding small initial steps will be important to overall progress, and so maintaining intercultural focus in learning activities across a full learning programme is important.

A meta-analysis of over 500 studies relating to intergroup contact theory, and involving over 250,000 participants from 38 nations, found that intergroup contact typically reduces intergroup prejudice and that although the original theory was devised in respect of racial and ethnic encounters, evidence supports that it 'can be extended to other groups' (Pettigrew & Tropp, 2006, p. 751). Indeed, the largest impacts were found in research among heterosexuals and gay men and lesbians. Some insights emerging through the meta-analysis of particular relevance to establishing successful intercultural learning activities and spaces are:

▶ where participants had no choice about whether or not they engaged in intercultural contact, the impact on prejudice reduction was slightly higher than when they did have a choice;

▶ although any contact situation might reduce prejudice, those designed to meet the optimal conditions in Allport's original hypothesis 'achieved a markedly higher mean effect size than others' (p. 766);

▶ while 'authority support' is shown to be relevant, it is not clear that it is so when introduced in isolation from other factors (for example, institutional support within a *competitive* contact situation has a strong chance of increasing animosity); and

▶ uncertainty reduction and anxiety reduction may significantly enhance the outcomes.

Building from their 2006 meta-analysis, Pettigrew and Tropp (2008) sought to identify the processes by which successful intergroup contact might reduce prejudice. The three most commonly studied contributors to reducing prejudice were:

(i) enhancing knowledge about the other group;
(ii) reducing anxiety about intergroup contact; and
(iii) increasing empathy and taking others' perspectives.

Of these, affective factors like anxiety reduction and empathy are 'clearly major mediators relative to the more cognitively oriented mediator of knowledge' (op. cit., p. 929).

In multicultural education, culturally relevant or culturally responsive pedagogies are underpinned with similar criteria, but are also deliberately geared to:

▶ create a sense of learner community 'camaraderie, kindredness, and reciprocity' (Gray, 2000, p. 215);

▶ engender a belief in academic success; and

▶ promote social justice beyond the learning environment and into the wider community.

Attention to the conditions within learning activities and spaces is a *significant determiner* of the learning which is likely to occur within them. In addition to conditions proposed within extended versions of the Intergroup Contact Hypothesis, other priorities for successful intercultural learning among diverse others include building a sense of community-belonging and mutual responsibility, as well as belief in success. The diverse students and contexts of the post-national university mean that learning activities and spaces may need to be differently designed to achieve those conditions for each of our learners. Specifics of these approaches are considered within the sections on formal curricula and pedagogy below.

▶ 5.3 Designing the Formal Curricula

This section explores four key principles set out in good practice literature with regard to their applicability for academics designing curricula in post-national universities in a multicultural and globalizing world:

- ▶ Relevance to the student
- ▶ Relevance to the 'real world'
- ▶ Meaningful intended learning outcomes
- ▶ Alignment across the curriculum

Principle 1 – Relevance to the Student

A key good practice principle is that curriculum content should be 'relevant' to the student. In curriculum internationalization and in multicultural education, there is particularly focus put upon integrating content which is *culturally* relevant – be that with regard to a student's national and regional cultures, or to his ethnicity, socio-economic group, gender, or religion. Currently, students may find, like participants in one American study, 'racism and sexism in course materials, sometimes because of what is present and sometimes because of the absence of materials created by anyone other than white men' (Caplan & Ford, 2014, p. 43). International students may find content and examples based exclusively in Western or first-world contexts, which are difficult to connect to their own experiences or priorities. Whatever the particular bias within a curriculum, when one cultural perspective dominates, relevance to many students is diminished, and it 'may hamper inclusivity and inhibit the realisation of positive educational outcomes which cultural diversity offers, but does not guarantee' (Dunne, 2011, p. 611).

One approach to building relevance into curricula for diverse students, therefore, is to incorporate content from a range of sources and perspectives. However, there are dangers that this process can be limited to inserting the occasional alternative case study or citation into what remains a fundamentally majority-culture curriculum, a 'one-shot injection of an add-on that remains the same even after treatment' (Mestenhauser, 2002, p. 58). Banks (1999) presents a three-tier model of cultural content, moving from this kind of *add-on* approach, through *infusion* to *transformation* approaches. The infusion approach presents a range of information from other countries and cultures, but continues to require students to engage with them through traditional Western majority conceptual frameworks. The shift in the transformation approach is not about which cultures are *represented* within the source material, but of the critical approach in which students engage with the materials – being encouraged, enabled, and rewarded for doing so from a range of perspectives, and building a 'pedagogy of recognition' within which students engage in 'a critical relationship with texts and theories, enabling them to deconstruct their own lives and to imagine alternatives' (Caruana, 2007, p. 18).

Early work by Marcuse (1970, cited in Brookfield, 2007) positioned the 'add-on' kind of response as 'repressive tolerance', since:

> an alternative idea, concept or text can be inserted into a curriculum of familiar, mainstream materials in such a way that it serves only to underscore the normality of the center while positioning the alternatives as exotic others. As a result, the attempt to diversify actually undercuts the serious consideration of diverse perspectives.
>
> (Brookfield, 2007, p. 557)

Marcuse essentially argued for the removal of *all* references to majority culture within a curriculum. This radical proposal arises from a belief that majority-cultural positionings within a curriculum risk not only making it *irrelevant* for minority students but also risk perpetuating structural prejudices and discriminations. However, I would propose that majority culture curriculum content needs to be included *in order that* it might be interrogated by all students, including those from the majority culture concerned. Removing it risks diminishing the relevance of the curriculum for majority students, and perhaps also risks implying to them that their perspectives need not be opened to critical scrutiny.

One of Gray's (2000, p. 214) 18 precepts for culturally relevant pedagogy (CRP) is that all work should be 'informed by the contexts and content of the cultures and lived experiences of different groups of color'. As already discussed, there is danger in assuming that macro-cultural values, norms, and practices can be applied to deliver a kind of cultural 'fit' between an individual student and the curriculum. Just as Ryan (2013, p. 283) cautions us not to ignore 'the considerable differences within cultures as well as between them' within transnational education (TNE) contexts, the same must be true of 'different groups of color', and for the design of curricula across any dimensions of diversity within our learning communities, at home, overseas, or online. Given the intersectionality playing out among the range of contexts, cultures, and individual biographies of diverse students across diverse local and global contexts, predetermining what will be 'relevant' to individual students or seeking to represent all perspectives within the content of a curriculum is simply not feasible. However, critiquing all the perspectives which are present from some perspectives which are absent might be.

Rather than achieving relevance by infusing the curriculum with values, perspectives, and experiences from a range of cultures per se, some advocates for an internationalization which is situated in global citizenship propose 'the development and infusion of a world view and perspective' (Bartell, 2003, p. 49). Although a 'world view' approach might rather beg questions of 'whose world' and 'whose view', I interpret this to mean embedding and critiquing the views of diverse global peoples, *whether or not* they are present on the campus or in the cohort. A global-selfhood approach argues that any perspective is worthy of respectful critique because a global-self is grounded in the world view that others are equally human, and their capabilities to live a life they have reason to value are the concern of each of us. This includes the perspectives and capabilities of people belonging to majority and minority groups, locally and globally. Where we are fortunate to have diverse students in our physical and virtual learning spaces, a curriculum which gives full voice to their values, perspectives, and experiences in dialogue with their peers can establish relevance and also build most effectively towards 'world views' consistent with global-selfhood – since a world view is an abstraction, but the diverse perspectives of our students are not. Where the diversity mix is more locally based, world view will need to derive from incorporating diverse content and the interrogation of that content from diverse perspectives, including those of peoples not physically present in the classroom or the community at large. Curricula designed to be relevant to all our students, then, needs to include content which is drawn from a range of sources, including those which relate to locally dominant culture(s). Care must be taken, though, to ensure that these alternative perspectives are not ad hoc or tokenistic, but are given equal status, considered with equal regard, embedded not appended. When a piece of curriculum is 'transported' to a new context or delivered to a differently diverse cohort, it needs to be interrogated afresh with regard to the diet of perspectives which are presented and interrogated. The intention is not to seek to 'teach' all different views or experiences so much as to enable students to see that differences exist, and that there is also 'difference within difference' (Luke, 2010, p. 61), that diverse perspectives and priorities hold validity within the discipline, and that they can *all* also be opened to critique. A curriculum designed with relevance to students in a multicultural and globalizing world entails enabling each student to *identify that* there is relevance in the perspectives of others, including the perspectives of others *not present* within his immediate cohort or community and to accept that his perspective is only one among many, and is equally open to critique as any.

Given the very real challenges identified in determining in advance what cultural referents, experiences of discrimination, possibilities for application, or contested positions might be salient to each of our diverse students in diverse contexts today, and within cohorts over time, an individual academic will need to draw upon expert informants to shape her 'relevant' curriculum. Such informants may be found among her peers, particularly when working in new cultural contexts (several examples can be found in the case studies in Chapter Six), and they can also be found among her diverse students.

Enabling each student to establish his own relationships with the curriculum is the most powerful way of ensuring relevance to him. Exploring citizenship education in the UK higher education context, Fryer (2005, p. 99) notes that within adult learning there is an established position of recognizing the 'value and authenticity of learners' own experiences', arguing that it is the role of faculty to 'bring those experiences into critical articulation with the experiences of others, and with concepts, theories and evidence' through a *negotiated curriculum* which involves students establishing areas of focus.

Relating CRP to critical race theory, Brown-Jeffy and Cooper (2011, p. 70) note how this approach 'recognizes the value of lived experience by marginalized groups in understanding and making meaning'. To reiterate, I do not situate race as a *necessarily* more salient identity marker than other dimensions of diversity. In the context of the 'reality of race and racism in American society' (op. cit., p. 69), it may well be appropriate to do so, but for differently diverse students in diverse contexts, race may be less salient than other local marginalized identities. This is only to say that principles established for CRP or within critical race theory need not be limited to contexts where race is the major 'issue', but may be applicable across other contexts where other minorities are subjected to similar structural discriminations. By way of a further example, Chopra et al., identify *ten* groups who are not equally served through the current higher education system in India: 'diverse socio-economic, caste and religious groups … women, people with special educational needs and disability, marginalised caste and socio-economic groups, religious minorities (such as Muslims) and those who live in rural areas' (Chopra et al., 2013, p. 176).

Whether group marginalization is based on race or other identities, then, insights within critical race theory, critiques of color-blind ideologies, and approaches developed in CRP can guide the academic work of curriculum design. Curriculum which is 'relevant to the student' is curriculum which engages with the lived experience of the student, whoever she is. That is, a curriculum in which the shapings of her individual biography are deliberately brought forward to develop her understanding and meaning-making, a position widely recognized in critical pedagogy from Freire's (1970, 1972) work onwards. All students, marginalized or not, will bring their unique lived experience to the table, and a relevant curriculum needs to (i) value each student's experience and (ii) enable her to situate that experience and critique the perspectives she has drawn from that experience, in the wider milieu of a multicultural and globalizing world. Doing one without the other will not serve her well:

▷ a curriculum of equalization will allow each student's meaning-making to be *voiced* and *valued*; and
▷ a curriculum for global-selfhood will require, also, that her meaning-making is *challenged* in the light of others' lived experience.

Interrogating the sources of curriculum content, the perspectives they represent, and the values they convey is important work, but it is the ways in which we structure engagement with that content which will enable individual students to make it personally relevant. Although schools-based, this short example from Ladson-Billings' early work on CRP (1995a, p. 162) offers a good example of making relevant by taking a critical approach to mandated content:

> Rather than merely bemoan the fact that their textbooks were out of date, several of the teachers in the study, in conjunction with their students, critiqued the knowledge represented in the textbooks, and the system of inequitable funding that allowed middle-class students to have newer texts. They wrote letters to the editor of the local newspaper to inform the community of the situation. The teachers also brought in articles and papers that represented counter knowledge to help the students develop multiple perspectives on a variety of social and historical phenomena.

Curriculum can be designed to engender similar approaches to any content, and at university level, students can be entrusted (and required within the design of the curriculum) to identify and bring in representations of 'counter knowledge' from their own experience and from that of others. A crucial role of faculty in this case, again borrowed from CRP, is to ensure that when students do so, they do so believing (and finding) they can succeed academically through the lenses they deploy, that is, they can 'maintain their cultural integrity while succeeding academically' (Ladson-Billings, 1995b, p. 476, cited in Schmeichel, 2012, p. 221).

There are, then, two dimensions to designing a curriculum for the post-national university which is *relevant to the student*:

(i)   ensuring the *content* of that curriculum is drawn from diverse perspectives, cultures, and traditions, and integrated into the curriculum in ways which allow full opportunity and 'reward' for our diverse students to also integrate personally relevant content; and

(ii) framing *engagement* with that content (*whatever* its origins) which demands critique from diverse perspectives, dialogic engagement with the perspectives of others (present or not), and the recognition of differential outcomes deriving from diverse approaches to meaning-making.

Principle 2 – Relevance to the 'Real World'

A second good practice principle is that curriculum should not only be relevant to the learner, but it should also be relevant to the contexts in which the learning will come to be applied. In some disciplines, particularly those based within specific professions, this is expressed as being relevant to the world of work. Although the neo-liberal thrust may seek to align all disciplines within an employability frame, it is much less easy to identify immediate employment contexts for the application of, say, the humanities. Even in strongly vocationally/professionally oriented provision, as illustrated by the Fashion and the Speech and Language Science programme development outlined in Case Studies 1 and 4 in Chapter Six, relevance to the world of work needs to be interpreted as opening wider global disciplinary perspectives or life opportunities. For all courses, relevance to the 'real world' must now beg such questions as:

▶ where-in-the-world will the student come to find himself employed, or married, or dispersed, or in need, or able to help?
▶ among what peoples?
▶ to what ends?

Where students are located in diverse TNE contexts from the outset, embedding 'real-world' relevance needs to be developed with the expertise of those within those contexts, academics and students.

The shift from academic-as-knower was suggested in Chapter Three to challenge what is for many academics a cherished professional identity. The 'swift obsolescence of knowledge' (Chun & Evans, 2009, p. 14), while perhaps more immediate in some disciplines than others, means the ways in which some students identify themselves as learners, and then as graduates, are also being challenged – shifting from one of student as knowledge-consumer to that of knowledge-constructor. Such an identity aligns directly with constructivist theories of the learning process as outlined in Chapter Three, and with the kinds of transformative education philosophies alluded to at several points through this book. Curriculum relevant to the 'real world' is curriculum directed towards enabling students-as-graduates to *interrogate* the current world and *keep up with* and *influence* the shifting sands of their disciplinary, professional, and social roles – each of which increasingly sits within a global as well as a local context. Relevance to the real world entails developing a 'global imagination' – a 'capacity to determine how knowledge is globally linked, no matter how locally specific its uses' (Rizvi, n.d., pp. 4–5).

In somewhat prescient work, Case (1993, p. 319) identified that a curriculum designed to develop 'appropriate conceptual and moral lenses through which to view global interactions may be more crucial than acquiring extensive information'. In the same era, advocating for multicultural citizenship, Kymlicka pointed out that:

> Since we can be wrong about the worth or value of what we are currently doing, and since no one wants to lead a life based on false beliefs about its worth, it is of fundamental importance that we are able rationally to assess our conceptions of the good in the lights of new information or experiences, and to revise them if they are not worthy of our continued allegiance.
>
> (Kymlicka, 1995, p. 81)

In her examination of agency, Archer makes a similar point, but with specific reference to examining *ourselves and our actions* within the contexts of those new lights, making it 'incumbent upon everyone to exercise more and more reflexivity in increasingly greater tracts of their lives' (Archer, 2007, p. 5).

Proposing the ever-changing 'supercomplexity' of the (real) world to require radical change in the ways in which universities define and achieve their goals for student learning, Ron Barnett proposes a threefold set of pedagogical priorities:

> Firstly, it has to create epistemological and ontological disturbance in the minds and the being of students: it has to pose cognitively and experientially the radical uncertainty presented by supercomplexity. Students have to come to feel in every sense the utter insecurity of the post-modern world. Secondly, higher education has to enable students to live at ease with this perplexing and unsettling environment. Thirdly, it has to enable them to make their own positive contributions to this supercomplex world, while being sensitive to the unpredictability and uncontrollability of the consequences of what they say and do.
>
> (Barnett, 2000)

I suggest that 'utter insecurity' is not a healthy state within which to learn or develop. Nonetheless, as rehearsed in Chapter Two, the diversities our students and graduates encounter, with the intrusions of different and often disturbing ontologies and epistemologies, and discomforting alternative behavioural norms, do indeed make the world at times perplexing and unsettling. Progressing to Barnett's third stage (and as he points out, should we fail our students at the second stage, we would be simply producing voyeurs without agency), relevance to the real world requires curriculum design through which a student regularly *experiences* herself *successfully being herself* among diverse others and their diverse perspectives within her university experience. Lacking experience and confidence in such encounters or lacking critical lenses on self and others will deprive her of the capabilities to make contributions among diverse others, or to view consequences from the perspectives of those others.

Good practice for twenty-first century 'real-world' curriculum development, then, means building a curriculum designed not for the reproduction of established ways of knowing, the performance of established ways of working, or the continuation of established ways of being. Curriculum which is relevant to the real, global and multicultural, world needs to be focussed upon developing global-self capabilities such as being comfortable and confident with:

▷ critically engaging with all current knowledge and behavioural norms;
▷ recognizing all truths to be variable and mutable;
▷ recognizing that 'cutting edge' can be 'dead wood' in less than a decade;
▷ knowing that every significant act has impacts on others, which need to be interrogated from the perspectives of those others; and
▷ being mindful and reflexive, in and for action.

As global-selves, the cognitive capabilities advanced for 'real-world relevance' need to be founded within attitudes and behaviours cultivated among culturally and otherwise diverse others and their worldviews, since it is these which underpin critical engagement in a real world which is multicultural and globalizing. This represents, I think, a significant shift in the way real-world relevance has, under the neo-liberal interpretation adopted by many disciplines and universities, come to be conceptualized. It is also a shift which has a real urgency in emerging post-national universities with their diverse local and global stakeholders. Where engaging with diverse others cannot be readily achieved within a largely mono-cultural or single-gendered (for example) cohort of a specific course or institution, it can be approached through curriculum design involving online contacts, as illustrated in some examples in Section 6.2, and described in Case Study 1, and through embedding international learning and experience within new programme requirements, as in the internationalized STEM (Science, Technology, Engineering, and Mathematics) programme described in Case Study 5.

Above all, in a real world which is rapidly changing and likely to be lived by many of our graduates in diverse locations and cultures, the greatest real-world relevance lies in a curriculum which encourages and enables a student to be willing to assess and revise the truths she holds, including her conceptions of what the good might be. This, of course, is the underpinning of lifelong learning.

The good-practice principle of real-world relevance, then, holds true, but much current good-practice thinking on what that means is entrenched in the development of current (or already defunct) and local work-based skills, rather than in those global-self-based capabilities which enable critical engagement with current ways of doing and ways of being, informed through local and global others, their perspectives and their priorities.

Principle 3 – Meaningful Intended Learning Outcomes

Within current dominant good practice models, intended learning outcomes (ILOs) are *fundamental* to the design and the subsequent delivery and assessment of any university course. Here, we focus on the design principles of ILOs and how they sit within the aspirations for internationalization and equalization set out in this book.

The notion of graduateness, and then of levelness within the stages of the graduate journey, are clearly articulated in many national systems of higher education. They are usually expressed as subject *benchmark statements* (or similar), written into national policy documents, and often also within the expectations and requirements set down by professional bodies and accrediting agencies. Institutional and national quality assurance offices are often very concerned with the interrogation of programme documentation against such expressions of what it means to be 'a successful second-year BSc student in Biology' (for example). As currently formulated, such statements, intended to 'standardize' disciplinary understanding of and requirements for 'graduateness', do not sit comfortably, in very many subjects at least, with the kinds of student- and real-world relevance criteria discussed above. Another significant source for notions of graduateness in some anglophone contexts derives from a long-established taxonomy of educational objectives in the cognitive domain, originally developed by Bloom and colleagues (Bloom, 1956). The fact that experts in curriculum design and benchmarking from these same anglophone contexts have often been consulted to advise on the development of benchmark statements and programme learning outcomes in diverse global contexts means that there has been a significant dispersal of the precepts within these models – a process which is now encroaching on local practice at more levels, as university regulations and national quality assurance requirements demand that international TNE partners and students comply with (typically anglophone) home institution programme specifications. As noted in the opening chapter of this book, the degree to which such processes reflect the homogenizing 'commodification of nothing' (Ritzer, 2004) is something that an internationalizing higher education industry should be reflecting upon.

The fact that Bloom's work on the cognitive domain has had such significant impact may have helped to build a degree of common language for discussing, describing, and agreeing more international notions of graduateness. If so, the neglect of companion taxonomies for the psychomotor (Simpson, 1972) and affective domains (Krathwohl et al., 1964) may at the same time have risked impoverishing some rather more holistic local conceptualizations of the graduate, and of the role that higher education should play in his development. An outcome of efforts to standardize notions of graduateness and align these within the curriculum has brought about a strengthening of focus on those attributes which are visible, measurable, and susceptible to differentiation through valid and reliable assessment mechanisms (Biggs, 1999; Biggs & Tang, 2011). As already alluded to, and re-examined below, this necessarily means a lack of focus upon affective attributes, such as 'willingness to', 'confidence in', 'respect for', or 'intolerance of', for example. Such affective attributes are necessary components in any social justice education (Adams, 2015), and also for any graduate who must make her way in a diverse multicultural and global world. Finding ways to embed their development within the learning experience is necessary work, made more difficult by an outcomes-based educational paradigm.

Capturing what it is which a student is *required* to learn within a finite number of statements is a challenging task, and doing so in ways which are transparent to all stakeholders in the process, *including diverse students locally and internationally,* is doubly complex. In determining the ILOs for a module, good practice guidance would include considering in the process:

▶ what is the content (subject matter) which the ILOs cover?
▶ what does the student have to be able to *do* with this content?
▶ are these two appropriate to the level of study and learning time available?
▶ is the way the learning is set down observable and measurable?
▶ is the way the learning is set down clear and unambiguous?
▶ when set beside the ILOs of other modules – is there sufficient differentiation between modules and coverage across modules?

These general good-practice questions would apply even if the curriculum were being designed for a single student in a single context. However, some modification or extension is needed if they are to be helpful when seeking to build ILOs which are equitable for our diverse learners and diverse contexts:
With regard to my diverse learners in their diverse contexts:

▶ what is the content (subject matter) which the ILOs cover?
  ▶ how is that content represented, valued, relevant to each student?
  ▶ how does that content reflect the values and lived experiences of each student?
  ▶ how is each student enabled to bring his own perspectives and experiences which relate to that content to the table?
▶ what does a student have to be able to *do* with this content?
  ▶ are each of them equally able, and equally accustomed to *doing* that?
  ▶ is this socio-culturally acceptable in his communities?
  ▶ are critical and diverse perspectives on the content encouraged/required?
▶ are these two appropriate to the level of study and learning time available?
  ▶ is each student likely to have the same prior learning, such that levels of study present equitable learning stages?
  ▶ will she have similar skill levels to her peers, such that equal time will be needed on task?
▶ is the way the learning is set down observable and measurable?
  ▶ will each student be equally accustomed to observing and measuring her own performance and that of others with respect to this learning?
  ▶ does the framing of required learning allow for alternative perspectives and experiences to be equitably measured and rewarded?

▶ is the way the learning is set down clear and unambiguous?
  ▶ is it equally clear and unambiguous to each student?
  ▶ do the concepts employed translate across cultures?
  ▶ is the language equally accessible to any student for whom it is not a first language?
▶ when set beside the ILOs of other modules – is there sufficient differentiation between modules and coverage across modules?
  ▶ have we considered any modules studied elsewhere which contribute to the programme?

Within a culturally responsive teaching frame, 'meaningfulness' for *each of the above* would be considered with regard to the integration of 'the cultural knowledge, prior experiences, frames of reference and performance styles of ethnically diverse students' (Saint-Hilaire, 2014, p. 598). In the post-national university, to highlight once more, a student's ethnicity is one among many dimensions to human diversity which needs to find ILOs to be meaningful and equitable.

Good-practice principles require that ILOs are transparent and meaningful to students, showing clearly what they are required to *do* with *what* content. As academics devise ILOs, consideration of how different students may interpret them, relate their own capabilities to them, and find meaning within them needs to be embedded in the design process. Too frequently, ILOs are written for other academics within the same academic tradition – rather than for the diverse students who are responsible for achieving them. This unsatisfactory situation is compounded when students come from diverse sociocultural backgrounds, or speak different first languages, or are studying in international contexts where the tacit knowledge needed to find the *intended meaning* may not be commonly present.

Principle 4 – Alignment across the Curriculum

Aligning curricular objectives set down in ILOs, with the learning experience and the assessment of the learning achieved, has come to be commonly referred to as 'constructive alignment' (Biggs, 2003; Biggs & Tang, 2007), a construct which has become a powerful driver and quality measure for curriculum design in several national contexts.

Significant attention is paid in current learning and teaching literature to this deceptively simple idea that what is set out for a student to learn in a module or course should be what is assessed, and what is assessed should be what is taught. The situation is made more complex than it might at first appear, however, because, as discussed in Chapter Three, learning theory points to learning being something actively constructed by the learner rather than transmitted by the teacher. This constructivist learning paradigm means that an academic is less able to predict what a student may (or may not) learn on a course, since it may, or may not, be the same as what she has 'taught'.

However difficult, it is the job of a university to measure and certificate that a specified package of learning has indeed taken place – so, whatever else may have been learned on the journey, if the curriculum ILOs have been successfully demonstrated, the student can claim to be a graduate of subject x from University Y. Good practice in curriculum design is, in this view, a matter of carefully aligning three components:

(i)   ILOs, which accurately convey what is required;
(ii) learning experiences, which maximize the likelihood that students will construct their learning appropriately; and
(iii) assessments, which enable the *intended* learning to be verified and quantified.

We all, faculty and students, build our learning from what we already know, what our lives have already enabled us to construct. In the post-national university this means that, increasingly, faculty are designing curricula for students whose life experiences are radically different to their own. Constructive alignment means that such students risk not only being faced with content which has limited relevance, but also experiencing learning and assessment mechanisms which do not align to their prior learning or epistemologies. If we are to enable our diverse students' own cultures and histories to create relevance in the curriculum, the alignment process requires that the relevance a student creates is present not only within the learning outcomes but also throughout the learning experience and the assessment process. This requires the global academic to be willing and able to challenge her own frames of reference in order to recognize value in the work presented by a student from a different cultural or biographical perspective.

As already explored, a fully aligned assessment process becomes especially problematic with regard to affective/attitudinal learning, such as 'being willing to', since we can only measure performance within the assessment context, not a willingness to perform beyond that. This makes several of the attributes of global-selfhood and the kinds of social justice outcomes underpinning CRP *impossible to require or to acknowledge through the certificated curriculum*. Curriculum design can, though, create learning activities and assessments which are *aligned to* learning outcomes along the lines of:

> students must develop a broader sociopolitical consciousness that allows them to critique the cultural norms, values, mores, and institutions that produce and maintain social inequities.
>
> (Ladson-Billings, 1995a, p. 162)

The ability to 'critique' is visible and measurable, but a *commitment* to continued engagement in that critique to the betterment of those suffering from social inequities cannot. With appropriately designed and experienced learning activities, though, some of the learning which is constructed *outwith* the assessed curriculum has a stronger chance of being aligned with broader objectives.

Overall, then, curriculum design for graduates in a multicultural and globalizing world can retain the good-practice principles set out above, but needs to re-conceptualize these to match the realities of diverse students and the diverse contexts in which they study and will go on to make their ways as global graduates. The proposed framing of the four principles of relevance to student, relevance to real world, meaningful learning outcomes, and alignment outlined in this section are summarized in Table 5.2.

Table 5.2 Proposals for Making Good Practice Principles for Curriculum Design Appropriate for a Curriculum Which Responds to Student Diversity and Builds towards Global Selfhood

Good-practice principle for curriculum design	Suggested re-conceptualization of this principle to enable diverse students in diverse contexts to graduate as global-selves
The curriculum must be *relevant to the student*	When designing or reviewing the curriculum, faculty need to ensure that majority cultural perspectives do not dominate; meaningful content needs to be drawn from *and critiqued from* varied sources/contexts. Additionally, curriculum design needs to ensure that students have full opportunity to draw upon/integrate/critique from their own cultural perspectives and those of others; these need to be recognized as a valuable addition to the curriculum.
The curriculum must be *relevant to the real world*	'Real worlds' are changing rapidly, and are varied across contexts in terms of the values held dear, the behavioural norms expected, and the priorities for social and professional action. Curriculum for the 'real world' needs to be designed to enable students to live interculturally, to be tolerant of ambiguity and uncertainty, to identify and critique different truths and emerging interpretations from local and global perspectives, and to be mindful and reflexive. These require affective as well as cognitive and behaviour learning.
Learning outcomes must be *meaningful* – i.e. clearly articulated, measurable, appropriate to level, developed with reference to other programme components	Each of these needs to be achieved in ways which are consonant with *relevance* as outlined in the first two principles, *equally achievable* by diverse learners in diverse contexts, presented in language which is *equally understandable* to all learners (including those whose first language may not be English), and allow reward for diverse ways of meaning-making and meaning-showing.

(Continued)

Table 5.2 (Continued)

Good-practice principle for curriculum design	Suggested re-conceptualization of this principle to enable diverse students in diverse contexts to graduate as global-selves
Learning activities and assessment mechanisms should be *constructively aligned* with the intended learning outcomes for the course	This should be rigorously applied, taking into account each of the other principles with regard to cognitive and behavioural outcomes. Recognising the fundamental importance of affective outcomes and constructively aligning *learning activities* and the ways in which they are experienced by diverse students in diverse contexts is critical to the achievement of these un-assessable attributes of the global self.

It is the application of such principles through approaches to pedagogy which give shape to the student learning experience.

▶ 5.4 Pedagogy

This section explores some dominant good-practice principles relating to the 'delivery' of the curriculum, and seeks to elaborate on those principles for a pedagogy of inclusion and globally and culturally relevant learning. Conditions for optimal intercultural learning set out in the first section of this chapter and principles for curriculum design set out above relate to all modes of delivery.

Designing Learning Activities – Voice and Choice

As noted in Chapter Three, in order for our students to learn effectively they need to be engaged in learning experiences which are *appropriately* challenging. Faculty are familiar with structuring the *content* of a course on the basis of anticipated prior knowledge, and the ways in which a student is expected to be able to engage with that content on the basis of their maturity as a learner (as represented by their level of study), but doing so for diverse learners in diverse contexts may challenge this familiarity. The subsequent task of devising and delivering learning *activities* which also provide appropriate and equitable challenge to learners is also more difficult when students and their learning contexts are more diverse.

As post-national universities work with wider cultures in more countries, the many factors which may contribute to how an activity 'fits' a student are un-certificated, less known, and less reliably assumed. As we create learning activities for diverse learners in diverse contexts, specifics of their prior experience of modes of engaging with that knowledge are, similarly, less predictable. Our students are individuals, and the appropriateness of the level of challenge within a learning activity will be different for each of them. Challenge which is too low will not create the kind of 'dilemma' needed to stimulate learning; challenge which is too high will create anxiety and may lead to disengagement, or to 'mis-learning'. An equitable pedagogy approach seeks to create learning activities which enable the individual student to experience an optimal level of challenge for her. Here we explore some of the pedagogical questions this raises for the global academic, drawing particularly on perspectives within CRP. CRP is not without its critics, and has been suggested to replace overt deficit modelling with a more covert process which, nonetheless, positions minority groups as 'other' to the norms of the majority (Schmeichel, 2012). There is a danger that in arguing for higher education pedagogies which are built around the diverse perspectives and priorities of culturally varied students, this book is similarly culpable. However, I see the principles of CRP as very appropriate for higher education within and for a multicultural and globalizing world, while acknowledging the need for vigilance in how those principles translate into practice. Arguably, in moving CRP beyond its origins in racial demarcations of difference to a recognition that we are all diverse in a global world, there is less scope for it to become an alternative mechanism for reproducing existing deficit models of any group.

The foundational principles for CRP are that:

(a) Students must experience academic success; (b) students must develop and/or maintain cultural competence; and (c) students must develop a critical consciousness through which they challenge the status quo of the current social order.

And

The trick of culturally relevant teaching is to get students to 'choose' academic excellence.

(Ladson-Billings, 1995a, p. 160)

Choice framed in these terms is rarely found in dominant good-practice literature on higher education, but is entirely in line with the social constructivist interpretation of learning outlined in Chapter Three. Dominant good-practice literature calls for learning activities which are interactive, experiential, and 'student-centred'. Student-centredness is often misinterpreted (and sometimes misrepresented) to mean simply 'doing what students want'. However, pedagogical approaches which help our students to understand the learning process and their role within it can also help them 'want' more sophisticated modes of participation than they may initially find attractive. Wanting and 'choosing' academic excellence is a transformative move, with additional challenge added when our students hold diverse expectations of how academic excellence is to be interpreted and validated. Reference was made in Chapter Three to academic value differences between China and the UK, and how these might lead to different interpretations of student and faculty behaviours. Following on from this, experience of different academic traditions may similarly impact upon the level of challenge posed by (for example) an interactive, student-centred learning activity. A *deliberate and explicit* focus on the affective and behavioural challenges within the *process* of engaging with a learning activity (as well as the difficulty of the subject matter and the 'level' of cognitive work involved) enhances the likelihood that it will be appropriate for diverse learners. These recommendations for enabling students who prefer more individually oriented learning tasks to derive benefits from the kind of cooperative learning advocated for within a CRP approach are a very clear example of what such a focus on *process* might look like:

> (1) create a climate and ethos of valuing cooperation and community in the classroom that operates at all times, not just when cooperative tasks are performed; (2) start small and phase cooperative learning into instruction gradually on the levels of both frequency and magnitude; (3) allow time and provide opportunities for students and teachers to become comfortable with and skilled at cooperative learning; (4) initially use a combination of individual, small group, and whole-class learning activities; and (5) use multi-tiered task assignments and be very clear in explicating these to students.
>
> Gray (2000, p. 168)

Thompson (2014, p. 5) identifies 15 strategies and perspectives which underpin a non-color-blind orientation in education. Of these, considerations which impact upon pedagogy beyond perspectives already introduced include (my emphasis):

> [The study of anti-racism] must now include multiple examples of oppression. *Addressing* non-race forms of *discrimination must not be done in trivial ways;*
>
> Because it is impossible to cover all [cultural] groups in a ... course, students will need to learn basic social justice principles from a sampling of diversity populations, then *apply the general themes and principles learned to all groups;*

Controversy should not be shunned, but rather embraced. Good learning happens when instructors face problems head on and skilfully address, not avoid, controversy;

The instructor must become adept at *releasing majority group students from historical guilt*, while at the same time recruiting them to become change agents;

Partisan political pandering is viewed as counter-productive to the ultimate goals of a diverse society. Eclectic *collaboration between* political groups and *competing ideologies is highly encouraged.* Common ground can be found;

Student reflection and on-going self-assessment make for a better professional. *Self-analysis is not our enemy.*

How a student is required to behave as part of a planned learning activity can make that activity differentially challenging depending upon his prior experience, and his expectations of how learning activities are performed. This in turn may (i) lead to disengagement and/or mis-learning because the level of challenge is inappropriate, and/or (ii) impact negatively on how he sees value in engaging at all, since the required behaviour does not fit his schema for 'valid learning activities'. Pedagogical approaches involving interactive learning, critical discussion, personalization, and other currently favoured learning activity design features, risk creating unequal learning challenge for diverse students in diverse contexts. This can be ameliorated by a deliberate focus on process and the staged introduction of unfamiliar activity types. This does not imply that, ultimately, learning activities should not embrace challenge, controversial issues, extension from specific examples to more general understandings, and critical self-reflection on a learner's individual responses to diverse others and new perspectives.

As touched upon in Chapter One, much has been written, and disputed (Haggis, 2003; Marshall & Case, 2005), about creating learning experiences which cater for students with different preferred learning styles (of many models, Kolb, 1976 has possibly had the most direct impact on best-practice thinking in higher education). At risk of over-simplification, the basic proposition is that individuals have preferred ways of engaging with new knowledge (preferring, for example, to reflect on it before acting, or to act upon it before reflecting), and, therefore, learning experiences should incorporate activities which allow for engagement in a variety of ways. A different area of theory which attaches to learning styles proposes that individuals have a preferred learning 'channel' – perhaps auditory or visual (see Fleming, 2006 for the popular VARK model). This also supports the provision of a variety of learning activities which will, collectively, provide stimulation across the range of learning channels – and will also thereby cater for diverse preferences while building individual strengths in less preferred channels. It is possible that a student's preferred learning styles and channels are themselves developed in part through the culture(s) in which she has experienced learning (which is to say, through the cultures in which she has experienced life) (Joy & Kolb, 2008; Yamazaki, 2005). To the extent that this is true, the premise that learning activities should offer varied ways of engaging is made *stronger* as the cultural diversity of our student body expands. In summing up her brief review of the applicability of learning styles theory to TNE contexts, O'Mahony (2014, p. 16) concludes that faculty 'need to understand other learning styles without assuming that these are inherently deficient', because through exploring and evaluating what may be unfamiliar approaches to learning among new student populations, an academic can then enhance his practice to better meet the needs of those students. Some evidence points to a correlation between the degree of fit between a student's learning style and an instructor's teaching style and enhanced student performance (Felder & Brent, 2005). With diverse students at home and online, though, finding the best fit within any single teaching style is unlikely, and so avoiding practice which caters to a limited range of learning styles or approaches and being willing to explore and evaluate alternatives are relevant also to faculty working outside TNE contexts.

Although learning-styles theories are contested, and any suggested links between cultural heritage and preferred learning styles must be approached with great care, the principle of providing varied learning activities which require and reward varied modes of performance from our students is fundamental to working with diverse students in diverse contexts. The current dominant best-practice paradigm of interactive, experiential learning activities may serve to disadvantage some students if applied as the predominant approach from the start. Many students may struggle to perform well in such learning activities without planned support and scaffolding over a period of time. This may be even more the case when part of the challenge within the activity relates to working with diverse others for the first time, as rehearsed in Chapter Two.

Another factor which attracts significant emphasis in pedagogy literature is *motivation* within the learning process, with *intrinsic* motivation (a student wants to learn something because she feels its value) being a stronger force than *extrinsic* motivation (a student needs to learn something because others say it has value). And associated with that distinction, it is common to find students being driven primarily or exclusively by the extrinsic motivator of their assessments.

Illeris (2002, p. 74) proposes that the 'dynamic in [any] learning process emanates from the affective, emotional, and motivational patterns' which 'provide the psychological energy for learning'. Ginsberg and Wlodkowski (2009, p. 27) examine motivation from a culturally responsive pedagogy perspective. They argue that *psychological* interpretations of motivation overly dominate the educational literature (and, hence, policy and good practice models); other disciplines, including 'cultural studies, critical race theory, anthropology, religion, philosophy, physics, and biology' also have perspectives to offer, and since dominant psychological perspectives are in any case drawn from Eurocentric assumptions and values, psychology 'provides an incomplete understanding of the many cultural groups that live within the United States'. However, intrinsic motivation remains a key aspect of their interpretation of culturally responsive teaching, and key to this approach is that faculty avoid imposing their interpretation of what such motivation might be, and seek instead to 'elicit, or encourage the learner's natural capacity to make meaning from experience' (op. cit., p. 29). These authors offer a motivational framework based on four conditions as a heuristic upon which faculty might build their teaching strategies. I represent this, along with the reflective question set by the authors with regard to each condition, in Table 5.3. These are proposed as dynamic, interactive, and reciprocal conditions which impact on the learner 'at the moment' within a learning activity and over time across learning activities.

Table 5.3 Conditions and Related Reflective Questions for Intrinsic Motivation within a Culturally Responsive Teaching Model, Adapted from Ginsberg & Wlodkowski (2009, pp. 34, 35 & 40)

Condition	Requires	Reflective Question
Establish inclusion	Norms and practices are woven together to create a learning environment in which learners and teachers feel respected and connected to one another	What do we need to do to feel respected by and connected to one another?
Develop attitude	Norms and practices that create a favourable disposition toward the learning experience through personal relevance and volition	How can we use relevance and volition to create a favourable disposition towards learning?
Enhance meaning	Norms and practices that create challenging and engaging learning experiences that include learners' perspectives and values	How do we create engaging and challenging learning experiences that include learners' perspectives and values?
Engender competence	Norms and practices that help learners understand how they are effectively learning something they value and is of authentic value to their community	How do we create an understanding that we are effectively learning something we value and perceive as authentic to our real world?

Faculty reviewing the reflective questions in Table 5.3, may find it difficult to set aside responses which apply to themselves, but which may not apply to some of their students. So, for example, with regard to the first question, what an individual academic needs to happen *in order to feel respected* may not align with what a particular student needs to happen for her to feel respected. As discussed in Chapters Three and Four, values *may* be common across cultures, but the behaviours through which they are expressed and interpreted are not. As well as pedagogic planning with a mind to process, these questions demand also the kind of mindfulness *within* the learning activity which asks:

▶ Does this student feel respected in this activity?
▶ How do I know?
▶ How can I find out?

In developing students as global-selves within an ethos of mindfulness and reciprocal learning, learning activities also need to engage a student in asking such questions during her real or virtual interactions with diverse others.

In subsequent pages, Ginsberg and Wlodkowski (2009) offer more detailed recommendations relating to each of their four conditions. Many of these are reflective of established good-practice models as discussed in this chapter, for example, the importance of clearly defined goals, fair and clear criteria of evaluation, relevant learning models, challenging learning experiences, or critical inquiry addressing real-world issues. But there are also some significant additions. For example, with regard to *Relevance & Volition*, not only are activities to be contextualized in the learner's experience, but 'the entire academic process' also 'encourages learners to make choices based on their experiences, values, needs, and strengths' (op. cit., p. 44).

With regard to *Engagement and Challenge*, not only are learners to participate in challenging, real-world learning experiences, but also student and teacher 'expression and language' are to be joined 'to form a "third idiom" that enables the perspectives of all learners to be readily shared and included in the process of learning' (op. cit., p. 46).

With regard to *Authenticity and Effectiveness*, not only is the assessment process to be connected to the learner's world, frames of reference, and values, but also how he may demonstrate that learning must include 'multiple ways to represent knowledge and skill' (op. cit., p. 47).

This section has proposed that a pedagogy for diverse students needs to be approached and designed to allow for meaning-making from individual perspectives, and offer students choices about their approach to engagement with the task. Intrinsic motivation and successful experiences can enhance the will and the confidence to engage in potentially challenging encounters with others, and different students will find such motivation in different places. A theme of an *individualized* pedagogy has emerged, in which students have choices and voices; the role of the academic is then to design activities which allow for, recognize, and place value on those choices, and to focus on process and scaffolding to bring students to points of equal engagement. The principles outlined in previous sections of the chapter need to be borne in mind when structuring a learning activity and the conditions within it.

Assessing and Giving Students Feedback

In Chapter One, I proposed that universities can lay no claim to being post-national, international, or global if their programmes lack significant international/multicultural learning; universities cannot know whether or not they do so unless they assess those aspects of their students' performance. Nor will students see their intercultural learning as valued and valuable unless it features in their assessment. As outlined earlier, although in tension with current good practice guidance concerning constructive alignment, the kind of aspirations we have for our graduating students to be global-selves require that we deliberately design learning *activities* with the intention that they will develop positive affective dispositions and capabilities towards diverse others in a multicultural and globalizing world. However, we cannot formally assess that affective learning. We can assess how students *relate* the affective learning they have experienced (for example, through reflective writing and learning logs), but developments in their true *willingness, confidence, resilience, affinity towards,* and so forth are hidden from view. Building *required* assessments which, for example, engage students in examining an issue from diverse perspectives, identifying the impacts of an action on diverse peoples in diverse locations, and critiquing own/dominant perspectives, add considerably to the message that such approaches are valued and valuable. Key good-practice principles for student assessment have been implied in earlier discussions; explicitly, they include:

(i)   what is assessed should be only what is articulated in the ILOs (which have been written for diverse students in diverse contexts);
(ii) assessment should include a varied range of performance types, creating opportunities which cater to different individual areas of strength; students, like faculty, may need support if they are to *believe* in the validity of some assessment performance requirements;

(iii) opportunities for students to become familiar with performance expectations need to be planned into their learning activities; this should include formative tasks upon which they receive feedback;

(iv) assessment should be made against explicit and transparent criteria, which are shared with students;

(v) creating 'explicit and transparent' criteria requires conscious attention to the linguistic and cultural capabilities and experiences of students, and needs to enable students to demonstrate achievement in ways which resonate with their own 'real worlds';

(vi) assessments should cover learning in the cognitive and behavioural domains, and be framed to demonstrate support for aspirational affective learning, even though this cannot be formally assessed.

There are varied opinions on the merits of anonymously marking assessed work, but evidence does generally indicate that where a range of information about the student is known (e.g. gender, ethnicity, performance on a previous task, physical appearance), unconscious bias can lead to work from those students being under- or over-graded (Malouff et al., 2014). Just as we should not imagine universities to be 'immune from institutional racism' (Singh, 2011), nor are they free from sexism or homophobia. This suggests that, where feasible given the nature of the assessment task and the cohort, whatever reasonable steps can be taken to facilitate anonymous grading should be taken to help equalize the assessment process. Beyond this, raising faculty awareness, and thence mindfulness within their grading process, might help alleviate bias in either direction.

For students, in the space between engaging in learning activities and undertaking formal assessments lies the experience of receiving feedback on their performance. Feedback which enables a student to enhance her work prior to summative assessment is presented in good-practice literature as facilitating learning, and as such it is part of the 'teaching' process. Many would suggest that feedback on summatively assessed work which does not enable a student to enhance her future work is something of a waste of everybody's time, though it may be very common practice. Dominant good-practice thinking would say that *all* feedback should offer a student opportunities to improve his future performance. If feedback on his summative work is based upon clear and transparent criteria, it should at the very least help him to relate his own performance to published criteria. Being better able to do so because of his experience with the current piece of assessed work should then support him in the same process (even with different criteria) prior to submitting his next piece of work.

The impact which success or failure within one activity can have upon a student's attitudes towards future engagement with similar activities is an important dimension to learning. There have been repeated references through early chapters to 'successful engagement in intercultural encounters', or similar. By witnessing himself being successful in an activity, a student can experience a powerful growth in his *self-efficacy* (Bandura, 1997), broadly his self-identification that 'I am a person who can do this'. A student who sees himself as someone who *has* successfully engaged in learning activities among diverse peers develops enhanced motivation to do so again because of its influence on his self-efficacy model for that activity – the reverse being the case if he sees himself as someone who has *unsuccessfully* done so. It is also possible that seeing others who he identifies as being 'similar to me' successfully engaging in a particular activity will enhance his own self-efficacy. Although a student will employ a range of mechanisms through which he judges his 'success or failure', feedback from his tutor is a deliberate educational intervention which carries significant weight, if done 'well'. Feedback which fails to give value to successful engagement with others, with other perspectives, with critiquing own perspectives, and so forth risks driving students to the safer world of established peers and world views. This relationship between engagement, feedback, and self-efficacy emphasizes the importance of providing students with feedback on intercultural learning activities through which they can recognize successes which will motivate future intercultural interactions. The absence of recognition within feedback may cause students to see positive performance as being irrelevant, lacking any academic value. This may reduce motivation to try again or go further in future, and the student loses valuable opportunities to extend intercultural self-efficacy. Low intercultural self-efficacy may then lead to disengagement with opportunities for intercultural learning which arise outside as well as inside the formal learning environment.

Time and resources are required for the best application of good-practice *principles* for feedback to inform student performance, which advocate at least four significant factors:

(i)   the existence of clearly articulated and available assessment criteria for each piece of assessed work;
(ii) faculty regularly making explicit and helpful reference to those criteria in their feedback;
(iii) providing feedback at a time and in a format which is most useful to the student; and
(iv) students being willing and able to engage with their feedback and the criteria.

With increasingly diverse students and diverse faculty, there are added complexities to each of these:

(i) *the existence of clearly articulated and available assessment criteria for each piece of assessed work* is made significantly more difficult to achieve when students and faculty have a range of first languages and competences in the language of instruction; criteria may be devised which reflect dominant culture perspectives on what constitutes good academic discourse, even where this is not an explicit requirement within any ILOs or support in achieving this;

(ii) *faculty regularly making explicit and helpful reference to those criteria in their feedback* may be confined to a familiar formula which has worked with previously less-diverse cohorts, and shaped by conventions within the academic traditions they have experienced as learners;

(iii) *providing feedback at a time and in a format which is most useful to the student* is technically more difficult when students are more dispersed, and the process may require communications between dispersed faculty, and requires faculty to be willing and *able* to deliver feedback in a variety of formats; and

(iv) *students being willing and able to engage with their feedback and the criteria* may, again, be constrained by lack of familiarity with this approach depending upon the academic traditions they are most familiar with, and it is likely that most will benefit from *learning* about how to engage with feedback as part of their programme of study.

As in other areas of pedagogy, different students will find different feedback mechanisms more meaningful and conducive to their learning. Feedback in writing may be more accessible to one student, his peers may find the more personal experience of oral feedback more helpful. The greater intimacy of face-to-face feedback may be intimidating to one student, while conveying, instead, empathy and support to others. Providing a range of feedback approaches across a semester is one approach to equalizing the learning value which diverse students derive from the process. Offering student choices, where this is administratively feasible, would be another. However, as with other aspects of pedagogy, a student who only experiences feedback mechanisms which are in alignment with what she currently prefers is being given limited opportunity to develop her broader capabilities (in this case, capabilities in receiving and responding to a range of feedback approaches which might be part of how she experiences her life as a graduate in a multicultural and globalizing world). Feedback should facilitate learning about successfully engaging in the learning *process* as well as about the specific performance at which it is directed.

▶ 5.5 Non-formal Curricula

Because this is a book principally directed at the academic community, attention is focussed on formal curriculum and pedagogy, but, given the continuous and incidental nature of much learning, as explored in Chapter Three, impacts of the hidden and extended curricula which surround it impact upon planned, mainstream learning and teaching activities and experiences.

The hidden curriculum (Giroux & Purpel, 1983), with its 'incidental lessons … about power and authority and about what and whose knowledge is valued and not valued' (Leask & Carroll, 2011, p. 652) often fails to feature in internationalization literature, despite its very obvious relevance to the often challenging 'foreign' environments within which diverse international students on our campuses and in our online provision experience their learning. Within multicultural education, the hidden curriculum has tended to be much more fully acknowledged, relating as it does to structural inequalities, wider social representations of, and discriminations against, minority groups. By way of illustration only, I include below some brief examples of university actions, beyond those of the formal curriculum, which can impact on student learning gain.

Research among home and international students in the UK cites a range of campus-based events and societies designed to promote inclusion of international students, with 'the general consensus' among participants being that:

> whilst building cohesion among and between groups of international students such arrangements served to '…separate the international students from the home students…' and celebrations of culture could be '…counter-productive…' if not accompanied by events which addressed the common ground between home and international students.
>
> (Caruana & Ploner, 2010, p. 85)

One university's proud identification with, and celebrations of, its 'tradition' were seen by its Black students to be 'based in Whiteness', with traditions relating to the experiences of Black students being 'largely ignored in the everyday life of the institution', contributing to Black students experiencing 'alienation and isolation' (Bourke, 2010, pp. 128 & 129).

Individual intimate intercultural pairings in friendships, dating relationships, and roommate situations have been found to have *the most substantial* contact effects (Sidanius et al., 2008). Such relationships can reduce prejudice towards *and beyond* the groups directly represented within the pairings. Summarizing research specifically investigating mixed-race rooming among university undergraduates in the USA, Sorensen et al. (2009, pp. 10 & 11) highlight the differential impacts of mixed- and same-race student accommodation arrangements, with cited research suggesting positive and negative effects of mixed-race arrangements from both groups:

Positive:

▶ more positive attitudes toward various ethnic groups;
▶ less symbolic racism;
▶ more heterogeneous friendship groups;
▶ reduction in intergroup anxiety;
▶ reduction in automatically activated (implicit) prejudice;
▶ more positive attitudes toward affirmative action;
▶ greater comfort with minorities several years later; and
▶ African Americans showing higher GPAs after the first academic quarter.

Negative:

▶ White students spend less time with, are less satisfied with, spend less time in shared activities with their roommate;
▶ White students interact less across networks; and
▶ roommate relationships are less likely to remain intact a semester and a year later.

Students in many countries, of course, do not share rooms at all, so are denied opportunities to experience the intense roommate contact which such arrangements afford. However, these studies point to the potential value (and risk) of establishing student residence arrangements in which intercultural contact is as intimate as possible, something which runs against policy in some institutions. An Australian study (Nesdale & Todd, 2000) among international and domestic students in halls of residence also suggests that when universities engineer planned interventions to encourage intercultural mixing within accommodation spaces, these positively impact on the learning gain.

The 'extended' or 'co-curricular' opportunities which might be available to students also impact on their intercultural learning. Most obviously, these include study, work, and volunteering abroad or, as in the 'internationalization at home' model, in different local social or cultural communities. One hidden curriculum message conveyed by universities setting up international and multicultural experience opportunities for students as optional and extracurricular is '*if intercultural learning is to take place, it is to take place "out there'"*, beyond standard campus spaces and disciplinary learning environments. This seems to present a double jeopardy for the, still vast majority of, students who do not participate in such activities – since it offers their programme and module designers the opportunity to escape responsibility for building such learning into their subject-based design, delivery, and assessment; it also tells students that such learning, anyway, is not something of significance to their disciplinary studies. Elective courses in diversity offered by multicultural education centres may send similar messages. While not intentional, all transformative extended curricular activities, which are in reality open only to a minority, represent an infringement of academic equity.

Where international mobility and volunteering activities, community-based activities, and diversity courses are fully integrated with the formal curriculum (by which I mean they are a required and credit-bearing component) – such as in 'service learning' or course-mandated work placements (for example, Case Study 5 in Chapter Six) – then they are part of the formal rather than the extended curriculum, and issues explored in this chapter with regard to how that curriculum, pedagogy, and assessments are framed and experienced apply to their design and delivery also.

▶ 5.6 Faculty Development

The emerging milieu of the post-national university is having 'profound implications on academic identities and roles of teachers' (Kosmützky & Putty, 2016, p. 18, as identified through their extensive literature review). Dealing with these requires cognitive, behavioural, and affective capabilities, and the reactions to engaging with this kind of work may include emotional distress and denial. Australian faculty working in TNE contexts were quoted as feeling 'scared', knowing 'absolutely nothing, not even basic stuff', and being 'terrified I wouldn't be good enough' (quotes from Australian faculty respondents, extracted from Hoare, 2013, p. 4). UK faculty discussing the value of equality and diversity training asked, '[w]hen there is no problem, why waste your time showing there is no problem? We have work to do', and called it 'a distraction for intelligent people from work of value' (quotes from UK faculty respondents, extracted from Nightingale et al., 2015), and faculty in another UK study spoke of '"other staff" being unwilling to discuss issues around ethnic minority students, either for reasons of "political correctness" or for fear of "saying the wrong thing"' (Stevenson, 2012, p. 8). Perhaps surprisingly, given the *idea* of universities as liberal spaces dedicated to learning, faculty development in these areas may need to begin with work to 'out' the issues and to establish spaces in which academics feel secure to explore them openly.

Good teaching in any context with any group of students needs to be framed with regard to the intended outcomes, the particular students, and the learning environment and resources available to support them, so it might be concluded that an academic's professional development need not be any different just because she is teaching more diverse students or in more diverse contexts. Egege and Kutielah (2004) argue that setting out to teach in culturally appropriate ways in different contexts is 'incoherent and theoretically flawed', since (i) there is diversity within learner populations everywhere, (ii) sound practice principles should be transferrable, (iii) it is beyond the capabilities of faculty to do so, and (iv):

> Students are empowered by new ways of teaching and exposure to this kind of academic difference. It is part of the international transformative experience they desire.
>
> (op. cit., p. 76)

On my reading, this seems to rather miss several points, each of which has been raised several times already:

▶ Yes – student diversities of many kinds exists in many contexts – and this is an argument *for* faculty engaging with culturally appropriate pedagogies in all contexts, but cultural appropriateness will manifest differently in different contexts;
▶ Yes – sound practice principles should be transferrable – but principles developed as 'good practice' in one context may not be 'sound' when transferred, and faculty being enabled to re-examine them for *these students in this context* can lead to sounder principles;
▶ Yes – the task may be beyond the capability of faculty – but that is a clarion call for faculty development not a reason to indulge poor practice; and
▶ Yes – students are empowered by new ways of teaching – but (i) when faculty expect one student to sink or swim amidst new ways while another can coast because those ways are familiar to her, this is inequitable, and (ii) where faculty allow some students to coast, they are denied the same empowerment as those who do manage to swim in a new milieu (the authors do not say, by the way, whether they advocate transferring *culturally inappropriate* teaching into their Australian classrooms to present their domestic students with similar transformative opportunity).

In the field of CRP, the focus is predominantly upon ensuring relevance to racial minorities, and transferring from that, perhaps, lies a presumption that it is White faculty who have the most work to do. However, recognizing the complex diversities among her own learners, Saint-Hilaire (2014, pp. 598–600) sought to advance her own professional development so as to 'figure out how a Black educator from the Caribbean' could best teach and support the learning of her diverse, including White, students. From her own learning journey, she was able to conclude that 'every teacher, regardless of race and culture' required development (and resources) if they were to be able to enact culturally relevant instruction. This discussion, then, relates to the development of all faculty, regardless of ethnicity, gender, or disability. This is particularly relevant to note with regard to TNE work because much of what has been written for that context has tended to focus either on intercultural work for 'home' institution faculty, or within a deficit model of faculty in the 'overseas' institution. However, as Wang (2008, p. 64) concluded following research among Chinese educational leaders undertaking an Australian Master's programme in China:

> it is inappropriate for Western academics to regard themselves as the privileged holders of Western ideas who can impose radical prescriptions for the situations of developing countries. It is advisable that they be flexible reflectors, ready to cater to the needs of learners from different cultures, and critical helpers of their capacity building. It is therefore important for them to develop their intercultural competence and intercultural learning. They should endeavour to respect and value the knowledge that their students have, and construct the course as a reciprocal learning situation.

Research focussed on Western (Australian) faculty responsible for coordinating and teaching on a new offshore programme in Singapore concludes that 'the personal and pedagogical adaptation required of academics is significant' (Hoare, 2013, p. 2). Hoare notes that TNE arrangements usually require a 'steep learning curve' which is 'likely to intensify personal, professional and ethical challenges for individual academics' (op. cit., p. 1). Institutions need to look carefully at the specifics of their TNE arrangements regarding pre-engagement support for *all* faculty involved – after all, faculty in the TNE partner institution overseas are also being asked to work interculturally across the curriculum.

An Australian 'good practice' guide for 'offshore delivery' (IEAA, 2008, p. 64) proposes that:

> Offshore pedagogies should relate to the culture of the student rather than to the teacher. If a student cohort is disadvantaged by a teacher's methods, choice of language, pace of speech or cultural frame of reference, no

one is learning. Student-centred teaching offshore will require strategies different from those used teaching onshore. International students and 'their' educational traditions are not the problem.

Certainly, students' traditions are not to be framed as the problem, but nor should those of the travelling academic. Global higher education demands a reciprocal approach to the development of the practices of learning and teaching. Good practice develops offshore, onshore, or online, through being subjected to ongoing review. It may be that even the best thought-through approach needs changing, or it may be that more needs to be done to help students to engage with the approach. Faculty development directed at facilitating learning among diverse students, colleagues, and contexts in the emerging global and differently multicultural higher educa-tion landscape needs to focus on strategies for *establishing* what may be best practice – strategies which need to include engaging the expertise of colleagues and students.

Much of what follows in this section concerns how academic staff might enhance their own practice for changing contexts of practice, but such work must be supported by their institutions and professional organizations. Development requires guidance and appropriate resources, including the time to reflect, enhance, and evaluate, and an internal culture reflective of a learning organization. The risks of inadequate development in TNE contexts include putting unwarranted stress on the academic, inappropriate teach-ing strategies and relationship-building with students, and institutional reputational damage through culturally inappropriate behaviours when among colleagues or when within the wider community. Similar conse-quences apply if working ineffectively with minority students on home cam-puses; if faculty lack the confidence or the capabilities to protect students from discrimination and harassment, for example, not only is the institution at risk of failing in its legal responsibilities, but academic staff again suffer increased stress and become 'vulnerable to complaint' (Nightingale et al., 2015, p. 1).

Working in new contexts or with diverse students are in themselves spaces for personal professional development if approached with openness. A UK academic's experiences teaching in Zambia led her to recognize opportuni-ties for faculty to 'critically reflect on their assumptions about learning and teaching': working in unfamiliar contexts 'compels us to reconsider what is familiar and come up with new ideas [and] to challenge ourselves and reconsider the academic rules and conventions with which we have grown comfortable. We need to embark on a journey of uncertainty' (Whittaker,

2008, p. 99). Embarking on such a journey may benefit from explicit strate-gies and a community of fellow travellers, as explored below.

Leask (2008b, p. 124) identifies three strategies for teachers embarking on work in TNE contexts, which I reproduce below with my own text in brackets to indicate that these same strategies are appropriate, also, to faculty working with diverse students at home or online:

- ▶ Develop your own international [and multicultural] perspectives through engagement with international [and culturally diverse] contacts in the professional area, including some in the transna-tional [and multicultural] contexts in which you teach. This might include shared planning of curriculum and teaching and learning activities as well as joint projects.
- ▶ Become informed on international [and multicultural] issues, stand-ards and practices in the discipline/professional field and how they are interpreted and enacted in the transnational environments [and multicultural communities] in which you teach. You might, for example, source and read journal articles written by academic staff working in the transnational [and culturally diverse] context.
- ▶ Seek out and incorporate into the course a range of international as well as local examples and perspectives from the transnational [or multicultural local] contexts in which you teach ... Examples are often available in the local media and from local staff.

The intercultural conversations with colleagues which underpin Leask's recommendations need to be enacted in ways which validate everybody's professional expertise and help to equalize everybody's status – something reportedly frequently lacking in both TNE contexts and among diverse fac-ulty and student services colleagues in local contexts, but also something which is emerging among practitioners on the ground, as several case studies presented in Chapter Six illustrate. The kind of reciprocal learning involved, gaining the requisite cultural understandings, 'can take years to develop' and needs to be based in '[c]andid discussions among stake-holders on both ends of the partnership – both *before the program is launched*, and on an ongoing basis' if they are to establish 'mutually acceptable solutions' (ACE, 2015, p. 21, emphasis added). As within student-student intercul-tural dialogue, 'candid' discussion means respectful, listening, and mindful conversations among equals. Such conversations might be conceived of as taking place within *intercultural* communities of practice (iCOPs) (Lave & Wenger, 1998; Wenger, 1998). If so modelled, the criteria set down for effective intergroup contact in Section 5.2 of this chapter are reflected in the characteristics of iCOPs in TNE contexts. Keay et al. (2014, p. 265) set out three principles for such work, in summary:

▶ *Joint enterprise* – coming together around a common goal with every-body's commitment and competence 'acknowledged and celebrated as well as enhanced';
▶ *Mutual engagement* – partnership working, joint activity, shared responsibility for communication and mutual support, and including 'the proactive participation of all parties, including senior management, teaching and administrative staff, and students'; and
▶ *Shared repertoire* – creating and sharing 'contextually appropriate' practices resources and practice through collaboratively interaction.

Others have also identified that for professional development in TNE contexts to be effective, it must be 'collaboratively designed and negotiated' and that stronger connection between faculty 'extends their capacity to create collaborative learning spaces amongst students studying in diverse cultural contexts, different places and shared cyberspaces' (Keevers et al., 2014, p. 233).

Some authors propose building iCOPs so that teachers *and students* in TNE contexts 'become partners in intercultural construction' Wang (2008, p. 59). UK faculty enabling students in Malaysia to create relevance in their postgraduate certificate, although admitting to difficulties in collaboration arising from pre-established prestige differentials, note the significant value of the 'interface between cultures, contexts and practices' in advancing understanding 'of how learners learn and teachers teach in the global village universities are helping to create' (Davidson & Scudamore, 2008, p. 118). Mitchell notes the power of student-faculty research partnerships in Qatar to 'alleviate concerns about the power imbalance' associated with TNE working. Through moving towards 'a partnership model of knowledge creation and dissemination in tandem with the local population', foreign faculty deficiencies were overcome and a 'contextually relevant, culturally sensitive, and accurately translated survey instrument' was produced (Mitchell, 2014, pp. 74, 80, 84).

Key to faculty development, then, is collaborative working and reciprocal learning among faculty and students across national and cultural boundaries. Faculty development is a continuous process, based upon evidence from practice, reflection, peers, students, and 'experts'. There are few 'Western' faculty development experts yet in best practice within TNE contexts, perhaps partly because relevant expertise from diversity education seems to have gained little traction in much 'mainstream' development activity. Expertise is to be found, though, among those faculty who have been doing the job, on the ground, with diverse students in diverse contexts, be they TNE colleagues or multicultural educators. Our diverse students also carry expert perspectives – their participation in collaborative learning with faculty resonates well with precepts for culturally relevant pedagogies. Building iCOPs for global higher education begins with conversations, and because these conversations take place among culturally diverse individuals, the resistances, the inhibitors, and the communication glitches which have been discussed throughout this book with respect to students also pertain in the spaces where diverse faculty meet.

Personal professional development in conversations among diverse peers and students requires, also, engagement in reflection upon experiences, responses, impacts, and so forth. A global academic's reflection on her practice needs to include a specific focus upon how effectively she is enabling the learning of the diverse learners she meets in the diverse contexts in which she works. This, in turn, requires her to become aware of how her own background and identity find expression in her practice and 'to recognise [her] affinities and prejudices and consider how they affect students' experiences of [her] course' (ECU, 2013a, p. 3). In her guide to practice on Teaching for Inclusion in Higher Education, Griffiths begins with 'reflection', before elaborating a further 13 strategies to assist academics to foster inclusive learning; the faculty development aspects of these include examining own values and beliefs, using feedback and peer observation, and listening carefully (Griffiths, 2010).

Hoare (2013, p. 11) offers a list of possible reflective questions to help faculty develop their own cultural self-awareness, reproduced below (adaptations of which might provide good discussion points for students):

- ▶ What do I value?
- ▶ Why do I value that?
- ▶ How might my culture and norms have contributed to that value?
- ▶ How might x (whatever I am considering) translate into another cultural context?
- ▶ In awareness of the preceding, what can, or should, I do differently?
- ▶ How can I adapt my:
  - ▶ expectations of students
  - ▶ questioning techniques
  - ▶ group processes
  - ▶ flexibility, and my understanding of what flexibility means?
- ▶ What can I do to ensure that I remain in a state of awareness of my own cultural biases and those of the students?

▶ What is a culturally responsible (e.g., realistic, ethical, unburdened by my own socialisation) expectation in terms of 'genuine dialogue'?

▶ How can I encourage my students to consciously join with me in this intercultural learning?

This section has suggested that faculty development needs to focus on establishing what good practice looks like for international and intercultural teaching, that the spaces of the post-national university are rich places for exploring such practice, that conversations and reciprocal learning among peers and students are the appropriate mechanisms for such exploration, and that openness and reflection are necessary for the development of new practice. Specific areas for individual faculty development to enable iCOPs to develop and for these processes to take place will vary across individuals, but may include:

▶ Becoming more open to alternative perspectives and norms;

▶ Becoming more willing to suspend judgement;

▶ Becoming better able to take critical global perspective on personal, professional and disciplinary norms and activities;

▶ Enhancing emotional recognition and resilience;

▶ Enhancing tolerance of ambiguity and uncertainty;

▶ Becoming more fluent in intercultural communication strategies;

▶ Developing greater capabilities in using English as a lingua franca/ international language; and, perhaps above all,

▶ Becoming more mindful.

Faculty development can significantly enhance equalized internationalized learning. It is also work which can be progressed despite any deficiencies in wider institutional practices, priorities, or resourcing; despite wider structural inequalities across the diverse societies in which we and our students live, and despite any neo-liberal assaults on higher education. However, provision of support, guidance, and appropriate development for locally and globally diverse faculty requires leaders who are willing to raise it on institutional agendas, and who are capable of delivering it; 'culturally responsive leadership' (Santamaria & Santamaria, 2016) is as necessary for faculty development as appropriate learning and teaching approaches are for students. Capabilities for international and intercultural teaching reach deep into each academic's identity, whoever she is and wherever she is, and span all dimensions of her learning. The complexity of faculty development and support involved in her journey highlights the unsuitability of any approach which is ad hoc, peripheral, or couched as human resources 'training', as well as the need for faculty development programmes to be designed in full partnership with those with expertise in the multicultural classroom and in the transnational classroom.

▶ 5.7 Chapter Summary

This chapter has explored practice for internationalizing and equalizing the learning experience to enhance positive learning gain across our students. It has drawn upon the theoretical, ethical, and experiential perspectives from internationalization and diversity education discussed in earlier chapters. Criteria have been posited, and in some contexts extensively researched, for optimizing opportunities for learning gain within intercultural learning experiences and environments, with 'equality' being the most important, but not the only one. With these in mind, it has considered 'good practice' perspectives on curriculum design and pedagogy, suggesting where these might be adjusted for the emergence of the post-national university and the aspirations for our graduates. In brief, curriculum, learning activities, feedback approaches, and assessment mechanisms need to be designed *with detailed, conscious reference to:*

- ▶ creating conditions of equality, cooperation, common goal orientation, and authority support, as set out in Intergroup Contact Theory;
- ▶ reducing any anxieties students may have about intergroup contact;
- ▶ establishing an ethos of reciprocity;
- ▶ enabling individual meaning-making, and validating those meanings;
- ▶ incorporating content from diverse cultures, perspectives, and social contexts;
- ▶ developing critical approaches to engaging with all content, and requiring critiques of content from diverse perspectives;
- ▶ supporting and validating the development of necessary affective learning, even though absent from ILOs and formal assessments;
- ▶ building confidence and abilities for interactive learning through a phased introduction of challenge and with tasks which allow choices through 'multi-tiered' design;
- ▶ supporting engagement across a variety of learning styles and learning channel preferences;
- ▶ recognizing the importance of intrinsic motivation, and understanding that students may find their motivation in different places and display their motivation in different ways;
- ▶ facilitating learner choice which builds from their experience and their values;

▶ utilizing and developing communication styles and strategies which are equally accessible to all students; and

▶ developing own capabilities to recognize alternative ways in which students may be demonstrating their learning.

The final section on faculty development has suggested that each academic needs to take a mindful and critically reflective approach towards her own capabilities and influences when working with diverse students in diverse contexts. Institutions, through the planned provision of appropriate resources and faculty development, can carry out their responsibilities to support her in advancing those capabilities. As proposed for all aspects of intercultural learning, conversation, critical reflection, and building communities across cultures, among faculty and students, are advocated to be the most productive spaces for reciprocal learning to take place.

6 Global Grounded Practice

▶ **6.1 Chapter Introduction**

Different perspectives explored in previous chapters have built towards a pedagogical approach for the emerging post-national university which seeks to be:

▶ more inclusive and appropriate for students from diverse backgrounds studying in diverse contexts, and
▶ more effective in developing students-as-graduates for a multicultural and globalizing world.

Intercultural learning activities in which diverse perspectives are presented and critiqued have been proposed as the ideal spaces for such inclusive and appropriately developmental pedagogies. Where groups or cohorts are somewhat homogeneous, the challenge when planning learning activities is to find ways in which diverse issues and perspectives can be 'made live' to students, and their own perspectives can be recognized as challengeable and, indeed, challenged by others. The era of globalization is providing enabling technologies through which this might be achieved.

The first section of this chapter cites examples of ongoing, and often small-scale, developments to pedagogy, of research within multicultural and transnational learning spaces, and of guidelines drawn up to support those working within such spaces. These offer brief illustrations of approaches which resonate with discussions in earlier chapters, and are included here to ground those discussions and provide ideas which might be of help when thinking about changes to current practice. Reflective questions are offered for each of the illustrated areas.

The concluding section is devoted to case studies kindly submitted for this volume. Aspects of these have been referenced at relevant points throughout the book because each of the cases, whatever its principal focus, illustrates a variety of aspects of internationalization and equalization. None of the authors would wish to claim the work they present is complete, or perfect, or a blueprint for others. However, each case describes both issues and 'solutions' which are relevant to other learning environments, overseas, online, or at home. I thank each contributor for taking the trouble, and the risk, to include them. While they all speak for themselves, I have added a few reflective questions prompted by each case study.

▶ 6.2 Illustrative Examples

This section offers illustrative examples of culturally inclusive and relevant pedagogies being taken forward in practice. They are addressed through four themes which apply across different types of learning activity:

- ▶ Establishing an inclusive learning culture;
- ▶ Embedding global-self outcomes;
- ▶ Engaging diverse voices; and
- ▶ Enabling intercultural interactions.

Within many of the sources cited below, further examples and perspectives can be found. The selected examples are not intended to be representative, nor are they necessarily offered as *exemplars,* or as tips or techniques to be *adopted.* Rather, they provide varied examples of good practice *in practice* to be approached as ideas upon which to reflect. Some may work in your learning spaces with your students, some will not. Some may work this semester, and fail next.

Establishing an Inclusive Learning Culture

Establishing an inclusive, safe, and expansive culture for intercultural working and multicultural learning is the most important condition for the kind of collaborative, reciprocal, and, at times, vulnerable work of the global student.

Building such a culture from the very start of a student's university journey is important, and while this cannot be achieved only through 'welcome' or 'induction' sessions, what a student experiences in the early days of his university life is likely to have lasting impact.

A case study from the University of the Liberal Arts Bangladesh (contributed by Haque, Roberts and Shoesmith to Brown, 2014, pp. 28–30) shows how orientation activities, as part of a wider process, have been framed to enable students to begin to transition to more student-centred approaches (away from the dominant local 'teacher-as-guru' paradigm):

> Sessions are interspersed with games designed to encourage participation and communication, mingling groups of people from disparate backgrounds … [and] … a number of other university-wide activities designed

to engage the student, encourage self-confidence and collaboration, and motivate them to take leadership roles.

(op. cit., p. 29)

A comprehensive guide for enhancing domestic:international student inter-actions includes suggestions for group-forming tasks which get students to explicitly explore together the 'challenges we might have working together' (UKCISA, 2009, p. 3). The materials to support the activity include examples to highlight the relevance of intercultural working, and others to show that it is not an easy task. There are also several scenario tasks in the same guide to prompt further reflection and discussion on what might go wrong and why. Bringing the topic to attention rather than, as often, pretending it does not exist can be liberating in itself and gives voice to the concerns of everybody rather than only majority students.

Reflective question: To what extent are your induction processes designed to deliberately encourage 'mingling groups of people from disparate backgrounds' and encourage 'collaboration'?

Reflective question: Do you take steps to explicitly enable all students to voice and discuss issues which might arise across group members before groups begin to work on a task?

Following through from induction and group formation, it is important to continue to support the process of collaboration and group working, which requires, '[faculty] making clear to their students that mixing with other students is a necessary and normal part of their study' (HEA, 2014c, p. 3). 'Making clear' does not happen simply by 'announcing' this to be the expectation; it needs re-enforcement – challenging students when it is not happening, recognizing when it is by '[r]ebalancing the value of process and product' such that it 'encourages students to see their *efforts* at "mixing" as worthwhile and valuable' (op. cit., p. 5, emphasis added), and by faculty modelling and being explicit about their own collaborative and reciprocal engagement among diverse colleagues and students.

The following good-practice recommendations, extracted from a study among Canadian faculty (Bond et al., 2003, p. 11), are particularly relevant for early encounters:

- ► Find out how many students have lived or worked abroad, and where;
- ► Make it known in your course outline and in your first meeting with your students that you invite them to contribute their ideas and experience;

▶ Describe your own experiences in living and working in different cultures;
▶ Tell your students about yourself, including your cultural heritage;
▶ Disclose in your course outline what you believe about respect, diversity and inclusivity.

Bond et al. (op. cit.) also recommend:

▶ Ask students what teaching strategy seems to work for them;
▶ Discuss with students your choice(s) of teaching strategies and your reasons for making the choices.

Reflective question: Are students on your course rewarded or challenged for the ways in which they engage with peers from different backgrounds?

Reflective question: How do you make it explicit to your students that the perspectives of all are valued and valuable, and that international and intercultural experience provide valued sources of global knowledge?

Reflective question: Do you devote time to discussing teaching strategies with your students, and how prepared would you be to modify your own approach to match their preferences? Would this be different if teaching overseas or with multicultural or international cohorts at home? If so, why?

As students progress into working with peers in their modules, continued explicit focus on intercultural grouping and processes is needed. An Australian study (Arkoudis et al., 2013, p. 12) into interactions between domestic and international students noted that in establishing environments which are conducive to interaction, it is important to create effective interaction conditions, and:

▶ Purposefully generate situations, within learning and teaching activities that require students to interact;
▶ Actively encourage students to move out of their established groups; and
▶ Support students to develop the confidence in interacting with other peers from diverse cultural and linguistic backgrounds.

An engineering lecturer is cited in the same report as structuring his course such that small-group problem-solving is required from the start, and then throughout, his course. The report writers note that:

Because students are instructed to form groups on the basis of a diverse set of skills and experiences, the objective and the logic behind interaction are made explicit. And, importantly, because groups are formed at course commencement and continued throughout the course, interaction becomes a core component of the curriculum.

(Arkoudis et al., 2013, p. 11)

Reflective question: In what ways do you deliberately seek to formulate or reformulate student groups which are diverse in nature, and which require interaction across all group members?

Much has been said about *language* within intercultural communication, but it is worth repeating that the words and phrases used need ongoing mindful attention. The ways in which language use is approached by faculty and students, particularly those for whom the dominant language and the language of instruction matches their own, are significant for establishing an inclusive culture, and are also important in the development of attributes for living within multilingual local and global contexts. How faculty and students exhibit inclusive language is, as discussed in the previous chapter, in part about mindfulness within spoken interactions, but it is also about *planning* so that key words, disciplinary jargon, and the like are not just glossed over. Recommendations for helping students understand the language faculty introduce include (adapted from HEA, 2014b; Scudamore, 2013):

- ▶ provide a written glossary of new terms and refer to it in lectures;
- ▶ write new terms, acronyms and abbreviations on the board/slides and point them out when you first use them;
- ▶ explain new words and concepts in several ways;
- ▶ use simple and complex terminology to help students build specialist subject language;
- ▶ listen to yourself and explain idiomatic language – terms such as 'shelf life' and 'reading up';
- ▶ plan sessions to allow time for reading new material before discussions;
- ▶ establish a mechanism whereby students can signal in class if they do not understand a term (and respond 'respectfully' when they do so);
- ▶ allow 'silences' – thinking time for students to process and/or to formulate responses;
- ▶ respond to students' *ideas* in class – not to their use of language (avoid overt corrections of language, but seek clarifications if you have not understood).

Although these recommendations were devised with regard to teaching students whose first language is not English, as Scudamore also notes, working in this way will also help others, including students with dyslexia or hearing-impairment. Similar recommendations could be given as guidance to students whose first language *is* English to help them in their communications with others.

Messages are also communicated through the images which are included in our learning materials or within the wider learning environment. Often these convey unintended 'hidden curriculum' messages which can support or conflict with inclusive, multicultural, or global learning aspirations. An ongoing critical review of images within institutional and course materials, including on lecture slides, handbooks and hand-outs, can be as simple as asking 'Who is visible and who is absent?', though concomitant questions concerning *how* those who are present are depicted is likely also necessary.

Written communications (handbooks, feedback, hand-outs, and slides) can be made more accessible to students with dyslexia, visual impairments, or whose first languages do not employ a Roman alphabet through a few thoughtful design features, such as using the following (extracted from Rodrquez-Falcon et al., 2010, p. 10):

- an accessible font (notably sans-serif fonts such as Arial or Tahoma);
- 12+ font size for paper, 24+ for slides;
- text colour which contrasts with background; and
- text left aligned rather than justified.

Reflective question: How much attention do you pay to the language you use and the language your students use in lectures, seminars, or classroom discussions? Do you build protocols into classroom interactions which allow for silences?

Reflective question: Do you routinely check that course information, lecture slides, and assessment briefs are clear, concise, and produced in accessible fonts, and that the images you use show diverse peoples in affirmative ways?

Embedding Global-Self Outcomes

Intended learning outcomes (ILOs) can capture many attributes appropriate to global-selfhood. There are two broad approaches to incorporating such outcomes within a programme of study: either develop dedicated modules, or embed aspects of these attributes across disciplinary learning outcomes throughout the mainstream curriculum. Where structurally possible, the second approach has the largest impact on the greatest number of students. However, it may be that only the former approach is feasible. There are many examples of learning outcomes designed for dedicated modules of this kind.

The following are selected, with minor changes for stylistic consistency, from a module within a recently developed programme to support the learning of students engaged in European student exchange programmes (Beavan & Borghetti, 2015). At the end of the module, students will be able to:

▶ recognize and explain the variety and complexity that exists among individuals in social groups;
▶ explain ways in which different types of identities (gender, age, racial, ethnic, national, geographical, historical, linguistic, etc.) impact on communication with others;
▶ describe ways in which people (re)construct and/or (re)negotiate their own and others' multiple identities depending on experiences, encounters, contexts, and interlocutors;
▶ explain the problematic nature of using certain terms (e.g. ethnicity, race, nation) to frame identity; and
▶ set realistic objectives in relation to intercultural encounters, including language and communication expectations for their stay abroad.

Reflective question: Is there space within any of the programmes you teach on to incorporate a module with learning outcomes similar to those outlined above? Do you think that such outcomes are relevant for your students? Do they?

Less work has been reported which seeks to take a whole curriculum approach to embed global-self learning within disciplinary outcomes. The following examples are extracted from a more detailed review of one such project at a large university in the UK (Jones & Killick, 2013; Killick, 2011). These are 'generic' outcomes in the sense that they could be modified to fit many disciplinary courses or modules.

At the end of this module, students will be able to [make appropriate subject-specific substitutions to the bracketed sections]:

▶ explain how [specific aspects of practice] impact upon the lives of people locally and in diverse global contexts;
▶ critically review [current UK practice] through reference to practice in [two] other countries;
▶ present an analysis of [the subject] appropriately for an audience of diverse cultures and first languages;
▶ make a significant positive contribution as a member of a multicultural/international team work project;
▶ effectively conduct primary research involving participants from a range of cultural backgrounds;

> ▶ synthesize a range of international data sources as the basis for an analysis of potential problems and benefits associated with [the expansion of this practice];
> ▶ critique the themes presented in [this area] from [two] alternative international perspectives;
> ▶ find commonly acceptable ethical solutions to complex global problems relating to [this area];
> ▶ present a critically reasoned and respectful argument in favour of one specific socio-cultural response to [this area];
> ▶ detect bias, stereotypical thinking and prejudicial opinion in published material relating to [this issue];
> ▶ advance creative solutions for [this problem] which demonstrate appropriate consideration of at least one global (non-UK) context in which they will be applied.

A related approach involves the development of 'linked assignments' in which an existing assignment is modified to include ILOs, so that working on it 'explicitly engages students with diverse backgrounds in collaboration' requiring 'authentic intercultural communication' – contributing to the 'relational outcomes', while retaining its disciplinary 'content' outcomes (Whalley, 2000, p. 10). The challenge for faculty is to create clear, *manageable* learning outcomes which 'can be achieved within a single assessment [and are] assessable' (op. cit., p. 20). A significant feature of this approach is that it does not require a huge initial project or significant resources, but can be taken forward 'one assignment at a time'. However, echoing messages at several points in this book, Whalley points out that this kind of work 'involves a shift from conceiving the instructor's expertise not primarily as a content expert [but] as a designer of learning activities' (op. cit., p. 8).

Reflective question: Could you make subject-specific substitutions to some of the above to make them relevant to modules and students you teach? How would you 'defend' learning outcomes such as these to your students?

Reflective question: What further development would help you to become more expert as principally a designer of learning activities? To what extent are you comfortable with such a shift in role?

In a rare (perhaps hitherto unique) example of an institutional project seeking to bring together multicultural education and global learning outcomes, student affairs staff and faculty from across a range of courses at Northern Arizona University (NAU) devised learning outcomes to reflect their aspirations for their students. See Charles et al. (2013) for a review of the wider project, from which the following examples are extracted. Students will:

▶ be able to demonstrate global citizenship by developing a diverse living and learning community with opportunities for intercultural interaction;
▶ be able to demonstrate familiarity with the history, theory, and contemporary practices of grassroots democratic organizing and engagement across a wide range of issues pertaining to environmental sustainability, social justice, diversity, equality, globalization, and the common goods of community;
▶ be able to explain, both orally and in written form, how human diversity affects the definition, use, and management of forested landscapes; and
▶ understand relationships between professional engineering and public and private organizations, and the mutual impacts that global environments and diverse societal and political systems of the world can have on one another.

These come out of the work of NAU's Global Learning Initiative, and Case Study 5 describes in more detail the provision of a double major programme in which STEM subjects have been allied with foreign languages and an overseas work placement (internship). The programme develops STEM graduates with greater global capabilities, and has also proved successful in attracting and graduating women and minorities typically underrepresented in STEM courses.

Reflective question: Are any student 'types' underrepresented on programmes you are involved with? Would a more globally oriented, intercultural curriculum, such as that reflected in the learning outcomes above, be helpful in widening participation in that programme?

Implied in any work to establish ILOs is that assessments and assessment criteria will be constructively aligned to ensure students are rewarded to the extent that they achieve them.

Engaging Diverse Voices

Leask (2008b, p. 130) advocates that curriculum 'for the transnational classroom needs to be both internationalized and localized'. While this is true, *any* classroom – transnational, local, or virtual – will have diverse learners within it, and this requires a personalized kind of localization, one which enables individual students to find or create personal relevance, acting as 'meaning makers rather than passive recipients' of established 'truths'

(Ambrosio, 2003, p. 34). Embedding diverse perspectives within curricular content, engaging critically with own and others' norms and values, and exploring an issue or an action from alternative global perspectives have been cited in earlier chapters as components of both internationalization and equalization. Below are large and small examples of introducing more globally relevant source materials, and of how faculty and student voices can bring 'living diversity' into learning activities.

Carroll reports a number of examples of actions taken by course teams intent on internationalizing their curricula. For example, when seeking to introduce a greater international focus within source materials, a team for an undergraduate statistics course introduced a *simple, but impactful change* by moving from local database sources to UN-generated data, and then adjusting 'the content of three courses to emphasise their international context' (Carroll, 2015, p. 107). A UK lecturer in Jurisprudence reported that although available texts often did refer to ethnic minority and British Muslim cases, they did so 'from a very neutral perspective...always very passive, always in an observing position', so he developed his own case studies in which his ethnic minority and his British Muslim students 'see names and scenarios that are familiar to them' to help them 'to feel a part of the module' (participant cited in Jabbar & Hardaker, 2013, p. 278). Another participant in the same study illustrated how students might be asked to 'think out of their current environment and question the world around them' by considering a case set initially within a familiar context from other perspectives (op. cit., p. 280):

> students were discussing the case of a priest abusing a boy within his parish. I asked the students to consider what would be the consequences if this happened in a mosque or a synagogue?

Reflective question: How diverse are the case studies, citations, and perspectives represented in your current curriculum content? Do you require students to reimagine ideas and actions from the perspectives of others?

UK faculty are advised that they 'are more likely to engage and motivate all students' by (extracted from ECU, 2013a, p. 3):

- ▶ illustrating points with examples that reflect the diversity of your students;
- ▶ recognising how the dynamics of relations between different groups have impacted on your subject field; and
- ▶ acknowledging which voices/issues are not represented.

Reflective question: Do you provide examples which speak to the diversity in your student body, and to wider diversities across a multicultural and globalizing world??

The personal experiences and perspectives of diverse international students and Australian students on exchange in a range of international contexts were used to develop two film resources which:

> address the question of how internationalisation affects students on a personal, social and institutional level by giving the audience the opportunity to hear how other students develop skills in dealing with the pleasures and pitfalls of living in an overseas environment.
>
> (Eisenchlas & Trevaskes, 2007, pp. 118–119)

This content, generated from student experiences, formed the basis for further learning activities (the publication contains three further practical case studies in intercultural learning).

Thom reports an example of a UK Events Management module in which faculty and students from the UK and India were brought together (also across disciplines) to support an international award ceremony. Within the collaborative project:

> They designed a week-long cultural awareness program for key workers in hospitality, retail, transport and security services. They made a film, devised and presented activities, and organised events. Students shared personal experiences of learning living, visiting and working in other countries, with each other and with the audiences. Each gained greater insight and deeper understanding of each other's cultural traditions, history, beliefs and lifestyle.
>
> (Thom, 2010, p. 162)

Reflective question: Could you develop learning resources in direct collaboration across international or local cultural groups? How might this add value to your module?

In a Canadian programme, domestic students were linked with international students to undertake cultural research as part of their Ethnographic Research Methods module. The programme worked well, with international students getting opportunity to improve their English through conversations with Canadians and to learn more about aspects of Canadian culture. Both international and Canadian students reported undertaking their own research into their own culture in order to be able to be better informed 'experts'. However, the organizers recognized that awarding credit for this to the Canadian Anthropology students while providing international student volunteers with no academic reward was leading to attrition. This inequitable framing of the intercultural encounters was rectified by creating a credit-bearing course in parallel for the international participants. The organizers report that:

> All who participated would agree that they learned something beyond the subject matter of the course. They learned how to communicate with and better understand one another in being members of a global community.
>
> (BCCIE, 2003, p. 16)

And a Japanese student participant quoted in the case study (op. cit., p. 11) illustrates the 'own culture' learning which the process encouraged:

> By sharing my own culture, I realized that I had not known about it very well. So I looked back at my life in my country, and researched it well. I would not have [done so] if there had not been [this] opportunity ... Knowing other cultures helps people to look back at their own culture and know about it more.

Reflective question: *How might you link diverse students in learning activities which value their voices and encourage them to examine disciplinary issues and representations within their own cultures with fresh eyes?*

Students may play a significant part as expert informers when invited to critically reflect upon, and then give shape to, the wider objectives and approaches within their curriculum. From experiences of assessing local educators within an established Western model of reflective practice in Zambia, Whittaker found the reflective model she was employing was itself deficient, specifically in its failure to allow for emotion in a context where 'significant issues of poverty and disease ... shape the lives of these Zambian students' (Whittaker, 2008, p. 99), and then in the reliance which her students and she 'conspired to undermine' real-live local issues in order that requirements/ expectations for the inclusion of Western expert sources be integrated to give validity to their reflective work. The model she developed in response (which she feels will need further review) is based in collaborative critical thinking, and the recognition that in this context these students become the experts (op. cit., p. 106):

▶ *Reflective thinking* is a suitable point for exploring professional development, but, as expectations of deeper reflection move towards critical thinking we should also expect that the complex nature of thinking to be reflected [*sic*] in more provisional and conditional conclusions – which may be subjected to further scrutiny.

▶ *Notions of power and autonomy* need to be critically explored. We know that trauma makes demands on coping strategies, and that this, in turn, will affect our ways of thinking. A learning community can be endowed with the power to confront academic hegemony and gently challenge assumptions about professional and personal development.

▶ *Theories and hypotheses* about professional development need to emerge from the learning community, rather than being simply 'borrowed' from Western literature. The learning community needs to be given the authority to use existing literature where and when it suits its needs, rather than simply to add weight and validity to its own words. Ideas that emerge from the group are accepted as being provisional and tentative. Both tutor and group members need to work to counter the competitive and combative ethos of assessment and professional development.

Educational developers from a UK university exported their Postgraduate Certificate in Learning and Teaching in Higher Education, developed for their faculty 'at home', to local academics working at an offshore campus in Malaysia. Following early work with their Malaysian colleagues, they reflected that 'the wholesale transmission' of ideas, research, and good practice had not been appropriate, and that to make the programme relevant to the student-academics:

> What was needed was the creation of spaces in which to contest the issues, values and ideas embedded not only in inter-disciplinary conversations, but also in the inter-national concerns of transnational teachers.
>
> (Davidson & Scudamore, 2008, p. 114)

Despite difficulties in fully engaging their Malaysian colleagues in a critical process to reformulate the course, changes were made to the mode of delivery (while retaining the same learning outcomes in the UK and Malaysia), in particular 'finding ways to make sure that academics studying the course can still focus on issues that concern them in their own teaching context' (op. cit., p. 117).

Reflective question: If you are involved with professional or postgraduate programmes, to what extent do you actively engage the participants in critiquing and establishing relevance to their own cultures, contexts, and priorities within the curriculum and its assessment?

Reflective question: How could you, practically, build critical reflection on their course experience into your course design to engage diverse students and students studying in diverse contexts?

Significant elements of these types of collaboration, with student as 'expert' knower, can bring greater relevance and equity to the assessments of diverse learners. Across a number of good-practice principles and guides, Leask (extracted from 2015, pp. 96–103) offers recommendations concerning assessment, including:

▶ Requiring that all students investigate case studies from different places rather than only selecting case studies close to home;
▶ Assessing group work processes as well as outputs;
▶ Assessing the development of intercultural skills and individual students' participation in intercultural group work at regular intervals;
▶ Encouraging self-reflection and self-assessment by students as they engage in cross-cultural group assignments.

Reflective question: Even if your curriculum content is drawn from diverse sources, to what degree are all students required to and rewarded for including them in their assessments? Do current assessments include an explicit focus on how students interact among diverse peers?

Although we are concerned with formal learning activities, it is worth mentioning one example of an institutional response which brought diverse voices directly into the wider learning spaces of the university. When the question, 'Why isn't my professor black?' was raised by students, University College London (UCL) organized a series of speakers to discuss the question, and then captured the discussion in a blog space to enable further debate. The initial blog space is open for all to view (UCL, 2014c), and is being followed up with a further discussion with student and faculty voices on the related issue of 'Why is my curriculum white?' (UCL, 2014b). Willingness to bring these topics to open, public debate evidences an institutional commitment to inclusion, with a recognition that there is work yet to be done. Several other resources are linked from the UCL 'community of academics, administrative staff *and students* at UCL, committed to righting racialised wrongs in our workplace and the wider world' (UCL, 2014a). In the UK, the National Union of Students' (NUS) commitments to 'liberating the curriculum' are directed towards giving equal recognition to black, queer, disabled, and feminist contributions to knowledge within the curriculum (Ali et al.; 2014); indicating that this remains a live issues across the student body. The three elements of their campaign are (summarized from op. cit. p. 2):

▷ **Liberation** – working to challenge and reverse the effects of structural oppression in society;
▷ **Equality** – ensuring that the curriculum does not disadvantage any student or group of students because of their background or characteristics; and
▷ **Diversity** – building curriculum which represents the diversity of contemporary society and facilitation of an environment in which all students feel welcome in the learning community.

Reflective question: How could you bring wider diversity concerns into a more public forum within your department or institution? How could international and community partners be encouraged to contribute to any such conversations?

Reflective question: How successfully would your current curriculum address each of the three elements of the NUS campaign? How can local or national student bodies in other contexts support work to liberate the curriculum?

Enabling Intercultural Interactions

The kinds of learning experiences described in this section are based in the premise that successful intercultural interactions are the most effective spaces for global-self development. In the previous section we saw examples of diverse contexts and learners becoming sources, even principal informants, within learning spaces and learning activities. Here, we see examples of work to enhance the quality of the intercultural interactions in which those learners may be engaged. Such interactions might take place within a lecture, a seminar, a 'flipped' classroom, an online discussion forum, while on a field trip, in a lab setting, during independent group work, and so forth. There are examples of student interaction within the kinds of learning activities in which the tutor might be most directly involved (such as lectures, seminars, and group tutorials) and, so, able to monitor and 'manage', and of more student-controlled activities. The latter tend to involve more extended interaction, but also may hold greater possibilities for student exclusion. Many of the examples below are transferrable to other activity types. Some generic procedures can be taken which will give more students the space they might need to participate in any of these forums, perhaps beginning with:

- establish an ethos of 'turn-taking', and 'enforce' this through requiring respectful listening and non-interruption;
- allow (setting a pattern of) a 'thinking pause' before anybody can respond to a point or a question;
- have pairs/small groups write an agreed response to a question before you ask for comments/answers.

Recommendations on asking direct questions include:

- Ask several students the same question in turn, perhaps leaving those who might need time to later 'slots'. Of course, this needs to be a question where hearing many views or takes on the issue will be of benefit.
- As you ask, make eye contact with the student using his/her name, then pause for a few seconds to watch the reaction – is silence a sign of thinking or withdrawal? Is there any sign of readiness to reply? You could re-phrase the question and ask again if you judge the student as preparing to reply.
- Once the student starts to answer, let the student complete what he or she wishes to say. Use supplementary / follow-up questions with care, especially in the early days. Follow ups for clarification ('When you mention child adoption, are you thinking about....?') will be likely to encourage whereas challenging questions ('So, what else should you be thinking about besides x?') might deter future attempts.
- If a student seems not to understand a question, you could either repeat it verbatim or rephrase it. Both approaches can help though the challenge comes in knowing which best fits the situation. Either way, understanding is a joint responsibility between you and the student.

(HEA, 2014d, p. 5)

When students are voicing and critiquing own and others' perspectives, areas of significant disagreement may emerge, and strategies to avoid these becoming conflictive and counterproductive include:

- providing opportunities for a range of views to be identified, without necessarily asking students to own or defend those views;

▷ offering frameworks and principles for positioning opinions on individual issues;

▷ setting each ethical issue in a wider conceptual approach to the topic.

(Scudamore, 2013, p. 21)

Within a postgraduate Chemistry programme, the course team report (Carroll, 2015, p. 108) that rather than change curriculum content, they 'put more emphasis on students' collaboration skills, especially involving work across cultural and language differences' and that they 'built towards' interactive group work 'with support and skills teaching in early modules'.

Reflective question: To what extent do you formalize the protocols and the support you provide to students for their interactions with each other and with yourself? Can you identify if any of your students would find any of the above protocols particularly unhelpful to equalize their participation?

Group work activities, face-to-face or online, particularly where they contribute to or build towards an assessment, are the activities most commonly cited as problematic in research into student experiences and attitudes with regard to domestic:international and majority:minority student integration. Yet they are also the learning spaces in which students may experience the most meaningful and protracted interactions, and gain the greatest cognitive learning gain (Bowman, 2010, p. 20). Group work activities may be particularly sensitive to the kinds of intergroup contact conditions outlined in the previous chapter. Brief examples of approaches are given below, and apply variously to short 'one-off' learning activities and more extended group projects and the like. Single one-off tasks need careful structuring and planning, but cannot be expected to achieve very much if left to 'stand alone'. Projects can offer more sustained opportunities for contact than in-class group work activities, potentially providing more meaningful and longer-term relationships to emerge, and encouraging students to commit to the relationship-formation work which might be needed 'up front'.

General advice on approaches to group formation differs, but tutor allocation is suggested to be more successful than self-selection, and building in focussed reflections *on process, task experience* and *diversity issues* which have been experienced is also needed (ECU, 2013a, p. 3). This process of reflection is argued to be key by many writers, echoing the view that:

unless students are given the opportunity to reflect on their feelings and their attitudes towards what is happening as they encounter another culture (the creation of the 'aha' moment), they will not gain much in respect of their intercultural competences.

(Coelen, 2013, p. 23)

Reflective question: At what points in your group work learning activities could you introduce critical reflection from your students? If your cohort does not include significantly diverse students, could you introduce reflective exercises which draw upon their wider experiences of diversity in their community or when travelling internationally?

Before reflection can take place, an activity needs to have been experienced, and maximizing participation within the activity is fundamental if there is to be anything positive to reflect on. In addition to the kinds of protocols illustrated above, arranging group tasks which follow a specific structure (rather than simply asking students to 'discuss' an issue) can enhance the likelihood that everybody might engage. Some other examples of structured group work formats are (Surgenor, 2010, cited in Scudamore 2013, p. 16):

Buzz groups: Small group discussions, within a larger group, about a precise task or issue.

Silent reflection: A set time to identify, alone, the key points/most surprising thing/question to ask, etc.

Three minutes each way: Set time to take turns, in pairs, to explain key principles/analyse images/describe phenomena, etc.

Brainstorms: Collection of ideas to the board with no immediate discussion on their validity.

Fishbowls: Small number of students demonstrating a task/debate, etc. with all other students watching.

Rounds: Each student/group in turn adds a new answer to a collection on the board.

A more extended structure is the *jigsaw task* in which information generated by each group during an initial task is carried by each individual in the original group into a new group, where it is needed to move onto the next task (and so forth). Stages within the full set of jigsaw tasks can also be conducted outside class by individuals for subsequent sharing, if preferred. Jigsaw tasks give each stage *purpose* (without completing it, the second stage cannot be achieved), a *collaborative ethos* through individual and group responsibility (there is a degree of reciprocity because students will let each other down if not completed), and *inclusivity* (students forming each new group carry 'expert knowledge' from their previous task, unknown to other participants). For any group work, task focus can be disciplinary based, but can also be designed to require engagement with different perspectives and a critique of dominant solutions or currently accepted practice.

Six lecturers collaborated to provide a group work experience to under-graduate Arts and Educations students undertaking a 13-week elective module in Australia. The class had 28 domestics students and 14 international students, and the subject-focussed group work was structured with the intention of researching how group working mechanics facilitated intercultural working. Protocols designed into group working included (for greater detail, see Cruickshank et al., 2012, from which the following is summarized):

▶ organizing students into random groups which were re-structured weekly so they engaged with different peers;
▶ initially, each student interviewed a partner and introduced him/her to the group;
▶ in each session students were asked if they remembered and could pronounce correctly the names of other group members;
▶ two structured activities started each session: (i) students in turn read a short extract from a required text which they felt important, and other students commented in turn prior to the first student responding, with no cross-discussion; the process then repeated with each student taking the lead role in turn; (ii) again in turn, from a tutor-prepared grid, students directed a question on out-of-class work to one other student, whose response must satisfy the group before he/she takes on the role of questioner; and
▶ following a break, a 'Think, Pair, Share' task was completed, which had been designed for different students to assume 'expert' roles on the basis of previously identified individual strengths.

Reflective question: Which of your current learning activities could be given a more formalized structure, employing any of the suggested formats, in order to ensure that interactions more fully involve minority or international students?

Intercultural learning is disruptive and can add significantly to critical education; approaches to interactions can be derived from principles within critical education. Sorensen et al. (2009, p. 12) advocate the use of a 'critical dialogic' approach to intergroup dialogue (IGD), but caution that:

> Although students are often eager to jump into the controversial hot topics, anticipating provocative discussions, IGD is not merely a space to talk about issues, opinions, and perspectives. It is an educational program

that provides students with opportunities to learn how to communicate effectively across different perspectives in order to prevent the fatal pitfalls that can characterize intergroup interactions while promoting positive relationships, understanding, and collaboration. Consequently, IGD progresses through a series of stages, each building on prior learning and experiences.

Facilitators involve students in the beginning of the dialogue to discuss their hopes and fears and to co-create a shared understanding of their needs and expectations for the dialogue, formulating ground rules or guidelines for engagement.

They use a planned and principled process of intergroup communication itself as the mechanism by which to develop relationships and build collaboration. The process includes:

(i)   intentional *structured interaction across group differences*, with small groups of students selected on the basis of their 'diverse identities';
(ii) *facilitative leadership* in which trained facilitators model dialogic communication and focus their attention on group dynamics; and
(iii) *critical reflection* by which students dialogue with others to examine perspectives, experiences, assumptions, power, privilege, and inequality.

These authors are very clear (op. cit., p. 29) that these type of programmes require the provision of 'training and supervision about how to process the disagreements and emotions that IGDs inevitably surface'.

Exploring how intergroup dialogue might advance 'critical whiteness' (i.e. making Whiteness the object of study to move learners to critically question the dominant framing of White privilege and its attenuating attitudes and actions), researchers in the USA found factors within the dialogue activity which students identified as constructive to the process to include (Yeung et al., 2013):

► fostering discussing rather than argument;
► listening to peers enabled others to be less defensive;
► having Black students in the class (with concern also that these students might have been put into a position of 'spokesperson' for their race, and that their presence inhibited honesty/openness on the part of some);
► having a Black and a White tutor to facilitate (with concern that having a Black tutor also may have inhibited some discussions within assignments); and
► tutors making clear that they, too, continued to struggle with racial issues.

Bell et al. (2015, p. 407) highlight the importance of group dynamics within social justice education because participants 'deal with emotional reactions, and negotiate asymmetric power relations and historically and culturally embedded patters of interaction'. They illustrate how faculty facilitating dialogue in such highly charged contexts may, by virtue of their own cultural norms and positionings, be ill-prepared to recognize or respond to group member behaviours:

▶ White people are socialized to view the world from a white normative frame and thus may not notice the racial dynamics when a white participant interrupts or minimizes comments made by classmates of color.
▶ Women are often socialized to harmonize and keep the peace, and may smooth over conflict rather than name and address it directly.
▶ Native English speakers may overlook participants for whom English is a second language, further marginalizing them in class discussions.

Such limitations are more evident as our students are drawn from more diverse groups and groups are being facilitated in more diverse contexts. Limitations among faculty apply also among our diverse students.

Reflective question: Do you feel equipped to deal effectively with critical dialogue and the potentially 'fatal pitfalls'? Is relevant faculty development available to support you in designing and running this type of learning activity?

Reflective question: How comfortable are you with sharing your own 'struggles' with your students?

Online group work can enable faculty to create intercultural encounter and learning opportunities which extend the experience of students beyond the diversity immediately available within a particular cohort, and ensure that non-mobile students 'are able to develop an informed international perspective of their discipline area and its associated professional practices' (Middlemas & Peat, 2015), as in Case Study 1 in the final section of this chapter. Such work offers wider diversity experience, and might also enable students to collaborate on early work across diversity areas which are less contested than those which pertain in their immediate group. For example, if race is a significant issue in the communities from which students are drawn, working online with students from another country can allow initial explorations and experiences to focus on national perspectives and approaches to an issue. A follow-up activity might then ask students to explore which areas of similarity and difference appeared most relevant to them from different racial perspectives.

Alternatively, online collaboration can enable students to see how theoretical aspects of their studies assume different dimensions when considered in relation to the lived experience of other students in different global (or local) contexts. For example, a second-year project developed by UCL's Medical School and the Nelson Mandela School of Medicine used online connection to enable students to 'investigate ethical and social issues in reproductive medicine and their impact on reproductive rights in a global context' (Noble, 2006, p. 18). Students in KwaZulu Natal and students in London interacted online through facilitated study groups, discussion boards, and other media, with editorial groups in the first term producing a magazine article or radio programme on a module topic. Faculty in the USA and Bolivia established a virtual collaborative 'classroom exchange', connecting students in both locations including both personal engagement (posting and comment upon each other's profiles) and structured academic project work in cross-national teams. The authors report on technical and administrative glitches and some of their solutions, and also recommend an explicit focus on the cross-cultural aspects of group interactions at the beginning of the programme. Notwithstanding areas identified for improvement, the virtual exchange took both student groups 'out of their comfort zones', gave them 'a true taste of the academic culture and expectations of their counterparts', and experienced learning outcomes 'greater than those in a regular classroom' (Abrahamse et al., 2015, pp. 152–154).

Reflective question: What opportunities can you identify for linking your own cohorts virtually with others who have alternative perspectives and experiences?

▶ 6.3 Case Studies

The case studies with which the chapter concludes illustrate many of the complex issues addressed in the preceding chapters. The first four case studies are drawn from transnational education (TNE) contexts, and demonstrate particularly the collaborative work of individual faculty to enhance practice, while the fifth focusses on a wider project within a single institution, and illustrates how moving beyond traditional and locally focussed disciplinary boundaries can both build global capabilities and create learning spaces which are more open to diverse students. Each case study showcases particular innovations to practice. However, in discussing the contexts and showing how specific issues were identified or addressed, each one also references broader questions concerning internationalization and equalization, as illustrated below (CS1 refers to Case Study 1, and so forth):

Collaborative approaches among faculty and students

▶ CS1 describes a collaborative project involving students in London, Hong Kong, and Singapore, and shows tutors in Hong Kong and London working together;

▶ CS2 shows the importance of involving local faculty 'from an early stage', and how it was, initially, faculty in the overseas college who carried expertise in two academic traditions, within 'professional exchanges in which all colleagues had recognition';

▶ CS3 identifies the impact of a change initially implemented by a Chinese academic;

▶ CS4 illustrates collaborative working through dialogue which 'was an educational process for all the academics involved in the partnership', with issues being 'resolved through effective cooperation, communication, team spirit and flexibility'; and

▶ CS5 gives an example of how engaging with women and minority students on one successful programme has advanced understanding to inform future inclusivity work.

Equalizing the student voice

▶ CS1 describes 'validating non-UK students' cultural capital' with students providing information to inform the assignments of their distant peers;

▶ CS2 describes introducing changes to assessment dates and deadlines in response to cultural requirements within the new delivery context, and describes the need to 'anchor design exercises in contexts which are meaningful in [students'] worlds';

▶ CS3 describes how re-establishing more teacher-led activities enabled a focus on process to help students bridge between their previous educational experience and expectations within their new programme;

▶ CS4 shows that it is possible to eliminate the potential power bias created by requirements to study and be assessed through the medium of English; and

▶ CS5 shows how changes to a traditional programme of study can create greater participation from women and minority students.

Technologies to equalize learning spaces

▶ CS1 describes using Facebook as a space which was 'equally familiar and accessible to each cohort';

- ▶ CS2 shows how technical solutions to resource sharing can be approached in ways which provide 'the best fit to local contexts'; and
- ▶ CS3 shows how 'remote delivery' was blended to enable enhanced face-to-face work.

Global perspectives on self and disciplinary practice

- ▶ CS1 describes collaboration which challenged 'perceived fixation on Western fashion trends'; and
- ▶ CS5 shows international internships can be particularly impactful for women and minority students as they see 'how they themselves may be differently represented and positioned'.

Equity issues in post-national university contexts

- ▶ CS2 acknowledges equity issues where faculty in one context are locally employed 'by a third party academic service provider';
- ▶ CS2 describes how having to 'deal with the duality of Eastern and Western expectations' presented ongoing challenges for their students in China;
- ▶ CS3 acknowledges that initial arrangements were 'not offering the students the same learning opportunities';
- ▶ CS4 showcases one example where a TNE collaboration with a private provider has widened access to a professional degree in the context of highly competitive public university admissions; and
- ▶ CS5 demonstrates how greater inclusivity can encourage women and minority students into STEM-related studies.

Enhancing global graduate opportunities

- ▶ CS4 illustrates how a TNE collaborative programme can extend professional opportunities for successful students in one location; and
- ▶ CS5 shows how programme focus and structure can bring greater global competences to participating students.

Each case also shows how the *academic community* can act, notwithstanding structural inequalities and neo-liberal agendas, to enable more equitable learning gain, which is at the same time better suited for graduates who will make their way in a multicultural and globalizing world. The reflective questions were prompted by reading the cases, and are not intended to capture their full value.

CASE STUDY 1

Dr Natascha Radclyffe-Thomas, Fashion Business School, London College of Fashion

Dr Ana Roncha, Fashion Business School, London College of Fashion

Dr Anne Peirson-Smith, City University of Hong Kong

Adrian Huang, LASALLE College of the Arts, Singapore

As the world is increasingly globalised, our students' future lives and workplaces require cross-cultural capabilities, yet curricula often remain situated within home cultures. This case study describes a collaborative project between students in London, Hong Kong and Singapore, initiated to explore discipline-specific local and global industry practices, as well as to internationalize the curriculum. The genesis of what has become a truly 'global classroom' had several influencing factors; a shared belief in the responsibility of higher education to foster interculturally capable, socially responsible graduates; an understanding of the potential of digital technologies to reimagine teaching in the 21st century; and a curiosity about how discipline-specific knowledge is created and understood in disparate geographic locations operating under different educational systems. The London College of Fashion attracts students from around the world to study, and as part of the University of the Arts London, which has 36% non-UK students, London College of Fashion has one of the most diverse student bodies, yet, reflecting the biases of the wider fashion industry, the curriculum focus was mostly Western Europe and North America. So, one desired outcome was to expose UK students to non-homogenous markets at the same time as validating non-UK students' cultural capital. The majority of CityU students are Hong Kong Chinese, learning in a second-language context, with each class having on average three to four exchange students from Europe, North America or Australia.

Informal discussions at a pedagogic conference on popular culture chimed with the authors' objectives to widen students' awareness of their own and others' cultural capital, gradually crystallising into a planned pilot collaboration. The pilot ran between 35 London College of Fashion students studying a Fashion Branding unit and 65 CityU Hong Kong students studying Popular Culture (30 students) and Advertising units (35 students). The collaboration brought geographically diverse students together to work on separate but aligned projects which specifically addressed issues around global and local marketing communications. Tutors in Hong Kong and London worked together to adapt existing projects to incorporate a collaborative international aspect which was designed to supplement a full programme of classroom delivery with an online element, allowing students access to peers in non-homogenous markets. Students in each location had a brief requiring them to evaluate business opportunities in international markets and also to suggest marketing strategies. Additionally, the tutors wanted to be able to record and collate the students' findings and interactions, thus a key decision was around how to share resources and facilitate interactions between the two cohorts. Debate on the relative merits of institutional versus commercial platforms led to the setting up of a private Facebook group: The International Fashion Panel. Facebook was identified as being a space which was equally familiar and accessible to each cohort.

Through scheduled seminar and private study assignments, staff and students shared learning resources and critiques around brand identity, cross-cultural marketing and city branding, and the Facebook platform also allowed the sharing of relevant fashion and business articles. The platform was used both separately and collaboratively to support students' learning e.g. carrying out primary research on the Hong Kong fashion industry via online surveys and focus groups, mirroring many contemporary working patterns, and allowed co-creation of educational experiences beyond the geographic and time constraints of working internationally. Having established that the collaboration should explore how fashion marketing communications are interpreted in diverse locations, tutors selected a sample of 12 fashion brands operating internationally, for which our students would be likely target customers. Tutors from both institutions ran asynchronous focus groups on the 4Ps of marketing with visual prompts relating to each brand posted into the Facebook group, against which students in both locations posted their seminar discussion responses, thus sharing perceptions from different perspectives and locations. Another seminar activity was for students in one location to provide local market information which would inform the partner students' assignments. This local intelligence was presented 'live' in their own seminars and also posted to the group in the form of pdf reports.

The digitally-mediated collaboration allowed for flexibility around when and how education took place, providing a third space for co-creation of learning. The ten-week collaborative pilot project succeeded beyond expectations with regard to fostering a global attitude; this student's comments are typical of the feedback received: 'the importance of cultural differences within the market place is one of the lessons I will take with me for a long time'. Students enjoyed the opportunity to choose to research cultures with which they had personal connections, and, furthermore, Asian students in London appreciated their classmates' enhanced interest in their home cultures: 'I hope there are more chances for home students (English students) to know more about other cultures and studies.'

Following the success of the initial collaboration, both the size and the scope of the project were expanded – 93 first-year students on the BA (Hons) Fashion Marketing at the London College of Fashion and 40 CityU Hong Kong Fashion Communication students were joined online by 48 students from the BA (Hons) Fashion Media & Industries programme at LASALLE College of the Arts, Singapore. Tutors at LASALLE saw the collaboration as a concrete way to counter a perceived fixation on Western fashion trends, and develop their students' sensitivity to the issues pertinent to development of the fashion industry in Singapore and the region, whilst also being aware of the global nature of fashion business.

The second global classroom started with an ice-breaker where students introduced themselves to their peers by sharing three places in the world they would like to live and three companies they aspired to work for. This activity was successful in expanding students' recognition of global opportunities their future life might afford and also showed how many of them shared the same ambitions. The project followed the previous outline with additional points of contact including peer critiques of each other's work in progress which proved to be one of the most popular activities.

Benefits of the collaboration included enhanced digital literacies, the facilitation of research in remote markets and the raising of awareness of cross-cultural issues in product design and fashion marketing. One outcome that has encouraged the future expansion of this international collaboration is how students conceive of the experience as a virtual exchange programme with a survey of the LASALLE students showing that 76% believed that cross-cultural e-learning projects are beneficial to their education.

> Through interacting on the International Fashion Panel I have been enlightened and inspired by how fashion can get people together and share a common interest. Hearing different views and seeing different ideas on fashion and the fashion industry has allowed me to not limit myself to thinking about what I'm used to but stepping outside the box. (UK student)
>
> The constant updates on UK, Singapore, Indonesian and HK brands allow me to explore more in-depth insights from different students. The most useful part is the frequent interactions on International

Fashion Panel because it is very constructive in understanding the fashion market and culture in other parts of the world. It is a very convenient and effective platform to receive and share multimedia information including images, videos, documents and external links. This also stimulates a sense of international collaboration and 'give and take' among the students. (HK student)

Reflective questions

To what extent do courses you are currently involved in reflect the observation of these writers that 'curricula often remain situated within home cultures'?

Would students on courses you are involved in benefit from exposure to 'non-homogeneous' contexts for their discipline and related professions?

How do you 'validate' the cultural capital of international or minority students on your course?

Can you identify one significant element of a course you are involved with which would benefit from bringing together students from different nationalities or communities in a similar way to that outlined in this case study?

CASE STUDY 2

Danny Toohey, School of Engineering and Information Technology, Murdoch University

Murdoch University (MU) in Perth, Western Australia, has had a transnational education (TNE) presence since the early 1990's. In common with the experience of many Australian universities, MU's involvement in TNE has changed from being driven and administered by individuals at School and/or Program level to one that is more closely aligned with organizational governance processes and broader strategic aims.

The Information Technology (IT) discipline at MU has been actively engaged in TNE since its establishment at Murdoch, initially as a provider of service teaching for the Business disciplines. Since the mid 2000's, IT has been offering its own courses at locations in Singapore, Dubai and Malaysia. These partnerships have operated under what could loosely be termed a 'franchise' model, where the students are taught using the Murdoch curriculum, by local academics employed by a third-party academic services provider, an equity issue in itself, but not explored here. Assessments, including examinations, are all created by academics at the Australian campus. In-term assessments are marked by the local staff and moderated by the home campus academics. Final examinations are marked by the home campus academics.

Over the period of IT's involvement in TNE, a broad range of issues have arisen. However, two of relevance here include marked inconsistencies in terms of computing infrastructure at the TNE locations and the Australian campus, and issues associated with localization of content.

The author teaches in the areas of database theory and business intelligence. Both require a high degree of technical skill and understanding, as well as the more abstract skills associated with design as the basis of practical implementation. In order to develop proficiency in terms of the technical skills in these areas, students are required to create, manage and manipulate sample datasets. In building skills in design, students are required to create designs on the basis of textual case studies or interaction with real-life clients.

Common to many TNE partnerships, resources and available technologies were identified as providing unequal opportunities for students in TNE contexts compared with their Australian peers. Unlike the case in many TNE partnerships worldwide, we have attempted to overcome the issues associated with inconsistent infrastructure and provide equitable access to learning and teaching resources. To that end, all resources used in both subjects are made equally available to all students through the use of virtual and online resources. Depending on the best fit to local contexts, some students are provided with access to a virtual desktop environment that can be run on any computer at any location; this ensures that the computing environment in which the student is working is identical to all other students, regardless of their location or physical infrastructure. In other cases, access to computing resources is provided online, with students being able to access those resources using free or open source software. As such, the TNE students have equal access to all resources as those who choose to study off-campus, or, who choose not to attend face-to-face classes for whatever reason. It also means that, conceivably, a student could complete these subjects using the most inexpensive hardware resources as long as they have access to the Internet.

Localization of content has been more problematic, particularly in terms of the creation and contextualization of the assessment items, many of which rely on the use of case studies in design exercises. While students are still developing competencies in design, it is important to anchor design exercises in contexts which are meaningful in their 'worlds', thus allowing the student to concentrate on the learning rather than being inhibited by the context. As all students' (in Australia or overseas) experience and understanding of design techniques improves, it becomes more appropriate to expose them to more complex and unfamiliar contexts in order to develop their skills in requirements determination.

Use of language, local experience and context, then, are all-important in the creation of these design activities. It became apparent from an early stage that involvement of the local staff was required if the activities were to be useful for the students. Small but impactful examples of items that caused issues for students in Singapore include the use of 'mobile' number ('hand phone' number in Singapore) and salaries being specified in terms of annual amount (monthly in Singapore) and paid fortnightly (monthly in Singapore). Many of the case studies used in design exercises at the Australian campus are based around domestic students' experiences and not the experience of the Singapore students.

In a broader context there are other issues that can impact on the students' capacity to be successful in their study. For example, male students in Singapore can be recalled to fulfill National Service obligations at any time during the year. Similarly, various religious and celebratory festivals in Singapore impact on the academic calendar that is designed around the Australian calendar. For these reasons, it was important to include more flexibility in assessment dates and deadlines. While none of these issues are necessarily large in themselves, when taken together they were observed to be negatively impacting on the students' learning processes.

Given the author's (initially at least) limited experience of Singapore, it was fortunate that several of the local staff had expertise in teaching Australian curriculum to local students and, indeed, in dealing with Australian academics. It was also fortunate that we were able to create opportunities in the early stages for the author to meet face-to-face with the local academics. These professional exchanges in which all colleagues had recognition, formed the foundation of ongoing and collegial relationships that have lasted the duration of the partnership. These relationships have allowed for discussion regarding both the conduct and the content of the subjects. Where appropriate, for example, the local academics have added a number of local case studies to replace those more focused on the Australian experience. Identified issues of language and culture have been addressed, and being alert to these means that others continue to be addressed in the design of teaching materials, assessments and the timing of those assessments. Practically, this will often take the case of a draft being released to the local academics for comment, or correspondence about how a given artefact could be amended for subsequent offering of the subject. Post hoc amendments of assessments or submission dates have also been able to be made on the basis of the relationships established between the home and local academics.

The outcome of these relationships has been a more focused and relevant curricula that allows the focus of the students to be more squarely, and so equitably, on the content rather than it being their sole responsibility to adjust for the context.

Reflective questions

Are you aware of any students accessing a course you teach on with 'marked inconsistencies in terms of computing infrastructure', or their access to that infrastructure? How do you, or could you, address the associated educational inequalities?

If you were preparing a course currently delivered on your home campus for delivery in another country or to a significantly different student cohort, what changes would the 'localization of content' involve?

Could your assessment requirements be made more flexible to accommodate the needs of diverse students, be they based in cultural, geographical, or personal circumstances?

CASE STUDY 3

Dr Leonie Ellis, School of Engineering and ICT, University of Tasmania

Dr Erin Roehrer, School of Engineering and ICT, University of Tasmania

In 2002 a transnational bi-lateral agreement was signed between the University of Tasmania and the Shanghai Ocean University and included the establishment of an International Education Institute within Shanghai Ocean University. Under the joint venture, around 400 Chinese students enrol annually for one of two double degrees, each studied over a four-year period, with no transfer to Tasmania. A contractual condition of the partnership was that the Tasmanian degrees would be taught using Western teaching methods and delivered in English. Students, therefore, study their Chinese degree with a more traditional teacher-centred approach, while simultaneously studying the Tasmanian degree by more collaborative approaches. The Tasmanian program was to be taught in partnership with Chinese faculty.

From the outset, a number of issues were identified, with the potential to create unequal learning experiences between students studying in Tasmania and those studying in China. Firstly, cultural differences in student learning approaches and interaction styles created a challenge for Chinese students when required to engage within the expectations of the Tasmanian curriculum. These challenges aligned with learner models presented in much learning and teaching literature; specifically, that students trained under a Chinese education system are accustomed to more passive roles with no experience of interactions in class. In contrast, the Tasmanian programmes rely on students becoming interactive learners as they progress through the degree. Dealing with the duality of Eastern and Western expectations presented ongoing challenges for these students as they were progressing along parallel, rather than convergent, study paths. This meant that students needed opportunities to develop into the learning models required by the Tasmanian curriculum if they were to have equal opportunity to succeed. The second set of issues related to the arrangements surrounding the design and delivery of their learning experience. The teaching teams collaborated to identify solutions which afforded the students better opportunities to undertake the identified learner development within their study programme. Three examples follow.

i) It became clear that a third year unit was not offering the students the same learning opportunities in China as in Tasmania. The Tasmanian curriculum was presented utilising online 'Learning Objects' to deliver the theory, supported by intensive two-hour workshops, in which students would work in groups to complete weekly tasks. In China, the delivery model involved a two-hour weekly lecture and a 45-minute weekly tutorial. The unit was redeveloped for remote delivery from Tasmania, and additionally supported by increasing the teaching visits from one to two – achievable through resource savings from the remote delivery. Students now work in self-managed groups with each student taking leader responsibility. Leaders attend a weekly workshop that is video-conferenced between Tasmania and China, discussing the week's activities and highlighting key learning areas. In this way, students are supported individually to work independently, develop critical thinking and have effective time management skills. This unit now reflects the onshore unit, and more importantly, supports learner development that was missing from the original model of delivery.

ii) Initially, the classes in China were supported by class monitors who reported on student attendance and behaviour to the management of the Chinese institution. Class monitors would even be sent to get students out of bed if they did not attend an early morning tutorial. This cultural practice did not sit well with the Tasmanian educational philosophy of independent learning, and as the Tasmanian degree became embedded, one of the changes observed was the reduced influence of classroom monitors, leading to a fall in tutorial attendance, especially those scheduled for early morning. The solution to this problem was founded within a change implemented by a Chinese lecturer. Frustrated with the lack of discussion in his tutorials, he insisted that the students must complete the tutorial work prior to attending class. Students were to provide dot point answers to the tutorial questions on a paper which was handed in at the end of the tutorial. This change had the dual effect of preparing the students for the tutorial and providing evidence of attendance. It can be seen as re-asserting a more teacher-centred approach to help students negotiate the gap between their educational experience to date and expectation within their new degree. As a teaching team, we could see how this principle could be extended to resolve low tutorial attendance more generally. The idea of a Just In Time (JIT) classroom was developed, in which students were required to complete tutorial work in advance of the class and to submit the work to the Learning Management System prior to attending class. In class, the students were called upon randomly to answer the questions for that week, and marked on the quality of their answer. If they were not in class or had not completed the work, they received zero. This resolved the lack of attendance through a more directed approach, and at the same time provided a basis for students to interact in a structured way in class. Its success in providing a structured way to bridge the two learning cultures and give students the opportunity to develop their familiarity with interactive learning led us to implement it in the majority of program units.

iii) Quality Assurance processes identified concerns about lecture formats which effectively repeated information which the students had read in advance. Our initial solution was to reformulate the lectures as a short overview of the key points of the week's reading, thereby creating time to introduce a Problem Based Learning approach, with a case study presented in week one and expanded on in further weeks. At the outset, the lecturer was asked to use a 'think aloud methodology' to provide answers to questions posed within the weekly case study and explain to the students how s/he had arrived at those answers. This approach was then further developed by a member of Chinese faculty, who engaged the students in the lecture *before* presenting her own reasoning and response. The interactions related to the case study, and were scaffolded week by week, in effect familiarising the students with case study analysis within the lecture space.

In the changes outlined above, the teaching teams sought to provide learning activities which would lead to a more equitable experience for students in China. The focus was largely about bridging the gaps between their established culture of learning and that required within the Tasmanian degree. In some cases, this meant re-formulating learning spaces to align with more teacher-led and structured interaction spaces. The success of the changes can be observed in improved engagement and better learning outcomes. The program produces quality graduates, equipped to continue their education and participate in their global futures.

Reflective questions

To what extent are you aware of any 'cultural differences in student learning approaches and interaction styles' presenting challenges for any of your current students? How might you respond if faced with students for whom the challenges were a significant bar to their participation and learning?

How much attention is given in your course design and delivery to enabling students to 'develop into the learning models' expected?

Could some of your students benefit from more teacher-directed or rule-bound learning as a step towards more independent modes of engagement?

Are international or minority group faculty routinely involved in shaping the delivery of learning experiences for students whose cultural and educational background they may be more familiar with? What networks or communities could you engage with to help achieve this?

CASE STUDY 4

K. Afantenou, Aegean Omiros College, Athens

F. Nasika, Aegean Omiros College, Athens

M. McCormick, Canterbury Christ Church University, Canterbury

Education in Greece is considered a highly valued asset and an investment in an individual's professional future. Parents encourage their children to finish school and pursue higher education studies in order for them to obtain a degree. A potential obstacle to this ambition can be the difficulty of entering a higher education institute via the Panhellenic State Exams – a highly competitive process through which only a relatively small number of potential students gain access to state-funded tertiary education. Consequently, many young people turn to the private sector to continue their education. The institutes that widen access by offering higher education opportunities in Greece outside the public University system are referred to as 'the Colleges', and they frequently collaborate with international educational partners. This case study describes a collaboration between Aegean Omiros College (AOC) and Canterbury Christ Church University (CCCU), which started in 2014 with the development of an undergraduate, pre-registration BSc (Hons) in Clinical Speech and Language Science (BSc CSLS), as one of three programmes in the first phase of the partnership.

The purpose of this collaboration was for AOC to create both local and international education opportunities so that their students could be offered a wider range of professional opportunities and the potential for some, if they wished to pursue it, to become eligible to work in the UK. In order to achieve this, there were a number of complexities, common to many TNE arrangements, that needed to be addressed in terms of quality assurance and professional regulatory requirements in both countries. The partnership required that in order for the College to offer programmes validated by a UK University, they had to meet (UK) QAA standards and also professional benchmark statements. These should be evidenced in the learning outcomes that formed standards of specific EU professional bodies. In addition, the programmes had to conform to Greek legislation and meet specific requirements in order for the students to have their professional qualifications recognized by the Ministry of Education in Greece.

The Greek programme team for the BSc CSLS consisted of staff from various academic backgrounds, and a clinical team comprising Speech and Language Therapists with specialist professional expertise and experience gained from work and studies in a number of countries, including the UK. The team familiarized themselves with the academic, regulatory, and professional standards required for setting up the programme modules. The Greek team collaborated with an Academic Link Tutor from Canterbury Christ Church University: an experienced member of the academic staff who would identify any potential issues or problems from the UK programme team perspective. The critical focus of this collaboration was to help define the required structures and processes and establish how these could be best adapted to suit the cultural and academic differences that shape both the learning and teaching environment and student needs and expectations.

During the formation of the degree, there was continuous communication and exchange of ideas between the programme team at the College and the Academic Link Tutor. This process was stimulating due to the constant need to find a balance between meeting the requirements of the quality assurance processes and procedures, and identifying opportunities to generate innovative responses and implement new ideas. This dialogue was an educational process for all the academics involved in the partnership, as it enabled the acquisition of new skills, knowledge and understanding that were then applied to the creation of the new degree programme.

Educational developments in a transnational context bring challenges which cannot always be anticipated ahead of time, as they often arise from wider political, economic, and institutional contexts, as well as evolving needs and responses required at a programme level. There were some key challenges that the collaborating programme teams faced in bringing the BSc CSLS to validation: negotiations in the wider institutional context, and the emerging needs for College to respond to significant political and economic shifts. Consequently, the BSc CSLS went through different iterations before teaching started in January 2015, each change designed to ensure it was meeting both the needs of the college as an educational provider, and of the students in terms of their future employability.

A key issue to be resolved concerned the language of teaching and assessment. Initially, the BSc CSLS was envisaged as a programme that would run fully in English. However, as Speech and Language Therapy education involves students engaging in clinical placement modules which would be carried out with Greek-speaking clients, it was deemed necessary for them to be taught and assessed in Greek. As a result, adjustments were made to ensure that UK QAA requirements that students should be taught in the language in which they are going to use in their professional context, were met. This change enabled the majority of participants to meet their own objectives of professional employment locally, while those with strong English-language skills would still be able to pursue their more international objectives.

This decision had significant implications for the running and structure of the programme and resulted in all documentation regarding the programme (i.e. assignment briefs, module handbooks, module specifications, exams, etc.) being first written in Greek, then translated into English and sent to the Academic Link Tutor who would provide his/her feedback in English. This feedback would be incorporated into both the Greek and the English version of the documents, with both these versions being accessible to the students and staff from Canterbury Christ Church University. This enabled a Greek speaking member of the academic staff at Canterbury Christ Church University to go through the Greek versions and ensure that they semantically matched their English translations. Finally, an external examiner was appointed who was fluent in Greek in order to examine the students' assessments and provide feedback, all in Greek.

This procedure was trialed in 2014–2015 for first-year students studying the BSc CSLS. As a result of the positive feedback and results from the running of this format in the first year, it was decided that the Greek-speaking format of the programme be extended to the other two years.

The first year of the BSc CSLS received very positive feedback from the external examiner, internal moderator, staff and students. It is now in its second year and continues to develop in both scope and impact.

The creation and evolution of the programme is an example of successful transnational collaboration in education, and shows that such a project is both achievable and realistic as a goal. There were challenges along the way; however, these were resolved through effective cooperation, communication, team spirit and flexibility within the cross-functional programme team which enabled the adjustment of elements of the UK educational model to the local demands and needs of the Greek educational context. A way of working has been established that will move the partnership towards an increasingly transformative relationship, which holds opportunities to explore further initiatives and ideas to put into practice as a transnational programme team.

Reflective questions

Do your academic regulations impede the development of equitable learning experiences for students whose first language is not English, or for any other identifiable group?

If you have been involved in developing programmes for delivery elsewhere, to what extent have faculty from the new providers been engaged in the process? Is their engagement a requirement within the academic regulations for developing such provision?

This case study focussed on a solution to an identified problem of English-language proficiency among a cohort with a different single first language. What approaches to assessment might be applied if you had a multinational, multilingual cohort?

CASE STUDY 5

Harvey Charles, Ph.D., University at Albany, State University of New York

Melissa Armstrong, Northern Arizona University

The importance of technological innovation to the globalizing world helps explain why the President of the United States has made STEM education a priority (US Department of Education, 2015). This call is particularly urgent for women and minorities, populations that are underrepresented in STEM disciplines in the USA (National Science Foundation/National Center for Science and Engineering Statistics, 2013) and globally. In fact, 'underrepresented minority groups comprised 28.5 per cent of our national population in 2006, yet just 9.1 per cent of college-educated Americans in science and engineering occupations' (National Academy of Sciences, 2011). Furthermore, diverse representation among STEM professionals brings added relevancy to the global research agenda and the solutions proposed to address global challenges.

It seems natural, therefore, that a commitment to diversity and internationalization should be integrated within STEM education to prepare students for the future. There remains, however, a disconnect between STEM education and the pressing need to prepare future professionals for the increasingly global nature of STEM careers and the problems they seek to address (Charles & Doerry, 2013).

Inspired by the increasing importance of STEM education, and the need to prepare STEM majors with the capabilities (skills, knowledge and dispositions) to negotiate and succeed in a global environment, Northern Arizona University (NAU) launched the Global Science and Engineering Program (GSEP) in 2011. Open to all STEM majors, students on this program are required to complete a second major in French, German, Spanish or Asian Studies (with emphases in Chinese and Japanese). Students begin the program in their freshman year and study both majors for three years while participating in monthly cultural and professional development workshops. Students spend the entire fourth year abroad in a country where the native language corresponds with their language/culture major, engaged in study for half of the year and an internship (work placement) for the second half. Students complete capstone requirements for both the STEM major and the language/culture major in the fifth year and have a chance to serve as a peer mentor to upcoming GSEP students.

Although the motivation for this program was the development of global capabilities rather than being to explicitly attract women and minority STEM majors, three years after the launch of the program, we were encouraged to discover high numbers of women and minorities in this program. In fact, with an enrolment currently at 230 students, more than 50% are women and more than 40% are minority students. We conducted five focus groups with 20 women and minority GSEP students in the spring semester of 2015 to better understand their views of and experiences in the program. The findings of these focus groups have helped us to understand the following as important factors that may explain the presence of underrepresented students in the GSEP.

Accessibility – The program is not advertised as exclusive or elite, but, rather, as a program that provides opportunities which will enrich the college experience. The veneer of exclusivity that may exist, say with an honors program, and might serve as a disincentive for some underrepresented students to elect to affiliate is simply not associated with the GSEP program. Indeed, students confirmed in the focus groups that they found the program welcoming and the application process straightforward.

Affordability – GSEP students pay no more than their peers who are not in this program; there are no program fees or added costs. They may apply for university-sponsored funding to assist with airfare for the year abroad. The biggest expense of this program is in a fifth year of tuition. However, the fifth year of the program is treated as part of the Pledge program, which freezes tuition for the first four years of college, meaning that there is no increase in tuition for the fifth year. The benefits of GSEP seem to outweigh the fifth year of tuition expense for students and their families, especially when no program costs are added and scholarship support is available.

Academic Rigor – No adjustments are made in the rigor of the coursework as GSEP students sit side by side other non-GSEP students. In fact, additional rigor comes from the substantially higher course load each semester when pursuing two majors at once. The program signals success in disparate subjects is realistic, and students indicated that their language/culture major enabled them to 'use a different part of their brain'. Combining the sciences and the humanities with high academic rigor enabled students to envision and then realize an undergraduate experience that added further spark to their STEM major, a holistic approach that improves retention of women and minority students (Ovink & Veazey, 2011). Packaging STEM education together with international education has attracted more women, as is consistent with reporting from the IIE annual Open Doors survey since the mid-1980s; twice as many US women study abroad each year than do male students (IIE, 2015).

Personalized Advising – Academic advising is a dominant feature of this program. Notwithstanding the existence of progression plans for all integrated double majors, students receive individualized support to address whatever challenges arise as they move through the program. Every effort is made to ensure that students stay on track, are able to pursue their preferred internship experience, and are prepared for the abroad experience. Additionally, students are guided through the essential capabilities for navigating their global careers – networking across cultures, learning the tools to take charge of their own education, socialization into the academic culture – vital elements for all, but particularly for minority student success in STEM (Ovink & Veazey, 2011; Wang, 2013).

Internships – A major draw of GSEP is the semester-long internship abroad, immersed in their language and culture of study. Applied, practical research and internship experience has been shown to be particularly beneficial for minority students in STEM fields (Thiry et al., 2011). In addition, internships in an international setting give women and minority students a chance to recognize that culture can be a powerful mediator in how problems are defined (Downey et al., 2006), and how they themselves may be differently represented and positioned in different cultures and contexts. Understanding how challenges can be seen and negotiated from perspectives that are different to how they may be understood in one's own culture imparts critical skills necessary for navigating the ambiguities of culturally heterogeneous communities and the globalized character of STEM disciplines and professions.

GSEP demonstrates that it is possible to design STEM education in a manner that prepares students to be globally competent upon graduation. Just as important, this design shows that women and students of color can be drawn to STEM programs that are academically rigorous and even more demanding, if they are structured with the experiences and support that such students want and need. We believe that a dynamic has already been set in place with the current numbers of underrepresented students in the program that will feed on itself and generate new and continued interest among this population as we move forward. We are also interested to discover if (i) the stronger presence of women and minority peers, and (ii) the structured integration of global learning within STEM programs, will become institutionalized over time so that students will enrol in STEM majors with the expectation of being prepared to be globally competent and having learning experiences in a more diverse context.

Reflective questions

To what extent would you identify a 'disconnect' between the current teaching of your own subject and the 'pressing need to prepare future professionals for the increasingly global nature' of related professions?

Would it be realistic to incorporate an international internship into any of your current programmes? If you were to do so, what problems might this present to any identifiable student group, and how might these be resolved?

Are any courses you are involved in currently promoted or described in ways which make them appear elitist or in any other way inappropriate or unwelcoming for minority, international, female, or otherwise diverse students?

Would you or your colleagues be concerned that opening your course to more diverse students would somehow compromise academic rigour? Is there evidence to support such a view?

▶ 6.4 Chapter Summary

This chapter has provided examples from practice, research, and guidelines related to internationalizing and equalizing university learning spaces and activities. Much more can be found within and beyond the cited sources, but reflecting on some of the examples may support responses to current and ongoing challenges and opportunities afforded by the emerging post-national university.

Whatever the specific aspect of practice, fundamental messages which come from the practitioners in this chapter are:

- ▶ the value of all our learners *to their peers* and to the academics they work with;
- ▶ the importance of attending to the learning *process* as well as to the product;
- ▶ the need to establish an inclusive learning culture in which *all voices are sought* and heard;
- ▶ the benefit of establishing a *cooperative and collaborative* rather than a competitive learning ethos;
- ▶ the necessity of *assessing and rewarding* our students for diverse and critical perspectives;
- ▶ the *relevance of inclusive practice* to all learning contexts, all modes of study, and all learners;
- ▶ the need for practice to be *research-informed* and itself researched, reflected upon, evaluated, and continually refreshed;

▶ the *benefits which accrue* to all learners when programmes are designed in order to encompass global and multicultural learning;

▶ the issues and solutions for internationalized and for equalized learning often *have much in common*; and, perhaps above all,

▶ when faculty with diverse experience and expertise collaborate, they create solutions which enhance the learning experiences of their students for a multicultural and globalizing world.

Concluding Thoughts

This book has covered extensive ground in an attempt to:

▶ frame the emergence of post-national universities as new spaces in which academics and students enact learning;

▶ illustrate how student and faculty diversity take on newly complex forms within those new spaces;

▶ argue that internationalization and equalization of student learning are necessary and complementary areas of focus within those new spaces;

▶ present global-self capabilities as the basis for building global social justice, and propose this to be a legitimate aspiration for all higher education graduates in a richly diverse multicultural and globalizing world;

▶ demonstrate that learning for global-selfhood and learning in inclusive ways requires overcoming cultural, social, and personal 'inhibitors', and developing affective as well as cognitive and behavioural capabilities;

▶ present evidence that current university learning spaces and practices are often not experienced as inclusive or conducive to the development of global-selfhood;

▶ present evidence that successfully engaging with diverse others and diverse perspectives can be achieved, and where it is achieved can lead to positive learning gain;

▶ review capabilities and development for the global academic, including knowledge areas concerning culture, learning, and intercultural working;

▶ revisit good-practice principles for designing and delivering learning experiences which will facilitate such learning gain for diverse learners in diverse contexts, with a recurrent focus on culturally responsive pedagogies and mindfulness;

▶ offer illustrative examples from practice which reflects those principles.

Nonetheless, there are inevitably many aspects of internationalization and equalization within emerging post-national universities which have not been explored. One concerns the degree to which the emerging global higher education enterprise will contribute *equally* to the capabilities of global human beings and their societies. I have argued that the post-national university be defined in terms of balances between its international and national risks, stakeholder impacts, and the learning it sets out to achieve. This last concerns the:

- ▶ *subjective capabilities* for global living among peoples beyond its immediate stakeholders; and
- ▶ *objective capabilities* afforded through greater global social justice, levelled playing fields, and reciprocal valuing of diverse ways of being.

For many in higher education, these are not new in their underlying principles, and national and regional universities have been working to achieve them locally on different fronts. Widening participation initiatives have sought to provide greater access to higher education for minority and 'underrepresented' groups; those advocating the internationalization of the student experience have often situated it within global citizenship agendas or with a focus on equitable practice for international students; and multicultural educationists have sought to provide more relevant learning experiences and transformative outcomes for the minority students who do make it into the system. As illustrated, although success has not always been as we might hope, progress continues to be achieved in each of these areas. Despite this excellent work, though, the massive expansions in numbers of students participating in higher education locally and globally are, in large measure, accounted for by larger numbers of majority students rather than significant increases among minority groups.

In light of this continuing imbalance across the emerging global arenas in which post-national universities are opening their virtual and physical doors, we must continuously re-examine whether, rather than challenging and dismantling global injustices and inequalities, higher education might be contributing to their proliferation – principally enhancing capabilities among those whose global cultural capital already offers significant advantage (Waters, 2005).

If the benefits of higher education are not to be limited to 'international social elites', we need to be vigilant to ensure that 'issues of access and equity in higher education' are addressed 'globally as well as nationally' (James, 2012, p. 103). And we also need to be vigilant to ensure that the curriculum, learning environments, and learning experiences we provide are appropriate, relevant, and inclusive for the diverse students and contexts we serve.

Bibliography

Abrahamse, A., Johnson, M., Levingson, N., Medsker, L., Pearce, J.M., Quiroga, C., & Scipione, R. (2015). A virtual educational exchange: A North-South virtual shared class on sustainable development. *Journal of Studies in International Education, 19*(2), 140–159.

ACE. (2015). International Higher Education Partnerships: A Global Review of Standards and Practices. Washington, DC: American Council on Education.

Adams, M. (2015). Pedagogical foundations for social justice education. In M. Adams, L.A. Bell, D.J. Goodman & K.Y. Joshi (Eds.), *Teaching for Diversity and Social Justice* (3rd ed., pp. 27–53). London: Routledge.

Adams, M., Bell, L.A., Goodman, D.J., & Joshi, K.Y. (Eds.). (2016). *Teaching for Diversity and Social Justice* (3rd ed.). Abingdon: Routledge.

Adams, M., Hopkins, L.E., & Shlasko, D. (2015). Classism. In M. Adams, L.A. Bell, D.J. Goodman & K.Y. Joshi (Eds.), *Teaching for Diversity and Social Justice* (3rd ed., pp. 213–253). London: Routledge.

Ahmed, S. (2006). The nonperformativity of antiracism. *Meridians: Feminism, Race, Transnationalism, 7*(1), 104–126.

Al Jazeera. (2015). Al Jazeera TV Viewers Demographics. Retrieved Jan 2016, from http://www.allied-media.com/aljazeera/al_jazeera_viewers_demographics.html

Alghamdi, A.K.H. (2014). The road to culturally relevant pedagogy: Expatriate teachers' pedagogical practices in the cultural context of Saudi Arabian higher education. *McGill Journal of Education, 49*(1), 201–226.

Ali, U., Baars, V., Bailey, A., Hart, E., Kaur, R., & Sesay, K. (2014). Liberation, Equality, and Diversity in the Curriculum. Retrieved June 2016, from http://www.staffs.ac.uk/assets/NUS Liberation Equality and Diversity in the Curriculum 2011_tcm44-65179.pdf

Allport, G. (1979/1954). *The Nature of Prejudice*. Cambridge, MA: Perseus Books.

Alred, G., Byram, M., & Fleming, M. (Eds.). (2006). *Education for Intercultural Citizenship: Concepts and Comparisons* (Vol. 13). Clevedon: Multilingual Matters.

Altbach, P.G. (2013). The prospects for the BRICs: The new academic superpowers? In P.G. Altbach, G. Androushchak, Y. Kuzminov, M. Yudkevich & L. Reisberg (Eds.), *The Global Future of Higher Education and the Academic Profession. The BRICs and the United States* (pp. 1–27). Basingstoke: Pagrave MacMillan.

Altbach, P.G, Reisberg, L., & Rumbley, L.E. (2009). Trends in Global Higher Education: Tracking an Academic Revolution: UNESCO.

Altbach, P.G, & Teichler, U. (2001). Internationalization and exchanges in a globalized university. *Journal of Studies in International Education, 5*(1), 5–25.

Amaluisa Fiallos, C. (2006). Adult education and the empowerment of the individual in a global society. In S.B. Merriam, B.C. Courtenay & R.M. Cervero (Eds.), *Global Issues in Adult Education: Perspectives from Latin America, Southern Africa, and the United States* (pp. 15–29). San Francisco: Jossey-Bass.

Ambrosio, J. (2003). We make the road by walking. In G. Gray (Ed.), *Becoming Multicultural Educators: Personal Journey Toward Professional Agency* (pp. 17–41). San Fransisco: Jossey-Boss.

Appadurai, A. (1997). *Modernity at Large. Cultural Dimensions of Globalisation*. Minnesota, MN: University of Minnesota Press.

Appadurai, A. (2006/1966). Disjuncture and difference in the global cultural economy. In H. Lauder, P. Brown, J.-A. Dillabough & A.H. Halsey (Eds.), *Education, Globalisation & Social Change* (pp. 179–188). Oxford: Oxford University Press.

Archer, M.S. (2007). *Making our Way through the World. Human Reflexivity and Social Mobility.* Cambridge: Cambridge University Press.

Arkoudis, S., Baik, C., Yu, X., Borland, H., Chang, S., Lang, I., Lang, J., Pearce, A. & Watty, K. (2013). Enhancing peer interaction between domestic and international students: A guide for academics. Stawberry Hills: Australian Learning and Teaching Council.

AUCC. (2014). Canada's Universities in the World: AUCC Internationalization Survey. Ottawa: Association of Universities and Colleges of Canada.

Australian Government (2016) Australia Global Alumni Engagement Strategy 2016–2020, Minister's foreword. Retrieved Aug 2016 from http://dfat.gov.au/about-us/publications/Pages/australia-global-alumni-engagement-strategy-2016-2020.aspx

Australian Government. (2014). Summary of the 2014 first half year higher education student statistics. Retrieved Jan 2016, from http://www.education.gov.au/selected-higher-education-statistics-2014-student-data

Australian Government. (2015). International student survey 2014: Overview Report. Canberra: Department of Education and Training.

Backhouse, J., & Adam, F. (2013). The student experience in South Africa. In C.B. Kandiko & M. Weyers (Eds.), *The Global Student Experience. An international and comparative analysis* (pp. 278–246). Abingdon: Routledge.

Bakhtin, M.M. (1984). *Problems of Dostoyevsky's Poetics* (C. Emerson, Trans.). Minneapolis, MN: University of Minnesota Press.

Bandura, A. (1997). *Self-Efficacy: The Exercise of Control.* New York, NY: Freeman.

Banks, J. (1999). *An Introduction to Multicultural Education.* Boston, MA: Allyn & Bacon.

Barnes, B. (2000). *Understanding Agency.* London: Sage.

Barnett, R. (2000). *Realizing the University in an Age of Supercomplexity.* Buckingham: Society for Research into Higher Education & Open University Press.

Barrie, S.C. (2004). A research-based approach to generic graduate attributes policy. *Higher Education Research & Development, 23*(3), 261–275.

Barrie, S.C. (2006). Understanding what we mean by the generic attributes of graduates. *Higher Education, 51,* 215–241.

Barron, P., Gourlay, L.-J., & Gannon-Leary, P. (2010). International students in the higher education classroom: Initial findings from staff at two post-92 universities in the UK. *Journal of Further and Higher Education, 34*(4), 475–489.

Bartell, M. (2003). Internationalisation of universities: A universities culture-based framework. *Higher Education, 45,* 43–70.

Baskerville, S. (2013). A guide to UK higher education and partnerships for overseas universities. London: UK Higher Education International Unit.

Baxter Magolda, M. (2001). *Making Their Own Way: Narratives for transforming higher education to promote self-development.* Sterling, VA: Stylus.

Baxter Magolda, M. (2009). Educating Students for Self-Authorship. Learning Partnerships to Achieve Complex Outcomes. In C. Kreber (Ed.), *The University and its Disciplines. Teaching and Learning within and Beyond Disciplinary Boundaries* (pp. 143–156). London: Routledge.

BCCIE. (2003). International Students: Contributing to the Internationalization Process. Victoria, BC: The British Columbia Centre for International Education.

Beavan, A., & Borghetti, C. (Eds.). (2015). *Intercultural Education Resources for Erasmus Students and their Teachers.* Koper: Annales University Press.

Beck, U. (2006). *Cosmopolitan Vision.* Cambridge: Polity Press.

Beelen, J. (2011). Internationalisation at home in a global perspective: A critical survey of the 3rd Global Survey Report of IAU. *Globalisation and Internationalisation of Higher Education, 8*(2), 249–264. Retrieved June 2016, from http://rusc.uoc.edu/ojs/index.php/rusc/article/view/v8n2-beelen/v8n2-beelen-eng

Beelen, J. (Ed.). (2007). *Implementing Internationalisation at Home.* Amsterdam: European Association for International Education (EAIE).

Bell, L.A. (2016). Theoretical foundations for social justice education. In M. Adams, L.A. Bell, D.J. Goodman & K.Y. Joshi (Eds.), *Teaching for Diversity and Social Justice* (3rd ed., pp. 3–26). London: Routledge.

Bell, L.A, Funk, M.S., Joshi, K.Y., & Valdivia, M. (2015). Racism and White privilege. In M. Adams, L.A. Bell, D.J. Goodman & K.Y. Joshi (Eds.), *Teaching for Diversity and Social Justice* (3rd ed., pp. 135–181). London: Routledge.

Bell, L.A, Goodman, D.J, & Varghese, R. (2015). Critical self-knowledge for social justice educators. In M. Adams, L.A. Bell, D.J. Goodman & K.Y. Joshi (Eds.), *Teaching for Diversity and Social Justice* (3rd ed., pp. 397–418). London: Routledge.

Bernal, D.D, & Villalpando, O. (2002). An apartheid of knowledge in academia: The struggle over the 'legitimate' knowledge of faculty of color. *Equity and Excellence in Education, 35*(2), 169–180.

Berry, J., & Loke, G. (2011). Improving the degree attainment of Black and minority ethnic students. London: Equality Challenge Unity/HEA.

Berry, J.W, & Sabatier, C. (2010). Acculturation, discrimination, and adaptation among second generation immigrant youth in Montreal and Paris. *International Journal of Intercultural Relations, 34*(2), 191–207.

Berry, J.W. (1990). Psychology of acculturation. Understanding individuals moving between cultures. In R. W. Brislin (Ed.), *Applied Cross-Cultural Psychology* (pp. 232–253). London: Sage.

Berry, J.W. (2005). Acculturation. In W. Friedlmeier, P. Chakkarath & B. Schwarz (Eds.), *Culture and Human Development* (pp. 291–302). New York: Psychology Press.

Biggs, J. (1999). *Teaching for Quality Learning at University.* Buckingham: Society for Research into Higher Education/Open University Press.

Biggs, J. (2003). *Aligning teaching and assessing to course objectives.* Paper presented at the Teaching and Learning in Higher Education: New Trends and Innovations, University of Aveiro, 13–17 April 2003.

Biggs, J., & Tang, C. (2007). *Teaching for Quality Learning at University.* Maidenhead: Open University Press/McGraw Hill.

Biggs, J., & Tang, C. (2011). *Teaching for Quality Learning at University* (4th ed.). Maidenhead: Open University/McGraw Hill Education.

BIS. (2013). *International Education: Global Growth and Prosperity.* London: HM Government.

BIS. (2014). *The Value of Transnational Education to the UK.* London: HM Government.

Bloom, B.S. (1956). *Taxonomy of Educational Objectives. Handbook I: The cognitive domain.* New York, NY: David McKay.

Bond, S.L., Qian, J., & Huang, J. (2003). The Role of Faculty in Internationalizing the Undergraduate Curriculum and Classroom Experience. Ottawa: Canadian Bureau for International Education.

Bourdieu, P. (2006/1986). The forms of capital. In H. Lauder, P. Brown, J.-A. Dillabough & A.H. Halsey (Eds.), *Education, Globalization & Social Change* (pp. 105–118). Oxford: Oxford University Press.

Bourke, B. (2010). Experiences of Black students in multiple cultural spaces at a predominantly White institution. *Journal of Diversity in Higher Education, 3*(2), 126–135.

Bowman, N.A. (2010). College diversity experiences and cognitive development: A meta-analysis. *Review of Educational Research, 80*(1), 4–33.

Brighouse, H., & Swift, A. (2014). The place of educational equality in educational justice. In K. Meyer (Ed.), *Education, Justice and the Human Good. Fairness and equality in the education system* (pp. 14–33). London: Routledge.

British Council. (2014). Exploring the impacts of transnational education on host countries: A pilot study. London: British Council.

Brookfield, S.D. (2007). Diversifying curriculum as the practice of repressive tolerance. *Teaching in Higher Education, 12*(5–6), 557–568.

Brown, S. (2014). *Learning, Teaching and Assessment in Higher Education: Global Perspectives.* Basingstoke: Palgrave MacMillan.

Brown-Jeffy, S., & Cooper, J.E. (2011). Toward a conceptual framework of culturally relevant pedagogy: An overview of the conceptual and theoretical literature. *Teacher Education Quarterly, Winter,* 65–84.

Caplan, P.J, & Ford, J.C. (2014). The voices of diversity: What students of diverse races/ethnicites and both sexes tell us about their college experiences and their perceptions about their institutions' progress toward diversity. *Aporia, 6*(3), 30–70.

Carroll, J. (2015). *Tools for Teaching in an Educationally Mobile World.* Abingdon: Routledge.

Caruana, V. (2007). *Internationalisation of HE in the UK: 'Where are we now and where might we go?'.* Paper presented at the Education in a Changing Environment Conference, Salford.

Caruana, V., & Ploner, J. (2010). Internationalisation and equality and diversity in higher education: merging identities. London: Equality Challenge Unit.

Case, R. (1993). Key elements of a global perspective. *Social Education, 57*(6), 318–352.

Charles, H., & Doerry, E. (2013). Essential elements for internationalizing science,technology engineering and math education: Lessons from an American perspective. In E. Beerkens, M. Magnan, M. Söderqvist & H.-G. van Liempd (Eds.), Internationalization of Higher Education Handbood. Retrieved June 2016, from http://www.handbook-internationalisation.com/index.php?option=com_content&task=view&id=22&Itemid=61: EAIE/ Duz Verlags und Medienhaus GmbH.

Charles, H., Longerbeam, S.D., & Miller, A.E. (2013). Putting old tensions to rest: Integrating multicultural education and global learning to advance student development. *Journal of College and Character, 14*(1), 47–58.

Chopra, P., Datta, S., & Mishra, V. (2013). The student experience in India. In C.B. Kandiko & M. Weyers (Eds.), *The Global Student Experience. An international and comparative analysis* (pp. 172–191). Abingdon: Routledge.

Chun, E., & Evans, A. (2009). Special issue: Bridging the diversity divide – globalization and reciprocal empowerment in higher education. *ASHE Higher Education Report, 35*(1), 1–144.

Clifford, V., & Montgomery, C. (Eds.). (2011). *Moving towards Internationalization of the Curriculum for Global Citizenship in Higher Education.* Oxford: Oxford Centre for Staff and Learning Development.

Coelen, R.J. (2013). The Internationalisation of Higher Education, 2.0. Inaugural Lecture. Retrieved Jan 2016, from https://stenden.com/fileadmin/user_upload/documenten/research/Inauguration_Speech_Robert_J._Coelen.pdf

Coffield, F., Moseley, D., Hall, E., & Ecclestone, K. (2004). *Learning Styles and Pedagogy in Post-16 learning: A systematic and critical review.* London: Learning and Skills Research Centre.

Cole, D., & Zhou, J. (2014). Diversity and collegiate experiences affecting self-perceived gains in critical thinking: Which works, and who benefits? *The Journal of General Education, 63*(1), 15.

Coleman, J.A. (1998). Evolving intercultural perceptions among university language learners in Europe. In M. Byram & M. Fleming (Eds.), *Foreign Language Learning in Intercultural Perspective* (pp. 45–75). Cambridge: Cambridge University Press.

Coleman, J.A. (1999). *Language learner attitudes and student residence abroad: New qualitative and qualitativeInsights*. Paper presented at the Poetics and Praxis of Language and Intercultural Communication, Leeds Metropolitan University.

Colvin, C., Fozdar, F., & Volet, S.E. (2015). Intercultural interactions of monocultural, mono-lingual local students in small group learning activities: A Bourdieusian analysis. *British Journal of Sociology of Education, 36*(3), 414–433.

Cotton, D., George, R., & Joyner, M. (2013). The Gender and Ethnicity Attainment Gap Research Project *PedRIO paper 2*. Plymouth: Plymouth University.

Council of Europe. (2016). Competences for democratic culture. Living together as equals in culturally diverse democratic societies. Strasbourg: Council of Europe.

Cousin, G. (2011). Rethinking the concept of 'Western'. *Higher Education Research & Development, 30*(5), 585–594.

Crenshaw, W. (1991). Mapping the margins: Intersectionality, identity, politics, and violence against women of color. *Stanford Law Review, 43*(6), 1241–1299.

Cribb, A., & Gewirtz, S. (2013). The hollowed-out university? A critical analysis of changing institutional and academic norms in UK higher education. *Discouse: Studies in the Cultural Politics of Education, 34*(3), 338–350.

Crisp, R.J., Bache, L.M., & Maitner, A.T. (2009). Dynamics of social comparison in counter-stereotypic domains: Stereotype boost, not stereotype threat, for women engineering majors. *Social Influence, 4,* 171–184.

Crisp, R.J., & Meleady, R. (2012). Adapting to a multicultural future. *Science, 336*(6083), 853–855.

Crisp, R.J., & Turner, R.N. (2011). Cognitive adaptation to the experience of social and cultural diversity. *Psychological Bulletin, 137*(2), 242–266.

Cruickshank, K., Chen, H., & Warren, S. (2012). Increasing international and domestic student interaction through group work: A case study from the humanities. *Higher Education Research & Development, 31*(6), 797–810.

DAAD. (2016). International Programmes in Germany 2016. Retrieved Jan 2016, from https://http://www.daad.de/deutschland/studienangebote/international-programs/en/

Davidson, M.R., & Scudamore, R. (2008). Training new transnational teachers. In L. Dunn & M. Wallace (Eds.), *Teaching in Transnational Higher Education. Enhancing Learning for Offshore International Students* (pp. 110–119). Abingdon: Routledge.

De Vita, G. (2000). Inclusive approaches to effective communication and active participation in the multicultural classroom: An international business management context. *Active Learning in Higher Education, 1*(2), 168–180.

De Vita, G., & Case, P. (2003). Rethinking the internationalisation agenda in UK higher education. *Journal of Further and Higher Education, 27*(4), 383–398.

de Wit, H. (2000). Changing rationales for the internationalization of Higher Education. In L.C. Barrows (Ed.), *Internationalization of Higher Education: An Institutional Perspective* (pp. 9–21). Bucharest: UNESCO.

Deardorff, D.K. (2006). Identification and assessment of intercultural competence as a student outcome of internationalization. *Journal of Studies in International Education, 10*(3), 241–266.

Denson, N., & Bowman, N. (2013). University diversity and preparation for a global society: The role of diversity in shaping intergroup attitudes and civic outcomes. *Studies in Higher Education, 38*(4), 555–570.

DEST. (2005). *Values for Australian Schooling: Professional Learning Resources*. Carlton South, Victoria: Australian Government.

Devlin, M. (2011). Bridging socio-cultural incongruity: Conceptualising the success of students from low socio-economic status backgrounds in Australian higher education. *Studies in Higher Education, 38*(6), 939–949.

Dewey, J. (1916/2012). *Democracy and Education.* Start Publishing LLC. Kindle e-book edition.

Di Napoli, R., & Barnett, R. (2008). Introduction. In R. Barnett & R. Di Napoli (Eds.), *Changing Identities in Higher Education. Voicing Perspectives* (pp. 1–8). London: Routledge.

Diamond, A., Walkley, L., Forbes, P., Hughes, T., & Sheen, J. (n.d.). Global Graduates. London: AGR, CFE, CIHE.

Djerasimovic, S. (2014). Examining the discourses of cross-cultural communication in transnational higher education: From imposition to transformation. *Journal of Education for Teaching, 40*(3), 204–216.

Dodds, A. (2008). How does globalization interact with higher education? The continuing lack of consensus. *Comparative Education, 44*(4), 505–517.

Downey, G.L., Lucena, J.C., Moskal, B.M., Parkhurst, R., Bigley, T., Hays, C., Jesiek, B.K., Kelly, L., Miller, J., Ruff, S., Lehr, J.L. & Nichols-Belo, A. (2006). The globally competent engineer: Working effectively with people who define problems differently. *Journal of Engineering Education, 95*(2), 107–122.

Duggan, M., Ellison, N.B., Lampe, C., Lenhart, A., & Madden, M. (2015). Demographics of Key Social Networking Platforms. Retrieved Jan 2016, from http://www.pewinternet.org/2015/01/09/demographics-of-key-social-networking-platforms-2/-facebook

Dunne, C. (2011). Developing an intercultural curriculum within the context of the internationalisation of higher education: Terminology, typologies and power. *Higher Education Research & Development, 30*(5), 609–622.

Easthope, H. (2009). Fixed identities in a mobile world? The relationship between mobility, place, and identity. *Identities: Global Studies in Culture and Power, 16*, 61–82.

ECA. (2013). Frameworks for the assessment of quality in internationalisation: European Consortium for Accreditation.

ECU. (2013a). Equality and diversity for academics: Inclusive practice. London: Equality Challenge Unit.

ECU. (2013b). Unconscious bias and higher education. London: ECU.

ECU. (2013c). Unconscious bias in colleges and higher education. Handbook for trainers. London: Equality Challenge Unit.

ECU. (2014a). Equality in higher education: Statistical report 2014. Part 1: Staff. London: Equality Challenge Unit.

ECU. (2014b). Equality in higher education: Statistical report 2014. Part 2: Students. London: Equality Challenge Unit.

ECU. (2015). The experience of black and minority ethnic staff in higher education in England. London: Equality Challenge Unit.

Egege, S., & Kutieleh, S. (2004). Critical thinking: Teaching foreign notions to foreign students. *International Education Journal, 4*(4), 75–85.

Eisenchlas, S., & Trevaskes, S. (2007). Developing intercultural communication skills through intergroup interaction. *Intercultural Education, 18*(5), 413–425.

Elevations Networks Trust. (2012). Race to the Top. The Experience of Black Students in Higher Education. Retrieved May 2016, from https://www.abdn.ac.uk/careers/resources/documents/4854.pdf

Elkington, J. (1997). *Cannibals with Forks: The Triple Bottom Line of Twenty-First Century Business.* Oxford: Capstone.

Ellenwood, A.E., & Snyders, F.J.A. (2010). Virtual journey coupled with face-to-face exchange: Enhancing cultural sensitivity and competence of graduate students. *Intercultural Education, 21*(6), 549–566.

Entwistle, N.J., & Peterson, E.R. (2004). Conceptions of learning and knowledge in higher education: Relationships with study behaviour and influences of learning environments. *International Journal of Educational Research, 41*, 407–428.

Erikson, E.H. (1959). *Identity and the life cycle*. New York: W.W. Norton.

Fanghanel, J. (2012). *Being an Academic*. Abingdon: Routledge.

Fantini, A.E. (2003). Academic mobility programs and intercultural competence. *SIT Occasional Papers Series, Winter*, 14–19.

Featherstone, M. (1995). *Undoing Culture*. London: Sage.

Felder, R.M., & Brent, R. (2005). Understanding student differences. *Journal of Engineering Education, 94*, 57–72.

Fleming, N.D. (2006). *Teaching and learning styles: VARK strategies* Retrieved June 2016, from http://vark-learn.com/product/teaching-and-learning-styles/

Fong, E., & Shibuya, K. (2005). Multiethnic cities in North America. *Annual Review of Sociology, 31*, 285–304.

Freire, P. (1970). *Pedagogy of the Oppressed*. New York, NY: Continuum.

Freire, P. (1972). *Cultural Action for Freedom*. Hammondsworth: Penguin.

Fryer, R.H. (2005). Universities and citizenship: The forgotten dimension? In S. Robinson & C. Katulushi (Eds.), *Values in Higher Education* (pp. 74–106). St Bride's Major: Aureus/University of Leeds.

Gerson, M.G., & Neilson, L. (2014). The importance of identity development, principled moral reasoning, and empathy as predictors of openness to diversity in emerging adults. *SAGE Open*. Retrieved June 2016, from http://sgo.sagepub.com/content/4/4/2158244014553584

Ghazarian, P.G., & Youhne, M.S. (2015). Exploring intercultural pedagogy: Evidence from international faculty in South Korean higher education. *Journal of Studies in In International Education, 19*(5), 476–490.

Ginsberg, M.B., & Wlodkowski, R.J. (2009). *Diversity and Motivation: Culturally Responsive Teaching in College* (2 ed.). San Fransisco: Jossey-Bass.

Giroux, A., & Purpel, D. (1983). *The Hidden Curriculum and Moral Education: Deception or Discovery?* Berkeley, CA: McCutchan Publishing.

Glass, C.R., Wongtrirat, R., & Buus, S. (2014). *International Student Engagement: Strategies for Creating Inclusive, Connected, and Purposeful Campus Environments*. Sterling, VA: Stylus.

Goffman, E. (1959). *Presentation of Self in Everyday Life*. New York, NY: Doubleday.

Goffman, E. (1967). *Interaction Ritual: Essays on Face-to-face Behavior*. New York, NY: Pantheon Books.

Gray, G. (2000). *Culturally Responsie Teaching. Theory, Research & Practice*. New York, NY: Teachers College Press.

Griffiths, S. (2010). Teaching for inclusion in higher education: A guide to practice: HEA, AISHE, Higher Education Authority.

Group of Lisbon. (1995). *Limits of Competition*. Cambridge, MA: MIT Press.

Gudykunst, W. (1995). Anxiety/uncertainty management (AUM) theory. In R.L. Wiseman (Ed.), *Intercultural Communication Theory* (pp. 8–58). Thousand Oaks, CA: Sage.

Gudykunst, W. (2002). Intercultural communication theories. In W. Gudykunst & B. Mody (Eds.), *Handbook of International and Intercultural Communication* (pp. 183–205). Thousand Oaks, CA: Sage.

Gurin, P., Dey, E., Hurtado, S., & Gurin, G. (2002). Diversity and higher education: Theory and impact on educational outcomes. *Harvard Educational Review, 72*(3), 330–366.

Haggis, T. (2003). Constructing images of ourselves? A critical investigation into 'approaches to learning' research in higher education. *British Educational Research Journal, 29*, 89–104.

Hall, C. (2010). Advancing LGB equality. Improving the experience of lesbian, gay and bisexual staff and students in higher education. London: Equality Challenge Unit.

Harland, T., & Pickering, N. (2011). *Values in Higher Education Teaching*. London: Routledge.

Harris, A. (2009). Shifting the boundaries of cultural spaces: Young people and everyday multiculturalism. *Social Identities, 15*(2), 187–205.

Harrison, N., & Peacock, N. (2010). Cultural distance, mindfulness and passive xenophobia: Using Integrated Threat Theory to explore home higher education students' perspectives on 'internationalisation at home'. *British Educational Research Journal, 36*(6), 877–902.

Harvard University. (n.d.). Project Implicit. Retrieved January 2016, from https://implicit.harvard.edu/implicit/takeatest.html

Hase, S., & Kenyon, C. (Eds.). (2013). *Self-Determined Learning*. London: Bloomsbury.

He, L. (2016). Transnational higher education institutions in China: A comparison of policy orientation and reality. *Journal of Studies in In International Education, 20*(1), 79–95.

HEA. (2011). The UK Professional Standards Framework for teaching and supporting learning in higher education. https://http://www.heacademy.ac.uk/sites/default/files/downloads/ukpsf_2011_english.pdf

HEA. (2014a). Internationalising Higher Education Framework. York: Higher Educationa Academy.

HEA. (2014b). Language. York: Higher Education Academy.

HEA. (2014c). Mixing, Learning and Working Together. York: Higher Education Academy.

HEA. (2014d). Seminars and Tutorials. York: Higher Education Academy.

Hee, Y.S., Matsamoto, D., & LeRoux, J. (2006). The influence of emotion recognition and emotion regulation on intercultural adjustment. *International Journal of Intercultural Relations, 30*, 345–363.

HEFCE. (2015). Differences in employment outcomes. Equality and diversity characteristics. London: Higher Education Funding Council for England.

Herdzfeldt, R. (2007). Cultural competence of first-year undergraduates. In H.E. Higson (Ed.), *Good Practice Guide in Learning and Teaching* (Vol. 4, pp. 23–29). Birmingham: Aston University.

Higson, E., & Liu, K. (2013). Business lessons without business: Can arts-based training enhance cultural competence? In J. Ryan (Ed.), *Cross-Cultural Teaching and Learning for Home and International Students* (pp. 110–124). London: Routledge.

Ho, E., Holmes, P., & Cooper, J.E. (2004). Review and Evaluation of International Literature on Managing Cultural Diversity in the Classroom: University of Waikato.

Hoare, L. (2013). Swimming in the deep end: Transnational teaching as culture learning? *Higher Education Research & Development, 32*(4), 561–574.

Hofstede, G.H. (1991). *Cultures & organisations: Software of the mind*. Maidenhead: McGraw Hill.

Holliday, A. (1999). Small cultures. *Applied Linguistics, 20*(2), 237–264.

Hudzik, J. (2014). *Comprehensive Internationalization*. London: Routledge.

Hurtado, S. (2001). Linking diversity and educational purpose: How diversity affects the classroom environment and student development. In G. Orfield (Ed.), *Diversity challenged: Evidence on the impact of affirmative action* (pp. 187–203). Cambridge, MA: Harvard Educational Publishing Group.

IEAA. (2008). Good practice in offshore delivery. Hawthorn, VIC: International Education Association of Australia.

IIE. (2015). Open Doors Data – U.S. Study Abroad. Retrieved Jan 2016, from http://www.iie.org/Research-and-Publications/Open-Doors/Data/US-Study-Abroad

Illeris, K. (2002). *The Three Dimensions of Learning.* Roskilde, Denmark: Roskilde University Press/Leicester, UK: NIACE.

Ippolito, K. (2007). Promoting intercultural learning in a multicultural university: Ideals and realities. *Teaching in Higher Education, 12*(5), 749–763.

Irizzary, J. (2009, December 2015). Characteristics of the cultural deficit model. Retrieved Jan 2016, from http://www.education.com/reference/article/cultural-deficit-model/

Jabbar, A., & Hardaker, G. (2013). The role of culturally responsive teaching for supporting ethnic diversity in British University Business Schools. *Teaching in Higher Education, 18*(3), 272–284.

James, R. (2012). Social inclusion in a globalised higher education environment: The issue of equitable access to university in Australia. In T.N. Basit & S. Tomlinson (Eds.), *Social Inclusion and Higher Education* (pp. 83–107). Bristol: Polity Press.

Jarvis, P. (2006). *Towards a Comprehensive Theory of Human Learning. Lifelong Learning and the Learning Society* (Vol. 1). London: Routledge.

Jones, E., & Killick, D. (2007). Internationalisation of the curriculum. In E. Jones & S. Brown (Eds.), *Internationalising Higher Education* (pp. 109–119). London: Routledge.

Jones, E., & Killick, D. (2013). Graduate attributes and the internationalised curriculum: Embedding a global outlook in disciplinary learning outcomes. *Journal of Studies in International Education, 17*(2), 165–182.

Joy, S., & Kolb, D.A. (2008). Are there cultural differences in learning style? *International Journal of Intercultural Relations, 33*, 69–85.

Keay, J., May, H., & O' Mahony, J. (2014). Improving learning and teaching in transnational education: Can communities of practice help? *Journal of Education for Teaching, 40*(3), 251–266.

Keevers, L., Lefoe, G., Leask, B., Sultan, F., Dawood, K.P., Ganesharatnam, S., Loh, V. & Lim, J.S.Y. (2014). 'I like the people I work with. Maybe I'll get to meet them in person one day': Teaching and learning practice development with transnational teaching teams. *Journal of Education for Teaching, 40*(3), 232–250.

Kember, D. (1997). A reconceptualisation of the research into university academics' conceptions of teaching. *Learning and Instruction, 3*, 225–275.

Killick, D. (2006). *Cross-Cultural Capability & Global Perspectives. Guidelines for Curriculum Review* Retrieved June 2016, from http://www.leedsbeckett.ac.uk/publications/files/Cross_Cultural_Capability_Guidelines.pdf

Killick, D. (2011). *Embedding a Global Outlook as a Graduate Attribute at Leeds Metropolitan University.* Leeds: Leeds Metropolitan University.

Killick, D. (2012a). Seeing ourselves-in-the-world: Developing global citizenship through international mobility and campus community. *Journal of Studies in International Education, 16*(4), 372–389.

Killick, D. (2012b). *Students As Global Citizens: Being and Becoming through the Lived Experience of International Mobility.* Saarbrücken: Lambert Academic Publishing.

Killick, D. (2014a). Bringing a global outlook into course curricula. In H. Spencer-Oatey, D. Dauber & S. Williams (Eds.), *Promoting Integration on Campus: Principles, Practice and Issues for Further Exploration* (pp. 36). London: UKCISA.

Killick, D. (2014b). *Developing the Global Student: Higher Education in an Era of Globalization.* London: Routledge.

Killick, D. (Forthcoming). Self-in-the-world identities: Transformations for the sojourning student. In L.T. Tran & C. Gomes (Eds.), *International Student Connectedness and Identity in Tertiary Education: Trans-National and Trans-Disciplinary Perspectives.* New York: Springer.

Killick, D. (Ed.). (2014c). *Embedding a Global Outlook as a Graduate Attribute at Leeds Beckett University* (2 ed.). Leeds: Leeds Beckett University.

Killick, D. (Ed.). (2014d). *Enabling your Students to Develop their Global Outlook* (2 ed.). Leeds: Leeds Beckett University.

Kim, U. (2001). Culture, science, and indigenous psychologies. In D. Matsumoto (Ed.), *The Handbook of Culture and Psychology* (pp. 51–75). Oxford: Oxford University Press.

Knight, J. (2015). International universities: Misunderstandings and emerging models? *Journal of Studies in International Education, 19*(2), 107–121.

Knight, J. (2016). Transnational education remodeled: Toward a common TNE framework and definitions. *Journal of Studies in International Education, 20*(1), 34–47.

Knowles, M.S. (1980). *The Modern Practice of Adult Education* (Revised ed.). Chicago, IL: Associated Press.

Kolb, D.A. (1976). *The Learning Styles Inventory: Technical Manual.* Boston: McBer.

Kosmützky, A., & Putty, R. (2016). Transcending borders and traversing boundaries: A systematic review of the literature on transnational, offshore, cross-border, and borderless higher education. *Journal of Studies in International Education, 20*(1), 8–33.

Krathwohl, D.R., Bloom, B.S., & Masia, B.B. (1964). *Taxonomy of Educational Objectives. The Classification of Educational Goals. Handbook II: Affective Domain.* London: Longman.

Kymlicka, W. (1995). *Multicultural Citizenship.* Oxford: Clarendon Press.

Ladson-Billings, G. (1995a). But that's just good teaching! The case for culturally relevant pedagogy. *Theory into Practice, 34*(3), 159–165.

Ladson-Billings, G. (1995b). Toward a theory of culturally relevant pedagogy. *American Educational Research Journal, 32*(3), 465–491.

Langer, E. (1989). *Mindfulness.* Reading, MA: Addison-Wesley.

Lave, J., & Wenger, E. (1998). *Situated Learning. Legitimate Peripheral Participation.* Cambridge: Cambridge University Press.

Lawton, W., & Jensen, S. (2015). An early-warning system for TNE. Understanding the future global network connectivity and service needs of UK higher education. London: Observatory on Borderless Higher Education/JISC/i-graduate.

Leask, B. (2008a). Internationalisation, globalisation and curriculum innovation. In M. Hellstén & A. Reid (Eds.), *Researching International Pedagogies: Sustainable Practice for Teaching and Learning in Higher Education.* Hong Kong: Springer.

Leask, B. (2008b). Teaching for learning in the transnational classroom. In L. Dunn & M. Wallace (Eds.), *Teaching in Transnational Higher Education. Enhancing Learning for Offshore International Students* (pp. 120–131). Abingdon: Routledge.

Leask, B. (2009). Using formal and informal curricula to improve interactions between home and international students. *Journal of Studies in International Education, 13*(2), 205–221.

Leask, B. (2010). 'Beside me is an empty chair'. The student experience of internationalism. In E. Jones (Ed.), *Internationalisation and the Student Voice. Higher Education Perspectives* (pp. 3–17). London: Routledge.

Leask, B. (2015). *Internationalizing the Curriculum.* London: Routledge.

Leask, B., & Carroll, J. (2011). Moving beyond 'wishing and hoping': Internationalisation and student experiences of inclusion and engagement. *Higher Education Research & Development, 30*(5), 647–659.

Lee, J.C., Zhang, Z., Song, H., & Huang, X. (2013). Effects of epistemological and pedagogical beliefs on the instructional practices of teachers: A Chinese perspective. *Australian Journal of Teacher Education, 38*(12), 120–146.

Lee, J.J., & Rice, C. (2007). Welcome to America? International students' perceptions of discrimination. *Higher Education, 53*(3), 381–409.

Lewis, J.A., Neville, H.A., & Spanierman, L.B. (2012). Examining the influence of campus diversity experiences and color-blind racial ideology on students' social justice attitudes. *Journal of Student Affairs Research and Practice, 49*(2), 119–136.

Lewis, R. (2012). *When Teams Collide*. London: Nicholas Brealey.

Lilley, K., Barker, M., & Harris, N. (2015). Educating global citizens: A good 'idea' or an organisational practice? *Higher Education Research & Development, Online, DOI 10.1080/07294360.2015.1011089*.

Lindsay, B., & Blanchett, W.J. (2011). *Universities and Global Diversity. Preparing Educators for Tomorrow*. Abingdon: Routledge.

Lindsay, B., & Scales Williams, T. (2011). Historically Black universities and colleges in New Orleans: Domestic and global engagement in the post-Katrina era. In B. Lindsay & W.J. Blanchett (Eds.), *Universities and Global Diversity. Preparing Educators for Tomorrow* (pp. 105–126). Abingdon: Routledge.

Liu, S. (2013). The student experience in China. In C.B. Kandiko & M. Weyers (Eds.), *The Global Student Experience. An International and Comparative Analysis* (pp. 192–211). Abingdon: Routledge.

Loes, C., Pascarella, E., & Umbach, P. (2012). Effects of diversity experiences on critical thinking skills: Who benefits? *Journal of Higher Education, 83*(1), 1–25.

Logan, S., Steel, Z., & Hunt, C. (2015). Investigating the effect of anxiety, uncertainty and ethnocentrism on willingness to interact in an intercultural communication. *Journal of Cross-Cultural Psychology, 46*(1), 39–52.

Luke, A. (2010). Educating the other: Standpoint and theory in the 'internationalization' of higher education. In E. Unterhalter & V. Carpenter (Eds.), *Global Inequalities and Higher Education. Whose Interests Are We Serving?* (pp. 43–65). Basingstoke: Palgrave Macmillan.

MacLean, P., & Ransom, L. (2006). Building intercultural competencies: Implications for academic skills development. In J. Ruyan & J. Caroll (Eds.), *Teaching International Students: Improving Learning for All* (pp. 45–61). London: Rotledge.

Mak, A.S., Brown, P.M., & Wadey, D. (2014). Contact and attitudes toward international students in Australia: Intergroup anxiety and intercultural communication emotions as mediators. *Journal of Cross-Cultural Psychology, 45*(3), 491–504.

Malouff, J.M., Stein, S.J., Bothma, L.N., Coulter, K., & Emmerton, A. (2014). Preventing halo bias in grading the work of university students. *Cognet Psychology, 1: 988937*. Retrieved June 2016, from http://dx.doi.org/10.1080/23311908.2014.988937

Marcuse, H. (1970). *Five Lectures*. Boston, MA: Beacon Press.

Marginson, S. (2007). Globalisation, the 'idea of a university' and its ethical regimes. *Higher Education Management and Policy, 19*(1), 31–45.

Marginson, S., & Sawir, E. (2011). *Ideas for Intercultural Education*. New York, NY: Macmillan.

Marshall, D., & Case, J. (2005). Approaches to learning research in higher education: A response to Haggis. *British Educational Research Journal, 31*(2), 257–267.

Matsumoto, D., & Juang, L. (2004). *Culture & Psychology* (3 ed.). Belmont, CA: Wadworth/Thompson Learning.

Matsumoto, D., LeRoux, J., Berhard, J.A., & Gray, H. (2004). Unravelling the psychological correlates of intercultural adjustment potential. *International Journal of Intercultural Relations, 28*, 281–309.

Matsumoto, D., LeRoux, J., Robles, Y., & Campos, G. (2007). The Intercultural Adjustment Potential Scale (ICAPS) predicts adjustment above and beyond personality and general intelligence. *International Journal of Intercultural Relations, 31*, 747–759.

Matsumoto, D., & Yoo, S.H. (2005). Culture and applied nonverbal communication. In R.E. Riggio & R.S. Feldman (Eds.), *Applications of Nonverbal Communication* (pp. 255–278). Mahwah, NJ: Lawrence Erlbaum Associates.

May, H., & Bridger, K. (2010). Developing and embedding inclusive policy and practice in higher education. York: Higher Education Academy.

McNaught, C. (2012). SoTL at cultural interfaces: Exploring nuance in learning designs at a Chinese university. *International Journal for the Scholarship of Teaching and Learning, 6*(2), Article 3.

Mehrabian, A. (1971). *Silent Messages*. Belmont, CA: Wadsworth.

Meissner, F., & Vertovec, S. (2015). Comparing super-diversity. *Ethnic and Racial Studies, 38*(4), 541–555.

Mendez Garcia, M d C. (2006). Citizenship education in Spain: Aspects of secondary education. In G. Alred, M. Byram & M. Fleming (Eds.), *Education for Intercultural Citizenship: Concepts and Comparisons* (pp. 187–212). Cleveland: Multilingula Matters.

Mestenhauser, J. (2002). Creative, critical and comparative thinking in internationalization. In S. Bond & C. Bowry (Eds.), *Connections and Complexities: The Internationalization of Higher Education in Canada* (pp. 55–77). Winnipeg: Centre for Higher Education Research & Development, The University of Manitoba.

Mezirow, J. (1991). *Transformative Dimensions of Adult Learning*. San Francisco: Jossey-Bass.

Mezirow, J. (2000). Learning to think like an adult. Core concepts of Transformational Theory. In J. Mezirow & Associates (Eds.), *Learning as Transformation* (pp. 3–33). San Fransisco: Jossey-Bass.

Middlemas, B., & Peat, J. (2015). 'Virtual internationalisation' and the undergraduate curriculum in UK and overseas universities. *Journal of Perspectives in Applied Academic Practice, 3*(3), 46–49.

Mitchell, J.S. (2014). Beyond bricks and mortar: Creating knowledge through student partnerships. *Journal of General Education, 63*(2–3), 73–93.

Montgomery, C. (2009). A decade of internationalisation: Has it influenced students' views of cross-cultural group work at university? *Journal of Studies in International Education, 13*(2), 256–570.

Montgomery, C. (2010). *Understanding the International Student Experience*. Basingstoke: Palgrave Macmillan.

National Academy of Sciences, National Academy of Engineering, Institute of Medicine. (2011). Expanding Underrepresented Minority Participation. Washington, DC: National Academies Press.

National Intelligence Council. (2008). Global Trends 2025: A Transformed World. Washington, DC: National Intelligence Council.

National Science Foundation/National Center for Science and Engineering Statistics. (2013). Women, Minorities, and Persons with Disabilities in Science and Engineering. *Special Report NSF13-304*. Retrieved June 2016, from http://www.nsf.gov/statistics/2015/nsf15311/archives.cfm

National Taiwan University Course Information System. (2015). Courses Conducted in English. Retrieved Jan 2016, from https://nol.ntu.edu.tw/nol/coursesearch/?lang=EN

NCES. (2010). Status and Trends in the Education of Racial and Ethnic Groups. Washington, DC: National Center for Education Statistics.

Nesdale, D., & Todd, P. (2000). Effect of contact on intercultural acceptance: A field study. *International Journal of Intercultural Relations, 24*, 341–360.

Nesdale, D., & Todd, P. (1993). Internationalising Australian universities: The intercultural contact issue. *Journal of Tertiary Education Administration, 15*(2), 189–202.

Ngalomba, S. (2015). China-Africa: Reviewing higher education's gains, *University World News, 14 December*.

Nightingale, C., Law, C., & Webb, H. (2015). Academic teaching staff: Developing equality and diversity skills, knowledge and values. London: ECU.

Nilsson, B. (2003). Internationalisation at home from a Swedish perspective: The case of Malmö. *Journal of Studies in International Education, 7*(1), 27–40.

Noble, R. (2006). University College London (UCL) Medical School: Reproductive medicine, science and student society. In D. Bourn, A. McKenzie & C. Shiel (Eds.), *The Global University. The Role of the Curriculum.* London: Development Education Association.

Northedge, A., & McArthur, J. (2009). Guiding students into a discipline: The significance of the teacher. In C. Kreber (Ed.), *The University and its Disciplines. Teaching and Learning Within and Beyond Disciplinary Boundaries* (pp. 109–118). London: Routledge.

Nussbaum, M. (1998). *Cultivating Humanity: A Classic Defense of Reform in Liberal Education.* Cambridge, MA: Harvard University Press.

O'Mahony. (2014). Enhancing student learning and teacher development in transnational education. York: Higher Education Academy.

Oberg, K. (1954). Culture shock. *The Bobbs-Merrill Reprint Series, Np. A-329.*

OECD. (2005). Guidelines for Quality Provision in Cross-border Higher Education. Retrieved June 2016, from http://www.oecd.org/education/innovation-education/35779480.pdf

OECD. (2008). Higher Education to 2030. Demography (Vol. 1). Paris: OECD.

OECD. (2015a). Education at a Glance: OECD Indicators. OECD Publishing.

OECD. (2015b). OECD StatExtracts – Inward Activity of Multinationals. Retrieved Jan 2016, from http://stats.oecd.org

Olson, C.L., Evans, R., & Shoenberg, R.F. (2007). *At Home in the World: Bridging the Gap Between Internationalization and Multicultural Education.* Washington, DC: American Council on Education.

Ovink, S., & Veazey, B.D. (2011). More than 'getting us through:' A case study in cultural capital enrichment of underrepresented minority undergraduates. *Research in Higher Education, 52*(4), 370–394.

Pascarella, E.T., Martin, G.L., Hanson, J.M., Trolian, T.L., Gillig, B., & Blaich, C. (2014). Effects of diversity experiences on critical thinking skills over 4 years of college. *Journal of College Student Development, 55*(1), 86–92.

Pettigrew, T.F. (1998). Intergroup Contact Theory. *Annual Review of Psychology, 49,* 65–85.

Pettigrew, T.F., & Tropp, L.R. (2006). A meta-analytic test of Intergroup Contact Theory. *Journal of Personality and Social Psychology, 90*(5), 751–783.

Pettigrew, T.F., & Tropp, L.R. (2008). How does intergroup contact reduce prejudice? Meta-analytic tests of three mediators. *European Journal of Social Psychology, 3,* 922–934.

Piaget, J. (1954). *The Child's Construction of Reality.* London: Routledge and Kegan Paul.

Pöllmann, A. (2013). Intercultural Capital: Toward the Conceptualization, Operationalization, and Empirical Investigation of a Rising Marker of Sociocultural Distinction. *SAGE Open, April–June,* 1–7.

Pon, K., & Ritchie, C. (2014). International academic franchises: Identifying the benefits of international academic franchise provision. *London Review of Education, 12,* 104–120.

Preisler, B., Klitgård, A., & Fabricius, A. (Eds.). (2011). *Language and Learning in the International University: Practicing Diversity in the Face of English Language Uniformity.* Cleveland, OH: Multilingual Matters.

Prosser, M., Trigwell, K., & Taylor, P. (1994). A phenomenographic study of academics' conceptions of science learning and teaching. *Learning and Instruction, 4,* 217–231.

QAA. (2011). Quality Code for Higher Education. Chapter B10: management of collaborative arrangements. London.

Ramos, M.R., Cassidy, C., & Haslam, S.A. (2016). A longitudinal study of the effects of discrimination on the acculturation strategies of international students. *Journal of Cross-Cultural Psychology, 47*(3), 401–420.

Richardson, J.T.E. (2008). The attainment of ethnic minority students in UK higher education. *Studies in Higher Education, 33*(1), 33–48.

Richardson, S. (2016). *Cosmopolitan Learning for a Global Era. Higher Education in an Interconnected World.* Abingdon: Routledge.

Ritzer, G. (2002). *McDonaldization: The Reader.* London: Pine Forge.

Ritzer, G. (2004). *The Globalization of Nothing.* Thousand Oaks, CA: Sage.

Rizvi, F. (n.d.). Internationalisation of Curriculum. Retrieved Jan 2016, from http://www.teaching.rmit.edu.au/resources/icpfr.PDF

Robinson, M., & Picard, D. (2006). Tourism, Culture and Sustainable Development. Paris: UNESCO.

Rodrquez-Falcon, E., Evans, M., Allam, C., Barrett, J., & Forrest, D. (2010). *The Inclusive Learning and Teaching Handbook.* Sheffield: University of Sheffield.

Rogers, C.R. (1961). *On Becoming a Person: A Therapist's View of Psychotherapy.* Boston, MA: Houghton-Mifflin.

Rogers, C.R. (1969). *Freedom to Learn: A View of What Education Might Become.* Columbus, OH: Charles E. Merrill.

Ross, S.N. (2014). Diversity and intergroup contact in higher education: Exploring possibilities for democratization through social justice education. *Teaching in Higher Education, 19*(8), 870–881.

Ryan, J. (2013). Listening to 'other' intellectual traditions. Learning in transcultural spaces. In J. Ryan (Ed.), *Cross-Cultural Teaching and Learning for Home and International Students* (pp. 279–293). London: Routledge.

Saint-Hilaire, L.A. (2014). So, how do I teach them? Understanding multicultural education and culturally relevant pedagogy. *Reflective Practice, 15*(5), 592–602.

Salzman, M., & D'Andrea, M. (2001). Assessing the impact of a prejudice prevention project. *Journal of Counseling and Development, 79*(3), 341–346.

Sanderson, G. (2008). A foundation for the internationalization of the academic self. *Journal of Studies in International Education, 12,* 276–307.

Santamaria, L.J., & Santamaria, P.S. (Eds.). (2016). *Culturally Responsive Leadership in Higher Education.* London: Routledge.

Saucier, G., Kenner, J., Iurino, K., Bou Malham, P., Chen, Z., Thalmayer, A.G., Saucier, G., Kemmelmeier, M., Tov, W., Boutti, R., Metaferia, H., Çankaya, B., Mastor, K.A., Hsu, K-Y., Wu, R., Maniruzzaman, M., Rugira, J., Tsaousis, I., Sosnyuk, O., Regmi Adhikary, J., Skrzypińska, K., Poungpet, B., Maltby, J., Salanga, M.G.C., Racca, A., Oshio, A., Italia, E., Kovaleva, A., Nakatsugawa, M., Morales-Vives, F., Ruiz, V.M., Braun Gutierrez, R.A., Sarkar, A., Deo, T., Sambu, L., Huisa Veria, E., Ferreira Dela Coleta, M., Kiama, S.G., Hongladoram, S., Derry, R. Zazueta Beltrán, H., Peng, T.K., Wilde, M., Ananda, F.A., Banerjee, S., Bayazit, M., Joo, S., Zhang, H., Orel, E., Bizumic, B., Shen-Miller, S., Watts, S., Pereira, M.E., Gore, E., Wilson, D., Pope, D., Gutema, B., Henry, H., Dacanay, J.C., Dixon, J., Köbis, N., Luque, J., Hood, J., Chakravorty, D., Pal, A.M., Ong, L., Leung, A. & Altschul, C. (2015). Cross-cultural differences in a global 'survey of world views'. *Journal of Cross-Cultural Psychology, 46*(1), 53–70.

Savicki, V. (Ed.). (2008). *Developing Intercultural Competence and Transformation: Theory, Research and Application in International Education.* Sterling, VA: Stylus.

Schmeichel, M. (2012). Good teaching? An examination of culturally relevant pedagogy as an equity practice. *Journal of Curriculum Studies, 44*(2), 211–231.

Scholte, J.A. (2000). *Globalization: A Critical Introduction*. Basingstoke: Palgrave.

Schön, D.A. (1983). *The Reflective Practitioner*. New York, NY: Basic Books.

Schwartz, S.H. (1994). Are there universal aspects in the structure and content of human values? *Journal of Social Issues, 50,* 19–45.

Scott, I., Yeld, N., & Hendry, J. (2007). A case for improving teaching and learning in South African higher education. *Higher Education Monitor* (Vol. 6). Pretoria: Council on Higher Education.

Scudamore, R. (2013). Engaging home and international students: A guide for new lecturers. York: Higher Education Academy.

Sen, A. (1993). Capability and well-being. In M. Nussbaum & A. Sen (Eds.), *The Quality of Life* (pp. 30–53). Oxford: Clarendon Press.

Sen, A. (1999). *Development as Freedom*. Oxford: Oxford University Press.

Sen, A. (2003). Development as capability expansion. In S. Fukudo-Parr & A.K. Kumar (Eds.), *Readings in Human Development* (pp. 3–16). Oxford: Oxford University Press.

Shannon-Little, T. (2013). Developing the multicultural community of practice. Starting at induction. In J. Ryan (Ed.), *Cross-Cultural Teaching and Learning for Home and International Students* (pp. 265–278). London: Routledge.

Sheil, C. (2006). Developing the global citizen. *Academy Exchange: supporting the student learning experience, Internationalisation special issue, 5*(Winter).

Sherry, M., Thomas, P., & Chui, W. (2010). International students: A vulnerable student population. *Higher Education, 60*(1), 33–46.

Shupe, E.I. (2007). Clashing cultures: A model of international student conflict. *Journal of Cross-Cultural Psychology, 38*(6), 750–771.

Sidanius, J., Levin, S., vanLaar, C., & Sears, D.O. (2008). *The Diversity Challenge: Social Identity and Intergroup Relations on the College Campus*. New York, NY: Russell Sage Foundation.

Simpson, E.J. (1972). *The Classification of Educational Objectives in the Psychomotor Domain*. Washington, DC: Gryphon House.

Singh, G. (2011). A synthesis of research evidence. Black and minority ethnic (BME) students' participation in higher education: Improving retention and success: EvidenceNet/Higher Education Academy.

Singh, P., & Doherty, C. (2008). Mobile students in liquid modernity. In N. Dolby & F. Rizvi (Eds.), *Youth Moves. Identities and Education in Global Perspective* (pp. 115–130). New York, NY: Routledge.

Smit, R. (2012). Towards a clearer Understanding of student disadvantage in higher education: Problematising deficit thinking. *Higher Education Research and Development, 31*(3), 369–380.

Smith, K. (2014). Exploring flying faculty teaching experiences: Motivations, challenges and opportunities. *Studies in Higher Education, 39*(1), 117–134.

Sorensen, N., Nagda, B.A., Gurin, P., & Maxwell, K.E. (2009). Taking a 'hands on' approach to diversity in higher education: A critical-dialogic model for effective intergroup nteraction. *Analyses of Social Issues & Public Policy, 9*(1), 3–35.

Spencer-Oatey, H. (2013). *Promoting dialogue: Challenges and opportunities*. Paper presented at the Warwick Integration Summit, University of Warwick.

Spencer-Oatey, H., & Stadler, S. (2009). *The Global People Competency Framework. Competencies for Effective Intercultural Interaction*. Warwick: The Centre for Applied Linguistics, University of Warwick.

Spencer-Rodgers, J., & McGovern, T. (2002). Attitudes toward the culturally different: The role of inter-cultural communication barriers, affective responses, consensual stereotypes, and perceived threat. *International Journal of Intercultural Relations, 26,* 609–631.

Spiro, J. (2014). Learning interconnectedness: Internationalisation through engagement with one another. *Higher Education Quarterly, 68*(1), 65–84.

Steele, C.M., Spencer, S.J., & Aronson, J. (2002). Contending with group image: The psychology of Stereotype and Social Identity Threat. *Advances in Experimental Social Psychology, 34*, 379.

Stevenson, J. (2012). Black and minority ethnic student degree retention and attainment. York: Higher Education Academy.

Strauss, P., U-Mackey, A., & Crothers, C. (2014). 'They drag my marks down!' – challenges faced by lecturers in the allocation of marks for multicultural group projects. *Intercultural Education, 25*(3), 229–241.

Strijbos, Sytse. (2002). Citizenship in our globalising world of technology. In N. Dower & J. Williams (Eds.), *Global Citizenship: A Critical Reader* (pp. 224–230). Edinburgh: Edinburgh University Press.

Study in Holland. (2015). Retrieved Jan 2016, from http://www.studyinholland.co.uk

Surgenor, P. (2010). Teaching Toolkit: Large and small group teaching. Retrieved June 2016, from http://www.ucd.ie/t4cms/UCDTLT0021.pdf

Sutherland, A., Edgar, D., & Duncan, P. (2015). International infusion in practice – from cultural awareness to cultural intelligence. *Journal of Perspectives in Applied Academic Practice, 3*(3), 32–40.

Tajfel, H. (1981). *Human Groups and Social Categories.* Cambridge: Cambridge Press.

Tajfel, H., & Turner, J.C. (1986). The social identity theory of intergroup behavior. In S. Worchel & W. G. Austin (Eds.), *Psychology of intergroup relations* (pp. 33–47). Chicago: Nelson-Hall.

TARGET. (2014). Studying in Malaysia. Retrieved Jan 2016, from http://targetpostgrad.com/advice/studying-abroad/studying-malaysia

Taylor, J. (2004). Toward a strategy for internationalisation: Lessons and practice from four universities. *Journal of Studies in International Education, 8*(2), 149–171.

Tema, B. (1985). Academic support: Its assumptions and its implications. *South African Journal of Higher Education, 2*(1), 29–31.

Testa, D., & Egan, R. (2014). Finding voice: The higher education experiences of students from diverse backgrounds. *Teaching in Higher Education, 19*(3), 229–241.

THES. (2015). The 100 most international universities in the world 2015. Retrieved Jan 2016, from https://http://www.timeshighereducation.com/news/the-100-most-international-universities-in-the-world-2015/2018125.article

Thiry, H., Laursen, S., & Hunter, A.-B. (2011). What experiences help students become scientists? A comparative study of research and other sources of personal and professional gains for STEM undergraduates. *Journal of Higher Education, 28*(4), 357–388.

Thom, V. (2010). Mutual cultures. Engaging with interculturalism in higher education. In E. Jones (Ed.), *Internationalisation and the Student Voice* (pp. 155–165). Abingdon: Routledge.

Thompson, F.T. (2014). Effective multicultural instruction: A non-color-blind perspective. *SAGE Open, January–March*, 1–5.

Tian, M., & Lowe, J. (2010). Intercultural experience in English universities: A case study of Chinese students. In F. Maringe & N. Foskett (Eds.), *Globalization and Internationalization in Higher Education* (pp. 291–304). London: Continuum International.

Tienda, M. (2013). Diversity & inclusion: Promoting integration in higher education. *Educational Researcher, 42*(9), 467–475.

Ting-Toomey, S. (1999). *Communicating Across Cultures.* New York, NY: The Guilford Press.

Ting-Toomey, S. (2005). Identity negotiation theory: Crossing cultural boundaries. In W. Gudykunst (Ed.), *Theorizing About Intercultural Communication* (pp. 211–234). Thousand Oaks, CA: Sage.

Tran, L.T., & Nguyen, N.T. (2015). Re-imagining teachers' identity and professionalism under the condition of international education. *Teachers and Teaching*, 1–16.

Triandis, H.C. (1994). *Culture and Social Behavior.* New York, NY: McGraw-Hill.

UCL. (2014a). Dismantling the Master's House. Retrieved Jan 2016, from http://www.dtmh.ucl.ac.uk

UCL. (2014b). Why is my curriculum white? Retrieved Jan 2016, from https://blogs.ucl.ac.uk/events/2014/11/21/ucl-faces-race-why-is-my-curriculum-white/

UCL. (2014c). Why isn't my professor black? Retrieved January 2016, from http://blogs.ucl.ac.uk/events/2014/03/21/whyisntmyprofessorblack/

UKCISA. (2009). Discussing Difference, Discovering Similarities: A toolkit of learning activities to improve cross-cultural exchange between students of different cultural backgrounds. London: UKCISA.

UN-DESA & OECD. (2013). World Migration in Figures. Retrieved Jan 2016, from http://www.oecd.org/els/mig/World-Migration-in-Figures.pdf

UNESCO. (2004). *Higher Education for a Globalized Society. UNESCO Education Position Paper.* (ED-2004/WS/33). UNESCO.

UNESCO. (2015). Global flow of tertiary-level students. Retrieved Jan 2016, from http://www.uis.unesco.org/Education/Pages/international-student-flow-viz.aspx

UNESCO/COUNCIL OF EUROPE. (2002). *Code of Good Practice in the Provision of Transnational Education.* Riga: UNESCO/COUNCIL OF EUROPE.

UNWTO. (January 2015). World Tourism Barometer. Vol. 13. Retrieved Jan 2016, from http://dtxtq4w60xqpw.cloudfront.net/sites/all/files/pdf/unwto_barom15_01_january_excerpt_1.pdf

Urry, J. (2002). *The Tourist Gaze: Leisure and Travel in Contemporary Society* (2 ed.). London: Sage.

Urry, J. (2003). Globalising the tourist gaze. Retrieved June 2016 from http://www.lancaster.ac.uk/fass/resources/sociology-online-papers/papers/urry-globalising-the-tourist-gaze.pdf

US Department of Education. (2015). Science, Technology, Engineering and Math: Education for Global Leadership. Retrieved Jan 2016, from http://www.ed.gov/stem

Valenzuela, A. (1999). *Subtractive Schooling: US–Mexican Youth and the Politics of Caring.* Albany, NY: State University of New York Press.

Valverde, L.A. (2003). *Leaders of Color in Higher Education: Unrecognized Triumphs in Harsh Institutions.* Walnut Creek, CA: AltaMira Press.

Vertovec, S. (2007). Super-diversity and its implications. *Ethnic and Racial Studies, 30*(6), 1024–1054.

Vinther, J., & Slethaug, G. (2013). The influence of internationalisation and national identity on teaching and assessments in higher education. *Teaching in Higher Education, 18*(7), 797–808.

Volet, S.E., & Ang, G. (1998). Culturally mixed groups on international campuses: An opportunity for inter-cultural learning. *Higher Education Research & Development, 17*(1), 5–23.

Volet, S.E., & Ang, G. (2012). Culturally mixed groups on international campuses: An opportunity for inter-cultural learning. *Higher Education Research & Development, 31*(1), 21–37.

Vygotsky, L.S. (1978). *Mind in Society: The Development of Higher Psychological Processes.* Cambridge, MA: Harvard University Press.

Wang, T. (2008). Intercultural dialogue and understanding. Implications for teachers. In L. Dunn & M. Wallace (Eds.), *Teaching in Transnational Higher Education. Enhancing Learning for Offshore International Students* (pp. 57–66). Abingdon: Routledge.

Wang, X. (2013). Why students choose STEM majors: Motivation, high school learning, and postsecondary context of support. *American Education Research Journal, 50*(5), 1081–1121.

Ward, C. (2001). The A, B, Cs of acculturation. In D. Matsumoto (Ed.), *The Handbook of Culture and Psychology* (pp. 411–445). Oxford: Oxford University Press.

Waters, J.L. (2005). Transnational family strategies and education in the contemporary Chinese diaspora. *Global Networks, 5*, 359–377.

Welikala, T. (2013). Beyond 'enculturation': Culture, learning and international contexts of higher education. In C.B. Kandiko & M. Weyers (Eds.), *The Global Student Experience. An International and Comparative Analysis* (pp. 27–45). Abingdon: Routledge.

Wenger, E. (1998). *Communities of Practice: Learning, Meaning, and Identity.* Cambridge, UK: Cambridge University Press.

Whalley, T. (2000). Internationalizing learning through linked assignments. An instructor's manual. Vancouver,BC: BCCIE.

Whittaker, G. (2008). Inside thinking/outside issues. In L. Dunn & M. Wallace (Eds.), *Teaching in Transnational Higher Education. Enhancing Learning for Offshore International Students* (pp. 99–109). Abingdon: Routledge.

Wilikins, S. (2016). Editorial for Special Edition on transnational higher education in the 21st century. *Journal of Studies in International Education, 20*(1), 3–6.

Winkle-Wagner, R., & Locks, A.M. (2014). *Diversity and Inclusion on Campus.* Abingdon: Routledge.

Yamazaki, Y. (2005). Learning styles and typologies of cultural differences: A theoretical and empirical comparison. *International Journal of Intercultural Relations, 29*(5), 521–548.

Yershova, Y., DaJaeghere, J., & Mestenhauser, J. (2000). Thinking not as usual: Adding the intercultural perspective. *Journal of Studies in International Education, 4*(1), 39–78.

Yeung, J.G., Spanierman, L.B., & Landrum-Brown, J. (2013). 'Being White in a multicultural society': Critical Whiteness pedagogy in a dialogue course. *Journal of Diversity in Higher Education, 6*(1), 17–32.

Zhou, Y., Jindal-Snape, D., Topping, K., & Todman, J. (2008). Theoretical models of culture shock and adaptation in international students in higher education. *Studies in Higher Education, 31*(3), 63–75.

Index